上海高校知识服务平台建设项目(编号：ZF1209)资助
Sponsored by Shanghai Higher Education Institutions' Intellectual Service Platform Construction Project (No. ZF1209)

2017年上海航运政策与法律发展
Shanghai Shipping Policy and Law Development 2017

编著/Authors　　林　江（John LIN）
　　　　　　　　　Peter MURRAY（彼得·马瑞）
　　　　　　　　　王雨茗（WANG Yuming）
　　　　　　　　　陈瑞瑛（CHEN Ruiying）
　　　　　　　　　韩赟斐（HAN Yunfei）
　　　　　　　　　贾杨慕凡（JIA Yangmufan）

上海浦江教育出版社
Shanghai Pujiang Education Press

图书在版编目（CIP）数据

2017年上海航运政策与法律发展：汉英对照/林江等编著.—上海：上海浦江教育出版社有限公司,2021.6
ISBN 978-7-81121-716-2

Ⅰ.①2… Ⅱ.①林… Ⅲ.①水路运输政策—研究—上海—2017—汉、英 ②航运—法律—研究—上海—2017—汉、英 Ⅳ.①F552.0②D927.510.229.6

中国版本图书馆 CIP 数据核字（2021）第 109138 号

2017 NIAN SHANGHAI HANGYUN ZHENGCE YU FALÜ FAZHAN
2017 年上海航运政策与法律发展

上海浦江教育出版社出版发行

社址：上海海港大道 1550 号上海海事大学校内　邮政编码：201306
电话：(021)38284912（发行）　38284923（总编室）　38284910（传真）
E-mail：cbs@shmtu.edu.cn　URL：http://www.pujiangpress.cn
上海商务联西印刷有限公司印装
幅面尺寸：170 mm×228 mm　印张：33.5　字数：619 千字
2021 年 6 月第 1 版　2021 年 6 月第 1 次印刷
责任编辑：丁　慧
定价：168.00 元

编写组特此感谢下述机构、单位给予的帮助：

中国(上海)自由贸易试验区管理委员会保税区管理局
中国(上海)自由贸易试验区管理委员会陆家嘴管理局
上海陆家嘴金融城发展局
中国(上海)自由贸易试验区管理委员会金桥管理局
中国(上海)自由贸易试验区管理委员会世博管理局
中国(上海)国际贸易单一窗口
上海一网通办平台
中国电子口岸数据中心上海分中心
上海市发展和改革委员会
上海市商务委员会
上海市经济和信息化委员会
上海市财政局
上海市人力资源和社会保障局
国家税务总局上海市税务局
国家税务总局上海市电子税务局
上海市国有资产监督管理委员会
上海市金融工作委员会
中华人民共和国洋山海关
国家外汇管理局上海市分局
上海市审计局
上海市统计局
上海市人民政府参事室
上海市人民政府发展研究中心
上海市工商业联合会
中国船舶代理及无船承运人协会上海办事处
上海亿通国际股份有限公司
上海海事大学
华东政法大学
复旦大学
上海交通大学

序

  2017年,国际航运市场有所回暖,似乎跳出了多年螺旋下行的轨迹。中国航运业人士的信心升至近三年来的高点,但大部分航运企业仍在通过"抱团取暖"的方式渡过黎明前的黑暗。联营、整合以及并购事件不断涌现:如中远海运、东方海外、长荣海运和达飞轮船的 Ocean Alliance 联盟,协力开展全球集装箱干线业务;又如中远海运携手上港集团收购东方海外的部分国际业务,提高资源利用率、降低营运成本。

  为帮助航运企业解困,保持航运这一支柱产业的稳步发展,中国政府推出系列扶持政策。如,国家发改委、交通运输部对港口垄断进行行政调查,促使相关企业主动整改、调整收费标准,为航运、贸易企业降低负担。在推出的政策中,最为重要的当数《全面深化中国(上海)自由贸易试验区改革开放方案》。

  上海自贸区始建于2013年,在初期发展过程中即取得了举世瞩目的成绩。截至2017年,上海自贸区内新注册企业累计超过5万户,其中:约10%为航运企业;外商投资负面清单减少到95条;区内关检"三个一"查验平台全面建成运行,货物状态分类监管试点企业扩大至39家;"证照分离"改革全面铺开,事中事后监管体系初步建成,实现21家监管部门全覆盖;政务信息"全域共享"加快推进,海关特殊监管区实现与口岸、金融等监管部门的信息共享。

  2017年,借"一带一路"春风,上海自贸区建设进入全新时代。在此关键时刻,国务院发布《全面深化中国(上海)自由贸易试验区改革开放方案》,提出对照国际最高标准、最好水平的自由贸易区,全面深化上海自贸区改革开放,加快构建开放型经济新体制。该方案中含有诸多有利航运企业发展的措施:

  (1) 建立同国际投资和贸易通行规则相衔接的制度体系,促进贸易转型升级和通关便利的贸易监管服务体系,形成法治化、国际化、便利化的营商环境和公平、统一、高效的市场环境。

  (2) 实施市场准入负面清单和外商投资负面清单制度,最大限度缩减自贸试验区外商投资负面清单,放宽投资准入,优化、简化办事环节和流程,推进航运服务等专业服务业和先进制造业领域对外开放。

  (3) 全面深化商事登记制度改革,开展企业名称登记制度改革,放宽住所(经营场所)登记条件,有效释放场地资源,优化营业执照的经营范围等登记方式,推行全程电子化登记和电子营业执照改革试点。

(4) 全面实现"证照分离",能取消的审批事项全部取消,需要保留审批的,按照告知承诺和加强市场准入管理等方式进一步优化调整,进一步扩大实行告知承诺的领域。

(5) 借鉴联合国国际贸易"单一窗口"标准,实施贸易数据协同、简化和标准化,纳入海港、空港和海关特殊监管区域的物流作业功能,推动将国际贸易"单一窗口"覆盖领域拓展至服务贸易。推进上海国际贸易"单一窗口"与"一带一路"沿线口岸的信息互换和服务共享。

(6) 建立安全高效便捷的海关综合监管新模式,深化实施全国海关通关一体化、"双随机、一公开"监管以及"互联网+海关"等举措,对接国际贸易"单一窗口",建立权责统一、集成集约、智慧智能、高效便利的海关综合监管新模式。

(7) 优化口岸通关流程,推进各环节监管方式改革,探索公布涵盖各通关环节的货物平均放行时间,最大限度实现覆盖船舶抵离、港口作业、货物通关等口岸作业各环节的全程无纸化,推进贸易领域证书证明的电子化管理。

(8) 在风险可控的前提下,深化国际船舶登记制度创新,进一步便利国际船舶管理企业从事海员外派服务。

(9) 在洋山保税港区和上海浦东机场综合保税区等海关特殊监管区域内设立自由贸易港区,依托信息化监管手段,取消或最大程度简化入区货物的贸易管制措施,最大程度简化申报手续。

(10) 建立综合性对外投资促进机构和境外投资公共信息服务平台,在法律查明和律师服务、商事纠纷调解和仲裁、财务会计和审计服务等方面开展业务合作。

(11) 大力发展海外投资保险、出口信用保险、货物运输保险等业务,为企业海外投资、产品技术输出、承接"一带一路"重大工程提供综合保险服务。

(12) 健全完善更加符合社会主义市场经济规律、人才成长规律和人才发展流动规律的人才认定标准和推荐方式,标准统一、程序规范的外国人来华工作许可制度及高效、便捷的人才签证制度。

(13) 探索具有国际竞争力的离岸税制安排,适应企业参与国际竞争和服务"一带一路"建设的需求,在不导致税基侵蚀和利润转移的前提下,基于真实贸易和服务背景,结合服务贸易创新试点工作,创新试点扩围的税收政策安排。

为了给航运业在上海自贸区茁壮成长构建良好的法制环境,最高人民法院颁布《关于为自由贸易试验区建设提供司法保障的意见》,其中与航运企业相关的保障措施简述如下:

(1) 各级人民法院应平等保护中外当事人合法权利,为自贸试验区的建设提供优质高效的司法保障。

（2）各级人民法院应在准确适用法律的基础上，注重及时调整裁判尺度，积极支持政府职能转变，尊重合同当事人的意思自治，维护交易安全。

（3）加强海事审判，规范航运市场建设，支持自贸试验区航运服务业开放、提升国际航运服务能级和增强国际航运服务功能。关注与船舶登记制度改革及其他与航运有关的新类型案件，研究新型海事法律关系的法律适用和专门管辖问题。及时通过典型案件的审理确认有关规则，引导行业行为，促进行业发展。

（4）积极支持自贸试验区内的融资租赁企业在核准的经营范围内依法开展融资业务。充分尊重中外当事人对融资租赁合同纠纷有关管辖和法律适用的约定。正确认定融资租赁合同效力，不应仅以未履行相关程序等事由认定融资租赁合同无效。

（5）鼓励运用仲裁、调解等多元化机制解决自贸试验区民商事纠纷，进一步探索和完善诉讼与非诉讼相衔接的矛盾纠纷解决机制。支持仲裁机构、商事和行业调解组织的创新发展。

（6）在自贸试验区内注册的外商独资企业相互之间约定商事争议提交域外仲裁的，不应仅以其争议不具有涉外因素为由认定相关仲裁协议无效。一方或者双方均为在自贸试验区内注册的外商投资企业，约定将商事争议提交域外仲裁，发生纠纷后，当事人将争议提交域外仲裁，相关裁决作出后，又以有关争议不具有涉外因素为由主张仲裁协议无效，并以此主张拒绝承认、认可或执行的，人民法院不予支持。

（7）境外民事主体在自贸试验区设立企业或办事处作为业务代办人的，可以向其业务代办人送达。境外民事主体概括指定其分支机构工作人员或者境内律师事务所律师作为特定时间、特定区域或者特定业务的诉讼代理人的，可以向其送达诉讼文书。

（8）人民法院审理的涉自贸试验区的涉外民商事案件，当事人约定适用外国法律，人民法院了解查明途径的，可以告知当事人。当事人不能提供、按照我国参加的国际条约规定的途径亦不能查明的外国法律，可在一审开庭审理之前由当事人共同指定专家提供。

在上海自贸区深化改革、为打造航运中心提供历史契机之时，《2017年上海航运政策与法律发展白皮书》又与读者见面了。本书聚焦过去一年上海国际航运中心建设中所历经的法治发展，共分六章。第一章航运法律、法规及政策，关注航运立法，对2017年国家及上海人大、政府部门出台的航运政策与法律进行梳理，并对影响较大或具有创新意义的法规进行简要的介绍及评析。第二章航运政策与法律的司法执行，将视线转向航运司法，简析上海航运司法机构进行航运政策与法律司法工作的情况，并精选案例彰显他们为完善航运司法服务、保障航运企业合法权益所做出的努力。第三章航运政策与法律的行政执行,侧重于执法,介绍上海航运执法机构进行航运政策与法律执法工作的情况,并选取2017年内重大海事、海洋、航运市场执法案件,结合相关的法规进行分析。第四章航运政策与法律的书文评析,以法治教育为观察视角,对2017年中航运法律学者及业界人士发表在各个核心期刊的文章以及出版的著作进行点评。第五章年度航运聚焦,整理并简析过去一年中与航运法治相关的业界亮点、热点,特别是上海航运市场发生的重要事件、关注的热点问题、实施的创新举措以及取得的主要成绩,以便广大读者了解上海国际航运中心建设、法治环境建设的进程。第六章为展望。

本书由上海国际航运研究中心政策与法律研究所副所长、上海海事大学法学院副教授、美国杜兰大学法学院外聘副教授林江组织撰写,并具体负责本书第一至六章的撰写工作。上海国际航运研究中心外国专家、上海海神律师事务所高级顾问Peter MURRAY先生负责本书英文部分的校对工作。上海国际航运研究中心政策与法律研究所王雨茗和陈瑞瑛,以及上海海事法院韩赟斐参与本书的撰写及翻译工作。

本书由上海国际航运研究中心出资、上海海神律师事务所赞助出版。本书的撰写和出版得到了上海海事大学和上海国际航运研究中心领导的关心指导,特此感谢上海海事大学原党委书记、校长於世成教授,上海国际航运研究中心秘书长真虹教授、副秘书长张婕姝教授,上海海事大学法学院院长王国华教授,以及上海国际航运研究中心政策与法律研究所所长叶红军先生、副所长沈秋明教授。此外,本书的撰写还得到来自航运、司法系统等社会各界人士的关心和支持,编写组走访了数十家机构、单位进行调研,保证了本书所提供信息与数据的真实性和准确性,同时也丰富了本书的内容,在此一并表示感谢。

本(系列)书的目的在于,通过回顾历年上海在航运政策与法律方面的发展,与社会各界有识之士共同探求上海航运法治建设的方向、路径和抓手,并尝试为上海国际航运中心的建设献策,特别是在航运政策制定、航运立法、执法、司法、法治文化教育等方面。编写组期望本(系列)书能起到抛砖引玉的作用,为航运、法律界业界人士带来启示,引发对航运法治环境整体建设的深层次思考。由于撰写时间紧迫,书中难免疏漏与不足之处,敬请业界同仁、广大读者指正(发送电邮至john.lin@hisunlaw.com),这将鼓励和鞭策我们继续勤勉、不断创新,把工作做得更好,让本(系列)书无愧于"上海、中国、世界首创"这一称号。

《上海航运政策与法律发展》编写组
上海国际航运研究中心政策与法律研究所
二〇一七年十二月三十一日

目　　录

Contents

第一章　航运法律、法规及政策 …………………………………………… 1
　一、航运法律、法规及政策汇总 ………………………………………… 2
　二、航运法律、法规及政策评析 ………………………………………… 4
　三、小结 ………………………………………………………………… 30

第二章　航运政策与法律的司法执行 …………………………………… 31
　一、2017年海事司法情况简介 ………………………………………… 32
　二、司法案例精选 ……………………………………………………… 36
　三、小结 ………………………………………………………………… 70

第三章　航运政策与法律的行政执行 …………………………………… 71
　一、上海海事局行政执法案例 ………………………………………… 72
　二、上海救助及打捞部门行政执法案例 ……………………………… 80
　三、上海市渔政监督管理处行政执法案例 …………………………… 83
　四、上海出入境边防检查总站行政执法案例 ………………………… 86
　五、小结 ………………………………………………………………… 90

第四章　航运政策与法律的书文评析 …………………………………… 91
　一、2017年出版的航运政策与法律类书籍评析 ……………………… 92
　二、2017年发表的航运政策与法律类论文评析 ……………………… 101
　三、小结 ………………………………………………………………… 113

第五章　年度航运聚焦 …………………………………………… 114
　　一、热点关注 ……………………………………………………… 115
　　二、自贸区与现代航运服务产品 ………………………………… 124
　　三、航运法治建设 ………………………………………………… 130
　　四、航运文化建设 ………………………………………………… 138
　　五、航运人才服务 ………………………………………………… 142
　　六、交流活动及会议 ……………………………………………… 146
　　七、小结 …………………………………………………………… 157

第六章　展　望 …………………………………………………… 158

附　录 ……………………………………………………………… 161
　　一、船舶修理合同 ………………………………………………… 161
　　二、全面深化中国(上海)自由贸易试验区改革开放方案 ……… 170
　　三、上海市邮轮旅游合同示范文本(2015 版) …………………… 176

Chapter 1　Shipping Laws, Regulations and Policies …………… 196
　　1　Laws, Regulations and Policies Judicial Interpretations ……… 198
　　2　Analysis and Comments of Laws, Regulations and
　　　　Judicial Interpretations ………………………………………… 201
　　3　Summary ………………………………………………………… 248

Chapter 2　Judicial Execution of Shipping Law …………………… 250
　　1　A Brief Introduction of Maritime Judicial Situation in
　　　　Shanghai in 2017 ……………………………………………… 253
　　2　Selection of Maritime Judicial and Arbitration Cases ………… 259
　　3　Summary ………………………………………………………… 317

Chapter 3 Administrative Enforcement of Shipping Policies and Laws 318
   1 Administrative Enforcement Cases of Shanghai Maritime Safety Administration 320
   2 Administrative Enforcement Cases of Shanghai Rescue and Salvage Department 337
   3 Administrative Enforcement Cases of Shanghai Fishery Supervision and Administration Division 342
   4 Administrative Enforcement Cases of Shanghai General Station of Immigration Inspection 348
   5 Summary 355

Chapter 4 Literature Review with regard to Shipping Policy and Law 356
   1 Book Review for Publication in 2017 358
   2 Journal Article Review for publication in 2017 376
   3 Summary 398

Chapter 5 Annual Shipping Focus 399
   1 Yearly Hot Issues 401
   2 Free Trade Zone and Modern Shipping Service Products 417
   3 Legal Construction of Shipping 429
   4 Shipping Culture Construction 443
   5 Shipping Talent Service 450
   6 Exchange Activities and Meetings 458
   7 Summary 478

Chapter 6 Prospect 479

Appendix ·· 483
  1 Contract for Ship Repairs ·· 483
  2 Notice of the State Council on Issuing the Plan for Comprehensively Furthering the Efforts of Reform and Opening Up in the China (Shanghai) Pilot Free Trade Zone ············· 497
  3 Shanghai Cruise Travel Contract Model Text (Edition 2015) ·· 509

第一章 航运法律、法规及政策

  航运业不仅是奠定国民经济健康发展的基石,也是建立对外贸易交流的重要桥梁。我国作为一个航运大国,一直致力于根据市场经济的发展变化,建立与时俱进的航运法规体系。自2014年,国务院把握国内外友好贸易交流之大势作出的重大战略决策,提出"一带一路"倡议。在"一带一路"建设中,航运是互联互通的纽带,法治是航运发展的保障。"一带一路"倡议为航运法治发展提供了新契机,也提出了新挑战。因此,航运法律与航运法规政策的创新、更新在指导航运经济运行当中有着相当重要的作用。

  2017年是实施"十三五"规划重要的一年,是供给侧结构性改革的深化之年,也是全面贯彻落实党中央国务院推进安全生产领域改革发展的开局之年。国务院、交通运输部以及其他相关部门协同合作,通过取消和下放多项行政审批事项、建立权利清单、清理港口收费等政策来保障航运业的健康持续发展。

  2月14日,交通运输部发布《关于印发2017年交通运输安全生产工作要点的通知》,明确要求:深入贯彻落实党的十八大和十八届三中、四中、五中、六中全会精神以及中央经济工作会议精神,坚决贯彻落实习近平总书记关于安全生产重要指示精神,按照国务院安委会和全国安全生产电视电话会议的部署,牢固树立红线和底线意识,以"平安交通"为统领,以改革发展为动力,以落实安全责任为核心,坚持问题导向,突出隐患排查治理和风险管控,扎实推进安全生产基础设施设备建设,扎实推动安全生产工作系统化、规范化、标准化,不断提高安全生产工作管理水平,坚决遏制重特大事故,全力保障交通运输安全生产形势持续稳定。

  6月20日,国家发展和改革委员会、国家海洋局制定并发布《"一带一路"建设海上合作设想》(以下简称设想)。该设想是自2015年3月28日发布《推动共建丝绸之路经济带和21世纪海上丝绸之路的愿景与行动》以来,中国政府首次就推进"一带一路"建设海上合作提出中国方案,也是"一带一路"国际合作高峰论坛的领导人成果之一。设想提出,愿与21世纪海上丝绸之路沿线各国一道开展全方位、多领域的海上合作,共同打造开放、包容的合作平台,建立积极务实的蓝色伙伴关系,铸造可持续发展的"蓝色引擎"。

  "一带一路"建设是我国相当长时期对外开放和对外合作的管总规划,对于全面提升我国全方位开放水平具有重大意义。把中国(上海)自由贸易试验区(以下简称上海自贸试验区)建设成为服务国家"一带一路"建设、推动市场主体走出去的桥头堡,是习近平总书记在全局高度对上海提出的新要求。10月11日,上海市政府发布《上海服务国家"一带一路"建设发挥桥头堡作用行动方案》,这对强化体制保障、整合政策资源,形成服务国家"一带一路"建设发挥强大的作用。

2017年,国家通过制定各项法律和政策来完善我国海运发展政策体系,营造参与国际竞争的公平环境;健全法规制度和标准,完善船舶技术政策和标准规范,清理规范行政审批事项,健全权益保障机制,为我国航运业发展提供重要支撑。这对推进航运企业深化改革,调整运力结构,实现转型升级,以及大力发展现代航运服务业,加快推进国际航运中心建设都将具有重要的指导意义。

一、航运法律、法规及政策汇总

(一)法律、法规及规范性文件

1. 航运管理

中华人民共和国国际海运条例实施细则(修正案)
交通运输部关于推进特定航线江海直达运输发展的意见
中华人民共和国海上海事行政处罚规定
水路运输市场信用信息管理办法(试行)
中国(上海)自由贸易试验区航运法治建设公约

2. 港口航道

国内水路运输管理条例(2017年修正)
中华人民共和国港口法(2017年修正)
港口危险货物安全管理规定
交通运输部办公厅关于印发《港口岸电布局方案》的通知
水路运输市场信用信息管理办法(试行)
中华人民共和国水污染防治法

3. 船舶管理

交通运输部关于修改《中华人民共和国船舶及其有关作业活动污染海洋环境防治管理规定》的决定
中华人民共和国船舶安全监督规则
交通运输部办公厅关于水路运输建设综合管理信息系统航运管理部分功能投入试运行的通知

交通运输部办公厅关于印发2017年交通运输安全生产工作要点的通知
2007年内罗毕国际船舶残骸清除公约
4. 船员管理
中华人民共和国船员培训管理规则(2017年修正)
交通运输部海事局关于进一步加强海员外派备用金管理有关事项的通知
交通运输部海事局关于征求《船员信誉管理办法》等三个办法意见的通知
交通运输部海事局关于实施《海船船员培训大纲》的通知
中华人民共和国船员条例(2017年修正)
5. 财政、税收
中华人民共和国海关法(2017年修正)
交通运输部关于印发《靠港船舶使用岸电2016—2018年度项目奖励资金申请指南》的通知
交通运输部办公厅关于明确享受中资"方便旗"船税收优惠政策船舶转挂五星红旗后兼营国内运输管理问题的通知
中华人民共和国船舶吨税法
港口收费计费办法
6. 自贸区和"一带一路"
国务院关于印发全面深化中国(上海)自由贸易试验区改革开放方案的通知
国务院关于在自由贸易试验区暂时调整有关行政法规、国务院文件和经国务院批准的部门规章规定的决定
国务院办公厅关于印发自由贸易试验区外商投资准入特别管理措施(负面清单)(2017年版)的通知
关于进一步引导和规范境外投资方向的指导意见
关于开展支持中小企业参与"一带一路"建设专项行动的通知
最高法发布第二批涉"一带一路"建设典型案例
中国保监会发布《关于保险业服务"一带一路"建设的指导意见》
最高人民法院关于为自由贸易试验区建设提供司法保障的意见
《中国(上海)自由贸易试验区航运法治建设公约》
国务院关于扩大对外开放积极利用外资若干措施的通知
上海服务国家"一带一路"建设发挥桥头堡作用行动方案
7. 其他
上海市人民政府关于进一步扩大开放加快构建开放型经济新体制的若干意见
交通运输部海事局关于印发《海事行政许可裁量权控制办法》的通知

中华人民共和国海洋环境保护法(2017年修正)
最高人民法院《关于进一步保护和规范当事人依法行使行政诉权的若干意见》

二、航运法律、法规及政策评析

(一) 最高人民法院关于为自由贸易试验区建设提供司法保障的意见

2016年12月30日,最高人民法院印发《关于为自由贸易试验区建设提供司法保障的意见》(以下简称《意见》)。

1. 出台背景

自由贸易试验区是我国改革开放的试验田,是我国构建开放型经济新体制的重要窗口。人民法院承担着为自由贸易试验区建设提供司法保障的重大职责,适时总结审判经验,为全国各级人民法院提供审判指导,已成为司法实践的迫切需要。为充分发挥人民法院的审判职能作用,保障我国自由贸易试验区(以下简称自贸试验区)的建设,最高院结合审判实践,针对人民法院涉自贸试验区案件的审判工作制定《意见》。

2. 主要内容

《意见》共12条,涉及内容:一是正确行使刑事、民事、行政等审判职能作用;二是依法支持自贸试验区企业的创新,鼓励探索新的经营模式;三是探索审判程序的改革与创新;四是注重总结审判经验,加强前瞻性研究工作。

(1) 关注船舶登记制度改革及航运新类型案件

海事审判对保障自贸试验区建设有特别的意义。《意见》提出要关注与船舶登记制度改革及其他与航运有关的新类型案件,研究新型海事法律关系的法律适用和专门管辖问题。及时通过典型案件的审理确认有关规则,规范航运市场建设,支持自贸试验区航运服务业开放、提升国际航运服务能级和增强国际航运服务功能。

(2) 支持融资租赁、跨境电子商务

为支持自贸试验区企业的创新,鼓励探索新的经营模式,《意见》充分尊重当事人对管辖和法律适用的约定,依法维护合同效力,依法支持融资租赁、跨境电子商务等行业创新性经营模式。

(3) 建立多元化纠纷解决机制

在积极探索审判程序的改革与创新方面,《意见》支持在自贸试验区建立多元化纠纷解决机制,鼓励各级人民法院在总结审判经验的基础上形成符合涉自贸试验区案件特点的审判机制。要求加大对仲裁的支持力度,提高商事纠纷仲裁国际化程度。同时对正确认定仲裁协议效力、探索审判程序创新、建立合理的外国法查明机制等方面作出规定。

(4) 加强前瞻性研究工作

《意见》规定:"审理好涉自贸试验区案件,总结可复制经验。各高级人民法院应当充分重视涉自贸试验区案件的审理,加强前瞻性研究工作。各地人民法院对在审理与自贸试验区相关的案件中发现的热点、难点问题,应当及时研究总结,形成应对意见,并及时向最高人民法院提出建议。"不断总结涉自贸试验区案件的审判经验,及时发现问题、解决问题,充分发挥人民法院的职能,为自贸试验区建设提供更优质、高效的司法保障。

3. 法规综述

在自贸试验区运行三周年之际,适时总结审判经验,为全国各级人民法院涉自贸试验区案件的审判工作提供审判指导,已成为司法实践的迫切需要。《意见》旨在发挥最高人民法院的业务指导作用,统一认识,更新审判理念,以实际举措支持自贸试验区内实施的各项改革措施,解决涉自贸试验区司法实践中迫切需要解决的、带有普遍性的问题。在新的历史时期,人民法院将充分发挥审判职能作用,为促进自贸试验区健康发展提供坚实可靠的司法保障。

(二)《2007年内罗毕国际船舶残骸清除公约》

1. 出台背景

沉船不仅在不同程度上威胁着过往船舶和船上船员的安全,更会对海洋和海岸环境造成严重的危害。近年来由于为加强船舶运输安全所作出的持续努力,海洋灾害的发生率急剧下降。但据报道,被遗弃的残骸数量有所增加,这给沿海国和航运业带来严峻的挑战。《2007年内罗毕国际船舶残骸清除公约》(以下简称《公约》)于2007年5月在肯尼亚内罗毕召开的国际海事组织外交大会上通过,2015年4月14日正式生效。经国务院批准,我国于2016年11月11日向国际海事组织递交《公约》加入书,《公约》于2017年2月11日起对我国生效。

2. 主要内容

1)《公约》明确缔约沿岸国对其专属经济区内残骸清除的权利和义务

(1) 缔约国的义务。《公约》第5条规定,缔约国应要求悬挂其国旗的船舶的船长和经营人,在海上事故导致其船舶成为残骸时,及时向受影响国家报告。作为缔约国的受影响国应根据《公约》第6条的规定,对残骸是否构成危害进行评估和确定。《公约》第7条和第8条进一步规定,如果受影响国家有理由相信残骸构成危害,应确保采取一切可行措施以确定残骸的准确位置并进行标记,并采取一切适当办法公布残骸标记的具体细节。《公约》第9条第1款还规定,为便利残骸的清除,受影响国确定残骸构成危害时,应立即通知船舶登记国和登记所有人,并就对残骸采取的措施与船舶登记国和受到残骸影响的其他国家进行协商。

(2) 缔约国的权利。《公约》第9条规定限期对残骸进行清除、强制清除和立即清除。受影响国应首先设定一个合理期限,要求船舶所有人在该期限内对残骸进行清除,并以书面方式将其所设定的期限通知船舶所有人,并说明如船舶所有人在该期限内不清除残骸,该国可以对残骸进行清除,费用由船舶所有人承担。如果船舶所有人在设定的期限内不清除残骸,或是无法联系到船舶所有人,或在需要立即行动且受影响国家已经相应地通知船舶登记国和船舶所有人的情况下,受影响国家可以采用现有最切实可行和最迅速且符合安全和海洋环境保护考虑的方式对残骸进行清除。

2) 强制责任保险或财务保证

悬挂缔约国国旗的船舶所有人应就残骸清除根据其有权享受的责任限制金额进行强制保险或提供财务保证;缔约国应确保驶入该国内水或领海的船舶符合强制保险或财务保证的要求。根据《公约》第12条第1款的规定,300总吨及以上且悬挂一缔约国国旗的船舶的登记所有人,应持有残骸清除责任保险或其他财务保证,数额等同于所适用的国内法或国际公约规定的责任限制金额,但无论如何不超过根据经修正的《1976年海事赔偿责任限制公约》第6条第(1)(b)款所计算的数额。

3) 对保险人或财务保证人的直接诉讼

《公约》规定对残骸清除责任保险人或财务保证人的直接诉讼制度,即有权索赔残骸确定、标记和清除费用的主体对残骸清除责任保险人或财务保证人具有直接的损害赔偿请求权。《公约》第12条第10款规定,根据《公约》产生的任何费用的索赔,可向为船舶所有人承保残骸清除责任的保险人或提供财务保证的其他人直接提出。保险人或财务保证人可以援引船舶所有人有权援引的免责事由和赔偿责任限制。

3. 法规综述

《公约》为计划清除或已清除可能威胁航行安全、海洋环境的船舶残骸的国家提供了法律依据,并提供统一的国际规则,以迅速和有效地清除位于领海之外的船舶残骸,以及在各国领土,包括领海中,选择性地适用规则。一方面明确了缔约沿岸国对其专属经济区内残骸清除的权利和义务,保证各国及时、有效地清除残骸并获得资金保障;另一方面规定了船舶登记所有人有义务对公约区域内被认为具有危害的船舶残骸进行定位、标记和移除。为了确保船舶所有人的履约能力,《公约》

规定船东严格责任和强制保险制度,取得缔约国签发的《证书》,意味着船舶的履约能力由主管机关出具《证书》以证明。

今后 300 总吨以上的中国籍船舶需持有符合《公约》要求的保险或其他财务担保,并申请办理《残骸清除责任保险或其他财务保证证书》随船携带,以满足船舶履约要求。《公约》的实施,一方面保障了我国海域内的船舶残骸可以及时有效清除,另一方面也增加沿海运输业的经营成本。同时,也需要更有针对性的保险产品。

(三)《中华人民共和国国际海运条例实施细则》(修正案)

交通运输部于 2017 年 3 月 13 日发布《中华人民共和国国际海运条例实施细则》(以下简称《实施细则》)(修正案)(以下简称《修正案》),自发布之日起施行。

1. 出台背景

为推进"先照后证"改革工作,落实 2016 年 2 月份发布的《国务院关于修改部分行政法规的决定》(国务院令 666 号)的内容,国务院决定对包括《国际海运条例》在内的行政法规进行修改。同时为国际海运领域深入贯彻落实"放管服"改革要求,强化国际海运市场监督检查等事中事后监管手段,以制度创新,激发市场活力。就《实施细则》本身,需要删除或修改部分不适应目前税费、发票和统计制度改革的条款以适应改革形势。

2. 主要内容

《修正案》主要对《实施细则》32 条内容进行修订,主要围绕以下几个方面作出修改或调整:

(1) 落实国务院"先照后证"改革部署进行的修改。根据修订后的《国际海运条例》关于申请人须事先"取得企业法人资格"的要求,明确申请国际船舶运输业务和国际船舶管理业务的主体统一为中国企业法人。删除了"先证后照"的内容以及对申请材料作了相应修改。修改内容涉及 7 个条款。

(2) 落实"放管服"改革要求进行的修改。一是强化安全管理,在提交的申请经营国际船舶运输业务的材料中增加国际船舶保安证书、安全管理证书、安全运营与防污染能力符合证明等材料;二是简化相关申请材料;三是针对国内企业经营国际船舶代理业务的许可已取消;四是增加执行运价报备制度的相关要求;五是为无船承运业务经营者增加了保函、责任保险等财务责任保证方式。修改内容涉及 12 个条款。

(3) 落实"营改增"税费改革及发票和统计制度改革方面,主要删除了不再使用国际海运业专用发票,已被国家统计局废止的统计报表。同时补充了报送相关统计信息的原则性要求。修改内容涉及 5 个条款。

(4) 在与《港口法》及配套规章衔接方面,删除了国际海运货物仓储、国际海运集装箱站和堆场业务有关内容。共涉及 9 个条款。

(5) 其他完善性修改内容,主要对部分条款的表述进行修改。如结合交通运输部授权上海航运交易所在其网站发布相关经营者名单及提单样本的实际,将"对外贸易经济合作部"修改为"商务部"等。共涉及 12 个条款。

3. 法规综述

《修正案》作为对《实施细则》这一行政法规的修改,为深入推进"先照后证"改革工作提供了便利,这项改革在航运领域主要涉及国际船舶运输业务和国际船舶管理两项业务。《修正案》的最大亮点是:获许从事国际船舶运输流程三步变两步。根据行业特点,切实做到简政放权,吸引资金流入市场,有利于激发航运市场活力。

除了上述改革,《修正案》进一步厘清了监管边界,国际海运及其辅助业务经营人在经营期间可以自查相关证书是否合法有效的程序便利赋予了企业更大的自主空间。2008 年以来航运低潮持续弥漫,不少从事无船承运业务的企业的流动资金受到影响。为了减轻企业负担,交通运输部于 2010 年、2013 年试行了保证金责任险和保证金保函制度,为无船承运人提供了多种可供选择的财务责任保证方式,在保障托运人利益的同时,有效缓解了无船承运人的资金压力。《修正案》的出台以部令的形式将相关制度固化下来,能够有效激发市场活力、促进行业发展,使减负举措更有力。

(四) 交通运输部关于推进特定航线江海直达运输发展的意见

交通运输部水运局于 2017 年 4 月 18 日发布《交通运输部关于推进特定航线江海直达运输发展的意见》(以下简称《意见》)。

1. 出台背景

推进江海直达运输发展,是深化交通运输供给侧结构性改革的重要内容,对于提升长江黄金水道功能和构建现代综合交通运输体系具有重要作用。为落实长江经济带发展规划纲要,认真落实依托黄金水道推动长江经济带发展决策部署,以推进交通运输供给侧结构性改革为主线,坚持深化改革、创新发展;依法依规、安全发展;示范引领、市场推动的总体原则,努力推进江海直达运输安全、高效和绿色发展,加快水运提质增效升级,更好地服务长江经济带发展,水运局出台了《意见》。

2. 主要内容

《意见》围绕以下主要任务和保障措施两个方面展开:

1) 主要任务

(1) 制定完善江海直达船舶法规规范:根据特定海域、特定航线的实际情况,制定实施长江经济带特定航线江海直达船舶法定检验暂行规则及建造规范。

（2）加强江海直达船型系列研发应用：鼓励航运企业与科研院校和设计单位等开展联合攻关，优先推进长江干线至宁波舟山港和长江干线至上海港洋山港区江海直达集装箱船等船型研发及应用。

（3）加强港口航道等基础设施建设：加强长三角地区主要港口集疏运体系建设，江海直达运输配套码头、锚地等设施以及桥梁改造的前期工作。

（4）积极培育江海直达运输市场：优先发展长江干线及长三角地区干散货、集装箱江海直达运输，发挥大型航运企业带动作用，加强运输上下游产业链资源整合。

（5）促进江海直达运输安全绿色发展：强化船舶运输法规制度的执行，严格落实企业安全主体责任。

（6）优化江海直达运输管理：研究制定江海直达船舶船员配备标准，制定江海直达船舶安全管理规定。

（7）提升江海直达运输应急能力：推进实施《国家水上交通安全监管和救助系统布局规划》，优化救助保障和应急处置布局。

2）保障措施

一是加强组织领导，各相关省级交通运输主管部门和海事管理机构要高度重视江海直达运输工作，加强领导，明确分工，强化协调。

二是加大政策扶持，优先支持江海直达运输相关港口集疏运项目建设，鼓励各地出台发展江海直达运输的优惠政策。

三是强化科技信息服务，相关科研部门要加强对江海直达运输的技术支持与指导，加强市场分析，及时发布信息，引导市场有序发展。

3. 法规综述

随着以上海为龙头的长江流域经济快速发展，上海港作为一个兼具经济腹地型与航运中枢特征的港口城市，通过长江这一黄金水道与长江流域的6省2市实现了有效沟通。长江流域集装箱货运量和疏运能力以及战略地位为加快长江腹地经济发展提供了有利条件。江海直达运输发展受航道、政策以及其他运输方式分流制约的影响而发展缓慢，《意见》的出台一定程度上加快长江流域江海直达集装箱运输的发展。

《意见》要求根据航行内河和特定海域的特点，突破现行制度体系，科学制定江海直达船舶法规制度优化运输组织，促进船舶、航道、港口协调发展。江海直达运输中需要强化法规制度的引领和规制作用，力求实现到2020年，建立健全长江经济带江海直达运输法规规范和管理制度，基本形成长江和长三角地区至宁波舟山港和上海港洋山港区江海直达运输系统,水路集疏运比重进一步提升,江海直达运输经济社会效益得到显现。到2030年,建成安全、高效、绿色江海直达运输体系,江海直达运输的经济社会效益显著提升,为长江经济带发展提供有力支撑。

(五)《中华人民共和国海上海事行政处罚规定》

《交通运输部关于修改〈中华人民共和国海上海事行政处罚规定〉的决定》已于2017年5月17日经第8次部务会议通过,并于2017年12月27日公布。

1. 修订背景

交通运输部按照简政放权的要求,取消和下放了一批行政许可,海事法律法规体系也发生了重大变化,本次修改是在2015年版《海事行政处罚规定》(以下简称《规定》)的基础上作出的修订。

2. 主要内容

(1)将16条第三款的规定由"国内航行船舶进出港口未按照规定办理进出港签证,国际航行船舶未按照规定办理进出口岸手续"变更为"国内航行船舶进出港口未按照规定向海事管理机构报告船舶的航次计划、适航状态、船员配备和载货载客等情况,国际航行船舶未按照规定办理进出口岸手续",由此可见,船舶进出港口签证制度正式取消,并以法律的形式规定,《船舶签证簿》和船舶IC卡亦同步取消,内河航行船舶及进入内河航行海船施行新的进出港报告制,船舶进出港更加便利,船舶运营亦明显降低,惠及船舶30余万艘。

(2)删除了原2015年版的第21条中关于违反征收港务费行为的处罚规定,第38、39条中的有关机动船舶违法违规排放污染气体的处罚规定。交通运输部公布,我国于2016年1月起在珠三角、长三角、环渤海(京津冀)水域设立船舶排放控制区,控制船舶硫氧化物、氮氧化物和颗粒物排放,为全面控制船舶大气污染奠定基础。在排放控制区作业的船舶可采取连接岸电、使用清洁能源、尾气后处理等与排放控制要求等效的替代措施。

3. 法规综述

此次修订适应了海事行政审批制度的发展形势,在行政许可的修改方面保证新《规定》的适宜性。同时对上位法发生变化的规定作出修改并逐条比对与其他规章的协调性,避免了出现冲突和法律竞合。

适时取消了船舶进出港签证制度,海事管理机构将通过船舶进出港报告服务网查看船舶进出港报告情况,必要时结合GPS,AIS,CCTV等多种手段核实船舶航行动态和在船人员信息,与相关单位建立信息共享和联合检查机制,加大船舶安全监督力度,保障水上交通安全形势稳定。我国在控制船舶排放污染气体方面采取《国际防止船舶造成污染公约》框架下且被国际公认的船舶大气污染控制措施，船舶减排措施方面采取较为严格的规定，船舶污染防治取得显著进步。

(六)《中华人民共和国水污染防治法》

《全国人民代表大会常务委员会关于修改〈中华人民共和国水污染防治法〉的决定》已由第十二届全国人民代表大会常务委员会第二十八次会议于 2017 年 6 月 27 日通过并公布。

1. 修订背景

当前我国水环境质量仍不容乐观，水污染防治任务艰巨。根据国务院印发的《水污染防治行动计划》确立的一系列新制度新措施，有必要修改水污染防治法，将《水污染防治行动计划》确立的各项制度措施规范化、法治化。

2. 主要内容

(1) 强化地方政府责任。各级政府，特别是县级以上地方政府，要对本行政区域的水环境质量承担实实在在的责任。

(2) 加强流域水污染联合防治与生态保护。规定国务院环境保护主管部门应当会同有关部门和省级政府，建立重要江河、湖泊的流域水环境保护联动协调机制，加强水污染联合防治并开展定期监测。

(3) 完善水污染防治监督管理制度。一是做好排污许可与总量控制、达标排放等制度的衔接，规定排污许可证应当明确水污染物种类、浓度、总量和排放去向等要求。二是完善环境监测制度，明确排污单位的自行监测义务。三是建立有毒有害水污染物名录制度，加强风险管理。

(4) 强化重点领域水污染防治措施。在工业废水管理，地下水、农业和农村水和船舶的污染防治等方面均作出具体规定。

(5) 强化饮用水安全保障制度。为确保城乡居民饮用水安全，在立法宗旨中明确增加"保障饮用水安全"的规定，并专门增设"饮用水水源和其他特殊水体保护"一章，进一步完善饮用水水源保护区的管理制度。

(6) 严格法律责任。根据《环境保护法》的精神，对无证或者不按证、超标、超总量排放水污染物等违法行为，规定严格的法律责任，并与《环境保护法》规定的按日连续处罚和拘留措施进行衔接。

根据《环境保护法》和行政审批制度改革要求，删除排污申报登记、船舶作业审批等有关规定。

3. 法规综述

这一次对《水污染防治法》的修订是根据水资源匮乏的实际情况进行的，更有利于保护水资源：针对水资源现状做了相应的调整，加大了对水资源的保障力度，弥补原先法律保障的不足之处，从而使《水污染防治法》的实施更加全面。

（七）《港口收费计费办法》

《交通运输部、国家发展改革委关于印发〈港口收费计费办法〉的通知》于2017年7月12日发布，新《港口收费计费办法》（以下简称《办法》）将于从2017年9月15日起实施，有效期是5年。

1. 修订背景

按照党中央关于全面深化改革的总体部署，为贯彻落实国务院关于进一步清理规范涉企经营服务性收费、减轻企业负担的要求，交通运输部会同国家发展改革委遵循市场化原则，以进一步减少政府定价项目、优化计费方式为主要任务，以拖船收费改革为重点，继续深化港口价格形成机制改革，进一步促进物流降本增效。

2. 主要内容

（1）改革拖船费计费方式。将拖船费由按拖船马力和使用时间计收调整为按被拖船舶的大小和类型计收，统一制定拖船费艘次单价。

（2）优化船舶引航收费结构。进一步优化引航收费结构。各引航机构要积极推进"阳光引航"，进一步提升引航服务水平。明确引航服务以外引领海上移动式平台在我国水域航行的技术服务费实行市场调节价，由引领服务单位与委托方协商确定具体收费标准。

（3）进一步减少政府定价收费项目。将国内客运和旅游船舶港口作业费纳入港口作业包干费范围，该费用由国内客运企业向港口经营人支付，不再直接向旅客收取。

（4）理货服务费实行市场调节价。明确理货服务费实行市场调节价，并要求各省级交通运输主管部门加快引入竞争机制，促进理货平稳、有序发展，不断激发市场活力，加强市场监管和行业自律。

（5）不再对国际航线船舶多点挂靠停泊费优惠和免费堆存保管期统一规定。政策背景发生重大变化，从促进公平竞争的角度，政府不宜过多干预市场，考虑停泊费为政府指导价上限管理，堆存保管费为市场调节价，是否优惠和给予多少优惠，应由企业协商，无需政府统一规定。

3. 法规综述

此次《办法》修订后，又减少1项政府定价收费项目，进一步减轻企业负担，预计港口企业每年可再减轻航运企业负担2亿元，市场化、规范化的港口收费体系进一步完善。《办法》的落实有利于进一步规范港口收费行为。各级价格主管部门监督收费政策实施,督促指导港口经营人、引航机构落实港口收费各项规定,遵循公平、合法和诚实信用的原则提供服务。

(八)《港口危险货物安全管理规定》

新修订的《港口危险货物安全管理规定》(以下简称《规定》)于2017年8月29日经交通运输部第14次部务会议通过,并于2017年9月4日予以公布。

1. 修订背景

随着港口的快速发展,港口危险货物的吞吐量和仓储量越来越大,品种越来越多,安全管理压力日益加大。经全面梳理危险品管理法规,认真查找和分析安全管理、制度建设中存在的薄弱环节和突出问题,发现在安全管理制度、企业主体责任落实等方面还有不够完善的地方。

2. 主要内容

(1)完善安全管理职责体系。进一步明确各级交通运输(港口)管理部门的职责,强化省级交通运输主管部门对下级部门的指导督促。

(2)调整优化部分许可管理权限。一是将危险货物港口建设项目的安全条件审查权限划分标准由立项层级调整为危险程度。二是由所在地港口行政管理部门统一实施危险货物港口经营资质管理和监督检查。

(3)落实企业安全生产主体责任。增加了危险货物港口经营人应当健全安全生产组织机构,提取和使用安全生产经费,加强从业人员安全生产教育培训等方面的内容,强化了装卸管理人员取得从业资格、配备专职安全生产管理人员的有关要求,明确了危险货物港口经营人应当开展安全生产风险辨识、评估,针对不同风险,制定具体的管控措施,落实管控责任。

(4)建立健全安全管理制度。新增了信息化管理制度、重点环节管理制度和信用管理制度这三个方面的管理制度。

(5)强化对企业违法行为的行政强制和处罚。补充完善了港口行政管理部门可以依法采取停止供电措施强制危险货物港口经营人履行决定,同时对6种其他情形在规章权限内设定了处罚条款。

3. 法规综述

此次《规定》的修订在许多方面都作出了完善,为各地更好地做好港口危险货物安全管理打下坚实的基础。在安全生产方面根据2014年新修订的《安全生产法》作出调整。在解决了各地在近几年港口危险货物安全管理中发现的一些新问题的同时,也融合了不少新的管理经验。这是加快完善港口危险货物安全监管体制和安全生产责任体系的重要环节,有利于双重预防控制和联合监管机制的健全。

(九)《水路运输市场信用信息管理办法(试行)》

2017年9月6日,交通运输部制定印发了《水路运输市场信用信息管理办法(试行)》(交办水〔2017〕128号,以下简称《办法》)。

1. 出台背景

社会信用体系是经济社会发展的重要基础。党中央、国务院高度重视社会信用体系建设,2015年5月,交通运输部发布《关于加强交通运输行业信用体系建设的若干意见》(交政研发〔2015〕75号),提出了完善信用制度标准体系等5个方面主要任务,切实加强交通运输行业信用体系建设,推动交通运输科学发展。目前,我国水路运输领域信用体系建设尚属于起步阶段,为加强水路运输市场信用体系建设,借鉴相关行业信用信息管理的成功经验和做法,交通运输部制定出台了《办法》。

2. 主要内容

《办法》共包括五个章节、二十一条具体内容和两个附表,明确了水路运输市场信用信息管理的目的依据、适用范围和管理原则,规定了相关管理部门、行业协会、从业单位及从业人员相应的权利、责任和义务,对水路运输市场信用信息归集、公开、应用提出了规范要求,建立了信用信息管理过程中的异议处理和权益保护机制,提出了从业单位和从业人员违法违规失信行为主要内容。

(1) 关于部省职责分工。在职责分工方面,水路运输市场信用信息管理实行统一管理、分级负责,按照权责清晰、有序高效的原则,对部省定位、权限和责任进行明确界定。部省两级信用信息系统实现互联。

(2) 关于信息归集范围和方式。根据《政府信息公开条例》等规定,依法明确信用信息归集范围主要包括交通运输管理部门履职过程中生成的信用信息。为保证信息归集的及时准确,坚持源头归集和属地管理,基本信息、良好行为信息和失信行为信息分别由相应层级的交通运输管理部门、行业协会等组织归集。

(3) 关于失信行为的管理。为加强对失信行为的管理,《办法》以列表形式明确从业单位和从业人员的违法违规失信行为主要内容。建立严重失信名单管理制度,提出严重失信行为的界定标准,明确严重失信名单的列入、更新和退出规则、对外发布机制和相关惩戒措施。

(4) 关于信用信息应用。根据《国务院关于建立完善守信联合激励和失信联合惩戒制度加快推进社会诚信建设的指导意见》等文件精神,结合行业实际,从日常监管、财政资金补贴、评优评先等方面对良好行为和失信行为实施信用奖惩。

3. 法规综述

水路运输在我国综合运输体系中占有重要地位,承担了我国90%以上的外贸货物运输量。水路运输行业点多、面广、线长,经营门类较多,且经营主体的规模差别较大。该《办法》的出台指明了今后一段时间我国水路运输市场信用信息管理方向,明确了管理任务。层层落实的方式,负责信息的录入和归集工作,明确职责分工,建立"部门参与,点面结合"的长效工作机制,有序推进水路运输信用信息管理工作。这将有力提升我国水路运输市场信用信息管理水平,充分发挥信用管理在事中事后监管和维护市场秩序中的作用,进一步支撑社会信用体系建设。

(十) 最高人民法院《关于进一步保护和规范当事人依法行使行政诉权的若干意见》

2017年8月31日,最高人民法院印发《关于进一步保护和规范当事人依法行使行政诉权的若干意见》(以下简称《意见》)。

1. 出台背景

新《行政诉讼法》实施和立案登记制改革取得重大成效,但在新法实施过程中,出现两种不良倾向:一是随着行政案件的大幅增长和办案压力的不断加大,少数法院限制当事人诉权的情况有所出现;二是个别当事人曲解立案登记制的立法含义,滥用诉权、恶意诉讼,浪费司法资源和行政成本。《意见》指出,各级人民法院要高度重视诉权保护,对于依法应当受理的行政案件,一律登记立案,做到有案必立、有诉必理。严禁在法律规定之外,以案件疑难复杂、部门利益权衡、影响年底结案等为由,不接收诉状或者接收诉状后不出具书面凭证;对于需要当事人补充起诉材料的,各级法院应当一次性全面告知当事人需要补正的内容、补充的材料及补正期限等,并做好诉讼引导和法律释明。

2. 主要内容

《意见》主要包括强化诉权保护意识和引导当事人依法行使诉权两大方面,主要包括:

(1) 在涉及强化群众保护诉权意识方面,《意见》要求各级人民法院要以实质化解行政争议为目标,切实转变观念,严格贯彻新《行政诉讼法》的规定;不断提高公民、法人和其他组织依法行使诉权的意识,要坚决清理限制当事人诉权的"土政策",避免在立案环节进行过度审查,违法将当事人提起诉讼的依据是否充分、事实是否清楚、证据是否确凿、法律关系是否明确等作为立案条件。人民法院要正确确定案件管辖权,应当进行认真审查可能超过起诉期限的案件。各级法院充分利用"大数据""互联网+""人工智能"等现代技术,继续推进诉讼服务大厅、诉讼服务网络、12368热线、智能服务平台等建设,不断创新工作理念,完善服务举措。要依法保障经济困难和诉讼实施能力较差的当事人的诉权。针对司法机关内部人员责任追究制度,及时制止和纠正违法违规行为。

(2) 各级人民法院要正确引导当事人依法行使诉权,以"一事不再理"为原则,并应当向当事人说明不予立案的理由,做好释明工作,避免给当事人造成不必要的诉累。人民法院要正确理解立案登记制的精神实质,在防止过度审查的同时,也要注意坚持必要审查。人民法院要准确把握新《行政诉讼法》第二十五条第一款规定的"利害关系"的法律内涵,依法审查行政机关的行政行为是否确与当事人权利义务的增减得失密切相关。在救济当事人权利时,上级行政机关可以监督和纠正下级行政机关的行政行为,或者针对行政机关的行政行为提起诉讼。当事人与其投诉、举报、检举或者反映问题等事项之间是否具有利害关系应当由法院认真审查。并且要正确区分当事人请求保护合法权益和进行信访之间的区别,防止将当事人请求行政机关履行法定职责当作信访行为对待。要依法制止滥用诉权、恶意诉讼等行为,要充分尊重和保护公民、法人或者其他组织的知情权,依法及时审理当事人提起的涉及申请政府信息公开的案件,在认定滥用诉权、恶意诉讼的情形时,应当从严掌握标准,要从当事人提起诉讼的数量、周期、目的以及是否具有正当利益等角度,审查其是否具有滥用诉权、恶意诉讼的主观故意。

3. 法规综述

诉讼权利是公民、法人和其他组织的基本权利。"有权利必有救济"是法治时代的必然要求。基于"民告官"的制度架构,加之"官本位"观念的长期影响,行政审判容易受到各方面的干扰。过去一些地方出台限制受理行政案件的"土政策""潜规则",将老百姓的诉求拒之门外。全面推行立案登记制就是为了解决"立案难"的痼疾。立案登记制施行后,行政诉讼"立案难"问题基本得以解决。因此,为巩固新法实施和改革成果,《意见》的出台,一方面对坚持保护诉权、坚定不移推行立案登记制有所助益;另一方面针对依法规制滥用诉权、恶意诉讼问题,防止当事人行使诉权偏离新行政诉讼法的规定,并且与立案登记制改革的精神实质十分契合。

(十一)《中华人民共和国海关法》(2017 修正)

《中华人民共和国海关法》(2017 修正)(以下简称《海关法》)已于 2017 年 11 月 4 日经第十二届全国人民代表大会常务委员会第三十次会议通过。

1. 出台背景

"一带一路"建设的优先领域是降低自由流动成本和解决影响互联互通的制度、标准,而海关治理所涉及的对外贸易关税税率、通关监管流程和要求以及保障准入安全等内容则成为当前海关管理进程中的关键环节。为维护国家的主权和利益,加强海关监督管理,促进对外经济贸易和科技文化交往,保障社会主义现代化建设,为进一步推进简政放权、放管结合、优化服务改革,更大程度上激发市场、社会的创新创造活力,立足于国家经贸宏观调控和"一带一路"的大局,《海关法》(2017版)经四次修正并通过。

2. 主要内容

1) 简化程序

《海关法》第三十三条第三款"加工贸易保税进口料件或者制成品内销的,海关对保税的进口料件依法征税;属于国家对进口有限制性规定的,还应当向海关提交进口许可证件"。该条规定商务部、海关总署于2016年联合发布的第45号公告中正式取消了加工贸易业务审批的规定有了更充分的法律依据,对不同职能部门之间相关业务的操作流程加以统一,便于企业顺利开展相关业务。同时取消了保税加工料件或成品转内销的申请原因,这也符合目前加工贸易企业的实际需求。减轻审批压力,提高企业效率,在一定程度上拉动了内需。

2) 提高效率

海关总署于2017年12月8日公布了新版的《中华人民共和国暂时进出境货物管理办法》(海关总署令第233号),根据《海关法》第四次修订作出了相应调整,取消了暂时进出境货物的部分行政许可事项,将其修改为事前选择性办理确认申请,使程序相对简化,同时也缩短办理时间,为企业提供了充分的选择余地和准备时间。

3. 法规综述

随着我国对外经济贸易关系的不断发展扩大,科技文化国际交流的日益增加,海关因其联结国际和国内两个市场的职能作用,是"一带一路"倡议的重要实施机构。为了维护国家主权和利益,海关加强监督管理是非常必要的,响应社会的发展变化,简政放权、转变职能、深化行政审批制度改革也是非常重要的。建立现代海关制度成为现实的需要,新的《海关法》成为建立现代海关制度的法律依据和有力保障。在立法层面,中央政府不断致力于简政放权的改革,促进企业的健康发展,《海关法》充分体现了简化手续、提高效率的政策导向,也使海关管理的行政措施得到贯彻推进。

(十二)《中华人民共和国船舶吨税法》

《中华人民共和国船舶吨税法》(以下简称《船舶吨税法》)已于2017年12月27日经第十二届全国人民代表大会常务委员会第三十一次会议通过,自2018年7月1日起施行。

1. 出台背景

响应"一带一路"建设号召,中国作为海洋大国更要加强海洋综合管理、坚决维护国家海洋权益,妥善处理海上纠纷,积极拓展双边和多边海洋合作,向海洋强国的目标迈进。李克强在政府报告中说道：要把"一带一路"建设与区域开发开放结合起来,加强新亚欧大陆桥、陆海口岸支点建设。《船舶吨税法》的前身是2011年12月5日国务院公布的《中华人民共和国船舶吨税暂行条例》,为了响应十八届三中全会"落实税收法定原则"及党的十九大"深化税收制度改革",经反复研究修改制定《船舶吨税法》。《船舶吨税法》是根据船舶吨税条例规范未作大调整平移上升为法律的。2018年7月1日起《船舶吨税法》实施后《中华人民共和国船舶吨税暂行条例》同时废止。

2. 主要内容

1) 征税对象

《船舶吨税法》第一条即规定"自中华人民共和国境外港口进入境内港口的船舶,应当依照本法缴纳船舶吨税"。该条规定明确依照《船舶吨税法》的征税对象包括所有由我国境外港口进入境内港口的船舶。

2) 设置优惠税率和普通税率

根据《船舶吨税法》第三条规定"中华人民共和国籍的应税船舶,船籍国（地区）与中华人民共和国签订含有相互给予船舶税费最惠国待遇条款的条约或者协定的应税船舶,适用优惠税率。其他应税船舶,适用普通税率"。该规定明确指出与我国签订相互给予船舶税费最惠国待遇条款的条约或者协定的国家经过我国境内港口需要依法交税的船舶可以享受优惠的税率,这一规定一定程度上促进我国在海洋上的多边和双边合作。

3) 税目税率

吨税税目按船舶净吨位划分为不超过2 000净吨、2 000～1万净吨、1万～5万净吨、超过5万净吨四个档次,维持了原有的税目税率,吨税税率根据船舶净吨位和吨税执照期限长短分别设置。在附表中清晰地划分了船舶吨税税目税率表,并且根据《船舶吨税法》第四条规定明确说明吨税按照船舶净吨位和吨税执照期限征收,吨税执照的期限可以在每次申报纳税时选择。

4) 免征税情形

在《船舶吨税法》第九条中列出包括应纳税额在人民币五十元以下、捕捞养殖渔船、警用渔船等十项内容是免征吨税的船舶。对征税单位、吨税申报纳税程序、纳税义务发生时间、纳税期限等也做了规定。

3. 法规综述

为了落实税收法定原则、深化税收制度改革,全国人大常委会将船舶吨税法安排在10月初次审议并且在《国务院2017年立法工作计划》中将其列为全面深化改革急需的项目。我国目前是国际化的航运大国,但是走向航运强国的路程还是很艰辛的,船舶吨税是海关代表国家交通管理部门在设关口岸对进出中国国境的船舶征收的用于航道设施建设的一种使用税,随着航运业日新月异的发展,把船舶吨税的基本制度用法律确定下来对于我国加强海洋管理并且维护海洋权益有着极其重要的影响。

(十三) 中华人民共和国海洋环境保护法

《中华人民共和国海洋环境保护法》根据 2017 年 11 月 4 日第十二届全国人民代表大会常务委员会第三十次会议《关于修改〈中华人民共和国会计法〉等十一部法律的决定》进行修订,由全国人大常委会通过中华人民共和国主席令第 81 号于 2017 年 11 月 4 日发布,自 2017 年 11 月 5 日起实施。

1. 出台背景

《中华人民共和国海洋环境保护法》自 1982 年 8 月 23 日第五届全国人民代表大会常务委员会第二十四次会议通过以来,根据 2013 年 12 月 28 日第十二届全国人民代表大会常务委员会第六次会议《关于修改〈中华人民共和国海洋环境保护法〉等七部法律的决定》第一次修正;根据 2016 年 11 月 7 日第十二届全国人民代表大会常务委员会第二十四次会议《关于修改〈中华人民共和国海洋环境保护法〉的决定》第二次修正;此次修改是根据 2017 年 11 月 4 日第十二届全国人民代表大会常务委员会第三十次会议《关于修改〈中华人民共和国会计法〉等十一部法律的决定》进行的第三次修改。

2. 主要内容

此次修改对海洋环境保护的重点放在对排污标准的严格规范。具体条款的修改如下:

(1) 将第三十条第一款修改为:"入海排污口位置的选择,应当根据海洋功能区划、海水动力条件和有关规定,经科学论证后,报设区的市级以上人民政府环境保护行政主管部门备案。"

第二款修改为:"环境保护行政主管部门应当在完成备案后十五个工作日内将入海排污口设置情况通报海洋、海事、渔业行政主管部门和军队环境保护部门。"

这一条的修改涉及入海排污口未知的选择。入海排污口位置是否合理,直接关系到对海洋环境影响的程度。因此,选择入海排污口位置应当根据海洋功能区划、海水动力条件和有关规定,经科学论证后,需报设区的市级以上人民政府环境保护行政主管部门备案,将原条款中的"报主管部门审查批准"改为"报主管部门备案"放宽了对排污口设置的监管。但同时在第二款的修改中增加"备案后十五个工作日内将情况通报有关主管部门",实际是更明确地规范了设置入海排污口之前,必须征求海洋、海事、渔业行政主管部门和军队环境保护部门的意见。

(2)第七十七条增加一款,作为第二款:"海洋、海事、渔业行政主管部门和军队环境保护部门发现入海排污口设置违反本法第三十条第一款、第三款规定的,应当通报环境保护行政主管部门依照前款规定予以处罚。"

此条的修改在第三十条修改的基础上增加了违反相应法则后的处罚规范。明确在违反入海排污口设置的备案制度以及在海洋自然保护区、重要渔业水域、海滨风景名胜区和其他需要特别保护的区域,不得新建排污口的规定的情况下将受到环境保护行政主管部门的相应处罚。这是对我国海洋环境以及除海洋自然保护区、重要渔业水域和海滨风景名胜区以外,具有环境保护上的特殊价值,而划出一定范围加以特别保护的区域的最大限度地保护。

3. 法规综述

海洋环境保护法是调整人们在利用海洋环境、保护海洋环境的活动中所发生的社会关系的法律规范,是进行海洋环境保护的基本依据。我国早在20世纪70年代就开展了海洋环境保护工作。1983年实施的《中华人民共和国海洋环境保护法》标志着我国海洋环境保护工作开始步入法制的轨道,它的出台对于促进沿海经济建设,推进海洋环境保护事业的发展起到积极的作用。但是,随着我国改革开放的不断深入,沿海经济的快速发展,以及保护海洋环境实践的发展变化,法本身的不适应性和实施过程中暴露出的问题愈加明显。从我国海洋环境的整体状况看,由于城市生活污水和工农业废水大量排海,赤潮、溢油、病毒以及养殖污染等海洋环境灾害发生频率持续增加,加上其他严重破坏海洋环境的活动,使得我国海洋环境污染损害不断加剧,海洋资源基础条件破坏严重,部分海域生态系统退化失衡,近海海域污染程度日趋严重,污染区域不断向外扩展,污染范围日趋扩大。为了保护和改善海洋环境,保护海洋资源,维护生态平衡,促进经济和社会的可持续发展,修订《海洋环境保护法》是十分必要的。此次的修改对于保护和改善海洋环境以及防治由于人类海洋活动的增加,向海洋中排放大量的物质和能量,使海洋环境受到不同程度的污染损害都具有重要影响。

(十四)《中华人民共和国港口法》(2017修正)

《中华人民共和国港口法》根据2017年11月4日第十二届全国人民代表大会常务委员会第三十次会议《关于修改〈中华人民共和国会计法〉等十一部法律的决定》进行修订,由全国人大常委会通过中华人民共和国主席令第81号于2017年11月4日发布,自2017年11月5日起实施。

1. 出台背景

《中华人民共和国港口法》自2003年6月28日第十届全国人民代表大会常务委员会第三次会议通过以来,根据2015年4月24日第十二届全国人民代表大会常务委员会第十四次会议《关于修改〈中华人民共和国港口法〉等七部法律的决定》第一次修正;此次修改是根据2017年11月4日第十二届全国人民代表大会常务委员会第三十次会议《关于修改〈中华人民共和国会计法〉等十一部法律的决定》进行的第二次修改。

2. 主要内容

《中华人民共和国港口法》(以下简称《港口法》)作出以下修改:

(1) 将第十七条中的"经依法办理有关手续,并经港口行政管理部门批准后,方可建设"修改为"经依法办理有关手续后,方可建设"。

(2) 将第四十六条修改为:"在港口建设的危险货物作业场所、实施卫生除害处理的专用场所与人口密集区或者港口客运设施的距离不符合国务院有关部门的规定的,由港口行政管理部门责令停止建设或者使用,限期改正,可以处五万元以下罚款。"

(3) 删去第五十六条第一项中的"违法批准建设港口危险货物作业场所或者实施卫生除害处理的专用场所"。

(4) 主要是针对港口行政管理部门在监管过程中认定合法的执法区域和执法事项,切实加强港口管理,达到立法目的具有重要法律意义。

3. 法规综述

《港口法》在加强港口管理、维护港口安全与经营秩序、促进港口建设发展等方面发挥了重要作用,但随着港口一体化改革等发展形势的变化,原先的一些条款需要修订:自2004年《港口法》颁布实行以来,一些条款已经不适应新时代港口发展的需求。现行的《港口法》对于港区、港口设施、港口工程项目的法律定义尚未十分明确,在港口布局的编制和审批上也要作出明确的规定。此次的修改一定程度上规范了港口行政管理部门的一部分执法事项,但上述提到的现行《港口法》存在的问题仍未得到彻底的解决:

《港口法》出台时,侧重于解决政企分开、港口下放属地管理问题,对省级交通运输主管部门在行业管理上的法律地位及职权不明确,未体现交通运输行业分级管理,造成上下协调不畅。随着港口一体化改革试点工作的开展,浙江、江苏等省级层面整合而成的港口集团相继组建,其他多个省份也在积极筹备。根据《港口法》现有的设定,省级港口行政管理部门的职权有限,难以与当前省级港口管理部门担负的任务相匹配,港口的管理职责层级不明。同时,《港口法》缺少综合协同的管理体系,不适应港口协同管理的要求。港口管理涉及多个部门和机构。但作为港口法规体系中的基本法,《港口法》仅明确了交通运输主管部门对港口管理的职责,对其他相关监管部门的职责未予明确,这就会造成港口监管工作难以全面开展。另外,港口岸线资源的稀缺所引发的岸线资源保护的问题需要加强对环境的保护,并结合《环境保护法》再进行修改。

(十五) 中华人民共和国船员条例(2017 修正)

《中华人民共和国船员条例》根据 2017 年 3 月 1 日《国务院关于修改和废止部分行政法规的决定》进行修订,由总理李克强通过中华人民共和国国务院令第 676 号于 2017 年 3 月 1 日发布,自发布之日起开始施行。

1. 出台背景

《中华人民共和国船员条例》自 2007 年 4 月 14 日中华人民共和国国务院令第 494 号公布。根据 2013 年 7 月 18 日《国务院关于废止和修改部分行政法规的决定》第一次修订;根据 2013 年 12 月 7 日《国务院关于修改部分行政法规的决定》第二次修订;根据 2014 年 7 月 29 日《国务院关于修改部分行政法规的决定》第三次修订,此次修改是根据 2017 年 3 月 1 日《国务院关于修改和废止部分行政法规的决定》的第四次修订。

2. 主要内容

将《中华人民共和国船员条例》第七十条修改为:"引航员的培训依照本条例有关船员培训的规定执行。引航员管理的具体办法由国务院交通主管部门制订。"主要就引航员培训的规定以及引航员的主管部门进行修改。

3. 法规综述

随着我国航运业的发展,船员对顺利完成运输任务,保障水上交通安全,防止船舶污染环境,促进国民经济发展和对外交往发挥着重要作用。船员工作比较艰苦、风险大,职业素质要求高。因此,许多国家都通过立法加强对船员的管理和保护船员的权益,国际海事组织和国际劳工组织也制定相应的公约。我国自 2007 年出台《船员条例》以来,从实质上实现了中国海事管理与现代国际海事管理理念的接轨,有效地规范了船员工作,为保障水上交通安全和防治船舶污染以及航运业的健康发展创造了积极的条件。但就船员的培训制度、就业环境、职业保障以及管理制度上的规定仍不够完备。就船员的培训制度而言,应当明确船员在上船前必须接受哪些专业培训、特殊培训以及适任培训,并且规定船员任职资格和培训许可等制度以便更好地发展船员队伍,提高船员的素质;船员权益的保护方面,现行条例中存在着对船员的职业保障不够完善,保障未能落到实处的问题。对此在《条例》

未来的修改中应当借鉴国际劳工组织和国际海事组织关于船员保护有关公约的规定在工资、保险以及工作环境中加以详细规定。现行条例的修改还远远跟不上航运业的发展和船员的现实需求,以上涉及的内容是未来《船员条例》修改中需要思考和改进的。更完善的《船员条例》才能使现有的船员认真完成本职工作,并吸引更多的年轻船员投身船员事业,从而推动船员事业的可持续发展,为航运业的稳定持续发展提供人才支撑。

(十六) 交通运输部办公厅关于印发《港口岸电布局方案》的通知

2017年7月24日,交通运输部印发《港口岸电布局方案》(以下简称《方案》),便于各级交通运输主管部门、港航管理机构和有关企业更好地理解相关内容,切实做好贯彻实施工作。

1. 出台背景

船舶靠港使用岸电,是减少船舶污染物排放的有效手段。我国自2010年首次采用高压岸电系统开始,靠港船舶使用岸电技术逐步在全国推开。"十二五"期,交通运输部先后出台《"十二五"水运节能减排总体推进实施方案》《关于港口节能减排工作的指导意见》,在岸电标准规范、试点示范、技术研发、资金扶持、宣传培训等方面开展大量工作,为岸电技术的推广应用奠定了良好基础。

2. 主要内容

《方案》包括总体要求、布局方案和保障措施三部分。总体要求明确《方案》编制的指导思想、基本原则、布局范围和布局目标。布局方案提出2020年全国主要港口和船舶排放控制区内港口的岸电泊位布局数量。保障措施包括科学组织实施、加大政策扶持、建立供售电机制和完善法规标准四个方面。几个主要问题说明如下:

1) 基本原则

按照法律法规和相关文件要求,结合当前港口岸电设施建设和船舶靠港使用岸电的现状、需求及发展前景,《方案》确定了"统筹协调、有效衔接""突出重点,分类推进""规模适度,科学布局"的原则,提出岸电布局要与现有相关环保规划和要求保持衔接,以重点区域港口和重点类型泊位为抓手推进岸电设施建设,港口岸电建设规模要与港口发展水平和区域污染防治要求相适应。

2) 布局范围

对新建港口,按照《大气污染防治法》要求,应当同步规划、设计和建设岸电设施。因此,《方案》只对已建港口进行布局。

关于纳入布局的港口范围。《方案》在《行动方案》基础上,按照突出重点的原则,结合排放控制区政策和区域大气污染防治要求,提出2020年前重点推动主要港口和排放控制区内港口的岸电设施建设,解决船舶污染排放较为集中和严重的港口靠港船舶使用岸电需求,减少重点区域港口的污染排放。主要港口和排放控制区港口共69个,按照2015年底的港口统计数据,布局范围内港口货物吞吐量占全国货物总吞吐量的75%,其中集装箱吞吐量约达全国集装箱吞吐量的90%。

关于纳入布局的泊位类型。《方案》在《行动方案》基础上,按照分类推进原则,除对适宜船舶靠港使用岸电的集装箱、邮轮和客滚三类专业化泊位进行布局外,为适应近年来长江上大型旅游船(大都在3 000吨级以上)和全国大型散货专业化码头快速发展的需要,充分考虑大型旅游船和散货船靠港使用岸电的适宜性、较好的推广基础和较大减排潜力,明确将3 000吨级以上客运和5万吨级以上干散货专业化泊位一并纳入岸电布局范围。

3) 布局目标

《方案》提出2020年实现全国沿海和内河主要港口以及船舶排放控制区内港口50%以上已建的集装箱、客滚、邮轮、3 000吨级以上客运和5万吨级以上干散货专业化泊位具备向船舶提供岸电的能力。此岸电覆盖率目标保持与《行动方案》的衔接,基本做到与2020年的港口发展水平和区域污染防治水平相适应。《方案》提出,对岸电需求较大、基础条件较好的港口,鼓励其加快岸电设施建设,争取实现100%的泊位岸电覆盖率,加大靠港船舶使用岸电的力度。

4) 布局方案

以主要港口和排放控制区内已建的5类专业化泊位的总数为基础,以实现总体覆盖率50%的布局目标为导向,考虑各港口的不同地理区位、泊位能力、吞吐量等多种因素,综合运用数学规划与筛选相结合的方法确定岸电布局方案:到2020年底前,在全国主要港口和排放控制区共布局493个具备向船舶供应岸电能力的专业化泊位,其中沿海366个,内河127个。经测算,《方案》实施后船舶靠港期间二氧化硫、氮氧化物和$PM_{2.5}$排放量预计每年可分别减少6.0万t、11.0万t和0.8万t,其中沿海港口分别减少5.3万t、9.1万t和0.7万t,内河港口分别减少0.7万t、1.9万t和0.1万t,减排效果显著。

3. 法规综述

近年来,国家生态文明战略和法律法规对靠港船舶使用岸电提出新的更高要求。2016年1月1日实施的《中华人民共和国大气污染防治法》规定:"新建码头应当规划、设计和建设岸基供电设施;已建成的码头应当逐步实施岸基供电设施改造。船舶靠港后应当优先使用岸电。"国务院《"十三五"生态环境保护规划》《"十三五"节能减排综合工作方案》和交通运输部《船舶与港口污染防治专项行动实施方案(2015—

2020年)》都对推动船舶靠港使用岸电提出明确要求。船舶排放控制区政策提出船舶可采取连接岸电等替代措施。《交通运输节能环保"十三五"发展规划》和《推进交通运输生态文明建设实施方案》明确要"制定港口岸电布局建设方案"。

《方案》是我国针对港口岸电设施建设的第一份顶层设计文件,其出台对推动我国港口岸电设施有序建设、引导船舶靠港使用岸电将起到积极作用,对促进水运供给侧结构性改革和绿色发展具有重要意义。

(十七) 中华人民共和国船舶安全监督规则

1. 出台背景

2016年11月7日,人大常委会通过对《海上交通安全法》的修改决定,取消海船进出港签证。2017年3月1日,国务院修改《内河交通安全管理条例》,取消内河船舶进出港签证。签证制度取消后,对船舶进出港的管理由事前审批调整为事中事后监管。为保证行政审批取消后管理不断不乱,海事管理机构需要一部新的法规对事中事后安全监管的制度予以细化完善。

2. 主要内容

①定义了船舶安全监督的适用范围、概念和行为。②规定了各相关方的责任和义务。③规定了船舶报告制度的具体要求。④运用了综合质量管理的理念。⑤完善了安全监督目标船舶选择标准。⑥明确和丰富了船舶安全监督的内容。⑦明确了船舶安全缺陷的处理和复查事宜。⑧突出了船舶安全责任的划分。⑨法律责任规定了违规行政处罚的法律依据。

新颁布的《船舶安全监督规则》具有以下几个特点:

一是及时与上位法进行衔接。《国务院关于修改和废止部分行政法规的决定》(国务院令676号),取消了船舶进出港签证,明确实施船舶进出港报告制度。新颁布的《船舶安全监督规则》进一步明确了船舶进出港报告的时机和方式。明确规定船舶应当在预计离港或者抵港4小时前向将要离泊或者抵达港口的海事管理机构报告进出港信息;航程不足4小时的,在驶离上一港口时报告。船舶在固定航线且单次航程不超过2小时的,可以每天至少报告一次进出港信息。船舶可以通过互联网、传真、短信等方式报告船舶进出港信息,并在船舶航海或航行日志内作相应的记载。

二是强化船舶安全主体责任。建立船舶开航前自查制度,明确船舶在离泊前应当对船舶安全技术状况和货物装载情况进行自查,填写《船舶开航前安全自查清单》并由船长签字确认,海事管理机构应将船舶自查情况作为执行船舶现场监督的重要内容。

三是实行船舶综合质量管理。明确建立船舶综合质量管理信息平台和船舶综合质量档案,对船舶的9大类信息进行收集、处理和评定,以便对不同船舶实施有针对性的监管措施,促进船舶、船员、船公司自觉遵守法律规定。

四是强化船舶安全监督。将船舶安全监督分为船舶现场监督和船舶安全检查,明确船舶现场监督和船舶安全检查的内容及船舶安全缺陷的处理,明确制定安全监督目标船舶选择标准,以便合理选择船舶实施船舶安全监督。

3. 法规综述

2014年1月1日东京备忘录组织在亚太地区实施港口国监督新检查机制,纳入全新的风险评估机制和检查策略,实现"基于数量"的检查机制到"基于风险"的检查机制的转变,对航运业发展影响巨大。为了满足新检查机制实施的需要,原《船舶安全检查规则》需要修订。新的《船舶安全监督规则》以便利运输、强化监管为宗旨,以实施船舶进出港报告制度为基础,以"保障水上人命、财产安全,防止船舶造成水域污染,规范船舶安全监督工作"为目标,以"依法、公正、诚信、便民"为原则,构建了新的船舶安全监督管理模式。随着安全生产法治化和依法治理全面推进,海事部门作为水上安全监管的主管机关,要严格履行法定职责,新形势下亟需制定规章对履职情况进行精准定位。

(十八)《中国(上海)自由贸易试验区航运法治建设公约》

2017年3月7日,中国(上海)自由贸易试验区商务委员会(航运办)举办《中国(上海)自由贸易试验区航运法治建设公约》(以下简称《公约》)签署仪式,来自航运各界的22家相关机构代表签署了公约。

1. 出台背景

随着航运领域不断扩大开放和制度创新,海事、航空纠纷的数量迅速增长,案件受理类型覆盖面明显扩大。在国际贸易和运输方式发生深刻变化的前提下,国际航运法律规则也在酝酿着新的变化和发展。鉴于此,签署《公约》推进航运法治环境建设从而促进上海国际航运中心软环境建设。

2. 主要内容

(1) 根据上海自贸区总体方案中关于"建设具有国际水准的投资贸易便利、监管高效便捷、法制环境规范的自由贸易试验区"的要求,积极参与和支持各项工作。

(2) 秉持独立、公正、共享的原则,公约成员应当牢固树立依法建设上海自贸区法制营商环境的意识,平等维护中外当事人的合法权益,共同提升上海自贸区航运服务的能级。

(3) 树立法律服务意识,公约成员应当为国内外航运机构、企业和组织在自贸区内的投资、经营等活动,提供包括但不限于海洋运输、船舶管理、内河航运、邮轮经营、港口服务、航空运输、仓储物流、航运融资、绿色航运、航运保险、新技术发展等内容的专业法律保障。

(4) 引领行业积极健康发展,公约成员应当在法治建设意见征询、合同标准研究和制定、行业法律风险预警、典型案例剖析、法律专业培训等方面作出积极贡献。

(5) 助推上海国际航运中心建设,公约成员应当一致努力,为航运资源高度集聚、航运服务功能健全、航运法制规范和完善发挥应尽的责任,确保"长江经济带""海运强国"等国家战略有序实施。

3. 法规综述

《公约》的制定是上海自贸区进一步深化改革的产物。随着航运领域不断扩大开放和制度创新,海事、航空纠纷的数量迅速增长,案件受理类型覆盖明显变广。据上海海事法院的统计数据,2016年其受理各类涉自贸区海事海商案件740多件,涉案标的额约8亿元。与此同时,国际贸易和运输方式也在发生深刻变化,新的国际航运法律规则正在形成中。为了更好地参与国际竞争,进一步加强航运法治环境建设,平等维护中外航运企业利益成为上海建设国际航运中心的重要任务。

(十九) 国务院关于扩大对外开放积极利用外资若干措施的通知

1. 出台背景

截至2016年底,我国累计吸引外资超过1.77万亿美元。2016年,在全球跨国投资总量有所下滑的背景下,我国吸引外资8 132.2亿元人民币,同比增长4.2%,特别是美国、欧盟28国对华实际投资大幅增长,同比分别增长52.6%和41.3%。外资在我国经济发展和深化改革进程中发挥积极作用,促进对外贸易、技术进步、产业升级和市场竞争。出台《关于扩大对外开放积极利用外资若干措施的通知》(以下简称《若干措施》)能进一步全面部署利用外资实现我国互利共赢开放战略。

2. 主要内容

一是进一步扩大对外开放。近年来,我国积极扩大开放领域,开放水平不断提高。但与高水平对外开放的目标相比,还需加快开放步伐、加大开放力度。《若干措施》明确提出,要以开放发展理念为指导,重点推进服务业、制造业、采矿业等领域放宽外资准入限制,积极吸引外商投资以及先进技术和管理经验《若干措施》同时提出,支持外资参与"中国制造2025"战略,促进外资深入融入制造业转型升级。构建开放的创新体系,国家科技计划项目向外资企业开放,支持外资企业加大研发投资、申报设立博士后科研工作站。拓展利用外资方式,支持外资以特许经营方式参与基础设施建设。

二是进一步创造公平竞争环境。外资企业和国有企业、民营企业一样,都是国民经济的重要组成部分。只要是在我国境内注册的企业,都要享受同等待遇。党中央、国务院明确部署,要加快形成企业公平竞争的现代市场体系,对内外资企业一视同仁、公平对待。为此,《若干措施》提出,外资政策必须进行公平竞争审查,事先公开征求意见,各地区各部门不得擅自增加对外资企业的限制。这就从制度上保证了政策的透明度、稳定性、可预期性以及执行上的一致性。《若干措施》要求,在业务牌照审核、标准制定、政府采购、融资渠道、注册登记等方面,对内外资企业实行统一标准,促进各类企业公平参与。

三是进一步加强吸引外资工作。《若干措施》提出,允许地方政府在法定权限范围内制定出台招商引资优惠政策,对就业、经济发展、技术创新贡献大的项目予以支持,降低企业投资和运营成本。这是给地方授权,希望各地更加积极主动开展工作,在发展中不断规范,在规范中实现更好发展。需要说明的是,这条措施不仅适用于外资,也适用于内资。《若干措施》提出,已有的外商投资产业、区域的鼓励政策保持不变,积极支持中西部、东北地区吸引外资,深化外商投资管理体制改革,提高投资便利化程度。

3. 法规综述

《若干措施》是当前和今后一段时期我国利用外资工作的指导性文件。主要政策导向:一是坚持开放发展,推动实施新一轮高水平对外开放,以开放促改革、促发展。二是致力于优化营商环境,进一步促进内外资企业公平竞争。三是促进引资引技引智相结合,增强对制造业外资的吸引力,构建开放的创新体系,提高利用外资质量和水平。四是建设统一的市场体系,加强和优化服务,鼓励外资企业深耕发展。五是加大改革力度,按照内外资一致原则,简化对外资的审批监管制度,提高投资便利化程度。

《若干措施》提出全面、系统的政策措施,不仅涉及外商投资准入前阶段,也涉及准入后企业经营阶段,不仅涉及中央层面的政策问题,也涉及地方政府的执行问题,可以说,充分反映了有关方面的关切。希望《若干措施》的贯彻实施,着力推进新一轮高水平对外开放,为外资创造更加开放公平便利的投资环境;也希望各国共同努力,促进经济全球化和跨国投资更好地发展。

(二十)上海服务国家"一带一路"建设发挥桥头堡作用行动方案

1. 出台背景

"一带一路"建设,是我国相当长一个时期对外开放和对外合作的管总规划,对于全面提升我国全方位开放水平具有重大意义。把中国(上海)自由贸易试验区

(以下简称上海自贸区)建设成为服务国家"一带一路"建设、推动市场主体走出去的桥头堡,是习近平总书记在全局高度对上海提出的新要求。上海在国家"一带一路"建设中发挥桥头堡作用,有利于进一步提升上海城市综合服务功能,发展更高层次的开放型经济;有利于推动形成我国全方位开放、东中西联动发展的新格局,更好地参与全球竞争与合作。为贯彻落实"一带一路"国际合作高峰论坛精神和中央要求,上海市政府制定此行动方案。

2. 主要内容

行动方案提出具体的实施路径,落实到各项可操作、能实施的具体行动上,分为6大专项行动。

(1) 贸易投资便利化专项行动。共提出15项举措,主要是围绕对接国家自由贸易区战略,构建"一带一路"多层次贸易和投资合作网络,促进贸易和投资自由化便利化。最核心的是要发挥上海自贸区的制度创新优势,提出两方面措施,即以上海自贸区为载体,加强与沿线国家(地区)制度和规则对接;以"区港一体、一线放开、二线安全高效管住"为核心,加快推进自由贸易港区建设。

(2) 金融开放合作专项行动。共提出10项举措,要把握国家金融开放和人民币国际化机遇,在风险可控前提下,依托上海自贸区金融改革创新,对接"一带一路"金融服务需求,加强与上海国际金融中心建设联动,目标是把上海建设成为"一带一路"投融资中心和全球人民币金融服务中心。

(3) 增强互联互通功能专项行动。共提出6项举措,主要围绕加强与上海国际航运中心建设联动,畅通内外连接通道、拓展综合服务功能,巩固提升上海全球城市门户枢纽地位。

(4) 科技创新合作专项行动。共提出6项举措,主要围绕全面对接国家"一带一路"科技创新行动计划,加强与科技创新中心联动,利用优势科技资源,依托功能性平台和项目,促进科技联合攻关和成果转化。

(5) 人文合作交流专项行动。共提出10项举措,依托国际文化大都市建设,发挥好重大"节、赛、会"作用,搭建更多文化艺术、教育培训、卫生医疗、旅游体育等交流机制和平台,全面提升人文合作交流水平。

(6) 智库建设专项行动。共提出7项举措,明确要发挥上海各类智库研究优势、网络优势和资源优势,为"一带一路"建设提供专业智力支撑。

3. 法规综述

上海服务国家"一带一路"建设的过程,也是培育发展新动能、代表中国参与全球竞争合作的过程,测试压力、防控风险、转型升级的过程,传播中国发展新理念、凸显上海全球城市价值的过程。因此,在"一带一路"桥头堡行动方案中,上海明确提出桥头堡的目标定位,把服务国家"一带一路"建设作为上海继续当好改革开放排头兵、创新发展先行者的新载体,服务长三角、服务长江流域、服务全国的新平台,联动东中西发展、扩大对外开放的新枢纽,努力打造能集聚、能服务、能带动、能支撑、能保障的桥头堡。

三、小结

随着上海国际航运中心建设的加快推进,以航运金融、海上保险、航运经纪、航运信息等为内容的现代航运服务业正逐步成为上海国际航运中心发展的核心驱动力。发展现代航运服务业需要法治的保障,建设国际航运中心需要法治的支撑。党的十九大把全面依法治国作为新时代坚持和发展中国特色社会主义的基本方略之一,强调要厉行法治,推进科学立法、民主立法,以良法促发展,保证善治。多年来,上海市人大高度重视以法治引领"四个中心"建设。"一带一路"建设为推动上海航运市场发展带来新的机遇和空间。上海成功出台的全国第一部航运中心建设的地方立法——《上海市推进国际航运中心建设条例》,标志着上海国际航运中心建设进入法治领航的新阶段。

第二章 航运政策与法律的司法执行

2017年,是党和国家事业进入新时代的一年。党的十九大胜利召开,习近平新时代中国特色社会主义思想成为党的指导思想,为胜利实现两个"一百年"目标和中华民族伟大复兴的中国梦提供了理论指引。在习近平新时代中国特色社会主义思想引领下,最高人民法院着力构筑新时代发展的战略优势,在海事审判领域深入实施国家战略和服务保障海事审判工作水平,完善创新海事诉讼机制,促进海事审判发展和航运纠纷解决。

2017年上海海事法院将自身发展与建设国际海事司法中心目标主动对接,明确以建设国际航运纠纷解决中心为核心功能,以建设国际海事司法高端智库和国际海事司法交流平台为辅助功能的国际海事司法中心建设的工作目标。积极开展路径探索,以服务国家重大战略和国际航运中心建设为着力点,以国际化、专业化、法治化为方向,以司法能力建设为核心,以制度机制创新为突破,以大数据战略、"互联网+"、"人工智能+"为支撑,加快形成与国际接轨的海事司法工作新局面,全面提升上海海事司法的国际公信力和影响力。

为更好地服务和保障海洋强国战略、"一带一路"倡议、上海自贸区(港)和"十三五"时期上海国际航运中心建设,推动各项工作持续创新发展,上海海事法院于2017年4月制定发布了《上海海事法院五年发展规划纲要(2017—2021)》(以下简称《规划纲要》)。《规划纲要》针对经济社会发展对海事司法提出的新的更高要求,立足工作实际,通过强化海事司法职能,提升战略定位和服务层级,从指导思想、发展目标、规划任务、实施要求四个方面对今后五年工作作出全面规划。上海海事法院在工作中认真贯彻落实《规划纲要》确定的各项目标和任务,努力把上海建设成为具有全球影响力的国际海事司法中心,为国家重大战略实施和上海及周边地区经济社会发展提供坚强有力的海事司法服务和保障。

2017年6月,最高人民法院在上海海事法院正式设立"智慧海事法院(上海)实践基地"。这是最高人民法院批准建设的全国第一家智慧法院实践基地,是落实人民法院信息化建设五年发展规划,服务保障海洋强国、长江经济带等国家重大战略,加快建设国际海事司法中心的必然要求,与上海打造国家人工智能发展高地的目标高度契合。"实践基地"致力于打造智慧海事法院的"样板间",建设一批符合海事司法规律、能够向全国海事法院推广的数据信息系统,研发海事审判执行、协作联动、诉讼服务等领域的新机制、新应用,形成和推广制度化、专业化的海事法院智慧审判模式,努力实现海事审判体系和审判能力的现代化。作为智慧法院实践基地的重要组成部分,上海海事法院海事联动指挥中心实体化运作,促进海事司法服务保障水平提升,有利于推动智慧海事法院建设。

上海海事法院与上海保监局在全国率先推出海事诉讼保全责任险以及保证函推荐格式文本,这一保险产品由上海航运保险协会开发推出,用于承保因错误保全造成的海事保全被申请人或第三人的直接经济损失。产品正式推出后,已在一大批案件中得到应用,其丰富了海事诉讼保全的担保形式,拓宽了诉讼保全的担保渠道,在司法实践和航运实务中具有积极作用。截至2018年1季度,海事诉讼保全责任保险提供相关保险金额共计3.646 9亿元,约60%的案件当事人在保全案件中选择海事诉讼保全责任险作为担保方式,海事诉讼保全责任险通过海事法院审查、被海事法院接受的比例达到100%。

2017年,海事仲裁服务更加多元化,在提供传统仲裁服务的基础上,中国海事仲裁委员会举办各类培训和研讨会,开展针对性宣传活动,落实仲裁条款。中国海事仲裁委员会继续提供延伸仲裁服务,将仲裁服务前置,充分发挥仲裁在多元化纠纷解决机制中的作用。

"加强海事审判工作,建设国际海事司法中心"被正式写入最高人民法院2016年工作报告。2017年,中国法律界正在致力于"两个中心"建设:国际海事司法中心和国际海事仲裁中心,这"两个中心"堪称服务海上丝绸之路的"并蒂莲花"。

2017年中国海事仲裁委员会积极参与并推动航运、造船及保险等相关行业协会起草标准格式合同,规范企业经营,落实仲裁条款。深入航运、修造船、货代、港口、保险、银行等行业进行调研,举办座谈会,了解企业需求,探讨合作方式,有针对性地开展仲裁宣传拓展工作,就企业普遍关注的海事海商、海事仲裁等领域的热点问题进行专题讨论,同时加强联系,主动协调与社会各界的关系,有针对性地为企业提供法律服务,扩大海事仲裁委员会的宣传范围和力度,努力创造有利于海事仲裁发展的软环境。

在"一带一路"倡议、建设国际海事仲裁中心目标的大环境、大背景、大战略下,中国海事仲裁事业的发展面临前所未有的历史机遇。

一、2017年海事司法情况简介

(一)上海海事法院

2017年,上海海事法院共收各类案件5 207件,同比上升3.03%;结案5 213

件,同比上升 2.20%;截至年底存案 296 件,同比下降 1.00%;立案标的总额 289 959.51 万元,结案标的总额 227 488.27 万元。

其中,上海海事法院自由贸易试验区法庭(洋山深水港派出法庭)、洋口港派出法庭和连云港派出法庭共收各类案件 1 468 件,结案 1 470 件。派出法庭收结案总数分别占全院收结案总数的 28.19% 和 28.20%,同比均略有下降。2015—2017 年一审案件收、结、存情况见图 2-1。

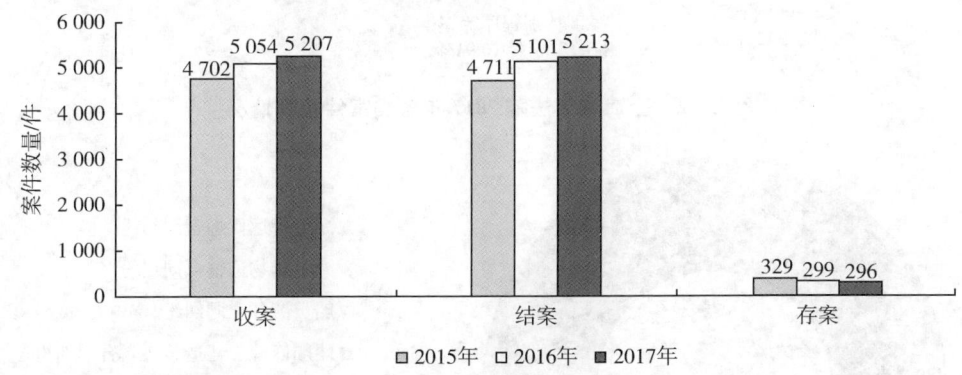

图 2-1 2015—2017 年上海海事法院案件收、结、存情况

2017 年一审共收案 4 274 件,同比上升 2.47%;结案 4 279 件,同比上升 1.66%。截至年底存案 263 件,同比下降 1.87%。

其中,一审海事海商案件收 3 914 件,结 3 904 件。受理案件中:海上、通海水域货运代理合同纠纷数量最多,共计 2 828 件;海上、通海水域货物运输合同纠纷数量位居其次,共计 487 件。上述两类案件合计占一审海事海商案件收案总量的 84.70%。其他具有代表性的案件数量与 2016 年度相比基本持平,其中:船员劳务合同纠纷 146 件,船舶修理、建造、买卖合同纠纷 35 件,租船合同纠纷 43 件,海上保险合同纠纷 25 件,海上人身损害责任纠纷 45 件,船舶碰撞及触碰损害纠纷 23 件。海事法院受理案件范围扩大以后可以受理的新类型案件又出现了一些新的纠纷形式,例如船舶专用物品买卖合同纠纷、码头租赁合同纠纷、船舶工程合同纠纷等案件数量均较少。此外,2017 年度还受理了一起海事行政案件。各类案件收案情况见图 2-2 和图 2-3。

在结案中:判决结案的 355 件,占 9.09%,同比下降 3.25 个百分点;撤诉结案的 3 260 件,占 83.50%,同比上升 6.55 个百分点;调解结案的 277 件,占 7.10%,同比下降 2.88 个百分点;其他方式结案(包括驳回起诉、移送等)的 12 件,占 0.31%,同比下降 0.42 个百分点。

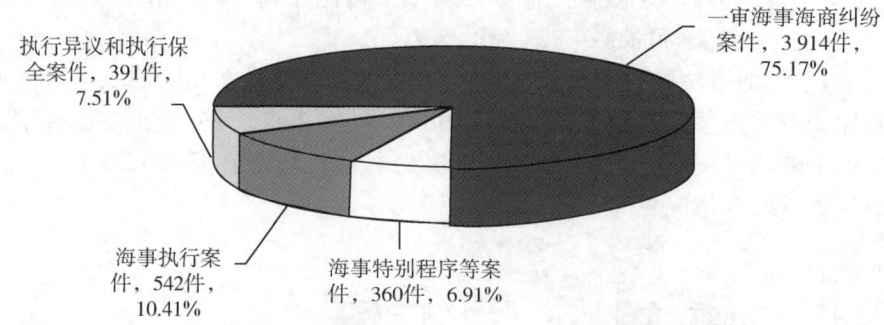

图 2-2　上海海事法院 2017 年各类案件收案情况

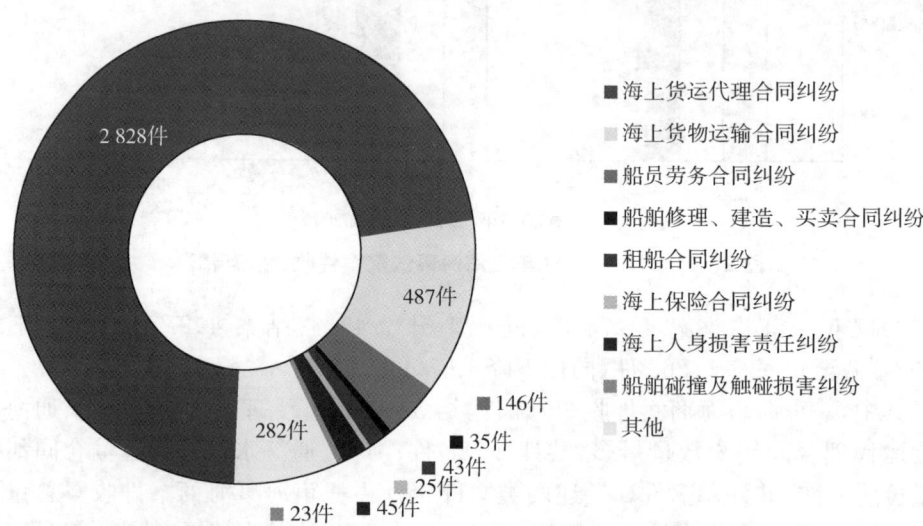

图 2-3　上海海事法院 2017 年一审海事海商案件收案类型分布

海事特别程序等案件收案 360 件,结案 375 件。收案类型主要包括申请海事债权登记 91 件、申请诉前财产保全 68 件、申请证据保全 10 件、申请扣押船舶(诉前)84 件、申请确认调解协议效力 64 件。

(二) 中国海事仲裁委员会上海分会

2017 年,中国海事仲裁委员会上海分会继续服务国家海洋强国战略及"一带一路"倡议,做好整体发展规划,推动仲裁法治建设,完善仲裁服务体制机制;创新思路,改善作风,用新制度、新机制、新方式激发新活力,提高核心竞争力;发挥引领作用,放大公务服务职能,加强海事仲裁理论研究;大力培养国际型的海事仲裁法律人才;深化国际仲裁交流与合作,打造一流海事仲裁机构,不断促进海事仲裁事业发展,扩大中国的国际影响力,提升话语权,提高我国航运软实力。

配合"一带一路"倡议,为重点经济区提供法律服务。海洋是各国经贸文化交流的天然纽带,共建"21世纪海上丝绸之路",为我国海洋经济的发展带来新的机遇。中国海事仲裁委员会利用已建立的分支机构、办事处所形成的海事仲裁服务网络,加大对上海、天津、舟山、广州、深圳、青岛、大连等重点港口城市的支持力度,主动为企业和相关部门提供专业法律服务,加快推进自由贸易试验区、"21世纪海上丝绸之路"核心区、海洋经济发展示范区等建设。

推进与海事法院的诉调对接工作。与海事法院的诉调对接业务是海仲委业务的重要环节。在巩固与上海海事法院诉调对接机制的基础上,联系并开拓与天津海事法院、武汉海事法院、大连海事法院等的诉调对接工作。

推动仲裁法制的发展与建设。随着仲裁事业不断进步,我国仲裁法需要进一步修改与完善。推动《仲裁法》修订工作,同时向有关部门反映我国《海商法》修改的必要性和紧迫性,积极推动《海商法》的修改进程,加快我国法律与世界接轨的步伐,更好地维护我国的航运利益。

利用与国际海事委员会(CMI)联络及参会的机会,逐步与CMI及其国家会员单位建立友好合作关系,提升海事仲裁委员会的国际性。

新形势下,中国海事仲裁委员会上海分会勇于作为,敢于担当,引领我国仲裁事业不断前进,有效应对国内外仲裁市场的竞争和挑战,实现更加国际化的一流仲裁机构的目标,为把中国建设成为国际海事仲裁中心作出新的贡献。

(三) 上海仲裁委员会国际航运仲裁院(即上海国际航运仲裁院)

2017年度,上海国际航运仲裁院(以下简称航运院)继续落实航运仲裁工作的推介,从多渠道宣传推介航运仲裁。这一年,除了坚持对部分案件当事人结案后的回访、听取当事人对于仲裁工作的建议,以及拜访、接待航运界专业人士外,航运院还积极参与了业界的各项活动,包括与浦东金融学会对接,就"浦东自贸试验区"、"一带一路"倡议、"长江经济带"国家战略、推进上海国际航运中心建设、人员培训、跨行业交流、"互联网金融+互联网仲裁"等院会合作方面进行探讨和交流;航运院与中国(上海)自贸试验区商务委员会(航运办)、东盟法律联盟、中国(上海)自由贸易试验区境外投资服务平台、上海海事大学法学院及上海市律师协会共同合作,举行了"一带一路"框架下上海自由贸易试验区与东盟航运投资法律研讨会,围绕"一带一路"建设面临的机遇与挑战这一主线,从如何促进国际合作、协助地方政府和企业积极融入"一带一路"建设布局入手,聚焦产经联盟的方法与对策,着力研究打造自贸试验区与东盟航运投资的交流对话平台以及实现政策与资源之间的推荐,共同探索新形势下的实践模式;航运院与上海航运交易所、浦东金融学会合作,就"智慧仲裁在航运金融衍生品交易中的运用"进行课题研究,力争服务于上海国际航运中心和国际金融中心建设,支持中国航运经济转型发展。

2017年度,航运院还应各机构和组织的邀请,参加了大量的航运论坛与交流活动,扩大航运院的仲裁影响力;全球最具影响力的法律媒体之一《亚洲法律杂志》刊登有关航运院参与共建的东盟法律服务上海合作中心的报道。

经上海市人民政府2017年12月6日批准,上海仲裁委员会第六届委员会正式成立。2017年12月26日,上海市委副书记、市长应勇在市政府办公厅为第六届委员颁发聘书。原第五届委员、上海航运交易所党委书记、总裁张页续聘为第六届委员。

作为上海仲裁委员会特设的专业仲裁审理航运交通、物流运输、海事海商、港口建设等争议案件的专门机构,航运院自成立以来已受理近千起涉及物流仓储、海上货物运输、船舶租赁、船舶配件及造船材料购销、船舶设计、陆上与航空交通工具交易等类型纠纷,积累了丰富的仲裁成果。第六届委员会除聘任大量的法律、经济界人士为仲裁员外,还吸纳了一大批海事海商、航空、物流运输等领域的专业人士,为上海国际航运仲裁院提供强有力的仲裁员队伍。航运院将积极践行党的十九大精神,以行业惯例为支撑,尊重法律与客观事实,为上海的国际航运中心建设、为上海"自由贸易港"建设保驾护航。

二、司法案例精选

(一) 海事法院案例
1. 无单放货损害赔偿纠纷
【案情】
上诉人(原审原告):XH国际物流有限公司
被上诉人(原审被告):智利NM轮船有限公司

2012年3月,XH物流委托上海XH向NM轮船的代理人NM轮船(中国)船务有限公司进行订舱,将一批医疗器械用品从中国上海港分别运往委内瑞拉卡贝略港和拉瓜伊拉港。嗣后,NM轮船先后签发了15套正本海洋提单。其中,13套提单的托运人记载非XH物流,15套提单记载的收货人均为瑞西卡公司,承运人为 NM 轮船。上述 15 套正本海洋提单均由 XH 物流持有。

2012 年 3 月 26 日,NM 轮船通过其代理人向中国国内各订舱代理发送电子邮件:"委内瑞拉海关和港务局签署新规定,收货人可以无需凭正本提单提货。鉴于此,现规定委内瑞拉货物订舱及提单特别要求如下:提交 EDI 订舱时出具发货人签署的保函;不得接受订舱的收货人或通知人即黑名单的客户暂停货运的保函要求;……"之后,NM 轮船收到一份保函,该保函抬头为 HIN‐PRO INTERNATIONAL LOGISTICS LIMITED(与 XH 物流英文名称一致),内容为:"……我们特此确认我们仍愿意将货物发往委内瑞拉,并自行承担它们在目的港被无单放货的风险。……我们特此不可撤回地承诺、保证和同意就赔偿和保证 NM 轮船免于因无单放货而直接或间接遭受的任何损失、索赔、费用、花费、损害和责任。"

上述 15 套提单项下集装箱货物分别于 2012 年 4 月 26 日至 8 月 14 日期间在目的港被卸下船舶,并于 2012 年 5 月 25 日至 8 月 30 日期间被瑞西卡公司等案外人提取。为此,XH 物流提起诉讼,请求判令 NM 轮船赔偿 XH 物流因无单放货而遭受的货值损失及利息。

【判决】

法院认为:双方之间成立海上货物运输合同法律关系。因涉案货物在目的港已被提走,XH 物流作为涉案正本提单的持有人,有权向作为承运人的 NM 轮船主张民事责任。关于 NM 轮船能否依据涉案保函或者我国相关法律规定免除其无单放货的法律责任,即使该保函如 XH 物流所称未进行授权,但其加盖公章的行为对外具有拘束力。然而,保函的内容并非当然免除承运人在目的港无需凭单放货的法律责任。同样地,根据《无单放货司法解释》第七条的规定,本案中 NM 轮船并未提供充分有效证据证明其可依照提单载明的卸货港所在地法律规定,必须将承运人到港的货物交付给当地海关或者港口当局。据此,NM 轮船无法依据涉案保函或者我国法律,免除其在目的港无单放货的法律责任。由于 XH 物流不能举证证明其系涉案货物的所有权人,也无法证明其遭受货款损失,故其提出的损害赔偿于法无据。为此,法院驳回了 XH 物流的诉讼请求。

【评析】

(1)承运人因无正本提单交付货物造成正本提单持有人损失的,正本提单持有人可以要求承运人承担违约责任或侵权责任。以涉案货物所有权人的身份向承运人主张货款损失,须证明其货主身份。持有提单的事实不能够免除提单持有人证明其遭受实际损失的义务。

承运人依照提单载明的卸货港所在地法律规定,必须将承运到港的货物交付给当地海关或者港口当局的,不承担无正本提单交付货物的民事责任,但承运人需承担证明卸货港当地法律规定的义务。①

2. 海上货物运输合同纠纷

【案情】

上诉人(原审被告):GRF 船务公司

被上诉人(原审原告):大连 JY 进出口有限公司(以下简称 JY 公司)

原审被告:LH 船舶代理有限公司(以下简称 LH 公司)

2013 年 11 月 25 日,JY 公司与案外人 YF 公司签订代理进口协议,约定 YF 公司委托 JY 公司进口印尼产红土镍矿 40 000(＋/－10%)吨。2013 年 11 月 30 日,JY 公司作为买方与 HY 公司签订了红土镍矿的货物买卖合同。GRF 公司系承运船舶所有人。2013 年 11 月 29 日,HY 公司(承租人)和 GRF 公司(出租人)签订租船合同。合同约定运费应在签订合同后支付 100 000 美元,剩余运费在船到卸港前支付。合同约定的放货条件为仅在提供正本提单后放货。2013 年 12 月 27 日,GRF 公司签发清洁已装船提单。提单上载明托运人为 HY 公司,收货人凭指示。

JY 公司通过信用证议付取得了涉案货物的全套正本提单。2014 年 1 月,涉案货物被卸下船后存放于连云港。此后,JY 公司向 GRF 公司的卸港代理人联合公司出具正本提单要求提货。2014 年 3 月 1 日,GRF 公司声明确认,LH 公司为其在卸港的代理,LH 公司依照 GRF 公司的指示,行使了涉案货物的留置权。GRF 公司至今未向 JY 公司交付涉案货物。

【判决】

本案中,JY 公司受 YF 公司委托进口涉案货物,但根据 JY 公司与 YF 公司签订的代理进口协议,在 YF 公司支付全部货款前,涉案货物的所有权归 JY 公司所有。JY 公司以自己的名义签订合同,开立信用证,付款赎单并对货物进口报关。涉案提单积载托运人为 JY 公司,向 HY 公司支付货款后合法取得涉案货物的全套正本提单,JY 公司与 GRF 公司之间存在海上货物运输合同关系。JY 公司作为提单权利人,有权以自己的名义对合同履行过程中发生的争议和所遭受的损失对外进行索赔。JY 公司基于其与 GRF 公司的货物运输合同关系,要求 GRF 公司履行承运人的交货义务,并非基于货物的所有权来主张权利。在 JY 公司已向 GRF 公司、LH 公司出示正本提单要求放货的情况下,其有权提取涉案货物。

---

① 《委内瑞拉海关组织法》第 22 条、《委内瑞拉海商法》第 203 条规定,货物交付对象有公共仓库、私人仓库或收货人三种。

GRF公司、LH公司以HY公司拖欠其运费和滞期费为由主张留置涉案货物。证据不足以证明存在运费及滞期费欠付的事实以及准确的金额。即使运费和滞期费欠付事实存在，相应的运费和滞期费也是基于HY公司与GRF公司之间的租船合同而产生，JY公司并非租船合同的当事人，并无支付上述款项的义务。根据《海商法》第六十九条的规定，托运人与承运人可以约定运费由收货人支付，但此项约定应在运输单证中载明。涉案提单中载明"运费预付"，并未载明由收货人支付运费；根据《海商法》第七十八条的规定，收货人、提单持有人不承担在装货港发生的滞期费、亏仓费和其他与装货有关的费用，但是提单中明确载明上述费用由收货人、提单持有人承担的除外，涉案提单中也无相应的记载。JY公司并非GRF公司所主张运费和滞期费的支付义务人，GRF公司无权留置涉案货物。涉案货物具备交付条件，如GRF公司未能向JY公司履行交货义务，则应按上述金额进行赔偿。

LH公司为GRF公司的卸港代理人，其根据GRF公司的指示代为处理在卸货港的相关事项，相应的法律后果应由其委托人承担。

【评析】

外贸代理，通常是代理人以自己的名义对外签订合同，合同权利义务由代理人对外承担，因合同产生的争议由代理人对外索赔或者采取其他补救措施，代理人与被代理人之间权利义务由委托代理合同确定。

根据《海商法》第八十七条的规定，应当向承运人支付的运费、共同海损分摊、滞期费和承运人为货物垫付的必要费用以及应当向承运人支付的其他费用没有付清，又没有提供适当担保的，承运人可以在合理的限度内留置其货物。托运人未支付任何一个航次的运费、滞期费、空仓费和承运人为货物垫付的必要费用，托运人对托运物品叙述不当或私自托运危险物品致使承运人或其他货物、财产受损，货物以多式联运方式运输时由承运人收取的陆上运费或其他费用，或者对承运人有其他任何债务未按期履行，承运人有权对货物进行留置。但是承运人留置权的不得对为此费用无支付义务的收货人行使。

3. 船舶碰撞损害责任纠纷案

【案情】

上诉人（原审被告）：TH海运有限公司（以下简称TH公司）

被上诉人（原审原告）：CPIC航运保险事业营运中心（以下简称TB）

2013年4月8日，CF公司所有的"长福6"轮与TH公司所有的"太行118"轮于长江的下行通航分道内发生碰撞事故，造成"太行118"轮破损、"长福6"轮沉没。经上海市高级人民法院调查并调解，由TH公司承担85%的赔偿责任，CF公司承担15%的赔偿责任。2012年4月28日，CF公司为"长福6"轮向太保投保沿海、内河船舶一切险。2013年7月5日,太保就"长福6"轮碰撞事故所致抢险救助费、货物清除费、沉船下水探摸费以及按责任比例承担的且属于承保范围内的"太行118"轮损失的保险赔偿同意一概支付,太保向CF公司实际赔付保险赔款后,取得代为求偿权,就上述损失起诉要求TH公司赔偿。

TH公司诉称:①碰撞和打捞作业共同造成船舶全损,TH公司不承担船舶全损及相应残骸清除损失。②本案部分事实认定有误:委托评估船舶市价无法律和事实依据,船舶残值应从船舶价值损失中扣除。

太保辩称:①"长福6"轮的损失与事故存在直接因果关系。②"长福6"轮的承保价值能够客观反映船舶的市场价值。③关于TH公司先行支付给CF公司的款项与太保无关,不应抵扣。

【判决】

本案系船舶碰撞损害赔偿纠纷。碰撞事故后,由CF公司支付的沉船打捞清除费用的合理性以及TH公司向太保承担的船舶价值损失和上述各项费用的具体数额引起上诉当事人的争议。

本案中,经法院双方一致选定公估机构对船舶价值损失进行评估,推定船舶全损。船舶价值损失计算问题当事人争议较大,法院确认:船舶碰撞所致财产损害赔偿应尽量达到恢复原状的原则,不能恢复原状的应以恢复原状为准折价赔偿,故船舶全损的折价赔偿应以寻找替代船舶恢复受损船舶相关营运为准,以弥补碰撞所致的船舶全损。

关于"长福6"轮船舶残值抵扣问题,因涉案碰撞事故所致该轮沉没于长江通航分道内,已严重影响船舶通航安全。相关海事主管机关要求CF公司限期打捞清除,否则将实施强制打捞清除,费用由CF公司承担。打捞合同关于船舶未能整体打捞时将打捞作业变更为清除残骸作业的约定是为了避免损失进一步扩大以及考虑打捞的必要性,该约定合法有效。残值已按打捞合同约定最终抵作船舶残骸打捞清除费用,不应在船舶价值损失中予以扣除。关于船舶价值损失,损失由双方共同委托公估机构估算,双方当事人对评估的船舶价值并未明确提出异议,依据《最高人民法院关于审理船舶碰撞和触碰案件财产损害赔偿的规定》(以下简称《船舶碰撞规定》)以及考虑到二手船舶购入后投入实际运营前产生成本及费用的船舶行业惯例,再结合船舶全损后受损方应以寻找替代船舶以弥补营运损失的惯常做法。因此,船舶价值损失为船舶市价加作为二手船的税费、维修、检验费用。

综上,鉴于太保自愿放弃沉船水下探摸费的诉请,二审法院撤销沉船水下探摸费的判决,TH公司关于不承担船舶全损和残骸清除费用的请求不能成立,应予驳回。二审法院支持太保关于船舶价值损失、抢险救助费、货物清除费、沉船下水探摸费的请求,驳回太保的其他诉讼请求。

【评析】

本案系保险人在向被保险人赔付后要求碰撞另一方对碰撞按照过失比例承担赔偿责任的船舶碰撞损害赔偿纠纷案件。《海商法》第一百六十九条规定碰撞事故中碰撞双方按照过失程度负比例责任,以及《中华人民共和国保险法》第六十条规定赋予保险人以代位求偿权。对此,本案并无争议。案中争议焦点为如何准确、合理地计算船舶价值损失。

根据《船舶碰撞规定》第三条规定:"船舶损害赔偿还包括:合理的救助费,沉船的勘查、打捞和清除费用,设置沉船标志费用。"第八条规定:"船舶价值损失的计算,以船舶碰撞发生地当时类似船舶的市价确定;碰撞发生地无类似船舶市价的,以船舶船籍港类似船舶的市价确定,或者以其他地区类似船舶市价的平均价确定;没有市价的,以原船舶的造价或者购置价,扣除折旧(折旧率按年 4%~10%)计算;折旧后没有价值的按残值计算。船舶被打捞后尚有残值的,船舶价值应扣除残值。"船舶价值损失的计算,对于正确处理船舶碰撞损害赔偿具有十分重要的意义。

本案涉及船舶推定全损,实务中,船舶全损价格的评估有市价折余法、市场售价类比法、重置价格法、收益现值法、外汇换算法等多种方法;具体项目采用何种方法,必须根据船舶的实际情况而定。且船舶估价必须由当事人向法院申请,或由法院委托一个由双方当事人共同选定的估价机构进行估价,这是为了防止当事人自行委托估价,而估价人易受当事人的影响而出现偏差。本案中考虑到此目的,采取与涉案碰撞事发当时最为匹配的国内船舶成交价格信息,并结合此时间节点前后更具代表性的多个国内船舶挂牌价格信息,综合比对取最合适的价格。

4. 海上保险合同纠纷案

【案情】

上诉人(原审被告):广东 RK 海运有限公司(以下简称 RK 公司)

被上诉人(原审原告):ZY 保险有限公司广东分公司(以下简称 ZY 保险)

2010 年 11 月 1 日,RK 公司和 ZY 保险签订沿海内河船舶保险合同,承保 RK 公司所有的"某某 1"轮。保险单约定承保条件为 ZY 保险沿海内河保险条款(一切险)、ZY 保险沿海内河保险附加四分之一碰撞、触碰责任保险条款,以及约定免赔:部分损失、全损、推定全损,包括碰撞、触碰及救助责任,每次事故绝对免赔额为 150 000 元或损失金额的 10%,两者以高者为准。

保险合同所附的《ZY 保险沿海内河保险条款》第二条"一切险"约定仅对碰撞或触碰所致的直接损失和费用负担,同时第十一条约定:"保险人对每次赔款均按保险单中的约定扣除免赔额(全损、碰撞、触碰责任除外)。"

2011年2月2日,"某某1"轮发生触碰码头事故,造成码头部分损毁并沉入江底,码头上所建综合楼一同损毁,楼内两名值班人员一死一伤,码头上架设的三台输油臂落水受损。事故发生后,RK公司向法院申请设立海事赔偿责任限制基金。

现码头公司和RK公司的纠纷已经过一审、二审和再审程序,并作出判决。但RK公司和ZY保险对触碰事故所产生的码头清障费用、事故现场及航道看护费、设标费、倒塌综合楼内财物损失、码头临时值班房购置费用等5个项目损失是否属于保险责任范围;保险金如何计算,是否按照享受海事赔偿责任限制后与之前承担责任的比例折算保险赔偿金;各项保险赔偿是否扣除免赔额;另案和本案中的律师费和诉讼费负担问题;双方之间的诉讼是否超过诉讼时效问题产生争议。

【判决】

法院认定,本案是海上保险合同纠纷,对当事人争议的几个问题法院认定如下:①诉讼时效问题:依据诉讼时效的司法解释第十二条和《海商法》第二百六十七条的有关规定——诉讼时效中断可以因当事人起诉以及被请求人同意履行义务而中断,因此双方签订《预赔付协议》,RK公司的起诉并未超过诉讼时效。②费用问题:涉案码头清障看护费用、设标费来源于海事局的行政强制措施,来由清晰,性质上是为保障航道安全与畅通所发生的费用,属于保险合同附件中的除外责任范围。但其他费用皆属于保险条款所约定的"碰撞、触碰责任限定为受碰撞的其他船舶和受触碰的码头、港口设施、航标""发生的直接损失和费用"的范围。③关于ZY保险是否按照责任限制后的范围承担保险金:依据《海商法》二百零六条,保险人享受的赔偿责任限制与被保险人相同,因此,ZY保险的保险金数额在未超过责任限制金额时全额赔付。④一审和二审法院均认为对于另案诉讼的律师费和诉讼费用在性质上属于RK公司为减少与保险责任有关的索赔而支出的费用,结合抗辩事项与保险责任的关系认定应由ZY保险承担。⑤对保险金和诉讼费用是否适用免赔额问题,虽然保险合同中特别约定和附件第11条有关免赔额的约定矛盾,但法院认为,特别约定优先于附件约定——因为"特别约定"包括"免赔条件"是双方协商一致的结果,被保险人知悉相关约定的内容,涉案投保单是双方订立保险合同的书面要约,其中包含的免赔条款与保险单亦相一致。

【评析】

本案中有两大问题值得注意:

(1)保险人与被保险人的海事赔偿责任限制相同的解释,从赔偿限额的角度看:在具体金额的确定上,保险人的赔偿限额与被保险人的赔偿限额适用相同的计算方法,即根据《海商法》第二百一十条的规定,以船舶总吨位为依据分级计算;

从最终体现的结果来看,具体数额上保险人的赔偿限额与被保险人的赔偿限额在数值上是相等的。因此,本案中,作为保险人的 ZY 保险广东公司所享受的海事赔偿责任限制金额与作为被保险人的 RK 公司所享受的海事赔偿责任限制金额一致,在保险人承担的赔偿责任未超过该金额的情况下,排除免赔等扣减因素,保险人应全额向被保险人承担保险赔偿责任。此外,保险人先行支付了限制基金金额,并不意味着其对外赔付的最终金额就是基金的数额。除了对责任限制抗辩理由的审查外,保险人与被保险人在保险单中的约定,也是处理双方对外赔付以及内部实际承担金额的重要依据。

(2) 保险合同本身对于免赔额的约定出现矛盾时,法院会依据保险合同和保险单结构及内容解释合同。相互矛盾的是哪个足以引起保险合同双方当事人的注意,合同双方商定保险事宜的其他材料例如"保单",将其作为保险合同订立的书面要约,决定是否适用免赔额。

5. 海事担保合同纠纷

【案情】

原告:CZ 船业集团有限公司

被告:新加坡 DL 海外有限公司

2012 年 4 月 27 日,原告将其所有的"成路 58"轮光船租赁给中成国际海运有限公司。2012 年 7 月初,"成路 58"轮在中国鲅鱼圈港受载货物,目的港为泰国高世昌港,托运人系中石油国际公司,收货人凭泰国暹罗商业银行股份公司指示,通知人为泰国马哈旺公司,承载货物为 12 250 吨散装颗粒尿素。案外人 HB 国际船舶代理有限公司代表"成路 58"轮船长签发提单,签发日期为 2012 年 7 月 10 日。提单正面注明有租约并入。

涉案 12 250 吨散装尿素于 2012 年 7 月 12 日装载完成。因信用证的装运期限为 2012 年 7 月 10 日,被告作为"成路 58"轮的承租人向"成路 58"轮的船东、光船租船人及船舶管理公司出具一份担保函,请求将大副收据和提单倒签至该日,以使提单的装运日期与信用证相符。担保函中记载,"作为你司遵照我司指令签发倒签提单的对价,我司承诺如下:①赔偿你司或你司雇员、代理任何性质的赔偿责任或遭受损失或损害,并保证使你司免于承担此类损失,如果此种损失是由于你司应我司要求签发倒签提单给中国石油国际事业有限公司所引起的;②如因为签发倒签提单所引起的任何针对你司、雇员、代理人的诉讼,我司将不时地提供足额的资金帮助你司抗辩此类诉讼;③如果'成路 58'轮或你司其他船舶或财产被扣押、留置或者被威胁扣押、留置,我司将提供保释金或其他保证以释放该船舶或财产,并赔偿你司因船舶被扣押或留置所引起的一切损失或费用,无论这种扣押、留置是否合理;④本赔偿函下对任何人或者任何方的责任都是连带和不可分的,不以你司诉讼第三方为前提条件,无论该第三方是否是合同一方或者对本赔偿函下的事故承担责任;⑤本赔偿函将依据英国法进行解释,与此免责函有关的人员需受英格兰高等法院管辖。"

2012年8月6日,泰国中央知识产权及国际贸易法庭(以下简称泰国法庭)根据收货人马哈旺公司的申请以运输事故导致货物减损为由在泰国高世昌港锚地扣押"成路58"轮。2013年8月7日,泰国法庭作出释放船舶命令,解除对"成路58"轮的扣押,并于8月14日实际释放船舶。2014年3月6日,泰国法庭对马哈旺公司诉本案原告及魏日亚保险股份公司民事索赔案作出判决,驳回马哈旺公司的诉讼请求,各方各自承担相关费用。

原告诉称,"成路58"轮遭扣押系因原告遵从被告指示倒签提单所至,且被告已明确承诺赔偿因倒签提单而发生的一切损失,故请求判令被告赔偿其损失。

被告未应诉答辩。

【判决】

法院认为,本案系海事担保合同纠纷。涉案海运保函的担保对象,即倒签提单行为是违法行为,其担保内容亦具有违法性,不能因为保函接受人自称不是违法行为的实施主体而使原本非法的担保行为产生合法效力。涉案担保函不具有相应的法律效力,但并不影响保函接受人在按照保函出具人指示实施违法行为或默认被告实施违法行为并遭受损失时向被告请求损害赔偿的权利。本案中原告(保函接受人)的船舶虽被扣押,但并非由于倒签提单的行为所致,两者之间没有必然的因果关系,故原告以该担保函主张被告承担赔偿责任缺乏事实和法律的依据。原告目前的证据尚不能证明其在涉案海上货物运输合同中系承运人或是实际承运人,更不能证明其与被告建立了海上货物运输合同关系。原告以船舶所有人,即为海上货物运输合同中实际承运人的身份主张被告承担涉案船舶被扣押期间的损失亦缺乏事实和法律的依据。最终,法院判决对原告的诉讼请求不予支持。

【评析】

倒签提单行为是海上货物运输中的违法行为,托运人为换取承运人倒签提单而出具海运保函,两者行为均非善意,应为无效。海运保函虽无效,但海运保函的接受人在按照保函出具人指示实施违法行为或默认其实施违法行为并遭受损失时,可以向保函出具人请求损害赔偿,其前提是倒签提单行为与损害后果之间存在必然的因果关系。此外,保函接受人与保函出具人根据过错大小承担相应责任。

6. 保证合同纠纷

【案情】

原告:HS船务有限公司

被告：上海 PF 银行股份有限公司

2006 年 12 月 6 日，中国-坦桑尼亚联合海运公司（以下简称中坦公司）与南通惠港造船有限公司（以下简称惠港公司）签订了一份造船合同。合同约定，中坦公司在船舶建造中按时间节点向惠港公司分期支付造船款，而惠港公司向被告申请开立退款保函，由被告向中坦公司提供退款担保，即根据合同条款终止造船合同时，如惠港公司在一定期限内未向中坦公司偿还造船款，则由被告承担担保还款责任。此后，中坦公司以更新协议的形式将造船合同转让给原告。被告于 2008 年 9 月 11 日出具退款保函，随后于 2010 年 3 月 16 日进行修改。根据保函记载，如果卖方未能在收到买方书面还款请求后 15 个工作日还款，被告不可撤销地、绝对地及无条件地作为主债务人而非仅作为保证人支付卖方应支付的金额；保函自惠港公司收到第一期分期付款之日起生效；任何保函引起的或与保函有关的争议应根据伦敦海事仲裁员协会的规则与规定在伦敦进行仲裁。原告依合同于 2009 年 11 月 30 日向惠港公司支付第一期款项，于 2010 年 4 月 22 日支付第二期款项。因惠港公司未按合同约定在原交船日 2011 年 6 月 30 日后的 180 日内交付船舶，构成延迟交付，原告于 2012 年 1 月 10 日发出取消通知，要求惠港公司退还原告支付的所有款项及利息，但惠港公司并未退还。同年 2 月 17 日，原告向被告发出退款请求，被告未支付任何款项。

2012 年 3 月 16 日，原告向被告发出仲裁申请书，表示已根据退款保函第十条向伦敦海事仲裁员协会提起仲裁。原告认为其已根据退款保函条款提出退款要求，而被告作为退款保证人未能根据退款保函条款向买方支付应偿付的分期付款及产生的利息，构成违约，故要求裁决被告偿还债务。

仲裁庭认定造船合同及保函不可执行，于 2013 年 7 月 8 日裁决驳回原告的索赔请求。

原告诉称，被告在订立退款保函时存在过失，请求被告赔偿退款保函确定的还款金额。

被告提起主管异议称，涉案纠纷已在伦敦仲裁解决，故法院不应受理。即便原告以缔约过失提起诉讼，缔约过失责任纠纷亦属于合同纠纷，仍然系仲裁协议约定的仲裁事项，法院不应受理。原告系恶意诉讼，应当驳回起诉。

【判决】

法院经审理认为，原告起诉的依据是被告于 2008 年 9 月 12 日签发的保函。该保函第十条约定，"本保函应由英国法律进行解释和管辖，本保函产生的或与之有关的任何争议应根据伦敦海事仲裁员委员会的规则和程序在伦敦提交仲裁"。原告确认依据该仲裁条款于 2012 年 5 月 17 日在伦敦提起仲裁，其仲裁请求被伦敦仲裁庭驳回。原告虽主张被告签署保函过程中的重大过错造成其损失,但其诉请内容亦属于与保函相关的争议,应当提交仲裁解决。原告选择伦敦仲裁的行为既确认了仲裁条款的有效性,又表明其接受仲裁条款的约束,并非其起诉时所称仲裁条款系被告单方意思表示。根据法律规定,当事人达成仲裁协议,一方向人民法院起诉未声明有仲裁协议,人民法院受理后,另一方在首次开庭前提交仲裁协议的,人民法院应当驳回起诉。涉案纠纷已由伦敦仲裁委员会仲裁解决,法院对本案没有管辖权。

【评析】

作为主合同的造船合同中的仲裁条款的效力并不必然及于保证合同项下的争议。纠纷发生后,债权人依照保证人单方出具保函中的仲裁条款提起仲裁的行为也确认了仲裁条款的有效性,表明其愿意接受仲裁条款约束,双方达成仲裁合意。合同中的仲裁条款一经成立,非经缔约方同意撤销自始有效。合同中的有效仲裁条款对于当事方关于缔约过失责任的争议仍然适用。《合同法》第五十七条规定,无论缔约过失最终结果是合同未订立、合同无效或被撤销等,均不影响已合法成立的仲裁条款的效力。

7. 海上人身损害责任纠纷

【案情】

原告:卞某

被告:东某

2015年3月24日,卞某在东某所有的"苏启渔01319"船上工作时,被船尾脱落的缆绳击中背部,造成颈部脊髓损伤。同年3月26日渔船回港,卞某被家人送至启东市第二人民医院,经检查,确定为高位截瘫,建议送上海医院诊治。当日下午,卞某被送至上海市东方医院治疗,被诊断为颈脊髓损伤伴四肢瘫。3月31日卞某在上海市东方医院进行手术,手术后卞某突发呼吸困难、咳痰不出、发热等症状,4月18日后卞某一直昏迷。

11月11日,司法鉴定科学技术研究所司法鉴定中心出具鉴定意见书,认为卞某在船上因故受伤,具有引起高位截瘫的损伤基础。在医院进行手术治疗后,卞某身体状况发展为丧失意识及四肢瘫。比照GB 18667—2002《道路交通事故受伤人员伤残评定》标准之规定,其遗留四肢瘫的后遗症相当于道路交通事故一级伤残。卞某在自身颈椎退行性病变的基础上遭遇本次外伤,导致颈髓损伤并经治疗后遗留肢体瘫痪,外伤系主要因素,外伤参与度拟为60%~80%。

卞某之子卞小某代理卞某诉称,卞某系在东某所有的渔船上工作时发生事故受伤,东某应予赔偿,故请求判令东某承担医药费、伤残补偿金、精神抚慰金、误工费、工资、交通费、护理费、被抚养人生活费等。

东某辩称,卞某本身的伤病以及医院治疗行为与卞某目前的病情之间的因果关系不明,东某不应承担卞某自身伤情以及医疗失当行为的赔偿责任。对于医疗费用,卞某并未实际支付,也未能区分其中治疗其自身疾病的费用,卞某无权向其追索。

【判决】

法院认为,卞某受东某雇佣在东某渔船上工作,应视为双方之间建立劳务关系。东某作为船舶所有人及实际经营人,对于船舶作业安全以及船员人身安全具有管理和保障的义务。卞某在为东某提供劳务过程中受伤,东某作为雇主依法应承担赔偿责任。

卞某因住院而实际支出的医疗费、护理费、交通费等费用,应由东某承担。因卞某并未实际支付医疗费,且还在住院治疗过程中,可待支付相应费用后一并另行主张。伤残赔偿金根据卞某的伤残等级,按司法鉴定意见书给出的外伤参与度60%~80%取中间值计算。

【评析】

船员在船工作时受伤,入院治疗过程中又发生医疗损害,致最终伤残结果加重。海事法院在处理该类海上人身损害责任纠纷案件时,应注意:第一,对于向医疗机构提出医疗损害赔偿部分的诉请,属于医疗损害责任纠纷,不属于海事法院管辖范围,不应予以受理或附带进行审理;第二,虽然医疗损害纠纷非由海事法院管辖,但海事法院在处理海上人身损害责任纠纷过程中可能涉及对因海上损害和医疗损害致残比例的区分问题,在委托司法鉴定时,应选择具有医疗损害鉴定资质的鉴定机构,对海上损害致伤残的结果参与度进行鉴定,以确保裁判结果的准确性,并保障相关权利人对可能存在的医疗损害责任另行主张的权利;第三,船舶所有人或实际经营人的赔偿责任,应根据船员在船受伤与最终损害结果的因果关系,按比例承担。

8. 海上货物运输合同纠纷

【案情】

原告:YG保险股份有限公司杭州中心支公司

被告:上海LS交易中心有限公司

2013年8月21日,案外人WC公司与被告签订物流服务交易合同。其中"合同概况"条款约定:WC公司委托被告进行货物运输;被告提供综合物流解决方案,并根据方案提供专业物流供应商;由被告同其指定的物流供应商签订有效的运输合同,为货物运输提供必要的担保,保证货物安全、及时、准确送达;被告提供第三方支付以及开具运输发票服务。"服务内容及价格"条款约定：货物名称带钢，总重量5 334.76吨；起运地京唐港，目的地江阴黄田，运输方式水运，船名新华。"结算方式"条款约定：WC公司选择被告作为第三方支付平台；WC公司需支付被告运费人民币33 884.84元，以及交易服务费人民币169.42元；WC公司确认运输完成后，指示被告在5日内向物流供应商转付上述运费。涉案运输并未实际开具运单。

涉案货物于2013年8月20日装上"新华"轮，并于同月26日到达江阴港。WC公司于同月29日发现货物受损，并于次日同港口经营人共同盘点。据盘点情况记载，涉案货物带钢系在卸货时即存在变形和散件的现象。同年9月22日，原、被告与WC公司三方共同出具损失确认书，确认由WC公司委托被告运输涉案货物，在卸货时发现大批带钢因挤压碰撞导致变形，对后期销售和加工造成影响。三方共同确认，受损货物共计113件重290.41吨，按照人民币200元/吨计算贬值，损失共计人民币58 082元。该损失确认书上显示被告身份为承运人以及责任人。

原告于2013年8月29日签发涉案运输保险单，记载投保人与被保险人均为WC公司，被保险货物名称热轧普碳钢带，运输路线自京唐港至江阴黄田港。WC公司于同年8月30日向原告申请保险赔偿，原告按照上述三方损失确认书中确认的金额，于10月18日向WC公司赔付人民币58 082元。

原告诉称：涉案货物在运输过程中发生损坏，被告系涉案运输的承运人，原告系取得代位求偿权的保险人，请求判令被告赔偿原告货物损失人民币58 082元及利息损失。

被告未应诉及答辩。

【判决】

上海海事法院经审理认为：本案系海上货物运输合同纠纷。原告作为保险人，在进行保险赔付后已依法取得代位求偿权。本案的主要争议焦点为：①被告在涉案运输中的法律地位；②被告就货物损失应承担的责任。

关于被告在涉案运输中的法律地位。首先，被告接受WC公司的委托运输涉案货物，并承诺保证货物安全、及时、准确送达，被告身份符合承运人的法律特征。其次，被告虽收取的是交易服务费，但被告并未实际促成WC公司与物流供应商直接订立合同，而是由WC公司先委托被告进行货物运输，被告再以自己的名义同物流供应商订立合同，故WC公司与被告之间存在运输合同关系，被告是承运人而非居间人。最后，涉案货损事故发生后，被告在三方损失确认书中已明确承认自己的承运人身份，而本案亦无运单等其他证据显示另有他人同WC公司订立运输合同，故法院认定被告系涉案海上货物运输合同项下的承运人。

关于被告就货物损失应承担的责任。根据三方损失确认书记载,涉案货物在卸货时即发现存在货损,货物因为运输中的挤压碰撞导致变形,在确认上述事实的基础上,被告还以责任人的身份确认货损金额,故被告应就其确认的金额即人民币58 082元向原告承担赔偿责任。

【评析】

作为航运业与互联网相结合的新产物,物流电商在海上货运业务中的身份识别是审判实践中面临的新问题。交易平台型的物流电商,虽初衷是为托运人和实际物流供应商提供订约媒介,但若以自己的名义分别同托运人和实际物流供应商签订合同,明确约定其接受托运人委托进行货物运输,再委托实际物流供应商提供运输服务的,应认定该物流电商是海上货运业务中的承运人而非居间人。

9. 船员劳动纠纷①

【案情】

异议人(案外人):南京市GR贷款有限公司(以下简称GR公司)

申请执行人:谭××

被执行人:南京LR贸易有限公司(以下简称LR公司)

LR公司所有的"LR6"轮船员谭××因工资遭拖欠,向上海海事法院申请扣押该轮。法院于2015年10月9日裁定准许,并于次日登轮实施扣押。同年11月3日,法院受理谭××诉LR公司船员劳务合同纠纷案,并于12月18日判决LR公司在判决生效之日起十日内向谭××支付工资报酬人民币419 431.05元及利息(按照中国人民银行同期六个月至一年贷款利率标准,自2015年10月8日起计算至判决生效之日止),并确认谭××就LR公司的上述给付义务对"LR6"轮享有船舶优先权。宣判后,双方均未上诉,判决已生效。因LR公司未履行生效判决确定的义务,谭××于2016年3月8日向上海海事法院申请执行,法院于同日立案执行,后LR公司逾期未履行义务。除"LR6"轮等五艘船舶外,LR公司未申报其他财产,且未与法院联络。同月28日,法院作出执行裁定,冻结、划拨LR公司的相应存款,查封、扣押、冻结、拍卖或变卖LR公司的相应财产。因LR公司始终未履行生效判决确定的义务,亦未对"LR6"轮被扣押后所产生的看管、移泊、维持等费用进行清偿或提供担保,法院决定拍卖"LR6"轮,同时成立"LR6"轮拍卖委员会。5月6日,南京市六合区人民法院(以下简称六合法院)受理GR公司申请LR公司破产清算,并向上海海事法院申请中止执行LR公司的财产。后5月10日,谭×

---

① 该案经过上海海事法院一审,案号为(2015)沪海法商初字第2938号。

×向上海海事法院申请继续拍卖实现其船舶优先权。上海海事法院审查后决定不予中止拍卖。拍卖成功后先后支付了扣押期间产生的各项费用。六合法院裁定GR公司不享有债务人LR公司船舶抵押权。

【判决】

上海海事法院经审理认为,异议人GR公司对"LR6"轮并不享有优于申请执行人(船舶优先权人)谭××的权利,故在执行程序中拍卖该轮并以船舶拍卖款优先清偿申请执行人的债权并不损害异议人的权益。海事诉讼中,为保护和实现船舶优先权而司法强制拍卖船舶的程序具有相对独立性,在船舶拍卖程序已经启动的情况下,不因船舶所有人进入破产程序而中止,因此LR公司关于破产清算申请受理后,涉及债务人财产的执行程序应当中止的异议不能成立。"LR6"轮拍卖程序严格依法进行,从组成拍卖船舶委员会到组织船舶检验、评估、确定拍卖方式和平台,从在多方媒体上发布拍卖公告到实际拍卖,再到最后拍卖成交、买受人付款、船舶交接,环节齐备、程序合法,故LR公司关于网络拍卖船舶违反法律规定,拍卖应予撤销的异议亦不能成立。综上,裁定驳回LR公司提出的异议。被执行人LR公司不服该裁定,申请复议。上海市高级人民法院以(2016)沪执复8号执行裁定驳回LR公司的复议申请。

【评析】

担保物权的实现与破产程序的关系、破产程序对担保物权的行使是否应有限制、限制程度如何是破产法理论与实务中颇有争议的问题。海事法院拍卖船舶程序及其所涉及的船舶优先权实现(拍卖船舶所要实现的债权大多具有船舶优先权担保)问题,相较一般担保物权的实现又更有其特殊性。该案中,以实现船员工资为目的的船舶司法拍卖程序启动在先,船舶所有人破产程序启动在后。在拍卖船舶公告已经发布,即将进入竞拍环节的情况下,是否应当中止船舶司法拍卖程序,将被拍卖船舶移交受理破产申请的法院处理。两级法院一致认为,海事诉讼中,保护和实现船舶优先权的船舶司法拍卖程序具有相对独立性,在船舶拍卖程序已经启动的情况下,不因船舶所有人进入破产程序而中止。

10. 船舶买卖合同纠纷

【案情】

原告:ZG有限公司

被告:XXY(上海)投资管理有限公司(以下简称XXY公司)

2013年12月30日,原告与QY(香港)有限公司(以下简称QY公司)签订船舶买卖合同,船舶买受人为QY公司,出卖人为原告。合同约定QY公司向原告购买自行耙吸挖泥船"航浚9002",标的船舶"现状交船"转让价款或合同价款,计为

第二章 航运政策与法律的司法执行

人民币 53 000 000 元。2014 年 4 月 24 日,原告与 QY 公司签订补充协议二,就前述买卖合同项下未尽事宜进行约定。协议第 3 条约定,双方同意以下未付款项应按照人民币结算,其中包括出口手续代理费、燃、润油料及留置费用、船舶维修及相关测试费用,共计为人民币 3 166 375 元;协议还约定,若 QY 公司未能在 5 月 23 日后的五个工作日内支付上述三项费用,由 XXY 公司担保支付。

2014 年 4 月 24 日,XXY 公司向原告出具一份担保函,其中记载"尽管在合约编号为:船舶买卖合同项下的买受人与出卖人于 2014 年 4 月 24 日签署补充协议壹与补充协议贰,并作出承诺,但 XXY(上海)投资管理有限公司进一步承诺如下:鉴于本公司已转账人民币 16 098 353 元至出卖人账户作为买受人完成付款义务的保障,但根据出卖人要求,本公司承诺若买受人在上述两份补充协议约定的日期内未能完成还款,本公司愿代为支付其中的人民币 3 166 375 元"。

因 QY 公司未能履行补充协议二约定的付款义务,自 2014 年 6 月 15 日起,原告通过电子邮件和信件等多种方式向 XXY 公司主张权利,要求 XXY 公司支付欠款人民币 3 166 375 元。

原告诉称,XXY 公司作为上述债务的连带保证责任人,当债务人 QY 公司未能履行付款义务时,应当承担相应的保证责任。

被告辩称,XXY 公司向原告提供的担保,属于境内机构为境外机构提供担保,应经国家有关主管部门和机关批准或者登记,但上述担保未经国家主管机关批准或登记,因此担保合同无效。

【判决】

上海海事法院经审理认为,《担保法司法解释》第六条第二项全面吸收了《境内机构对外担保管理办法》和《境内机构对外担保管理办法实施细则》等部门规章中关于合同无效情形的内容,初衷在于维护社会经济秩序和保护公共利益,其适用的主体和事由是中国境内机构(境内外资金融机构除外)作为担保人按照法律规定的要求,以保证、抵押、质押方式,向作为债权人或受益人的中国境外机构或者中国境内的外资金融机构承诺,当作为债务人的被担保人未按照合同约定偿付债务时,由担保人履行偿付义务。本案中,虽然是中国境内企业为注册在香港特别行政区的机构提供担保,但债权人为境内的国资企业法人,因此,本案担保合同关系的主体和法律事实并非属于《担保法司法解释》以及其吸收的上述部门规章关于合同无效情形的调整和适用范围。基于上述原因以及本案中查明的事实,原告与 XXY 公司在形成保证合同关系时双方均主体适格,且意思表示真实,保证合同关系的内容合法,故涉案保证合同依法有效,具有法律约束力。现原告已按约履行船舶买卖合同以及补充协议二中的各项义务,然而债务人 QY 公司至今仍然未向原告履行补充协议二中约定的付款义务。因此,原告依据XXY公司出具的担保函以及相关法律规定,要求XXY公司对QY公司在补充协议二中尚未履行的债务承担连带保证责任并无不当,对此予以支持。

【评析】

对外担保产生于国际经济交往和国际资本流动的需要,随着我国资本流动规模的快速增加及流动性的不断提高,调整对外担保的政策法规必然要与时俱进。对外担保并不是一个纯粹的民商事制度,其既要符合相关担保法律规定,同时还要符合外汇管制和外债管理的行政规定,因而其在担保主体、担保方式、担保效力等方面与国内担保存在着显著差别。由于行政机关对境内机构对外担保的监管要求在不断调整,同一类型的对外担保在不同时期会有不同的规范要求,从而相应的合同效力也会出现不同的认定结果。2014年5月12日国家外汇管理局发布《跨境担保外汇管理规定》(以下简称新规)及《跨境担保外汇管理操作指引》,并废止了《境内机构对外担保管理办法》和《境内机构对外担保管理办法实施细则》,对司法实践中有关担保合同的效力认定造成一定影响。

新规的发布及旧的管理规章的废止,导致《担保法司法解释》第六条第二项的适用前提现已不复存在。将未经批准、登记的对外担保认定为无效的主流裁判思路不宜继续适用。一方面,在外汇管理实践中未登记的对外担保合同合规生效,而司法审判却认定合同无效,必然产生司法实践与社会实践脱节的矛盾;另一方面,该裁判思路必将严重损害基于信赖新规而签订对外担保合同的债权人利益,变相鼓励背信行为。面对相互矛盾且层级不同的规范,最高法院已注意到这一规范冲突,其在《关于全面推进涉外商事海事审判精品战略为构建开放型经济体制和建设海洋强国提供有力司法保障的意见》中提出,法院要密切关注外汇管理体制改革、金融业开放对跨境融资、对外担保等法律行为效力认定思路的影响,适时调整裁判思路,适时出台或修改司法解释、指导性意见,保障相关改革的顺利进行。

11. 海上货物运输合同纠纷案

【案情】

原告:XSY公司

被告:HJ海运有限公司

2014年7月10日,XSY公司接受SG股份有限公司(以下简称SG公司)委托承运18个集装箱货物,并签发联运提单,装货港为上海,卸货港为加拿大鲁珀特王子港,交货地为加拿大埃德蒙顿。同日,HJ公司接受XSY公司委托承运该批货物,并向XSY公司签发海运单,货物描述及装货港、卸货港、交货地等运输信息均与 XSY 公司出具的联运提单记载一致。同年 7 月 24 日,该批货物卸离船舶后,HJ 公司委托加拿大铁路公司将其中的 17 个集装箱通过火车运往交货地埃德蒙顿。7 月 25 日,该 17 个集装箱货物因火车出轨遭受货损。

2015 年 7 月 14 日,涉案货物的保险人 PICC 天津市分公司(以下简称人保天津公司)以代位求偿权人身份向法院起诉,要求 XSY 公司赔偿涉案货物损失。

【判决】[①]

一审法院认为:查明 XSY 公司接受 SG 公司的委托,制作并出具了多式联运提单,收取全程运费,后委托他人向 HJ 公司订舱、支付运费,赚取运费差价,而且其为 HJ 公司海运单记载的托运人,HJ 公司海运单记载的收货人系其目的港代理人点线公司,故 XSY 公司系涉案运输的承运人即多式联运经营人。XSY 公司系涉案运输的契约承运人,根据 XSY 公司出具的海运单 HJ 公司系涉案运输的实际承运人。涉案事故发生后天津人保对 SG 公司进行赔付获得了代位求偿权,故天津人保有权依法向托运人 XSY 公司行使代位求偿权要求赔偿。

涉案运输方式为多式联运且应适用中华人民共和国法律。经查明 HJ 公司认为涉案货损发生于加拿大境内的铁路运输区段,因此主张多式联运经营人的赔偿责任和责任限额应依据加拿大法律确定,并就相关加拿大法律进行举证。但因其提供的证据和相应判例规定与货损实事及提单条款存在不同,故不足以证明其可以适用加拿大的赔偿责任和责任限额。又其因涉案货损发生在铁路运输段是在 HJ 公司的责任期间内,根据中华人民共和国相关法律规定涉案货损及相关费用应由 XSY 公司和 HJ 公司共同承担。后 XSY 公司和 HJ 公司不服该判决向上海市高级人民法院提起上诉,上海市高级人民法院于同年 11 月 2 日作出判决,驳回上诉,维持原判。

【评析】

本案系海上货物运输多式联运合同纠纷。SG 公司系涉案运输的托运人,XSY 公司签发涉案多式联运提单;HJ 公司向 XSY 公司签发海运单,除了托运人、收货人和通知方的信息外,其他信息与 SXY 公司签发的多式联运提单的记载一致。SG 公司与人保天津公司之间系海上货物保险合同关系,涉案事故发生后,人保天津公司向被保险人 SG 公司支付保险赔款,并取得涉案保险代位求偿权有权向 XSY 公司要求赔偿,另外 HJ 公司作为 XSY 公司的实际承运人就海运单上记载的全程运输向 XSY 公司承担责任。综上所述,XSY 公司系涉案多式联运合同项下的多式联运经营人,根据海运提单记载,HJ 公司和 XSY 公司成立海上货物多式联

[①] 上海海事法院审理,经上诉,上海市高级人民法院二审驳回上诉,维持原判(2016)沪民终 321 号。

运合同关系,HJ公司为实际承运人对运输全程负责。

因为合同当事人没有就法律适用作出一致选择,根据最密切联系原则,涉案当事人XSY公司及涉案船舶装货港均位于我国境内,故本案适用中华人民共和国法律审理。又XSY公司提供的HJ公司出具的海运提单,根据相关记载可以证明两者成立海上货物多式联运合同关系。尽管涉案货物损失发生在铁路运输段,但根据海上货物多式联运合同货损发生在其责任期间,XSY公司作为多式联运经营人应该对由此造成的损失承担赔偿责任,HJ公司作为全程承运人,货损发生在其责任期间故就涉案货物在加拿大铁路运输区段发生的灭失和损坏应向收货人承担连带责任。

12. 供应合同纠纷

【案情】

原告(反诉被告):LB涂料(上海)有限公司(以下简称LB公司)

被告(反诉原告):上海AYD船务有限公司(以下简称AYD公司)

2013年1月,LB公司向AYD公司发送配套报价要约,该笔业务中的防污漆ECOLOFLEXSPC2000BROWNA和ECOLOFLEXSPC600PLUM有载明防污漆有效期按36个月配套,每月航行0~6 000海里的说明。

2013年2月AYD公司的"丽天"轮涂刷了防污漆且原告向被告支付了包括两种防污漆在内的油漆款。2014年11月"丽天"轮在韩国被发现船底附着海生物。11月17日,AYD公司通过电子邮件的方式将船舶污底情况通知被告,并要求被告安排勘验。12月8日,AYD公司再次通过电子邮件方式与被告沟通防污漆问题,要求被告采取解决措施或提出补偿方案,被告LB公司庭审过程中确认未派员进行勘验。2014年11月25日至12月11日,"丽天"轮停靠锚地。其间,Amir公司在韩国釜山锚地对"丽天"轮船底进行清污并出具清污报告,清污报告记载了清污工作情况及船底被海生物覆盖比例。2015年10月,"丽天"轮靠泊上海港吴淞船厂进行修理,AYD公司委托YS公司就防污油漆失效进行检验。根据YS公司出具的检验报告显示,"丽天"轮水线以下船体附着大面积、高密度海生物。YS公司认为海生物附着部分防污漆未发现脱落现象,可以断定防污漆失效是导致船体被海生物污损的原因。AYD公司提前通知LB公司"丽天"轮进港坞修时间且LB公司于10月14日派员登轮查看。

船舶在停轮做清底时产生清底费13 307.91美元,"丽天"轮停靠锚地期间产生锚地使用费(含代理费)6 364.57美元、引水费696.42美元,移泊产生的燃油费用,"丽天"轮检验报告评估为重油费2 100美元、轻油费3 352.50美元。"丽天"轮检验报告还就清污期间的船期损失估算为13 650美元。此次修理时根据YS公司报告中登轮证费用人民币 500 元和船员更换费用人民币 1 600 元与防污漆重做无关，产生人民币 5 928 元的港口使用费。与防污漆重做相关的坞修费用为人民币 203 390 元、服务费为人民币 194 667 元，共人民币 398 057 元。

2013 年 5 月，LB 公司向 AYD 公司发送"开某"轮油漆配套报价，载明"防污漆有效期按 36 个月配套，每月航行 0～6 000 海里"。2013 年 6 月，"开某"轮进行防污漆涂刷施工。2014 年 5 月，油漆出现脱落情况。根据 2014 年 5 月 LB 公司出具的 CHEXXXX 进坞油漆检验报告（以下简称 2014 年 5 月检验报告）的记载，脱落面积主要为：直底有少量防污漆脱落，平底有 40% 左右的防污漆脱落。2016 年 6 月，"开某"轮靠泊上海港吴淞船厂，座坞××1 号船坞，进行修理。AYD 公司委托上海 YZ 保险公估有限公司（以下简称 YZ 公司）就防污油漆失效进行检验。根据 YZ 公司出具的"开某"轮检验报告显示，"开某"轮水线以下船体附着大面积海生物。AYD 公司就"开某"轮进港坞修时间提前通知 LB 公司，但 LB 公司未登轮参与检验。

此次船舶修理产生与防污漆失效相关的费用：①重做油漆费用，发票金额为 49 084.10 美元，实际支付金额为 47 246.14 美元。②进出港口使费，发票金额为人民币 84 536 元，"开某"轮检验报告认为与防污漆失效相关项目费用计人民币 73 236 元，因发票金额不符，故 AYD 公司实际支付港口使费 12 658.93 美元，共计人民币 72 851.34 元。③船厂坞修费，发票金额为人民币 688 047 元。④主机备件费和修理人工费，发票金额分别为人民币 708 842 元和人民币 185 276 元。

【判决】

一审法院认为：本案系船舶物料和备品供应合同纠纷。LB 公司向 AYD 公司发送配套报价构成要约，AYD 公司根据该份配套报价涂刷了相应防污漆且支付了价款构成承诺，双方之间的船用防污漆供应合同关系成立有效。本案一审争议焦点为 LB 公司是否存在违约以及违约责任的范围及赔偿数额。

本案中 LB 公司发来的报价明确有"防污漆有效期按 36 个月配套，每月航行 0～6 000 海里"的内容，此外在涂刷油漆过程中 LB 公司应提供技术服务。"丽天"轮和"开某"轮均在未满 36 个月即出现大面积海生物附着情况可以初步判断是 LB 公司提供的防污漆未能达到双方约定的使用效果。关于"开某"轮，根据 AYD 公司提供的资料可以初步证明：因为 LB 公司供错产品以致使用错误工艺涂刷防污漆。LB 公司主张油漆脱落系施工条件不合格引起，但却未能提交有效证据证明确实存在不宜施工情况，也未能证明已告知 AYD 公司施工条件不适宜，故法院不支持其抗辩。

关于责任的范围及赔偿数额。AYD 公司主张的重涂油漆费用包含不同种类的油漆,而涉案损失系因防污漆失效所引起,故 LB 公司仅应承担防污漆费用,对于其他油漆产品费用不应承担,"开某"轮检验报告亦采用此标准评估损失。

(1) 对于"丽天"轮:AYD 公司主张的损失主要有六项,包括韩国清污费用、重涂油漆费用、港口使费、船厂坞修费用、主机备件费、运费和修理费,以及租金、燃油损失。AYD 公司提交了清底费用、锚地使用费(含代理费)、引水费发票及支付凭证,"丽天"轮检验报告对于进出锚地重油及轻油消耗量的评估也较为合理,而该五项费用因船底清污产生,系防污漆失效引起,故法院对该五项费用共计 20 580 美元予以认可。LB 公司认为一般服务费的分摊不合理,一审法院认为就一般服务费的分摊,公估人员确实无法给出明确、合理的分摊依据,LB 公司也提不出具体计算方法,因船舶在船厂期间涉及检验、油漆重做等多个项目,故酌定由 AYD 公司与 LB 公司各担一半,即由 LB 公司负担人民币 118 251 元。关于港口费,因为船舶进出港口同时进行检验和重涂油漆项目,故就与防污漆相关的港口使费酌定为 AYD 公司与 LB 公司各担一半,即 LB 公司负担人民币 27 505.50 元。就重涂油漆费用,"丽天"轮检验报告认为与防污漆相关费用为 24 883 美元,LB 公司对此亦认可,一审法院予以支持。就公估费及翻译费,因 LB 公司表示若一审法院采信相关证据材料,则愿意承担相应部分公估费和翻译费,故酌定由 LB 公司负担公估费人民币 3 650 元和 1 431.25 美元,以及翻译费人民币 1 080.50 元。

但是清底期间"丽天"轮并无租约在身,故对 AYD 公司主张的船期损失不予支持。就主机备件费、运费和修理费,一审法院认为:第一,AYD 公司提交的"丽天"轮检验报告不能有效证明主机提前维修确系必需,主机提前维修与船舶污底具有必然因果关系;第二,即使防污漆失效与主机磨损相关,AYD 公司在已知防污漆失效情况下,未及时采取合理措施避免损失扩大,也不应就扩大损失部分向 LB 公司予以主张;第三,因防污漆失效造成主机损坏已超出 LB 公司订立合同时所能预见的损失范畴,据此对 AYD 公司关于主机备件费、运费及修理费损失的主张不予支持。就 AYD 公司主张的公估、公证认证费及翻译费,一审法院认为,公证认证费系 AYD 公司为进行诉讼的必要支出,故不予支持。

(2) 对于"开某"轮:AYD 公司主张的损失主要有四项,包括重涂油漆费用、港口使费、船厂坞修费用和主机备件费、修理费。LB 公司应承担的重做防污漆费用为 23 312.12 美元。就港口使费,LB 公司认为"开某"轮系为进行强制检验而进坞,因此该笔费用必然发生不应由 LB 公司承担,一审法院认定与防污漆相关的港口使费酌定为 AYD 公司与 LB 公司各担一半,即 LB 公司负担人民币 36 425.67 元。就船厂坞修费用 LB 公司仍对一般服务费的分摊提出异议,与"丽天"轮同理,法院认为由 AYD 公司与 LB 公司各担一半,即 LB 公司负担一般服务费人民币

188 073元。

关于主机备件费及修理费,法院同"丽天"轮的意见一致,不予支持。

后LB公司不服该判决,向上海市高级人民法院提起上诉,且双方均未提交新证据。上海市高级人民法院认为:一审认定事实和佐证证据均清楚明确,予以认定,争议焦点仍在LB公司是否存在违约以及违约责任的范围及赔偿数额。LB公司认为涉案两份检验报告不能作为定案证据。二审法院认为,YZ公司和YS公司均有经营保险公估业务许可证,公估人员均持有保险公估从业人员执业证书。两份检验报告可以作为认定本案事实的证据。另外,LB公司关于检验报告应当由3名公估人员签字盖章的上诉理由没有事实和法律依据,故不予支持。从LB公司的报价内容来看,"丽天"轮和"开某"轮均在未满36个月时出现大面积海生物附着情况,LB公司存在违约事实。LB公司认为两轮进坞的时间均为油漆涂刷后36个月,故进港重涂油漆是必然发生的,且该时间也恰是船舶例行检查时间,故港口使费和船厂坞修费用中的一般服务费不应由LB公司来分摊。法院认为LB公司违约在先,应当承担由此导致的违约损失。AYD公司的安排并没有扩大立邦联邦公司应当赔偿的违约损失,反而有利于防止因违反租约而可能导致的损失进一步扩大,符合减损的原则。由于AYD公司确认涉案两轮进坞时除进行防污漆重涂外,还进行了船舶检验,一审法院综合考虑船舶在船厂期间进行了检验、重涂油漆等多个项目的事实,酌定双方当事人各半负担港口使费和船厂坞修费用中的一半服务费,并无不当,对LB公司关于一审法院分摊船厂坞修费中的一般服务费、港口使费不公平、不合理的上诉理由不予支持。关于LB公司主张一审判决以发票金额为依据确定LB公司负担费用的金额,系认定事实错误问题,故认为一审法院根据具体实付金额已作出详尽计算并充分释明。

综上,LB公司的上诉请求无事实和法律依据,不予支持。故驳回上诉,维持原判。

【评析】

本案系船舶物料和备品供应合同纠纷。LB公司作为报价人向AYD公司发出报价,且AYD公司接受并支付了价款,二者之间船用防污漆供应合同关系成立有效。LB公司的约定中关于"防污漆有效期按36个月配套"的内容和实际AYD公司"丽天"轮和"开某"轮未满36个月内即发现船底有大批海生物的事实现状存在出入,LB公司存在违约事实。

AYD公司主张的重涂油漆费用包含了不同种类的油漆,而涉案损失系因防污漆失效所引起,故LB公司仅应对涉案船舶承担防污漆费用,对于其他油漆产品费用不应承担。双方对涉案船舶主要就重涂油漆费用、港口使费、船厂坞修费用、主机备件费、运费和修理费等费用展开辩诉。涉案船舶均不是在发现海底附着物且存在油漆脱落的问题后立即进行重涂油漆等挽救方法,而是在涂满36个月之后进坞同时进行防污漆重涂和船舶检验,但LB公司违约在先,且AYD公司的安排并没有扩大LB公司应当赔偿的违约损失,反而有利于防止因违约而可能导致的损失进一步扩大,符合减损的原则,相关的服务费等也酌情由双方均摊。关于主机备件费已经超过LB公司的合理预期也AYD公司也并不能证明其与防污漆失效有必然联系,故不予支持。在赔偿损失额上,法院坚持落实具体支付金额且坚持公正、合理原则,使涉案双方各自承担应有的责任。

(二)海事仲裁案例精选
1. 船舶修理合同争议案
【案情】

2014年7月16日,申请人与被申请人签订合同。由被申请人委托申请人修理J轮船舶。2014年7月18日,J轮到申请人的船厂进行修理。申请人依约完成该轮修理义务。2014年7月31日,申请人与被申请人就J轮的修理费用又签订结算及付款协议(以下简称协议)。双方当事人确认该轮修理费为人民币390 618元。被申请人已支付人民币100 000元,船舶出厂前再支付人民币100 000元,余款人民币190 618元于2014年8月31日前一次性汇入申请人的银行账户。但被申请人只支付了船舶修理费人民币20万元,剩余人民币190 618元经申请人多次催讨,被申请人仍拖欠至今。

因此,申请人请求仲裁庭裁决:

(1)被申请人向申请人支付船舶修理费人民币190 618元,并从2014年9月1日起按银行同期贷款利率支付利息,至实际履行之日止。

(2)本案仲裁费用由被申请人承担。

被申请人答辩称:

(1)协议是被申请人在被逼无奈之下签署的。在申请人执意要求下,只有被申请人签署了该协议后,J轮才能出厂。因该轮在期租合同期内,为了减少损失被申请人只得签署该协议。

(2)申请人没有按照修理项目单上的要求做"锅炉烟管检查疏通并根据船检要求做相关检验"的修理项目。J轮出厂后,因锅炉问题导致主机熄火。申请人拒绝J轮停靠其码头,被申请人只能联系舟山应氏船舶修理有限公司修理锅炉,花费人民币16 661元。

(3)《合同》第十一条约定,供电费为人民币2.2元/千瓦时,但是,申请人在完工结算时,供电费按人民币 2.5 元/千瓦时计算。被申请人认为,应扣除多计电费金额人民币 1 951.2 元。

(4) 因申请人修理调配和统筹管理不当,造成 J 轮二次进出坞,第二次进出坞费人民币 21 351 元应予扣除。

另外,被申请人提出仲裁反请求称:

J 轮坞修时间从 7 月 21 日至 7 月 27 日。该轮锅炉和尾轴修理本应在此期间完成。但是,由于申请人未按照合同要求办理,致使 J 轮 7 月 27 日出坞,隔两天即 7 月 29 日再次进坞。7 月 31 日修理完毕出厂后,被申请人又寻找其他修理厂修理锅炉直至 8 月 8 日完成。综上所述,由于申请人修理怠慢和管理不善,导致 J 轮修理时间拖延 12 天,致使被申请人的营运损失达人民币 32 万元。

被申请人请求仲裁庭裁决:

(1) 申请人赔偿被申请人营运收入损失人民币 320 000 元;

(2) 本案仲裁费由申请人承担。

【仲裁庭意见】

1) 关于船舶修理合同和结算及付款协议的效力

2014 年 7 月 16 日,申请人与被申请人就 J 轮船舶修理事宜,经双方当事人协商,签订合同。仲裁庭认为,双方当事人在平等、自愿的基础上,经协商签订的涉案合同,无论从内容还是从形式上,均符合法律的规定。应认定该合同合法有效,对双方当事人均有约束力。

仲裁庭认为,J 轮修理项目全部完工后,经双方当事人验收、结算,于 2014 年 7 月 31 日签署协议。同日,J 轮随即出厂。据此,双方当事人签署协议的程序是符合合同第四条的约定。未发现因申请人实施胁迫行为而导致被申请人是在被逼无奈之下签署协议的情况。被申请人完全具有对该协议提出异议或拒签的选择权。但是,被申请人并未提出异议或拒签。因此,被申请人关于协议是在被逼无奈之下签署的说法是不成立的。仲裁庭认为,协议签订的程序是合法的,协议约定的内容是真实的,也是符合合同的约定。协议是双方当事人真实的意思表示,应认定合法有效。双方当事人均应受协议的约束,应予认真履行。

2) 关于增加、减少修理项目和电费单价问题

(1) 关于尾轴测量和尾轴更换配件修理项目。仲裁庭认为,该修理项目是经双方当事人口头协商同意并实际施工完成的。事后,又经被申请人签字确认的新增加修理项目。虽然双方当事人在新增加该修理项目的当时,没有按照合同约定"如影响坞期或影响修理总周期的经双方代表协商,根据实际情况,增加修理周期,并另订书面补充合同"的要求。但是,在 J 轮修理完工后,双方当事人经协商并签

字、盖章签署的协议,是双方当事人根据实际情况,对 J 轮修理周期及修理项目的费用作了最后的确认。因此,该协议是原合同的补充合同。

(2) 关于锅炉烟管检查疏通并根据船检要求做相关检验的修理项目。仲裁庭认为,经双方当事人协商一致签署的协议已最后确认该修理项目未被列入修理项目的范围内,也未收取该修理项目的修理费用。事实上,该修理项目也未实际施工。据此,应当认定该修理项目是经双方当事人协商一致确认减少的修理项目。

(3) 关于电费单价问题。仲裁庭认为,虽然双方当事人在合同中约定电费单价为人民币 2.2 元/千瓦时。但是,被申请人在 J 轮修理项目费用汇总表上,确认申请人以 2.5 元/千瓦时计算,且双方当事人签署协议时,被申请人并未提出异议。这是双方当事人对合同相关条款的内容变更,是双方当事人对各自权利义务的处分。据此,电费单价 2.5 元/千瓦时,予以认可。

3) 关于逾期欠款金额及利息

申请人确认在协议签署后,被申请人又向申请人支付人民币 100 000 元。现在,被申请人拖欠金额应为人民币 190 618 元。据此,仲裁庭对该事实予以认定。

关于申请人提出按银行同期贷款利率计算利息。仲裁庭认为,申请人提出的计息方法不够明确,且也不尽合理。因为银行有央行及数量众多的商业银行,申请人未明确按哪一家银行公布的利率来计算利息。且申请人也未提供贷款合同、贷款合同与涉案款项的关联性以及该贷款合同是否实际履行等相关的证据材料。因此,仲裁庭认为,应按中国人民银行公布的同期壹年期定期存款利率计算,自 2014 年 9 月 1 日起至实际履行之日止产生的利息损失。这对双方当事人是相对比较公平合理的。

4) 关于被申请人的仲裁反请求

被申请人称,J 轮坞修时间为 2014 年 7 月 21—27 日,尾轴和锅炉修理本应在该期间完成,由于申请人未按船舶修理合同要求办理,致使 J 轮在 7 月 27 日出坞,隔两天即 7 月 29 日进坞。7 月 31 日出坞离厂后,又寻找其他修理厂修理锅炉直至 8 月 8 日完成。因尾轴和锅炉两项修理致使 J 轮修理时间拖延 12 天,致使被申请人营运收入损失约计人民币 32 万元。要求申请人赔偿被申请人的损失。

【评析】

本案的争议焦点在于合同的效力问题。案件审理中,当事人有时会以提出其做出的某项意思表示是由于受到对方的逼迫或胁迫下的无奈之举,非其真实的意思表示作为抗辩的理由。《合同法》第五十四条第二款规定,一方以欺诈、胁迫的手段或者乘人之危,使对方在违背真实意思的情况下订立的合同,受损害方有权请求人民法院或者仲裁机构变更或者撤销。《合同法》中的胁迫是指以将要发生的损害或以直接施加损害相威胁,使对方产生恐惧并因此而订立合同。胁迫的构成要件包括:①胁迫人具有故意;②胁迫人实施了胁迫行为;③被胁迫人因胁迫而订立合同;④胁迫行为是非法的。《合同法》第七十七条规定:"当事人协商一致,可以变更合同。"据此,如当事人需要对合同内容重新修改或者补充,应当本着协商的原则进行。如果双方当事人就变更事项达成一致意见,变更后的内容就取代原合同的内容,当事人就应当按照变更后的内容履行合同。

本案中,被申请人提出其与申请人签订的结算及付款协议是在被逼无奈之下签署的,但被申请人并没有提供相应的证据来证明申请人故意实施了非法胁迫行为。故,仲裁庭无法认同被申请人的抗辩理由。

2. 船舶修理合同争议案

【案情】

2014年5月4日,被申请人将其所经营的J轮委托申请人进行修理。双方约定在船舶修理期间靠厂码头费为人民币500元/天。同时约定,开工之前被申请人支付工程修理费的30%(计人民币30万元),合同完工日期之前完成结价并在开船之前全额付清尾款。双方于2014年5月5日签署J轮借靠合同,约定船舶定于2014年5月5日进厂,暂定8月6日离厂。2014年5月12日,被申请人向申请人预先支付修理工程费用人民币30万元。2014年7月15日、2014年7月26日、2014年9月28日,双方分别签订两份备忘录及一份补充合同,最终将J轮借靠合同终止日期延后至2014年10月15日。被申请人同意修船资金若在此日期内无法落实,应服从申请人的安排,对前期的费用进行结算付清并离厂。

然而,虽经申请人多次催促,被申请人一直未支付其所拖欠的修理费,由此产生的停靠服务费用及其他费用,申请人对该轮行使留置权,但被申请人仍未支付上述费用。

基于以上事实和理由,申请人提出仲裁请求如下:

(1) 请求裁决被申请人向申请人支付其拖欠的全部修理工程费用人民币4 177 519元(包括修理前准备工作服务费用人民币163 460元、船舶靠泊服务费用人民币2 891 500元、船舶停靠船厂期间的移泊费用人民币756 000元、船舶停靠船厂期间的日常看管维护费用人民币595 800元、船舶停靠船厂期间的安全维护费用人民币70 759元),并支付滞纳金(滞纳金应按照1.5%/月,自每笔未付款项应付之日的次月起计算至裁决生效之日止)。

(2) 请求裁决确认申请人对J轮享有船舶留置权。

(3) 请求裁决被申请人承担申请人的律师费用,暂计人民币5万元。

(4) 请求裁决被申请人承担本案的全部仲裁费用及其他相关费用。

【仲裁庭意见】

1) 关于本案修船工程合同及其他合同的效力

根据仲裁庭认定的案件事实,涉案修船工程合同明确约定生效的条件,上述合同没有被申请人的签字和盖章,因此仲裁庭无法认定该合同已经生效。同时,仲裁庭注意到,J轮借靠合同、两份J轮备忘录、J轮借靠合同补充合同都有双方当事人的签章;双方对于涉案船舶进行有限修理的意思表示未发生变化;申请人所主张的请求都与上述三份合同有关。

仲裁庭认为,修船工程合同并未生效。J轮借靠合同、两份J轮备忘录、J轮借靠合同补充合同真实有效。

2) 关于申请人的仲裁请求

(1) 申请人关于全部修船工程费用的请求。双方当事人在J轮借靠合同第三条中明确约定"借靠船舶以外产生的工程项目参照报价书的报价标准,其结算价格依据为中船总公司92年黄本(中国船舶工业总公司1992年编制的《国内民用船舶修理价格表》)修理价格$K=1.0$"。申请人主张的修船工程费用包括:修理前准备工作服务费、船舶靠泊服务费(双方合同约定的借靠码头费、靠泊费)、船舶停靠船厂期间的移泊费用、船舶停靠的日常看管维护费用和安全维护费用等五项,仲裁庭认定如下:

① 修理前准备工作服务费:包括拉、割锚链产生的费用,使用拖船配合船舶进厂、船舶离靠码头、安排引水、护航费用,修理前的现场勘验费用,生活区绝缘检测工程费用。

仲裁庭认为,船舶进厂、切割锚链和"前期准备工作"已完成,申请人和被申请人已经确认,由此产生的费用是合理的费用。有关费用的计算方式应当按照双方当事人的约定,没有约定的,仲裁庭将根据公平合理且兼顾双方当事人利益的原则酌定。

上述前期准备工作中,船舶离靠码头时解缆2次、搭拆上下船舷梯2次的项目符合合同约定的92黄本第一项和第十一项。对于涉案船舶,靠离码头系解缆单价应当为人民币256元,搭拆上下船舷梯单价应当为人民币350元。申请人请求的船舶靠离码头系解缆2次,计人民币512元,搭拆上下船舷梯2次,计人民币700元,两项共计人民币1212元的请求有明确的合同依据,应当予以支持。

仲裁庭认为,申请人所主张的费用实际发生且合理。上述修理前准备工作服务费用共计人民币163 460元应当予以支持。

② 船舶靠泊服务费用。申请人请求的船舶靠泊费用分为3部分,其计算依据

和计算标准并不相同：自 2014 年 5 月 5 日起（涉案船舶进厂之日）至 2014 年 8 月 5 日止，涉案船舶的靠泊服务费用按照人民币 500 元/天计收；2014 年 8 月 6 日至 2014 年 10 月 15 日止，涉案船舶的靠泊服务费用按照人民币 5 000 元/天计收，并应在 2014 年 10 月 18 日之前安排船舶离厂，未依约安排离厂的 10 月 16 日、17 日仍按 5 000 元/天计。2014 年 10 月 18 日至 2016 年 2 月 25 日（原仲裁开庭之日），涉案船舶的靠泊服务费用按照人民币 5 000 元/天计收。

2014 年 5 月 5 日至 2014 年 8 月 5 日，共计 93 天，金额共计人民币 46 500 元；2014 年 8 月 6 日至双方约定的合同终止时间 10 月 15 日为 71 天，靠泊服务费用计人民币 355 000 元；2014 年 10 月 16 日至 2016 年 2 月 25 日为船舶延迟离厂时间，共计 498 天，靠泊服务费用金额共计人民币 2 490 000 元。

仲裁庭认为，申请人请求的船舶靠泊服务费用应认定为兼具违约惩罚和损失赔偿的性质，该约定是双方当事人的真实意思表示，于法不悖。上述申请人请求至 2016 年 2 月 25 日的费用共计人民币 2 891 500 元，应当予以支持。

③船舶停靠船厂期间的移泊费用。申请人在 2014 年 5 月 5 日至 2016 年 2 月 25 日止的 662 天内，共安排涉案船舶移泊 21 次，每次移泊费用为人民币 36 000 元，共计请求移泊费用人民币 756 000 元。

仲裁庭认为，船舶移泊费用人民币 36 000 元/次是合理的，上述费用确系实际发生。但申请人对涉案船舶连续多日移泊的安排存在不合理之处。仲裁庭基于公平合理地保护双方当事人的利益考量，酌情支持申请人船舶停靠船厂期间的移泊次数为 15 次。

④船舶停靠船厂期间的日常看管维护费用。仲裁庭注意到，J 轮船长为 91.5 米，参照 92 黄本第三项和第四项，日常消防值班及消防巡查的费用为人民币 112 元/人（85 元+27 元）。仲裁庭认为，申请人派驻 3 名工作人员是合理的，但是主张按照每天人民币 300 元/人的标准发放报酬明显高于合同的约定，双方对修船工程收费项目适用 92 黄本已有明确约定，仲裁庭尊重双方当事人的约定。日常消防值班及消防巡查的费用应当按照每天人民币 112 元/人计算。仲裁庭支持申请人主张的船舶停靠船厂期间的日常看管维护费用共计人民币 222 432 元，其中借靠合同期内 164 天，计人民币 55 104 元，合同期外船舶延迟离厂期间 498 天，计人民币 167 328 元。

⑤船舶停靠船厂期间的安全维护费用。仲裁庭认为，船舶停靠船厂期间的安全维护费用虽然合同没有约定，但是申请人实际支付了上述费用，避免被申请人船舶价值的减损，使被申请人获益。而且被申请人的这种获益与申请人的付出存在直接的因果关系。因此，申请人请求的船舶停靠船厂期间的安全维护费用共计人民币 70 759 元，仲裁庭予以支持。

上述各项因修理而产生费用共计人民币 3 888 151 元,扣除被申请人已经支付的人民币 300 000 元,被申请人还应当向申请人支付人民币 3 588 151 元。

(2) 关于申请人对拖欠修理工程费用的"滞纳金"的请求。仲裁庭认为,按稍后签订的借靠合同补充合补充合同为依据,确定 J 轮的全部工程款项最晚应于 2014 年 10 月 15 日的合同终止日前结算付清更符合双方合同目的和最终意愿,届时,被申请人必须付清全部工程费用,逾期付款则应根据借靠合同约定,由被申请人承担滞纳金。

仲裁庭认为,被申请人因 2014 年 10 月 15 日的合同终止日之前未结算付清全部费用合计人民币 798 823 元,应自次月起按合同约定承担支付滞纳金的责任,即对欠款金额每月承担 1.5% 的滞纳金(不足一月按一月计),直至本案裁决生效之日止。实际计算滞纳金的基数应为扣减 30 万后的人民币 498 823 元。此外,船舶因被申请人自身原因继续滞留船厂,其又未结算付清此后继续产生的靠泊服务费等费用合计人民币 3 089 328 元(截至 2016 年 2 月 25 日),按照双方合同约定,被申请人对该部分欠款仍然应当承担支付滞纳金的责任。综上,仲裁庭认为,申请人关于"滞纳金"的请求符合双方当事人的约定,于法不悖。仲裁庭予以支持。

(3) 关于申请人的"留置权"的请求。根据 J 轮借靠合同第五条第 5 项约定,申请人关于"留置权"的请求符合双方当事人的约定,应当予以支持。

【评析】

双方的争议焦点清楚明确,即关于本案修船工程合同、J 轮借靠合同、两份 J 轮备忘录、J 轮借靠合同补充合同的效力。仲裁庭认为,涉案修船工程合同没有被申请人的签字和盖章,因此无法认定修船工程合同已经生效。但 J 轮借靠合同、两份 J 轮备忘录、J 轮借靠合同补充合同都有双方当事人的签章;双方对于涉案船舶进行有限修理的意思表示未发生变化。因此,这四份合同真实有效。

3. 合同代位权诉讼的仲裁协议纠纷

【案情】

上诉人(次债务人)与原审第三人(债务人)之间订有载有约定提交香港国际仲裁中心、按照联合国国际贸易法委员会(UNCITRAL)仲裁规则并按美国纽约州实体法进行仲裁之仲裁条款的股票购买协议及股东协议。被上诉人(债权人)以其对原审第三人存有投资合作协议、投资合作终止协议、股东协议案等合同项下的到期债权,而原审第三人怠于行使其在股票购买协议及股东协议项下对上诉人之到期债权为由,以上诉人为被告,向上海市第二中级人民法院提起代位权诉讼。

【判决】

上诉人向上海市第二中级人民法院提出管辖权异议,上海市第二中级人民法院作出《民事裁定书》,驳回上诉人的管辖权异议。此后,上诉人就前述《民事裁定书》向上海市高级人民法院提起上诉。

上海市高级人民法院审理后认为:"我国《民事诉讼法》规定,涉外经济贸易、运输和海事中发生的纠纷,当事人在合同订有仲裁条款或者事后达成仲裁协议,提交中华人民共和国涉外仲裁机构或者其他仲裁机构仲裁的,当事人不得向人民法院起诉。本案中,上诉人与原审第三人之间明确约定双方涉案纠纷应当提交香港国际仲裁中心按照联合国国际贸易法委员会仲裁规则进行,并按美国纽约州实体法,因此,上诉人与原审第三人之间排除法院的管辖。本案系涉外债权人代位权纠纷,我国《合同法司法解释》规定,次债务人对债务人的抗辩,可以向债权人主张。这种抗辩既包括实体上的抗辩,也包括程序上的抗辩。被上诉人在本案中提起的债权人代位权诉讼,其实质是代债务人向次债务人主张到期债权,基于保护次债务人管辖利益立场,代位权人应当受该仲裁条款的约束。根据在案证据表明,被上诉人与原审第三人签署商谈备忘录时已明确知晓原审第三人与上诉人之间存有仲裁约定,故人民法院对本案没有管辖权。"据此,上海市高级人民法院裁定撤销上海市第二中级人民法院的《民事裁定书》,并裁定驳回被上诉人的起诉。

【评析】

关于在债务人与次债务人之间存在有效仲裁协议的情况下,债权人的代位权诉讼是否会因次债务人的抗辩而被驳回,仲裁理论界对此存在支持和反对两种观点,司法实践中亦曾出现过对立的认定结论。就此问题产生不同观点的原因系基于:①代位权的行使方式是否包括仲裁,债务人与次债务人之间的仲裁协议能否延长到仲裁协议之外的第三人;②《合同法司法解释一》第十八条("在代位权诉讼中,次债务人对债务人的抗辩,可以向债权人主张")应该如何理解,即次债务人的抗辩是否包括对程序上的争议解决方式的抗辩,此亦涉及如何协调我国现行《合同法》与《仲裁法》下相关制度设计背后的根本理念冲突问题,而仅依靠人民法院在个案审理中作出的相关认定,似无法从根本上解决该等冲突,以保障相关当事人权利的充分实现。因此,仍需相关部门通过明确的修法意见,对该冲突予以弥补。

4. 租船合同纠纷

【案情】

被申请人于2008年8月25日就运输巴西铁矿事宜向申请人发出招标书,列出具体要约邀请条款,并提出回盘截止时间为2008年8月27日上午10:00时;申请人于2008年8月27日按招标书的条件向被申请人发出投标书;被申请人于2008年8月27日向申请人发出运输招标确认书确认申请人中标的运价。在前述整个招投标的过程中,双方当事人均以电子邮件、传真等数据电文的形式表达各自的意见,并到达对方的收件系统。

【仲裁庭意见】

1) 关于租船合同是否成立的问题

被申请人认为:本案中的租船协议经过招投标的程序,应当以书面形式订立。2008年8月27日申请人向被申请人提交的租船协议草本是合同书形式的纸质合同必须由双方签字盖章合同方可成立。对2008年9月5日申请人提供的租船协议最后修改稿,被申请人没有作出任何承诺的意思表示,双方对"额外保险"问题未达成一致意见。该租船协议是谈判文本而非依法成立的合同,因此租船合同没有成立。申请人认为:申请人向被申请人发出的投标书构成要约,被申请人发给申请人的运输招标确认书构成承诺,本案的租船合同自运输招标确认书到达申请人时成立,即在2008年8月27日依法成立。《海商法》第四十三条要求租船合同以书面形式订立。《合同法》第十一条要求的书面形式包括以电报、电传、传真、电子邮件等数据电文的形式订立合同。本案申请人的投标文件以及被申请人的运输招标确认书都以传真的方式发送给对方当事人。因此租船合同符合法律上"书面形式"的要求,合法有效。

在申请人收到被申请人的运输招标确认书以后,双方当事人就航次租船合同的"合同条款后续问题"进行磋商。其中草本租船协议第27条的草案原文是:"额外保险:如果由于船龄超过20年而产生超龄险,则应由租家承担。但船东应一次性补偿租家USD10 000并从运费中扣除。"申请人将该草案修改为:"如果船龄超过20年而产生超龄险,则应由租家承担。船东不负责超龄额外保险。"这两款草案虽然不尽相同,但它们的共同之处是:船龄超过20年的船舶可以使用,只是对船舶的超龄保险应由谁承担的问题有分歧意见。关于船龄问题,在这以前的招投标的过程中,被申请人的招标书中是"……五,船龄要求:20年MAX……",申请人的投标书中是"…MAX 20 YEAR OLD…"。很明显双方约定中标的船舶船龄最高为20年。也就是说,船龄20年以上的船舶不能成为涉案航次租船合同的承运船舶。《招标投标法》第四十六条规定,"……招标人和中标人不得再订立背离合同实质性内容的其他协议。"由于当事双方后续磋商的租船协议第27条的内容背离招标书和投标书中双方关于最高船龄为20年的约定,即使当事双方最终对此条款达成一致意见,这样的条款也是无效的,其行为也是违反法律规定的。

仲裁庭认为,当事双方进行磋商这样的条款违反《招标投标法》第四十六条的规定,不予支持。关于船龄问题应以中标结果为准,即最高船龄不得超过20年。除此以外,双方当事人对草本租船协议的其他条款均未提出异议。仲裁庭认为,双方当事人对其他条款已达成一致意见,因此依据招投标结果订立的航次租船合同已经成立。

2) 关于租船合同生效问题

被申请人认为:在涉案租船协议第 33 条约定"本租船协议由中,英语书写,签字生效"。双方签字是该协议生效的要件。由于双方未在该协议上签字,对双方没有合同约束力。被申请人不承担任何违约责任。申请人在租船协议草本尚未正式成立前自行提前指派船舶,导致的任何损失应当属于申请人自愿承担的商业风险。

申请人认为:本案通过招投标的方式,双方以交换电函、数据电文形式订立的合同,法律上并不要求以签字盖章作为合同成立并生效的要件。本案租船合同的成立符合《海商法》关于书面形式的要求,是合法有效的合同。此外,自从 2008 年 9 月 5 日申请人向被申请人发出派船通知起,双方已开始履行租船合同,这也表明该合同是有效合同。

在租船协议第 33 条中有关于签字生效的条款。仲裁庭认为,本案中的租船合同是当事双方根据中标的结果订立的合同。该租船合同的条款由两部分组成:①招投标文件中的内容和中标结果中约定的条件。在本案中它们是货名货量、运价、装/卸港、受载期、滞期/速遣、船龄、船舶代理等方面的约定条件。这些条件构成租船合同的核心条款。根据《招标投标法》第四十五条规定,"中标通知书对招标人和中标人具有法律效力"。这部分的租船条款已经生效并对双方当事人具有约束力。谁违反这些生效的约定,谁就要承担相应的法律责任。②中标后双方订立的租船合同后续条款。但这部分条款必须符合《招标投标法》第四十六条的规定,即"招标人和中标人不得再行订立背离合同实质性内容的其他协议"。其目的就是确保中标结果的落实,即确保前述①中的合同核心条款能顺利得到履行。涉案租船协议的第 33 条属于本案租船合同的后续条款,并不是招投标书中的条件和中标结果,也不是法律的强制性规定,因此它必须符合《招标投标法》第四十六条的规定,不得有任何"背离"。对于"本租船协议由中、英文书写,签字生效"的条款,其含义很清楚,在双方签字之前,整个租船合同内容都没有法律效力。也就是说,不仅租船合同的后续条款没有法律效力,就连前期中标产生的并且已经生效的合同核心条款也成了没有法律效力的条款。这样就否定了通过招投标而产生的中标结果的法律效力。这样的条款违反《招标投标法》第四十五、四十六条的规定,因此对于被申请人非签字不生效的主张,仲裁庭不予支持。

【评析】

本案主要讨论了经过招投标程序所订立的航次租船合同关于书面形式的认定以及生效要件。

关于航次租船合同的书面形式的认定,仲裁庭认为:本案中的航次租船合同由当事双方通过招投标的方式订立。根据《合同法》的相关规定,被申请人发出的招标书构成向申请人的要约邀请;申请人向被申请人发出的投标书构成了申请人的要约;被申请人向申请人发出的运输招标确认书实质应为运输中标确认书,构成被申请人对申请人的承诺,并且到达了申请人。承诺到达要约人时生效,承诺生效时合同成立,即本案的招标投标法律关系成立,产生包括招投标书内容在内的中标结果。《招标投标法》第四十五条规定"中标通知书对招标人和中标人具有法律效力。中标通知书发出后,招标人变更中标结果的或者中标人放弃中标项目的,应当依法承担法律责任"。因此本案中含有航次租船合同主要条款的中标结果对当事双方都具有法律效力。第四十六条规定:"招标人和中标人应当自中标通知书发出之日三十日内,按照招标文件和中标人的投标文件订立书面合同。招标人和中标人不得再行订立背离合同实质性内容的其他协议。"当事双方应该根据该条的规定订立本案的书面航次租船合同。

根据《海商法》第四十三条规定"航次租船合同应当书面订立。电报、电传和传真具有书面效力"。对于本案中的航次租船合同形式,这些法律都规定必须是"书面形式"。至于使用何种"书面形式",法律没有作出强制性选择规定。此外,在整个招投标的过程中当事双方也没有约定事后的航次租船合同必须以合同书形式订立。因此,被申请人认为根据招投标结果订立的合同必须是"合同书"形式,这一主张既不是法律规定的强制要求也不是当事双方的合意,仲裁庭不予支持。仲裁庭认为,本案中的航次租船合同以非"合同书"的书面形式订立没有违反法律的规定。

关于航次租船合同的书面形式的生效要件,仲裁庭认为:本案的双方当事人通过招投标过程建立对双方具有约束力的中标法律关系。根据《合同法》的规定,当事双方经过该过程建立的法律关系就是合同关系。就涉案合同内容而言,它就是一份航次租船运输合同。其建立的方式是当事双方通过电子邮件、传真等数据电文的交换。这完全符合《海商法》第四十三条的规定,"航次租船合同应当书面订立。电报、电传和传真具有书面效力"。对于用前述形式订立的合同,法律并没有规定这类合同的成立必须经由当事双方的签字盖章。因此本案租船合同的订立符合法律的规定。"依法成立的合同,自成立时生效。"此外,根据《招标投标法》第四十五条的规定,在被申请人发出中标通知书时,中标通知书对"招标人和中标人具有法律效力",即中标结果生效并对当事双方都具有约束力。

5. 修船责任保险合同纠纷

【案情】

2005年9月6日,申请人与被申请人签订修船责任险保险单,约定由被申请人承保申请人的修船责任险,保险期限自 2005 年 9 月 11 日零时起至 2006 年 9 月 10 日 24 时止。该保险单的第十五条约定争议由北京中国海事仲裁委员会进行仲裁解决。2005 年 9 月 11 日至 2005 年 10 月 28 日,涉案船舶在申请人处修理,其中一项修理工程为主机五号缸检修。

2005 年 11 月 25 日,涉案船舶从新加坡开往马六甲海峡时,经检修的主机五号缸发生机损事故。申请人在得知事故后,及时与被申请人联系,被申请人随之委派公估人调查、查勘。其后申请人与涉案船舶船东磋商并于 2007 年 5 月 29 日达成和解协议,由申请人向船东支付 145 000 美元作为经济补偿。申请人就该过程也及时向被申请人报告并提出索赔。被申请人于 2008 年 3 月 6 日向申请人发来保险拒赔通知书,称事故不属于保险责任范围。

申请人认为,本案保险为职业责任保险。按修船责任保险协议书第三条的约定,被申请人所承保的基本风险是"按修船合同及有关协议规定应由被保险人(申请人)负责的,对承修船舶所造成的损失"。在修船合同下申请人对船东负有赔偿责任,申请人就有权按照修船责任保险协议书从被保险人获得保险赔偿。

被申请人认为,根据修船责任保险协议书第三条保险责任范围约定,"按修船合同及有关协议规定应由被保险人负责的,由于修船工人或技术人员的过失而引起的火灾事故或船舶机损对承修船舶所造成的直接损失,但机器本身的损坏不予负责"。本案主机五号缸确实发生机损事故,但未造成除机器本身以外的船舶任何部分损失。至于主机五号缸本身的损坏,保险责任范围已明确规定"机器本身的损坏不予负责"。本案事故的原因是,在修理的过程中,申请人发现主机五号缸的缺陷,并向船东提出上车床校调,船东拒绝校正并拒绝在备忘录上签字。有关的部件在船东的要求下组装,整个组装过程在船东代表的监督下进行。另外单缸没有足够的冷却,以及船员未能及时发现该缸温度异常,致使事故发生和扩大。这些均属船东自身原因,并无任何一项属于申请人应当承担的责任事项。因此,申请人并无承担责任的事实基础和法律基础。

【仲裁庭意见】

在本案修船合同中,船厂(申请人)所承担的修船责任是修船责任保险协议的承保基础。修船责任的大小或范围由船厂和船东在修船合同中约定。在修船责任保险协议中,保险公司(被申请人)对属于船厂的全部修船责任或部分修船责任进行承保。修船责任保险的范围大小则由保险公司和船厂在修船责任保险协议中约定。就本案而言,申请人与船东订立的修船合同中,船厂的修船责任范围相应比较宽,责任的种类也相应多,而申请人(船厂)与被申请人签订的修船责任保险协议中的保险责任范围相应比较窄。修船责任保险协议是一份以申请人与被申请人约定责任的修船责任保险合同。其承保的风险是"火灾事故"和"机损事故",赔偿责任是"对承修船舶所造成的直接损失",并非对船厂的所有修船风险都承保并承担相应的赔偿责任。因此,对申请人的主张,即"在修船合同下申请人对船东负有责任,申请人就有权按照修船责任保险协议从被保险人获得保险赔偿",仲裁庭不予支持。

【评析】

关于修船责任保险合同保险赔偿范围的认定,仲裁庭认为,修船合同与修船责任保险协议是两个性质不同的合同,但两者之间有一定的联系。在保险实务中,修船合同中的"修船责任范围"和修船责任保险合同中的"修船责任保险范围",可以相同也可以不相同。这完全取决于不同当事人之间的合同约定。

三、小结

海事法治是建设国际航运中心重要的组成部分,提高我国的海事法治建设水平及其在国际航运中的话语权,并且在未来全球国际航运中心建设竞争中取得优势是我们的目标。不断完善海事司法机制,提高我国海事审判的司法能力,重点研究关于"一带一路"争端解决中心的设立,更好地服务于海洋强国战略,同时上海为建设国际航运金融法治中心应当发挥核心凝聚力,提升研究水平及影响力,更好地保障"一带一路"建设。

第三章 航运政策与法律的行政执行

海事行政是国家行政管理的一部分,它是海上安全监督管理机关及其工作人员为了维护国家主权、维护水上交通安全、保护水上人命和财产安全、防止船舶污染水域,依法采取行政许可、行政处罚、行政强制等手段所进行的管理活动。这种管理活动涉及船舶、船员以及海域管理的方方面面,主要有:船舶登记与安全管理、船员管理、同行水域管理、航标配布及管理、船舶载运危险货物管理、海上搜寻与救助等。本章将对2017年上海海事局、东海救助局、交通运输部上海打捞局、上海市渔政监督管理处、上海出入境边防检查总站等行政执法案例进行介绍。

2017年上海海事局紧紧围绕市委、市政府重大决策部署、局中心工作和人民群众关注关切,推进落实《上海市人民政府办公厅关于印发2017年上海市政务公开工作要点的通知》,根据水利部、住建部、国家海洋局政务公开工作要求,结合上海市海事、水务行业实际,坚持改革创新和需求导向,进一步完善政务公开制度体系建设,推进决策、执行、管理、服务、结果"五公开",加强解读回应,扩大公众参与,不断增强公信力、执行力,进一步提升水务、海洋公共服务能力和行业管理水平。

上海海事局积极推进行政权力运行信息公开,努力打造"法治海事"。贯彻"互联网政务服务"的相关要求,以公开推动"放管服"改革举措落实,做到权力公开透明、群众明白办事。根据权责事项取消和调整情况,及时更新权力清单、责任清单。推动编制公布中介服务评估评审办法。进一步推进行政审批事项办理过程公开。推进政务服务事项接入网上政务大厅,并通过中国上海门户网站和局门户网站集中公开。探索行政审批网上办理服务举措,持续深化网上办理,优化网上办事服务体验,推进线上线下一体化联动。

上海海事局积极推进信用和监管信息公开透明。根据行政许可和行政处罚"双公示"要求,及时向社会公示行政许可和行政处罚信息。配合市相关部门,进一步扩大法人信息的覆盖范围,实时更新应公示的企业信息。协同推进事中事后综合监管平台建设和失信被执行人跨部门协同监管。拓展信用信息在水务、海洋行政管理领域的应用,加强主动查询信用信息,创新行政审批管理和服务方式;根据行政相对人信用情况,探索建立随机抽查、分级分类、动态检测频率等信用分级监管方式,探索开展部门协同监管、联合惩戒、预警机制,进一步提高事中、事后监管水平。

十九大报告明确,"坚持陆海统筹,加快建设海洋强国",充分体现党中央对海洋事业建设发展的新要求,充分体现决胜全面建成小康社会、夺取新时代中国特色社会主义伟大胜利赋予海洋事业的新目标、新任务,为海洋事业建设发展指明了前进方向。2017年上海海事局按照十九大战略部署,深刻领会新时代新形势新战略新要求,加快推进海洋强国建设。

2017年,东海救助局共完成海上值班8 368艘天,执行各类救助抢险任务629起,出动救助力量850次,救助各类遇险人员1 035人,救助遇险船舶42艘,直接获救财产价值估算19.03亿元。东海救助局管理体制改革成效明显,救助中心工作成绩突出。其用实际行动践行了国家海上"德政工程",筑牢了海上安全最后一道防线。

一、上海海事局行政执法案例

(一)崇明口岸查验单位首次通过"单一窗口"实施联合登临检查

2017年12月6日,崇明海事局、崇明海关、崇明出入境检验检疫局以及崇明出入境边防检查站四家口岸单位的10余名执法人员登上位于崇明华润大东船厂的意大利籍邮轮"歌诗达新浪漫号"进行联合登临检查,这是崇明口岸首次通过"单一窗口"实施的联合登临检查。

近年来,随着上海港邮轮经济的发展,崇明华润大东船厂作为首家打入邮轮厂修市场的中国修船企业,已先后完成"歌诗达大西洋""歌诗达赛琳娜""天海新世纪"等10艘次豪华邮轮进港维修工作,成为远东地区重要的邮轮维修基地。此次"歌诗达新浪漫号"豪华邮轮是首次在上海进行维修养护。

检查过程中,针对船舶安全状况、货物和人员等检查内容,四家单位坚持联合登临机制"依法高效、方便船舶、分工合作"的原则,在同一时间针对不同项目登轮开展现场检查,减少了重复登临检查次数,缩短了口岸检查的总体时间。同时按照"信息互换、监管互认、执法互助"的要求,避免检查内容重复,提升了口岸查验的通关效率,最大限度地降低对邮轮维修作业的影响。

此次"单一窗口"联合登临检查为崇明口岸船舶修造企业响应国家供给侧结构性改革加快实施转型升级,开展豪华邮轮维修、特种船舶修造等新业态提供了有力支持。崇明海事局作为联合登临召集单位,将进一步总结经验,优化崇明口岸单位联合登临检查机制,不断提高口岸查验能力和服务水平,为即将到来的出游旺季打好"前哨战"。

(二) 30只集装箱落水,上海海上搜救中心紧急交通组织

2017年11月18日15时25分,上海海上搜救中心接报,载有400余只集装箱的多用途船"鹏安盛"轮(福建公司,长148.78米,总吨9 977,船上17人,载20英尺箱153只、40英尺箱258只,烟台—上海)在长江口D3灯浮附近北侧水域,受寒潮大风影响,船上30只40英尺集装箱落水。箱内所装汽车配件,无危险品箱。上海海上搜救中心指派吴淞海事局"海巡012"、协调"东雷5""东雷12""东雷16""东南起12"等4艘打捞船赶往现场。上海海上搜救中心通知洋山港、崇明、浦东海事局协助,播发航行警告。

截至当晚,长江口深水航道通航正常,进口国际邮轮计划正常。上海海上搜救中心在事发水域进行交通组织,提醒过往船舶谨慎驾驶,听从交管指挥。

针对此类集装箱坠海事故频发,上海海事局提示:①船舶应重视每一装卸港口的集装箱系固方案,并切实按照方案实施集装箱系固操作,并对船舶可移动系固装备定期检查维护;②当船舶遇到大风浪时,船长应及早采取有效措施,如减速、改向,以减少船舶正面受浪的冲击,降低船舶水平和减轻船舶的横摇等。通过以上措施减免船舶受损、集装箱坠海事故的发生。

(三) 上海海事局全面开展2017年"中秋""国庆"船舶安全大检查活动

2017年"中秋""国庆"佳节将至,为便捷人民群众安全出行,保障辖区水上交通安全形势稳定,上海海事局根据上级部门有关通知精神,结合《上海海事局客运船舶安全管理长效机制》等要求,于2017年9月11日起在辖区全面开展船舶安全大检查活动。

大检查活动主要针对局辖区投入运营的客运、危险品船舶进行检查,重点对所有投入运营的客运船舶、交通艇和其他载客超过12人的船舶实施船舶安全检查,对检查出的所有缺陷须进行纠正和跟踪复查,确保客运船舶检查率100%,缺陷纠正率100%。

此次大检查活动检查的重点是船员实际操作能力、值班制度落实情况、船舶消防救生设备等是否按要求配备并保持可用状态及开展应急演练等。对客运船舶的安全检查将持续到9月底,督促全面落实安全生产主体责任,加强对所属船舶的安全管理和岸基支持,督促其切实执行客运船舶落实恶劣天气禁限航工作和公司管理人员值班值守和应急处置工作。上海海事局通过加强与政府、交通、安监等部门联合执法力度,维护正当营运秩序,全力保障客运船安全营运。

(四) 违章船舶哪里逃,科技手段抓现行

2017年6月21日,杨浦海事局指挥中心在电子巡航过程中发现船舶"＊＊

207"轮进入辖区复兴岛木材公司码头进行装卸作业,系统显示该船舶此前已多次涉嫌未按规定航路及未按规定航速航行的违法行为却尚未处理。针对此情况,指挥员当即再次核实该船位置并通知现场执法人员对其进行违法行为调查,通过对航行日志和 AIS 轨迹等证据的提取核对,船方最终承认违法行为。当日下午,该轮船东主动到杨浦海事局接受调查处理,并承认前期接到违法通知后存在侥幸心理,想通过拖延时间逃避处罚。

这是杨浦海事局依托电子巡航系统新增的"协查船舶到港报警功能"所查获的首艘存在多次违法行为未处理的船舶。此后杨浦海事局继续深入开展电子巡航,加强与现场执法的协作联动,严厉打击各种违法行为。

(五)闵行海事局查获上海港首例外轮滞留缺陷未纠正、带病航行案件

2017 年 5 月 15 日,闵行海事局查获一起外轮港口国监督检查滞留缺陷未纠正、带病航行至上海港的案件。这是新版 PSC Manual 中的新缺陷行动代码"46"实施以来,上海港查获的首例外国籍船舶滞留缺陷应用了代码"46"但未实际纠正的案件。

当日,闵行海事局在利用上海海事局开发的"船舶安全监督辅助决策支持系统"对辖区适检外轮进行检查时发现:辖区关港 4 泊位靠泊的一艘外轮的过往 PSC 检查记录中有一项遗留项目属于滞留缺陷,但系统显示该缺陷并无纠正记录,存在重大安全缺陷未纠正、带病航行至上海港的嫌疑。闵行海事局当即指派执法人员对该轮开展港口国监督检查做进一步核实。

经检查发现,该外轮曾经在日本大阪因为"舱盖板无法风雨密"的缺陷被滞留,且滞留缺陷行动代码为新版 PSC Manual 中的新代码"46"。代码"46"不代表解除船舶滞留,船舶应在适当的时间范围内驶往当时指定的修理港烟台进行修理以纠正滞留缺陷。然而执法人员经检查发现,该船并未驶往烟台对该严重缺陷进行修理,依然"带病航行",严重违法港口国监督程序新代码"46"的相应要求。同时,该滞留缺陷未纠正也显示船舶严重违反了 ISM 规则的有关要求。鉴于问题的严重性,闵行海事局依法对该外轮实施了滞留。

(六)吴淞口 37 只集装箱落江,上海海上搜救中心全力组织主航道清障

2017 年 5 月 10 日 2157 时,上海海上搜救中心接报,吴淞口警戒区有 37 只集装箱落江,箱内无危险品。中心立即组织搜救及应急力量至现场,搜寻、定位、打捞集装箱,并优先对主航道进行扫测,确保进出长江船舶安全航行。

10 日夜间,装有 129 个集装箱的"顺港 19"轮航行至吴淞口警戒区时 37 个集装箱翻倒落江,箱内载有废纸屑。据核实,落江集装箱中无危险品。接报后,中心向周边水域船舶播发航行警告,水上交通管控中心(VTS)加强安全信息广播和交通组织,开辟应急处置专台,相关水域实行临时交通管制。中心组织11艘海事巡逻艇、6艘拖船、11艘打捞船、2艘测量船在事故现场搜寻、定位、打捞,当时打捞起6个落江集装箱。

东海航海保障中心测量船"海巡1668"对相关水域进行扫测,优先扫测长江主航道、吴淞口水域,确保进出长江、黄浦江船舶安全航行。现场东南风3级,轻浪,能见度良好。

吴淞海事局已开展事故调查。上海海上搜救中心制定细化扫测清障方案,加大扫测力度,增派打捞力量加速清障进程。

(七)上海海事局全面启动入厦船舶专项安全监管工作

根据《交通运输部海事局关于对近期入厦船舶开展专项安全监管工作的通知》要求,上海海事局经过前期认真研究、周密部署,于2017年6月1日起正式启动对进入厦门管控水域船舶的专项安全监管工作,扎实推动各项监管措施的落实。

一是加强组织领导。结合上海海事局工作实际制定具体工作方案,合理调配人力资源和执法装备,明确各项工作要求,确保入厦船舶专项安全监管工作领导到位、责任到位、措施到位、人员到位。

二是开展内部学习。组织现场执法人员认真学习关于入厦船舶专项安全监管工作的有关要求,统一工作标准,重点对实施日期、专项安检要求、保安检查要求等进行细化和明确。

三是广泛对外宣传。通过VTS广播、政务窗口、现场登轮以及微博微信等途径,向行政相对人广泛宣传入厦船舶专项安全监管要求,并设立咨询电话热线,做好相关宣传解释工作。

四是加强船舶监控。通过电子巡航、进出港报告系统等手段加强对入厦船舶的动态监控和报告信息核查,对未按规定接受专项检查的船舶及时采取有效管控措施。

上海海事局持续严格落实入厦船舶专项安全监管工作各项要求,并结合以往远端管控工作经验,认真落实,监管到位,使专项安全监管工作顺利完成。

(八)上海海事局服务自贸区建设取得重大成果:颁发上海第一家外商独资海员外派机构资质证书

上海海事局服务自贸区建设取得重大成果,经上海海事局受理、初审的中英中船船舶管理(上海)有限公司取得交通运输部海事局签发的外商独资海员外派机构资质证书。

2017年5月24日,中英中船船舶管理(上海)有限公司到上海海事局政务中心领取交通运输部海事局签发的海员外派机构资质证书,成为中国(上海)自由贸易试验区内第一家外商独资海员外派机构,这是交通运输部海事局、上海海事局服务中国(上海)自由贸易试验区建设的重大成果。

根据交通运输部海事局核准,中英中船船舶管理(上海)有限公司限于为中英中船(香港)有限公司管理的船舶派遣船员。允许外商独资企业在自贸区内开展海员外派试点,是交通运输部海事和上海海事局服务自贸区建设的重要举措,希望借助国际先进船舶管理公司船员管理的先进经验、管理优势和丰富资源,促进更多的中国海员走向世界,同时带回国际船舶管理经验,实现企业自身发展和自贸区建设的共赢。

(九)吴淞海事局积极开展涉渔船舶专项整治,有力保障长江口深水航道安全畅通

长期以来,吴淞海事局始终坚持将保障"两口一线"水上交通安全,特别是长江口深水航道的安全、畅通作为"三化"建设的主要任务以及履职尽责的核心使命。3—4月是渔业捕捞旺季,长江涉渔船舶渔网占用航道和锚地的情况频频发生,对来往船舶通航安全造成影响。对此,吴淞海事局切实履行职责,发挥多方合力,创新工作方法,积极开展涉渔船舶专项整治,有效保障了长江口深水航道安全、畅通、高效运行。

一是下好"先手棋",摸清规律再行动。2017年初,吴淞海事局组织对辖区锚地、航道水域进行拉网式排查,对于长期或经常停泊驻靠的涉渔船舶开展信息登记,掌握船主信息和联系方式,了解掌握相关涉渔船舶停泊、航行及作业规律等各类信息,并进行系统分析研究,为后续行动有序开展打下扎实基础。

二是念好"紧箍咒",先礼后兵有章法。根据排查情况,吴淞海事局组织力量有针对性地深入到相关锚地、集中停靠点等水域,向相关涉渔船舶就违规穿越航道或设置渔网等行为可能引起的水上安全事故风险及法律后果进行宣传教育;对于不听从劝导的涉渔船舶,联合水上公安、渔政部门等实施重点管理。

三是抓好"关键点",长效管理显成效。为防止涉渔船舶违法作业现象反弹,吴淞海事局联合渔政等相关部门,积极建立完善长效管理机制,着力加强水域巡航、联合执法和宣传教育。在2017年第一季度中,吴淞海事局在整治中共出动执法人员132人次,巡逻艇巡航190小时,航行1 780海里,驱离教育违规涉渔船舶48艘次,清理阻碍航道渔网渔具10次,整治工作取得阶段性成效。

2017年,吴淞海事局紧紧围绕保障长江口深水航道安全、畅通、高效运行的目标,进一步深化整治工作,对涉渔"三无"船舶和小型渔船在航道内设置渔网等违法现象实施重点打击,积极营造良好通航环境,为"三化"建设全面推进构筑坚实基础。

(十) 500 余艘船舶滞留上海港,优先安排邮轮有序疏港

2017 年 4 月 15 日傍晚,一场大雾降临上海港,局部水域能见度不足 500 米,吴淞辖区实施临时交通管制。直至 2017 年 4 月 17 日上午,大雾才缓缓散去。持续了几天的大雾导致包括大型邮轮"歌诗达赛琳娜""蓝宝石公主""天海新世纪"在内的 500 多艘船舶滞留长江口水域。2017 年 4 月 17 日 1100 时开始,吴淞海事局开启紧张、有序的疏港工作。

疏港工作按"客轮优先;先航道,后锚地;先出口,后进口;先货船、集箱船,后危险品、油轮"的总原则安排船舶进出口。为更加安全、有序地开展疏港工作,吴淞海事局不断加强与上下游兄弟单位的联动,并设置 VTS 加强班协助值班员进行疏港。南北槽船舶采取报备排队制度,最大限度提高航道的通航效率。

大雾期间,有三艘邮轮同时滞留上海港,涉及上万名乘客,但吴淞邮轮码头只有两个泊位,如何妥善安排这三艘邮轮靠泊,是这次疏港工作的重中之重。吴淞海事局密切关注水域能见度恢复情况,第一时间为邮轮开辟绿色通道,结合通航环境优先安排其进港。"蓝宝石公主""天海新世纪"首先前往邮轮码头靠泊,"歌诗达赛琳娜"在三角区应急锚地抛锚等候,待泊位空出后起锚靠泊。海事部门在最短的时间内完成了三艘邮轮的安全靠泊。

(十一) 闵行海事局通航环境专项治理初见成效

随着黄浦江上游浮吊整治工作的有力推进,闵行海事局辖区浮吊已经全部撤离,砂石料船舶改靠辖区码头卸货。因码头卸货能力有限,导致大型砂石料船舶在局辖区滞留,最多时有 42 艘大型砂石料船舶。针对浮吊整治后出现的新动态,闵行海事局高度重视、积极行动,组织开展通航环境专项治理工作,确保辖区通航安全形势稳定。

第一,用 CCTV,AIS 等电子巡航系统实时监控辖区航道情况,发现违规锚泊情况,第一时间指派巡逻艇前往现场宣传和比对,对未明确作业计划、作业时间和作业码头的大型砂石料船舶予以驱离,2017 年 4 月份累计驱离大型砂石船舶 31 艘次,有效改善了通航环境。

第二,加强与码头管理中心的信息沟通,落实大型砂石料船舶报备工作,有效减少砂石料船舶盲目进港、无序锚泊现象,滞留在局辖区的大型砂石料船舶已减少至 15 艘。

第三,加强巡逻艇水域现场巡查力度,对违章锚泊的砂石船舶坚决予以查处,严厉打击影响通航安全的违法违规行为,2017年3—4月累计查处砂石料船舶各类违章53艘次。

第四,严格落实码头管理制度,督促码头经营企业强化对船舶靠泊秩序的管理,根据码头卸货能力科学合理安排船舶进港计划,杜绝砂石料船舶盲目无序进港。

闵行海事局将持续开展辖区通航环境综合治理,消除安全隐患,全力维护好后浮吊时期黄浦江通航秩序。

(十二)减少轮渡停航,方便群众出行——吴淞海事局积极开展黄浦江通航秩序整治

为有效缓解船舶航行高峰与水上客流高峰重叠期轮渡被迫停航对百姓生活的影响,切实为浦江两岸人民群众水上安全出行提供更多便利。吴淞海事局正式启动2017年度黄浦江通航环境专项整治,严厉打击吴淞海事局辖区黄浦江段各类水上交通违法行为。

在专项整治中,吴淞海事局立足辖区通航环境现状,按照"教育与处罚相结合、维护与治理相结合"的方针,从三方面积极推进治理活动的有序开展。

一是定计划,明职责,全局上下织成一张网。活动开展前,精心谋划,周密制定活动方案,进一步细化治理活动的重点时段和各阶段工作侧重点,明确各有关部门的职责分工,将VTS监管、现场巡航、政务受理、后勤保障等各方面工作有机结合起来,为治理活动的开启定好总基调,细织责任网。

二是重宣传,抓治理,千方百计下好一盘棋。在前期宣传教育阶段,充分利用横幅标语、电子显示屏、微信短信平台等多种宣传方式,发布宣传教育资料,对船舶加强警示教育。在集中治理阶段,一方面重点对每日黄浦江船舶进口高峰时段水上交通违法行为加强查处力度,另一方面现场巡逻艇适时开展分流引导和秩序维护,防止船舶同时过量进入黄浦江造成航道拥堵,确保已进入黄浦江船舶航行安全,努力下好该水域安全监管这盘棋。

三是强联动,建机制,千头万绪拧成一股绳。整治活动期间,各执法部门密切配合形成合力,各执法轮艇间信息互通及时补位,并综合运用电子巡航系统轨迹、CCTV实时画面监控、VTS监控回放以及现场海事巡逻艇照片拍摄等方式实现违法证据的采集和固化。同时,将各执法部门的每日违章查处行为进行汇总统计和分析对比,每周对整治活动进行评估,及时修正具体方案,进一步探索和建立长效治理的工作机制。

整治活动旨在为辖区轮渡通航打造安全通畅、稳定有序的水域环境。吴淞海事局持续按照方案要求，压实责任，严格履职，确保整治活动有序推进，治理成果长久有效，并做好下一步到相关轮渡公司的走访工作，督促企业在落实安全主体责任、确保航行安全的前提下，合理缩短停航时间，为浦江两岸人们的出行提供切实的便利。

（十三）上海海事局启动船舶载运危险货物安全综合治理行动暨国内航行油船和散装液体化学品船舶专项整治活动

2017年4月，交通运输部和部海事局分别发布《交通运输部关于印发〈船舶载运危险货物安全综合治理行动方案（2017—2018年）〉的通知》和《交通运输部海事局关于印发〈国内航行油船和散装液体化学品船舶专项整治活动方案〉的通知》，计划通过为期一年的专项活动，有效防范遏制船舶载运危险货物重特大事故发生，保障人民生命财产安全，巩固"平安船舶"活动成果。

上海海事局迅速落实上级文件要求，结合工作实际，制定安全综合治理行动和专项整治活动工作方案，明确各单位/部门的职责分工，并提出相关工作要求。根据该工作方案，上海海事局自2017年4月1日至2018年5月31日，分三个阶段开展专项行动，通过专项行动，实现国内载运危险货物船舶专项安全检查覆盖率100%、危险货物船舶安全管理的航运公司安全管理体系或制度专项检查率100%、督促国内航行油船和散装液体化学品船舶自查率100%、督促船舶检验机构实现油船的防止油污证书和散装液体化学品船舶的适装证书检验核查率100%。

上海海事局相关业务处室将指导协助各分支海事局，通过加强领导、精心组织、明确权责、强化监管、综合治理、联防联控、加强宣传、做好总结等举措，有效开展安全综合治理行动和专项整治活动，集中实施对公司安全管理、船检质量、船舶作业、船员素质等方面的监督检查，形成源头管理和现场检查有效结合的监管模式；集中查处瞒报谎报危险货物、违法排放洗舱水、不适航船舶承载危险货物等行为，形成打击船载危险货物违法行为的高压态势，实现船载危险货物安全形势持续稳定好转的目标。

（十四）上海海事局认真落实内河航行船舶进出港签证取消要求

为便利船舶进出港口，依据《中华人民共和国内河交通安全管理条例》的修改决议，交通运输部海事局下发《关于实施内河航行船舶进出港报告制度有关事项的通知》，明确自2017年3月22日起，取消内河航行船舶进出港签证，改为实施船舶进出港报告制度。为保证该项工作开展平稳有序，上海海事局发布通知，多措并举，积极落实上级通知要求。

一是要求各窗口单位做好宣传工作，利用多种有效方式，向行政相对人全面宣传船舶进出港报告制度的重要意义和便利措施、船舶进出港报告的操作流程以及需要注意的事项，同时对外公布便于行政相对人咨询的联系方式。

二是做好船舶进出港报告平台注册工作，各窗口单位对前来办理海事业务的船舶，将指导其完成船舶进出港报告平台注册申请。对上海海事局登记船舶的注册申请，将尽快予以核验审批。

三是建立健全船舶进出港报告信息核查机制，加大对船舶现场核查力度，通过多种手段全程掌握船舶航行动态。

四是对船舶管理质量体系文件进行调整，删除原船舶进出港签证的相关体系文件，建立健全船舶进出港报告的相关体系文件。

（十五）上海港在港外锚地水域开展联合检查

2017年3月9日，吴淞海事局联合吴淞海关、浦江检验检疫局、吴淞出入境边防检查站、洋山出入境边防检查站的执法人员，同时登上停泊于绿华山锚地的国际航行船舶"张謇"轮实施联合检查。这是上海港首次在港外锚地水域实施联合登轮检查。

根据交通运输部、公安部、海关总署、质检总局《关于建立国际航行船舶联合登临检查工作机制的通知》的要求，各口岸单位执法人员秉承依法高效、方便船舶、分工合作的原则，依照各自职责分别对该轮的船舶设备、货物装载、人员情况等项目开展现场检查，并分别出具相关文书，办理相关手续。联合登轮检查按照"信息呼唤、监管互认、执法互助"的原则，大大缩短了口岸查验时间，有效提高了船舶出入境查验效率，将进一步增强上海口岸竞争力，助力国际航运中心建设。

吴淞海事局联合各家口岸单位，不断完善联合登轮检查工作机制，进一步提高国际航行船舶出入境查验效率和港口运营效率，使船舶联合登临检查更加便民高效。

二、上海救助及打捞部门行政执法案例

（一）救助"闽龙渔66822"轮

2017年2月6日，福建漳州籍渔船"闽龙渔66822"轮在厦门东南约60海里处因大风浪导致机舱进水，船舶不断下沉，船上11名渔民遇险，情况十分危急。此

外,该险情发生在春节和春运重点保障时段,遇险位置位于台湾的敏感水域,具有协调难度大、区域敏感性强等特点,东海第二救助飞行队接报后立即启动应急预案,紧急出动B-7310和B-7328两架救助直升机,进行急救。

2月6日1553时,直升机B-7310首先从厦门高崎机场起飞。1617时,直升机B-7328跟进起飞前往事发海域。当时,东海第二救助飞行队将2架直升机出动的情况通报台湾中华搜救协会,台方表示暂不出动直升机。1634时,直升机B-7310距离目标2 n mile范围时,由于现场能见度只有3 km左右,为了方便搜寻目标,直升机降低空速到80节左右,并打开机载雷达辅助发现目标,开始进行搜救程序。距目标1 n mile左右,机组发现2点钟方位有一艘渔船在风浪的作用下有些倾斜,随即前往并确定此船为遇险船,同时立即开始救援。由于在航路上机组已经完成了所有搜救/吊运任务前检查的内容,机组直接下降高度到等待点(距遇险船舶4～5个单位)开展救援。考虑到渔民未有吊运经验,机组先尝试进行下放一名救生员到遇险倾斜船舶上,让救生员协助渔民使用救生套的方式进行吊运,但是救生员下放到船舶上后发现风浪太大,且渔船前舷已下锚,船尾部上下浮动太大,救生员无法安全站立作业,在成功协助一名船员吊起后,机组决定尝试使用高绳协助吊运的方式进行作业,第一次高绳吊运由于渔民操纵使用高绳力度过大导致高绳崩断,机组马上准备备份高绳进行作业。此时,直升机B-7328到达现场。双机根据分工开展救援,直升机B-7328在直升机B-7310左后方向做备份保障和观察提示,直升机B-7310正常吊运作业,两架直升机互为保障,保持目视飞行安全间隔,确保作业安全。

1650时,遇险渔船在风浪影响下倾覆角度更大,有可能随时沉没,经过B-7310剩余功率确认安全后,直升机B-7310和B-7328默契配合,将11名遇险人员全部被救上直升机B-7310直升机。此时,遇险渔船已经呈90°倾斜状态。1705时,直升机B-7310返场。1715时,直升机B-7328返场。

1737时和1751时,直升机B-7310和B-7328先后安全降落厦门高崎机场,将11名遇险人员全部移交海事部门。救助圆满结束。

在本次救助中,遇险位置为台湾海峡,是我国东南沿海的交通要道,船舶流量大,受"峡管效应"影响,多大风大浪,气象海况复杂。这次成功救助主要得益于遇险渔民的及时报警和相关救助力量的快速反应、协调配合,否则在气温水温较低的情况下,后果将不堪设想。

(二)"东海救102"轮前往长江口北堤口救助沉没中"启程先锋"轮
2017年12月4日凌晨0400左右,长约54 m的"启程先锋"轮在长江口北堤附近搁浅,主甲板浸水,船上9人遇险,急需救助。东海救助局获知后立即启动应急救助预案,指令在长江口鸡骨礁附近待命的"东海救102"轮前往救助,"东海救102"轮经过一个小时的全速航行,于当天0500时抵达现场。航行途中,"东海救102"轮实时保持与遇险船沟通,了解遇险船舶及人员状况,结合现场海况,制定救助方案,并及时指导船上人员关闭所有阀门、管路,防止船内溢油泄露等次生灾害的发生。

由于遇险船搁浅在岛礁区,正值落潮,水深太浅,"东海救102"轮和专业救助艇均无法靠近。"东海救102"轮按照既定的救援方案,指导遇险人员身着救生衣和救生圈后,沿遇险船和救助艇间搭建的援救生命导引绳,一个接一个地安全牵引至"东海救102"轮救助艇。经过两个半小时的努力,9名遇险人员全部接上救助艇,并被安全转运至东海救助局"东海救102"轮妥善处置。

长江航道上大小船舶往来十分频繁,每天过往船舶达千余艘,这些船舶不仅携带为船舶提供动力的燃油,还有废油,有的还是专门运输柴油、汽油或食用油的船舶,这些船舶一旦发生意外,可能造成油料外泄,污染水资源。在此次救援过程中,东海救助局不但快速制定救援方案救助遇难船员,而且很好地防治了船舶溢油情况的发生,体现了东海救助局面对可能突发的船舶污染事故的应急保障能力。

(三)"东海救111"轮前往定海湾东南约12 n mile处救助倾斜货船"福顺67"轮

2017年8月20日凌晨,渔船"滨海渔19868"轮在江苏盐城外海10 n mile处遇险翻扣,多人遇险,1名渔民随船翻扣在舱内待救。接到险情后,东海救助局指令"东海救112"轮和连云港救助基地应急队员赶赴江苏盐城海域。搜救人员克服流急、夜间能见度差、渔网多等重重困难,现场勘查,清理渔网,翻扣固定,应急队员潜水进舱,最终从翻扣渔船船舱内成功救起1名被困21小时的遇险人员。

受强对流天气影响,东部海区近日险情不断,发生多起事故,在有关省市搜救中心的协调下,东海救助局成功处置多起险情,有效保障东海辖区的安全。

8月18日和8月20日,专业救助直升机分别在温州和舟山救助2名遇险渔民;8月19日起,"东海救111"轮、专业救助直升机"B-7345"、福州救助基地应急队员在平潭澳前南面水域搜寻沉没货船"新东远"轮9名落水失踪人员;8月20日,"东海救204"轮、专业救助直升机"B-7361"在上海吴淞4号锚地附近水域搜救沉没货船"顺航9688"轮上2名落水失踪人员。

东海救助局专业救助力量快速出动化险为夷,归功于东海救助局积极探索新形势下加强救助基地综合管理和发展模式,不断拓宽救助基地功能。但同时也应当注意恶劣天气情况下的防抗措施:一是加强应急值班值守,进一步配置优势值班力量、提高人员责任意识;二是密切跟踪天气变化、加强与港航企业信息沟通,及时发布安全信息;三是加强锚泊秩序管理,强化重点船舶监管,严格旅游船艇监管,防止碰撞事故发生;四是专门部署破冰工作,有效应对海冰影响。

(四)上海打捞局奋战590天,"世越"号三年后重见天日

韩国"世越"号渡轮船长145 m、宽22 m、型深14 m,空船重6 113 t,载重量3 794 t,排水量9 907 t。2014年4月,"世越"号在全罗南道珍岛郡附近水域沉没,导致295人遇难,9人下落不明。2015年7月,在全球19家实力最强的打捞公司共同参与的国际商业竞标中,上海打捞局以整体实力和"钢梁托底"的人性化打捞方案中标,与韩方签署打捞合同,并于同年8月12日赴韩实施打捞任务。

"世越"号沉船整体起浮采用驳船抬浮方式完成,包括抬浮提升出水、拖航移位、移放半潜驳和整体起浮出水四个作业环节。沉船整体出水后,在作业现场进行绑扎,随后运往韩国木浦新港进行最终的滚卸上岸。

历时590天的打捞作业中,上海打捞局共投入作业船舶3 000余艘次,施工作业人员2 170人次。其中,作业所占比重较大的潜水作业累计完成逾6 000人次,水下作业总时间近1.3万小时,工程时间之长、任务之艰巨创造了世界之最。"世越号"打捞的成功出水,在世界打捞史上创造了奇迹,体现了中国救捞的实力。

三、上海市渔政监督管理处行政执法案例

(一)渔政水务联合出击,清理河道违规网具

为加强河湖水域渔业资源管理,2017年10月,闵行区农委执法大队(渔政站)联合浦锦街道水务部门共同对重点河道开展"清网"专项行动,不断夯实水域生态文明基础。

专项行动出动执法船艇3艘、人员26人次,重点巡查周浦塘沿岸1.8 km违法捕捞现象,联合执法队员们冒雨耗时2.5小时对河道两岸细致排查,共查获地笼网37张,有效取缔了非法网具,还河道以清洁通畅的生态环境。

闵行区农委执法大队(渔政站)持续联合街镇相关职能部门对在辖区河道内违法捕捞行为保持严厉打击的高压态势,共同保护管辖水域范围内的渔业资源和生态环境。

(二) 上海浦东渔政专项整治违规渔网具,还内陆河道清洁顺畅

为进一步加强浦东新区内陆河道管理,整治中小河道,2017年7月11—18日,浦东渔政联合南汇新城镇相关职能部门主要针对区域河道内违规渔网具开展河道专项整治工作。渔政执法人员顶着三伏天的烈日,共出动执法人员77人次、车辆11辆次、执法船艇11艘次,清除区域内地笼网150余条。

清理违规渔网具是落实河道管理长效机制的重要举措。2017年度浦东渔政通过增加巡查次数、严控严管等多项措施,加大对内河河道的监管,彻底清除各类违规渔网具。对违规渔网具的专项整治行动,进一步改善河道环境,还河道顺畅、河水清洁,从而达到维护河道生态健康以及保持航道畅通的目的。

(三) 市渔政处组织开展"2017清江4号"渔业专项执法行动

为严厉打击上海市内陆水域非法捕捞行为,切实加强渔业资源和水域生态环境保护,2017年9月12—13日,市渔政处组织各级渔政部门,集中力量开展"2017清江4号"渔业专项整治行动。行动累计出动执法人员301人次,执法船(艇)56艘次,执法车(辆)40辆次,共查获案件22起(其中电捕鱼案件10起),没收各类违规网具138顶(件),电捕工具9台(套),渔获物33 kg,已结案15起,罚没款15 350元,另外7起案件正在处理当中。

行动前,针对市民群众举报非法网具较集中、非法捕捞案件查获较多的水域,渔政部门确定重点、精心策划、周密部署。行动中突显了三方面特点:一是行动市、区渔政部门衔接,通过对近阶段非法捕捞行为事发时间、地点、违法人员构成的综合分析,划分出执法重点时段和重点水域,合理调配执法资源,优化执法手段,提升执法效能。二是在行动中,渔政部门联合崇明区当地公安、市容、水务等部门协调配合共同开展渔政执法工作,做到多部门联动。对东平镇和陈家镇等河道水域中发现的非法捕捞网具予以及时清理,对附近居民宣传有关法律法规并得到他们的支持和理解,打击各类非法捕捞行为,保护内陆水域渔业资源和水域生态环境。三是在两天一夜的连续行动中,执法人员基本上采取从白天到夜间连续执法的行动方案,特别是在下半夜及凌晨的非法捕捞高发时段进行重点检查,增强执法行动的针对性,有效打击相关违法人员,起到较好效果。

(四) 上海渔港监督局开展水上执法和应急演练工作

2017年8月29日至9月2日,上海渔港监督局开展"利剑-2017"渔业水上专项执法行动,执法人员在横沙渔港、北港及深水航道等水域,重点检查船长未按规定保证渔业船舶符合最低配员标准以及未按规定确保渔业船员携带符合法定要求

的证书等违法违规行为。该航次共办理渔业行政执法案件5件,罚款人民币1万元。在办案过程中,执法人员使用新版电子执法文书,用执法记录仪全程记录执法过程,确保执法行动严格、规范、公正、文明。

中国渔政31005、中国渔政31006船结合本次水上专项执法行动,组织进行船副的操纵训练和全船应急演练。在操纵训练中,船副通过在不同气象条件下的靠泊和航行训练,提高独立操纵水平。两艘执法船的应急演练包括救生、消防和拖带(旁拖和尾拖)部署训练等内容。通过训练,船员的整体训练水平得到提高,为执行各种抢险救助任务打下坚实的基础。

上海渔港监督局不断加强渔业安全生产执法检查,继续强化应急演练工作,着力提升执法人员法治意识,全面履行渔业安全监管职责,发挥安全执法检查工作在渔业安全生产中的积极作用,推动上海市现代渔业健康发展。

(五)上海渔港监督局对杭州湾水域开展联合执法行动

2017年8月15日,为切实做好开捕后杭州湾水域渔业安全生产工作,进一步排查渔业安全生产隐患,上海渔港监督局芦潮港分局联合浦东渔政,在杭州湾水域开展海上联合执法行动。

本次执法行动检查重点包括:船员临水作业是否穿戴救生衣,救生、消防和通导设备的配备情况,船舶配员情况以及船舶进出港签证等。在检查过程中,执法人员发现,经过近几年的宣传教育和常态化执法检查,本市渔民的安全生产意识有了较大提高,主要表现在:船员在临水作业时能够主动穿戴好救生衣,保障自身安全;遇到检查时,船长积极配合,相关证书资料提交齐全。但同时执法人员也发现部分外地渔船存在配员不齐、临水作业未穿戴救生衣的情况。

作为杭州湾水域休渔开捕后的首次联合执法,本次行动有效排查渔业生产过程中的安全问题,有力保障渔民群众生命财产安全,为该水域渔业生产有序开展奠定良好基础。上海渔港监督局联合各区渔政,加强执法力度,进一步做好杭州湾水域的渔业安全生产监管工作。

(六)上海铁路运输法院宣判非法电捕鱼案

2017年7月27日,上海铁路运输法院第二法庭上3名非法捕捞长江水产品的犯罪人员张某、胡某和沈某被集中宣判,三人分别被判处有期徒刑缓期执行、拘役等刑罚,这标志着长江航运公安局上海分局在2017年打击非法捕捞、维护长江生态环境工作中取得阶段性成效。

2017年上半年,长江航运公安局上海分局不断强化对长江非法捕捞行为的打击力度,联合渔政等部门多次开展联合执法行动,并通过积极调查取证,先后在长江崇明、长兴、横沙等水域,连续破获75起涉嫌非法捕捞水产品案件,抓获张某、胡某等违法犯罪嫌疑人17名,当场缴获长江刀鲚、凤尾鱼、青鱼、鲈鱼等非法渔获物数百公斤、起获非法网具百余顶。7月27日上午,张某等3人被集中宣判,其他涉案人员法院将择日进行判决。通过渔政部门行政执法与公、检、法司法工作的衔接,形成"案件查办""统一起诉""集中宣判"的办案模式,不仅有力打击了非法捕捞违法犯罪行为,还提升了法律的震慑力。

自2002年以来,为更好保护长江水域环境,推动渔业绿色发展,农业部每年都会发布长江禁渔期公告,禁渔期期间禁止一切针对长江水产品的捕捞作业。即便如此,仍有少数不法之徒基于巨大的利益驱使,无视相关规定,在长江上海段水域多次使用深水张网、电捕等"杀鸡取卵""断子绝孙"的方式捕捞长江刀鲚等水产品,并从中牟利,这无疑给长江带来灾难性的后果——不仅可能影响船舶在航道内的通航安全,还会因滥捕造成长江流域生物链恶化,渔业资源严重衰退,导致珍稀鱼类灭绝。

生态环境问题关乎经济社会发展全局,长江航运公安局上海分局今后将继续联合相关行政执法部门采取有效措施,严厉打击辖区内各种破坏环境资源的犯罪行为,保护长江母亲河,促进人水共和谐。

四、上海出入境边防检查总站行政执法案例

(一)吴淞边检站开展锚地水域巡检工作

为切实做好锚地船舶管理工作,防范和打击各类违法违规行为,推动锚地巡检工作常态化、制度化,2017年11月16日,吴淞边检站执法检查组乘坐"边检3166"艇赴吴淞锚地、宝山锚地等辖区水域开展巡检工作。

其间,该站执法检查组搭乘"边检3166"艇对吴淞锚地、宝山锚地等水域进行警戒巡航,对沿线锚泊船舶信息进行比对,注意发现有无违法违规情况,对埃塞俄比亚籍某轮进行重点巡检,对该轮人员上下、船员在位等情况实施询问检查。

巡检过程中适逢阴雨天气,能见度低、出航条件差、巡检任务较以往难度加大,执法检查组全体人员和"边检3166"艇全体船员克服不利因素,顺利完成各项工作任务,为在恶劣天气完成锚地巡检任务奠定坚实基础。

(二)外高桥边检站签发上海港首张电子登轮证

2017年10月23日,外高桥边检站通过上海"单一窗口"边检许可服务平台签

发了上海港首张电子登轮证,船务代理公司员工叶某持电子登轮证及本人身份证件,在接受执勤民警查验后,顺利登上中国香港籍某轮工作。

根据上海边检总站相关部署,外高桥边检站多措并举,扎实推进平台实测工作。一是开展内部培训,确保民警熟练掌握平台各项功能。二是组织部分航运企业、船务代理单位开展平台实测工作,指导相关单位开展信息登记。三是及时反馈意见,对实测运行中发现的各类问题进行收集整理上报。

(三)吴淞边检站开启"绿色通道"救助受伤船员

2017年7月6日0600时,吴淞边检站接新海丰代理公司电话,称该公司所代理的帕劳籍"吉星9"轮上一名越南籍船员不慎受伤,经船上医务人员初步诊断为手指粉碎性骨折,需要紧急送往医院救治,希望边检机关提供紧急救助。

接报后,该站立即响应,派出民警迅速赶赴交通艇码头,在船员抵达后第一时间对受伤船员实施人证对照。经核实相关情况,允许受伤船员先行下地进行治疗,并补办相关入境手续,为伤者争取到宝贵的救治时间。

(四)外高桥边检站与海事部门联合执法查处首起船舶同时违反边检、海事法律规定案

2017年5月,外高桥边检站和浦东海事局对靠泊于上海外高桥一期码头的某外国籍船舶实施联合登临检查。检查中,发现该轮外档搭靠了一艘无明显船名、船籍港标识的小型油船。经查,该船实为中国籍"苏××"号油船,冒用"沪××"轮搭靠外轮许可证搭靠外国船舶。在查明案件事实后,外高桥边检站依据《中华人民共和国出境入境管理法》相关规定,对该船舶负责人进行处罚。浦东海事局依据海事法律相关规定,对该船舶违法行为进行处罚。

该起案件是上海外高桥口岸相关工作机制建立以来,口岸单位联合执法查获的首起船舶同时违反边检、海事法律规定案件。

(五)上海边检总站开展"一带一路"国际合作高峰论坛安保锚地巡检工作

为确保"一带一路"国际高峰论坛期间锚地水域管控安全,2017年5月9—10日,上海边检总站统一部署派遣执法小组搭乘"边检3166"艇赴吴淞、金山锚地等水域执行锚地巡检和警戒巡航任务。此次任务历时2天1夜,累计航程近300海里。

巡检过程中,执法小组通过"边检3166"艇无线电呼叫核查、AIS航迹跟踪、雷达搜索等多种方式对停靠锚地国际船舶进行巡检。对停泊于金山联检引航锚地的巴拿马籍"横滨先锋"轮和韩国籍"皇家三富"轮进行信息问询和警示提醒,强调出入境管理法律法规和锚泊期间的边检管理规定。巡检结束后,执法小组搭乘"边检3166"艇对相关水域实施警戒巡航。

此次巡检,进一步提升了边检机关对吴淞、金山锚地靠泊外轮的管理力度,增强水上执法执勤能力,达到警示效果,为确保"一带一路"国际高峰论坛期间锚地水域的安全有序奠定扎实基础。

(六)浦江边检站和江浙沪皖四地旅游局、文化市场行政执法总队开展联合执法

2017年4月26日,浦江边检站和江浙沪皖四地旅游局、文化市场行政执法总队组成26人的联合执法组在吴淞口国际邮轮港开展联合执法行动。

行动前,联合执法组听取浦江边检站关于上海港运营邮轮的基本情况、邮轮入境简化和出境自助通关等创新便民举措的介绍,重点了解上海邮轮口岸旅行团通关流程、通关方式以及存在的问题,并就密切信息互通、加强行政执法力度、深化区域执法合作进行深入交流。

行动中,根据该站前期掌握的邮轮组团旅行社信息和旅行社在收客、带团中存在的问题,联合执法组重点就当日组团旅行社领队导游资格证、团体旅客名单表、领队是否随团出境等进行全面检查,对发生的问题责令旅行社进行整改。

自建立联动协作机制以来,浦江边检站和市文化执法总队开展多次联合执法,有效将包船旅行社纳入口岸综合治理范围,取得实质性成效。此次联合执法,更进一步整合了江浙沪皖的优势资源,增强各方在邮轮旅游执法中团结协作的能力。

(七)外高桥边检站参加上海外高桥口岸首次国际航行船舶联合登临检查

2017年4月26日,外高桥边检站与外港海关、外高桥检验检疫局、上海浦东海事局对停靠上海外高桥二期码头的美国籍"美森菲弗"轮实施联合登临检查。

外高桥边检站精心组织、周密部署,提前制定工作方案,派出骨干力量与联合登临检查单位组成联合检查小组,共同对船舶、船员实施相关检查,取得预期效果。此次检查是上海外高桥口岸部门首次对国际航行船舶实施联合登临检查,是落实国务院相关措施,强化大通关协作机制,全面推进"一站式作业"的重要举措之一。

(八)吴淞边检站积极做好大雾天气下边检执勤工作

2017年4月6日,上海气象局发布大雾黄色预警,长江口水域因迷雾导致船舶能见度降至不足百米,长江口锚地、吴淞锚地等大部分国际航行船舶入出境(港)受

到影响。原计划于凌晨进港的"海洋统治"轮等16条船舶因雨雾变更进出港计划。

吴淞边检站积极应对,采取有效措施确保恶劣天气下口岸通关顺畅:一是严密勤务组织,增加巡检频率,加大码头巡查力度,确保管理措施到位。二是密切关注船舶动态变更,加强与船舶代理、海事部门及兄弟海港边检站的沟通联系,切实掌握船舶动态信息。三是通过服务大厅电子公告牌、微信公众号等信息平台适时发布船情动态信息,提醒服务对象及时调整行程安排,避免在口岸长时间等待。四是根据大雾持续时间和潮水时间,提前做好警力部署,确保大雾消除后,船舶出入境高峰时段边检手续办理迅速,口岸通关顺畅。

(九)浦江边检站顺利完成"爱达贝拉"号邮轮边防检查任务

2017年4月2日,意大利籍访问港邮轮"爱达贝拉"号从日本石垣入境靠泊上海港国际客运中心码头,随轮载有旅客1 900余名、船员600余名。该轮在港停留3天,并在上海整船换客,于2017年4月4日载运近2 000名旅客出境前往日本那霸。

该轮隶属歌诗达邮轮公司,本航次系首次访沪。为确保旅客通关顺畅,浦江边检站多措并举,保障旅客顺畅通关:一是做好准备工作。提前与船方及代理联系,准确掌握需要办理24小时或144小时过境人员信息及是否有旅客申办15天免签手续等情况,部署充足警力,开足人工验证通道。二是加开备用通道。鉴于近2 000名旅客均为外国籍,且600余名船员需要采集证件资料页,该站除开足全部人工查验通道外,设置隔离措施,临时调整旅客走向,并启用4条备用通道,大幅缩短旅客候检时间。三是增加台外警力。针对该轮"老年旅客多,行动不便"的特点,现场检查队增加咨询、引导等岗位警力,协助旅客填写入境卡片,并提供必要的帮助。四是确保口岸安全。梯口执勤民警使用相关信息系统精确统计登离轮人员,做好人证对照工作,确保该轮在港期间人员上下安全有序。

(十)金山边检站与金山海事局开展联合执法行动

为进一步加强锚地管理,确保化工码头沿岸水域安全稳定,2017年3月16日,金山边检站与金山海事局开展联合执法行动。

行动中,边检民警和海事执法人员乘坐巡逻艇巡视金山沿岸水域,结合金山锚地管理现状和当前口岸管控形势,对联合打击违反搭靠、无证登轮等违法行为和协同应对化工口岸突发状况进行详细讨论推演。随后,双方人员共同登上停靠金山锚地的中国香港籍"大西洋女神"轮,按照各自分工,仔细查看船体各部位,全面检查船舶安全管理情况,并将发现的问题及时向船方进行反馈,督促整改落实。

此次联合执法行动是双方协作协议和执法协作机制的具体落实,也为下一步开展的国际航行船舶联合登临检查工作奠定基础。联合执法进一步增进沟通交流,提升执法合力,为更好地应对口岸突发状况,共同防范恐怖极端事件,维护口岸安定有序提供有力保障。

五、小结

海事行政执法部门维护水上交通秩序,负责船舶的监督管理,调查调解船舶发生的水上交通事故,组织水上安全巡逻和护航,指挥、协调水上搜救工作等。业务覆盖行政许可、行政强制、行政处罚等各方面,海事行政执法机构和执法队伍在不断加强,执法和执法监督制度日趋完善。海事行政执法部门的规范化有利于全面提升海事文化建设水平,同时将"人文生态管理"的理念融入海事管理,构建一个健康的海事内外环境,为海事加快现代化建设提供有力支撑。

第四章　航运政策与法律的书文评析

2017年是中国实践"十三五"规划的第二年，也是上海进一步建设国际航运中心的关键时刻。在建设"长江经济带"、实施"一带一路"倡议和"海运强国"国家战略以及建设上海自贸区的重大实践的同时也带动学术界对于航运政策的研究发展，专业学者紧跟航运业发展进程，结合实践进行深入研究，并取得可喜的研究成果，为航运业提供理论支持，也为政策与法律制度的制定和创新提供有力支撑。

《"一带一路"建设发展报告(2017)》从多个角度对"一带一路"5周年做了阶段性总结，为今后发展提出建设性构想。该书研究中国与"一带一路"沿线国家在央企合作、中亚合作、带盟对接、海外利益保护及国际舆情等领域的问题和前景。《中国自贸区发展报告(2017)》对我国自贸试验区的发展进行回顾和展望。在介绍世界及我国经济发展背景的基础上，对我国当前自贸区战略进行分析和展望。重点分析我国自贸试验区在金融创新领域的发展情况，对扩容的自贸试验区的发展进行展望，同时结合"一带一路"倡议对我国自贸区战略进行分析，最后重点对上海自贸试验区成立三周年以来的成绩及今后的发展进行综述和展望。《全球视野下的国际航运中心发展》在研究分析国际航运中心的概念、特征、构成要素、驱动力和产业链的基础上，以案例分析的方式研究比较新加坡、香港、上海以及国内等不同的国际航运中心的关键特征，通过建构科学的指标体系对具有全球影响力的国际航运中心进行评估，从而探寻未来国际航运中心的发展方向、趋势和核心竞争力，为上海建设具有全球资源配置能力的国际航运中心提供参考和借鉴。《航运金融手册》基于宏大的视角，全方位、多角度地介绍船舶融资概念和运营模式，收集多种常规实用的船舶融资模式和实际操作案例，内容涵盖股权资本市场融资、船舶融资贷款等的法律处理、德国KG模式、船舶估值定价及风险控制，对各类型船舶融资手段进行梳理，提供海事和船舶融资行业的新想法和新概念，对行业面临的共同难题提供解决思路。

《海商法基础理论的内涵、研究现状与研究意义》通过对海商法基础理论内容的介绍说明中国海商法学界对于海商法基础理论缺乏全面、系统和深入的研究，而民法、刑法、经济法等其他法律部门的基础理论研究对海商法基础理论研究具有借鉴价值。说明研究海商法基础理论对于完善海商法理论体系、提升海商法理论研究品位，正确引导海事立法与海事司法实践和正确指引航运实践具有重要意义。《"一带一路"背景下的国际海事司法中心建设》分析国际海事司法中心提出的原因并借鉴英国经验,对我国建立海事司法中心提出建议。呼吁我国应积极稳妥推进国际海事司法中心建设,努力实现从海事司法大国向海事司法强国的转变。

一、2017 年出版的航运政策与法律类书籍评析

1.《"一带一路"建设发展报告(2017)》[①]

《"一带一路"建设发展报告(2017)》分为总报告、国际合作篇、国内区域篇、专题篇四部分。总报告指出,"一带一路"建设成绩初现。国际合作篇重点分析中国与土耳其、伊朗、捷克、乌兹别克斯坦、阿塞拜疆以及东盟等国家和地区在"一带一路"建设上的合作。国内区域篇研究甘肃省、河南省、黑龙江省、海南省及云南省参与"一带一路"的规划与实施。专题篇研究中国与"一带一路"沿线国家在法律风险、产能合作、跨境贸易、铁路交通以及融资投资等合作领域的问题与前景。

报告由共 25 篇组成,从多个角度对"一带一路"5 周年做了阶段性总结,为今后发展提出建设性构想。

在"一带一路"倡议提出五周年之际,中国和沿线国家在投资合作领域取得显著成就,不仅大幅提升我国投资的自由化与便利化,中国对外投资还成为拉动全球对外直接投资增长的重要引擎。

"一带一路"建设是统筹国内与国际两大格局重大举措。报告着重分析北京、江苏、福建、四川、陕西、内蒙古、广西及宁夏参与"一带一路"的规划和实施情况。北京立足城市定位,发挥自身优势,继续加快城市功能转变,将在"一带一路"建设中发挥示范和排头兵作用。江苏围绕"一带一路"交汇点建设,着力推进设施互联互通,加强江海联动、陆海统筹。福建坚持经贸合作与人文交流并重,全方位开展与"一带一路"沿线国家和地区多领域合作。四川以建设完备的交通网络为基础,把自身的经济、文化资源和"一带一路"沿线国家有机的结合起来,实施四川的"251"经济发展。"一带一路"倡议的提出让陕西由内陆变成开放的前沿。在国家"一带一路"倡议全局中,内蒙古被赋予"发挥联通俄蒙的区位优势"的时代任务。广西在推动国际陆海贸易新通道、中国—东盟信息港等方面取得积极的成效。宁夏借内陆开放型经济试验区为契机,以中阿博览会为平台,不断加强与"一带一路"沿线国家的交流与合作。

在丝绸之路经济带沿线,各国参与"一带一路"建设的热情和愿望日益高涨,中亚、高加索和中东欧地区尤其如此。这些努力取得了积极成效。国家发改委新闻

---

① 李永全."一带一路"建设发展报告(2017)[M].北京:社会科学文献出版社,2017.

发言人曾经对媒体列举了"一带一路"建设的初步成就:一是强化战略对接,凝聚合作共识,加强与沿线国家的沟通磋商,推动与沿线国家战略对接、规划编制等工作,特别提到《建设中俄蒙经济走廊规划纲要》与波兰、捷克等国签署走廊规划纲要;二是强化互联互通,建设陆海通道,除中俄蒙经济走廊外,还提到中欧班列、中国-中亚-西亚经济走廊建设取得的成果;三是深化产能合作,扩大投资贸易,2016年各类双多边产能合作基金规模超过1 000亿美元,中国已与法国、德国、韩国、英国、西班牙等国就共同开拓"一带一路"沿线第三方市场达成重要共识,与俄罗斯、哈萨克斯坦、巴基斯坦、伊朗等国开展核电合作,中国企业已在"一带一路"沿线国家建设46个合作区;四是协同各方力量,形成共建合力,在地方合作、金融合作、人文教育合作领域取得显著成果。

报告还研究了中国与"一带一路"沿线国家在央企合作、中亚合作、带盟对接、海外利益保护及国际舆情等领域的问题和前景。

2.《中国自贸区发展报告(2017)》[①]

2016年世界经济仍未走出全球金融危机的阴影,总体表现为经济增速持续下降,潜在经济增长率不断降低,国际贸易投资不断下行,"黑天鹅事件"频发,贸易保护主义和反全球化趋势抬头,全球金融市场波动性和脆弱性加大,从而使世界经济面临更多的风险和挑战。

进入2016年以来,我国面临国际经济政治等方面形势变化带来的挑战。外贸方面,随着外部经济形势持续恶化,我国出口增速逐渐下滑,2015年甚至出现负增长;汇率方面,人民币升值的预期随着美联储加息周期的来临发生逆转,为稳定汇率避免人民币大幅贬值,我国的外汇储备也在不断减少;而国内经济方面,金融以及房地产市场的波动,加上实体经济一直以来未见明显好转,我国经济下行压力较大。

我国经济在进入以结构调整和发展方式转变为核心的新常态后,也亟待培育发展新动能,而"一带一路"与自贸区建设的结合则为我国通过进一步扩大开放来深化改革提供了思路和途径,尤其是在外部整体环境不利于贸易投资自由化发展的情况下,更需要通过推动多边、区域性贸易谈判来扩大国际市场,同时大力建设自由贸易试验区,通过自主扩大开放,探索制度创新、服务国家战略、打造改革开放新模式。

报告主要对我国自贸试验区的发展进行回顾和展望,全书分为三个部分。第一部分是总报告,在介绍世界及我国经济发展背景的基础上,对我国当前自贸区战

---

① 王力.中国自贸区发展报告(2017)[M].北京:社会科学文献出版社,2017.

略进行分析和展望;第二部分是自贸试验区发展评述篇,对我国当前四大自贸试验区发展进行综述的基础上,重点分析我国自贸试验区在金融创新领域的发展情况;第三部分是自贸试验区发展展望篇,对扩容的自贸试验区的发展进行展望,同时结合"一带一路"倡议对我国自贸区战略进行分析,最后重点对上海自贸试验区成立三周年以来的成绩及今后的发展进行综述和展望。

3.《国外媒体看"一带一路"(2017)》①

《国外媒体看"一带一路"(2017)》摘录国外数十家媒体对"一带一路"的观点、看法和预测,为"他者"看"一带一路"提供重要视角,也帮助国内了解国外对"一带一路"的态度和反应,从而更好地为"一带一路"建设提供信息参考和资政服务。

"一带一路"倡议于2013年首次提出,2014年"一带一路"全面布局,2015年"一带一路"落地实施,2016年"一带一路"全力推进,建设成果丰硕。四年来,中国与"一带一路"建设参与国的政策沟通不断深化,设施联通不断加强,贸易畅通不断提升,资金融通不断扩大,民心相通不断促进。充满中国智慧的"一带一路"倡议得到越来越多国家和国际组织的积极响应,并已在世界范围内形成广泛共识。2017年10月,在党的十九大报告中五次提到"一带一路",强调积极促进"一带一路"国际合作,努力实现政策沟通、设施联通、贸易畅通、资金融通、民心相通,打造国际合作新平台,增添共同发展新动力。将推进"一带一路"建设写入党章,这充分体现了在中国共产党的领导下,中国高度重视"一带一路"建设、坚定推进"一带一路"国际合作的决心和信心。

媒体是"一带一路"的讲述者、传播者和阐释者。国内有关"一带一路"的报道铺天盖地。2016年,随着"一带一路"的落地生根,国外媒体对此反响也越来越强烈。百分点数据科学部2017年5月发布的《"一带一路"国际舆情大数据报告》显示,从2015年开始,"一带一路"国际讨论声量呈逐年递增趋势,2016年较2015年环比增长330.2%。中国提出"一带一路"倡议的目的何在,"一带一路"项目建设进展如何,是否应加入"一带一路","一带一路"有何风险与挑战,"一带一路"将带来怎样的影响等一系列问题成为海外媒体关注的焦点。

"一带一路"倡议提出后受到国际社会高度关注,大部分国外媒体对"一带一路"表示欢迎、赞许,认为"一带一路"倡议是文明冲突之际的一股清流,它将有利于创造就业,提高人民生活水平,促进贸易和经济往来,也有助于增进地区理解,消除偏见,实现融合发展;但个别媒体对"一带一路"表示质疑和警惕,认为"一带一路"是中国扩大其地区和世界影响力的工具,指出中国旨在通过单方决定实现联通目

---

① 王辉.国外媒体看"一带一路"(2017)[M].北京:社会科学文献出版社,2017.

的；也有媒体暗示，在"一带一路"项目建设过程中，中国企业忽视项目所在国的实际需求，对项目所在国的自主选择缺乏尊重；还有媒体对"一带一路"建设建言献策，提出独到善意的建设意见。

该书突出媒体的态度、观点和观察视角，可以帮助读者快捷地了解外媒对"一带一路"的报道和解读。该书旨在帮助国内了解国外媒体对"一带一路"的反应和态度，更好地为"一带一路"建设提供信息参考和资政服务。

4.《中国邮轮产业发展报告（2017）》[①]

习近平总书记在2017"一带一路"国际合作高峰论坛开幕式上的演讲中提出，"经济全球化、社会信息化、文化多样化深入发展"，"世界人民对美好生活的向往从来没有像今天这样强烈"，邮轮产业已然成为世界人民追求美好生活的重要支撑，成为经济转型升级重要推动力，成为生态文明建设重要引领产业，成为展示国家综合实力的重要载体。

2017年是党和国家事业发展中具有重大意义的一年，也是供给侧结构性改革的深化之年，更是我国邮轮产业稳健发展的关键一年。《中国邮轮产业发展报告（2017）》是由上海国际邮轮经济研究中心组织国内外业内专家，根据国际邮轮产业发展最新形势及变革趋势进行编写的年度研究报告。全书由总报告、"一带一路"专稿、产业篇、政策建议篇四部分组成、内容体系较之前更加丰富完善，更具研究深度。总报告全景式地对2016—2017年国内外邮轮产业环境、中国邮轮产业发展现状及问题进行全面深入解析，并对邮轮产业发展趋势进行研判，探寻邮轮产业内在规律，并探讨促进中国邮轮产业行稳致远的对策；对中国邮轮产业的最新动态以"十大热点"形式呈现，展现中国邮轮产业最新发展成果；在国家"一带一路"倡议下，特别设立"一带一路"专题，深度解析"一带一路"倡议下国际邮轮产业发展的新机遇、新路径、新模式、新战略；产业篇研究的是整个邮轮产业结构的变革战略路径，以求推进邮轮产业转型升级；政策建议篇主要是探讨在全球背景下探索中国邮轮产业政策的创新，实现中国邮轮产业的持续健康发展。

国际邮轮市场规模持续增长，预计游客总量将达到2 580万人次，中国在2016年首次超过200万人次规模的基础上继续稳步提升，邮轮旅游在我国旅游业中地位持续提高，国际影响力不断增强，邮轮全产业链的经济辐射效应也明显增强。上海在全球邮轮市场的影响力和美誉度得到强化，在2016年亚太第一、全球第四大邮轮母港的基础上，国际排名有望进入前三，成为全球最具影响力的邮轮母港之一。中国各级政府对邮轮产业的重视程度加大，对邮轮产业的关注和支持力度以

---

① 钱永昌.中国邮轮产业发展报告（2017）[M].北京：社会科学文献出版社，2017.

及对邮轮产业的信心持续提升,2017年新增福州、大连两大中国邮轮旅游发展实验区,全力支持中国邮轮产业的创新探索。国际邮轮公司加速在中国市场进行战略调整,18艘母港邮轮为中国服务,2017年诺唯真游轮开启中国全新航季,将全新"中国定制"的邮轮"喜悦号"投放中国市场,公主邮轮"为中国宾客量身定制"的"盛世公主号"经历49晚的"海上丝路之旅"来到中国,星梦邮轮"世界梦号"也于2017年11月投放中国,全新邮轮的到来为中国邮轮市场增添了新的活力和发展动力。

展望2018年,中国邮轮市场将在高速发展中逐渐全面转型走向成熟,全国邮轮旅游产业发展将更加注重整体性与协调性,更加注重稳健性与持续性,更加注重特色性与差异化。国际邮轮公司对中国邮轮市场的信心将持续提升,中国将持续成为亚洲邮轮经济的引领者和全球邮轮市场的重要推动者,逐渐成为全球邮轮市场的标杆,创造国际邮轮经济发展的新规律。中国乘势而上、顺势而为,参与全球邮轮产业治理和新型邮轮产品供给,推动"一带一路"倡议下的国际邮轮经济行稳致远,抓住时代发展的新机遇,培育国际邮轮经济新业态,保持国际邮轮经济增长活力,推进我国邮轮经济迈向更加美好的未来。

5.《中国海关发展前沿报告(2017)》[①]

中国(上海)自贸试验区成立三年以来,海关在参与这场国家试验的同时迎来了重要改革。在自贸区的法律地位方面,海关应当借鉴国际通行规则,确立自贸区"境内关内"的海关监管区地位,确立海关对自由区内货物(包括侵权货物问题)实施监管的充分权力。在立足周边、辐射"一带一路"的自由贸易区网络战略背景下,海关应当进一步拓展与区域物流企业合作的深度和广度,为国际性物流通道建设以及区域贸易发展提供良好环境支撑。同时,自贸区的设立对外贸监督管理部门的跨部门合作、监管制度创新提出新的要求,海关监管制度创新应着眼于法律依据、协同创新、创新路径方面的问题,在实践中应当以国际贸易单一窗口建设为抓手,探索建立新机制,打破协调创新瓶颈。在监管制度创新的基础上,随着自贸区制度创新对制造业、文化贸易发展促进作用的显现,海关应进一步利用上海自贸试验区这一试验田,继续推广明确涉及制造业的各项措施,对制造业转型升级发挥导向作用,借鉴发达国家文化贸易发展经验,从文化产品出口贸易与文化服务贸易两方面拓宽文化贸易的发展路径。

海关全面深化改革的推进同样需要建立在对我国近年来对外贸易形势分析的基础上。该书分为三个部分,从文化、制度、对外贸易等方面对海关监管政策进行总结并指出问题提出宝贵建议。第一部分从发展规模、文化服务与文化产品贸易

---

① 干春晖.中国海关发展前沿报告(2017)[M].北京:社会科学文献出版社,2017.

的比较、核心文化产品与服务的构成比例、与全国其他城市的比较四个方面分析上海文化贸易的发展现状,指出上海文化产业的发展势头不及北京、江苏等地且总体规模偏小,与国际大都市相比差距较大的问题。第二部分通过数据表明海关制度创新对促进制造业的转型升级起到重要作用,尤其是自贸区包括海关制度创新的政策引导和帮助,制造业外资的大量流入,给制造业的发展不仅带来资金这一在发展中所必备的基础,而且会带来国外的先进技术、生产管理经验,同时促进物流业等的发展,他们之间互相促进、共同发展,将会更好地促使制造业的发展和转型升级。第三部分强调推行现代船舶吨税制对推进我国贸易和航运发展具有积极意义。船舶吨税是海关对于进出一国关境的船舶征收的税收。现代船舶吨税制的实质是以船舶吨为基础的公司税,世界上主要的航运国家都已实行现代船舶吨税制。我国目前的船舶吨税制给航运企业的发展造成一定的阻碍。在我国推行现代船舶吨税制,对推进我国贸易和航运发展具有积极意义,海关应作为一个有建设性话语权的执行者,协同税务机关形成完善的航运税收体系,提高执法效能。

该书在立足周边、辐射"一带一路"的自由贸易区网络战略背景下,以"海关全面深化改革"为主题,采取理论研究和现实问题相结合的方式,运用最新理论成果对海关全面深化改革中的重大现实问题等进行深入分析,内容全面,数据翔实。

6.《自贸区背景下的航运业创新实践》①

全球主要经济体需求疲弱,国际贸易复苏缓慢,航运业运力过剩将趋于常态,加之运营成本持续增加,航运业长期不景气的格局很难打破。自贸区的建设以及全球供应链理念的引入,将给航运企业带来新的发展机遇。该书系统地介绍自贸区背景下航运业的政策和影响,基于供应链创新的航运业发展战略,精细化管理的航运运营优化,以及物联网技术在航运业的创新应用。

该书从解析自贸区航运政策入手,结合自贸区航运政策的应用案例引出:先行先试外贸进出口集装箱在国内沿海开放港口和上海港之间的沿海捎带业务,将引发一系列的沿海运输权限问题。此外,WTO服务贸易原则要求不能内外有别和外外有别而进行歧视。

第二部分聚焦航运管理问题:目前中国船舶管理企业面临诸多困难,首当其冲的是船员所得税问题。以某船舶管理企业为例,船员成本占运输总成本(包括油耗)的15%,占管理费用(不包括油耗)的50%。在船收入通常较客观,以船长为例每月5万～7万元,而在岸收入则是船员所属劳务工资所在地的最低收入。远洋船员的个税起征点为4 800元,以船长为例,每月需缴税25%～30%,即需缴税1.5

---

① 胡坚堃,郝杨杨.自贸区背景下的航运业创新实践[M].上海:上海浦江教育出版社,2017.

万元,而船员平均一年在船时间为8个月,每年需要缴纳的个人所得税很高。在国际航运全球化的情况下,中国管理五星红旗船舶的船舶管理企业竞争力不强。新加坡、菲律宾对船员实行完全免税,印度对在海外上船天数超过50%的(即一年内有183天在船上工作)船员免税。另一个棘手问题是,全外资船舶管理企业没有船员管理资质。对船舶管理企业而言,其主要业务包括:技术、商务以及船员管理。目前新注册的外资船舶管理企业没有外派资质,不能派遣管理自己的船员,影响其业务发展。此外,还有人才引进、代收代付的税收和维修备件过境问题;船舶管理企业高层出境签证以及海外船员入境签证的便利性问题;形成类似菲律宾的POEA的监管部门等,这些问题都给船舶管理企业带来很大困扰。虽然在上海自贸试验区开展业务有一定的便利性,但很多条款还未落地,政策落实速度明显过慢,很多领域还需进一步开放。

该书最后强调自贸区航运政策亟待突破:自贸区航运业总体上仍以港口依赖型航运产业为主,低端、传统航运功能(如港口装卸、船舶运输、货运代理、船舶代理、集疏运等)占主体,高端、新兴航运服务功能(如航运金融、国际中转集拼、融资租赁、供应链管理、航运交易、船舶管理、航运总部经济等)亟待拓展提升。业界普遍认为,航运业低端劳动力较多,高端专业人才严重缺乏(仅占从业人员总数的1%左右);国际化高端航运组织集聚不足,中国航运组织和企业的国际化水平较低;市场主体缺乏多样性,创新发展活力不足。

航运专业服务方面,包括航运金融、保险、法律服务、信息服务等领域,普遍存在服务能力不强,市场规模不大,专业性、权威性不强,面临多重制度政策障碍等问题,总体处于发展的初级阶段,综合发展环境亟待提升。

7.《全球视野下的国际航运中心发展》①

开放、融合将成为国际航运中心发展的新趋势。国际航运中心是以优质的港口设施、发达的物流体系、关键的地缘区位为基础条件,以高度完善的航运服务为核心驱动,在全球范围内配置航运资源的重要港口城市。"一带一路"视野下国际航运中心发展面临新趋势,港口成为撑起"一带一路"海上合作的重要支点。

该书在研究分析国际航运中心的概念、特征、构成要素、驱动力和产业链的基础上,以案例分析的方式研究比较新加坡、香港、上海以及国内等不同的国际航运中心的关键特征,通过建构科学的指标体系对具有全球影响力的国际航运中心进行评估,从而探寻未来国际航运中心的发展方向、趋势和核心竞争力,为上海建设具有全球资源配置能力的国际航运中心提供参考和借鉴。

---

① 张婕姝.全球视野下的国际航运中心发展[M].上海:上海浦江教育出版社,2017.

该书指出目前国内各大港口企业仍面临着"走出去水土不服"等诸多挑战。对标国家任务,大部分港口国际化程度仍然偏低,尚未具备单独走出去的能力。未来需要探索如何加强地方政府和港口企业的协同努力,助力我国港口加速融入"一带一路"倡议,发挥好航运中心枢纽作用。同时当前经济处于重大转折调整期,海运和航运面临新趋势。以信息化、互联网为引领的技术高速发展,将进一步促进各行业之间融合发展。从全球来看,整个港口和航运业越来越重视安全和对环境的保护,企业大联盟渐成趋势,港口在沿海都开始启动港口资源的整合,极大改变航运和港口的生态。

该书提出:海上互联互通、港口城市合作机制以及海洋经济合作等途径,能够极大地拓展我国经济发展空间。这种开放的发展理念,一方面,有利于我国国际航运中心吸引跨国公司、研发中心、结算中心、物流中心落户,产生集聚效应;另一方面,我国国际航运中心通过其在金融、保险、物流等领域的竞争优势与海运、港口企业长期海外经营的经验结合,将成为中国企业走出去的"跳板"以及"一带一路"倡议的亮点,进而为我国国际航运中心建设提供更为广阔的市场与发展空间。

8.《长江航运发展报告(2017)》[①]

该书严格贯彻落实党的十九大精神与创新、协调、绿色、开放、共享五大发展理念,以及"交通强国"战略与新时代长江航运现代化发展的新思路、新战略、新目标,全面总结和展示2017年长江航运业运行和发展态势、亮点,聚集绿色发展、智能发展、行业治理等当前热点内容,剖析长江黄金水道服务国家战略的成效,展望新时代的发展前景与目标。

该书首先介绍2017年长江航运发展的进程:长航局系统完成32个项目"工可"批复,34个项目"初设"批复;完成15个项目"工可"部审,3个"初设"部审;安排建设项目80余个,预算执行率达到95%以上。长江航运基础设施面貌持续改善,服务长江经济带建设的基础不断夯实。一批重点工程让长江黄金水道焕发出更大的活力。"645工程"等重点项目稳步推进,武汉至安庆段6 m水深航道整治工程"工可"报告通过国家发改委审查;"3升2工程"项目有关渔评专题获环保批复;大埠街至浏河口段数字航道、三峡库区交管二期、镇江溢油应急设备库等在建项目主体完工;荆江航道整治工程被评为"内河航道生态环保示范工程"。

该书紧跟"一带一路"倡议步伐:介绍长江航运行政管理体制改革。该改革既是一招着眼黄金水道建设、服务沿江经济社会发展的"先手棋",更是一场贯彻国务院、交通运输部决策部署,必须打赢的"攻坚战"。以综合执法为基础,长航局行政

---

① 交通运输部长江航务管理局.长江航运发展报告(2017)[M].北京:人民交通出版社,2017.

管理体制改革工作也在稳步推进。推进长江干线四川段水监体制改革、江苏海事局管理关系调整和长江干线水上监管一体化工作,长江干线海事管理体制基本理顺;长江航道管理体制改革实现政事企分开,职能定位得到明确,职能转换实现推进,组织结构更加优化,服务效能进一步提升。

该书全面介绍长江航运发展成就,为行业管理部门的科学决策提供重要智力支持,为大众了解认识长江航运发展状况提供有益的帮助,也为从事长江航运发展理论研究学者和长江航运实际参与者提供一定的借鉴。

9.《航运金融手册》[①]

船舶融资作为一个涉及航运、金融、法律等大跨度、多专业的领域,其健康发展对正在"一带一路"倡议推动下打造航运和海洋强国的中国显得日益重要。该书基于宏大的视角,全方位、多角度地介绍船舶融资概念和运营模式,收集多种常规实用的船舶融资模式和实际操作案例,内容涵盖股权资本市场融资、船舶融资贷款等的法律处理、德国KG模式、船舶估值定价及风险控制,对各类型船舶融资手段进行梳理,提供了海事和船舶融资行业的新想法和新概念,对行业面临的共同难题提供了解决思路。

全书分为六大部分:第一部分介绍一些传统船舶融资的基础知识;第二部分侧重于股权融资;第三部分着眼于资产定价问题;第四部分专注于制度框架及其对船舶融资的影响;第五部分整理行业所共同面临挑战的现有解决方法,如重组、风险管理以及替代性船舶管理和融资方法;第六部分侧重于介绍与船舶融资密切相关的服务。内容集中30多位来自国际和汉堡的专家的观点,他们的知识和专长是从行业实践中转化而来。

该书介绍了航运企业运作过程中发生的融资、保险、货币保管、兑换、结算、风险管理等经济活动而产生的一系列相关业务,涉及航运业、船舶业、金融业。其中介绍的德国KG模式,是一种有限合伙模式。组成KG模式有五大元素:一是固定税率,这对投资者而言是一种有利的税收模式;二是有限责任的股份有限公司模式,这是KG模式的法律架构;三是德国的航运银行,为KG模式提供借款;四是航运企业,进行船舶管理;五是零散投资人,进行股权投资。KG模式是基于委托的利润天堂。KG基金的发起人保障银行利益和抵押权;经纪人和赞助商保障造船企业的利益;船舶管理人保障资产;租船经纪人保障期租合同;KG基金保障投资人、信托和有限责任的一般合伙人的利益。

书中还提到:与欧美国家已相对成熟的航运金融产业相比,中国航运金融产

---

① 奥勒提斯·席纳斯.航运金融手册[M].北京:中信出版社,2017.

业仍处于起步发展阶段,研究和借鉴欧美国家在航运金融领域的丰富经验和失败教训是发展中国航运金融产业的重要途径之一。该书借鉴国外的成功经验,有利于中国建立有效的航运产业组织结构,优化升级航运产业结构,合理布局产业生产力和提高效益;吸取国外的失败教训,可适当地规避航运业的周期性和不稳定性,避免重蹈国外金融机构在船舶融资领域的覆辙。

10.《中国航运信托基金操作指引与法律解读》[①]

航运信托基金是航运金融创新的重要方式之一。研究航运信托基金有利于拓展航运融资渠道,促进航运产业升级和产业链整合,促进我国"一带一路"倡议、建设国际航运中心与国际金融中心以及海洋强国战略的实现。

基于航运市场和我国资本市场的特殊性,该书对中国航运信托基金的法律地位以及设立中国航运信托基金所涉及的主体法律关系、信托基金财产所有权的归属、基金当事人的权利义务等问题进行深入分析。

该书对众多国外和国内在航运金融领域成功经验进行总结,是全面了解国外航运金融行业特点、投资运作、融资渠道、风险管理等方面的实用工具。将航运金融产业作为一个有机整体的"产业"并以此出发,探讨在以工业化为中心的经济发展中金融机构与产业的互动关系、产业本身的发展规律以及研究这些规律的方法。为促进航运金融产业的发展,我国需要强化针对航运金融业的金融政策扶持,鼓励和支持金融机构积极开展适合航运、船舶业特点的金融产品和服务方式创新,有效拓宽航运、船舶业企业融资渠道,特别是加大对高端船舶与海洋工程装备制造业的信贷支持力度。该书可以针对以上方面给读者提供具有参考价值的答案和思路。

船舶融资在我国仍然是一个相对较新的领域,文献资料非常少,理论和实践远未定性,该书在这方面填补了一个空白。书中提及的行业操作和动向可让国内航运企业看到更多的可能性,均将会引发航运金融领域的创新思维和史无前例的运作方式。

二、2017年发表的航运政策与法律类论文评析

1.《海商法基础理论的内涵、研究现状与研究意义》[②]

作者基于中国海商法基础理论研究现状,指出中国海商法学界对于海商法基

---

① 金海斯.中国航运信托基金操作指引与法律解读[M].北京:中信出版社,2017.
② 胡正良,孙思琪.海商法基础理论的内涵、研究现状与研究意义[J].中国海商法研究,2017(1):3-12.

础理论尚无全面、系统和深入的研究,其他法律部门的基础理论研究对海商法基础理论研究具有借鉴价值,同时,研究海商法基础理论对于完善海商法理论体系、提升海商法理论研究品位,正确引导海事立法与海事司法实践和正确指引航运实践,具有重要意义,呼吁中国应当重视海商法基础理论的研究。

特定法学学科的基础理论反映海商法学科的基本框架,对于海商法学科具有支撑性的基础作用,为本学科的理论研究、立法、司法乃至实务领域所遵循。自《中华人民共和国海商法》(以下简称《海商法》)于1992年通过以来,中国海商法的理论研究,尤其是在海商法的实用性方面,获得了长足的发展。然而,长期以来海商法学界缺乏海商法基础理论的系统研究,主要原因是对海商法基础理论重要性认识的不足。这一基础环节的缺失,影响中国海商法理论研究实现质的提升。

作者运用法理学中法律基础理论的相关原理,借鉴其他法学学科基础理论的研究,探讨海商法基础理论的内涵,分析中国海商法基础理论的研究现状,阐述海商法基础理论研究的意义。

作者认为中国海商法学界对海商法基础理论缺乏全面、系统和深入的研究。原因在于《海商法》出台后,海商法研究主要侧重于对以《海商法》条文为主的既存海商法律规则在适用中的解释,具有浓厚的中世纪罗马法学的"注释法学"色彩,且海商法律规范的解释论事实上主导海商法理论研究的情形至今并无明显改观,海商法基础理论研究未受到学界的重视。

因此作者详细介绍其他法律部门基础理论研究对海商法基础理论研究的借鉴价值。现行《海商法》的规定绝大多数属于调整平等主体之间权利义务的规定,属于民法的特别法。民法理论是海商法理论研究重要的理论给养,民法基础理论的研究成果为海商法基础理论的研究提供了良好的理论基础。对于基础理论研究作用的正确认识和重视,是经济法学得以在中国较快地形成相对完备的理论体系,且在法学研究中后来居上并占据一席之地的重要原因。此种基础理论研究意识,可能正是中国海商法基础理论研究缺失的根源所在。

最后总结海商法基础理论研究的意义在于:完善海商法理论体系,提升海商法理论研究品位;正确引导海商法律实践;正确指引航运实践。

2.《提单管辖冲突研究——以一起中英提单管辖冲突案件为例》[①]

作者以一起中英提单管辖冲突案件为例,分析中英两国法院对同一提单管辖条款效力不同认定的原因及各自取得管辖权的不同依据,指出它们是形成提单管

---

① 牛元,林爱民.提单管辖冲突研究——以一起中英提单管辖冲突案件为例[J].中国海商法研究,2017(1):60-70.

辖冲突的表面原因,并揭示提单管辖冲突的根本原因是各国对自身利益的考量。最后指出提单管辖冲突的协调必须依靠国际和国内两个途径。虽然国际层面的协调已经取得一定的成果,但受国际公约适用范围的限制,各国国内层面管辖冲突协调机制的完善仍具有有益的补充作用。

作者在介绍基本案情后提出案情所涉及的问题:一是提单管辖条款效力问题,属于当事人选择法院的视角;二是提单管辖权的取得问题,属于法院确定管辖权的维度。

作者针对提单管辖条款的概念进行介绍并就中英法院对其效力不同认定的原因解释。中英两国法院对内容相同的提单管辖条款的效力认定不同?主要是提单管辖条款的准据法问题。提单管辖条款在司法实践中常被视为协议管辖条款,而协议管辖条款的效力有可能受不同地方法律的调整。提单管辖条款本身是否有效的问题(也就是对提单管辖条款效力限制的问题)涉及不同国家对提单管辖条款效力的限制。常见的限制主要有:第一,排除内国法院管辖的提单管辖条款无效。第二,选择不具有客观实际联系地法院的提单管辖条款无效。第三,以"对等原则"对提单管辖条款的效力加以限制。第四,以免除或减轻承运人的责任为由对提单管辖条款的效力加以限制。提单管辖条款是否具有排他性是提单管辖条款效力的另一个重要方面。基于各国对本国司法管辖权的保护,大多数国家对提单中管辖权条款的排他效力不予承认。提单管辖条款具有一定的特殊性,它不完全是当事人的合意,如果条文本身没有明确"排他性",则不宜作出"排他性"推定,否则对被动接受提单管辖条款的货方不利。《鹿特丹规则》采取的观点为只有在管辖协议本身明确约定为排他管辖时,才具有排他的效力。

最后作者从国际和国内两个角度对管辖权冲突的解决提出自己的建议。在国际上建议统一提单管辖条款效力评判的标准,《鹿特丹规则》全面肯定了选择法院协议的效力,它不仅是对当事人意思自治的尊重,同样也是避免管辖冲突的有效手段。但存在签署国家有限,在适用范围上存在局限性。在各国国内的协调制度上建议坚持和完善先诉管辖制度,引入必要的拒绝管辖制度并优先中止本国诉讼,减少以"禁诉令"的方式对外国司法管辖权的不当干涉。

国际民事领域的管辖权冲突,是各国政治、经济利益冲突的表现。无论是国内立法还是国际条约,在解决和防止管辖权冲突方面都具有一定的局限性。因此,国际民事管辖权的冲突必须依靠国际和国内两个途径,相互配合,共同解决。提单管辖权冲突的协调同样如此。一方面,国际社会正致力于协调包括提单管辖冲突在内的海上货物运输领域内的管辖冲突问题,并且已经取得一定的成果;另一方面,由于国际公约适用范围的局限性,管辖冲突的协调又离不开各国自身管辖冲突机制的建立和完善,国内层面的协调是对国际层面协调的有益补充。作者通过具体的案例分析,针对海事诉讼过程中管辖权问题中英的不同认定,总结管辖冲突的协调需国际和各国国内共同完善。

3.《中国船员投诉机制研究》[①]

在船员投诉机制上,中国的相关法律规定与《2006年海事劳工公约》(MLC 2006)还有一定的差距。作者建议完善船上投诉,建立船上船舶投诉处理委员会,并且加强与岸上的联系。建立岸上配套投诉机制,健全投诉处理解决程序,面向社会提供咨询、调解、联络、仲裁等服务,切实保障投诉船员的隐私,为船员的权益保障提供全方位支持。

被称为"航运业第四大公约"的 MLC 2006 于 2013 年 8 月 20 日生效,全球 90%以上的船队已经按照该公约的要求来运行,全球 77 个国家已批准加入公约并按照该公约来保障海员的体面工作和生活条件,其船舶总吨位占全球船舶的 90% 以上。中国已于 2015 年 11 月 12 日向国际劳工组织总干事盖·莱德递交中国批准 MLC 2006 的批准书,根据公约规定,MLC 2006 将于 2016 年 11 月 12 日对中国正式生效。中国目前的任务就是修改相应的国内法以适应公约的要求。中国在船员权益保护方面还存在着较多的问题和难题,特别是在船员投诉处理机制方面与公约的要求有一定差距,中国规定船上投诉程序,但却没有明确岸上投诉程序。总结国内及英国船员投诉机制现状,并且与公约投诉相关规定进行比较,从而对公约转化为国内立法及中国船员投诉处理机制建设提出建议。

中国船员投诉机制存在的问题:第一,很多船员不知道如何投诉、向谁投诉、怎么投诉,船公司也没有提供船员可以投诉的方式渠道。第二,船员投诉之后,问题不能够得到解决,拖延处理,没有很好的投诉处理机制。第三,没有有效的保护机制。投诉船员往往面临被排挤、打击报复等难以继续留下来的严重问题。第四,主管机关的监督检查职责不清。建立积极有效的船员投诉和纠纷解决机制是一项重要任务。

作者详细介绍 MLC 2006 规则的优势:对于船员投诉的规定也是以前国际劳工组织从没有规定过的,分别规定船上投诉程序和岸上投诉程序。公约在内容方面全面吸收国际劳工组织和其他国际组织在立法方面的优秀成果,体现尊重并保护人权的人文精神。最大的优点是其执行机制。公约规定船旗国的检查和发证制度以及港口国的监督检查制度,通过检查向船舶发放《海事劳工证书》和《海事符合声明》,这是为了保证公约的切实履行而确立的强有力的执行体制,是一个为了遵

---

① 曹艳春,唐树源.中国船员投诉机制研究[J].中国海商法研究,2017(2):3-11.

守公约通过认证系统而支撑的执行体制。公约的"不予优惠条款"则明确了不给未批准国船舶更优惠的待遇,这也是确保公约执行的强有力规定。

将中国船员投诉程序与公约投诉程序对比后,作者认为借鉴公约同时应针对中国没有建立岸上投诉机制等问题,需要调研国内外争议解决机制的利弊,建立适应中国的岸上投诉机制。

最后作者提出建议:加强船员投诉处理队伍的建设;规范船员投诉处理程序,在完善船上投诉程序同时建立岸上配套投诉机制;规范统一船员相关立法。

作为特殊劳动者的船员,是支撑航运业的骨干,全面保障船员的权益并建立健全的投诉处理机制对推动航运业顺利发展具有重要意义。中国是航运大国和海员大国,以加入公约为契机,对比学习国外船员投诉处理相关经验,完善相关立法和制度,能够更好地使中国船员的权益得到保障,真正实现海员在船上的体面工作和生活,提高海员的经济和社会地位,对更好地促进中国航运业的发展具有重要意义。

4.《从近代航线班轮公会的兴衰看航运业反垄断豁免制度的合理性》[①]

航运业作为一个较为特殊的垄断行业,它的一些垄断组织对于国际贸易的稳定发展具有积极的促进作用,因此其被赋予一些反垄断豁免的特权,班轮公会便是其中最具典型的垄断组织。在世界近代航运发展史上,班轮公会的出现无疑是一个光环。作者通过班轮公会的兴起、鼎盛以及逐渐衰落的发展进程,对班轮公会对整个航运业产生的积极意义和消极意义进行详细分析,从而对航运业一些反垄断豁免制度的变迁进行深入探讨。

作者从近代航线班轮公会对于航运业的意义分析入手,近代航线班轮公会对航运业产生的积极意义在于:①班轮公会对运价进行统一,协定各企业共同应当遵守的费率,不允许公会成员私自增减运费。②班轮公会在其所控制的航线上,规定各会员公司的航次和挂靠港口,并统一安排运营;为了平衡各会员公司的利益,班轮公会将统筹分配收入,按比例将会员公司的收入集中分配。不仅将原来分散的队伍集中起来,避免了恶性竞争,有利于航运业的进一步发展。③班轮公会采取延期回扣制度,这一制度既有利于班轮公会中的各会员公司,使其能够获得稳定的货源来进行货运承载,同时也有利于货主,只要他们将自己的货物全部交于某一航线班轮公会的某一班轮公司运输,便能够在计算期届满时从班轮公会处获得相应的回扣。班轮公会的成立既有利于各公会成员公司,也有利于货主,达到一个"双赢"的局面。

---

① 王晖.从近代航线班轮公会的兴衰看航运业反垄断豁免制度的合理性[J].中国水运,2017(5):11-12.

但近代航线班轮公会对航运产业也存在消极意义：由于班轮公会的垄断性质，它的存在极大地抑制了许多发展中国家的民族航运企业。以近代的中国为例，当时中国的航线班轮公会中，其公会成员公司大多是外国的船公司或一些洋行，班轮公会只会对其会员公司有利，而当时中国国内的一些民族航运公司都被班轮公会拒之门外，因此许多游离于班轮公会之外的中国船公司便享受不到工会的优惠政策，反而会因为班轮公会实行的延期回扣制度失去大量的货源，致使经营举步维艰。这种垄断组织不仅违背公平竞争的基本原则，也不利于海上自由竞争体制的形成，对整个航运市场竞争具有较大的危害性。

作者基于班轮公会对航运业发展的积极意义和消极意义探讨是否取消反垄断豁免权。在欧洲，欧盟部长理事会于2006年9月25日宣布自2008年10月18日起取消班轮公会反垄断豁免权；在美国，其《1998年航运改革法》的规定开始对班轮公会实施有限度的反垄断豁免制度，规定公会会员公司进行国内运输时不得享有反垄断豁免权；在日本，其新出台的反垄断法规定应将班轮公会的反竞争行为降至最低限度。对我国来说，作为一个航运大国而非强国，航运业的国际竞争力仍有待提高，因此为了保持航运业的稳定，在一定时间内仍然需要班轮公会这样的垄断组织存在，也需要对航运业实施必要的反垄断豁免制度。我国取消班轮公会所享有的反垄断豁免权为时尚早，首要任务应当是尽快完善航运业反垄断豁免制度相关的法律法规，提高本国航运业的国际竞争力。

作者通过近代航线班轮公会兴衰的发展历程，对其整个航运业产生的意义进行分析，并对班轮公会所享有的反垄断豁免权的合理性以及是否应当对其取消进行国内国外不同方面的探讨。总的来说，作为航运业典型的垄断组织，班轮公会的兴衰历程折射出不同国情国家航运业反垄断豁免权的合理性，近代航线班轮公会的兴衰在航运业的整个发展史上都是不可或缺的一页。

5.《从油污染损害赔偿看船舶燃料企业租船供油风险与对策》[①]

船舶燃料供应企业面临的船舶油污染风险是不可回避的重大风险，作者从船舶污染赔偿的范围、原则谈起，介绍国际、国内船舶污染损害赔偿机制，对我国油污染损害赔偿现状作了分析研究，就租船供油面临的船舶污染损害赔偿风险作了探讨并提出有关对策建议。

作者介绍了国际上船舶油污损害赔偿机制主要的三个模式：①加入《油污损害民事责任公约》(CLC)和《油污损害赔偿基金公约》(FC)两个国际公约，依公约建立船舶油污损害赔偿机制。公约缔约国通过接受，以及加入国际油污基金的方

---

① 宋兆国.从油污染损害赔偿看船舶燃料企业租船供油风险与对策[J].中国远洋航务，2017(8)：74-76.

式,建立船舶油污损害赔偿机制。②通过本国立法建立国内船舶油污损害赔偿机制。这种模式最具代表性的是美国。美国没有参加国际油污基金,而是通过制定《1990年油污法》(OPA 90),建立自己的国家油污基金中心(NPFC)和溢油责任信托联合基金(OS LTF),设立高达10亿美元的国内油污基金,同时对船东规定了更加严格的责任。③既加入国际公约,又通过本国立法建立船舶油污损害赔偿机制。这种模式最具代表性的是加拿大。加拿大既接受了FC 92,加入国际油污基金,又通过对本国《航运法》的修正,建立国内油污基金(SOPF),两套机制同时运作,相辅相成。

《防治船舶污染海洋环境管理条例》对我国防治船舶污染损害具有重要意义,对照以往法律、法规对船舶油污染责任规定,条例进一步明确了船舶污染损害赔偿制度的归责原则、免责情形。将船舶污染损害的民事责任主体确定为船舶一方,按照"谁加害,谁负责"的原则,将船舶所有人、光船租船人作为民事责任主体,在无过错责任基础上对船舶污染损害承担连带责任。作者认为,期租状态下的供油操作,公司处于既是货主,又是船舶经营人的地位,因此如一旦产生油污染事故,其将作为民事责任主体而负有连带责任。

作者对租船实施供油作业安全与防污染工作提出相应对策与建议:①建立船舶状况评估机制。在租用前对船舶状况、船员操作水平、经验、公司安全管理资质及管理状况进行全面了解和评估,对租用船舶实施供油作业可能遇到的风险实施全面评价并提出相关控制措施的建议。②选择安全管理水平较高的出租人。在选择出租船舶时一定要认真分析和评估公司安全管理的状况。③加大油污保险投保额度。按《防治船舶污染海洋环境管理条例》及其配套法规《船舶油污损害赔偿基金征收使用管理办法实施细则》规定,载运持久性油类(重油)的船舶,应办理油污险的额度按国家加入的国际公约的责任限制要求进行,5 000总吨以下的重油船舶应投保的保险金额应为451 SDR(约合人民币4 800万元)。此保险额度的规定是建立在保护船东利益情况设定船舶责任限制基础上作出的,当前环保形势日益严峻,在污染事件容忍度越来越低的情况下,一旦发生较大污染事故,带来的污染损害赔偿必然巨大,船舶租赁人和货方难逃责任。

随着船舶燃料供应市场的发展和变化以及社会协作分工的必然趋势,船舶燃料供应企业减少自有船舶,实施租用船舶供油作为一种新型的开放式的操作模式,对于有效利用市场资源,提高效率,降低企业成本具有现实意义。但不可否认,租船供油相比公司自用船舶供油具有一定的特殊性和弊端,在租用船舶供油时应统筹考虑,权衡利弊,更好地发挥此种供油运作方式的作用。

船舶燃料供应企业时刻与油品打交道,企业运营中涉及油品储存、运输、配送、供应等诸多环节,船舶事故溢油造成海洋污染是企业一项重大安全环保风险,作者研究分析船舶污染损害赔偿相关责任,尤其是租赁船舶实施供油情况下船舶燃料企业面临的相关赔偿责任,对于做好租用船舶审核和管理具有一定现实意义。

6.《"一带一路"背景下的国际海事司法中心建设》①

我国是海洋大国,拥有广泛的海洋战略利益。海事司法是经略海洋、管控海洋工作的重要组成部分。目前,我国是世界上海事审判机构最多、海事法官数量最多、海事案件数量最多的国家。海洋强国、海运强国、国际航运中心建设等国家战略的推进给航运业发展提供了历史性机遇,也对海事司法提出更高的要求。作者分析国际海事司法中心提出的原因并借鉴英国经验,对我国建立海事司法中心提出建议。呼吁我国应积极稳妥推进国际海事司法中心建设,努力实现从海事司法大国向海事司法强国的转变。

党的十八大报告提出"提升海洋资源开发能力、发展海洋经济、保护海洋生态环境、坚决维护国家海洋权益、建设海洋强国"的战略任务和目标。十八届三中全会要求"推进丝绸之路经济带、海上丝绸之路建设,形成全方位开放新格局。"十八届四中全会提出全面推进依法治国总目标。到2020年,上海将基本建成具有全球航运资源配置能力的国际航运中心;中国要初步实现由造船大国向造船强国的转变;中国要实现建成具有国际竞争力的现代化海运体系的阶段性目标,并以此为基础向建设海运强国迈进。在以上背景下,作者认为提出建设国际海事司法中心是契合中国发展的,主要原因有二:①维护海洋权益需要海事司法保障。当前,我国海洋权益面临严峻的挑战。管辖地域、管辖案件的特殊性,使海事法院在维护宣示国家司法主权等方面具有特别重要意义。②推进"一带一路"建设需要海事司法护航。随着"一带一路"倡议的实施,海上经济活动将更为频繁,海洋生态环境问题将更加突出,海事纠纷数量上升的趋势难以避免。如果没有一个良好的海事司法环境,没有坚强的司法管辖权作为后盾,"一带一路"建设就会缺乏法治助力,我国的国家利益将得不到充分保障。

英国是世界公认的国际海事纠纷解决中心。英国法院的判决受到国际贸易界、海事界、司法界和学术界的广泛关注,并在一些国家得到援引或遵循。在海事仲裁领域,伦敦更是一家独大。世界上75%的海事仲裁在伦敦进行,90%以上的造船合同选择英国法律作为适用法律,80%以上的造船合同选择在伦敦仲裁。作者认为主要的原因在于:第一,法律的稳定性和裁判的可预见性强。英国是判例法国家,海事文化悠久,经历了多年的发展,英国法和重要的海运公约的含义都比

---

① 张文广."一带一路"背景下的国际海事司法中心建设[J].中国远洋航务,2017(11):68-70.

较明确，法官的整体水平较高，司法公信力较强。当事人愿意选择适用英国法解决纠纷。第二，大量的国际航运组织扎堆伦敦，由其制定并推荐使用的标准合同通常约定"适用英国法""伦敦仲裁"。第三，英国航运金融领域实力很强，银行是出资人，保险公司和互保协会通常是海事纠纷的最终买单人，其在合同条款的拟定方面具有很强的话语权，选择熟悉的法律并在"主场"解决纠纷是其理性的选择。第四，伦敦人才汇聚，产业链完整，能够发挥协同效应，迅速且经济地解决纠纷。第五，路径依赖短期内难以改变。为了澄清英国法和国际海运公约的具体含义，海事界、贸易界已经支付了巨额的律师费用。对商人而言，成本固然重要，但风险可控更加关键。除非其他选择具有明显的优势或是源于法律的强制性规定，商人通常不愿意改变原有做法。

作者对于中国建设国际海事司法中心的具体举措提出建议：第一，完善涉海法律制度。《海商法》《海事诉讼特别程序法》的修改应重视吸收中国司法经验，体现中国司法智慧，形成能被国际海事界普遍接受的"中国经验""中国规则"。第二，改革海事司法制度。设立海事高级法院，建立完整的海事专门法院体系，对进一步强化海事司法的专业性，更好地整合海事司法资源、统一海事司法的裁判尺度具有重要意义。

随着"一带一路"建设的推进，中国海事司法争取较高国际地位和国际影响力、积极参与国际规则的制定并引领国际规则的发展，已是紧迫的现实需求和大国的应有担当。中国应树立大国司法理念，加快推进国际海事司法中心建设。

7.《我国海事强制令颁发中程序性权利与实体性权利的冲突及解决办法》[①]

为解决海事法院在裁定颁发海事强制令时程序性权利与实体性权利的冲突，作者分析在司法实践中以及立法上因海事强制令的滥用使得被申请人实体权利行使受到阻却的因素，提出立法和司法层面存在的问题及建议：目前我国海事强制令的规定行文存在问题；《海事诉讼特别程序法》对海事法院就海事强制令申请的审查方面缺乏具体规定；海事强制令内容不够明确；海事强制令的实施可能阻却被请求人依法行使实体性权利；海事强制令案件立案须遵循一定的原则；适时引入听证程序；合理运用海事诉讼担保制度。

在司法实践中，一些申请人申请海事强制令时基本不考虑是应该通过申请海事强制令还是应该通过证据保全，或先予执行或通过实体审理来解决问题。作者认为造成这种现象的原因有：①当事人因素，因法律专业知识的欠缺而分不清海

---

① 沈晓明.我国海事强制令颁发中程序性权利与实体性权利的冲突及解决办法[J].水运管理,2017(7):22-25.

事请求保全与海事强制令制度之间的不同适用情形,从而造成滥用海事强制令;②我国在相关法律规定方面存在理解上的或然性,在证据保全与海事强制令的申请条件规定上存在重合性,两者都是在海事请求人因情况紧急时才被提起,都可在起诉或仲裁前向海事法院提出申请。

在司法实践中,申请人申请的海事强制令造成被申请人无法实现其合法的实体性权利,这种申请行为可以认为是一种滥用行为。滥用行为的情形有很多,其中强制放货是海事司法实践中常见的一种情形。在这种情形中,海事强制令的实施有可能导致被请求人无法行使其合法的实体性权利。作者认为主要是《海事诉讼特别程序法》在海事强制令立法上存在的问题。首先,我国海事强制令的规定行文存在问题。《海事诉讼特别程序法》第五十一条规定,海事强制令是指海事法院根据海事请求人的申请,为使其合法权益免受侵害,责令被请求人作为或者不作为的强制措施。该条规定最大的问题是将程序性的问题通过实体性规范方式解决,即在程序性规定中认为其"为使其合法权益免受侵害"而责令被请求人作为或不作为。其次,从程序法角度,作为启动海事诉讼特别程序的海事强制令程序,海事法院除了须对作出申请海事强制令程序的决定或裁定进行审查外,还要对拒绝作出海事强制令即驳回申请程序的决定或裁定进行审查。目前,《海事诉讼法》仅对申请作出海事强制令的条件作出规定,对海事法院在受理海事强制令申请等程序性规则没有任何规定。最后,海事强制令的实施可能阻却被请求人依法行使实体性权利。《海事诉讼特别程序法》虽然要求申请人提交相关证据,但是海事强制令具有程序性特征,不涉及当事人最终责任的分担定性,海事法院在审查申请人提供的证据时仅做一般表面证据审查即可,因而海事强制令的批准有可能因错误申请或错误审理而给被申请人或被告带来不应有的损失。

作者对海事强制令的实施有可能导致被请求人无法行使其合法的实体性权利的解决办法提出建议:适用听证制度来弥补我国有关海事强制令法律规定的空缺。这种听证制度的实施必须要有一个合理的适用听证程序规则,才有助于法官在全面分析事实的基础上作出公正的裁判,提高司法的透明度,真正维护双方当事人的利益。

海事强制令具有紧急性、密行性等特征,而我国有关的海事强制令相关立法和司法制度尚不健全,其作为一种法律给予当事人的程序性权利,颁发和行使都可能导致对方当事人实体权利的阻却,甚至实体权利的彻底丧失,或者给当事人造成诉累或造成司法资源的浪费。作者建议,应从立法和司法两方面对我国相关的海事强制令制度作出修改,以达到当事人实体权益与程序权益的平衡。

8.《〈民法总则〉对航运法律的影响》①

为进一步厘清《民法总则》的生效对航运法律可能产生的影响,作者分析:绿色原则的确立能够指导我国船舶污染损害赔偿等海洋环境保护制度的立法;对于习惯作为民法法源的规定,赋予航运惯例作为处理航运纠纷正式渊源的效力;《民法总则》与《海商法》等法律之间的适用关系需要在实践中进一步厘清。

《民法总则》第九条规定:"民事主体从事民事活动,应当有利于节约资源、保护生态环境。"该条规定的内容被称为"绿色原则",也是我国民商事立法首次将环境与资源保护确立为基本原则之一。《民法总则》第九条确立的绿色原则符合当代航运法律的发展方向。海洋环境保护作为当代国际海事立法的重点之一,航运法律尤其是《海商法》的价值目标呈现愈发重视海洋环境保护的趋势。作者认为:《海商法》缺失船舶污染损害赔偿制度,《中华人民共和国海洋环境保护法》也仅有第八十九条、第九十一条涉及海洋环境污染损害赔偿责任。法律具有引导人们行为的作用,民法基本原则的功能则在于填补法律漏洞、指导民事立法。因此,《民法总则》第九条确立绿色原则作为该法的基本原则之一,对引导人们在航运活动中更加关注海洋环境保护,以及指导未来我国《海商法》修改等海事立法中相关制度的创设具有积极意义。

《民法总则》的生效将对航运法律产生较为明显的影响,许多法律问题需要在实践过程中逐步厘清。作者认为此种影响主要表现在:①对于作为民事特别法的《海商法》未有规定的情形,《民法总则》的许多规定将直接适用于航运活动产生的社会关系;②对于《海商法》规定不明确的问题,法院在解释时将以《民法总则》为依据,或者适当考虑《民法总则》确立的基本原则和具体规定;③在今后对《海商法》进行修改时,将在维持所需的特别海事法律制度的前提之下,充分考虑与《民法总则》的接轨和协调统一,包括创设一些适应航运发展的特别规则。

由于《民法总则》是以"提取公因式"的方法对民事活动作出一般规定,因而对于航运法律的影响大多并不体现在对具体航运活动的法律规制之中。作者分析《民法总则》与《海商法》的法律使用关系显示民法典编纂对航运法律的影响。因此,航运界对于《民法总则》以及未来民法典分则各编的编纂,均应给予充分关注。

9.《完善我国船舶污染损害赔偿体系的建议》②

作者从船舶污染损害责任保险的作用入手,分析我国船舶污染损害赔偿体系现状,对现行的各船舶污染损害赔偿体系进行比较,指出完善我国船舶污染损害赔

---

① 孙思琪.《民法总则》对航运法律的影响[J].水运管理,2017(9):33-36.
② 周舫震,朱羿峰.完善我国船舶污染损害赔偿体系的建议[J].水运管理,2017(11):30-35.

偿体系的必要性和紧迫性,从开展课题研究、修订船舶污染损害赔偿相关法律、修改完善配套制度等三方面提出完善我国船舶污染损害赔偿体系的建议。

作者介绍我国海域和内河船舶油污损害赔偿体系。由于我国实行河海分治的管理体系,船舶污染损害责任赔偿体系也互相独立。以污染区域划分,体系可以分为内河水域船舶污染损害赔偿体系和海域船舶污染损害赔偿体系;以污染物划分,体系可以分为油污损害赔偿体系和危险化学品污染损害赔偿体系。海域船舶油污损害赔偿体系建设最早,为其他损害赔偿体系建设提供了良好的范例。

作者通过图表清晰展示完善我国船舶污染损害赔偿机制的必要性和紧迫性,我国将生态文明建设放在突出位置,将生态环境保护放在战略性高度,争从决策源头上防止环境污染和生态破坏,解决环境恢复问题。获得充分的环境损害赔偿是顺利实施环境恢复措施的前提条件。国际海事组织已通过《国际海上运输有毒有害物质损害责任和赔偿公约》,该公约建立了与国际油污损害赔偿机制类似的国际有毒有害物质赔偿体系。完善船舶污染损害赔偿机制既是我国航运业与海洋环境保护协调发展的迫切需要,也符合国际船舶污染损害赔偿体系发展趋势。

作者提出完善我国船舶污染损害赔偿机制的建议:①开展课题研究。开展船舶污染损害赔偿责任课题研究,摸清我国船舶污染损害情况,研究分析我国船舶污染损害赔偿工作现状,提出完善我国船舶污染损害赔偿机制的解决方案。②修订船舶污染损害赔偿相关法律。在《中华人民共和国环境保护法》的基础上,修订《中华人民共和国水污染防治法》《中华人民共和国海洋环境保护法》《中华人民共和国海商法》等法律,完善我国水域船舶污染损害赔偿体系的相关法律,增加与在我国内河水域实施油污损害赔偿责任保险、在沿海水域实施危险化学品污染损害赔偿责任保险等相关内容,为我国全面施行船舶污染损害民事责任保险制度提供法律依据。③修改完善配套制度。待上位法对船舶污染损害赔偿基本制度作出规定后,适时出台相应的配套实施细则,保障船舶污染损害赔偿责任保险制度及船舶污染损害赔偿基金制度顺利运行。

10.《东亚其他地区海上货物运输立法对于中国的借鉴价值》[①]

考察东亚其他地区海事立法的主要法域,韩国已于2007年完成本国海商法的修订,日本正在进行相关修订工作,其海运立法呈现承运人责任期间扩大、航海过失免责得以维持以及运输单证多元化的趋势。作者认为《中华人民共和国海商法》

---

① 曹珊,蒋正雄.东亚其他地区海上货物运输立法对于中国的借鉴价值[J].中国海商法研究,2017(3):32-39.

第四章"海上货物运输合同"修改时应当顺应此种趋势,将承运人责任期间扩展为"接收至交付",保留航海过失免责,并且规定海运单以及电子运输记录的相关规则。

作者介绍东亚地区国家海上货物运输立法能为中国借鉴的前提基础:即因任何法律的制定都需要结合本国(地区)的经济状况,航运相关法律的制定和修改也不能忽视本国(地区)的航运经济形势。东亚地区各国有相似的航运经济形势。东亚地区各国海事法律制度,以日本法律为例海商法总体结构相似。东亚其他地区的海上货物运输立法与中国存在相似性,具有较为充分的借鉴基础。

作者详细介绍承运人的责任期间、承运人责任的归责原则与免责事由、运输单证以及其他规则,将东亚地区海事法律与《海商法》比较,对《海商法》的修改提出建议:①关于承运人的责任期间,东亚其他地区的海运立法呈现扩大趋势,《海商法》修改时应将承运人责任期间扩展为"接收至交付"。②关于承运人责任的归责原则与免责事由,东亚其他地区的海运立法均保留了航海过失免责,《海商法》在当前以及今后的一个时期修改时也应维持以《海牙—维斯比规则》为基础的不完全过错责任原则。③关于运输单证,东亚其他地区的海运立法呈现多元化的趋势,《海商法》修改时应当规定海运单以及电子运输记录的相关规则。

由于航运经济形势以及海事法律制度的相似性,东亚其他地区的海上货物运输立法趋势对中国具有借鉴价值。

三、小结

本章中汇集了众多专家学者从国内外研究中汲取精华、苦心钻研的综合研究成果,涉及海商海事理论前沿问题探究和重大疑难问题的讨论,为海事司法规范以及海事纠纷解决提供宝贵贡献,加强理论研究和司法实践的联动性,为我国航运业健康发展提供智慧力量。

第五章 年度航运聚焦

2017年,低迷已久的国际航运市场走出谷底,出现复苏的迹象。持续成长的上海国际航运中心,积极探索建设自由贸易港、试水全自动化码头、完善航运高端服务产业链、加强与"一带一路"和长江经济带联动……一系列迈向"深蓝"的新举措,吸引了世界目光。

党的十九大报告提出"赋予自由贸易试验区更大改革自主权,探索建设自由贸易港"。上海抓紧编制自由贸易港建设方案,上海建设自由贸易港不仅可以推动贸易的繁荣,还将带动船舶供应、航运金融、保险和海事法律等一大批现代服务业的发展。

2017年初,中国第一家航运自保公司——中远海运财产保险自保有限公司在沪成立,航运保险形成完整产业链。10月,中国船东互保协会进驻上海国际航运服务中心。随着各类航运保险运营中心和中介服务机构相继落户,上海为国际航运业提供日益丰富的保险服务选择。

2017年5月,由中国商飞研制的国产大型客机C919在浦东国际机场首飞成功。12月,由外高桥船厂建造的首艘2.1万标箱集装箱船顺利出坞。在上海举行的中国国际海事展,已成为与汉堡海事展齐名的世界级海事展之一。以高端航运装备产业为基础,航运领域的"上海制造""上海服务"名片交相辉映,为上海国际航运中心建设提供了坚实的物质基础和技术支撑。

2017年6月和9月,中远海运集团先后与西班牙最大码头运营商、马士基集团签署协议收购相关码头资产。7月,上海航运交易所发布"一带一路"航贸指数,全面、及时反映"一带一路"倡议在贸易畅通和交通运输方面的发展成效。港口、码头等基础设施的建设和运营,直接关系到"一带一路"贸易大通道的畅通。在沪港航企业纷纷落子海外,既实现了企业国际化战略的突破,也助推"一带一路"沿线基础设施的互联互通。

上海持续吸引和培育国际航运功能性机构,海事服务体系日益完善。由联合国国际海事组织授权设立的亚洲海事技术合作中心,2017年5月在上海海事大学成立。这是中国第一个经国际海事组织授权设立的实体性功能机构,目标是成为引领全球海运业绿色发展的示范平台。最高人民法院已确立上海海事法院为国际海事司法上海基地。上海海事法院发布五年发展规划纲要,提出把上海建设成具有全球影响力的国际海事司法中心。通过建设亚洲海事技术合作中心、国际海事司法上海基地,上海不断吸引和培育国际航运功能性机构,加快形成完备的海事服务体系。

2017年航运文化建设取得长足发展。"一带一路"文化圆桌会议等活动的举办,相关展览展示及研讨座谈的开展,提升了航运文化的影响力,让全社会更加关注航运事业发展。

2017年上海航运法治建设不断推进。为更好地服务保障海洋强国战略、"一带一路"建设、上海自贸区和"十三五"时期上海国际航运中心建设,制定发布《上海海事法院五年发展规划纲要(2017—2021)》,全面规划上海海事法院未来五年工作。

2017年一系列会议、活动召开。为上海以及来自全国各地的航运人士提供了一个交流、分享和学习的平台,深化航运业界的合作和交流。汇集多方智慧,为当前新形势下的国际合作提供新思路、开拓新视野。

一、热点关注

(一) 中远海运财产保险自保有限公司正式宣告成立

2月17日,中远海运财产保险自保有限公司(以下简称中远海运自保公司)在上海正式宣告成立。中远海运自保公司是由中国远洋海运集团有限公司独资发起设立的集团二级子公司,注册地位于上海,注册资本20亿元人民币。国务院国有资产监督管理委员会监事会主席潘良、交通运输部水运局局长李天碧、上海市交通委主任谢峰等出席成立大会,并与中远海运集团董事长、党组书记许立荣,总经理万敏等共同为中远海运自保公司揭牌。

万敏在致辞中表示,作为中远海运集团航运金融战略板块的第一张真正意义上的金融牌照,中远海运自保公司的成立标志着中远海运集团在布局"6+1"产业集群的横向和纵深化改革更具成效。这是中远海运集团战略蓝图中极为重要的金融战略布局,对助力集团打造以航运、综合物流及相关金融服务为支柱,多产业集群、全球领先的综合性物流供应链服务集团具有里程碑式的意义。中远海运自保公司作为上海市第一家自保公司,也是国内第一家航运自保公司,对上海市乃至全国航运业和保险业都具有深远影响。自保公司作为中远海运集团的保险管理平台、风险管理工具和成本管理中心,将充分利用和整合集团内保险资源,为集团风险管理能力与水平的升级提供保障,为国家的战略安全和资产安全保驾护航,为国家"一带一路"倡议和"海洋强国"战略保驾护航。

上海市交通委员会张林在致辞中表示航运企业是"一带一路"倡议和"走出去"国家战略的重要参与者和执行者,在实现战略效能大目标的同时,一定要注重国家战略安全和人员安全、资产安全、环境安全,强化安全生产的风险识别,采取有效措施防控风险。自保公司作为我国航运业和保险业紧密衔接的新生事物,必将具备旺盛的生命力和发展前景,必将为中远海运集团风险管理水平的专业化、运营管理能力精细化和业务发展能力的链条化保驾护航,为我国航运业和保险业新形态的探索和推广积累更积极丰富的经验,更将为"一带一路"和"走出去"国家战略的执行提供更加有益的风险保障。希望中远海运自保公司能够逐渐成为国内保险业有特色、有能力、有高度的专业自保公司,也期望公司能够发展成为国内保险业的典范和全球自保领域的佼佼者。

最后,中远海运自保公司郑晓哲对与会嘉宾的到来表示感谢。对公司筹建过程中给予关心和支持的各级政府机关、集团及系统内单位以及各界同仁表示感谢!作为新集团成立一周年的献礼,中远海运自保公司一定会根据监管要求,依法合规创新经营,充分践行自保公司作为集团"风险管理工具、保险管理平台和成本管理中心"的战略定位,为集团及各成员单位提供更加贴合于公司实际的定制化风险管理专项方案,全心全意的做好服务工作,把自保公司打造成为国内领先,并引领国际航运业自保公司发展的标杆性公司。

(二) 9 大港口集团和 5 家航运企业联合在沪成立"长江经济带航运联盟"

2017 年 7 月 20 日,长江经济带航运联盟成立大会在上海举行。由上港集团、宁波舟山港集团等 9 家港口集团以及长航集团等 5 家航运企业共同发起成立的长江经济带航运联盟是一个非营利的行业性组织,旨在贯彻落实党中央、国务院关于推动长江经济带发展的重大战略部署,秉承生态优先、绿色发展理念,发挥联盟的协同联动作用。

联盟将重点加强区域港航信息一体化,集装箱、散杂货、液货和滚装等货物江海联运,船型标准化,绿色港口和航运体系建设以及维护航运市场有序稳定发展等领域交流合作,依托上海国际航运中心先行先试作用和沿江各航运中心的服务辐射功能,创新业务服务模式与服务内涵,满足长江航运便捷、高效、透明和低成本的市场需求,着力打造畅通、高效、平安、绿色的现代化长江航运体系,进一步提升对长江经济带发展的支撑作用。

联盟以长江经济带港口建设和航运发展为导向,推进长江航运资源优化配置和协同发展,着力提升黄金水道功能,实现航道畅通、枢纽互通、江海联通和关检直通,降低企业综合物流成本,更好地服务长江经济带贸易增长,促进经济发展。组建长江经济带航运联盟,发挥好上海国际航运中心的先行先试作用和服务辐射功能,推进长江航运资源优化配置和协同发展,加强港口分工协作,提升现代航运服务,对于加快绿色航运发展、充分发挥黄金水道功能、服务长江经济带国家战略具有重要意义。

(三) 全球最大的自动化码头上海港洋山深水港四期开港

2017年12月10日,上海港洋山深水港四期开港。

作为全球规模最大的自动化码头——上海洋山深水港四期码头正式开港投入试生产,为上海港加速跻身世界航运中心前列注入全新动力。由中国交建设计建设的、中国建筑参与承建的上海港洋山港区,是世界第一座海岛型深水集装箱港区,集装箱吞吐量占比上海港40%以上,是上海成为国际航运中心的重要支撑点。

洋山深水港是世界最大的海岛型人工深水港,也是上海国际航运中心建设的战略和枢纽型工程。洋山港工程一至三期现已完工,共有16个7万~15万吨级深水集装箱泊位,释放出年集装箱吞吐量超过1 500万TEU的生产能力。洋山港四期码头自2014年开始建设,可布置7个大型集装箱深水泊位,设计年通过能力初期为400万标准箱,远期为630万标准箱。已完成调试的首批10台桥吊、40台轨道吊、50台自动导引车(AGV)将投入开港试生产,根据规划,洋山四期最终将配置26台桥吊、120台轨道吊、130台AGV。规模如此之大的自动化码头一次性建成投运堪称史无前例。洋山港四期码头开港后上海港的年吞吐量将突破4 000万TEU,这个数字是全美国所有港口加起来的吞吐总量,也是目前全球港口年吞吐量的十分之一。

洋山四期也被称为"魔鬼码头"。这座无人的"魔鬼码头"相对于传统的集装箱码头,最大的特点是实现码头集装箱装卸、水平运输、堆场装卸环节的全过程智能化的操作。这就意味着整个码头和堆场内将不再有人,不仅岸桥不需要人驾驶,连集装箱卡车也不再需要,直接由自动运行的无人驾驶AGV小车把集装箱运到堆场,堆场的桥吊也是无人操作。原先的码头操作员全部转移到监控室,对着电脑屏幕就能完成全部作业。

四期全自动化码头将达到40箱/小时,远超人工码头的作业效率,减少人工70%。该码头能24小时不间断作业,保证操作工人人身安全,工作环境也得到极大改善,而且电力驱动,节能环保。由上港集团自主研发的码头智能生产管理控制系统(TOS系统)和振华重工自主研发的智能控制系统(ECS系统)指挥全自动化码头,两者组成洋山四期码头的"大脑"与"神经"。这两套系统的研制与应用,让国内全自动化码头真正用上"中国芯"。

洋山四期全自动化码头是全球最大的单体全自动化集装箱码头，也是全球综合自动化程度最高的码头。它的建成和投产标志着中国港口行业在运营模式和技术应用上实现里程碑式的升级，更为上海港巩固港口货物吞吐能力世界第一地位提供保障。

（四）上海航运交易所正式对外发布"一带一路"航贸指数

2017年7月11日，在上海市交通委指导下，中国航海博物馆、中国金融信息中心等单位联合主办的第二届"21世纪海上丝绸之路"建设高峰论坛在上海举行。上海航运交易所在论坛上正式对外发布"一带一路"航贸指数。

为全面、及时反映"一带一路"建设成果，特别是在贸易畅通和交通运输方面的发展成效，上海航运交易所在交通运输部和上海市"一带一路"推进工作小组办公室指导下，于2015年研发并对外试运行发布该指数。指数发布后，受到众多境内外政府、金融、媒体机构高度关注，也获得业界高度评价和认可，部分港航企业纷纷咨询指数、查阅指数、订购指数。经过2年的试运行，指数结构不断调整优化，并在2017年7月11日正式对外发布。

正式对外发布"一带一路"航贸指数由"一带一路"贸易额指数、"一带一路"货运量指数、"海上丝绸之路"运价指数等3大类指数组成，细分煤炭、矿石、原油、集装箱等4大货种，运输方式不仅限于海运，更包括铁路，未来还将拓展和增加航空等多种运输方式。"一带一路"航贸指数以2015年1月为基期，基期指数为100点。上海航运交易所在每个月的最后一周星期三对外发布。

"一带一路"货运量指数包含1个综合指数，5个成分指数（分别是中国至"一带"沿线国家铁路货运出口量指数，中国（上海）至"一路"沿线国家出口集装箱海运量指数，中国自"一路"沿线国家进口煤炭海运量、铁矿石海运量、原油海运量指数）及细分地区指数。"一带"货运量指数反映中国至丝绸之路经济带沿线蒙俄、中亚、东南亚、欧洲等地区主要国家的铁路货运量变化；"一路"货运量指数反映中国与沿线国家之间煤、矿、油、箱等主要货种海运量变化，涉及"海上丝绸之路"沿线东南亚、西亚、南亚、欧洲、大洋洲和北非等多个地区。

"海上丝绸之路"运价指数包括1个综合指数，4个成分指数（分别是"海上丝绸之路"出口集装箱运价指数、进口集装箱运价指数、进口干散货运价指数和进口原油运价指数）及细分航线指数。指数涵盖联通亚非欧的"海上丝绸之路"主要货种、主要航线。

上海航运交易所总裁张页表示，"'一带一路'倡议是中国构建全方位对外开放新格局的重要基础，它与自贸区建设、京津冀协同发展和长江经济带等战略有机衔接、互为支撑,与全面深化改革、海运强国战略也有着千丝万缕的关系。航运业在'一带一路'倡议中的体现最为关键的就是运量和运价。因而上海航交所从运量与运价出发,将'一带一路'倡议中的航运要素信息公开,增强了市场的透明度和影响力"。

"一带一路"航贸指数不仅反映贸易发展情况,还能直接反映贸易额、货运量、运输价格三者之间的变化和相互关系;不仅能充分发挥上海国际航运中心建设和"一带一路"桥头堡的优势,更能从国家层面全面反映"一带一路"倡议的实施效果。未来,以"一带一路"指数为依托,上海航运交易所将积极推广应用"一带一路"航贸指数,搭建"一带一路"国家共同参与的航贸指数合作平台。

(五)上海航运交易所发布远东干散货指数(FDI)

2017年11月28日,2017年上海航运交易论坛在沪举行,论坛的主题设定为"大数据时代的航运决策"。来自交通运输部、上海市交委、上海浦东新区以及航运产业等各界人士从多角度畅谈大数据时代的突破和创新。

经过近20年发展,"上海航运指数"已经覆盖集装箱、干散货、油轮、买卖船、"一带一路"、船员薪酬、航运企业景气度等航运相关各大细分市场领域,形成全面、权威、综合的指数体系。"上海航运指数"品牌系列已成为航运市场走势的风向标,为政府宏观掌握市场趋势和企业决策提供客观依据,其中部分指数在指数挂钩协议、以指数为结算标的的运价衍生品等多个领域发挥创新性、决定性的作用。

"上海航运指数"再添新成员——远东干散货指数(FDI)正式对外试运行。中国沿海成品油运价指数(CCTFI)从中国沿海(散货)运价指数(CBFI)中独立出来正式试运行,中国进口干散货运价指数(CDFI)也进行调整优化。

最近十年来,全球航运中心东移亚太,远东地区在全球干散货贸易中的地位越来越凸显,远东市场成为全球航运的重中之重。为适应航运中心东移的趋势,在交通运输部的指导下,在中国进口干散货运价指数编委单位的支持下,上海航交所构想在CDFI的基础上发展远东干散货指数。从中国走向远东的意义不仅在于给市场提供更多、更全面的信息参考,也为我国航运企业走出去,进一步参与国际分工,提升国际竞争力奠定基础;从中国走向远东的意义还在于以指数为基础,加快推动形成"远东价格",并在整个远东市场,乃至亚太市场形成影响力和话语权。

(六)长三角船舶排放控制区全面实施船舶靠岸换油

2017年9月1日起,长三角船舶排放控制区提前执行船舶排放控制区2018年相关要求,即所有船舶到港后应按要求换用低硫燃油,或采取使用岸电、尾气后处理等替代措施。

根据交通运输部出台的船舶排放控制区方案要求,2018年1月1日起,船舶在排放控制区内所有港口靠岸停泊期间应使用硫含量小于或等于0.5‰mm的燃油。长三角船舶排放控制区将这一要求提前至2017年9月1日起执行,比原方案提前4个月,进一步推进绿色航运发展和船舶节能减排。

加之长三角船舶排放控制区核心港口上海港、宁波舟山港、苏州港、南通港已于2016年4月1日率先实施船舶排放控制区方案,至此长三角船舶排放控制区已全面实施船舶靠岸换油措施。一年多来,环保部门监测数据显示,长三角各地空气质量均有所改善,临港地区二氧化硫浓度下降程度显著。2016年4—12月与2015年同期相比,上海市东高桥监测站二氧化硫浓度同比下降52%;新江湾城监测站二氧化硫浓度同比下降23%。2017年上半年,宁波镇海空气质量监测点的二氧化硫浓度同比下降31%;北仑空气质量监测点的二氧化硫浓度同比下降21%。

(七) 外高桥造船首艘 21 000 TEU 集装箱船下水

2017年12月25日,外高桥造船为中远海运集运建造的首艘21 000 TEU集装箱船(H1416)在长兴重工顺利出坞。这是迄今为止国内在建主尺度最大、载箱量最大的超大型集装箱船,再一次刷新国内最大集装箱船建造记录,这是中国造船业的又一次突破,标志着外高桥造船成功立足超大型集装箱船的国际"建造俱乐部"。

该集装箱船总长约400 m,型宽58.6 m,型深33.5 m,大约相当于4个足球场纵向并列布置,设计吃水14.5 m,结构吃水16 m,航速22节,载箱数为21 237 TEU,其中冷箱数1 000 TEU。

该集装箱船作为超大型集装箱船的典型代表,是中船集团为中远海运集团量身订造,由中国船舶及海洋工程设计研究院(MARIC)开发设计,全面考虑了船东的个性化要求,结合船东营运特点进行定制化设计,对其装载性能与水动力性能进行综合优化,突破超大型集装箱船结构设计的关键技术,具有优异的技术经济指标和环保指标。

为了提高船舶的智能化水平,国内首次在20 000箱级别集装箱船上实现智能系统的实船应用,配备智能化系统,并将取得CCS船级社的i-ship(N,M,E,I)智能船级符号。且该船符合LR船级社的GR(A,S,E(M))船级符号设计技术,满足未来以最小代价进行双燃料改装的可行性,同时采用高效主机和最优的推进设计,实现出色的能源效率和排放控制。

该集装箱船的建造,不仅顺利完成诸多技术攻关,如采用TOFD新技术,整船定位探伤零遗留;还成功积累了诸如坞内多岛式建造、大总段移位、数字化试箱、导轨架精度控制、中压电力测试、质量检测及控制等超大型集装箱船建造中的关键技术，为中国造船行业提供了宝贵的经验。

（八）上海成为世界第3个年航空货运量突破400万吨的城市

2017年12月15日，上海机场（包括浦东机场、虹桥机场）年航空货量首次突破400万吨，由此上海成为继中国香港、美国孟菲斯后全球第3个年航空货量400万吨以上的城市。

这是上海继2016年成为全球第5个航空旅客亿级城市的又一个大喜事，对上海机场航空枢纽建设具有里程碑意义，同时也是上海国际航运中心建设取得的重要成绩，是上海这座国际化大都市综合实力的重要体现。

1998年，上海机场集团建成之后就开始谋求航空货运业务发展。1999年，浦东国际机场建成投入使用，一期货运设施同步启动运营。2004年，制定《上海航空枢纽战略规划》，提出货运与客运并举、国际和国内并重发展战略，进一步明确航空货运在城市经济发展中的地位。2011年，编制"建世界级航空货运枢纽"行动方案。2012年，提出浦东机场货运争创"世界第一"目标。2015年，成立上海机场航空物流发展公司，整合机场内部货运资源，积极推进航空货运枢纽建设，提出建设最具吸引力的世界级航空货运枢纽目标。

2002年，上海机场货量突破100万吨；2005年，上海机场货量突破200万吨；2008年，浦东机场货量跃居全球机场第三；2010年，上海机场货量突破300万吨；2017年，上海机场货运量突破400万吨。

近年来，上海机场货邮运量复合增长率为5%，货邮吞吐量占全国机场货邮吞吐量的1/4，国际货邮吞吐量占全国机场国际货邮吞吐量的近1/2。上海航空口岸货邮量仅占上海口岸货物总吞吐量的比例约0.8%，但创造了上海口岸进出口货物价值总值总量的34.2%。

从硬件看，上海浦东、虹桥两场共拥有六条跑道、三个货邮国际（地区）转运中心，是全国首个货运功能区纳入综合保税区和自贸试验区的机场，货运专用基础设施建设领先于主要竞争对手。从软件看，2017年上海机场电子运单使用率达52%，居全球机场第二、全国第一，航空货运信息集成系统日趋成熟，智慧物流园区建设正积极推进。

上海机场集团"筑巢引凤"，1999年，上海浦东国际机场货运站有限公司（PACTL）和东航货站公司入驻浦东机场投入运营；2000年，浦东机场国际快件中心投入运营，Fedex、UPS、DHL、TNT齐聚浦东；2009年，亚洲单体最大公共货站运营主体上海浦东国际机场西区公共货运站有限公司正式成立并投入运营；2008

年,UPS 转运中心投入运营;2013 年,DHL 北亚枢纽投入运营,同年 11 月作为自贸区制度创新的航空快件国际中转集拼项目由 DHL 启动;2017 年,Fedex 国际货运快件中心投入运营,至此浦东机场成为世界上唯一一个全球三大国际物流集成商进驻的机场。

上海机场积极寻求与国内新型承运人战略合作。2016 年 5 月,上海机场与顺丰正式签署合同,顺丰国内快件分拨中心项目落地浦东机场快件中心。上海机场正在与邮政、顺丰等战略客户进行协商,探索未来其在浦东机场进一步建设航空货运设施的可行性。

上海机场通过打造世界级航空综合货运枢纽,正在进一步构建连接"一带一路"沿线主要空港的航线网络,服务于"一带一路"沿线的产业转移和经贸合作,提升"一带一路"国家的国际竞争力。上海机场近年来进出"一带一路"沿线主要空港的货量呈高速增长态势。2017 年上海机场集团与俄罗斯空桥航空签署战略合作备忘录,在共同助力中俄空中大通道建设等领域,将建立起更为紧密的协作机制。

浦东机场近年来多次获得全球最佳货运机场和亚洲最佳货运机场称号,2017 年又获得全球最佳绿色机场称号。

截至 2017 年底,共有 100 多家航空公司在上海运营定期航班开展货运业务。其中,浦东机场航线网络覆盖全球五大洲 279 个城市,虹桥机场航线网络覆盖日、韩、港澳台及 87 个国内城市。上海机场集团努力打造枢纽优势突出、高端要素集聚、功能布局完整的综合性国际航空枢纽,成为辐射全球、面向亚太的世界级航空综合货运枢纽,为上海迈向全球城市提供有力支撑。

(九)亚洲海事技术合作中心在上海成立

2017 年 5 月 15 日,由联合国国际海事组织授权设立的亚洲海事技术合作中心(MTCC Asia)在上海海事大学成立。

这是中国第一个经联合国国际海事组织授权设立的实体性机构,也是亚洲唯一具有全球海事技术协调资格和能力的合作中心,旨在促进中国航运业与全球航运业共同取得绿色发展、可持续发展。

服务"一带一路"建设将是亚洲海事技术合作中心的重要议题。该中心将推动上海成为建设"21 世纪海上丝绸之路"的主导城市,提升上海在全球航运智库和全球影响力科创中心建设方面的水平,将对上海国际航运中心乃至整个中国航运事业的发展产生深远影响。

中心旨在完成 5 项重任:实施国际海事组织使命和任务,把握航运环境保护的先进理念和文化,充分利用航运技术和管理的发展,聚焦亚洲航运业船舶减排和能效方面的能力建设以及实现全球社会经济可持续发展。

近30年来,联合国国际海事组织(IMO)致力于建设全球区域性海事技术合作中心,开展广泛的技术交流与合作,推广全球航运业减排和能效提升理念和战略。IMO决定构建全球船舶减排和能效技术合作中心网络,并于2016年4月15日,向全球发出申请主办海事技术合作中心的邀请。

该中心作为亚洲航运业的一个直通国际最高海事立法机构IMO以及其有关先进环保理念的国际平台,受IMO精心指导,与全球其他4个MTCC协调运作,计划建成为亚洲乃至全球航运专业技术领域国际交流与合作的重要平台。

(十) 上海海事法院确立为"最高人民法院国际海事司法上海基地"

2017年3月23日,上海海事法院正式召开《上海海事法院五年发展规划纲要(2017—2021)》(以下简称《五年规划纲要》)征求意见座谈会,来自航运部门、研究机构、大型航运企业以及上海高院的专家学者受邀参会,一场更大范围更深层次的征求意见活动再次展开。上海海事法院对座谈会上的所有反馈意见进行逐条梳理,在经过反复琢磨和研究后,最终制定出正式的《五年规划纲要》并于2017年4月12日发布。

这是全国海事法院首个出台的五年发展规划,独具前瞻性的指导思想、发展目标、令人耳目一新的规划任务、实施要求,全面、系统地提升未来上海海事法院的战略定位和服务层级。

这次制定《五年规划纲要》就是为了在服务大局中给上海海事法院提供一个战略性、前瞻性、导向性的行动纲领,更好地凝聚、提升、释放内在的活力,推动法院的持续创新发展。

《五年规划纲要》清晰地明确上海海事法院到2021年的发展总体目标:以现代、创新、专业、智慧、透明为特征,建成司法功能健全、司法公正高效、专业特色鲜明、人才基础坚实、信息技术先进,能够全方位适应服务保障国家重大战略实施和经济社会发展司法需求,与上海国际航运中心地位相匹配,与上海加快建成社会主义现代化国际大都市要求相符合,国内领先、国际一流的海事法院,率先全面实现海事审判体系和海事审判能力现代化。

上海海事法院在《五年规划纲要》中"自我加压",进一步明确今后海事审判工作的具体目标,努力做到"服务国家战略更有作为、司法公信力大幅度提升、司法国际影响不断扩大、司法供给能力明显增强、司法创新实践持续深化"。

近年来,上海海事法院致力于打造"互联网+海事审判"新模式,相继推出网上立案、网上调解、远程庭审、移动办案、在线境外证据审查、在线船舶数据分析、网上船舶拍卖一系列举措,全力打造集智能、网络、阳光、移动为一体的海事审判工作新格局。

2016年3月13日,最高人民法院院长周强在工作报告中明确指出,要继续深化司法公开,加快建设"智慧法院"。同年7月,上海高院研究制定《"数据法院"建设与发展规划(2017—2019)》,继续推进上海法院的信息化建设向纵深发展。上海海事法院紧紧围绕建设"数据法院"的要求,在《五年规划纲要》中也提出明确的发展目标。

2017年4月19日,上海海事法院海事联动指挥中心正式启用。海事联动指挥中心由审判管理、队伍建设、服务大局、信息集控、警务保障、指挥中心及深具海事特点的智能分析、联动协同等八大模块组成,其中,智能分析模块中的船舶数据分析系统在全国海事法院中尚属首创,具备船舶定位分析功能和海上船舶碰撞动态模拟功能。

上海海事法院将认真落实《五年规划纲要》确定的各项目标任务,努力把上海建设成为具有全球影响力的国际海事司法中心,为国家重大战略实施和上海及周边地区经济社会发展提供坚强有力的海事司法服务保障。

二、自贸区与现代航运服务产品

(一)商务部开展工作推动建立自由贸易港区

2017年10月26日,商务部会同相关省市和部门,在高标准高水平建设自贸试验区的基础上,围绕建立自由贸易港区积极开展工作。

十九大报告提出,赋予自由贸易试验区更大改革自主权,探索建设自由贸易港。商务部新闻发言人高峰说,这是对改革开放试验田的建设提出更高要求,指明新的方向,要求我们对标更高的标准,推动更全面、更深入的开放新格局。

在国务院3月份印发的《全面深化中国(上海)自由贸易试验区改革开放方案》中,明确提出设立自由贸易港区,对标国际最高水平,实施更高标准的贸易监管制度。商务部正会同上海市和相关部门研究制定有关的建设方案。

此外,浙江自贸试验区也制定初步建成自由贸易港区先行区的发展目标,对接国际标准,推动以油品为核心的国际大宗商品贸易自由化。

下一步,商务部将深入学习贯彻党的十九大精神,会同有关省市和部门,紧扣自贸试验区制度创新的核心任务,加大力度探索建设自由贸易港,进一步彰显全面深化改革和扩大开放试验田的作用。

（二）上海自贸区出台 2017 行动方案

国务院正式印发《全面深化中国（上海）自由贸易试验区改革开放方案》（3.0版）。2017年4月2日上海市政府新闻发布会上提到，上海将根据这一"3.0版"方案，明确主体责任和实施职责，以重点突破带动整体推进，进一步细化措施，拿出2017年行动方案，形成合力抓推进抓落实，在更大范围内全面深化改革。

在制定方案时，坚持以制度创新为核心，率先建立同国际经贸通行规则相衔接的制度体系，力争取得更多可复制可推广的制度创新成果，进一步彰显全面深化改革和扩大开放试验田作用。坚持对照最高标准，查找短板弱项，以建设开放度最高自由贸易园区为目标，对照国际最高标准、最好水平，全面深化推动贸易和投资自由化便利化的改革举措，向世界亮明我国全方位开放的鲜明态度。

"3.0版"方案提出，上海自贸试验区要对标国际最高水平，实施更高标准的"一线放开""二线安全高效管住"贸易监管制度。上海将结合自由贸易港区建设，进一步推进国际最高标准单一窗口建设，包括努力实现口岸执法和贸易管理全覆盖；与国家部委的单一窗口系统进行对接，把各类口岸的许可及资质证明全部纳入进来；全面贯通口岸物流的所有环节，将口岸物流全部环节纳入国际贸易单一窗口等。

同时，上海自贸试验区将更加突出改革的系统集成，增强制度创新的系统性、整体性、协同性，着力健全"四个体系"；各类市场主体平等准入和有序竞争的投资管理体系；促进贸易转型升级和通关便利的贸易监管服务体系；深化金融开放创新和有效防控风险的金融服务体系；符合市场经济规则和治理能力现代化要求的政府管理体系，形成综合性改革态势。

浦东新区副区长陆方舟表示，为加强贸易便利化改革举措的系统集成，推进贸易发展方式转变，上海自贸试验区将对标国际高标准，建立完善一整套与国际投资贸易通行规则相衔接的制度创新体系，使之逐步定型、成熟、完善，"重点工作包括推进通关综合监管改革、深化货物状态分类监管制度、全面优化国际贸易'单一窗口'、增强贸易航运功能，服务上海国际贸易中心和航运中心建设"。

市工商局副局长彭文皓表示，2017年进一步推进"多证合一"登记制度改革。根据国家工商总局出台的《关于推进"多证合一"登记制度改革的意见》，与市商务委、市公安局、中国人民银行上海分行、上海海关、上海出入境检验检疫局等部门进行对接，整合更多涉企证件，更深层次实现部门间信息共享，减少重复办证、重复提交材料，便利群众办事创业。

站在全新的起点，上海自贸试验区下一步更加突出联动发展，注重强化自贸试验区内改革同上海市改革的联动、同上海国际金融中心和科技创新中心的联动，主动服务"一带一路"建设和长江经济带发展等国家战略，充分发挥自贸试验区辐射带动作用。

"目前,上海自贸试验区已成为全国走出去的一个重要通道,企业需求非常旺盛,可以乘势而上,紧紧围绕服务'一带一路'建设,以全球资源配置为目的,以国际产能合作为核心,以基础设施互联为依托,以公共服务体系为支撑,将自贸区建设成为各类企业和要素走出去的一个重要枢纽"。市商务委副主任杨朝表示,上海继续完善以便利化为核心的对外投资合作管理体系,推动商务部放宽自贸试验区对"一带一路"沿线国家的高新技术、基础建设、生物医药、高端制造等投资建设的条件,探索突破以工程承包为主的经营资格管理体制,进行相关探索和试点。

针对金融改革领域,市金融办副主任李军表示,围绕推进落实"金改40条",上海进一步深化自贸试验区金融开放创新试点,同时对标国家战略和金融改革开放总体部署,服务"一带一路"建设和人民币国际化战略,加强与科创中心建设、国际航运中心建设等联动,不断放大自贸试验区"金改"效应,不断提升金融服务实体经济功能。

陆方舟透露,在上海自贸试验区与科创中心的联动上,2017年推动设立快速获权、快速确权、快速维权的中国浦东知识产权保护中心,推进公安部"双自"人才出入境新政落地,吸引更多海外高层次人才到区内创新创业。

(三) 2017中国自贸区发展指数发布

2017年9月16日举行的第五届中国自由贸易试验区论坛上,上海财经大学发布2017"上财中国自由贸易试验区发展指数"。结果显示上海自贸区指数为81.35,领先于广东、天津和福建自贸区,具有一定的先行先试优势,广东、天津和福建分别为80.58、79.71和79.90,后成立的自贸区与上海发展差距在缩小。

上海财经大学上海发展研究院/自由贸易区研究院院长赵晓雷教授介绍说,该指数是上海财经大学项目组综合调研2 000多家企业、社会公众、相关专家以及公开披露的经济数据得出的结果,同时考虑自贸区内投资、外贸、财政、金融、就业等各领域的变动及相互影响,结合自贸区发展的特点,来衡量自贸区综合发展状态及寻找自贸区周期性的发展规律。

"发展指数"从主观和客观两个维度来考察自贸区的发展,并分别从信心、创新和影响三个层面来界定评价指标体系,用来评估上海、天津、广东和福建四个自贸区的发展。"发展指数"包含发展信心指数、创新力指数和影响力指数。

信心指数根据企业和公众对自贸区发展的主观判断和心理感受进行编制,反映出大众和企业对自贸区未来发展的信心。结果显示,综合发展信心指数为80.96,显示出自贸区对改革开放、地区经济、企业发展和大众生活可以带来显著的正面影响,同时企业的获得感在进一步加强。

创新力指数用以衡量自贸区的营商环境的优化效果,主要针对政府职能转变、投资领域的扩大开放、金融创新、贸易便利化以及管理制度创新等五个方面。结果显示,自贸区发展的创新力指数为81.04,略高于信心指数,这说明自贸区在制度创新方面发展速度加快,获取的企业、大众和专家的一致认可。从四个自贸区来看,上海为81.98,广东为81.39,天津为80.49,福建为80.41,上海和广东处于领先地位,在采取"证照分离"和事中事后监管等制度创新中走在几个自贸区的前列。

影响力指数反映的是自贸试验区对区域经济发展和公众生活的影响及波及性。指数显示,自贸区的影响力指数为80.73,上海为81.62,广东为79.82,天津为77.88,福建为77.53。赵晓雷认为,上海自贸区作为首先的试点,其在经济发展上较为突出。自贸区对所在区域的经济发展推动力显著,但是对周边区域的影响尚需提高。

项目组在调研过程中也发现,位于自贸区内企业的信心与满意程度要显著高于区外,企业规模和成立年限对信心和评价有着负向的影响。

此外,公众对"证照分离""负面清单"以及"市场准入"等概念不甚了解,一定程度上反映出自贸区政策解读、发展规划以及宣传力度的透明度尚需提升。文化教育、旅游休闲等服务行业对自贸区发展的评价相对较低,这体现出自贸区对相关服务业开放的力度需要进一步提高。

整体上,要进一步加大改革开放的力度,完善自贸区相关制度的法制体系建设,提升自贸区的经济影响力是未来的重要发展方向。

(四)"一带一路"框架下上海自贸试验区与东盟航运投资法律研讨会在沪成功举办

2017年6月27日,由中国(上海)自贸试验区商务委员会(航运办)主办,上海仲裁委员会国际航运仲裁院承办,并由东盟法律联盟、中国(上海)自由贸易试验区境外投资服务平台、上海海事大学法学院及上海市律师协会共同合作的"一带一路"框架下上海自贸试验区与东盟航运投资法律研讨会在上海航运和金融产业基地成功召开。

该研讨会围绕"一带一路"建设面临的机遇与挑战这一主线,从如何促进国际合作、协助地方政府和企业积极融入"一带一路"建设布局入手,聚焦产经联盟的方法与对策,着力研究打造自贸试验区与东盟航运投资的交流对话平台以及实现政策与资源之间的对接,并共同探索新形势下的实践模式。

研讨会由中国(上海)自由贸易试验区商务委员会副主任、上海市浦东新区商务委员会副主任陆启星主持,上海浦东新区陈希副区长致开幕式欢迎辞。陈希副区长表示,根据中央对上海自贸区功能定位的最新要求和服务国家"一带一路"倡议的任务部署,浦东新区政府将围绕增强全球航运资源配置能力这一发展主线部署航运的相关工作,包括着力完善航运综合服务功能布局,加强集聚国际航运功能性机构和领军企业,进一步完善上海自贸区的营商服务软环境等工作。上海自贸区和浦东新区将以更加开放的姿态参与国际经济合作,欢迎更多的国际企业和机构到浦东寻找合作伙伴,拓展业务和市场。

上海市律师协会俞卫锋会长作"'一带一路'框架下的法律服务国际化思考"的主旨发言。如何在"一带一路"的框架下建立国际新的贸易准则、纠纷解决机制,这是整个中国法律界需要考虑的问题。中国律师面对国际化的大背景,应充分把握这样的机遇,勇敢地直面现代技术给传统法律服务业带来的挑战。

研讨会上,上海外联发商务咨询有限公司副总经理刘旭、上海海事大学法学院副教授于耀东就"中国资本境外投资的相关政策及创新""建设21世纪海上丝绸之路的风险、挑战与应对"这两个核心议题,与参会嘉宾进行积极地互动。来自中国、新加坡、马来西亚、菲律宾、柬埔寨和泰国等近二十位航运、金融、投资领域的法律专业人士还围绕"一带一路"与东盟经济区投资、争议管理,以及仲裁在上述活动中的作用、上海仲裁委员会国际航运仲裁院近年来的专业化发展特点,展开热烈的小组讨论。

研讨会的成功举办,切实加强东盟经济伙伴对"一带一路"倡议的深刻认识,进一步向业界展现上海自贸区良好的法治环境,加深各大经济交易主体对仲裁这一国际通行的纠纷解决机制的认同感。相信随着"一带一路"倡议的不断深化,以及上海自贸区建设的不断升级,仲裁必将为国内外航运和贸易主体提供更多的专业法律保障。

(五)上海市政府新闻发布会:介绍上海自贸试验区深化改革、创新发展有关情况

市政府新闻办2017年9月12日举行市政府新闻发布会,市发展改革委副主任朱民介绍上海自由贸易试验区成立以来深化改革、创新发展的举措和成果。浦东新区副区长、上海自贸区管委会副主任陆方舟介绍上海自贸试验区年度工作重点。市商务委副主任申卫华、市工商局副局长彭文皓、市金融办副主任李军、市口岸办副主任武伟出席发布会,共同回答记者提问。

建设中国(上海)自由贸易试验区,是以习近平同志为核心的党中央在新形势下全面深化改革和扩大开放的战略举措。到2017年9月底,上海自贸试验区挂牌

运作将满四年。四年来,在党中央、国务院的坚强领导下,国家各有关部门积极推动,主动服务,全力支持和协调上海自贸试验区总体方案、深化方案和全面深化方案的落实。上海坚持解放思想、大胆实践,紧紧抓住制度创新这一核心要务,加强整体谋划、系统创新,围绕服务国家战略,努力把上海自贸试验区建设成为在新形势下引领全面深化改革、加快创新驱动发展的标杆和引擎。近四年来,上海自贸试验区改革创新主要体现在三个方面。

第一,制度创新进一步激发市场创新活力和经济发展动力。

按照把扩大开放同改革体制结合起来,把培育功能同政策创新结合起来的要求,上海自贸试验区积极推进制度创新优势转化为产业功能优势、产业功能优势转化为产业发展优势的进程。

保税区域是上海自贸试验区最先运作的区域。四年来,制度创新在推动保税区域经济结构转型升级和提升经济运行质量效益方面发挥的显著作用。自2013年来,保税区域实现区域经济规模年均增长9%,进出口额年均增长5%的持续稳定发展。

上海自贸试验区扩区两年多来,制度创新显示出对新扩片区经济发展提质增效的积极作用。陆家嘴金融片区的金融开放创新功能更加完善,区域新增企业8 000多家,是扩区前同期的2倍多。金桥开发片区持续推动"金桥制造"和"金桥服务"协同发展,推动先进制造业向研发、设计、销售、服务等"微笑曲线"两端延伸,加快培育互联网+、物联网+、虚拟现实等跨界融合生产性服务业新兴业态,经济发展质量效益明显提升。张江高科技片区持续推进"双自联动",在药品上市许可人制度、海外人才出入境政策、知识产权保护机制等方面取得重大突破,创新创业的生态环境不断完善。

第二,构建与国际投资和贸易通行规则相衔接的制度体系。

中央要求上海当好标杆,发挥先发优势,率先建立同国际投资和贸易通行规则相衔接的制度体系。上海按照中央要求,全球视野,立足国情,保持锐意创新的勇气、敢为人先的锐气、蓬勃向上的朝气,以新发展理念为引领,聚焦投资、贸易、金融和事中事后监管领域,形成一批基础性和核心制度创新,并在实践中不断成熟、定型,以制度创新促进政府管理经济的方式发生根本性转变,在率先形成法治化、国际化、便利化的营商环境上取得重大进展。

第三,为全局性改革发挥示范引领和突破带动作用。

四年来,上海自贸试验区的改革创新理念和制度创新成果已分领域、分层次在全国复制推广。开展"证照分离"改革试点的116项行政许可事项,在全国其他10个自贸试验区,以及有条件的国家自主创新示范区、国家高新技术产业开发区推广实施。外商投资备案管理、企业准入"单一窗口"等37项投资领域改革措施在全国复制推广。先进区后报关、批次进出集中申报等34项贸易便利化改革措施,已在全国范围、长江流域范围、海关特殊监管区域等分阶段有序推广实施。跨境融资、利率市场化等23项金融制度创新改革成果分领域、分层次在全国复制推广。上海自贸试验区的主动开放、自主改革,探索新形势下推动全面深化改革和扩大开放的新路径,为全国自贸试验区建设提供可借鉴的经验和模式。

  2016年底,习近平总书记对上海自贸试验区建设作出重要批示,充分肯定了上海自贸试验区建设成效。2017年初,国务院印发《全面深化中国(上海)自由贸易试验区改革开放方案》,全面深化方案细化的98项改革任务和2017年的24项重点工作已经全部推开。

  上海深入学习好、领会好、贯彻好习近平总书记重要指示精神,以建设开放度最高的自由贸易园区为目标,以"三区一堡"和"三个联动"为抓手,对照国际最高标准、最好水平的自由贸易区,持续在深化自贸试验区改革上作出新作为,发挥好引领带动作用,更好地服务国家战略,进一步彰显上海自贸试验区全面深化改革和扩大开放试验田的作用。

三、航运法治建设

(一)上海海事法院与上海保监局合作促进航运保险业改革创新

  2017年10月13日,上海海事法院与上海保监局联合召开新闻发布会,在全国首次推出海事诉讼保全责任险以及保证函推荐格式文本。

  此次推出的海事诉讼保全责任险及保证函推荐格式文本,具有明显的海事诉讼特色。它是上海海事法院与上海保监局、上海航运保险协会多次磋商研讨的合作成果。

  该推荐文本中列明海事审判中常见的保全类型,便于保险公司根据不同保全类型存在风险的差异核定费率和收费方式,也便于海事法院进行审查。海事诉讼保全申请人向保险公司投保保全责任险,保险公司出具保证函,并在错误保全时依法向被申请人或第三人承担损害赔偿责任。同时,推荐文本对保证函名称及有效期的表述更为精准简洁,对出具保证函的保险公司层级也有明确规定。

  该推荐文本已在上海海事法院审理的一起金融借款合同纠纷中首次得到适用,效果良好。

（二）上海海事法院发布涉船员权益保护海事审判白皮书

2017年6月22日,在"6·25世界海员日"来临之际,上海海事法院召开新闻发布会,以涉船员权益保护为专题发布中英文版2016年度海事审判白皮书,重点通报近三年涉船员权益保护案件的审判执行情况。这是该院继2010年以来第七次向社会通报海事审判工作情况。

此次发布的白皮书,继续采用中英文双语发布的形式,延续"发布常态化、专题系列化、内容精细化"的特点,并聚焦航运民生领域热点问题,关注船员群体职业发展和权益保障,全面详实地反映该院涉船员权益保护案件的审判执行情况以及涉民生司法保障各项工作机制的实施状况,为规范、引导船员行业及航运业健康发展提供有效的司法实践经验。

白皮书显示:2016年上海海事法院共收案5 054件,结案5 101件,同比分别上升7.49%和8.28%;涉案标的总额人民币45.90亿元;其中涉外、涉港澳台案件983件,涉及36个国家和地区;海上、通海水域货物运输合同纠纷和货运代理合同纠纷仍为主要案件类型,占一审收案总数的69.79%。

在审判执行总体保持良好态势的基础上,上海海事法院还办结了一批精品案件。通过依法对发生在南海黄岩岛附近海域海难事故纠纷行使司法管辖权,向国际社会宣示我国对南海海域的国家主权;一起船舶碰撞损害赔偿责任纠纷案入选最高人民法院公报案例和"2016年全国法院海事审判十大典型案例""2016年度上海法院十大典型案例";两起海上货运代理合同纠纷案,被法国权威法律期刊《法国海商法杂志》登载,获法国业界高度评价。

白皮书还通报上海海事法院在深入实施审判精品战略,积极参与航运领域综合治理,深化专业审判机制,建立快立、快保、快审、快执"四快"绿色通道,完善船舶网络司法拍卖机制以及扩大网络信息技术应用等六方面情况的工作和取得的成效。

针对海事案件中的新情况新问题,白皮书通报船舶营运借款合同纠纷多发,《国内水路货物运输规则》废止后实际承运人的身份认定和责任承担发生困难,新兴市场纺织品出口运输纠纷多发,邮轮旅游引发的纠纷进入诉讼,船舶出险溢油引发清防污企业主张作业费用案件较为集中等问题,并进行相应的风险提示。

白皮书除通报上海海事法院2016年度海事审判工作基本情况外,还对该院2014—2016年审理的涉船员权益保护的相关案件进行专项总结和分析,发布涉船员权益保护的典型案例。开展审判执行工作,为船员群体提供更加完善的司法保护,营造良好法治环境,推动我国航运业健康发展。

白皮书显示,三年来,上海海事法院共受理各类涉船员纠纷案件2 000余件,其中船员劳务合同纠纷案件790件。受市场经营状况影响,每年受理案件数有较大幅度的波动,分布在涉案标的额6万元以下区间的案件较为集中,且多以船员集体诉讼的形式出现。同期审结的804件案件中,49.62%的案件以判决方式结案,55.47%的案件在一个月内审结。此外,涉外、涉港澳台的船员劳务合同纠纷案件增长明显。

白皮书发布的涉船员权益保护典型案例,分别涉及船员因伤致残、海难事故多名船员伤亡、外派船员人身损害等案件类型以及涉船员司法保护绿色通道、涉船员执行等工作情况,以成熟统一的司法裁判标准,规范和引导市场主体行为,优化船员履职法律环境,促进航运业有序发展。

上海海事法院在为船员权益提供司法保护方面开展大量工作,形成一套相对成熟的机制和经验。白皮书专门介绍该院依法保护船员权益的工作机制和主要做法,比如建立"四快"绿色通道,缩短船员权益实现周期,积极推进船舶网络司法拍卖工作,以更快更好地实现船员群体的胜诉权益。

(三) 首例"有主"船舶油污损害案件获得理赔

2017年6月15日,交通运输部在北京召开中国船舶油污损害赔偿基金管理委员会2017年度会议。会议审议通过3起船舶油污事故的理赔报告,涉及赔偿金额近1600万元。其中,"山宏12"轮油污事故理赔是我国船舶油污损害赔偿基金首次理赔"有主"船舶油污损害案件,标志着我国船舶油污损害赔偿基金工作取得新突破。

会议审议通过中国船舶油污损害赔偿基金管理委员会秘书处年度工作报告、中国船舶油污损害赔偿基金2017年度收支预算报告,以及《船舶油污损害赔偿基金专家管理办法》和首批理赔专家名单。中国船舶油污损害赔偿基金管理委员会秘书处秘书长、交通运输部海事局局长许如清向首批理赔专家代表颁发聘书。

许如清作总结讲话时指出,我国船舶油污损害赔偿基金的使用管理是一项崭新实践,必须结合实际、探索实践、循序渐进。通过两年的努力,基金的规章制度日趋完善、基金的惠民作用日趋体现、基金的管理体制日趋成熟、基金的社会影响日趋扩大。为更好地推进基金的使用工作,要未雨绸缪,进一步完善基金制度,并做好相关政策储备工作;要坚持问题导向,充分发挥专家智囊作用,推进基金使用管理工作的科学、健康发展;要加强宣传和沟通工作,发挥好基金的辐射效应;要总结经验,进一步完善决策和运行机制,增强基金的使用效果。

(四) 上海海事大学法学院获批设立全国首家海事仲裁研究中心

2017年5月19日,中国仲裁法学研究会正式批准在上海海事大学法学院设立海事仲裁研究中心,并将该中心作为中国仲裁法学研究会的专业委员会报请国家民政部主管部门、中国法学会以及中国国际贸易促进委员会备案。

上海海事大学法学院整合专业优势资源,力邀权威专家加盟,成功获批设立全国首家海事仲裁研究智库。海事仲裁研究中心将依托精干的科研团队和坚实的研究基础,在中国仲裁法学研究会的指导下开展学术交流、教学指导、课题研究、会员服务等工作,加强海事仲裁领域理论界与实务界的沟通和交流,跟踪各国立法与实践的前沿动态,探索学术创新,荟萃精品成果,促进我国海事仲裁制度的发展与完善,推动我国仲裁法治建设进程。

(五)上海海事法院与江苏省连云港市中级人民法院联合发布《服务保障"一带一路"建设合作框架协议》

2017年8月29日,上海海事法院与江苏省连云港市中级人民法院联合召开新闻发布会,发布两院签署的《服务保障"一带一路"建设合作框架协议》。上海海事法院副院长荚振坤、连云港市中级人民法院副院长顾长洲出席新闻发布会,通报相关情况并回答记者提问。

2017年5月,习近平总书记在"一带一路"国际合作高峰论坛上回顾了四年来"一带一路"建设取得的丰硕成果,并为"一带一路"的未来发展作出前瞻性部署。当前,"一带一路"建设不断深入推进,我国正在发挥沿海港口的地理优势,积极搭建跨境多式联运走廊,开展贯通海上丝路和丝路经济带的陆海联运大通道建设。上海是"21世纪海上丝绸之路"的重要港口城市,正在积极发挥国际经济、金融、贸易、航运"四个中心"、自由贸易试验区、科创中心建设的叠加优势,进一步提升对接"一带一路"建设的服务能级。连云港在"丝绸之路经济带"中地位独特,作为新亚欧大陆桥经济走廊首要节点城市、中哈物流中转基地和上合组织出海基地,正在积极构筑"一带一路"东西双向开放门户,并不断加强交汇点核心区先导区建设。上海与连云港在海上丝路和丝路经济带建设中区位优势明显,肩负的职责日益凸显。连云港派出法庭作为上海海事法院在江苏连云港的派出机构,在司法服务保障"一带一路"陆海联运大通道建设中与连云港中院形成有效对接。此次上海海事法院和连云港中院签署的协议,旨在深入贯彻习近平总书记关于"一带一路"倡议的重要指示精神,贯彻落实最高人民法院关于为"一带一路"建设提供司法服务保障的工作要求,通过发挥各自优势,形成工作合力,全方位对接海上丝路和丝路经济带陆海联运大通道建设中的司法需求,共同为"一带一路"建设提供更加优质高效的司法服务保障。

根据协议内容,双方将加强对涉"一带一路"案件审判工作的沟通交流,提高涉外审判工作水平,营造良好的营商法治环境;积极化解矛盾纠纷,共同推进多元化纠纷解决机制的构建,维护和谐稳定的社会环境;加强执行工作,建立全方位立体化执行协作机制,依法维护当事人胜诉权益;发挥两地管辖优势,推出巡回审判和方便当事人诉讼的互助举措,延伸司法服务职能。

新闻发布会介绍上海海事法院的基本情况、管辖范围、工作特点和连云港派出法庭工作情况,上海海事法院服务保障"一带一路"建设的工作计划及展望,以及上海海事法院和连云港中院双方合作情况和执行协作相关案例。

(六)上海海事法院与上海对外经贸大学签署合作协议共建"21世纪海上丝绸之路研究中心"

2017年11月28日,上海海事法院与上海对外经贸大学举行"21世纪海上丝绸之路研究中心"揭牌仪式。上海海事法院院长赵红和上海对外经贸大学副校长徐永林分别致辞,并代表两家单位签署合作协议,共同为研究中心成立揭牌。

根据协议,双方围绕服务"一带一路"、海洋强国、贸易强国、上海自由贸易区、自由贸易港和国际航运中心建设,合作成立"21世纪海上丝绸之路研究中心",在决策咨询和学术课题研究、中国海事司法案例国际化传播、对外学术交流、外国法查明、大数据服务共享等领域开展全方位合作。

近年来,上海海事法院积极探索建设国际海事司法高端智库,以一流智库促进海事审判理论和实践水平提升,先后与清华大学、上海海事大学等高校签署合作协议,不断深化拓展司法智库型研究平台建设。

上海海事法院以本次签约为契机,与上海对外经贸大学精诚合作、互相支持,高标准、高质量推动各项合作事宜落实,努力将中心建设成为研究资源集聚、研究活动繁荣、研究视野宽广、研究成果丰硕的一流法律政策智库,为国家重大战略实施和上海经济社会发展贡献更多的智慧和力量。

(七)上海海事法院被最高人民法院正式确立为"最高人民法院国际海事司法上海基地"

2017年4月,上海海事法院被最高人民法院正式确立为"最高人民法院国际海事司法上海基地"。

为充分发挥上海海事审判的工作优势,通过区域性先行先试的实践探索,完善创新海事诉讼机制和审判方法,形成更多可复制可推广的审判经验,上海海事法院制定出台《关于推进"最高人民法院国际海事司法上海基地"建设的实施意见》,进一步向"把我国建设成为具有较高国际影响力的国际海事司法中心"目标迈进。

该意见明确提出,上海基地以建设国际海事纠纷解决中心为核心功能,以建设国际海事司法高端智库和国际海事司法交流平台为辅助功能。

作为主功能的国际海事纠纷解决中心,是建设国际海事司法中心的主要和核心目标。上海海事法院依托在航运主体国际化、纠纷数量规模化和纠纷类型多样化等方面的优势,深入实施海事审判精品战略,着力提升海事司法国际公信力,以公正、透明、可预期的裁判引领规则创制,以与国际接轨、有较大吸引力、便利化的海事诉讼机制,吸引更多中外航运市场主体选择上海海事法院解决诉讼纠纷。

作为辅助功能之一的国际海事司法高端智库,旨在找准海事司法与国家重大战略的结合点和着力点,围绕国际社会普遍关注的海事司法理论与实践重大热点问题,集聚国际海事法律人才和资源,提供优质的海事司法服务保障和专业智库支持。

作为另一辅助功能的国际海事司法交流平台,旨在利用上海的国际化优势,搭建互联互通的海事司法信息交流共享平台,更好地与国际海事法律领域接轨,扩大中国海事司法的国际影响力。

上海海事法院近年来推进国际海事司法中心主要表现在:①充分发挥海事审判职能,积极推动航运营商环境法治化、国际化、便利化。②公正高效解决航运领域纠纷,提升海事司法国际公信力。③创新便利化诉讼机制,积极打造海事诉讼优选地。④深化国际海事司法交流合作,建设海事司法智库新平台。⑤加强海事法院队伍建设,培育国际化高端海事司法人才。

(八) 上海海事法院被最高人民法院确立为"智慧海事法院(上海)实践基地"

2017年6月,上海海事法院被最高人民法院确立为"智慧海事法院(上海)实践基地"。作为全国首家智慧法院实践基地,上海海事法院制定出台《关于推进"智慧海事法院(上海)实践基地"建设的实施意见》,充分运用现代科技手段,着力解决影响和制约海事审判发展的重点和难点问题,全面服务保障以执法办案为第一要务的法院各项工作。

该意见提出,智慧海事法院建设要促进人工智能的全面应用,以及与海事审判、海事诉讼服务深度融合,努力使"智慧海事法院"成为引领海事司法发展的重要举措,成为推动海事审判创新发展的重要手段。通过打造智慧海事法院建设"样板间",切实提升海事审判服务保障国家战略和上海经济社会发展的能力和水平。

该意见明确,智慧海事法院建设的主要任务是打造"1+2+X"的信息化建设模板。建设"一个中心",即构建安全、稳定、先进、可控的大数据交换处理中心,实现数据的采集、交换、处理、展示、发布等一体化集成。建设"两个平台",即建设智能化办案平台,提高审判执行质效,提升诉讼服务能力;建设智能化办公平台,提高司法行政能力,提升司法保障水平。建设若干个智能辅助系统,实现智慧海事法院"人工智能+"工作模式的转型升级。

上海海事法院近年来在建设海事特色大数据平台、探索"互联网+海事审判"、推进完善船舶网络司法拍卖工作、建设智能化辅助办案系统等方面有不少亮点工作。

(九)上海市浦东新区法院发布 2016—2017 年涉自贸案件审判工作白皮书

2017 年 11 月 19 日,浦东新区人民法院发布上海自贸区审判工作白皮书(2016 年 11 月—2017 年 10 月)及十大典型案例,并展示涉自贸案件司法大数据研究成果。

白皮书披露,2016 年 11 月—2017 年 10 月,浦东法院共受理各类涉自贸案件 33 708 件。从案件类型看,包括民商事案件 26 847 件、刑事案件 565 件、行政案件 12 件、执行案件 6 284 件。

浦东法院副院长胡永庆表示,浦东法院一直致力于为自贸区建设提供公正高效的司法服务,过去一年,随着自贸区建设的推进,浦东法院审理的涉自贸案件也呈现出相应特点和变化规律。首先,收结案数量增速放缓,涉诉纠纷趋于平稳;其次,案件调撤率上升,涉自贸多元化纠纷解决机制成效显著;再次,案件类型结构调整,反映自贸试验区法治环境持续完善;最后,涉外案件类型呈多样化态势,自贸试验区开放进一步深化。

在白皮书中,浦东法院专门对涉自贸案件作了类型化分析,就刑事、普通民事、投资贸易类商事、金融商事、知识产权、劳动争议、行政和执行等案件的审理概况、基本特点等进行深入分析。

2017 年 3 月,国务院印发《全面深化中国(上海)自由贸易试验区改革开放方案》。在此背景下,自贸区建设需要更为有力、高效的司法服务保障。一方面,要对不断出现的新类型疑难案件进行高质量审理,推动自贸区规则建立、价值引领;另一方面,要大胆运用"互联网+"、大数据等技术,提升审判质效,便利当事人。

2017 年 11 月 19 日,浦东法院还发布 2016—2017 年涉自贸十大典型案例,并对涉自贸案件司法大数据研究成果进行现场演示。

浦东法院自贸区法庭庭长曹克睿介绍,十大典型案例包括 4 件商事案例、2 件知识产权案例、1 件行政案例、1 件劳动争议案例、1 件刑事案例和 1 件执行案例。这些案例大多是新类型、疑难案件,审理结果具有较强的示范效应。

十大案例涉及股权转让纠纷、证券经纪合同纠纷、不正当竞争纠纷、竞业限制纠纷等多个案由。其中,"大众点评诉百度不正当竞争纠纷案"还曾入选"《中国审判》2016十大典型案例""2014年至2016年中国互联网法治十大影响性案例"。这些案例社会关注度较高,对促进行业健康发展及类案审理均有重要参考价值。

浦东法院演示涉自贸案件大数据分析系统。该系统为全国首创,可以自动收集、分析上海乃至全国涉自贸案件的分布、案件信息等数据,形成自贸案件分析数据库。系统还能以自贸区内各重点主体、重点行业及新型领域作为关键词,及时发现新型和典型案例,对自贸区内的风险实现动态监管和防控。

(十)最高人民法院发布第二批涉"一带一路"建设典型案例

2017年5月15日,最高人民法院召开新闻通气会,发布第二批10个涉"一带一路"建设典型案例,最高人民法院民四庭副庭长刘敬东介绍有关情况,最高人民法院新闻发言人林文学主持通气会。

此次发布的典型案例都是"一带一路"建设中常见的纠纷类型,涉及信用证开证、股权转让合同、居间合同、独立保函、海域污染损害赔偿、海上货物运输合同、承认和执行外国仲裁裁决、承认和执行外国商事判决等案件,案件所涉的法律问题均具有很强的代表性。如中国建设银行股份有限公司广州荔湾支行与广东蓝粤能源发展有限公司等信用证开证纠纷再审案是一起具有涉外因素的远期跟单信用证开证纠纷,最高人民法院通过合同体系解释的方法,依法保护了持有提单的开证行所享有的优先受偿权,同时澄清长期困扰司法实践的提单凭证法律属性之争。

涉"一带一路"建设的案件绝大部分为涉外案件,在此类案件的审理过程中,经常会遇到适用冲突规范确定准据法、查明和适用外国法、适用国际公约和国际惯例、公共秩序保留等问题。如在大连市海洋与渔业局海域污染损害赔偿纠纷一案中,涉及《1992年国际油污损害民事责任公约》的解释,该案严格依照《维也纳条约法公约》的规定,明确公约规定的环境损害赔偿限于合理恢复措施的费用。西门子公司申请承认与执行外国仲裁裁决一案则是自贸试验区内外商独资企业之间的合同纠纷,该案确认仲裁条款有效,并明确"禁止反言",践行《纽约公约》"有利于裁决执行"的理念。

在"一带一路"建设推进过程中,案件所涉的交易类型日趋丰富,一方面会出现更多的立法空白,需要我国完善相应的法律制度,另一方面则将更多地涉及我国和沿线国的法律冲突和协调问题。

2017年,最高人民法院将围绕司法服务和保障"一带一路"建设,就承认和执行外国民商事判决、对外担保等迫切需要解决的涉外审判疑难问题出台司法解释,并着手制定有关船员劳务纠纷问题、海洋资源与生态污染损害赔偿纠纷案件的司法解释。同时,出台关于涉外民商事案件诉讼管辖问题的规定,进一步完善涉外诉讼管辖机制,推进海事法院管辖海事刑事案件试点工作,维护蓝色国土安全,保障海上丝绸之路畅通。

四、航运文化建设

(一) 2017年"行舟致远"航海文化论坛成功举办

2017年7月10日,第九届"行舟致远"航海文化论坛在宁波博物馆成功举办。作为今年中国航海日专题论坛之一,该论坛由中国航海日论坛组委会主办,宝德中国古船研究所、庆安会馆、宁波博物馆和宁波市港航管理局共同承办。

论坛主要通过图片展览、主旨演讲、专家论坛等形式进行。"丝路帆影"英国皇家格林威治博物馆影像图片展在宁波庆安会馆开始其全球首展,图片展真实还原20世纪30年代中国沿海一带船、人与港口的融合共生。

论坛开幕式上,宁波市政府王建云副秘书长作致辞,阐述我国,尤其是宁波在航海历史文化中的发展和成就,并期盼宁波作为"一带一路"重要节点城市,作出新突破、新贡献。英国驻上海副总领事、英国皇家格林威治博物馆馆长Kevin Fewster和国家文物局水下文化遗产保护中的技术总监孙键分别作主旨演讲。来自英国国际博物馆、宁波博物馆、香港海事博物馆和中国海外交通史研究会的相关负责人对博物馆界的国际合作进行交流发言,并与现场嘉宾进行互动。在"中国近代航海与贸易"专场,20余位业界知名专家学者根据自己的研究领域展开专业的学术汇报交流。

此次论坛以"海丝视野下的中国近代航海与贸易"和"海上丝绸之路与博物馆"为主题,汇集专家智慧、凝聚各方共识,展开专业的学术交流与探讨,让大家在感受航海文化魅力的同时,增强航海和海洋意识,取得了良好社会效果。

(二) 北外滩码头文化博物馆开建

北外滩滨江区域将再添新亮点,一条反映上海百年码头文化历史的"长廊"——码头文化露天博物馆已经开建。

虹口区境内黄浦江沿岸曾经是上海重要的货运、客运集散地。早在1845年,英商东印度公司在徐家滩(今东大名路、高阳路)一带建造简陋的驳船码头。1860年,英商宝顺洋行建造宝顺码头,这是上海第一个轮船码头。1861年,美商旗昌洋行建造旗昌码头。1864年,英商蓝烟囱轮船公司重建虹口码头,由驳船码头改为轮船码头。

新中国成立之前,虹口区域内黄浦江沿岸主要有黄浦码头、杨树浦码头、汇山码头、华顺码头、公平路码头、高阳路码头、外虹桥码头、扬子江码头等八个码头。

虹口区开建的码头文化露天博物馆是个开放式的码头文化历史长廊,把上海的都市文化与码头文化、传统与现代有机地结合起来。博物馆以600米长的玻璃墙为展陈载体,加上雕塑、勒石铭碑、史地人物标志、建筑构件小品等,利用适当的声、光、电技术手段,结合虹口区丰富的历史人文资源,以1843年上海开埠为起点,到上海近代工业创办,再到先进的社会文明开启,以追忆上海城市发展历史为主线。码头文化露天博物馆不仅展示出上海海纳百川、大气谦和的城市精神,还是对海派文化的传承与发展。

根据规划,玻璃墙由三部分组成,即"码头衍变""西学东渐""名人踪迹",主要用历史图片及二维码,展示包括上海沿江码头的历史变迁,早期中国知识分子远涉重洋,在此踏上赴海外留学的道路,探求真理,学习国外先进知识,参与文化交流的场景,以及许多世界文化名人和科学家,如泰戈尔、爱因斯坦、卓别林等从这里上岸来华访问讲学的情景。

码头文化露天博物馆还设置若干个滨江景观点雕塑和模型,其中包括老上海黄浦江分布示意图、北外滩老码头分布示意图模型、码头栓绳桩、20块码头年轮等。同时还有一组题为"相对"的爱因斯坦和孩子景观雕塑,意为爱因斯坦发明相对论。

(三) 2017"一带一路"文化圆桌会议

2017年8月24—25日,由中国宋庆龄基金会与兰州大学联合举办的"一带一路"文化圆桌会议在兰州大学举行,来自中国、俄罗斯、美国、日本、印度、巴基斯坦、澳大利亚等21个国家的近百位专家学者与会,深入探讨如何发挥民间组织与高校的作用,推进"一带一路"区域内国家间的交流与合作,为和平发展、交流互鉴、合作共赢凝聚共识和智慧。

"共同捍卫人类的精神和文明价值,倡导各种文明之间的建设性对话,积极应对各类新挑战,是非政府组织的时代使命"。中国宋庆龄基金会党组书记、常务副主席齐鸣秋表示,在"一带一路"建设中,政府间的精诚合作、互利互信是主导,非官方的交流对话也具有独特而不可替代的作用。各国非政府组织作为沟通政府与社会的纽带、桥梁,在国际事务特别是人类共同关注的一些领域发挥着越来越重要的作用。

教育部原党组副书记、副部长杜玉波指出,在推进"一带一路"建设的过程中,要更好地促进沿线国家之间的教育交流,尤其是高等教育的交流合作,以发挥高等教育在沿线国家人文交流中的桥梁作用,发挥沿线各国高等教育界在"一带一路"建设中的智库作用,发挥高等教育在增强沿线国家互信中的催化作用。

兰州大学校长王乘表示,在丝绸之路经济带振兴的过程中,教育和文化科技等各项交流合作必将起到重要的先导作用。兰州大学作为地处丝绸之路经济带核心节点城市的国家重点综合性大学,今后将整合更多的科研力量,以更加广阔的视野和更多元的务实合作来开展研究、为之服务。

在主旨论坛上,中外专家学者围绕主题进行演讲,探讨务实开展文化、区域、高校合作的具体路径,分析如何推动"和平合作、开放包容、互学互鉴、互利共赢"的丝绸之路精神在沿线各国的弘扬。

会议期间还组织"文化交流""区域合作""高校合作"三个分论坛,与会专家就相关领域的话题展开深入的研讨与交流。

在为期两天的研讨和交流中,与会专家通过平等对话、坦诚交流、集思广益,达成以下共识:

一是以"共商、共建、共享"原则推进"一带一路"建设,不仅要积极推动区域间的经贸交流与合作,更要挖掘和领略蕴含其中的文化底蕴和人文精神。要进一步深化沿线各国的民间友好和务实合作,通过跨越国界、跨越文明的交流活动,推动"一带一路"沿线各国弘扬交流、融合、对话、合作和共赢的理念,使欧亚空间成为繁荣发展和和平安宁的地区。

二是推进"一带一路"建设必须跳出传统的区域经济模式,探索一种新型的区域合作模式。要在各国认同同一理念和规则的前提下,以平等、互利、共赢的方式扩大经济交流,倡导更高层次和更广泛内容的合作,不仅有产业转移,加强贸易往来,深化投资合作,而且要深化人文、教育、科技、生态、环境等领域的合作,并最终实现政策沟通的常态化,贸易投资的自由化。

三是在知识与经济结合更加紧密的时代,高等教育已经成为各国推动社会经济发展的重要力量。推进"一带一路"建设的过程中,更好地促进沿线国家之间的教育交流,尤其是高等教育的交流合作,具有格外突出的意义。沿线各国应当进一步鼓励和扩大高等教育界各种形式的人员交往,通过更高频率和层级的教育资源共享、科学技术合作、人员沟通交流,为"一带一路"建设提供更多的人才支持和创新驱动力。

(四)上海举行多项活动庆祝第 13 个中国航海日

2017 年 7 月 11 日是第 13 个中国航海日,以"船·港·人——互联互通"为主题,上海举行丰富多彩的宣传纪念活动,弘扬航海精神,宣传航海文化,营造全社会共同关心、支持航海事业的良好氛围。

7月11日,集聚航运功能性机构、承载航运历史文化的北外滩航运服务中心正式揭幕,进一步提升北外滩航运产业能级和地位;《上海航运文化地标手绘图》首发仪式、"驿路丝路复兴路　行走新丝路"主题邮展也在新落成的北外滩航运服务中心举行。

在新落成的北外滩航运服务中心,如今已有中国船东协会、中国船舶油污损害理赔事务中心、上海国际航运研究中心、中国航运50人论坛秘书处等一批全国性重点航运功能性机构入驻。2016年,航运产业在虹口区的整个财政收入中已占比达31%,成为名副其实的虹口支柱产业。为此,虹口区提出"一线两圈四中心"战略格局,临江沿线着力吸引航运业总部落户、邮轮、游艇、游船等产业发展;霍山路圈重点依托航运功能要素集聚,促进航运信息交流,吸引相关功能性机构以及各类航运会议论坛落户,上海外滩航运服务中心正是霍山路圈的形象标志;密云路圈则依靠国家级的上海船员评估示范中心,发展上海航海人才公共实训基地、上海港口安全培训基地,重点聚焦船员服务。

此次发布的《上海航运文化地标手绘图》,收集沪上约39处航运文化地标,集中展示上海的航运文化内涵与特色,于7月11日起在上海机场、码头、轮渡等处向市民免费发放,上海邮政还专门发行专属纪念封。

为积极呼应国家"一带一路"建设,探讨"21世纪海上丝绸之路"背景下,航海业如何抓住新机遇、谋求新动力、拓展新空间,上海如何在建设国际航运中心过程中对接国家战略、发挥支撑与引领作用,第二届"21世纪海上丝绸之路"建设高峰论坛在陆家嘴举行,来自航运界、金融界的近400位行业专家、企业代表、政府部门代表参加。

"2016年,全球经济规模达到约80万亿美元,其中世界贸易总额约为32万亿美元,占据约40%,这其中,绝大多数都依靠航运,这正是航运的重要价值与意义"。上海海事大学党委书记金永兴说,上海的历史,印证港因城用、城因港兴的发展轨迹。

21世纪海上丝绸之路,在共商、共建、共享的原则指导下,在建设成为"和平之路、繁荣之路、开放之路、创新之路、文明之路的"目标下,为交通方式、贸易内容、覆盖范围的拓展提供新机遇、新动力和新空间。探讨如何抓住新机遇、谋求新动力、拓展新空间,结合地区和行业实际,促进新丝路背景下的航海大发展,成为论坛的主旨所在。在论坛上,专家学者分别从宏观政策、航运发展、"一带一路"与自贸区、港口发展、海事法律、航运金融、国际合作等角度发表主旨演讲,共同探讨上海机遇。

论坛上,经过 2 年试运行,指数结构不断调整优化后,上海航运交易所正式发布"一带一路"航贸指数。这一指数由"一带一路"贸易额指数、"一带一路"货运量指数、"海上丝绸之路"运价指数等 3 大类指数组成,细分煤炭、矿石、原油、集装箱等 4 大货种,运输方式包括海运、铁路,未来还将增加航空等多种运输方式。

五、航运人才服务

(一)上海自贸区外籍高层次人才可直接申请"中国绿卡"

上海自贸试验区的外籍人才申请在华永久居留,如今有更为方便快捷的渠道。外籍人才认定标准和认定流程获公安部批准:从 2017 年 4 月 13 日起,外籍人才可凭上海自贸区管委会出具的《中国(上海)自由贸易试验区外籍高层次人才申请在华永久居留推荐函》,到市出入境管理局申请办理外国人永久居留证,其外籍配偶和未成年子女也可随同申请。

外国人永久居留证被称为"中国绿卡",为支持上海科创中心建设,公安部推出出入境政策"新十条"。其中第一条明确,"对符合认定标准的外籍高层次人才,经上海张江国家自主创新示范区或上海自贸试验区管委会推荐,可直接申请在华永久居留"。如今人才认定标准和认定流程出炉,意味着此项改革举措正式落地。2017 年 4 月 13 日起,上海自贸试验区区域内的高等院校、科研院所、企业等单位可向其所在自贸片区管理局提出申请,由新区人保局审核后,向相关部门推荐符合认定标准的外籍高层次人才。

外籍高层次人才的认定标准具体分为三类:一类是知名奖项获得者或高层次人才计划入选者,包括诺贝尔奖、菲尔兹奖、沃尔夫奖、克拉福德奖、图灵奖、普里茨克建筑奖等国际知名奖项获得者或提名者;中国政府"友谊奖""国际科技合作奖"等国家级对外表彰奖项获得者;中央"千人计划""外专千人计划"入选者;国家杰出青年科学基金获得者;教育部"长江学者"奖励计划、中科院"百人计划""引进杰出技术人才计划"入选者等。浦东新区"百人计划"入选者、浦东新区"500 首席科学家"计划当选者等重大人才计划入选者也纳入该类标准。

第二类是外籍知名专家、学者、专业技术人才,包括中国科学院或中国工程院外籍院士、外国国家科学院院士或工程院院士;"国家高技术研究发展计划"(863 计划)、"国家重点基础研究发展计划"(973 计划)首席科学家;获得国家技术发明奖、国家科学技术进步奖的主要完成人等。在上海自贸试验区内的国家实验室、国家重点实验室、国家工程实验室、国家工程研究中心、国家认定企业技术中心、国家工程技术研究中心、外商投资研发中心的负责人(副主任及以上)也可以提出申请。

第三类是企业创新创业外籍高层次人才。这类人才主要体现上海自贸区特色和需求,纳入自贸区内鼓励发展的不同类型企业人才,特别是重点金融、航运、贸易机构、总部型企业和"四新"企业,及其他具有特殊专长和高超技能并为上海自贸试验区紧缺急需的外籍人才。

此次上海自贸区永久居留政策开放力度非常大,相信该政策的落地实施,将为海外人才到浦东工作、创新创业提供便捷化的快速通道,也为海外人才提供更加便捷、高效、优质的服务,对提高上海自贸区开放度和国际人才集聚度,促进上海科创中心建设,将发挥积极的作用。

(二) 上海自贸区多措提升海外人才创业落沪成功率

2017年9月11日中国(上海)自由贸易试验区海外人才离岸创新创业基地工作协调小组办公室召开新闻通气会,通报"第二届海外人才上海自贸区创业汇"离岸基地大型对接交流活动情况。

上海自贸试验区海外人才离岸创新创业基地建设是中国科学技术协会与上海市合作的重要项目,是中国首批离岸基地试点之一,是一项在人才引进机制和创新创业模式上的全新探索和试验,于2015年8月揭牌,2016年下半年投入实体化运营,总部空间正式启用。

上海自贸试验区海外人才离岸创新创业基地仅一年就签约入驻或注册海外项目75个;引进海内外合作伙伴44个,其中专业团体28个、第三方服务机构16个;签约合作空间7个、发展意向合作空间2个,在以色列贝尔谢巴设立首个海外服务站。

以"创响自贸链动全球"为主题的第二届海外人才上海自贸区创业汇活动将于2017年9月17—20日在上海自贸试验区举行,作为国际化综合性创新创业平台,离岸基地引才引智、创业孵化、专业服务保障等优势功能正逐步发挥。

上海市浦东新区科技和经济委员会副主任徐敏栩介绍,创业汇旨在通过活动集聚一批优质海外人才和项目,实现"引才引智",离岸基地定位为面向海外人才、区内注册,海内外经营,以低成本、便利化、全要素、开放式、配套成熟的空间载体为基础,构建创业孵化,专业服务保障等功能的国际化综合创业平台。

2017年离岸基地着力打造升级版"1+N"创业汇系列活动,以1场大型对接交流活动为依托,结合N场系列专项活动,打造具有国际影响力的创业盛宴,形成海外项目与本土资本、技术常态化对接交流的机制,引导更多海外高端人才在自贸试验区创新创业,促进各类创新资源的跨境流动。

除政策推介、路演展示、园区考察及传统资本对接外,本次活动首设"世界500强企业技术需求发布及资本、技术对接"环节,邀请大中企业与投资机构共同参会,通过"资本＋技术"双重对接模式,促进小企业创新优势与大企业产业资源优势的协作共赢,提高海外项目落地成功率。

在项目征集遴选方面,强调技术创新,鼓励原创。活动要求项目必须具有一定技术优势且具有强烈的到上海自贸试验区创业的意愿,聚焦电子信息、生物医药、人工智能等自贸试验区重点发展行业领域。

在受邀参会人才方面,"年轻化、高学历、精英化"成为特色标签。活动参会人才来自全球12个国家和地区,外籍人士占2/3以上,平均年龄41岁,硕士及以上学历占83%,在国际知名企业有高管任职或知名高校有研究经验的达70%,对海外技术、经济环境十分熟悉。

创业汇每年都安排考察活动,通过不同环节的活动安排,来帮助海外人才来了解宏观政策,对接技术资本,感受创新氛围,对自贸区优质宽松的创业环境,有更全面认识,进而吸引更多海外人才前来创业。

(三) 2017面向"一带一路"人才培养和争端解决战略研讨会

2017年5月8日,中国航空工程科技发展战略研究院在北京航空航天大学召开面向"一带一路"人才培养和争端解决战略研讨会。来自中国工程院、最高人民法院、国家铁路局、国家遥感中心、中国国际贸易促进委员会、中国法学会学术交流中心以及中航工业集团、中国航天科技集团、中国远洋海运集团、浙江大学、石家庄铁道大学、一带一路国际研究院、北京航空航天大学等有关单位和部门40余人出席会议,会议由北京航空航天大学副校长、航空战略研究院副院长陶智教授主持。

张军院士在致辞中指出,"一带一路"沿线60多个国家,是法律制度、法治环境、历史文化特点多样化的国家,建立适合"一带一路"特点的争端解决机制和机构,是推动"一带一路"倡议实施的必要保障。为服务"一带一路"倡议和"北斗走出去"国家重大战略,北航与"一带一路"沿线国家一流大学共同建设北斗丝路学院,面向沿线国家培养国际化、高水平、创新性的人才。

黄海军教授介绍面向"一带一路"开展人才培养、建设北斗丝路学院的情况,围绕成立北斗丝路学院的背景、定位、目标、机制创新、现有基础和筹建进展等方面进行汇报。"一带一路"国际研究院院长王贵国教授从国际争端解决的现状,成立"一带一路"争端解决机构的必要性、紧迫性和可行性,以及方案和建议等方面作了汇报。

与会的院士专家围绕"一带一路"人才培养和争端解决的现状、迫切需求和紧迫性,以及成立"一带一路"争端解决机构的方案和建议等方面进行深入的交流和研讨。大家一致认为,在"一带一路"倡议实施过程中,论证"一带一路"争议解决机制意义重大,加快推进我国"一带一路"争端解决机构的论证和咨询研究工作。

(四) 2017年"一带一路"倡议实施与人才培养论坛

2017年6月4日,由同济大学经济与管理学院与校文科办共同主办的"一带一路"倡议实施与人才培养论坛召开。

该论坛围绕着如何面向"一带一路"建设,不断提升我国大学的国际化办学水平,打造适应"一带一路"建设的高素质人才展开深入而富有成果的研讨。

与会代表认为,"一带一路"建设是中国新一轮开放发展,应加强民心相通等软实力建设,通过系统性、长期性的社会责任实现中外民心的"软联通",推动当地经济发展与人才培养,以负责任受尊敬的企业品牌助力国家形象的塑造。

与会代表强调,海外发展离不开国际化人才的培养,国际化人才应具有全球视野和国际化思维模式,熟悉国际商务规则、技术标准及相关法律财务等知识,具备较强的跨文化沟通能力和具有较高的外语水平。此外,可资助所在国留学生来华留学,通过"传、帮、带"培养当地技术和管理人才。

论坛上与会者畅所欲言,集思广益,为"一带一路"建设与人才培养献计献策,共同研讨高校如何造就具有全球化视野的管理人才,从而为"一带一路"建设提供持续而坚实的人力资源支撑。

(五) "领航计划"2017年首次航运青年人才交流会顺利举办

2017年3月16日,上海陆家嘴金融城发展局支持开展的2017陆家嘴国际航运精英"领航计划"项目的首次活动航运青年人才交流会顺利举办。

本次活动主题为"航运女性领导力及职业发展",活动邀请业内3位女性代表专家出席,分别是瓦锡兰集团的Banu Kannu女士、亿海蓝的刘倩文女士和劳合社的谷佳谕女士,她们以小组讨论的形式与参会人员分享她们自己的职场经验与人生阅历。活动现场有包括中远海运集装箱、DHL、德路里海事服务、劳氏船级社、中航国际租赁、丹麦托克航运、德国赛尔重件运输等航运领域的近100位青年人才参加。

该活动为陆家嘴的航运青年人才创造与各专家、各领域同仁互动交流的机会,现场气氛活跃,获得与会人员的广泛认可与好评。

(六) 航运物流企业人才发展与人才培养访谈会

2017年11月9日,航运物流企业人才发展与人才培养访谈会在上海海事大学中远报告厅举行,此次活动由上海海事大学团委、宣传部、学生处、图书馆主办,交通运输学院团委、交通运输学院大学生职业发展协会协办。来自中菲行国际物流集团的黄羿华女士,来自得美行国际货运代理(上海)有限公司销售经理郑旭隆先生作为嘉宾出席现场。

访谈中探讨航运物流市场的问题,就目前市场低迷以及在航运界掀起一股整并风,这既是危机,也是转机。对于社会关心的人工智能进入航运领域以及阿里将涉足航运界是否带来冲击的问题,郑先生强调应该乐观面对,智能化的发展,替代一部分人力的同时也带来大数据的便捷,但最终这些智能还是以服务人为主,数据的分析、应用还是靠人。关于处理实习与学业二者的关系,黄女士就自身的经验给出宝贵的建议:重视理论学习与实践的有机结合。要有一颗愿意学习的心和一个谦逊好学的态度,将自己当成一个品牌去经营。

访谈提问环节,就 AI 对物流的影响、企业用人最为看中的素质、学历及海外学习经历被企业重视的程度等问题给予耐心解答,鼓励大家不要忽视专业知识的学习,学历是敲门砖,好学肯学、态度积极的人才是企业最为看中的。

六、交流活动及会议

(一)第四届国际航运与互联网高峰论坛在沪成功举行

2017 年 5 月 18 日,由航运界网主办,陆家嘴航运协会、陆家嘴航运互联网专业委员会协办,长江汇、运去哪、洲际船务作为支持方,以"共话数据航运、智慧航运的新征程"为主题的第四届国际航运与互联网高峰论坛会议在沪顺利召开。

论坛上,一海通供应链有限公司副总经理唐红斌以"无车承运人的思考与实践"发表主旨演讲,并详细指出理想中的物流行业应该是物流与信息流的重合,这也是未来物流行业的一个发展方向。互联网的基本精神是开放共享,企业通过运用互联网可以高效利用资源,提高效率并减少成本,信息技术的发展为传统企业带来创新和变革。

"运去哪"平台创始人、CEO 周诗豪以"变化的市场不变的逻辑"为主题,全面阐述互联网下的"新航运",他认为优秀的国际物流企业是在高效率并不断扩大规模的前提下产生的。"互联网能把一切卖不掉的商品卖掉",在原有场景卖不掉的东西+互联网就等于新场景的商品+满足更多市场需求,就造就新服务、新价值。

零一创投合伙人吴运龙,讲述"B2B 公司的投资逻辑"的思考与感悟,他认为 B2B 虽然目前遇到一些寒冬或瓶颈,但长远来看仍有转机。商业模式本身都是传统的,甚至长期都没有发生过变化。但是完成商业流程的手段随着技术的进步发生大幅度的进步,效率得到前所未有的提升。

中远海运集团法务与风险管理本部副总经理杨磊则以"航运互联网+的前景和风险"论述当前航运与互联网存在的风险与潜在隐患。互联网+航运的主要风险有:基于"交易"还是"可交易"的战略风险;基于"箱"还是基于"货"的策略风险;"能力"&"能力"的运营风险;"资源"VS"目标"的财务风险;合规监管的法律风险。

亿海蓝(北京)数据技术股份有限公司高级副总裁刘倩文,从大数据端全面阐述"航运物流大数据的创新与协同"的观点,在当下的航运市场中,大数据革命的正在进行,集装箱市场是一个非常有意思的市场,不仅在海上,在陆地上也是。希望通过更多透明的信息把这个市场做得更好,给客户真正需要的服务,并在服务客户的同时拿到产业链上面的数据,这些数据可以提供给上下游,让他们做他们应该做的事情。

南京长江船服电子商务科技有限公司董事长方保利,以"长江航运如何向智慧航运转型"为主题探讨从长江内河航运出发,什么样的智慧航运才是创新,才称得上转型。从多方面与多个角度讲述当下长江航运的现状与痛点。智慧航运的驱动三要素是平台化、智能化、共享化。发展"智慧航运"要拥抱时代技术,创新服务新路径、构建航运新生态。

携运网创始人陈志庆以"航运电商的创新升级之道"为主题发表主题演讲。他表示:"船公司+第三平台是航运电商未来发展的一个方向。成功与否,一方面取决于第三方平台的资源综合能力和综合物流服务能力,另一方面也取决船公司交易规定的制定,毕竟船公司在其传统的主流货量提供方——货代和新兴的货量不可预知的第三方平台之间做一个平衡和取舍。"

船老大网创始人黄贤明则从另一角度发表"长江内河与互联网的机遇"的主题演讲,他认为国内水运运费规模超过5 000亿,全产业链规模超3万亿,因此,互联网+长江内河面临难得的机遇。集吉运联合创始人王怡秋在具体到拼箱业务中详细地探讨"互联网如何助推拼箱发展新业态",他分享了在互联网深度运用整合方面的思考:建立在线交易的标准化体系和价格规则;实现人均效率和综合效能的提升;深入整个物流链基于云技术的应用,实现协同,交互和分享;结合第四方物流,构建物流柔性供应链;建立在大数据上客户定位,精准需求;结合B2B自带的金融属性,关联交易实现企业授信和金融服务。

(二) 2017年上海航运交易论坛成功召开

2017年上海航运交易论坛于2017年11月28日在中国金融信息中心举行,论坛的主题设定为"大数据时代的航运决策"。来自交通运输部、上海市交委、上海浦东新区,以及金融界、财经界、航运界等业内翘楚及宏观、行业专家从多角度畅谈大数据时代的突破和创新——从"一带一路"贸易数据看航运业的发展机遇与挑战、大数据时代背景下港航业未来发展趋势、"区块链"在供应链中的应用、港口布局与创新中的大数据、沿海集装箱运力布局的大数据逻辑、用大数据打造长江邮轮休闲小镇、从资本市场中港航上市公司的运行数据看港航业走势等。

　　站在大数据时代的潮头,上海航运交易所在论坛上宣布:远东干散货指数(FDI)和中国沿海成品油运价指数(CCTFI)正式对外试运行,"上海航运指数"再添新成员。

　　大数据已经与航运业深入融合,信息时代的经济长波即将到来。大数据的挖掘和航运科技的快速发展,带来信息服务平台的升级与转型,从而将引发航运业服务模式和盈利方式的革命,并最终实现航运业运作体系的跨越式发展。

　　上海航运交易论坛是上海航运交易所自2010年开始打造的专业化、国际化、大型化的航运精品论坛,论坛每年选择一个关乎航运未来的关键议题,各方精英汇聚一堂,其精彩观点以及创新实践将引领市场。

(三) 2017年中国航海日论坛在宁波举行

　　根据国家海洋强国战略实施的逐步推进,2017年航海日的主论坛议题和议程进行及时调整,使主论坛自觉融入国家战略。主论坛将宣传中国观点,倾听业界关注,广交国际朋友,营造合作氛围,为21世纪海上丝绸之路建设作出新的贡献。

　　2017年航海日论坛活动集中在2017年7月10—12日召开,其中于7月10日举办的专题论坛有2个:行舟致远航海文化论坛和航运50人论坛。7月11日有5个专题论坛,包括海员论坛、海丝港口论坛、引航论坛、中小航运企业论坛、国际航运服务业论坛。7月12日有1个专题论坛:海洋新兴产业论坛。8个专题论坛邀请的演讲嘉宾,主要由政府官员、企业高层、科研机构的知名专家组成。第三届港口管理机构圆桌会议和宁波舟山港与中东欧港口合作会议也在宁波同期召开。

　　论坛以"再扬丝路风帆　共筑蓝色梦想"为主旨,由1个主论坛及中国国际海员论坛、海丝港口国际合作论坛等8个专题性论坛组成。交通运输部副部长何建中在主论坛上发表主旨演讲。浙江省副省长高兴夫,宁波市委副书记、市长裘东耀出席主论坛并致辞。

　　中国航海学会理事长黄有方全程主持中国航海日论坛的主论坛,中国航海学会常务副理事长曹迪、秘书长王群、副秘书长顾维国等参加主论坛及有关活动。

　　何建中在演讲中指出,在新的发展时期,习近平主席提出"一带一路"倡议,为世界各国开辟了新的合作之路,得到国际社会积极响应和广泛支持。海运是"21世纪海上丝绸之路"的重要载体和保障,需要在加强基础设施互联互通等"硬件"建设的同时,加强海运发展制度、规则、政策、标准衔接融通等"软件"建设,深化合作机制,突出规划引领,推进项目落实,为"一带一路"建设当好先行。

高兴夫表示:"为贯彻习近平总书记在 G20 峰会期间提出的新要求和省第十四次党代会的精神,今后几年我省海洋港口工作的目标是奋战实战、引领新发展,重点实施'5211'海洋强省行动,大力实施五大战略举措,打造浙江海洋经济示范区、舟山江海联运服务中心、以上海合作开发洋山港等五家平台,着力建设海洋强省、国际强港,到 2020 年初步实现海洋经济综合实力、海洋科技创新能力、海洋生态保护能力、海洋管控能力强的海洋强省目标。实现全球一流现代化枢纽港、全球一流航运服务基地、全球一流大宗商品交易基地,并全面落实规划引领重大项目、海洋产业、海洋生态创新体制机制等 11 项中国措施。"

石青峰在演讲中说,"十二五"以来,我国海洋经济总体保持良好发展态势,海洋经济在拓展发展空间、建设生态文明、加快动力转换、保持经济持续稳定增长中发挥了重要作用。据统计,2016 年我国海洋生产总值达到 70 507 亿元,占国内生产总值比重达 9.5%,增速为 6.8%,高出同期国内生产总值 0.1 个百分点,海洋经济已经成为拉动国民经济增长的重要引擎。面向未来,随着海洋强国建设、21 世纪海上丝绸之路建设等重大战略的推进实施,我国海洋经济发展的空间将更加宽广,前景将更加美好,对国民经济发展的贡献率也将不断提升。

郑新立表示,习近平总主席在 2017 年 7 月 7 日二十国集团领导人峰会上讲话既为世界经济发展指明道路,也提出国内经济发展如何适应经济全球化要求的新任务。我们要在积极构建开放型世界经济中扩大对外投资贸易,通过发展互利共赢的对外经济关系引领经济全球化,努力在国内经济发展和全球经济治理两方面为世界各国做出榜样。

(四) 2017 年海事海商专题研讨会暨航运企业破产相关法律问题研究会召开

2017 年 5 月 12 日,中华全国律师协会海商海事专业委员会——"2017 年海事海商专题研讨会暨航运企业破产相关法律问题研究会"在浙江舟山召开,会议由中华全国律师协会海商海事专业委员会主办,瀛泰律师事务所、京衡律师事务所、大成律师事务所共同承办,浙江省律师协会企业破产管理专业委员会、上海市律师协会海事海商专业委员会、舟山市律师协会共同协办。

会议采取圆桌会议的形式,由各主题主持人、开题人作专题演讲后,出席会议的专家、学者就该主题进行讨论,围绕"航运与造船企业破产案件海事法院及人民法院管辖之冲突现状以及解决方案""仲裁程序与破产案件程序冲突""航运与造船企业银行债权人在破产案件中的困境""跨国航运企业破产法法律问题研究——从韩进破产事件解析"四个议题展开深入研讨,成果颇丰,对于推动完善航运企业破产相关制度的实践创新与理论研究具有深远的意义。

宁波海事法院吴胜顺法官主持,任一民律师、中国海事仲裁委员会上海分会张利荣仲裁员作开题演讲,围绕仲裁裁决的执行;撤销裁决的管辖法院;不予执行仲裁裁决的审查是否继续;破产撤销权、破产抵销权、破产取回权纠纷是否可以仲裁;涉外仲裁等问题及其解决思路进行探讨。

大成(宁波)律师事务所高级合伙人童登勇主持,大成(舟山)律师事务所主任董杰律师、大成(宁波)律师事务所任一律师和敬海(上海)律师事务所主任陈向勇律师作开题演讲,围绕银行债权人在航运与造船企业中相关权利的影响及行使问题进行探讨,从船舶留置权对在建船舶抵押权的影响、船舶优先权对抵押债权实现的影响、船舶价值贬损等方面进行深入的讨论。

上海海事大学胡正良教授主持,上海海事法院王蕾法官、中国远洋海运集团有限公司法务高级经理汪洋、瀛泰律师事务所律师方懿作开题演讲,王蕾法官就韩进破产案件中衍生诉讼在中国地区的审理情况进行介绍,瀛泰律师事务所方懿律师作为亲身经历者,介绍韩进破产案件的整体流程、债权申报程序和大致情况以及在韩进破产案中所遇到的问题与思考,与会代表就其中涉外破产案件在我国的承认与执行、涉外破产企业在我国的财产执行等问题进行重点探讨。

近年来,造船业和航运业持续低迷,船企破产进入高发期。船企破产重整或清算,一方面,造成众多船舶被扣押、拍卖,并因此引出大量海事海商纠纷;另一方面,破产程序与海事诉讼之间,从案件管辖及至清偿分配,无论在实体上还是在程序上,都存在着很大的差异和冲突,同时,破产与仲裁程序的冲突、涉跨国航运破产问题也日益突出,给破产工作的开展和相关审判工作带来许多难题和挑战。如何加深理论研究,加强沟通协调,妥善解决不同法律制度、不同国家破产制度之间的冲突和衔接,是法院、海事海商律师、船企破产管理人都面临的共同课题。

(五)第三届中国海事金融(东疆)国际论坛在津举行

2017年5月16日,第三届中国海事金融(东疆)国际论坛在天津召开,论坛由天津东疆保税港区管理委员会、波罗的海国际航运公会和金融时报社联合举办。天津市副市长阎庆民出席论坛并作开幕致辞,银监会、外汇管理局、海关总署、交通运输部海事局、中国船级社、中国船东协会、中国互联网金融协会、中国国际商会等相关领导出席。

本届论坛以"新机遇·新变革·新形态：中国海事金融多元化发展之路"为主题，秉承"开放、创新、务实、合作"的精神，深入探讨海事金融发展的新需求、新变化和新趋势，推动产业链各环节合作共赢，得到中国外商投资企业协会租赁业工作委员会、中国船东协会、中国融资租赁30人论坛的大力支持，吸引境内外250家机构和人民网等42家媒体与会，会议规模首次突破600人，引起业界高度关注。

参会企业层次提升显著，实现海事金融产业链上下游的全覆盖。包括47家租赁企业、49家金融机构、42家航运和制造企业、10家国际船级社、36家中介机构以及皇家加勒比、歌诗达邮轮、嘉年华集团、地中海邮轮等国际大型邮轮公司。中国海事金融（东疆）国际论坛已成为每年一度的蜚声海内外的海事金融专业盛会，为参会企业搭建高效的商务洽谈和交流合作平台。

在主论坛上境内外50多位发言嘉宾共同探讨60个议题，内容涉及全球航运经济形势分析、海事投融资新生态、创新海事金融服务、法律风险防控、海事资产管理、海事金融税务筹划、海事金融国际化战略、航运基金、航运保险等。

东疆作为国家租赁创新示范区，高度重视发展海事金融产业与国际资本深度融合，积极打造中国海事金融创新发展和先行先试的领军区，坚持政策创新、功能创新、模式创新、产品创新和服务创新，不断完善金融环境、司法环境、人才交流环境，营造与国际接轨的海事金融产业新生态，已经成为中国海事金融跨境租赁业务与离岸租赁业务的聚集地和中国海事金融租赁资产登记、债权公示、交易、流转的综合平台。截至2017年4月底，东疆共注册租赁公司2 230家，累计注册资本金达2 888亿元人民币；东疆累计注册单船公司160家，国际船舶租赁资产达52亿美元，占全国80%；海上钻井平台租赁资产25亿美元，占全国100%。

2016年《中国（天津）自由贸易试验区总体方案》90项改革任务全部启动，175项制度创新举措，151项落地实施，9项制度创新成为国家复制推广试点经验。伴随着自贸区的投资贸易便利化水平显著提高，以及国际化的营商环境日益完善，东疆海事金融迎来新发展。

在"一带一路"倡议及"中国制造2025"等国家战略下，东疆未来将积极探索、大胆创新，建设中国最大海外工程出口基地，打造中国海事金融和离岸金融创新区，持续推动中国海事金融产业快速发展。

（六）"一带一路"争端解决机制建设圆桌讨论会举行

为深入学习和践行十九大精神，落实习近平同志关于推进"一带一路"建设的系列讲话和指示，2017年10月24日，由最高人民法院和西安交通大学主办，最高人民法院民事审判第四庭、西安交通大学丝绸之路国际法与比较法研究所和西安交通大学"一带一路"自贸区研究院法律治理研究中心承办的"'一带一路'争端解决机制建设圆桌讨论会"在西安交通大学隆重召开。最高人民法院审判委员会副部级专职委员刘贵祥、陕西省委常委、省委政法委书记、副省长杜航伟，西安交通大学常务副书记王小力以及来自最高人民法院、商务部、陕西省委省政府、陕西省高级人民法院等政府部门，来自学术机构和来自中国国际经济贸易仲裁委员会等实务部门的40余位领军专家学者齐聚西安，围绕"一带一路"争端解决机制建设与司法保障建言献策、共襄盛举。

杜航伟在致辞中表示，陕西作为丝绸之路经济带的新起点，在融入"一带一路"倡议方面具有得天独厚的区位优势，陕西省委省政府高度重视对接"一带一路"在促进陕西省经济社会发展中的重要性，全省上下齐心协力，以习近平同志来陕重要讲话指示精神和十九大报告的要求，正在着力打造"一带一路"核心区，包括"一带一路"争端解决的核心区。杜航伟鼓励陕西相关部门、高校院所与最高人民法院等部门进一步密切联系与合作，共同推进"一带一路"争端解决机制与"一带一路"法律服务与法治创新示范区建设等重大议题的对接协调问题，为国家"一带一路"倡议和法治中国建设作出更大的贡献。

刘贵祥在致辞中表示，构建公正高效便利的"一带一路"纠纷解决机制，是"一带一路"法治化的核心，也是一项长期的系统工程。实务界和法学界要深入学习党的十九大报告精神，群策群力，共同加强研究，夯实"一带一路"争议解决机制的理论基础，加强国际司法合作，积极参与国际规则的制定，推动跨境纠纷解决机制的协调与整合，构建由调解、仲裁和诉讼有机衔接的"三位一体"的一站式纠纷解决机制，努力开创国际商事海事审判新局面，切实提升服务和保障"一带一路"建设的水平。

围绕"一带一路"争端解决机制建设，从需求与设计、配套法治创新、投资仲裁改革等三个专题进行研讨。与会专家一致认为建立一套公正、合理的争端解决机制，是"一带一路"法治化进程面临的一项重大紧迫课题；妥善处理和解决"一带一路"建设中发生的商事海事纠纷、投资贸易争端不仅是"一带一路"建设顺利进行的前提和保障，也是打造"一带一路"法治化营商环境的必然要求；构建"一带一路"争端解决机制是一项具有重大意义的系统工程，需要统筹国际、国内两大资源，需要国际法治与国内法治的良性互动，需要国际争端解决机制与内国司法的相互配合；"一带一路"争端解决机制建设应综合运用调解、仲裁、审判等机制，尤其要注重发挥调解机制的主导作用；为了更好地服务"一带一路"争端解决机制建设，我国需要在仲裁法修改、调解协议效力、仲裁裁决的承认和执行等问题上进行法律和制度创新。

鉴于陕西在"一带一路"中的突出历史地位与当代地缘优势,有必要积极探索依托陕西自贸区,在西安建立国家级的"一带一路"法律服务与法治创新示范区,在服务"一带一路"倡议争端解决的同时,为国家探索调解、仲裁与司法三位一体的具有国际竞争力的法律服务与法治创新之路。

(七) 2017"'一带一路'建设与海事司法应对"研讨会

2017年9月26日,中国审判理论研究会海事海商审判理论专业委员会2017年年会在上海海事法院召开,年会主题为"'一带一路'建设与海事司法应对"。

中国审判理论研究会海事海商审判理论专业委员会副主任、上海市法学会海商法研究会会长、上海海事法院院长赵红在会议上致欢迎辞。中国审判理论研究会常务理事、最高人民法院应用法学研究所副所长曹守晔,上海市法学会专职副会长施基雄出席会议并讲话。中国社会科学院国际法研究所、清华大学、上海市交通委、中国海事仲裁委员会上海分会和中国远洋海运集团五家单位,分别就"一带一路"倡议背景下上海国际航运中心建设、国际海事司法中心建设、海事仲裁发展等内容作了主旨发言。

与会代表围绕"'一带一路'与自贸区建设对接中的法治创新""海上法律体系完善和海事纠纷多元化解决机制""海事司法需求和审判热点问题"三个专题进行研讨。中国审判理论研究会海事海商审判理论专业委员会秘书长、上海市法学会海商法研究会副会长、上海海事法院副院长荚振坤主持会议。来自最高人民法院中国应用法学研究所、上海市法学会、上海市高级人民法院、全国各海事法院以及有关科研院校、主管部门、仲裁机构和港航企业等单位的代表约60人参加研讨会。

(八) 2017首届"一带一路"与海事法治建设高端论坛

2017年6月20日,首届"一带一路"与海事法治建设高端论坛在上海海事大学举行。来自中国法学会、国务院法制办、最高人民法院、中国仲裁法学研究会、上海市法学会、上海海事法院、中国海事仲裁委员会、中国船东互保协会、中国政法大学、大连海事大学、上海交通大学、中国远洋海运集团、中国航油集团等单位,以及多家知名律师事务所的专家学者出席活动。

中国法学会副会长、全国人大常委会委员、法律委员会副主任委员张鸣起,中国仲裁法学研究会顾问、国务院法制办中国仲裁协会筹备领导小组副组长卢云华,上海市法学会常务副会长林国平,上海海事大学校长黄有方等分别致辞。

黄有方校长表示,在"一带一路"倡议、建设国际海事司法中心目标的大环境、大背景、大战略下,举办本次"一带一路"与海事法治建设高端论坛,对推动上海海事大学的发展、推进上海国际航运中心建设具有重要意义。

林国平副会长指出,设立海事仲裁研究中心,将进一步深化多元化纠纷解决机制改革,提升我国航运软实力,助力上海国际航运中心建设。

卢云华顾问表示,海事仲裁制度是国家海洋战略实施的重要保障,海事仲裁研究中心的设立是贯彻海洋强国和"一带一路"倡议的重要举措。

张鸣起副会长指出,海事仲裁研究中心应充分发挥智库作用,有条不紊地开展学术交流、教学指导、课题研究工作,进一步推动我国海事仲裁事业的发展。

论坛上,全国首家海事仲裁研究智库——海事仲裁研究中心正式挂牌成立。中国仲裁法学研究会常务副秘书长郭峰宣读《关于在上海海事大学设立海事仲裁研究中心的批复》和中心聘任的首批高级研究员名单。张鸣起、卢云华、林国平、黄有方共同为海事仲裁研究中心揭牌,并为中心主任、顾问以及高级研究员颁发聘书。

最高人民法院民四庭副庭长刘敬东,中国海事仲裁委员会副秘书长、仲裁院副院长陈波分别围绕"充分发挥仲裁在一带一路建设中的作用""中国海事仲裁新发展——转型与新吸引力"主题,发表演讲。与会专家就"一带一路"与海事法治建设中的热点问题展开深入研讨。

(九)2017年度国际航运与金融高峰论坛在沪成功举行

2017年11月10日,由BIMCO和航运界网主办,陆家嘴航运协会协办,陆家嘴人才金港、青岛洲际船务、前海航交所及瀛泰律师事务所为支持方,以"市场复苏,航运金融何去何从?"为主题的2017年度国际航运与金融高峰论坛在沪成功举行,来自航运、金融、法律、保险、新闻媒体等航运产业链的150多位嘉宾出席会议,中国船东协会常务副会长张守国为本次论坛致开幕词。

主办方波罗的海航运公会(BIMCO)和航运界已连续成功举办四届国际船舶融资高峰论坛。在此基础上,主办方联合陆家嘴航运协会在上海举办该论坛,邀请到港口、航运、航运金融公司的各类专家,云集一堂,集思广益:共同探讨在航运业已经成为国家战略行业的大背景下,如何推动金融机构对航运业的有力支持,以及如何建设性地发展航运与金融的关系。

德鲁里海事咨询中国区董事韩宁从集装箱运输市场的供需数据分析指出,2.2万TEU型船或将是市场最大船型,但是船舶升级换代将导致所有航线的船舶规模扩大,供需平衡在2020年不会出现,市场运费会增长但是波动性会增加。菁英航运集团董事长季文元阐述大宗干散货市场的现状与特点。大宗干散货运输市场的运费呈现变化周期短、相对变化幅度大的特点,波动背后与大宗商品贸易(价格、进口量等)有着千丝万缕的关系。国家发改委综合运输研究所副主任陆成云则阐述中国航运企业的发展机遇。青岛洲际船务集团董事长郭金魁从经营、管理和资本等三个方面出发,阐述传统船东如何应对市场新常态。

尽管航运市场的未来前景并非一片坦途,但是航运与金融的链接和融合永远都是值得关注的话题。远海信达投资管理(天津)有限公司执行董事总经理金海坦言,尽管银行是最大的航运资本提供者,对于那些有兴趣、有能力投资航运业的资本来源来说仍旧有巨大机会。每一类航运投资金融机构都有一套独特的标准,寻求资金的船东必须理解从而决定选择哪一种正确的来源。金融船东已经成为航运市场不可忽视的重要力量,工银租赁航运事业部执行总经理郭芳萌表示,金融船东在投资方面,需要注意船型多样化组合,利用各船型周期可能不同的特点;需要有节奏的投放,尤其是经营租赁业务,避免大量船舶租约同时到期;需要重视客户选择,客户违约率控制在10%以下,不良租赁率控制在5%以下。成功转型成为航运金融公司的中远海发航运租赁事业部龚灵也认为,在航运弱周期之下,航运租赁产业迎来新机遇。瀛泰海事律师事务所合伙人刘雨佳则对航运融资的新业态和法律风险进行解读。

对于中小航运企业而言,面对严峻的生存挑战。上海鼎衡船务有限责任公司董事长李多珠对新时代航运产业链下,中小企业如何突破困局给出建议。内河航运市场参与主体多为个人船东,交易规模小、交易数据分散,而传统金融机构在细分行业下沉不足,缺乏对船舶等动态资产的有效监控,尤其是珠江、长江两大流域的内河航运融资市场存在比较严重的供需失衡。前海航交所副总裁黄逢霖在会上表示,前海航交所依托航运资产管理平台,通过开展航运金融服务、船舶资产技术服务及支付结算服务等,逐步积累并形成具有权威参考价值的内河航运风险数据库,从而初步搭建航运资产管理的业务模式。一方面,前海航交所为金融机构与内河中小航运企业之间搭建桥梁,另一方面,也为前海航交所后续打造我国最大无船承运人平台和船货智能匹配平台打下坚实的基础。

(十) 2017上海国际航运法治论坛举行

2017年10月25日,由上海市法学会、华东政法大学以及中国海事仲裁委员会共同主办2017上海国际航运法治论坛召开。专家学者共同探讨"一带一路"下国际航运纠纷解决机制的构建等问题。

华东政法大学校长叶青表示,本次论坛以"一带一路""航运""法治"为核心议题,紧密对接十九大报告中国家的发展蓝图。在"一带一路"建设中,航运是互联互通的纽带,法治是航运发展的保障。"一带一路"倡议为航运法治发展提供了新契机,也提出了新挑战。他表示华东政法大学将继续深化上海国际航运中心建设法治保障问题研究,为上海国际航运中心建设提供理论支撑和智力支持。

中国海事仲裁委员会秘书长顾超认为,在中国经济迎来新发展的时刻,中国航运法律服务业也迎来新机遇。中国国际海事司法中心和国际海事仲裁中心优势互补,有利于增强在国际舞台上的中国声音。中国海事仲裁迎来前所未有的发展机遇和空间,加强顶层设计建立完善多元化纠纷解决机制,发展海事仲裁事业,对促进上海国际航运中心建设具有重要意义。在专题讨论中,来自国内法学法律界和相关实务部门的百多位专家学者围绕论坛主题:"一带一路"背景下国际航运法治发展的新趋向、国际海事司法中心建设与海事审判理论研究、国际海事立法趋势与我国海商法律制度完善、"一带一路"下国际航运纠纷解决机制的构建等专题进行深入探讨和交流。

(十一)"一带一路"建设海上合作设想发布

2017年6月20日,国家发展和改革委员会、国家海洋局制定并发布《"一带一路"建设海上合作设想》。

该设想是自2015年3月28日发布《推动共建丝绸之路经济带和21世纪海上丝绸之路的愿景与行动》以来,中国政府首次就推进"一带一路"建设海上合作提出中国方案,也是"一带一路"国际合作高峰论坛的领导人成果之一。

该设想提出,愿与21世纪海上丝绸之路沿线各国一道开展全方位、多领域的海上合作,共同打造开放、包容的合作平台,建立积极务实的蓝色伙伴关系,铸造可持续发展的"蓝色引擎"。

思路上,设想提出,根据21世纪海上丝绸之路的重点方向,"一带一路"建设海上合作以中国沿海经济带为支撑,密切与沿线国的合作,连接中国-中南半岛经济走廊,经南海向西进入印度洋,衔接中巴、孟中印缅经济走廊,共同建设中国-印度洋-非洲-地中海蓝色经济通道;经南海向南进入太平洋,共建中国-大洋洲-南太平洋蓝色经济通道;积极推动共建经北冰洋连接欧洲的蓝色经济通道。

该设想明确5方面合作重点:围绕构建互利共赢的蓝色伙伴关系,创新合作模式,搭建合作平台,共同制订若干行动计划,实施一批具有示范性、带动性的合作项目,共走绿色发展之路,共创依海繁荣之路,共筑安全保障之路,共建智慧创新之路,共谋合作治理之路。

共创依海繁荣之路方面,设想提出,积极参与北极开发利用,中国政府愿与各方共同开展北极航道综合科学考察,合作建立北极岸基观测站,研究北极气候与环境变化及其影响,开展航道预报服务。支持北冰洋周边国家改善北极航道运输条件,鼓励中国企业参与北极航道的商业化利用。愿同北极有关国家合作开展北极地区资源潜力评估,鼓励中国企业有序参与北极资源的可持续开发,加强与北极国家的清洁能源合作。

该设想提出,要在5方面展开积极行动,包括高层引领推动、搭建合作平台、加大资金投入、推进内外对接、促成项目落地等。其中,针对资金投入,设想提出,中国政府统筹国内资源,设立中国-东盟海上合作基金和中国-印尼海上合作基金,实施《南海及其周边海洋国际合作框架计划》。亚洲基础设施投资银行、丝路基金对重大海上合作项目提供资金支持。

七、小结

经历了2016年的运价低谷,2017年航运业走上触底回升之路。2017年,国务院和交通运输部以及相关部门针对航运业长远发展和当前面临的严峻形势,作出重要批示。上海作为中国最大的港口城市,软硬条件较为优越,应责无旁贷地承担实现"一带一路"倡议的历史责任。大力发展现代航运建设,加强发展和创新航运技术、航运金融、航运交易、海事司法等现代服务业建设。提升航运业国际竞争力,构造国际航运交易中心,加快国际航运中心建设。

第六章 展　望

2017年是上海建设自由贸易试验区的第五个年头，也是上海自贸区深化改革开放的关键之年。在"一带一路"倡议全面展开之际，上海自贸区建设进入全新时代。上海自贸区的发展目标是货物自由进出、资金流动便利、运输高度开放、人员自由执业和信息快捷联通，发展核心为对标国际贸易、航运、金融中心，制定并实行自由化便利化制度，集聚国内外企业，打造资源要素配置平台。

纵观英国伦敦、新加坡、中国香港等国际贸易、航运、金融中心的发展历程，上海若要从中国中心蜕变成为国际中心，就必须大力发展离岸航运在内的离岸服务产业。所谓离岸服务指的是本国居民（如企业、组织、个人等）为他国居民之间进行的与本国无实际关联的货物、技术、服务等交易行为提供服务。离岸服务大体分为中介型、中间商型和交易所型。交易所型为离岸服务的高端业态，最佳实例为伦敦劳合社保险市场（以下简称劳合社），该市场积聚了200多个国家和地区的航运及其他保险公司和投保人，85%以上的保险交易在非英国企业间达成。

离岸服务产业的发展程度是区分国内、地区、国际贸易中心的主要指标。只有掌握了离岸（他国之间）交易，才能获得国际市场的话语权、定价权、规则制定权和最终利益分配权，进而对市场产生实质影响。如，2018年劳合社的保险交易金额约为人民币3 200亿元，其中离岸约为2 700亿元，占全球跨国总量的30%～40%。该市场的保费费率被视作国际市场标准，而制定的保险合同格式条款成为国际市场规范。

离岸服务产业是现代国际贸易的重要组成部分，大力发展该产业是党和国家批准设立新片区的题中应有之意，理由如下：

（1）离岸服务是实现自贸区建设目标的理想载体。自贸区目标为货物、资金、人才和信息的自由流动。离岸服务恰恰涉及前述四个要素进出中国国境、自贸区区域，离岸服务是唯一能够同时促进"四要素自由流动"的高端服务产业。

（2）自贸区以服务国家"一带一路"倡议为己任，而离岸服务的首要服务对象即是"走出去"、在"一带一路"沿线布局的中国企业。离岸服务将消除"走出去"企业在他国发展的后顾之忧，并使其能够运用合理手段降低中美贸易摩擦的不利影响。

（3）发展离岸产业契合国家赋予上海建设"五个中心"、提升我国国际影响力的历史使命。该产业的发展不仅能为上海经济转型创造新增长点,还能在一定程度上消弭我国巨额服务贸易赤字。离岸贸易、运输、金融、保险等相关产业的良性互动,将让我国站到世界舞台的中心。

与公认的国际贸易中心相比,上海的离岸服务产业处于萌芽阶段,尚未统计公布有关离岸产业数据。根据中央对上海自贸区提出的新要求,鉴于上海离岸服务产业的发展现状,编写组建议:上海市政府争取国家部委授权,将新片区作为沙盒,在风险可控前提下创设离岸服务产业中心,试点有利于离岸航运及其他离岸产业发展的便利化政策措施。具体建议如下:

(1) 顶层设计。上海市政府设立"上海离岸服务产业发展办公室"(以下简称办公室),与新片区管理委员会合属办公,推动离岸服务产业总体发展。办公室制定《上海自贸新片区离岸服务产业发展办法(试行)》,从商事主体登记、经营、外汇收付结算、税收、引进人才等各方面为离岸服务企业打造适宜的营商环境。

(2) 交易所型离岸服务。由办公室组织国有大型贸易公司,联合上海现有的20余家交易所、国内外大型贸易公司和电商平台,在新片区共同组建"上海离岸服务中心(交易所)"(以下简称中心),包括线上和线下交易平台,为参与离岸服务的国外企业和提供离岸服务的国内外企业提供展示咨询、中介代理、签约交割、期货交易、支付结算、融资租赁、物流运输、信用评估、保险风控、争议解决等各项服务。鼓励上海航运交易所、上海保险交易所、上海期货交易所(上海国际能源交易中心)、中国外汇交易中心等已具备离岸能力的机构发挥带头作用,在中心平台开发、提供离岸贸易、航运、金融等产品和服务模式。

(3) 企业引进。借助长三角一体化进程和长江流域宽阔的经济腹地,着力引进"一带一路"及"走出去"企业、长三角外资贸易型总部和国外贸易、电商企业,在自贸区设立离岸服务公司,在中心平台为他们的境外(关联、客户)公司提供贸易、航运、金融等离岸服务。鼓励国内外商贸企业和电商在中心平台上提供离岸贸易服务。积极探索与国外离岸贸易服务提供商的合作,特别是那些在中国有机构的境外交易所,如劳合社、伦敦波罗的海航运交易所等。

(4) 为便利国际收付结算,避免被中美贸易战误伤,中心可鼓励离岸交易者用离岸人民币进行交易;为避免汇率波动,可考虑发行锚定离岸人民币或特别提款权的数字、稳定货币或代币凭证,但必须以真实交易为基础,且仅限中心交易使用;为避免交易和系统性风险,可考虑购买政策或商业保险。

(5) 对在中心平台上提供离岸服务的企业所获得的外汇服务收入,上海税务机关可给予一定比例的"服务出口退税"。

编写组坚信,发展离岸服务产业是建设上海自贸区不可或缺的板块,也是打造上海国际贸易、航运、金融中心的重要一环,更是让中国重塑世界经济格局的重要切入点。

《上海航运政策与法律发展》编写组
上海国际航运研究中心政策与法律研究所
二〇一八年一月一日

附 录

一

船舶修理合同

本《船舶修理合同》（以下简称本合同）由以下双方于_____年_____月_____日签署。

委修方名称（以下简称船东）

和

承修方名称（以下简称船厂）

双方合称为双方，分别称为各方。

船东同意将船舶"_____"轮（_____，以下简称船舶）交由船厂修理，船厂同意为船东修理"_____"轮。双方因此达成以下条款：

第1条　船舶描述

船舶名称：_____

IMO号：_____

船旗国：_____

登记船东名称：_____

是否光船出租：□否

　　　　　　　□是，光船承租人名称：_____

　　　　　　　　光船租赁租期：_____

　　　　　　　是否登记：□无　□是

若船舶存在光租，船东应提供一份光船租赁合同复印件及光租登记证明复印件（若有）作为本合同附件1。

第2条　合同的履行

2.1　在签订本合同之前或之时，船东应当向船厂提供修理工程所需的工程项目单（该工程项目单及双方后续对其的变更和修改，以下统称为修理工程）、重要图纸（包括但不限于进坞图、总布置图、舱容图和舯横剖面图）和必要技术资料；船厂应当根据本合同约定及现行施工操作规范完成修理工程。

2.2　若一方要求变更或修改修理工程，要求变更或修改修理工程的一方应当立即书面通知对方，双方应共同决定该变更或修改是否列入修理工程范围。双方同意变更或修改修理工程的,本合同的价款及第 3.2 条约定的修理工期应作相应调整。

2.3 若变更或修改修理工程对于修理工程的开展是必须的或不可或缺的,船东不得无理拒绝同意船厂提出的对于修理工程的变更或修改;若船东未能在收到船厂变更或修改修理工程通知后 2 日内同意变更或修改,船厂有权中止修理工程并相应延长第 3.2 条所约定的修理工期,因此而产生的损失和费用,应当由船东承担。

2.4 在修理工期内,经船厂事先书面同意,船东可将与本船舶有关的,且在船厂能力范围之外的其他修理工程交由具备相应资质的船厂之外的其他修理服务供应商(包括但不限于船东自己、船长或船员)完成。船东应向船厂明确其他修理工程的具体范围,且应对前述其他修理工程负责;如前述其他修理工程妨碍或拖延了整个修理工程的正常进行,则船厂有权相应延长修理工期。船厂有权在相应修理工程开始之前提出合理理由拒绝接受船东指定的其他修理服务供应商,但由于船厂不合理地拒绝导致修理工期延误的,船厂无权延长修理工期。

2.5 在船东指定的其他修理服务供应商进行上述第 2.4 条所述的其他修理工程期间,船厂有权在其他修理服务供应商开始相应修理工程前向其收取合理的管理费。若前述其他修理服务供应商未支付管理费,则船厂有权拒绝其进行相应修理工程,因此导致修理工期延误的,船厂有权相应延长修理工期。

2.6 船厂有权委任分包方完成全部或部分修理工程,但船厂应为分包方完成的修理工程负责。船东有权在相应修理工程开始之前提出合理理由拒绝接受船厂指定的分包方,但由于船东不合理地拒绝导致修理工期延误的,船厂有权相应延长修理工期。

第 3 条　船东交船、修理工期及船厂还船

3.1 船东应在双方事先商定的日期和时间(＿＿＿＿年＿＿＿＿月＿＿＿＿日),将船舶驶达船厂指定的安全水域或施工地点(以下称修理场所)并向船厂交付船舶,此时船舶应正常漂浮、测爆合格、不含货载、不含油污水、污泥、过量的压载水或对人体健康有害的或有危险的物品(以下称交船)。经检查后,船厂接受船东交船并开始进行修理工程。在交船之前所进行的靠码头、拖航、引航、进船坞以及靠泊等的费用及风险均由船东承担。

3.2 预计修理工期为＿＿＿＿个日历日(包括进坞天数)(不保证,以下简称"修理工期")。修理工期自交船之日或船东提供了修理工程所需的全部重要图纸和必要技术资料之日(以较晚者为准)的次日 0800 时(船厂当地时间)起算。在船厂已经实际开始进行修理工程的情况下,如果船东延误提供修理工程所需的图纸和技术资料,船厂有权相应延长修理工期。

3.3 在船东履行合同义务的前提下,船厂应在修理工程完成后在修理场所或双方约定的其他地点及时向船东还船(以下称还船)。如还船地点为双方约定的其他地点,将船舶移动至该地点的费用及风险应当由船东承担。

3.4 应船东要求,船厂应及时向船东通报修理工程进展及预计还船日期。

3.5 若交船或还船日期有任何变更,请求变更的一方应当获得另一方的事先同意。

3.6 若船东无法按照第 3.1 条的约定将船舶驶达船厂指定的修理场所且未事先征得船厂书面同意,船厂有权解除合同。船厂解除合同不影响船厂向船东索赔因此遭受的损失。

3.7 若在还船日船东未能按照约定接收船舶,船厂有权自次日起按照每日【　　】的标准向船东收取费用,该费用应视为合同价款的一部分。如船厂有证据表明其实际损失高于前述费用标准的,该损失由船东承担。

第 4 条　进坞

4.1　双方可约定船舶进坞修理。但是,如果停泊在船厂船坞或码头或泊位的其他船舶发生不可预料的水下损坏或缺陷,为保证其安全船厂认为必须开展紧急的和连续的修理,则船厂有权调整船舶进坞时间。同时,在及时通知船东进坞受到影响的情况下,船厂有权相应延长修理工期。在此情况下,船厂应当安排船舶尽快进坞修理。

4.2　若双方同意对修理工程作出变更或修改并且因此船舶在坞期间需延长,在原先同意的在坞期间届满后,船厂有权根据其船坞使用计划令船舶出坞,之后尽早安排船舶重新进坞。船舶进出坞的额外成本和费用由船东承担。如修理工程仅能于在坞期间进行,因前述修理工程的变更或修改而导致的船舶出坞等待时间不计入修理工期。

第 5 条　修理工程的监督和验收

5.1　在整个修理工期内,船东应当委派船东代表在船厂监督修理工程。若在修理工期内,船东未能指定船东代表或船东代表不能或拒绝履行职责,船舶的船长应视为船东代表。

5.2　除非船东对船东代表的权限作出明确限制,否则船东代表有权全权代表船东处理与本合同有关的全部事宜,包括但不限于批准计划、图纸、计量、文件,就修理工程的变更或修改作出指示,确认修理工程完工情况,签署修理工程完工单、账单、关于最终合同价款的协议等。

5.3　若船东代表未能妥善履行其职责,包括但不限于在给出相关批准、指示、确认或意见时的故意或不合理的迟延等,船厂有权要求船东立即更换船东代表。因更换船东代表而影响修理工程顺利进行的,船厂有权相应延长修理工期。

5.4　在船厂还船之前,船东代表应签署船厂提供的修理工程完工单确认修理工程完工;船厂也可以在修理过程中按照具体单项修理工程提供相应修理工程完工单供船东代表签署。若船东代表在收到修理工程完工单后【　　】个工作日内未确认并签署,也未提出任何书面异议,则视为船东已认可并接受该修理工程完工单;若船东代表对修理工程完工单提出书面异议,双方应协商解决或共同指定第三方检验人员或检验机构(以下称检验人)对双方有争议的修理工程完工单的事项进行鉴定。检验人的鉴定结论对双方均有约束力。根据检验人的鉴定结论,若船东异议不成立,则船厂因此遭受的损失及检验人的费用应由船东承担;若船东异议成立,则船厂应对修理工程进行修改调整,并重新提交相应的修理工程完工单,且承担检验人的费用。

5.5　船东、船东代表船员以及船东的雇员有义务配合并协助完成全部修理工程;如其不履行协助义务致使修理工程不能按时完成的,船厂可以催告船东在合理期限内履行义务,并有权相应延长修理工期;仍逾期不履行的,船厂可以解除合同并有权请求赔偿。

第 6 条　废旧材料处理

6.1　所有因修理工程而产生的废旧材料,船厂有权处置;根据中国相关环保法律属于固体废物或危险废物的,船厂贮存、处置这些废物产生的成本和费用(包括委托有经营许可证的第三方贮存、处置废物产生的费用),由船东承担,但应扣减船厂处置这些废物而得到的收入。

6.2　船东要求带走修理中从船舶上拆卸的旧件和设备的,其应在拆卸前书面通知船厂并征得船厂同意,在拆卸后及时运走并且符合中国相关环保法律的规定;船厂因此而产生的贮存费用以及因前述旧件和设备未经妥善处理而遭受的损失(包括但不限于所遭受的当地环境保护主管部门的处罚)应由船东承担。

第7条 船东供应物料

7.1 船东应根据船厂的要求将船东供应项目中的所有物料及时提供到船厂指定地点。如船东迟延提供物料,船厂有权相应延长修理工期或对相应单项工程拒绝施工,并有权请求船东赔偿因此遭受的损失。

7.2 修理工程需要的所有油漆涂料应由船东提供。

7.3 对于应船东的要求由船厂保管的所有属于船东的物料,其风险及责任均由船东承担,船厂仅承担适当的看管义务。

7.4 对于修理工程过程中或完工之后,因船东供应的物料引起的任何故障、缺陷或损坏和/或任何事件,船厂不承担责任。

第8条 合同价款及支付

8.1 本合同的计价标准,除双方另行书面约定之外,应依照□本合同所附的价目表(附件2) □中国船舶工业行业协会制定的自2016年6月1日起生效的《中国修船价格指引(2016版)》(不包含其附件)执行,前述计价标准的折扣系数为【　　】。船东确认,在签订本合同时知悉并且同意上述计价标准内容及折扣系数。

8.2 根据上述计价标准,本合同的预计合同价款为【　　】。本合同的最终合同价款由船东签署的账单或双方签署的关于最终合同价款的协议确定。

8.3 在船东签署修理工程完工单之后,船厂应及时向船东出具账单或分期账单,船东应在收到账单或分期账单后【　　】个日历日内,确认并签署相应账单或与船厂签署关于最终合同价款的协议(关于最终合同价款的协议应视为本合同的一部分,其格式请见附件3)。

8.4 除非双方书面明确约定,船东应当以美元或者船厂可接受的其他币种全额支付合同价款。除折扣系数外,船东无权对合同价款进行抵消、扣减,且其支付行为不会受到外汇管制。与合同价款有关的任何税费、银行手续费等应由船东承担。

8.5 双方同意,船东应在本合同签订之日起【　　】个日历日内支付【　　】作为修理工程的预付款。若船东未能按时支付预付款,船厂可中止修理工程,亦有权解除合同并向船东索赔因此遭受的损失。

8.6 若双方同意对修理工程进行变更或修改,但船厂认为该变更或修改系对原修理工程的实质性变更或修改的,船厂有权要求船东在工程完工之前将预计合同价款分【　　】期支付给船厂。若船东未能按照船厂要求支付分期款,船厂有权中止执行该变更或修改,直至船东按照约定支付分期款,船厂因此遭受的损失应由船东承担。

8.7 船厂在修理工期前完工的,每提前一天(不足一天按比例计算),船东应支付给船厂按照最终合同价款的【　　】%计算的速修费;非因船东原因所导致,船厂在修理工期(包括船厂根据本合同约定相应延长后的工期)后完工的,每迟延一天(不足一天按比例计算),船厂应支付给船东按照最终合同价款的【　　】%计算的滞修费。但在任何情况下,前述速修费以及滞修费不得超过最终合同价款的【　　】%。船厂在修理工期前后 5 天内完工的,双方互不承担速修费或滞修费。

8.8　除非双方书面明确约定,船东应当在修理工程完工之日起【　　】个日历日内,在船厂还船之前(以较早者为准),向船厂支付全部最终合同价款或约定的【　　】%的最终合同价款。若船东未能按照上述规定支付合同价款,船厂有权留置或滞留船舶,直到船东按照合同有关规定支付合同价款;船厂对留置或滞留船舶的行为不承担任何责任,并且不影响船厂向船东请求因行使留置权或滞留船舶而产生的费用、损失和/或损害赔偿的权利;在船舶被留置或滞留期间,船东负有妥善保管船舶的义务,船东应按照第 10.4 条的规定对船舶的安全和防止船舶污染环境承担全部责任。如果船东在收到船厂留置通知后的 1 个月内不履行债务,船厂有权通过法院拍卖、变卖船舶来实现留置权并就拍卖、变卖船舶所得的价款优先受偿。

8.9　最终合同价款确认后,双方可约定分期支付。若船东没有按约定支付其中任何一期款项,则所有剩余分期款视为已到期,船东应立即支付所有到期款项及其按照第 8.10 条计算的利息。

8.10　如果船东未按期支付全部或部分款项,船东应按【　　】%的年利率支付未付款项自到期之日起至全部偿还之日止的利息。如合同价款以人民币以外的币种支付,且船东未按期支付合同价款的,船厂在船东实际支付之日将前述合同价款转换为人民币时所遭受的汇率损失应当由船东承担。

8.11　与修理工程相关的船级社服务、技术服务工程师以及试航等均由船东自行安排并承担费用,但双方另有约定的除外。

第 9 条　船厂的义务和责任

9.1　船厂对船舶及其部件、船上货物、船东其他财产和/或船东雇员遭受的或与之有关的损失或损害不承担责任,除非该损失或损害是由船厂或其雇员或其分包方在从事修理活动或雇佣活动或授权活动过程中的故意或重大过失直接造成的。

9.2　责任限制:对船东或任何其他方(包括保险人和所有第三方,不论该方是否与船舶所有或营运有利害关系)的所有损失或损害(包括但不限于所有直接或间接损失,包括但不限于人身伤亡赔偿),不论是否是产生于合同、侵权行为还是其他原因,也不论是否是由船厂、船厂的雇员、代理或分包方的过错所引起,船厂的全部赔偿责任以【　　】美元为限。该赔偿限额适用于由单个或多个原因或事件引起的单个或一系列的事故、损失或损害。船东同意并承诺对船厂超过【　　】美元赔偿限额的损失、损害、请求、索赔或费用承担责任并使船厂免受损害,不论前述赔偿责任如何产生,也不论是否是由船厂、船厂的雇员、代理或分包方的过错所引起。

9.3　船舶的任何测试、试航或移动,均应由船东自行承担风险。任何离岸修理的风险均应由船东承担。船厂或其雇员或分包方对船舶试航或移动或离岸修理中产生的费用(非指修理费)或导致的违约、损害赔偿、损失等不承担责任。

9.4　除以下第 9.5 条的约定之外,工程完工后,船厂即不再承担任何责任。

9.5　船厂对其提供的任何设备、零配件、材料或船厂工艺存在的缺陷承担质保责任。对于固定部件,船厂的质保责任期限为还船之日起【　　】个月;对于移动部件,船厂的质保责任期限为还船之日起【　　】个月。船东应在相关缺陷发生后的【　　】日内向船厂发出书面通知,描述该缺陷,并提供材料证明该缺陷完全是由于船厂的过失所造成的。如果船东不能在以上期限内发出书面的索赔通知,将被视为放弃索赔。

9.6　收到上述 9.5 条中的索赔通知后,船厂有权通过其授权代表对缺陷产生的原因进行调查,船东应提供必要的便利。如船厂确认该缺陷是由于船厂的过失所致,船厂应在其修理场所免费修理、更换材料或改正其工艺。如果船东将船舶驶往船厂的修理场所既不现实也不经济,船东可以在取得船厂事先书面同意后,在其他地点进行必要的修理或材料更换;在满足所有前述条件的情况下,船厂应根据船东的书面要求向船东支付在其他地点进行修理或材料更换的费用,但前述费用应不超过以下限额(合同当事方勾选其一):□不超过合同价款的【　　】倍;□不超过在中国领先船厂进行同样修理或材料更换价格的【　　】倍;□不超过在中国、新加坡或中东地区船厂进行同样修理或材料更换价格的【　　】倍。

9.7　船厂的保修责任只限于根据上述第 9.5 及 9.6 条的约定承担,船厂不负责任何其他损失、损害或费用(不论是直接的还是间接的),包括但不限于由故障或缺陷引起的救助费、拖带费、船坞使用费、码头费、实际维修船厂的任何其他非常规服务收费、港口规费、任何其他检验和监管费用、消耗品、保险费、运输费等以及船舶营运损失和/或船舶修理导致的时间损失或利润损失。船厂对船东受到的罚款、罚金、处罚不承担责任,船厂对任何与船舶所有、营运、船载货物等有利害关系的第三方的潜在性损害或将恶化的损害也不承担责任。

9.8　在任何情况下,有关保修的请求不影响船东的付款义务。任何尚未支付的合同价款必须按时支付,船东不得全部或部分扣留该款项或将该款项与保修请求进行抵消。

9.9　船东要求船厂进行与油漆生产厂家要求不一致的不适当的预处理时,船厂对该油漆施工的工艺、质量和/或状况不承担保证责任。

9.10　修理工期内,船厂应有足够的修船责任保险,并按照船东的要求及时向船东提供保险单复印件、证据和详细说明等相关文件材料。

9.11　船厂的义务和责任不限于本条规定。

第 10 条　船东的义务和责任

10.1　船东有义务办理与船舶有关的所有必须的认可文件和证书,并维持其效力。

10.2　修理工期内,船东应为船舶、船员、船上设备以及船上其他属船东所有或控制的财产购买相应的保险,包括但不限于保赔险、船壳和机械险以及战争险,并按照船厂的要求及时向船厂提供保险单复印件、证据和详细说明等相关文件材料。

10.3　船东或其船员或其雇员或船东指定的其他修理服务供应商忽视或违背附件 4 的"船厂规则"中的禁止规定或船厂关于船舶在船厂时的安全规则而引起的损失或损害,由船东完全负责。

10.4　无论何时,船东应始终对船舶的安全承担全部责任,船东应采取所有必要的保护船舶安全以及防治船舶污染环境的措施;本合同下的船东交船与船厂还船,不影响或免除船东的上述义务和责任。在船舶修理期间船厂可在船东的要求下协助船东维护船舶的安全及防治船舶污染环境,船厂因此而产生的费用由船东承担。前述费用包括但不限于船厂为维护船舶安全及采取污染防治措施而产生的人工及材料成本、为满足船舶安全及污染防治管理规范而代为支付的费用、因协助船东或根据船东指示采取必要措施而实际支出的费用及遭受的损失。

10.5 无论何时船东应对其雇员或船员或仍在船上的乘客或船东指定的其他修理服务供应商的雇员的死亡、伤害和疾病负责,且应使船厂在受到有关人身伤亡或疾病的索赔时免受损害或赔偿船厂的损失,但船厂和/或其雇员或其分包方在从事修理活动或雇佣活动或授权活动过程中的故意或重大过失所直接导致的除外。

10.6 在本合同期间内,如果船东拟出让船舶所有权,或拟终止对船舶的光船租赁,船东应提前书面通知船厂;船厂有权要求船东在船舶所有权变更及光船租赁终止之前全额付清已经产生的合同价款,或为未付的合同价款提供船厂可接受的担保;船厂有权终止本合同,停止尚未完成的修理工程,除非船东按照船厂要求提供担保。

10.7 船东的义务和责任不限于本条规定。

第 11 条 修理工期的延长

11.1 如遇不可抗力事件(指在订立合同时不能预见,对其发生和后果不能避免且不能克服的事项,如火灾、洪水、台风、地震、恶劣天气、政府命令等),船厂应在【   】个日历日内以书面形式通知船东,并且应在不可抗力事件结束后【   】个日历日内以书面形式通知船东。船厂有权相应延长修理工期,船厂为避免或减轻不可抗力事件对修理工程的影响而实际支出的费用应当由船东承担。

11.2 除本合同第 2.3 条、第 2.4 条、第 2.6 条、第 3.2 条、第 4.1 条、第 5.3 条、第 5.5 条和第 7.1 条的规定之外,其他因船东原因所导致的修理工期的延误,船厂均有权相应延长修理工期。

第 12 条 合同的解除

12.1 除本合同第 3.6 条、第 5.5 条、第 8.5 条和第 10.6 条的规定之外,本合同可在下列情况下解除:

12.1.1 因发生不可抗力事件致使合同目的不能实现,任何一方均可解除合同;

12.1.2 如存在要求一方解散、清算或破产的裁定、命令或有效决议,或就一方的全部或部分财产已经指定了接收人/管理人,或在任何司法辖区开始了类似的程序,或一方停止营业、与其债权人达成特别安排或和解协议,则另一方有权解除合同;

12.1.3 一方明确表示或者以自己的行为表明不履行本合同约定的,另一方有权解除合同。

12.2 即使合同被解除,船东仍应自解除日起【   】个日历日内向船厂支付合同解除前已产生的合同价款和船厂为完成修理工程而实际支出的全部费用,包括但不限于为完成修理工程而已购买的材料、已供应的物资。合同解除后,船厂有权将船舶从修理场所移至其他位置,由此产生的靠码头、拖航、引航、进船坞以及靠泊等的费用及风险均由船东承担。

第 13 条 商标和专利

对于修理工程中按照船东提供的图纸、说明书、模具和其他数据和信息制造或换新机器、设备、配件或部件,船东应对可能出现的对第三人商标权、专利权或其他类似权利的侵害完全负责,并且应使船厂在受到第三方关于上述侵权索赔时免受损害或赔偿船厂的损失。船厂有权停止此种制造或换新,并有权向船东索赔因此遭受的损失。

第 14 条　保密

船厂的图纸、设计、图表和其他由船厂制作的文件为船厂所有，未经船厂书面同意，不得泄露给第三方。同样，未经船东书面同意，船厂不得将船东的图纸或资料泄露给第三方。双方均有责任做好保密工作。

第 15 条　转让

除本合同第 2.6 条之外，未经对方的书面同意，双方均无权将其在本合同下的权利和义务转让给第三方。

第 16 条　对合法性要求的配合

如果船厂在履行合同时需要向政府办理一定的手续以满足法律法规的要求，船东应按照船厂的要求配合船厂履行该手续。

第 17 条　通知

17.1　本合同有关的通信和通知应当向如下地址送达：

致船东：

地　　址：

收 件 人：

电话号码：

传真号码：

电子邮件：

致船厂：

地　　址：

收 件 人：

电话号码：

传真号码：

电子邮件：

17.2　一方地址变更应当书面通知对方。未能通知对方的，对方发往其最后一次获知的地址即被视为是充分有效的送达。

17.3　本合同中的书面指所有字迹清楚的文字通信方法。一份有效的通知可以采取下列任一方法送达：电报、电传、传真、电子信件、挂号信、商业快递或电子邮件或人工递送件等。

17.4　向船东代表或船长的送达视为向船东送达。

第 18 条　合同的签署及生效

18.1　以下署名者承诺其具有合法授权代表各方签署本合同。

18.2　本合同可通过传真或电子邮件的方式签署，并具有完全法律效力。

18.3　本合同在船东方及船厂方代表签署后生效。如船长尚未签署的，不影响本合同效力。

18.4　如在签署本合同之前船东已经交船，船东与船厂之间所达成的任何书面协议均应视为本合同的组成部分;二者之间有冲突的,以本合同约定为准。

18.5 本合同的全部附件以及经签署的修理工程完工单、账单等均为本合同的组成部分,与本合同具有同等法律效力。

第 19 条 争议解决和适用法律

本合同应受中华人民共和国法律管辖并按其解释。凡因本合同引起的或与本合同有关的任何争议,均应提交中国海事仲裁委员会,按照申请仲裁时该会现行有效的仲裁规则进行仲裁。仲裁裁决是终局的,对双方均有约束力。

各方授权代表于文前日期签署本协议。

船东方代表:

_____(签字)

_____(公司名称)作为船舶管理人(/船舶经营人)(/代理)

代表船东(/船舶光租人)_____(公司名称)签订本协议

签字人:_____(签字人姓名及职位)

作为船舶管理人(/船舶经营人)(/代理)的授权代表在本协议上签字/加盖印章

签字/盖章:

日期:

_____(签字)

船长:_____(船长姓名)

代表船东(/船舶光租人)_____(公司名称)签订本协议

船章或船长章:

日期:

船厂方代表:

_____(签字)

_____(签字人姓名及职位)

代表船厂_____(船厂名称)

(船厂公章)

二

全面深化中国(上海)自由贸易试验区改革开放方案

建设中国(上海)自由贸易试验区(以下简称自贸试验区)是党中央、国务院在新形势下全面深化改革和扩大开放的战略举措。自贸试验区建设三年多来取得重大进展,总体达到预期目标。为贯彻落实党中央、国务院决策部署,对照国际最高标准、最好水平的自由贸易区,全面深化自贸试验区改革开放,加快构建开放型经济新体制,在新一轮改革开放中进一步发挥引领示范作用,制定本方案。

一、总体要求

(一)指导思想。全面贯彻党的十八大和十八届三中、四中、五中、六中全会精神,深入贯彻习近平总书记系列重要讲话精神和治国理政新理念新思想新战略,认真落实党中央、国务院决策部署,统筹推进"五位一体"总体布局和协调推进"四个全面"战略布局,坚持稳中求进工作总基调,坚定践行新发展理念,坚持以制度创新为核心,继续解放思想、勇于突破、当好标杆,进一步对照国际最高标准,查找短板弱项,大胆试、大胆闯、自主改,坚持全方位对外开放,推动贸易和投资自由化便利化,加大压力测试,切实有效防控风险,以开放促改革、促发展、促创新;进一步加强与上海国际金融中心和具有全球影响力的科技创新中心建设的联动,不断放大政策集成效应,主动服务"一带一路"建设和长江经济带发展,形成经济转型发展新动能和国际竞争新优势;更大力度转变政府职能,加快探索一级地方政府管理体制创新,全面提升政府治理能力;发挥先发优势,加强改革系统集成,力争取得更多可复制推广的制度创新成果,进一步彰显全面深化改革和扩大开放试验田作用。

(二)建设目标。到2020年,率先建立同国际投资和贸易通行规则相衔接的制度体系,把自贸试验区建设成为投资贸易自由、规则开放透明、监管公平高效、营商环境便利的国际高标准自由贸易园区,健全各类市场主体平等准入和有序竞争的投资管理体系、促进贸易转型升级和通关便利的贸易监管服务体系、深化金融开放创新和有效防控风险的金融服务体系、符合市场经济规则和治理能力现代化要求的政府管理体系,率先形成法治化、国际化、便利化的营商环境和公平、统一、高效的市场环境。强化自贸试验区改革同上海市改革的联动,各项改革试点任务具备条件的在浦东新区范围内全面实施,或在上海市推广试验。

二、加强改革系统集成,建设开放和创新融为一体的综合改革试验区

加强制度创新的系统性、整体性、协同性,围绕深化投资管理体制改革、优化贸易监管服务体系、完善创新促进机制,统筹各环节改革,增强各部门协同,注重改革举措的配套组合,有效破

解束缚创新的瓶颈,更大程度激发市场活力。

(三)建立更加开放透明的市场准入管理模式。实施市场准入负面清单和外商投资负面清单制度。在完善市场准入负面清单的基础上,对各类市场主体实行一致管理的,进一步优化、简化办事环节和流程,对业务牌照和资质申请统一审核标准和时限,促进公平竞争。进一步提高外商投资负面清单的透明度和市场准入的可预期性。实施公平竞争审查制度,清理和取消资质资格获取、招投标、权益保护等方面存在的差别化待遇,实现各类市场主体依法平等准入清单之外的行业、领域和业务。

(四)全面深化商事登记制度改革。保障企业登记自主权,尊重企业自主经营的权利。开展企业名称登记制度改革,除涉及前置审批事项或企业名称核准与企业登记不在同一机关外,企业名称不再预先核准。放宽住所(经营场所)登记条件,有效释放场地资源。优化营业执照的经营范围等登记方式。推行全程电子化登记和电子营业执照改革试点。探索建立普通注销登记制度和简易注销登记制度相互配套的市场主体退出制度。开展"一照多址"改革试点。

(五)全面实现"证照分离"。深化"先照后证"改革,进一步加大探索力度。把涉及市场准入的许可审批事项适时纳入改革试点,能取消的全部取消,需要保留审批的,按照告知承诺和加强市场准入管理等方式进一步优化调整,在改革许可管理方式、完善风险防范措施的基础上,进一步扩大实行告知承诺的领域。加强许可管理与企业设立登记管理的衔接,实现统一社会信用代码在各许可管理环节的"一码贯通"。实施生产许可"一企一证",探索取消生产许可证产品检验。

(六)建成国际先进水平的国际贸易"单一窗口"。借鉴联合国国际贸易"单一窗口"标准,实施贸易数据协同、简化和标准化。纳入海港、空港和海关特殊监管区域的物流作业功能,通过银行机构或非银行支付机构建立收费账单功能,便利企业办理支付和查询。实现物流和监管等信息的交换共享,为进出口货物质量安全追溯信息的管理和查询提供便利。推动将国际贸易"单一窗口"覆盖领域拓展至服务贸易,逐步纳入技术贸易、服务外包、维修服务等,待条件成熟后逐步将服务贸易出口退(免)税申报纳入"单一窗口"管理。与国家层面"单一窗口"标准规范融合对接,推进长江经济带跨区域通关业务办理,加强数据衔接和协同监管。

(七)建立安全高效便捷的海关综合监管新模式。深化实施全国海关通关一体化、"双随机、一公开"监管以及"互联网+海关"等举措,进一步改革海关业务管理方式,对接国际贸易"单一窗口",建立权责统一、集成集约、智慧智能、高效便利的海关综合监管新模式。综合应用大数据、云计算、互联网和物联网技术,扩大"自主报税、自助通关、自动审放、重点稽核"试点范围。深化"一线放开"、"二线安全高效管住"改革,强化综合执法,推进协同治理,探索设立与"区港一体"发展需求相适应的配套管理制度。创新加工贸易出口货物专利纠纷担保放行方式。支持海关特殊监管区域外的企业开展高附加值、高技术、无污染的维修业务。深入实施货物状态分类监管,研究将试点从物流仓储企业扩大到贸易、生产加工企业,具备条件时,在上海市其他符合条件的海关特殊监管区域推广实施。

(八)建立检验检疫风险分类监管综合评定机制。完善进口商品风险预警快速反应机制,加强进口货物不合格风险监测,实施消费品等商品召回制度。建立综合应用合格评定新机制,设立国家质量基础检验检疫综合应用示范园区。在制定发布不适用于第三方检验结果采信目录清单基础上,积极推进扩大商品和项目的第三方检验结果采信。探索扩大检验鉴定结果国际互认的范围。

(九)建立具有国际竞争力的创新产业监管模式。优化生物医药全球协同研发的试验用特殊物品的准入许可,完善准入许可的内容和方式。完善有利于提升集成电路全产业链国际竞争力的海关监管模式。研究制定再制造旧机电设备允许进口目录,在风险可控的前提下,试点数控机床、工程设备、通信设备等进口再制造。探索引入市场化保险机制,提高医药生产等领域的监管效率。

(十)优化创新要素的市场配置机制。完善药品上市许可持有人制度。允许自贸试验区内医疗器械注册申请人委托上海市医疗器械生产企业生产产品。健全完善更加符合社会主义市场经济规律、人才成长规律和人才发展流动规律的人才认定标准和推荐方式,标准统一、程序规范的外国人来华工作许可制度及高效、便捷的人才签证制度,吸引更多外籍高层次人才参与创新创业,为其提供出入境和停居留便利,并按规定享受我国鼓励创新创业的相关政策。根据法律法规规定,支持持有外国人永久居留证的外籍高层次人才创办科技型企业,给予与中国籍公民同等待遇。深化上海股权托管交易中心"科技创新板"试点,完善对科创企业的金融服务。支持外资企业设立联合创新平台,协同本土中小微企业开展创新成果产业化项目推进。深化推进金融中心与科技创新中心建设相结合的科技金融模式创新。

(十一)健全知识产权保护和运用体系。充分发挥专利、商标、版权等知识产权引领作用,打通知识产权创造、运用、保护、管理和服务的全链条,提升知识产权质量和效益。以若干优势产业为重点,进一步简化和优化知识产权审查和注册流程,创新知识产权快速维权工作机制。探索互联网、电子商务、大数据等领域的知识产权保护规则。建立健全知识产权服务标准,完善知识产权服务体系。完善知识产权纠纷多元解决机制。支持企业运用知识产权进行海外股权投资。创新发展知识产权金融服务。深化完善有利于激励创新的知识产权归属制度。

三、加强同国际通行规则相衔接,建立开放型经济体系的风险压力测试区

按照国际最高标准,为推动实施新一轮高水平对外开放进行更为充分的压力测试,探索开放型经济发展新领域,形成适应经济更加开放要求的系统试点经验。

(十二)进一步放宽投资准入。最大限度缩减自贸试验区外商投资负面清单,推进金融服务、电信、互联网、文化、文物、维修、航运服务等专业服务业和先进制造业领域对外开放。除特殊领域外,取消对外商投资企业经营期限的特别管理要求。对符合条件的外资创业投资企业和股权投资企业开展境内投资项目,探索实施管理新模式。完善国家安全审查、反垄断审查等投资审查制度。

(十三)实施贸易便利化新规则。优化口岸通关流程,推进各环节监管方式改革,探索公布涵盖各通关环节的货物平均放行时间。最大限度实现覆盖船舶抵离、港口作业、货物通关等口

岸作业各环节的全程无纸化,推进贸易领域证书证明的电子化管理。深化亚太示范电子口岸网络试点。推动实施原产地预裁定制度。根据自由贸易协定规定,推动实施原产地自主声明制度。推进企业信用等级的跨部门共享,对高信用等级企业降低查验率。深化完善安全预警和国际竞争力提升的产业安全保障机制。

（十四）创新跨境服务贸易管理模式。在风险可控的前提下,加快推进金融保险、文化旅游、教育卫生等高端服务领域的贸易便利化。提高与服务贸易相关的货物暂时进口便利,拓展暂时进口货物单证制度适用范围,延长单证册的有效期。探索兼顾安全和效率的数字产品贸易监管模式。大力发展中医药服务贸易,扩大中医药服务贸易国际市场准入,推动中医药海外创新发展。深化国际船舶登记制度创新,进一步便利国际船舶管理企业从事海员外派服务。在合适领域分层次逐步取消或放宽对跨境交付、自然人移动等模式的服务贸易限制措施。探索完善服务贸易统计体系,建立服务贸易监测制度。

（十五）进一步深化金融开放创新。加强与上海国际金融中心建设的联动,积极有序实施《进一步推进中国（上海）自由贸易试验区金融开放创新试点加快上海国际金融中心建设方案》。加快构建面向国际的金融市场体系,建设人民币全球服务体系,有序推进资本项目可兑换试点。加快建立金融监管协调机制,提升金融监管能力,防范金融风险。

（十六）设立自由贸易港区。在洋山保税港区和上海浦东机场综合保税区等海关特殊监管区域内,设立自由贸易港区。对标国际最高水平,实施更高标准的"一线放开""二线安全高效管住"贸易监管制度。根据国家授权实行集约管理体制,在口岸风险有效防控的前提下,依托信息化监管手段,取消或最大程度简化入区货物的贸易管制措施,最大程度简化一线申报手续。探索实施符合国际通行做法的金融、外汇、投资和出入境管理制度,建立和完善风险防控体系。

四、进一步转变政府职能,打造提升政府治理能力的先行区

加强自贸试验区建设与浦东新区转变一级地方政府职能的联动,系统推进简政放权、放管结合、优化服务改革,在行政机构改革、管理体制创新、运行机制优化、服务方式转变等方面改革创新,全面提升开放环境下政府治理能力。

（十七）健全以简政放权为重点的行政管理体制。加快推进简政放权,深化行政审批制度改革。以厘清政府、市场、社会关系为重点,进一步取消和简化审批事项,最大限度地给市场放权。推动实现市场准入、执业资格等领域的管理方式转变。深化大部门制改革,在市场监管、经济发展、社会管理和公共服务、改革和法制、环保和城建五个职能模块,按照精简高效原则形成跨部门的协同机制。

（十八）深化创新事中事后监管体制机制。按照探索建立新的政府经济管理体制要求,深化分类综合执法改革,围绕审批、监管、执法适度分离,完善市场监管、城市管理领域的综合执法改革。推进交通运输综合行政执法改革,加强执法协调。将异常名录信息归集范围扩大到市场监管以外的行政部门,健全跨部门"双告知、双反馈、双跟踪"许可办理机制和"双随机、双评估、双公示"监管协同机制。落实市场主体首负责任制,在安全生产、产品质量、环境保护等领域建立

市场主体社会责任报告制度和责任追溯制度。鼓励社会力量参与市场监督,建立健全会计、审计、法律、检验检测认证等第三方专业机构参与市场监管的制度安排。

(十九)优化信息互联共享的政府服务体系。加快构建以企业需求为导向、大数据分析为支撑的"互联网+政务服务"体系。建立央地协同、条块衔接的信息共享机制,明确部门间信息互联互通的边界规则。以数据共享为基础,再造业务流程,实现市场准入"单窗通办""全网通办",个人事务"全区通办",政务服务"全员协办"。探索建立公共信用信息和金融信用信息互补机制。探索形成市场主体信用等级标准体系,培育发展信用信息专业服务市场。

五、创新合作发展模式,成为服务国家"一带一路"建设、推动市场主体走出去的桥头堡

坚持"引进来"和"走出去"有机结合,创新经贸投资合作、产业核心技术研发、国际化融资模式,探索搭建"一带一路"开放合作新平台,建设服务"一带一路"的市场要素资源配置功能枢纽,发挥自贸试验区在服务"一带一路"倡议中的辐射带动作用。

(二十)以高标准便利化措施促进经贸合作。对接亚太示范电子口岸网络,积极推进上海国际贸易"单一窗口"与"一带一路"沿线口岸的信息互换和服务共享。率先探索互联互通监管合作新模式,在认证认可、标准计量等方面开展多双边合作交流。加快建设门户复合型国际航空枢纽。促进上海港口与21世纪海上丝绸之路航线港口的合作对接,形成连接国内外重点口岸的亚太供应链中心枢纽。建立综合性对外投资促进机构和境外投资公共信息服务平台,在法律查明和律师服务、商事纠纷调解和仲裁、财务会计和审计服务等方面开展业务合作。打造"一带一路"产权交易中心与技术转移平台,促进"一带一路"产业科技合作。积极推进能源、港口、通信、高端装备制造等领域的国际产能合作和建设能力合作。

(二十一)增强"一带一路"金融服务功能。推动上海国际金融中心与"一带一路"沿线国家和地区金融市场的深度合作、互联互通。加强与境外人民币离岸市场战略合作,稳妥推进境外机构和企业发行人民币债券和资产证券化产品,支持优质境外企业利用上海资本市场发展壮大,吸引沿线国家央行、主权财富基金和投资者投资境内人民币资产,为"一带一路"重大项目提供融资服务。大力发展海外投资保险、出口信用保险、货物运输保险、工程建设保险等业务,为企业海外投资、产品技术输出、承接"一带一路"重大工程提供综合保险服务。支持金砖国家新开发银行的发展。

(二十二)探索具有国际竞争力的离岸税制安排。适应企业参与国际竞争和服务"一带一路"建设的需求,在不导致税基侵蚀和利润转移的前提下,基于真实贸易和服务背景,结合服务贸易创新试点工作,研究探索服务贸易创新试点扩围的税收政策安排。

六、服务全国改革开放大局,形成更多可复制推广的制度创新成果

紧紧把握自贸试验区的基本定位,坚持先行先试,充分发挥各方面的改革创新主动性和创

造性,为全面深化改革和扩大开放,取得更多制度创新成果。

(二十三)加快形成系统性的改革经验和模式。把理念创新、体制机制创新、政策创新和加强风险防控等方面的改革试点经验作为重点,加强试点经验的总结和系统集成。对于市场准入、贸易便利化、创新发展体制机制等领域的改革,加快形成可以在全国复制推广的经验。对于进一步扩大开放、对接高标准国际经贸规则等压力测试事项,积极探索经验,为国家推进构建多双边经贸合作新格局做好政策储备。对于政府管理模式创新等改革事项,在改革理念和组织推进等方面总结形成可供其他地区借鉴的改革经验。

七、抓好工作落实

在国务院自由贸易试验区工作部际联席会议统筹协调下,充分发挥地方和部门的积极性,抓好改革措施的落实。按照总体筹划、分步实施、率先突破、逐步完善的原则,各有关部门要大力支持,及时制定实施细则或办法,加强指导和服务;对涉及法律法规调整的改革事项,及时强化法制保障,做好与相关法律立改废释的衔接,共同推进相关体制机制创新,并注意加强监管、防控风险。上海市要把握基本定位,强化使命担当,创新思路、寻找规律、解决问题、积累经验,完善工作机制,系统推进改革试点任务的落实,继续当好全国改革开放排头兵、创新发展先行者。重大事项要及时向国务院请示报告。

三

上海市邮轮旅游合同
示范文本
（2015 版）

上海市工商行政管理局和上海市旅游局制定

使用说明

一、本合同示范文本供旅游者参加邮轮旅游与旅行社签订包价旅游合同时使用。旅游者应选择具有经营旅游业务相应资格的旅行社。旅行社应具有旅游行政管理部门颁发的《旅行社业务经营许可证》和工商行政管理部门颁发的《营业执照》。经营出境旅游的旅行社应具有经营出境旅游业务资格；经营赴台湾地区旅游的旅行社除了应具有上述经营出境旅游业务资格外，还应具有组织大陆居民赴台湾地区旅游的经营资格。

二、旅游前，旅行社应当与旅游者签订书面旅游合同，本合同及其附件均应使用中文文本。旅游者在交纳旅游费用后，旅行社应开具发票。

三、旅游者在自行安排活动期间，应结合自身身体状况选择邮轮上的活动项目。旅游者应选择适合自身身体状况的岸上旅游产品及项目。

四、旅行社委托组团，须事先告知旅游者并在本合同中载明。

五、旅游者与旅行社也可使用本合同电子版。

六、在填写本合同第二条"行程与标准"和"旅游行程单"时，旅行社应以准确、明晰的语言表述，不得出现"准X星级"、"相当于X星级"、"仅供参考"、"与××同级"等模糊不确定性用语。

七、旅游者有权自主选择旅游产品和服务，有权拒绝旅行社的强制交易行为。

八、在签订合同时，双方应当结合具体情况选择本合同协议条款中所提供的选择项，条款前有"□"符号的，甲乙双方应当协商选定。双方选定的条款，应当在"□"中划"√"；双方不选的条款，应当在"□"中划"×"；条款中有空格处的，供双方自行约定并填写完整，对双方不予约定的空格处，应当划"×"以示没有特别约定。

九、旅行社制定补充条款等双方自行约定内容对本合同示范文本有关条款的内容进行补充、细化的，自行约定内容不得减轻或者免除应当由旅行社承担的责任。

十、本合同示范文本自 2015 年 8 月 25 日起使用。今后凡未制定新的版本前，本版本延续使用。

十一、旅游咨询与投诉机构：
1. 上海市旅游质量监督所
   地址：中山南二路 2419 号 B1 楼　邮编：200232
   投诉电话：64393615、962020
2. 上海市消费者申（投）诉举报中心
   举报投诉电话：12315
3. 上海市文化市场行政执法总队
   地址：永嘉路 383 号　邮编：200031
   旅游违法违规举报电话：12318

合同编号：_____

上海市邮轮旅游合同
（2015 版）

甲方(旅游者或旅游团体)：_____
乙方(旅行社)：_____
经营许可证编号：_____
经营范围：_____

根据《中华人民共和国合同法》、《中华人民共和国旅游法》、《旅行社条例》、《上海市旅游条例》及其它有关法律法规的规定，甲乙双方在平等自愿、协商一致的基础上，签订本合同。

第一条 合同标的
邮轮产品名称_____。
团号：_____。
组团方式（二选一）
□自行组团
□委托组团（委托社全称及经营许可证编号_____）。
出发日期_____,出发地点_____。
邮轮途中停靠港口_____。
岸上游览地点_____。
结束日期_____,返回地点_____。

第二条 行程与标准（乙方提供旅游行程单，须含下列要素）
邮轮上舱位类型及标准和住宿天数_____
邮轮上用餐次数_____,标准_____
岸上景点名称和游览时间_____
岸上往返交通_____,标准_____
岸上游览交通_____,标准_____
岸上旅游者自由活动时间_____,次数_____。
岸上住宿安排（名称）及标准和住宿天数_____
岸上用餐次数_____,标准_____
岸上地接社名称_____,
地址_____,
岸上地接社联系人_____,联系电话_____。

第三条 旅游者保险
乙方提示甲方购买人身意外伤害保险和邮轮旅游意外保险。经乙方推荐，甲方已经阅读并明确知晓上述保险的保险条款及其保单内容。甲方_____（应填同意或不同意，打勾无效）委托乙方办理个人投保的人身意外伤害保险；甲方_____（应填同意或不同意，打勾无效）

委托乙方办理个人投保的邮轮旅游意外保险。
　　保险公司及产品名称＿＿＿＿＿＿＿＿＿＿＿＿。
　　保险费人民币＿＿＿＿＿＿元/人。
　　相关投保信息和约定以保单及其保险条款为准。
　　第四条　旅游费用及其支付(以人民币为计算单位)
　　旅游费用包括：□邮轮船票费(含邮轮上指定的舱位、餐饮、游览娱乐项目和设施等)；□船上服务费(小费)；□港务费；□签证费；□签注费；□乙方统一安排岸上游览景区景点的门票费、□交通费、□住宿费、□餐费；□其他费用＿＿＿＿＿＿＿＿＿＿＿＿＿＿。
　　甲方应交纳旅游费用＿＿＿＿元,大写＿＿＿＿＿＿＿＿＿元。
　　旅游费用交纳期限＿＿＿＿＿＿＿＿＿＿＿＿＿＿。
　　旅游费用交纳方式：□现金；□支票；□信用卡；
　　　　　　　　　　　□其他＿＿＿＿＿＿＿＿＿＿＿＿。

第五条　双方的权利义务
(一)甲方的权利义务
1. 甲方有权知悉其购买的邮轮及岸上旅游产品和服务的真实情况,有权要求乙方按照约定提供产品和服务；有权拒绝乙方未经协商一致指定具体购物场所、安排另行付费旅游项目的行为；有权拒绝乙方未经事先协商一致将旅游业务委托给其他旅行社。

2. 甲方应自觉遵守旅游文明行为规范,遵守邮轮旅游产品说明中的要求,尊重船上礼仪和岸上旅游目的地的风俗习惯、文化传统和宗教禁忌,爱护旅游资源,保护生态环境；遵守《中国公民出国(境)旅游文明行为指南》等文明行为规范。甲方在旅游活动中应遵守团队纪律,配合乙方完成合同约定的旅游行程。

3. 甲方在签订合同或者填写材料时,应当使用有效身份证件,提供家属或其他紧急联络人的联系方式等,并对填写信息的真实性、有效性负责。限制民事行为能力人单独或由非监护人陪同参加旅游的,须征得监护人的书面同意；监护人或者其他负有监护义务的人,应当保护随行未成年旅游者的安全。

4. 甲方应当遵守邮轮旅游产品说明及旅游活动中的安全警示要求,自觉参加并完成海上紧急救生演习,对有关部门、机构或乙方采取的安全防范和应急处置措施予以配合。

5. 甲方不得随身携带或者在行李中夹带法律、法规规定及邮轮旅游产品说明中禁止带上船的违禁品。甲方应遵守邮轮禁烟规定,除指定的吸烟区域外,其余场所均禁止吸烟。

6. 在邮轮旅游过程中,甲方应妥善保管随身携带的财物。

7. 在邮轮上自行安排活动期间,甲方应认真阅读并按照邮轮方《每日须知》和活动安排,自行选择邮轮上的用餐、游览、娱乐项目等。在自行安排活动期间,甲方应在自己能够控制风险的范围内活动,选择能够控制风险的活动项目,并对自己的安全负责。

8. 甲方参加邮轮旅游以及岸上游览必须遵守集合出发和返回邮轮时间,按时到达集合地点。

9. 行程中发生纠纷,甲方应按本合同第八条、第十一条约定的方式解决,不得损害乙方和其他旅游者及邮轮方的合法权益,不得以拒绝上、下邮轮(机、车、船)等行为拖延行程或者脱团,不得影响港口、码头的正常秩序,否则应当就扩大的损失承担赔偿责任。

10. 甲方向乙方提交的出入境证件应当符合相关规定。甲方不得在境外非法滞留,随团出游的,不得擅自分团、脱团。

11. 甲方不能成行的,可以让具备参加本次邮轮旅游条件的第三人代为履行合同,并及时通知乙方。因代为履行合同增加或减少的费用,双方应按实结算。

(二)乙方的权利义务

1. 乙方提供的邮轮船票或凭证、邮轮旅游产品说明、登船相关文件、已订购服务清单,应由甲方确认,作为本合同组成部分。

2. 乙方提供旅游行程单,经双方签字或者盖章确认后作为本合同组成部分。

3. 乙方不得以不合理的低价组织旅游活动,诱骗甲方,并通过安排购物或者另行付费旅游项目获取回扣等不正当利益。

4. 乙方应在出团前,以说明会等形式如实告知邮轮旅游服务项目和标准,提醒甲方遵守旅游文明行为规范、遵守邮轮旅游产品说明中的要求,尊重船上礼仪和岸上旅游目的地的风俗习惯、文化传统、宗教禁忌。在合同订立及履行中,乙方应对旅游中可能危及甲方人身、财产安全的情况,作出真实说明和明确警示,并采取防止危害发生的适当措施。

5. 当发生延误或不能靠港等情况时,乙方应当及时向甲方发布信息,告知具体解决方案。

6. 乙方应妥善保管甲方提交的各种证件,依法对甲方信息保密。

7. 因航空、港务费、燃油价格等费用遇政策性调价导致合同总价发生变更的,双方应按实结算。

8. 甲方有下列情形之一的,乙方可以解除合同:

(1)患有传染病等疾病,可能危害其他旅游者健康和安全的;

(2)携带危害公共安全的物品且不同意交有关部门处理的;

(3)从事违法或者违反社会公德的活动的;

(4)从事严重影响其他旅游者权益的活动,且不听劝阻、不能制止的;

(5)法律规定的其他情形。

因前款情形解除合同的,乙方应当按本合同第七条扣除必要的费用后,将余款退还甲方;给乙方造成损失的,甲方应当依法承担赔偿责任。

9. 成团人数与不成团的约定(二选一)

□最低成团人数_____人;低于此人数不能成团时,乙方应当提前30日通知甲方,本合同解除,向甲方退还已收取的全部费用。

□本团成团不受最低人数限制。

第六条　甲方不适合邮轮旅游的情形

因邮轮上没有专科医师及医疗设施,邮轮离岸后无法及时进行急救和治疗,为防止途中发生意外,甲方购买邮轮旅游产品、接受旅游服务时,应当如实告知与邮轮旅游活动相关的个人健康信息,参加适合自身条件的邮轮旅游活动。如隐瞒有关个人健康信息参加邮轮旅游,由甲方承担相应责任。

第七条 甲方解除合同及承担必要费用

因甲方自身原因导致合同解除，乙方按下列标准扣除必要费用后，将余款退还甲方：

（一）甲方在行程前解除合同的，双方约定扣除必要费用的标准为：

1. 行程前_____日至_____日，旅游费用_____%；
2. 行程前_____日至_____日，旅游费用_____%；
3. 行程前_____日至_____日，旅游费用_____%；
4. 行程前_____日至_____日，旅游费用_____%；
5. 行程开始当日，旅游费用_____%。

甲方行程前逾期支付旅游费用超过_____日的，或者甲方未按约定时间到达约定集合出发地点，也未能在中途加入旅游的，乙方有权解除合同，乙方可以按本款规定扣除必要的费用后，将余款退还甲方。

（二）甲方因疾病等自身的特殊原因，导致在行程中解除合同的，必要的费用扣除标准为：（二选一）

□1. 双方可以进行约定并从其约定：

旅游费用一（　　）一（　　）一（　　）一（　　）

□2. 双方未约定的，按照下列标准扣除必要的费用。

旅游费用×行程开始当日扣除比例＋（旅游费用－旅游费用×行程开始当日扣除比例）÷旅游天数×已经出游的天数。

如按上述（一）或（二）约定标准扣除的必要费用低于实际发生的费用，按照实际发生的费用扣除，但最高额不应当超过旅游费用总额。

行程前解除合同的，乙方扣除必要费用后，应当在合同解除之日起_____个工作日内向甲方退还剩余旅游费用。

行程中解除合同的，乙方扣除必要费用后，应当在协助甲方返回出发地或者到达甲方指定的合理地点后_____个工作日内向甲方退还剩余旅游费用。

第八条 责任减免及不可抗力情形的处理

（一）具有下列情形的旅行社免责

1. 因甲方原因造成自己人身损害、财产损失或造成他人损失的，由甲方承担相应责任，但乙方应协助处理。
2. 因不可抗力造成甲方人身损害、财产损失的，乙方不承担赔偿责任，但应积极采取救助措施。
3. 在自行安排活动期间甲方人身、财产权益受到损害的，乙方在事前已尽到必要警示说明义务且事后已尽到必要救助义务的，乙方不承担赔偿责任。
4. 甲方因参加非乙方安排或推荐的活动导致人身损害、财产损失的，乙方不承担赔偿责任。
5. 由于公共交通经营者的原因造成甲方人身损害、财产损失的，由公共交通经营者依法承担赔偿责任，乙方应当协助甲方向公共交通经营者索赔。因公共交通工具延误，导致合同不能按照约定履行的,乙方不承担违约责任,但应向甲方退还未实际发生的费用。

(二)因发生不可抗力情形或者乙方、履行辅助人已尽合理注意义务仍不能避免的事件,可能导致邮轮行程变更或取消部分停靠港口等情况时,按以下约定方式处理。

1. 行程前发生的,甲方可以按(1)或(2)选择(二选一)

□(1)甲方同意邮轮行程变更或取消部分停靠港口等,按以下约定处理:

①在不减少行程自然天数的情况下,启航延迟、港口停靠时间缩短、返航延迟抵达:船方提供餐食和各项服务,乙方退还旅游费用总额的_____%。

②无法停靠目的地港口:退还该港口的港务费以及未发生的岸上观光费用。

③行程自然天数减少:扣除已实际支付且不可退还的费用后,按照减少行程的自然天数所占计划行程的百分比退还旅游费用。

□(2)甲方不同意邮轮行程变更或取消部分停靠港口等上述约定,解除本合同;乙方应当在扣除已实际支付且不可退还的费用后,将余款退还甲方。

2. 行程中发生的,按上述(1)的约定处理。

第九条　违约责任

(一)乙方在行程前30日以内(含第30日,下同)提出解除合同的,向甲方退还全额旅游费用(不得扣除签证/签注等费用),并按下列标准向甲方支付违约金:

1. 行程前_____日至_____日,支付旅游费用总额_____%的违约金;
2. 行程前_____日至_____日,支付旅游费用总额_____%的违约金;
3. 行程前_____日至_____日,支付旅游费用总额_____%的违约金;
4. 行程前_____日至_____日,支付旅游费用总额_____%的违约金;
5. 行程开始当日,支付旅游费用总额_____%的违约金。

如上述违约金不足以赔偿甲方的实际损失,乙方应当按实际损失对甲方予以赔偿。

乙方应当在解除合同通知到达日起_____个工作日内,向甲方全额退还已收旅游费用并支付违约金。

(二)甲方逾期支付旅游费用的,应当每日按照逾期支付部分的旅游费用的_____%,向乙方支付违约金。

(三)甲方提供的个人信息及相关材料不真实而造成的损失,由其自行承担;如给乙方造成损失的,甲方还应当承担赔偿责任。

(四)甲方因不听从乙方的劝告、提示而影响旅游行程,给乙方造成损失的,应当承担相应的赔偿责任。

(五)乙方未按合同约定标准提供交通、住宿、餐饮等服务,或者违反本合同约定擅自变更旅游行程,给甲方造成损失的,应当承担相应的赔偿责任。

(六)乙方未经甲方同意,擅自将旅游业务委托给其他旅行社的,甲方在行程前(不含当日)得知的,有权解除合同,乙方全额退还已收旅游费用,并按旅游费用的15%支付违约金;甲方在行程开始当日或者行程开始后得知的,乙方应当按旅游费用的25%支付违约金。如违约金不足以赔偿甲方的实际损失,乙方应当按实际损失对甲方予以赔偿。

（七）乙方未经与甲方协商一致或者未经甲方要求，指定具体购物场所或安排另行付费旅游项目的，甲方有权在旅游行程结束后三十日内，要求乙方为其办理退货并先行垫付退货货款，或者退还另行付费旅游项目的费用。

（八）乙方具备履行条件，经甲方要求仍拒绝履行合同，造成甲方人身损害、滞留等严重后果的，甲方除要求乙方承担相应的赔偿责任外，还可以要求乙方支付旅游费用_____倍（一倍以上三倍以下）的赔偿金。

（九）其他违约责任：_____。

第十条　自愿购物和参加另行付费旅游项目约定

1. 甲方可以自主决定是否参加乙方安排的购物活动、另行付费旅游项目。

2. 乙方可以在不以不合理的低价组织旅游活动、不诱骗甲方、不获取回扣等不正当利益，且不影响其他旅游者行程安排的前提下，按照平等自愿、诚实信用的原则，与甲方协商一致达成购物活动、另行付费旅游项目补充协议。

3. 购物活动、另行付费旅游项目安排应不与旅游行程单冲突。

4. 地接社及其从业人员在行程中安排购物活动、另行付费旅游项目的，责任由订立本合同的乙方承担。

5. 购物活动、另行付费旅游项目具体约定见《自愿购物活动补充协议》（附件1）、《自愿参加另行付费旅游项目补充协议》（附件2）。

第十一条　争议解决方式

双方发生争议的，可协商解决，也可在旅游合同结束之日90天内向旅游质监机构申请调解，或提请上海仲裁委员会仲裁（**不愿意仲裁而选择向法院提起诉讼的，请双方在签署合同时将此仲裁条款划去**）。

第十二条　附则

本合同自双方签字或盖章之日起生效，本合同附有的旅游行程单、邮轮旅游产品说明和补充条款、补充协议等均为合同的附件，与本合同具有同等法律效力。

补充条款

甲方签字(盖章):_____　　乙方签字(盖章):_____
住　　　所:_____　　营业场所:_____
甲方代表:_____　　乙方代表(经办人):_____
联系电话:_____　　联系电话:_____
邮　　编:_____　　邮　　编:_____
日　　期:_____　　日　　期:_____

附件 1

自愿购物活动补充协议

1. 甲方可以自主决定是否参加乙方安排的购物活动；
2. 乙方可以在不以不合理的低价组织旅游活动、不诱骗甲方、不获取回扣等不正当利益，且不影响其他旅游者行程安排的前提下，按照平等自愿、诚实信用的原则，与甲方协商一致达成购物活动的约定；
3. 购物活动安排应不与《行程单》冲突；
4. 具体购物场所应当同时面向其他社会公众开放；
5. 地接社及其从业人员在行程中安排购物活动，责任由订立本合同的乙方承担；
6. 购物活动具体约定如下：

具体时间	地点	购物场所名称	主要商品信息	最长停留时间(分钟)	其他说明	甲方签名同意
年 月 日 时						签名：
年 月 日 时						签名：
年 月 日 时						签名：

甲方签名：　　　　　　　　　　乙方(经办人)签名：
　年　月　日　　　　　　　　　　年　月　日

附件 2

自愿参加另行付费旅游项目补充协议

1. 甲方可以自主决定是否参加乙方安排的另行付费旅游项目;
2. 乙方可以在不以不合理的低价组织旅游活动、不诱骗甲方、不获取回扣等不正当利益,且不影响其他旅游者行程安排的前提下,按照平等自愿、诚实信用的原则,与甲方协商一致达成另行付费旅游项目的约定;
3. 另行付费旅游项目安排应不与《行程单》冲突;
4. 另行付费旅游项目经营场所应当同时面向其他社会公众开放;
5. 地接社及其从业人员在行程中安排另行付费旅游项目的,责任由订立本合同的乙方承担;
6. 另行付费旅游项目具体约定如下:

具体时间	地点	项目名称和内容	费用(元)	项目时长(分钟)	其他说明	甲方签名同意
年 月 日 时						签名:
年 月 日 时						签名:
年 月 日 时						签名:

甲方签名:　　　　　　　　　　　乙方(经办人)签名:
　年　　月　　日　　　　　　　　　年　　月　　日

The writing team hereby thanks the following organizations and units for their help (in order of investigation):

 China (Shanghai) Pilot Free Trade Zone Administration
 Lujiazui Financial and Trade Zone
 Lujiazui Financial City
 Jinqiao Administration of China (Shanghai) Pilot Free Trade Zone
 Expo Area Administration of China (Shanghai) Pilot Free Trade Zone
 China (Shanghai) International Trade Single Window
 Government Online Office Shanghai
 China (Shanghai) E-port Information Data Center
 Shanghai Municipal Development & Reform Commission
 Shanghai Municipal Commission of Commerce
 Shanghai Municipal Commission of Economy & Informatization
 Shanghai Municipal Finance Bureau
 Shanghai Municipal Human Resources and Social Security Bureau
 Shanghai Municipal Tax Service, State Taxation Administration
 Shanghai Municipal E-tax Service, State Taxation Administration
 State-owned Assets Supervison and Administration Commission of Shanghai
 Shanghai Municipal Financial Regulatory Bureau
 Yangshan Customs of the People's Republic of China
 Shanghai Administration of Foreign Exchange
 Shanghai Municipal Audit Bureau
 Shanghai Municipal Bureau of Statistics
 Counsellors' Office of Shanghai Municipal People's Government
 The Development Research Center of Shanghai Municipal People's Government
 Shanghai Federation of Industry and Commerce
 China Association of Shipping Agencies & Non-vessel-operating Common Carriers of Shanghai Office
 Shanghai E & P International
 Shanghai Maritime University
 East China University of Political Science and Law
 Fudan University
 Shanghai Jiao Tong University

Preface

In 2017, the international shipping market rose somewhat, and it seemed that it has jumped out of the spiral downward trajectory for many years. The confidence of the people in the Chinese shipping industry has risen to a high point in the past three years, but most shipping companies are still going through the darkness before dawn by means of "holding together to keep warm". Joint ventures, integration, and merger and acquisition events continue to emerge: such as the Ocean Alliance of COSCO SHIPPING, OOCL, Evergreen Marine, and CMA CGM, to jointly develop the global container trunk line business; and COSCO SHIPPING and SIPG to acquire part of OOCL's international business to increase resource utilization and reduce operating costs.

To help shipping companies alleviate their difficulties and maintain the steady development of shipping as a pillar industry, the Chinese government launched a series of support policies. For example, the National Development and Reform Commission and the Ministry of Transport carried out administrative investigations on port monopolies, prompting relevant companies to take the initiative to rectify and adjust the charging standards, and reduce the burden on shipping and trading companies. Among the policies introduced, the most important one is the *Proposal for Comprehensively Deepening the Reform and Opening-up of China (Shanghai) Pilot Free Trade Zone*.

Shanghai Pilot Free Trade Zone was established in 2013, and achieved remarkable results in the initial development process. As of 2017, the number of newly registered enterprises in Shanghai Pilot Free Trade Zone exceeded 50,000, of which: about 10% were shipping companies; the negative list of foreign investment was reduced to 95; the "three one" inspection platform for customs inspection in the zone was fully completed and operated, the number of pilot enterprises for the classification and supervision of goods status was expanded to 39; the reform of the "separation of licenses" was fully implemented, and the operational and post-operational oversight system was preliminarily completed to achieve the full coverage of 21 regulatory departments; the "global sharing" of government information was accelerated, and the special customs supervision area realized information sharing with regulatory authorities such as ports and finance.

In 2017, with the spring breeze of the "Belt and Road", the construction of Shanghai Pilot Free Trade Zone entered a new era. At the critical moment, the State Council issued the *Proposal for Comprehensively Deepening the Reform and Opening-up of China (Shanghai) Pilot Free Trade Zone*, proposing to comprehensively deepen the reform and opening-up of Shanghai Pilot Free Trade Zone against free trade zones with the highest international standards and the best level and accelerated the establishment of a new open economic system. The proposal contains many measures that are beneficial to the development of shipping companies:

(1) Establish a system that is in line with international investment and trade regulations, promote trade transformation and upgrading, and a trade supervision service system for facilitating customs clearance and form a legal, international, and convenient business environment and a fair, unified, and efficient market environment.

(2) Implement a negative list of market access and a negative list of foreign investment, minimize the negative list of foreign investment in the Pilot Free Trade Zone, relax investment access, optimize and simplify service links and processes, and promote professional services and advanced manufacture industry such as shipping services to open to the outside world.

(3) Comprehensively deepen the reform of the commercial registration system, carry out the reform of the enterprise name registration system, relax the registration conditions of residence (business premises), effectively release site resources, optimize the registration methods of business scope of business licenses, and implement full-range electronic registration and electronic business licenses reform pilot.

(4) Fully realize the "separation of licenses", all the approval items that can be canceled are canceled, and those that need to be kept for approval should be further optimized and adjusted according to the methods of notification

commitments and strengthening market access management, and further expand the scope of implementing notification commitments.

(5) Drawing on the "single window" standard of United Nations for international trade, implementing coordination, simplification and standardization of trade data, including the logistics operations of seaports, airports and customs special supervision areas, and promoting the expansion of the coverage of "single window" of international trade to service trade. Promote information exchange and service sharing of "single window" of Shanghai international trade and ports along the "Belt and Road".

(6) Establish a safe, efficient and convenient new model of comprehensive customs supervision, deepen the implementation of integration of national customs clearance, "double random, one open" supervision and "Internet + customs" and other measures, dock the "single window" of international trade, and establish rights and responsibilities unified, integrated and intensive, intelligent, efficient, and convenient new model of comprehensive customs supervision.

(7) Optimize the customs clearance process at the port, promote the reform of the supervision methods at each link, explore and publish the average release time of the goods covering each customs link, and maximize the paperless coverage of all aspects of the port operation such as ship arrivals and leave, port operations, and goods clearance, promote the electronic management of trade certification.

(8) Under the premise of controllable risks, deepen the innovation of the international ship registration system and further facilitate the international ship management enterprises to engage in seafarer assignment services.

(9) Set up a free trade port area in the special customs supervision areas such as the Yangshan Bonded Port Area and Shanghai Pudong Airport Comprehensive Bonded Area. Rely on information-based supervision methods, the trade control measures for goods entering the zone will be canceled or simplified to the greatest extent, and the declaration will be simplified to the maximum formalities.

(10) Establish a comprehensive foreign investment promotion agency and an overseas investment public information service platform to carry out business cooperation in legal investigation and lawyer services, commercial dispute

mediation and arbitration, financial accounting and audit services.

(11) Vigorously develop overseas investment insurance, export credit insurance, goods carriage insurance and other services, and provide comprehensive insurance services for enterprises' overseas investment, product technology output, and undertaking major projects of the "Belt and Road".

(12) Improve and perfect the talent recognition standards and recommendation methods that are more in line with the laws of socialist market economy, talent growth and talent development flow and licensing system for foreigners to work in China with unified standards and standardized procedures, and an efficient and convenient visa system for talents.

(13) Explore offshore tax arrangements with international competitiveness to meet the needs of enterprises to participate in international competition and services for the construction of the "Belt and Road". On the premise of not leading to base erosion and profit shifting, based on the background of real trade and services, and combined with the service trade innovation pilot work, innovate the tax policy arrangement for pilot expansion.

In order to build a good legal environment for the shipping industry to thrive in Shanghai Pilot Free Trade Zone, the Supreme People's Court issued the *Opinions on Providing Judicial Security for the Construction of Pilot Free Trade Zones*, and the guarantees which are relevant to shipping companies are briefly described as follows:

(1) People's courts at all levels shall equally protect the legal rights of Chinese and foreign parties, and provide high-quality and efficient judicial guarantees for the construction of free trade zones.

(2) People's courts at all levels shall, on the basis of accurately applying the law, focus on timely adjustment of the judgment scale, actively support the transformation of government functions, respect the autonomy of the parties to the contract, and maintain transaction security.

(3) Strengthen the maritime trial, standardize the construction of the shipping market, support the opening of the shipping service industry in the Pilot Free Trade Zone, enhance the level of international shipping services and enhance the functions of international shipping services. Pay attention to new types of cases relevant to the reform of the ship registration system and others which are

relevant to shipping, and study the legal application and special jurisdiction of the new maritime legal relationship. Confirm relevant rules through the trial of typical cases timely, guide industry behavior, and promote industry development.

(4) Actively support the financial lease enterprises in the Pilot Free Trade Zone to carry out financing business according to the law within the approved scope of business, and fully respect the Chinese and foreign parties' agreement on financial lease contract disputes regarding jurisdiction and application of law. Correctly recognize the validity of a financial lease contract, it shall not be used to invalidate a financial lease contract solely on the grounds of failure to perform relevant procedures.

(5) Encourage the use of diversified mechanisms such as arbitration and mediation to resolve civil and commercial disputes in the Pilot Free Trade Zone, and further explore and improve the dispute resolution mechanism that links litigation and non-litigation. Support the innovative development of arbitration institutions, commercial and industry mediation organizations.

(6) If a wholly foreign-owned enterprise registered in the Pilot Free Trade Zone agrees to submit a commercial dispute to arbitration outside the territory, the relevant arbitration agreement shall not be invalid only on the ground that the dispute does not have foreign-related factors. One or both parties are foreign-invested enterprises registered in the Pilot Free Trade Zone. They agree to submit commercial dispute to extraterritorial arbitration. After a dispute, the parties submit the dispute to extraterritorial arbitration. After the relevant arbitrament is made, they claim that the arbitration agreement is invalid and refuse to acknowledge, endorse or perform.

(7) If a foreign civil entity establishes an enterprise or office as a business agent in the Pilot Free Trade Zone, it can serve it to its business agent. If a foreign civil entity appoints the staff of its branch or the lawyer of a domestic law firm as an agent *ad litem* for a specific time, a specific area or a specific business, it can serve the litigation documents.

(8) For foreign-related civil and commercial cases involving pilot free trade zones tried by the people's court, the parties have agreed to apply foreign laws. If the people's court knows the way to find out, it may inform the parties. Foreign laws that cannot be provided by the parties and cannot be found out according to

the ways stipulated in the international treaties to which my country is a party can be provided by experts the parties jointly appointed before the trial of the first instance.

At the time when the Shanghai Pilot Free Trade Zone deepens reforms and provides a historical opportunity to build a shipping center, *Shanghai Shipping Policy and Law Development White Paper 2017* met with readers again. The book focuses on the development of the rule of law experienced in the construction of the Shanghai International Shipping Center in the past year and is divided into six chapters. Chapter 1 Shipping Policies and Laws, focuses on shipping legislation, sort out the shipping policies and laws issued by the country, Shanghai People's Congress and government departments in 2017, and briefly introduce and analyze the laws and regulations with greater impact or innovation. Chapter 2 Judicial Execution of Shipping Law turns our attention to shipping justice, briefly analyzes Shanghai shipping judiciary's work on shipping policies and legal justice, and selects cases to highlight their efforts to improve shipping judicial services and protect the legal rights and interests of shipping companies. Chapter 3 Administrative Execution of Shipping Policy and Law, focuses on law enforcement, introduces the shipping policy and legal enforcement of Shanghai Shipping Law Enforcement Agency, and selects major maritime, marine, and shipping market law enforcement cases in 2017, and analyzes them combined with relevant regulations. Chapter 4 Literature Review with regard to Shipping Policy and Law, from the perspective of rule of law education, reviews articles published by shipping legal scholars and professionals in various key journals and books published by major publishing houses in 2016. Chapter 5 Annual Shipping Focus, sorts out and briefly analyzes the industry highlights and hot spots relevant to the rule of law of shipping in 2016, especially the important events that happened in the Shanghai shipping market, the hot issues concerned, the innovative measures implemented, and the main achievements achieved, so that readers can understand the progress of the construction of the Shanghai International Shipping Center and the construction of rule of law environment. Chapter 6 is Prospect.

The book is written by LIN Jiang, Deputy Director of Shanghai International Shipping Institute Shipping Policy & Law Institute, Associate Professor of Law

School of Shanghai Maritime University, and External Associate Professor of Tulane University Law School, and he is specifically responsible for the job of writing of chapters 1—6. Mr. Peter MURRAY, a foreign expert of Shanghai International Shipping Institute and a senior consultant of Shanghai Hisun Law Firm, is responsible for proofreading the English version of the book. WANG Yuming and CHEN Ruiying of Shipping Policy & Law Institute of Shanghai International Shipping Institute, and HAN Yunfe of Shanghai Maritime Court participate in the writing and translation of the book.

  The book is funded by Shanghai International Shipping Institute and sponsored by Shanghai Hisun Law Firm. The writing and publication of the book have received the care and guidance of the leaders of Shanghai Maritime University and Shanghai International Shipping Institute. Hereby thank Professor YU Shicheng, former Party Committee Secretary and President of Shanghai Maritime University; Professor ZHEN Hong, Secretary of Shanghai International Shipping Institute, and Professor ZHANG Jieshu, Deputy Secretary of Shanghai International Shipping Institute; Professor WANG Guohua, Dean of Law School of Shanghai Maritime University, and Mr. YE Hongjun, Director of Shipping Policy & Law Institute of Shanghai International Shipping Institute and Professor SHEN Qiuming, Deputy Director of Shipping Policy & Law Institute of Shanghai International Shipping Institute. In addition, the writing of the book has also received the care and support of people from all walks of life from the shipping and judicial systems. The writing team visited dozens of institutions and units for research to ensure the authenticity and accuracy of the information and data provided in the book. At the same time, it also enriches the content of the book, thank you together.

  The purpose of the (series) book is to explore the direction, path and grasp of Shanghai's rule of law in shipping with the community of insight by reviewing the development of Shanghai in shipping policy and law over the years and try to provide suggestions for the construction of Shanghai International Shipping Institute, especially in the formulation of shipping policies, shipping legislation, law enforcement, justice, culture and education of the rule of law. The writing team expects that the (series) book will play a role as an inspiration, bring inspiration to the shipping and legal professions, and trigger a deep-level thinking on the overall construction of the shipping legal environment. Due to the tight writing time, there are inevitable omissions and deficiencies in the book, colleagues in the industry and readers can correct us (e-mail to john. lin @ hisunlaw. com), which will encourage and urge us to continue our diligence, continuous innovation, and work Better, make the (series) book worthy of the title of "Shanghai, China, the world's first".

Shanghai Shipping Policy and Law Development Writing Team
Shanghai International Shipping Institute Shipping Policy & Law Institute
December 31, 2017

Chapter 1 Shipping Laws, Regulations and Policies

The shipping industry is not only a cornerstone for the healthy development of the national economy, but also an important bridge for establishing foreign trade exchanges. As a major shipping country, China has always been committed to establishing a shipping law system that advances with the times according to the development and changes of the market economy. Since 2014, State Council has grasped domestic and foreign friendly trade exchanges and made a major strategic decision, proposing the "Belt and Road" initiative. In the construction of the"Belt and Road", shipping is the link of interconnection, and the rule of law is the guarantee for the development of shipping. The "Belt and Road" initiative has provided new opportunities for the development of the rule of law in shipping and also raised new challenges. Therefore, the innovation and renewal of shipping laws and shipping regulations and policies play a very important role in guiding the operation of shipping economy.

2017 is an important year for the implementation of the "13th Five-Year Plan", a year of deepening the supply-side structural reforms, and also the beginning of the comprehensive implementation of the Party Central Committee and State Council to promote the reform and development of the safe production field. State Council, Ministry of Transport and other relevant departments coordinates and cooperates to ensure the healthy and sustainable development of the shipping industry by policies like canceling and delegating a number of administrative approval matters, establishing a list of rights, and clearing port charges.

On February 14, Ministry of Transport issued the *Notice on Printing and Distributing the Main Points of Safe Production and Work of Transportation in 2017*, which clearly stipulated that: in-depth implementation of the spirit of the 18th National Congress of the CPC and the 3rd, 4th, 5th, 6th Plenary Session of the CPC's 18th National Congress and the spirit of the Central Economic Work Conference, resolutely implement the spirit of General Secretary XI Jinping's important instructions on safe production, according to the deployment of the

State Council's Security Committee and the national safe production video and telephone conference, firmly establish the awareness of the red line and the bottom line, with "safe traffic" being command, take reform and development as the driving force, take the implementation of safety responsibilities as the core, adhere to the problem-oriented, highlight hidden danger investigation and governance and risk management and control, solidly promote the construction of safe production infrastructure equipment, solidly promote the systematic, standardized and normalized work system of safe production, continuously improve management level of safe production, resolutely curb major accidents, and make every effort to ensure that the situation of transportation safe production continues to be stable.

On June 20, National Development and Reform Commission and State Oceanic Administration formulated and released the *Vision on the construction of the "Belt and Road" Initiative for Maritime Cooperation* (hereinafter referred to as Vision). The Vision is the first time that the Chinese government proposed a Chinese plan to promote the maritime cooperation in the construction of the "Belt and Road" since the *Vision and Action of Promotion of the Joint Construction of the Silk Road Economic Belt and the 21st Century Maritime Silk Road* was released on March 28, 2015. It is also one of the achievements of the leaders of the "Belt and Road" International Cooperation Summit Forum. Vision proposed that we are willing to work with all countries along the 21st Century Maritime Silk Road to carry out all-round and multi-disciplinary maritime cooperation, jointly create an open and inclusive cooperation platform, establish an active and pragmatic blue partnership, and create a "blue engine" for sustainable development.

The construction of the "Belt and Road" is a long-term management general plan for China's opening up and cooperation with foreign countries. It is of great significance for comprehensively improving China's level of all-round opening up. To construct China (Shanghai) Pilot Free Trade Zone (hereinafter referred to as Shanghai Pilot Free Trade Zone) into a bridgehead serving the construction of China's "Belt and Road" and promoting market players to go out is a new requirement that General Secretary XI Jinping put forward to Shanghai from a global perspective. On October 11, Shanghai Municipal Government issued the

Action Plan for Shanghai and Serve the Construction of China's "Belt and Road" to Play the Role of Bridgehead, which plays a powerful role in strengthening institutional guarantees, integrating policy resources, and forming the service of construction of the "Belt and Road" for the country.

In 2017, the state formulated various laws and policies to improve China's shipping development policy system and create a fair environment for participating in international competition; improve laws and regulations and standards, improve ship technology policies and standards, clean up and regulate administrative approval matters, and improve rights and interests protection mechanism, which provides important support for the development of China's shipping industry. It will have important guiding significance for promoting the deepening reform of shipping enterprises, adjusting the structure of shipping capacity, achieving transformation and upgrading, and vigorously developing modern shipping service industry, and accelerating the construction of international shipping centers.

1 Laws, Regulations and Policies Judicial Interpretations

1.1 Laws, Regulations and Rules
1.1.1 Shipping Management

Implementation Regulations of the People's Republic of China on International Shipping Regulations (Amendment)

Opinions of Ministry of Transport on Promoting the Development of Non-stop Transportation in Rivers and Seas on Specific Routes

Provisions on Administrative Penalties for Maritime Affairs of the People's Republic of China

Administrative Measures for Credit Information of Water Transport Market (Trial)

China (Shanghai) Pilot Free Trade Zone Shipping Law Construction Convention

1.1.2 Port Channel

Regulations on the Administration of Domestic Water Transport (2017 Amendment)

Chapter 1 Shipping Laws, Regulations and Policies

Port Law of the People's Republic of China (Amended in 2017)

Provisions on the Safety Management of Hazardous Goods at Ports

Notice of General Office of Ministry of Transport on Printing and Distributing the *Port Shore Power Layout Plan*

Administrative Measures on Credit Information of Water Transport Market (Trial)

Law on the Prevention and Treatment of Water Pollution of the People's Republic of China

1.1.3 Ship Management

Decision of Ministry of Transport on Amending the *Regulations on the Prevention and Treatment of Marine Environment Pollution by Ships of the People's Republic of China and Relevant Operations*

Ship Safety Supervision Regulations of the People's Republic of China

Notice of General Office of Ministry of Transport on Trial Operation of some functions of Shipping Management of the Integrated Management Information System for Water Transport Construction

Notice of General Office of Ministry of Transport on Printing and Distributing the Main Points of Safe Production and Work of Transportation in 2017

Nairobi International Convention on the Removal of Wrecks 2007

1.1.4 Crew Management

Crew Training Management Regulations of the People's Republic of China (Amended in 2017)

Notice of Maritime Safety Administration of Ministry of Transport on Further Strengthening the Management of Reserve Funds of Seafarers' Outgoing

Notice of Maritime Safety Administration of Ministry of Transport on Soliciting Opinions on the Three Measures including the *Credit Management Measures for Crew*

Notice of Maritime Safety Administration of Ministry of Transport on the Implementation of the *Outline of Seafarer Crew Training*

Crew Regulations of the People's Republic of China (Amended in 2017)

1.1.5 Finance, Tax

Customs Law of the People's Republic of China (Amended in 2017)

Notice of Ministry of Transport on Printing and Distributing the *Guidelines for the Application of Project Incentive Funds for Port Ships to Use Port Power in 2016—2018*

Notice of General Office of Ministry of Transport on the Management Issue of Defining that Ships Enjoying the Preferential Tax Policies for Chinese-Funded "Convenience Flag" Run a Domestic Carriage after Switching Hanging a Five-Star Red Flag

Ship Tonnage Tax Law of the People's Republic of China

Port Charges and Billing Methods

1.1.6　Free Trade Zone and "Belt and Road"

Notice of State Council on Printing and Distributing the Plan for Comprehensively Deepening the Reform and Opening up of China (Shanghai) Pilot Free Trade Zone

Decision of State Council on the Temporary Adjustment of Relevant Administrative Regulations, State Council Documents and Administrative Rules and Regulations Approved by State Council in Pilot Free Trade Zone

Notice of General Office of State Council on Printing and Distributing Special Administrative Measures for Foreign Investment Access (Negative List) (2017 Edition) in Pilot Free Trade Zone

Guidance on Further Guiding and Regulating the Direction of Overseas Investment

Notice on Launching Special Action to Support Small and Medium-sized Enterprises to Participate in the Construction of the "Belt and Road"

Supreme People's Court Released the Second Batch of Typical Cases involving the Construction of "Belt and Road"

Guiding Opinions of China Insurance Regulatory Commission on the Service of Insurance Industry for Construction of the "Belt and Road"

Opinions of the Supreme People's Court on Providing Judicial Guarantees for the Construction of Pilot Free Trade Zone

Convention on the Construction of Shipping Legal System in China (Shanghai) Pilot Free Trade Zone

Notice of State Council on Several Measures of Expanding Opening to Foreign Countries and Actively Using Foreign Investment

Action Plan for Shanghai to Serve the Construction of China's "Belt and Road" and Play the Role of Bridgehead

1.1.7 Other

Several Opinions of Shanghai Municipal People's Government on Further Expanding Opening and Accelerating the Construction of a New Open Economic System

Notice of Maritime Safety Administration of Ministry of Transport on Printing and Distributing the *Measures for the Control of Discretionary Powers in Maritime Administrative License*

Marine Environment Protection Law of the People's Republic of China (Amended in 2017)

Supreme People's Court *Several Opinions on Further Protecting and Regulating Parties' Performance of Administrative Action Rights according to the Law*

2 Analysis and Comments of Laws, Regulations and Judicial Interpretations

2.1 *Opinions of the Supreme People's Court on Providing Judicial Guarantees for the Construction of Pilot Free Trade Zone*

On December 30, 2016, Supreme People's Court printed and issued the *Opinions on Providing Judicial Guarantees for the Construction of Pilot Free Trade Zones* (hereinafter referred to as *Opinions*).

2.1.1 Background

Pilot Free Trade Zone is a test field for China's reform and opening up, and an important window for China to build a new open economic system. People's courts have taken on the important responsibility of providing judicial guarantees for the construction of the Pilot Free Trade Zone. Summarizing trial experience in a timely manner, and providing trial guidance to people's courts at all levels across the country, which has become an urgent need for justice practice. In order to give full play to the trial function of the people's courts and guarantee the construction of China's Pilot Free Trade Zone, Supreme Court combined the trial practice and formulated *Opinions* for the trial work of people's courts involved in Pilot Free Trade Zone.

2.1.2 Main content

There are 12 Articles in *Opinions*, covering the content: firstly, to correctly exercise the functions of criminal, civil, administrative and other judicial functions; secondly, to support the innovation of enterprises in Pilot Free Trade Zone according to law, and to encourage the exploration of new business models; thirdly, to explore the reform and innovation of trial procedures; fourthly, to focus on summarizing trial experience and strengthening forward-looking research.

1) Pay attention to the reform of ship registration system and new types of shipping cases

The maritime trial is of special significance to guarantee the construction of Pilot Free Trade Zone. *Opinions* proposes to pay attention to the reform of the ship registration system and other new types of cases relevant to shipping, and to study the legal application and special jurisdiction of the new maritime legal relationship. Promptly confirm relevant rules through the trial of typical cases, standardize the construction of the shipping market, support the opening of the shipping service industry in Pilot Free Trade Zone, improve the level of international shipping services and enhance the functions of international shipping services.

2) Support financial leasing and cross-border e-commerce

In order to support the innovation of enterprises in Pilot Free Trade Zone and encourage the exploration of new business models, *Opinions* fully respects the parties' agreement on jurisdiction and the application of the law, maintain the effect of the contract according to the law, and support innovative operations modes in industries such as financial leasing and cross-border e-commerce.

3) Establish a diversified dispute resolution mechanism

In actively exploring the reform and innovation of trial procedures, *Opinions* supports the establishment of a diversified dispute resolution mechanism in Pilot Free Trade Zone, and encourages people's courts at all levels to form trials mechanism that match the characteristics of cases involving Pilot Free Trade Zone based on the summary of trial experience. It is required to increase support for arbitration and increase the internationalization of arbitration in commercial disputes. At the same time, it provides that correctly determining the effect of arbitration agreements, exploring innovation in trial procedures, and establishing a reasonable foreign law review mechanism.

4) Strengthen forward-looking research work

Opinions stipulates that:"trying cases involving Pilot Free Trade Zone well, summarizing replicating experience. People's courts of high-level should pay full attention to the trial of cases involving Pilot Free Trade Zone, and strengthen forward-looking research work. The hot spots and difficult issues found by court of all places in the trial of relevant cases of Pilot Free Trade Zone should be studied and summarized in a timely manner to form a response opinion and make recommendations to Supreme People's Court in a timely manner." They should constantly summary trial experience in cases involving Pilot Free Trade Zone, identify and solve problems in a timely manner, give full play to the functions of the people's courts, and provide better and more efficient judicial guarantees for the construction of Pilot Free Trade Zone.

2.1.3 Summary

On the third anniversary of the operation of Pilot Free Trade Zone, it is timely to sum up trial experience and provide trial guidance for the trial work of people's courts at all levels in cases involving Pilot Free Trade Zone, which has become an urgent need for justice practice. *Opinions* aims to give full play to the guiding role of Supreme People's Court in work, to unify the understanding, update the trial concept, and support the various reform measures implemented in Pilot Free Trade Zone with practical measures to solve problems with the urgent need to be resolved and with universality in the justice practice involving Pilot Free Trade Zone. In the new historical period, people's courts will give full play to the role of trial, and provide solid and reliable judicial guarantees for the healthy development of Pilot Free Trade Zone.

2.2 *Nairobi International Convention on the Removal of Wrecks 2007*
2.2.1 Background

Shipwrecks not only threaten the safety of passing ships and crew to varying degrees, but also cause serious harm to the marine and coastal environment. In recent years, due to continuous efforts to enhance the safety of shipping carriage, the incidence of marine disasters has declined sharply. However, it has been reported that the number of abandoned wreckage has increased, which poses serious challenges to coastal countries and the shipping industry. The *Nairobi International Convention on the Removal of Wrecks 2007* (hereinafter referred to as *Convention*) was adopted at the International Maritime Organization Diplomatic Conference held in Nairobi, Kenya in May 2007 and entered into force on April 14, 2015. With the approval of State Council, China submitted the accession letter of *Convention* to International Maritime Organization on November 11, 2016, and *Convention* entered into force for China on February 11, 2017.

2.2.2 Main content

1) *Convention* clearly stipulates the rights and obligations of the coastal contracting states to remove wreckage in their exclusive economic zone

(1) Obligations of contracting parties. Article 5 of *Convention* stipulates that contracting parties shall require the captain and operator of a ship hanging its flag to report to the affected country in a timely manner when its ship becomes wreckage due to a marine accident. The affected states as contracting parties shall assess and confirm whether the wreckage constitutes a hazard according to Article 6 of *Convention*. Articles 7 and 8 of *Convention* further stipulate that if the affected country has reason to believe that the wreckage constitutes a hazard, it shall ensure that all feasible measures are taken to determine the exact location of the wreckage and mark it, and take all appropriate measures to publish the specific details of marks of wreckage. Article 9, Paragraph 1 of *Convention* also stipulates that, in order to facilitate the removal of wreckage, when the affected country confirms that the wreckage constitutes a hazard, it shall immediately notify the ship registration state and the registered owner, and shall negotiate with the ship registration state and other countries affected by the wreckage on measures taken against the wreckage.

(2) Rights of the contracting parties. Article 9 of *Convention* stipulates that the wreckage shall be removed, forcedly removed and immediately removed within a time limit. The affected country should first set a reasonable time limit, require the ship owner to remove the wreckage within that time limit, and notify the ship owner in writing of the set time limit, and state that if the shipowner does not remove the wreckage within this time limit, the country can remove the

wreckage and the fee should be borne by shipowner. If the shipowner does not remove the wreckage within the set time limit, or the shipowner cannot be contacted, or in the event that immediate action is required and the affected country has notified the ship registration state and shipowner, the affected country can remove wreckage in the most practicable and fastest way available and according to safety and marine environment protection considerations.

2) Compulsory liability insurance or financial guarantee

The shipowner of a ship hanging the flag of the contracting party should provide compulsory insurance or provide financial guarantees for the removal of the wreckage according to the amount of liability limitation to which it is entitled; the contracting party should ensure that ships sailing into the domestic waters or territorial sea meet the requirements of compulsory insurance or financial guarantee. According to Article 12, Paragraph 1, of *Convention*, the registered owner of a ship of 300 gross tonnage and above and hanging the flag of a contracting party shall hold wreckage removal liability insurance or other financial guarantees in an amount equivalent to the amount of limitation of liability stipulated in the applicable domestic law or international conventions, but in any case, not exceeding the amount calculated according to Article 6 (1) (b) of the amended the *Convention on Limitation of Liability for Maritime claims, 1976*.

3) Direct litigation against the insurer or financial guarantor

Convention stipulates for a direct litigation system against the wreckage removal insurer or financial guarantor, namely, a subject that has the right to claim for the confirmation, marking and removal of wreckage has a direct right to claim compensation for damage to the wreckage removal insurer or financial guarantor. Article 12 Paragraph 10 of *Convention* stipulates that claims for any fee happened under *Convention* can be brought directly to the insurer who covers responsibility for the removal of the wreckage or other person who provides financial guarantee for the shipowner. The insurer or financial guarantor can invoke the exemption and limitation of compensation liability that the shipowner has the right to invoke.

2.2.3 Summary

Convention provides a legal basis for countries planning to remove or has removed ship wreckage that may threaten the safety of navigation and the marine environment, and provides uniform international rules to quickly and effectively remove ship wreckage located outside the territorial sea, as well as in territories of countries, including territorial waters, selectively apply the rules. On the one hand, it clarifies the rights and obligations of the coastal contracting parties for the removal of wreckage in their exclusive economic zone, and ensures that all countries can remove the wreckage in a timely and effective manner and obtain financial guarantee; on the other hand, it stipulates an obligation of registered shipowner to locate, mark and remove wreckage deemed hazardous in the convention area. To ensure the performance capability of shipowner, *Convention* stipulates that strict liability of shipowners and compulsory insurance systems and obtain the *Certificate* issued by the contracting parties, which means that the ship's performance capability is proved by *Certificate* issued by the competent authority.

In the future, Chinese ships of more than 300 gross tonnage will need to hold insurance or other financial guarantees that meet the requirements of *Convention*, and apply for a *Wreckage Removal Liability Insurance or Other Financial Guarantee Certificate* to be carried with the ship to meet the requirements for ship performance. The implementation of *Convention* on the one hand guarantees that ship wreckage in China's sea areas can be effectively removed in a timely manner, on the other hand, it also increases the operating cost of the coastal carriage industry. At the same time, more targeted insurance products are also needed.

2.3 Implementation Regulations of the People's Republic of China on International Shipping Regulations (Amendment)

Ministry of Transport issued the *Implementation Regulations of the People's Republic of China on International Shipping Regulations* (Amendment) (hereinafter referred to as the *Amendment*) on March 13, 2017, which will take effect as of the date of publication.

2.3.1 Background

In order to promote the reform of "License before Certificate" and implementation of the contents of the *Decision of State Council on Revising Some Administrative Regulations* (State Council Order No. 666) issued in

February 2016, State Council decided to revise administrative regulations including *International Shipping Regulations*. At the same time, for the international shipping field, it will deeply implement the requirements for the reform of "releasing, supervising and serving", strengthen the post and formative supervision methods such as supervision and inspection of the international shipping market, and use system innovation to stimulate market vitality. As for the *Implementation Regulations* itself, it is necessary to delete or modify some of the articles that do not fit articles of reform of current taxes, invoices and statistical systems to adapt to the reform situation.

2.3.2　Main content

Amendment mainly revises the contents of 32 Articles of the *Implementation Regulations*, mainly making changes or adjustments around the following aspects:

(1) Implement the revision made by State Council's reform and deployment of "License before Certificate". According to the requirements of the revised *International Shipping Regulations* that applicants must "acquire corporation legal person qualifications" in advance, it is clear that the subjects applying for international shipping carriage services and international shipping management business are unified as Chinese corporation legal persons. The content of "License before Certificate" has been deleted and the application materials have been revised accordingly. The revised content involves 7 articles.

(2) Implement the revision required by the reform of "releasing, supervising and serving". Firstly, strengthen safety management, and add international ship security certificates, safety management certificates, compliance certification of safe operation and anti-pollution capabilities and other materials into submitted materials of applying to operated international ship carriage business; secondly, simplify relevant application materials; thirdly, licenses that target domestic enterprise to operate international shipping agency business have been canceled; fourthly, increase the relevant requirements for the implementation of the freight rate report system; fifthly, add letter of guarantees, liability insurance and other financial liability guarantee methods for NVOCC operators. The revised content involves 12 Articles.

(3) Implement the tax and fee reform of "replace business tax with VAT" and the reform of invoice and statistical system, mainly deleted the that no longer

using special invoices for the international shipping industry and the statistical reports that have been abolished by the National Bureau of Statistics. It also supplements the principle requirements for reporting relevant statistical information. The revised content involves 5 Articles.

(4) In connection with the *Port Law* and supporting regulations, the relevant contents of the international shipping goods storage, international shipping container station and yard business were deleted. The revised content involves 9 Articles.

(5) Other complete revision mainly modified the expression of some Articles. For example, "Ministry of Foreign Trade and Economic Cooperation" was changed to "Ministry of Commerce" combined with the fact that the Ministry of Transport authorized the Shanghai Shipping Exchange to publish the list of relevant operators and samples of bills of lading on its website. A total of 12 Articles are involved.

2.3.3 Summary

The *Amendment* as a revision to the *Implementation Regulations*, an administrative regulation, has facilitated the in-depth advancement of the reform of "License before Certificate", which mainly involves the international shipping carriage business and international ship management business in the shipping field. The biggest highlight of the *Amendment* is that it is allowed to engage in the international shipping carriage process in three steps and two steps. According to the characteristics of the industry, it is practical to simplify administration and decentralization, and attract funds to the market, which will help stimulate the vitality of the shipping market.

In addition to the above-mentioned reforms, the *Amendment* further clarified the regulatory boundaries. The international shipping and its auxiliary business operators can self-check whether the relevant certificates are legal and effective during the operation. This facilitates the enterprise to give itself more room for autonomy. Since 2008, the shipping low tide has continued to spread, and many enterprises engaged in NVOCC business have been affected by their liquidity. In order to reduce the burden on enterprises, Ministry of Transport tried out the margin liability insurance and margin letter of guarantee system in 2010 and 2013, which provided a variety of alternative financial liability guarantee methods for NVOCC. While protecting the interests of shippers, effectively alleviating the funding pressure of NVOCC. The promulgation of the *Amendment* solidified the relevant systems in the form of ministerial orders, which could effectively stimulate market vitality, promote industry development, and made the burden reduction measures more powerful.

2.4 Opinions of Ministry of Transport on Promoting the Development of Non-stop Transportation in Rivers and Seas on Specific Routes

On April 18, 2017, Water Transport Bureau of Ministry of Transport issued the *Opinions of Ministry of Transport on Promoting the Development of Non-stop Transportation in Rivers and Seas on Specific Routes* (hereinafter referred to as the *Opinions*).

2.4.1 Background

Promoting the development of non-stop carriage between rivers and seas is an important part of deepening the structural reform of the transportation supply side, and plays an important role in improving the function of the golden waterway of Yangtze River and constructing a modern comprehensive transportation system. In order to implement the outline of the development plan of Yangtze River Economic Belt, earnestly implement the decision-making and deployment of promoting the development of Yangtze River Economic Belt by relying on golden waterways, and use the main line of promoting the structural reform of the transportation supply side, to insist on deepening reform and innovative development; develop safely according to laws and regulations; the general principles of leading role and demonstration affect and market promotion, strive to promote the safe, efficient and green development of non-stop carriage between rivers and seas, speed up the improvement of quality and efficiency of water carriage, and better serve the development of Yangtze River Economic Belt. Water Transport Bureau issued the *Opinions*.

2.4.2 Main content

The *Opinions* revolves around two aspects as following main tasks and guarantee measures:

1) Main tasks

(1) To formulate and improve the regulations and rules for the non-stop

ships between rivers and seas: according to the actual situation of specific sea areas and specific routes, formulate and implement the interim rules and construction specifications for the legal inspection of the non-stop ships between rivers and seas in the specific routes of Yangtze River Economic Belt.

(2) Strengthen research and application of non-stop ship types between rivers and seas: encourage shipping enterprises and scientific research institutions and design units to carry out joint research and give priority to the promotion of research and application of non-stop container ships between rivers and seas and other types from Yangtze River trunk line to Ningbo Zhoushan Port and from Yangtze River trunk line to Shanghai Port Yangshan Port Area.

(3) Strengthen the construction of infrastructures such as port waterways: strengthen the construction of the main port collection and distribution system in Yangtze River Delta region, and the facilities such as supporting docks and anchorages for non-stop carriage between rivers and seas and preparations for bridge reconstruction.

(4) Actively cultivate the non-stop carriage between rivers and seas market: give priority to the development of non-stop carriage between rivers and seas of the dry bulk goods and container in Yangtze River Trunk Line and Yangtze River Delta region, give play to the leading role of large shipping enterprises, and strengthen the integration of the carriage upstream and downstream industry chain resources.

(5) Promote the safe and green development of non-stop carriage between rivers and seas: strengthen the implementation of ship carriage laws and regulations, and strictly implement the responsibility of corporation safety subjects.

(6) Optimize the management of non-stop carriage between rivers and seas: study and formulate the crewing standards of non-stop ships between rivers and seas, and formulate regulations on the safety management of non-stop ships between rivers and seas.

(7) Improve the emergency capacity of non-stop carriage between rivers and seas: promote the implementation of the *National Water Carriage Safety Supervision and Rescue System Layout Plan*, and optimize the rescue guarantee and emergency response layout.

2) Safeguards

First is to strengthen organizational leadership. All relevant provincial transportation authorities and maritime management agencies should attach great importance to the non-stop carriage between rivers and seas, strengthen leadership, clarify the division of labor, and strengthen coordination.

Second is to increase policy support, giving priority to supporting the construction of port collection, distribution and transportation projects relevant to non-stop carriage between rivers and seas, and encouraging local governments to introduce preferential policies for the development of non-stop carriage between rivers and seas.

Third is to strengthen scientific and technological information services. Relevant scientific research departments should strengthen technical support and guidance for non-stop carriage between rivers and seas, strengthen market analysis, timely release information, and guide the orderly development of the market.

2.4.3 Summary

With the rapid economic development of Yangtze River Basin with Shanghai as the leader, Shanghai Port, as a port city with both economic hinterland and shipping hub characteristics, has achieved effective communication with the six provinces and two cities in Yangtze River Basin through the golden channel of Yangtze River. The container freight volume, carriage capacity and strategic position of Yangtze River Basin provide favorable conditions for accelerating economic development in the hinterland of Yangtze River. The development of non-stop carriage between rivers and seas has been slow due to the influence of channels, policies, and Shunt restriction of other transportation modes. The *Opinions* has accelerated the development of non-stop container carriage between rivers and seas to a certain extent.

The *Opinions* requires that, based on the characteristics of sailing inland rivers and specific sea areas, break through the current regulations systems, scientifically formulate laws and regulations on non-stop ships between rivers and seas to optimize transportation organizations, and promote the coordinated development of ships, waterways and ports. In the non-stop carriage between rivers and seas, it is necessary to strengthen the guidance and regulation of laws and regulations, and strive by 2020, to establish and improve the regulations and management systems of non-stop carriage between rivers and seas in Yangtze River Economic Belt, and basically form the non-stop carriage system between rivers and seas from Yangtze River and Yangtze River Delta to Ningbo Zhoushan Port and Shanghai Yangshan Port Area. The proportion of waterway collection, distribution and carriage is further increased, and the economic and social benefits of the non-stop carriage between rivers and seas are shown. By 2030, construct a safe, efficient and green non-stop carriage system between rivers and seas, and the economic and social benefits of non-stop carriage between rivers and seas will be significantly improved, providing strong support for the development of Yangtze River Economic Belt.

2.5 *Provisions on Administrative Penalties for Maritime Affairs of the People's Republic of China*

The *Decision of Ministry of Transport on Revising the Provisions on Administrative Penalties for Maritime Affairs of the People's Republic of China* was adopted by the 8th Ministerial Conference on May 17, 2017, and announced on December 27, 2017.

2.5.1 Background

According to the requirements of simplified administration and decentralization, Ministry of Transport has canceled and delegated a batch of administrative licenses, and major changes have taken place in the maritime laws and regulations system. This revision was made on the basis of the 2015 edition of the *Provisions on Administrative Penalties for Maritime Affairs* (hereinafter referred to as the *Provisions*).

2.5.2 Main content

(1) Change the provisions of Article 16 Paragraph 3 from "domestic sailing ships do not apply for entry and exit visas according to regulations, and international sailing ships do not apply for import and export shore procedures according to regulations" to "domestic sailing ships which enter and exit ports do not reports the ship's voyage plan, airworthiness status, crewing, loading goods and passenger according to regulations to maritime management agency, and international sailing ships do not apply for import and export shore procedures

according to regulations", it can be seen that the visa system for ships entering and leaving the port has been formally canceled and stipulated in the form of laws that the *Visa for Ships* and the ship's IC card are also canceled at the same time. Inland navigation ships and sea ships that have inland navigation was implemented a new port entry and exit reporting system. Ship port entry and exit are more convenient. Ship operations are also significantly decreased, benefiting more than 300,000 ships.

(2) The penalties for violations of the collection of port fees in Article 21, and the penalties for violations of laws and regulations on the discharge of polluting gases by motor vessels in Article 38 and Article 39 of the original 2015 edition have been deleted. Ministry of Transport announced that China has set up ship emission control zones in the water areas of Pearl River Delta, Yangtze River Delta, and Bohai Rim (Beijing, Tianjin and Hebei) from January 2016 to control the emission of sulfur oxides, nitrogen oxides and particulate matter from ships, in order to lay the foundation for comprehensively controlling ships air pollution. Ships operating in the emission control area may adopt alternative measures equivalent to emission control requirements such as connection to shore power, use of clean energy, and tail gas post-treatment.

2.5.3 Summary

This revision adapts to the development situation of the maritime administrative examination and approval system and guarantees the suitability of the new *Regulations* in terms of the revision of administrative licenses. At the same time, the regulations that changed in the higher-level laws are revised and the coordination with other regulations is compared one by one to avoid conflicts and legal competition.

The ship entry and exit visa system was canceled in due course. The maritime management agency will check the ship port entry and exit report status through the ship port entry and exit report service network, and if necessary, combined with GPS, AIS, CCTV and other means to verify the ship's sailing dynamics and onboard personnel information and establishes information sharing and joint inspection mechanisms with relevant units, strengthens ship safety supervision, and ensures the stability of the water traffic safety situation. China adopts air pollution control measures that internationally recognized under the framework of the *International Convention for the Prevention of Pollution from Ships* in aspect of controlling the emission of pollution gas from ships, and adopts stricter regulations on ship emission reduction measures, and significant progress has been made in the prevention and control of ship pollution.

2.6 Law on the Prevention and Treatment of Water Pollution of the People's Republic of China

The *Decision of the Standing Committee of the National People's Congress on Revising the Law on the Prevention and Treatment of Water Pollution of the People's Republic of China* was adopted by the 28th meeting of the Standing Committee of the 12th National People's Congress on June 27, 2017.

2.6.1 Background

At present, the quality of China's water environment is still not optimistic, and the task of water pollution prevention is arduous. According to a series of new systems and measures established in the *Water Pollution Prevention Action Plan* issued by State Council, it is necessary to revise the water pollution prevention law to standardize and legalize the various system measures established in the *Water Pollution Prevention Action Plan*.

2.6.2 Main content

(1) Strengthen local government responsibilities. Governments at all levels, especially local governments at or above the county level, must bear real responsibility for the quality of the water environment in their administrative areas.

(2) Strengthen joint prevention and ecological protection of water pollution in river basins. It stipulates that the competent department of environment protection under State Council shall, in conjunction with relevant departments and provincial governments, establish linkage coordination mechanisms for water environment protection in important rivers and lakes, strengthen joint prevention and control of water pollution and carry out regular monitoring.

(3) Improve the water pollution prevention supervision and management system. First is to do a good job in linking up the discharge permit with the total amount control and discharge according to standards, and stipulate that the discharge permit should specify the requirements of the water pollutant type, concentration, total amount and discharge destination. Second is to improve the

environmental monitoring system and clarify the self-monitoring obligations of the polluting units. Third is to establish a list system of toxic and harmful water pollutants to strengthen risk management.

(4) Strengthen water pollution prevention measures in key areas. Specific regulations are made on industrial wastewater management, pollution prevention of groundwater, agriculture and rural water and ships.

(5) Strengthen the drinking water safety guarantee system. In order to ensure the safety of drinking water for urban and rural residents, the provisions of "guaranteeing the safety of drinking water" are clearly added to the legislative purpose, and a special chapter of "protection of drinking water sources and other special water bodies" is added to further improve the management system of drinking water source protection areas.

(6) Strict legal liability. According to the spirit of *Environment Protection Law*, strict legal liabilities are stipulated for illegal acts such as discharge of water pollutants without a certificate or non-certification, exceeding the standard, and exceeding the total amount, and are connected to continuous punishment daily and arrest measures stipulated in the *Environment Protection Law*.

According to the *Environment Protection Law* and the requirements of the reform of the administrative examination and approval system, the relevant regulations such as the declaration of pollution discharge registration and the examination and approval of ship operations should be deleted.

2.6.3 Summary

The revision of the *Water Pollution Prevention and Control Law* this time is based on the actual situation of lack of water resources, which is more conducive to the protection of water resources; according to the current situation of water resources, the corresponding adjustments have been made to ensure the strength of protection of water resources and make up for the original inadequacy of legal guarantees. which makes the implementation of the *Water Pollution Prevention and Control Law* more comprehensive.

2.7 Port Charges and Billing Methods

The *Notice of Ministry of Transport and National Development and Reform Commission on Printing and Distributing Port Charges and Billing*

Methods was announced on July 12, 2017. New *Port Charges and Billing Methods* (hereinafter referred to as the *Methods*) should be implemented from September 15, 2017 and the validity period is 5 years.

2.7.1 Background

According to the overall plan of the Party Central Committee for comprehensive deepening of reforms, in order to implement State Council's requirements to further clean up and regulate service charges relevant to enterprise operations and reduce the burden on enterprises, Ministry of Transport and National Development and Reform Commission followed the marketization principle to further reduce government pricing projects and optimizing billing methods, which are the main tasks. Focus on tugboat charging reforms, continue to deepen the reform of the port price formation mechanism and further promote logistics cost reduction and efficiency gain.

2.7.2 Main content

(1) Reform the tugboat fee billing method. The tugboat fee is adjusted from the tugboat horsepower and usage time to the tugboat size and type, and the tugboat fee unit price is uniformly set.

(2) Optimize the structure of ship pilot charges. Further optimize the structure of pilot charges. Pilot agencies should actively promote "sunshine pilot" to further improve the level of pilot services. It is clarified that the technical service fee for leading offshore mobile platforms to sail in China's water areas other than pilot services should be subject to market adjustment prices, and the leading service unit should negotiate with the entrusting party to confirm the specific charging standards.

(3) Further reduce government pricing and charging items. The port operation fee for domestic passenger transportation and tourist ships should be included in the scope of port operation contract fee, which is paid by the domestic passenger transportation enterprise to the port operator and is no longer directly charged to passengers.

(4) Tally service fee is subject to market-adjusted prices. It is clear that tally service fee are subject to market-adjusted prices, and all provincial transportation authorities are required to accelerate the introduction of competition mechanisms to promote the smooth and orderly development of tally, continuously stimulate

market vitality, and strengthen market supervision and industry self-regulation.

(5) No more unified regulations on more preferential berthing fees and free stockpiling and storage periods for ships on international routes. The policy background has undergone major changes. From the perspective of promoting fair competition, the government should not intervene in the market too much. Consider berthing fee as the government's guidance price ceiling management, and stockpiling and storage fee as market-adjusted prices. Whether and how many concessions should be negotiated by enterprises, and there is no need for uniform government regulations.

2.7.3 Summary

After the revision of the *Methods*, another government pricing and charging project was reduced to further reduce the burden on enterprises. It is expected that port enterprises can reduce the burden on shipping enterprises by another 200 million yuan per year, and the market-oriented and standardized port charging system will be further improved. The implementation of the *Methods* is conducive to further standardizing port charges. The competent pricing departments at all levels supervise the implementation of the charging policy, urge and guide port operators and pilot agencies to implement various regulations on port charges, and provide services according to the principles of fairness, lawfulness, honesty and credibility.

2.8 Port Dangerous Goods Safety Management Regulations

The newly revised *Port Dangerous Goods Safety Management Regulations* (hereinafter referred to as the *Regulations*) was adopted by the 14th Ministerial Conference of Ministry of Transport on August 29, 2017, and announced on September 4, 2017.

2.8.1 Background

With the rapid development of the port, the throughput and storage of dangerous goods in the port are getting larger, more and more varieties, and the pressure of safety management is increasing. After comprehensively sorting out dangerous goods management laws and regulations, carefully looking for and analyzing the weak links and outstanding problems in safety management and system construction, it is found that there are still inadequacies in the safety management system and the implementation of corporation responsibility.

2.8.2 Main content

(1) Improve the safety management responsibility system. The responsibilities of transportation (port) management departments at all levels are further clarified, and the provincial transportation authorities were strengthened to guide and supervise the subordinate departments.

(2) Adjust and optimize some license management rights. First is to adjust the standard for reviewing the safety conditions of dangerous goods port construction projects from the project level to the degree of danger. Second is that the local port administrative department should uniformly implement the management and supervision and inspection of dangerous goods port operation qualifications.

(3) Implement the responsibility of the subject of enterprise safe production. Increase the content of that dangerous goods port operators should improve the safe production organization, take and use safe production funds, strengthen the safety production education and training of practitioners, and strengthen relevant requirements for loading and unloading management personnel to obtain employment qualifications and allocate full-time safe production management personnel to clarify that port operators of dangerous goods should carry out safe production risk identification and evaluation, formulate specific control measures for different risks, and implement control responsibilities.

(4) Establish and improve the safety management system. Three new management systems including information management system, key link management system and credit management system have been added.

(5) Strengthen the administrative coercion and punishment for illegal acts of enterprises. It supplements and improves that the port administrative department can take measures to stop power supply according to law to force port operators of dangerous goods to fulfill their decisions, and at the same time set penalties within the scope of regulations for six other situations.

2.8.3 Summary

The revision of the *Regulations* has been improved in many aspects, laying a solid foundation for better safety management of dangerous goods in ports. In terms of safe production, adjustments were made according to the newly revised *Safe Production Law* in 2014. While solving some new problems found in the safety management of dangerous goods in ports in recent years in many places, many new management experiences have also been integrated. This is an important part of accelerating the improvement of the safety supervision system and safety production responsibility system for dangerous goods in ports, and is conducive to the improvement of dual prevention and control and joint supervision mechanisms.

2.9 Administrative Measures on Credit Information of Water Transport Market (Trial)

On September 6, 2017, Ministry of Transport formulated and issued the *Administrative Measures on Credit Information of Water Transport Market (Trial)* (Jiao Ban Shui [2017] No.128, hereinafter referred to as the *Measures*).

2.9.1 Background

The social credit system is an important foundation for economic and social development. The Party Central Committee and State Council attach great importance to the construction of the social credit system. In May 2015, Ministry of Transport issued the *Several Opinions on Strengthening the Construction of the Credit System in the Transportation Industry* (Jiao Zheng R & D [2015] No. 75), proposing standards for improving the credit system and main tasks of the five aspects to effectively strengthen the construction of the credit system of the transportation industry and promote the scientific development of transportation. At present, the construction of the credit system in the field of water transportation in China is still in its infancy. In order to strengthen the construction of the credit system in the water transportation market, drawing on the successful experience and practices of credit information management in relevant industries, Ministry of Transport has formulated and issued the *Measures*.

2.9.2 Main content

The *Measures* includes five chapters, 21 specific contents and two schedules, which clarify the purpose basis, scope of application and management principles of the credit information management of the water transportation market, and stipulate corresponding rights, responsibilities, and obligations of the relevant management departments, industry associations and practitioners and practitioners, and set requirements for the collection, disclosure, and application of credit information in the water transportation market, and establish mechanisms for objection handling and rights protection mechanism in the process of credit information management, and proposed the main content of violations of laws and regulations of practitioners and employees.

(1) Regarding the division of responsibilities between ministries and provinces. Regarding the division of responsibilities, the credit information management of the waterway transportation market implements unified management and hierarchical responsibility, and clearly defines the positioning, authority and responsibility of the ministries and provinces according to the principles of clear rights and responsibilities, order and efficiency. The credit information systems at the two levels of the ministry and the province are interconnected.

(2) Regarding the scope and method of information collection. According to the *Government Information Disclosure Regulations* and other regulations, according to law, the scope of credit information collection mainly includes the credit information generated during the performance of duties by the transportation management department. In order to ensure timely and accurate information collection, adhere to source collection and territorial management, basic information, good behavior information and dishonest behavior information are collected by corresponding levels of transportation management departments, industry associations and other organizations.

(3) Regarding the management of dishonesty. In order to strengthen the management of dishonest behaviors, the *Measures* clarifies the main content of violations of laws and regulations of practitioners and employees in a list. Establish a system for the management of serious dishonesty, put forward the definition criteria for serious dishonesty, and clarify the rules for the inclusion, update and withdrawal of the list of serious dishonesty, and mechanism and relevant disciplinary measures should be published.

(4) Regarding the application of credit information. According to the spirit of the *State Council's Guiding Opinions on Establishing and Improving the Joint Incentives for Trustworthiness and Joint Disciplinary System for Dishonesty to Accelerate the Construction of Social Honesty*, and combined with the actual situation of the industry, from the aspects of daily supervision, financial subsidies, and evaluation of good behaviors, advanced behavior to conduct credit rewards and punishments to good behaviors and dishonesty.

2.9.3 Summary

Waterway carriage occupies an important position in China's comprehensive transportation system, and bears more than 90% of China's foreign trade goods transportation. The waterway transportation industry has many points, wide areas, long lines, many business categories, and the scale of business entities varies greatly. The promulgation of the *Measures* indicates the direction of credit information management of China's water transportation market for a period of time in the future, and clarifies the management tasks. It is implemented in layers, is responsible for information input and collection, clarifies the division of responsibilities, establishes a long-term working mechanism of "departmental participation, combining points with aspects", and promotes the orderly management of waterway transportation credit information. This will effectively improve the level of credit information management in China's water transportation market, give full play to the role of credit management in post-event supervision and maintenance of market order, and further support the construction of a social credit system.

2.10 Supreme People's Court *Several Opinions on Further Protecting and Regulating Parties' Performance of Administrative Action Rights according to the Law*

On August 31, 2017, Supreme People's Court issued *Several Opinions on Further Protecting and Regulating Parties' Performance of Administrative Action Rights according to the Law* (hereinafter referred to as the *Opinions*).

2.10.1 Background

The implementation of the new *Administrative Procedure Law* and the reform of the case registration system have achieved significant results, but during the implementation of the new law, two undesirable tendencies have emerged: firstly, with the substantial growth of administrative cases and the increasing pressure to handle cases, the situation of that a few courts have restricted litigation rights of the parties has emerge; secondly, individual parties misunderstand the legislative meaning of the case registration system, abuse litigation rights and malicious litigation, wasting judicial resources and administrative costs. The *Opinions* pointed out that people's courts at all levels should attach great importance to the protection of the right to litigation, and all administrative cases that should be accepted according to the law should be registered and filed, so that the case must be established and the case must be settled. It is strictly forbidden to refrain from receiving the complaint or not to issue a written voucher on the grounds that the case is complicated, the weighing of the interests of the department, or affecting the closing of the case at the end of the year; for those that parties need to supplement action materials, courts of all levels should inform comprehensively the parties of the content to be corrected, supplementary materials and time limit for correction, and do well in litigation guidance and legal interpretation.

2.10.2 Main content

The *Opinions* mainly includes strengthening the awareness of protection of litigation rights and guiding parties to exercise the litigation rights according to law, mainly including:

(1) In terms of strengthening the awareness of the people to protect the right to litigation, the *Opinions* requires that people's courts at all levels should aim at substantively resolving administrative disputes, effectively change their concepts, and strictly implement the provisions of the new *Administrative Procedure Law*; continuously improve citizens, legal persons and other organizations' consciousness of exercising the right of litigation according to the law and must resolutely clean up the "local policy" that restricts the litigation rights of the parties, avoid excessive review in the case of accepting, and illegally bring that whether the basis of litigants' litigation issufficient, whether facts are clear, whether the evidence is conclusive, and whether the legal relationship is clear as conditions for accepting. The people's court must correctly determine the jurisdiction of the case and should conduct a careful review of cases that may exceed the statute of limitations. Courts at all levels make full use of modern technologies such as "big data", "Internet +" and "artificial intelligence", continue to promote the construction of litigation service hall, litigation service network, 12368 hotline, and intelligent service platform, constantly innovate work concepts and improve service measures. It is necessary to protect the litigation rights of parties with financial difficulties and poor law enforcement ability according to law. Aiming at the system of accountability of personnel

within the judiciary, timely stop and correct violations of laws and regulations.

(2) People's courts at all levels should correctly guide the parties to exercise the right of litigation according to the law, based on the principle of "the incident no longer", and should explain to the parties the reasons for not accepting the case, do a good job of interpretation, and avoid causing unnecessary litigation to the parties. The people's court must correctly understand the spirit of the case registration system, while preventing over-review, should also pay attention to insisting on the necessary review. The people's court must accurately grasp the legal connotation of "interests" as provided in Article 25 Paragraph 1 of the new *Administrative Procedure Law*, and review according to the law whether the administrative actions of the administrative agencies are closely relevant to the gain and loss of the parties' rights and obligations. When remedying the rights of the parties, the higher-level administrative agency may supervise and correct the administrative actions of the lower-level administrative agencies, or file an action against the administrative actions of the administrative agencies. Whether the parties have an interest in matters such as their complaints, reports, impeach, or problems reflected should be carefully reviews by the court. In addition, it is necessary to correctly distinguish between the parties' claim for protection of lawful rights and interests and the conduct of letters and visits, so as to prevent to treat the parties' claim for administrative agencies to perform their legal duties as letters and visits. To stop the abuse of litigation rights and malicious litigation according to law, fully respect and protect the right to know of citizens, legal persons or other organizations, and promptly review cases involving applications for government information disclosure initiated by the parties according to the law, when confirming the abuse of litigation rights and malicious litigation, it is necessary to strictly grasp the standards, and to review whether the parties have subjective and intentional abuse of litigation rights and malicious litigation from the perspectives of the number, period, purpose, and whether they have legitimate interests in the litigation.

2.10.3 Summary

Litigation rights are the basic rights of citizens, legal persons and other organizations. "There must be remedies for rights" is an inevitable requirement of the rule of law. Based on the institutional structure of "citizen against officials" and the long-term influence of the concept of "government-based", administrative trials are susceptible to interference from all sides. In the past, "local policies" and "unspoken rules" restricting the acceptance of administrative cases were issued in some places, which rejected the common people's claims. The full implementation of the case registration system is to solve the chronic problem of "difficult case accepting". After the implementation of the case registration system, the problem of "difficult case accepting" in administrative litigation was basically resolved. Therefore, in order to consolidate the achievements of the implementation and reform of the new law, the introduction of the *Opinions* on the one hand is helpful to uphold the protection of litigation rights and unswervingly implements the case registration system; on the other hand, it aims at regulating the abuse of litigation rights and malicious litigation according to law to prevent the parties from deviating from the provisions of the new administrative procedure law is in line with the spirit of the registration system reform.

2.11 *Customs Law of the People's Republic of China* (Amended in 2017)

The *Customs Law of the People's Republic of China* (Amended in 2017) (hereinafter referred to as the *Customs Law*) was adopted by the 30th Session of the Standing Committee of the 12th National People's Congress on November 4, 2017.

2.11.1 Background

The priority areas for the construction of "Belt and Road" are to reduce the cost of free movement and to solve the systems and standards that affect interconnection. However, the customs administration involves foreign trade tariff rates, customs supervision procedures and requirements, and guarantee of access to safety, which have become the key link in the management process current of customs. In order to safeguard the country's sovereignty and interests, strengthen customs supervision and management, promote foreign economic and trade and technological and cultural exchanges, and guarantee socialist modernization, in order to further promote simplified government, decentralization, integration of decentralization and management, and optimization of service reforms, to a greater extent, stimulate the market, the innovation and creativity of society, which is based on the national macroeconomic regulation and control of economy and trade and the overall situation of "Belt and Road". The *Customs Law* (2017 version) has been amended four times and passed.

2.11.2　Main content

1) Simplified procedures

The *Customs Law* Article 33 Paragraph 3"If the bonded imported materials is for processing trade or manufactured goods for domestic sale, the customs shall levy taxes on the bonded imported materials according to the law; where the import is restricted by the state, the import license shall also be submitted to the customs."This article provides more enough legal basis for that that Ministry of Commerce and General Administration of Customs officially canceled the provision of processing trade business approval in No.45 Announcement jointly issued in 2016. The operation procedures of relevant businesses between different functional departments are unified to facilitate enterprises to carry out relevant businesses smoothly. At the same time, the reasons for the application of bonded processing materials or finished products for domestic sales have been canceled, which is also in line with the actual needs of current processing trade enterprises. Alleviating the pressure on approval, improving the efficiency of enterprises, and stimulating domestic demand to a certain extent.

2) Improve efficiency

General Administration of Customs announced the new version of the *Administrative Measures for the Temporary Entry and Exit of Goods of the People's Republic of China* (No. 233 Decree of General Administration of Customs) on December 8, 2017, and made corresponding adjustments based on the fourth revision of the *Customs Law* and canceled it. Some administrative licensing items for temporary entry and exit of goods have been canceled and modified to selectively process recognition applications beforehand, which simplifies the procedures and shortens the processing time. It provides enterprises with sufficient choice and preparation time.

2.11.3　Summary

With the continuous development and expansion of China's foreign economic and trade relations and the increasing international scientific and cultural exchanges, customs is an important implementing agency for "Belt and Road" initiative because of its functional role in connecting the international and domestic markets. In order to safeguard national sovereignty and interests, it is very necessary for the customs to strengthen customs supervision and management. In response to social development and changes, it is also very important to simplify the decentralization of government, transform functions, and deepen the reform of the administrative approval system. The establishment of a modern customs system has become a realistic need, and the new *Customs Law* has become the legal basis and strong guarantee for the establishment of a modern customs system. At the legislative level, the central government is continuously committed to simplifying the reform of decentralization and promoting the healthy development of enterprises. The *Customs Law* fully reflects the policy guidance of simplifying procedures and improving efficiency, and also promotes the implementation of administrative measures for customs administration.

2.12 Ship Tonnage Tax Law of the People's Republic of China

The *Ship Tonnage Tax Law of the People's Republic of China* (hereinafter referred to as the *Ship Tonnage Tax Law*) was adopted by the 31st meeting of the Standing Committee of the 12th National People's Congress on December 27, 2017 and should become effective since July 1, 2018.

2.12.1 Background

Responding to the call for the construction of "Belt and Road", China, as a major maritime country, must strengthen integrated marine management, resolutely safeguard national maritime rights and interests, properly handle maritime disputes, actively expand bilateral and multilateral maritime cooperation, and move towards the goal of a maritime power. Li Keqiang said in the government report: we must combine the construction of "Belt and Road" with regional development and opening up, and strengthen the construction of the new Asia-Europe Continental Bridge and the fulcrum of land and sea ports. The predecessor of the *Ship Tonnage Tax Law* was the *Interim Regulations of the People's Republic of China on Ship Tonnage Tax* promulgated by State Council on December 5, 2011. In response to the "implementation of the principle of taxation legality" of the 18th CPC Central Committee and the "deepening of the reform of the taxation system" at the 19th CPC National Congress, the *Ship Tonnage Tax Law* was formulated after repeated study and revision. The *Ship*

Chapter 1　Shipping Laws, Regulations and Policies

Tonnage Tax Law is translated into law without major adjustments according to the provisions of ship tonnage tax regulations. The *Interim Regulations of the People's Republic of China on Ship Tonnage Tax* will be repealed at the same time after the implementation of the *Ship Tonnage Tax Law* from July 1, 2018.

2.12.2　Main content

1) Objects of taxation

The *Ship Tonnage Tax Law* Article 1 stipulates that "ships entering the domestic port from ports outside the People's Republic of China shall pay ship tonnage tax according to this Law". This article clearly stipulates that the taxable objects according to the *Ship Tonnage Tax Law* include all ships entering the domestic port from ports outside China.

2) Set preferential tax rates and ordinary tax rates

According to the *Ship Tonnage Tax Law* Article 3, "For taxable ships of the People's Republic of China's nationality, taxable ships of country of registration (regions) and the People's Republic of China have concluded treaties or agreements that contain mutual most-favored-nation treatment clauses on ship taxes and fees, preferential treatment applies. For other taxable ships, the general tax rate applies". The regulation clearly points out that countries that have concluded treaties or agreements with China on mutual most-favored-nation treatment clauses on ship taxes and fees can enjoy preferential tax rates for ships that need to pay taxes according to law when passing ports in China. This regulation to some extent promotes China's multilateral and bilateral cooperation on sea.

3) Tax rate

Tonnage tax items are divided into four grades of no more than 2,000 net tonnage, 2,000 to 10,000 net tonnage, 10,000 to 50,000 net tonnage, and more than 50,000 net tonnage according to the net tonnage of the ship, maintaining the original tax item tax rate and ton tax rate was set separately according to the net tonnage of the ship and the length of the tonnage tax license. In the attached table, the ship tonnage tax item tax rate table is clearly divided, and according to the *Ship Tonnage Tax Law* Article 4, it is clearly stated that the tonnage tax is collected according to the net tonnage of the ship and the tonnage tax license period. The tonnage tax license period can be chosen when declaring tax.

4) Tax exemption

In the *Ship Tonnage Tax Law* Article 9, ten ships includes that the tax payable is less than 50 RMB yuan, fishing and breeding fishing ships, and police fishing ships are listed as exempt from tonnage tax. It also stipulates taxation units, tax declaration procedures for ton taxes, the time when tax obligations happen, and the tax payment period.

2.12.3 Summary

In order to implement the principle of law-based taxation and deepen the reform of the taxation system, the Standing Committee of the National People's Congress arranged the ship tonnage tax law for the first time in October and listed it as a much-needed item in the comprehensive deepening reform in the *State Council's 2017 Legislative Work Plan*. China is currently a large international shipping country, but the journey to a strong shipping country is still very difficult. Ship tonnage tax is a kind of levy imposed by the customs on behalf of the national traffic management department on ships entering and leaving China's borders at port with tariff for the construction of waterway facilities. With the rapid development of the shipping industry, the determination of the basic system of ship tonnage tax by law has a very important impact on strengthening marine management and protecting marine rights and interests in China.

2.13 Marine Environment Protection Law of the People's Republic of China

The *Marine Environment Protection Law of the People's Republic of China* was revised according to the *Decision on Revising the Eleven Laws of including the Accounting Law of the People's Republic of China* at the 30th Session of the Standing Committee of the 12th National People's Congress on November 4, 2017, which was issued by the Standing Committee of the National People's Congress on November 4, 2017 through the No.81 Decree of the President of the People's Republic of China, and should be implemented from November 5, 2017.

2.13.1 Background

The *Marine Environment Protection Law of the People's Republic of China* was firstly revised according to the *Decision on Revising the Seven Laws of including the Marine Environment Protection Law of the People's Republic of China* at the 30th Session of the Standing Committee of the 12th National

People's Congress on December 28, 2013; secondly revised according to the *Decision on Revising the Marine Environment Protection Law of the People's Republic of China* at the 24th Standing Committee of the 12th National People's Congress on November 7, 2016; thirdly revised according to the *Decision on Revising the Eleven Laws of including the Accounting Law of the People's Republic of China* at the 30th Session of the Standing Committee of the 12th National People's Congress on November 4, 2017 since it was adopted on the 24th meeting of the Standing Committee of the 5th National People's Congress on August 23, 1982.

2.13.2 Main content

The focus of this revision on marine environment protection is to strictly regulate the discharge standards. The specific terms are modified as follows:

(1) Article 30 Paragraph 1 was revised to that: "the choice of the location of the sewage outfall into the sea shall be reported to the environment protection administrative department of the people's government at or above the municipal level where the district is established after scientific demonstration according to the marine functional zoning, seawater power conditions and relevant regulations."

Paragraph 2 was revised to that: "the environment protection administrative department shall notify the marine, maritime, fisheries administrative department and military environmental protection department of the establishment of sewage discharge ports within 15 working days after the completion of the filing."

The revision of this article involves an unknown choice of sewage outfalls into the sea. Whether the location of the sewage outfall into the sea is reasonable is directly relevant to the degree of impact on the marine environment. Therefore, the location of the sewage outfall into the sea should be selected according to the marine functional zoning, seawater dynamic conditions and relevant regulations. After scientific verification, the environment protection administrative department of the people's government at or above the municipal level where the district is established must be reported for filing, and the "report to administrative department for examination and approval" in the original clause was changed to "report to administrative department for filing" and the supervision on the establishment of sewage outlets was relaxed. But at the same time, adding "report to the relevant authorities within 15 working days after filing" in the revision of the Paragraph 2, in fact, it is more clearly regulated before setting up the sewage outfall into the sea, the administrative departments of marine, maritime and fishery and military environment protection department must be consulted for opinions.

(2) A new paragraph is added to Article 77 as the Paragraph 2:"the marine, maritime, fishery administrative departments and the military environment protection department have found that the establishment of sewage outfalls into the sea violates Article 30 Paragraph 1 and Paragraph 3 of this Law, it shall notify the environment protection administrative department to punish according to the provisions of the preceding paragraph."

The revision of this article adds the penalty rules after violating the corresponding rules on the basis of the revision of Article 30. It is clarified that in violation of the filing system for the establishment of sewage outfalls into the sea, and in the case of marine nature reserves, important fishery waters, coastal scenic spots and other areas that require special protection, new sewage outfalls will not be built, it shall be punished accordingly by the environment protection administrative department. This is of special environmental protection value to China's marine environment, and apart from marine nature reserves, important fishery waters and coastal scenic spots, and has maximum protection of an area designated for special protection to some scale.

2.13.3 Summary

The marine environment protection law is a legal regulation that regulates the social relationships that happen in people's activities in using and protecting the marine environment, and is the basic basis for marine environment protection. China has carried out marine environment protection work as early as the 1970s. The *Marine Environment Protection Law of the People's Republic of China*, implemented in 1983, marking the beginning of China's marine environment protection work on the orbit of rule of law. Its promulgation has played a positive role in promoting coastal economic construction and promoting the development of marine environment protection. However, with the continuous deepening of China's reform and opening up, the rapid development of the coastal economy, and the development and changes in the practice of protecting the marine environment, the incompatibility of the law itself and the problems exposed in the implementation process have become more and more obvious. From the overall situation of China's marine environment, due to the large amount of urban domestic sewage and industrial and agricultural wastewater discharged into the sea, the frequency of marine environment disasters such as red tides, oil spills, viruses and breeding pollution continues to increase, and other activities that seriously damage the marine environment, which make China's marine environment pollution has continued to intensify, the basic conditions of marine resources have been severely damaged, and the degradation of some marine ecosystems has become unbalanced. The degree of pollution in offshore waters has become increasingly serious. The polluted areas have continued to expand outward and the scope of pollution has expanded. In order to protect and improve the marine environment, protect marine resources, maintain ecological balance, and promote the sustainable development of the economy and society, it is necessary to revise the *Marine Environment Protection Law*. This revision has an important impact on the protection and improvement of the marine environment, as well as the prevention and control of the discharge of large amounts of material and energy into the ocean due to the increase in human marine activities, and the marine environment is subject to various degrees of pollution damage.

2.14 *Port Law of the People's Republic of China* (Amended in 2017)

The *Port Law of the People's Republic of China* was revised according to the *Decision on Revising the Eleven Laws of including the Accounting Law of the People's Republic of China* at the 30th Session of the Standing Committee of the 12th National People's Congress on November 4, 2017, which was issued by the Standing Committee of the National People's Congress through the No. 81 Decree of the President of the People's Republic of China on November 4, 2017, and should be implemented from November 5, 2017.

2.14.1 Background

The *Port Law of the People's Republic of China* was firstly revised according to the *Decision on Revising the Seven Laws of including the Port Law of the People's Republic of China* at the 14th Session of the Standing Committee of the 12th National People's Congress on April 24, 2015; secondly revised according to the *Decision on Revising the Eleven Laws of including the Accounting Law of the People's Republic of China* at the 30th Standing Committee of the 12th National People's Congress on November 4, 2017 since it was adopted on the 3rd meeting of the Standing Committee of the 10th National People's Congress on June 28, 2003.

2.14.2 Main content

The *Port Law of the People's Republic of China* (hereinafter referred to as the *Port Law*) makes the following revision:

(1) In Article 17, "construction was only after the relevant procedures have been completed according to law and approved by the port administrative department" was changed to "construction was only after the relevant procedures have been completed according to law".

(2) Article 46 was revised to that: "if the distance between a dangerous goods operation site, a special site for sanitary detoxification treatment and a densely populated area or a port passenger transportation facility constructed in a port does not comply with the relevant regulations of State Council, the port administrative department shall order the construction or use to be stopped, make corrections within a time limit, and shall impose a fine of not more than 50,000 yuan."

(3) Paragraph 1 of Article 56 was deleted, "illegal approval of construction of dangerous goods operation sites in ports or special sites for sanitary detoxification treatment".

(4) Mainly aiming at the law enforcement areas and law enforcement matters that the port administrative department has determined to be legal during the supervision process, it is of great legal significance to effectively strengthen port management and achieve legislative purposes.

2.14.3 Summary

The *Port Law* has played an important role in strengthening port management, maintaining port safety and operating order, and promoting port construction and development. However, as the development situation of port integration reform changes, some of the original provisions need to be revised: since the promulgation of the *Port Law* in 2004, some provisions have not adapted to the needs of port development in the new era. The current *Port Law* has not yet made clear the legal definitions of port areas, port facilities, and port engineering projects, and clear regulations must be made in the preparation and approval of port layout. This revision regulates a part of the law enforcement matters of the port administrative department to a certain extent, but the problems mentioned in the current *Port Law* have not been completely resolved.

When the *Port Law* was promulgated, it focuses on resolving the issue of separation of government and enterprises and decentralized management of ports. The legal status and powers of provincial transportation authorities in industry management were unclear, which did not reflect the hierarchical management of the transportation industry, resulting in coordination between the upper and lower not smooth. As the pilot work of port integration reform is carried out, port groups integrated at the provincial level in Zhejiang, Jiangsu and other provinces have been formed successively, and other provinces are also actively preparing. According to the current setting of the *Port Law*, provincial port administrative department has limited powers, and it is difficult to match the tasks undertaken by the current provincial port administrative department. The level of port management responsibilities is unknown. At the same time, the *Port Law* lacks a comprehensive and coordinated management system and does not meet the requirements of port cooperative management. Port management involves multiple departments and agencies. However, as the basic law in the port regulation system, the *Port Law* only clarifies the responsibilities of the transportation authority for port management, and the responsibilities of other relevant regulatory authorities are not clear, which will make it difficult for the port supervision to be fully carried out. In addition, the problem of shoreline resource protection caused by the scarcity of port shoreline resources needs to be strengthened to protect the environment, and revised again according to the *Environment Protection Law*.

2.15 *Crew Regulations of the People's Republic of China* (Amended in 2017)

The *Crew Regulations of the People's Republic of China* was revised according to the *Decision of State Council on the Revision and Abolition of Part of Administrative Regulations* on March 1, 2017, which was issued by Premier

LI Keqiang on March 1, 2017 through State Council Order No.676 of the People's Republic of China and was implemented from the date of announced.

2.15.1 Background

The *Crew Regulations of the People's Republic of China* was firstly revised according to the *Decision of the State Council on Abrogation and Revision of some Administrative Regulations* on July 18, 2013; secondly revised according to the *Decision of the State Council on Revising Some Administrative Regulations* on December 7, 2013; thirdly revised according to the *Decision of the State Council on Revising some Administrative Regulations* on July 29, 2014, which was fourthly revised according to the *Decision of the State Council on Abrogation and Revision of Some Administrative Regulations* on March 1, 2017 since it was promulgated by Decree No.494 of State Council of the People's Republic of China on April 14, 2007.

2.15.2 Main content

Revise Article 70 of the *Crew Regulations of the People's Republic of China* to that: "the pilot training shall be carried out according to the regulations on crew training. The specific measures for pilot management shall be formulated by the transportation department of State Council." The regulations of the pilot training and the competent authority of the pilot are revised.

2.15.3 Summary

With the development of China's shipping industry, crew play an important role in successfully completing carriage tasks, ensuring the safety of marine traffic, preventing ships from polluting the environment, promoting the development of the national economy, and promoting foreign exchanges. Crew work is harder, has greater risks, and requires high professional quality. Therefore, many countries have adopted legislation to strengthen the management of crew and protect the rights and interests of crew, and the International Maritime Organization and the International Labour Organization have also formulated corresponding conventions. Since the promulgation of the *Crew Regulations* in 2007, China has substantially realized the integration of China's maritime management and modern international maritime management concepts, effectively regulated the crew's work, created positive conditions to ensure the safety of water traffic and prevent ship pollution and the healthy development of the shipping industry. However, the regulations on crew training system, employment environment, occupational guarantee and management system are still not complete. As far as the crew training system is concerned, it should be clear which professional training, special training and qualified training the crew must receive before boarding, and regulations such as crew qualifications and training permits are required to better develop the crew and improve the quality of the crew; as far as the protection of the rights and interests of crew, there is a problem in the current regulations that the occupational guarantee of the crew is not perfect and the guarantee has not been implemented. For this, future revisions to the *Regulations* should draw on the provisions of the International Labour Organization and the International Maritime Organization on the protection of crew conventions in terms of wages, insurance, and work environment. The revision of the current regulations is still far from keeping up with the development of the shipping industry and the actual needs of the crew. The above-mentioned content is what needs to be considered and improved in the future revision of the *Crew Regulations*. Only a better *Crew Regulations* can make the existing crew complete their duties seriously, and attract more younger crew to join the crew business, thereby promoting the sustainable development of the crew business and providing talent support for the stable and sustainable development of the shipping industry.

2.16 Notice of General Office of Ministry of Transport on Printing and Distributing the *Port Shore Power Layout Plan*

On July 24, 2017, Ministry of Transport issued the *Port Shore Power Layout Plan* (hereinafter referred to as the *Plan*), which is convenient for transportation authorities at all levels, port and shipping management agencies and relevant companies to better understand the relevant content and effectively do implementation well.

2.16.1 Background

The use of shore power by ships at ports is an effective means to reduce the discharge of pollution from ships. Since China firstly adopted the high-voltage shore power system in 2010, the use of shore power technology for ships at ports has gradually been rolled out nationwide. During the Twelfth Five-Year Plan period, Ministry of Transport successively issued the *Twelfth Five-Year Plan for the Implementation of Water Transport Energy Conservation and Emission Reduction Overall Promotion* and the *Guiding Opinions on Port Energy Conservation and Emission Reduction Work*, and has carried out a lot of work in onshore power standards, pilot demonstration, technology research and development, financial support, publicity and training, which has laid a good foundation for the promotion and application of shore power technology.

2.16.2 Main contents

The *Plan* includes three parts: general requirements, layout plan and guarantee measures. The overall requirement is to clarify the guiding ideology, basic principles, layout scope and layout goals of the *Plan*. The layout plan proposes the number of shore power berths in 2020 in major ports and ports of ship emission control zones in the country. The guarantee measures include scientific organization and implementation, increased policy support, establishment of electricity supply and sales mechanism and improvement of laws and standards. Several main issues are explained as follows:

1) Basic principles

According to the requirements of laws, regulations and relevant documents, combined with the current situation, demand and development prospects of the construction of port shore power facilities and the use of shore power by ships at ports, the *Plan* has determined the principle of "integrated coordination, effective connection", "emphasis on key points, and classification promotion" and "proper scale and scientific layout", which proposes that the shore power layout should be kept in line with the existing relevant environmental protection plans and requirements. The key regional ports and key types of berths should be used as the starting point to promote the construction of shore power facilities. The construction scale of port shore power should be in line with the development level of port and regional pollution prevention and control requirements.

2) Layout scope

For newly built ports, according to the requirements of the *Air Pollution Prevention and Control Law*, shore power facilities should be planned, designed, and constructed simultaneously. Therefore, the *Plan* only lays out the built ports.

Regarding the scope of the port included in the layout. On the basis of the

Action Plan, the *Plan* proposes to focus on promoting the construction of shore power facilities in major ports and ports in emission control areas by 2020 according to the principle of emphasizing priorities, combined with emission control zone policies and regional air pollution control requirements to address the need for ships to use shore power in ports where pollution emissions from ships are concentrated and serious, and reduce pollution emissions from ports in key areas. There are 69 major ports and ports in the emission control area. According to the port statistics at the end of 2015, the port goods throughput within the layout accounted for 75% of the total national goods throughput, of which container throughput reached approximately 90% of the national container throughput.

Regarding the types of berths included in the layout. The *Plan* is based on the *Action Plan* and according to the principle of classification promotion. In addition to the layout of three types of specialized berths suitable for ships to use port power at ports, such as containers, cruise and passenger rolls, in order to adapt to the large-scale tourist ships on the Yangtze (most are above 3,000 tons) and the rapid development of large-scale bulk goods specialized terminals across the country, fully considering the suitability of large-scale tourist ships and bulk goods carriers to use shore power at ports, better promotion basis and greater emission reduction potential, it is clearly included in the scope of shore power layout for passenger carriage above 3,000 tons and dry bulk goods specialized berths above 50,000 tons.

3) Layout goals

The *Plan* proposes to achieve that more than 50% of the containers, passenger rolls, cruises, passenger carriage of more than 3,000 tons and dry bulk goods specialized berths of more than 50,000 tons of the ports in major coastal and inland rivers ports and ship emission control areas have the ability to provide shore power for ships in 2020. This shore power coverage target remains in line with the *Action Plan* and basically meets the port development level and regional pollution prevention and control level in 2020. The *Plan* proposes that ports with greater demand for shore power and better basic conditions are encouraged to accelerate the construction of shore power facilities, strive to achieve 100% berth shore power coverage, and increase the use of shore power by ships at ports.

4) Layout plan

Based on the total number of 5 types of specialized berths that have been built in major ports and emission control areas, and guided by the layout goal of achieving an overall coverage of 50%, considering the various geographic locations, berth capabilities, throughput of each port, comprehensively using a combination of mathematical planning and screening to determine the shore power layout plan: by the end of 2020, a total of 493 specialized berths with the ability to supply shore power to ships will be deployed in major ports and emission control areas of the country, including costal 366, inland rivers 127. It is estimated that after the implementation of the *Plan*, the emissions of sulfur dioxide, nitrogen oxides and $PM_{2.5}$ during the berthing period of the ship are expected to be reduced by 60,000 tons, 110,000 tons and 8,000 tons each year, of which, coastal ports are reduced respectively by 53,000 tons and 91,000 tons, and 7,000 tons, inland ports are reduced respectively by 7,000 tons, 19,000 tons and 1,000 tons, and the emission reduction effect is significant.

2.16.3 Summary

In recent years, national ecological civilization strategies and laws and regulations have placed new and higher requirements on the use of shore power by ships at ports. The *Air Pollution Prevention and Control Law of the People's Republic of China*, which was implemented on January 1, 2016 stipulates that: "newly built terminals should plan, design, and construct shore-based power supply facilities; completed terminals should gradually implement the transformation of shore-based power supply facilities. After ships arrive at the port, shore power should be given priority." State Council's *Thirteenth Five-Year Plan for Ecological Environment Protection*, *Thirteenth Five-Year Comprehensive Work Plan for Energy Conservation and Emission Reduction*, and the *Implementation Plan for the Special Action on Ship and Port Pollution Prevention and Control (2015—2020)* have made clear requirements to promote the use of shore power by ships at ports. The ship emission control zone policy states that ships can adopt alternative measures such as connecting shore power. The *Thirteenth Five-Year Development Plan for Transportation Energy Conservation and Environmental Protection* and the *Implementation Plan for Promoting the Construction of Ecological Civilization in Transportation* clearly state that "the plan for the construction of port shore power layout" should be clearly formulated.

The *Plan* is China's first top-level design document for the construction of port shore power facilities. Its promulgation will play an active role in promoting the orderly construction of port shore power facilities in China and guiding ships to use shore power at ports and is of great significance to supply side structural reform and green development to water carriage.

2.17 Ship Safety Supervision Regulations of the People's Republic of China

2.17.1 Background

On November 7, 2016, the Standing Committee of the National People's Congress passed a decision to revise the *Maritime Traffic Safety Law* to cancel the entry and exit visas for sea ships. On March 1, 2017, State Council revised the *Regulations on the Management of Inland Rivers Traffic Safety* to cancel the entry and exit visas for inland river ships. After the cancellation of the visa system, the management of ships entering and leaving the port was adjusted from prior approval to operational and post-operational supervision. In order to ensure continuous stable management after the cancellation of administrative examination and approval, the maritime management agency needs a new regulation to refine and improve the system of operational and post-operational safety supervision.

2.17.2 Main content

①The scope, concept and behavior of ship safety supervision are defined. ②The responsibilities and obligations of the relevant parties are stipulated. ③The specific requirements of the ship reporting system is stipulated. ④The concept of comprehensive quality management is applied. ⑤The selection criteria of target ships for safety supervision are improved. ⑥ The content of ship safety supervision is clarified and enriched. ⑦The handling and review of ship safety defects are clarified. ⑧The division of ship safety responsibilities is highlighted. ⑨Legal liability stipulates the legal basis for administrative penalties for violations.

The newly promulgated *Ship Safety Supervision Regulations* have the following characteristics:

First is to make timely connection with the higher-level law. The *Decision of*

State Council on the Revision and Abolition of Part of Administrative Regulations (State Council Order No. 676), canceled the entry and exit visas for ships, and clearly implemented the ship entry and exit reporting system. The newly promulgated *Ship Safety Supervision Regulations* further clarified the timing and methods of ship entry and exit reports. It clearly stipulates that the ship should report the entry and exit information to the maritime management agency that will leave or arrive at the port 4 hours before it is expected to leave or arrive at the port; if the voyage is less than 4 hours, it should be reported when leaving the previous port. If the ship sails on a fixed route and the single voyage does not exceed 2 hours, it can report the entry and exit information at least once a day. Ships can report the ship's entry and exit information via the Internet, fax, SMS, and make corresponding records in the ship's navigation or logbook.

Second is to strengthen the responsibility of the subject of ship safety. Establish a self-inspection system before the ship sails, clarify that the ship should conduct a self-inspection on the ship's safety technical status and goods loading before leaving the port, fill out the *Self-inspection Safety Checklist Before Sailing* and be signed by the captain to confirm, the maritime management agency should take the self-inspection of the ship as an important part of the on-site supervision of the ship.

Third is to implement comprehensive ship quality management. Clearly establish a comprehensive ship quality management information platform and a comprehensive ship quality file, collect, process and evaluate nine types of ship information, so as to implement targeted supervision measures for different ships, and promote ships, crew and shipping companies to consciously abide by the law.

Fourth is to strengthen ship safety supervision. Ship safety supervision is divided into ship on-site supervision and ship safety inspection, the content of ship on-site supervision and ship safety inspection and the treatment of ship safety defects are clarified, and the ship selection criteria for the target of safety supervision are clearly formulated so as to reasonably select ships to implement ship safety supervision.

2.17.3 Summary

On January 1, 2014, the Tokyo Memorandum Organization implemented a new port state supervision inspection mechanism in the Asia-Pacific region, incorporating a new risk assessment mechanism and inspection strategy to achieve the transformation from a "quantity-based" inspection mechanism to a "risk-based" inspection mechanism, which has a huge impact on the development of the shipping industry. In order to meet the needs of the implementation of the new inspection mechanism, the original *Ship Safety Supervision Regulations* need to be revised. The new *Ship Safety Supervision Regulations* aims to facilitate transportation and strengthen supervision, take the implementation of the ship entry and exit reporting system as the basis, and "ensure the safety of life and property on the water, prevent ships from causing water pollution, and regulate ship safety supervision" as the goal, based on the principle of "legal, fair, honest and convenient", a new ship safety supervision and management model has been constructed. With the legalization of safe production and comprehensive advancement of administration according to the law, the maritime department, as the competent authority for water safety supervision, must strictly perform its statutory duties. Under the new situation, it is urgent to formulate regulations to accurately position the performance of duties.

2.18 *Convention on the Construction of Shipping Legal System in China (Shanghai) Pilot Free Trade Zone*

On March 7, 2017, the Commercial Committee of China (Shanghai) Pilot Free Trade Zone (Shipping Office) held the signing ceremony of the *Convention on the Construction of Shipping Legal System in China (Shanghai) Pilot Free Trade Zone* (hereinafter referred to as the *Convention*). Representatives of 22 relevant institutions concluded the convention from various aspects of shipping industry.

2.18.1 Background

With the continuous expansion of the shipping field and the innovation of the system, the number of maritime and aviation disputes has grown rapidly, and the coverage of the types of cases accepted has expanded significantly. Under the premise of profound changes in international trade and transportation methods, new changes and developments are also brewing in international shipping laws and regulations. Whereas, the conclusion of the *Convention* promotes the construction of a legal environment for shipping and thus promotes the construction of a soft environment for the Shanghai International Shipping Center.

2.18.2 Main content

(1) Actively participate in and support various work according to the requirements of Shanghai Free Trade Zone Comprehensive Plan on "constructing a pilot free trade zone with international standards for investment and trade facilitation, efficient and convenient supervision and regulated and legal environment".

(2) Adhere to the principles of independence, fairness and sharing, parties of the convention should firmly establish the awareness of constructing a legal business environment in Shanghai Free Trade Zone according to law, equally safeguard the legal rights and interests of the Chinese and foreign parties, and jointly improve the shipping service level of Shanghai Free Trade Zone.

(3) Establish a sense of legal services, parties of the convention should provide investment, operations and other activities in the free trade zone of domestic and foreign shipping agencies, enterprises and organizations with professional legal guarantee including but not limited to marine carriage, ship management, inland shipping, cruise operations, ports services, air transportation, warehousing and logistics, shipping financing, green shipping, shipping insurance, new technology development.

(4) Lead the industry's active and healthy development. Parties of the convention should make active contributions in the consultation of construction of rule of law, research and formulation of contract standards, early warning of industry legal risks, analysis of typical cases, and professional legal training.

(5) Promote the construction of Shanghai International Shipping Center. Parties of the convention should make concerted efforts to fulfill their responsibilities for the high concentration of shipping resources, the perfect function of shipping services, the standardization and improvement of the shipping legal system, and to ensure the national strategy of "Yangtze River Economic Belt" and "Shipping Power" to be implemented in an orderly manner.

2.18.3 Summary

The formulation of the *Convention* is the product of further deepening reforms in the Shanghai Free Trade Zone. With the continuous expansion of the shipping field and the innovation of the system, the number of maritime and aviation disputes has grown rapidly, and the coverage of the types of cases accepted has significantly expanded. According to the statistics of Shanghai Maritime Court, in 2016, it accepted more than 740 cases of maritime and maritime business involving various free trade zones, and the subject matter involved was about 800 million yuan. At the same time, profound changes have taken place in international trade and transportation methods, and new international shipping legal rules are being formed. In order to better participate in international competition and further strengthen the construction of a shipping environment of rule of law, the equal protection of the interests of Chinese and foreign shipping companies has become an important task for Shanghai to construct an international shipping center.

2.19 Notice of State Council on Several Measures of Expanding Opening to Foreign Countries and Actively Using Foreign Investment

2.19.1 Background

As of the end of 2016, China has attracted more than 1.77 trillion USD of foreign investment. In 2016, against the backdrop of a decline in the total amount of global cross-border investment, China attracted 813.22 billion yuan of foreign investment, an increase of 4.2% year-on-year. In particular, the actual investment in China by the United States and the 28 EU countries increased significantly, a separate increase of 52.6% and 41.3 % year-on-year. Foreign investment plays an active role in China's economic development and deepening reform process, promoting foreign trade, technological progress, industrial upgrading and market competition. The issuance of the *Notice on Several Measures of Expanding Opening to Foreign Countries and Actively Using Foreign Investment* (hereinafter referred to as the *Several Measures*) can further fully deploy the use of foreign investment to achieve China's mutually beneficial and win-win opening strategy.

2.19.2 Main content

First is to further expand opening up. In recent years, China has actively expanded the field of opening up and the level of opening up has been continuously improved. However, compared with the goal of opening up to the outside world at a high level, it is necessary to accelerate the pace of opening up and increase the intensity of opening up. The *Several Measures* clearly states that it should be guided by the concept of open development, focus on promoting the relaxation of foreign investment access restrictions in the fields of services, manufacturing, mining, and actively attract foreign investment and advanced technology and management experience. The *Several Measures* stated simultaneously that it supports foreign investment to participate in the "Made in China 2025" strategy, and promote the deep integration of foreign investment into manufacturing transformation and upgrading. Build an open innovation system. National science and technology projects are open to foreign-invested enterprises, support foreign-invested enterprises to increase R & D investment, and apply for the establishment of post-doctoral research stations. Expand the use of foreign investment and support foreign investment to participate in infrastructure construction through franchising.

Second is to further create a fair competition environment. Like state-owned enterprises and private enterprises, foreign-invested enterprises are an important part of the national economy. As long as it is an enterprise registered in China, it shall enjoy the same treatment. The Party Central Committee and State Council have made clear arrangements to accelerate the formation of a modern market system for fair competition among enterprises, and treat domestic and foreign enterprises equally and fairly. For this, the *Several Measures* proposes that foreign investment policies must be reviewed for fair competition, and opinions must be solicited publicly in advance. Various regions and departments must not increase restrictions on foreign-invested companies without authorization. This systematically guarantees the transparency, stability, predictability of policies and consistency of implementation. The *Several Measures* requires the implementation of unified standards for domestic and foreign-invested enterprises in the areas of business license review, standard setting, government procurement, financing channels, and registration to promote the fair participation of various enterprises.

Third is to further strengthen the work of attracting foreign investment. The *Several Measures* proposes that local governments are allowed to formulate preferential policies for investment attraction within the scope of statutory authority, to support projects that contribute greatly to employment, economic development, and technological innovation, and to reduce enterprise investment and operating costs. This is to authorize the localities, hoping that all localities will work more proactively and constantly regulate in development, and achieve better development in the regulation. It should be noted that this measure applies not only to foreign investment, but also to domestic investment. The *Several Measures* proposes that the existing incentive policies for foreign-invested industries and regions remain unchanged, actively support the central and western regions, and northeast regions to attract foreign investment, deepen the reform of foreign investment management systems, and increase the degree of investment facilitation.

2.19.3 Summary

The *Several Measures* is a guiding document for China's current and future use of foreign investment. Main policy directions: Firstly, adhere to open development, promote the implementation of a new round of high-level opening to the outside world, and promote reform and development through opening up. Secondly, committed to optimizing the business environment and further promoting fair competition between domestic-invested and foreign-invested companies. Thirdly, promote the combination of attracting investment, attracting technology and attracting wisdom, enhancing the attractiveness of foreign investment in manufacturing, building an open innovation system, and improving the quality and level of foreign capital utilization. Fourthly, construct a unified market system, strengthen and optimize services, and encourage foreign-invested enterprises to deepen their development. Fifthly, intensify reform efforts, simplify the examination and approval and supervision system for foreign investment according to the principle of domestic and foreign unanimous investment, and increase the degree of investment facilitation.

The *Several Measures* proposes comprehensive and systematic policy measures, not only involving the pre-admission phase of foreign investment, but also the post-admission phase of business operation, not only involving central-level policy issues, but also involving local government implementation issues. It can be said that it sufficiently reflects the concerns of relevant parties. It is hoped that the implementation of the *Several Measures* will focus on advancing a new round of high-level opening to the outside world and create a more open, fair and convenient investment environment for foreign investment. It is also hoped that all countries will work together to promote the development of economic globalization and transnational investment.

2.20 Action Plan for Shanghai to Serve the Construction of China's "Belt and Road" and Play the Role of Bridgehead

2.20.1 Background

The construction of "Belt and Road" is a long-term management plan for China's opening up and cooperation with the outside world, and is of great significance for comprehensively improving China's all-round opening level. To construct China (Shanghai) Pilot Free Trade Zone (hereinafter referred to as Shanghai Free Trade Zone) into a bridgehead serving the construction of the country's "Belt and Road" and promoting market players to go out is a new requirement that General Secretary XI Jinping puts forward to Shanghai from a global perspective. Shanghai's role as a bridgehead in the construction of the national "Belt and Road" is conducive to further enhancing the city's comprehensive service functions of Shanghai and developing a higher level of open economy; it will help form a new pattern of all-round opening up and interconnected development between East-Middle-West of China, and better participate in global competition and cooperation. In order to implement the spirit of "Belt and Road" International Cooperation Summit Forum and the requirements of the Central Government, Shanghai Municipal Government has formulated this action plan.

2.20.2 Main content

The action plan proposes a specific implementation path and implements it into various operational and implementable specific actions, which are divided into 6 special actions.

(1) Special action on trade and investment facilitation. A total of 15 measures were proposed, mainly to construct a "Belt and Road" multi-level trade and investment cooperation network around the strategy of docking with national free trade zones to promote trade and investment liberalization and facilitation. The core is to give full play to the system innovation advantages of the Shanghai Free Trade Zone, and put forward two measures, namely, to use the Shanghai Free Trade Zone as a carrier to strengthen the docking with the systems and rules

of the countries (regions) along the route; "zone port integration, the first-line release, two-line safe and efficient control" is the core, and accelerate the construction of free trade port area.

(2) Special action on financial opening and cooperation. A total of 10 measures were proposed to seize the opportunities of national financial opening and RMB internationalization. Under the premise of controllable risks, relying on the financial reform and innovation of the Shanghai Free Trade Zone, to meet the needs of "Belt and Road" financial services, and strengthen the linkage with the construction of Shanghai International Financial Center. The goal is to construct Shanghai into a "Belt and Road" investment and financing center and a global RMB financial service center.

(3) Special action to enhance the interconnection function. A total of 6 measures were proposed, mainly focusing on strengthening the linkage with the construction of Shanghai International Shipping Center, unblocking internal and external connections, expanding comprehensive service functions, and consolidating and enhancing the status of Shanghai as a global city gateway hub.

(4) Special action on technological innovation cooperation. A total of 6 measures were proposed, mainly focusing on comprehensively docking with the national "Belt and Road" technology innovation action plan, strengthening linkage with science and technology innovation centers, using superior technology resources, and relying on functional platforms and projects to promote joint scientific and technological research and transformation of achievements.

(5) Special action on humanities cooperation and exchange. A total of 10 measures were proposed, relying on the construction of an international cultural metropolis, to play a major "festival, competition, meeting" role, construct more cultural arts, education and training, health care, tourism and sports and other exchange mechanisms and platforms to comprehensively enhance the humanities cooperation and exchanges level.

(6) Special action for the construction of think tanks. A total of 7 measures were proposed to make clear that Shanghai's various think tanks have research advantages, network advantages and resource advantages to provide professional intellectual support for the construction of "Belt and Road".

2.20.3 Summary

The process of Shanghai serving the country's "Belt and Road" construction is also a process of cultivating new dynamism, participating in global competition and cooperation on behalf of China, testing pressure, preventing and controlling risks, transforming and upgrading, disseminating new concepts of China's development, and highlighting the value of Shanghai's global city. Therefore, in the "Belt and Road" bridgehead action plan, Shanghai clearly put forward the goal positioning of bridgehead, and regard the service for the country's "Belt and Road" construction as a new carrier for Shanghai to continue to be a pioneer in reform and opening up, and a pioneer in innovation and development, a new platform for serving the Yangtze River Delta, the Yangtze River basins and the whole country, a new hub for interconnecting development between East-Middle-West, and opening wider to the outside world, and strive to construct a bridgehead that can gather, serve, drive, support, and guarantee.

3 Summary

With the acceleration of the construction of Shanghai International Shipping Center, the modern shipping service industry with the contents of shipping finance, marine insurance, shipping brokerage, and shipping information is gradually becoming the core driving force for the development of Shanghai International Shipping Center. The development of modern shipping service industry needs the guarantee of the rule of law, and the construction of an international shipping center needs the support of the rule of law. The 19th National Congress of the CPC regards comprehensively governing the country according to law as one of the basic strategies for upholding and developing socialism with Chinese characteristics in the new era, emphasizing that the rule of law should be enforced, scientific legislation and democratic legislation should be promoted, good law should be used to promote development, and good governance should be guaranteed. For many years, Shanghai Municipal People's Congress has attached great importance to leading the construction of "four centers" with the rule of law. The implementation of national strategies such as "Belt and Road" initiative has brought new opportunities and space for the development of the Shanghai shipping market. Shanghai successful issued first local legislation on the construction of the shipping center, the *Regulations of Shanghai on Promoting the Construction of an International Shipping Center* signifies that the construction of Shanghai International Shipping Center has entered a new stage of guidance of rule of law.

Chapter 2　Judicial Execution of Shipping Law

  2017 is a year when the cause of the party and the state entered a new era. The 19th National Congress of the CPC was successfully held, and XI Jinping Thought on Socialism with Chinese Characteristics for a new era became the party's guiding ideology, providing theoretical guidance for the successful realization of the two "100-year" goals and the Chinese dream of the great renaissance of the Chinese nation. Under the guidance of XI Jinping Thought on Socialism with Chinese Characteristics for a new era, the Supreme People's Court focused on building strategic advantages for the development of the new era, implementing national strategies and services in the field of maritime trials, ensuring the level of maritime trials, improving and innovating maritime litigation mechanisms, and promoting the development of maritime trials and shipping dispute resolution.

  In 2017, Shanghai Maritime Court proactively docked its own development with the goal of constructing an international maritime judicial center. It clearly defined the goal of constructing an international maritime justice center with the core function of constructing an international shipping dispute settlement center and the high-end think tank of international maritime justice and the international maritime justice exchange platform as auxiliary functions. It actively carries out path exploration, focuses on serving national major strategies and the construction of international shipping centers, takes internationalization, specialization, and rule of law as the direction, with judicial capacity building as the core, institutional mechanism innovation as the breakthrough, and is supported by big data strategy, "Internet $+$" and "Artificial Intelligence $+$", to accelerate the formation of a new situation in maritime justice work in line with international standards, and comprehensively enhance the international credibility and influence of Shanghai maritime justice.

  In order to better serve and guarantee the strategy of maritime power, the "Belt and Road" initiative, the construction of Shanghai Free Trade Zone (Port) and the construction of Shanghai International Shipping Center during the "13th Five-Year Plan" period, and promote the continuous innovation and development of various work, Shanghai Maritime Court in April, 2017, issued the *Outline of Shanghai Maritime Court Five-year Development Plan* (2017—2021) (hereinafter referred to as *Outline of Plan* was issued. The *Outline of Plan* addresses the new and higher requirements for maritime justice in the light of economic and social development, which is based on practical work, by strengthening the function of maritime justice, improving strategic positioning and service level, from four aspects such as guiding ideology, development goals, planning tasks, and implementation requirements and makes comprehensive plans for the work of next five years. Shanghai Maritime Court earnestly implements the goals and tasks set in the *Outline of Plan* in its work, and strives to build Shanghai into an international maritime justice center with global influence, providing strong maritime justice services and guarantees for the implementation of major national strategies and the economic and social development of Shanghai and its surrounding areas.

In June 2017, the Supreme People's Court formally established the "Smart Maritime Court (Shanghai) Practice Base" in Shanghai Maritime Court. This is the first smart court practice base in the country approved by the Supreme People's Court, and it is the inevitable requirements for the implementation of the five-year development plan for the informatization construction of the People's Court, serving major national strategies such as guaranteeing the maritime power and the Yangtze River Economic Belt, and speeding up the construction of the international maritime justice center, which are highly consistent with Shanghai's goal of building a national artificial intelligence development highland. The "Practice Base" is dedicated to building a "model room" for smart maritime courts, building a number of data information systems that conform to the law of maritime justice and can be promoted to the national maritime courts, and developing new mechanisms and applications in the areas of maritime trial enforcement, collaborative linkage, and litigation services, and forming and promoting institutionalized and specialized maritime courts smart trial model, and striving to modernize the maritime trial system and trial capacity. As an important part of the practice base of Smart Court, Shanghai Maritime Court's Maritime Linkage Command Center is substantively operated to promote the improvement of the maritime justice service guarantee level, which is conducive to promoting the construction of the Smart Maritime Court.

Shanghai Maritime Court and Shanghai Insurance Regulatory Bureau are the first in the country to introduce the maritime litigation preservation liability insurance and the recommended format text of the letter of guarantee. This insurance product was officially developed and launched by Shanghai Shipping Insurance Association to cover direct economic loss of the respondent and the third person of the maritime preservation due to wrong preservation. After the product was officially launched, it has been applied in a large number of cases, which has enriched the guarantee form of maritime litigation preservation, broadened the guarantee channels for litigation preservation, and played an active role in justice practice and shipping practice. As of the first quarter of 2018, maritime litigation preservation liability insurance provided a total of 3,646.9 million yuan of relevant insurance amount. About 60% of the parties in the preservation case chose maritime litigation preservation liability insurance as the guarantee method. The proportion of that the maritime litigation preservation liability insurance passed the review of the maritime court and was accepted by the maritime court reached 100%.

In 2017, maritime arbitration services became more diversified. On the basis of providing traditional arbitration services, the China Maritime Arbitration Committee held various trainings and seminars, carried out targeted publicity activities, and implemented arbitration clauses. China Maritime Arbitration Committee continues to provide extended arbitration services, advance arbitration services, and give full play to the role of arbitration in the diversified dispute settlement mechanism.

"Strengthening maritime trial work and constructing an international maritime justice center" was formally included in the 2016 work report of the Supreme People's Court. In 2017, the Chinese legal profession is working on the construction of "two centers": the international maritime justice center and the international maritime arbitration center. These "two centers" can be called the lotus that serves the Maritime Silk Road.

In 2017, China Maritime Arbitration Committee actively participated in and promoted relevant industry associations such as shipping, shipbuilding and insurance to draft standard format contracts, regulate business operations, and implement arbitration clauses. Conduct in-depth research in shipping, shipbuilding, freight forwarding, port, insurance, banking and other industries, hold seminars to understand the needs of enterprises, discuss cooperation methods, and carry out targeted arbitration publicity and expansion work. Conduct special thematic discussions on hot issues in maritime and maritime commerce and maritime arbitration and other fields that enterprises have widespread concern, at the same time strengthen contacts, proactively coordinate relations with all sectors of society, provide targeted legal services to enterprises, expand the publicity scope and intensity of maritime arbitration committees, and strive to create soft environment for maritime arbitration development.

Under the "Belt and Road" initiative and the overall environment, background, and strategy of constructing an international maritime arbitration center, the development of Chinese maritime arbitration is facing unprecedented historic opportunities.

1 A Brief Introduction of Maritime Judicial Situation in Shanghai in 2017

1.1 Shanghai Maritime Court

In 2017, Shanghai Maritime Court received 5,207 cases of various types, an increase of 3.03% year-on-year, and concluded 5,213 cases, an increase of 2.20% year-on-year. At the end of the year, 296 cases were filed, a decrease of 1.00% year-on-year. The total amount of the accepted subject matter was 2,899,595,100 yuan, and the total amount of the concluded subject matter was 2,274,882,700 yuan.

Among them, Shanghai Maritime Court Pilot Free Trade Zone Tribunal (Yangshan Deepwater Port Dispatched Tribunal), Yangkou Port Dispatched Tribunal and Lianyungang Dispatched Tribunal received a total of 1,468 cases of various types and concluded 1,470 cases. The total number of cases accepted and concluded by the dispatched tribunal separately accounted for 28.19% and 28.20% of the total number of cases accepted and concluded by the whole court, a slight decrease year-on-year. Fig. 2 – 1 shows the situation of the first-instance case accepted, concluded and filed in 2015—2017.

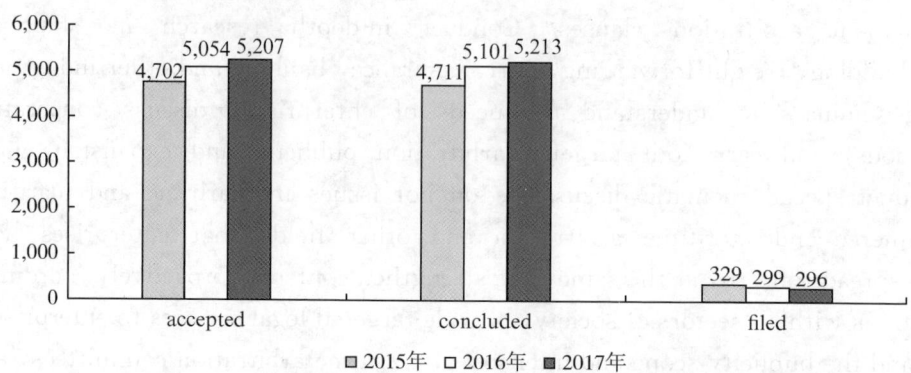

Fig. 2 – 1　Situation of Case Accepted, Concluded and Filed by Shanghai Maritime Court in 2015—2017

A total of 4,274 cases were accepted in the first instance in 2017, an increase of 2.47% year-on-year; 4,279 cases were concluded, an increase of 1.66% year-on-year. As of the end of the year, 263 cases were filed, a decrease of 1.87% year-on-year.

Among them, the first-instance maritime and maritime commercial cases were accepted as 3,914 cases and concluded 3,904 cases. Among the accepted cases: the largest number of disputes happened in maritime freight forwarding contract, in aggregation amount of 2,828 cases; the second largest number of disputes happened in contract of carriage of goods by sea, in aggregation amount of 487 cases. The above two types of cases together accounted for 84.70% of the total number of first-instance maritime and maritime commercial cases accepted. The number of other representative cases was basically the same as that in 2016, including: 146 disputes over crew labor contract, 35 disputes over ship repair, shipbuilding and sale contracts, 43 disputes over charter party, 25 disputes over marine insurance contract, and 45 disputes over personal injury liability and 23 disputes over ship collision and touching damage. After the expansion of the scope of cases accepted by the maritime court, new types of disputes that can be accepted have emerged in new types of cases, such as disputes on sale contracts of ship-specific goods, disputes over terminal leasing contracts, and disputes over ship engineering contracts. The number of cases was relatively small. In addition, a maritime administrative case was accepted in 2017. Fig. 2 – 2 and Fig. 2 – 3 show the acceptance of various cases.

Chapter 2 Judicial Execution of Shipping Law

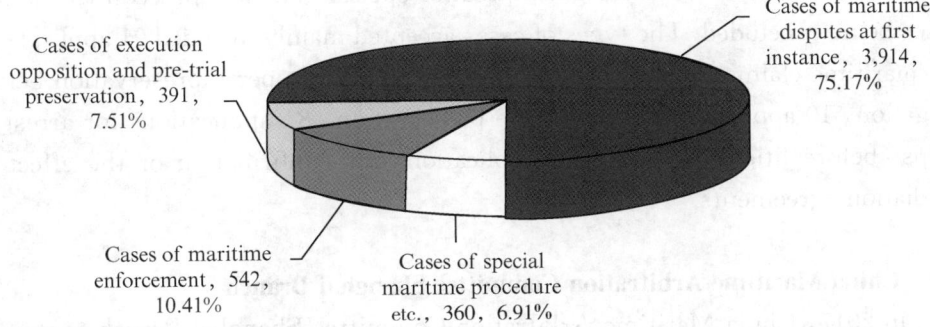

Fig. 2 – 2 Situation of Various Cases Accepted by Shanghai Maritime Court in 2017

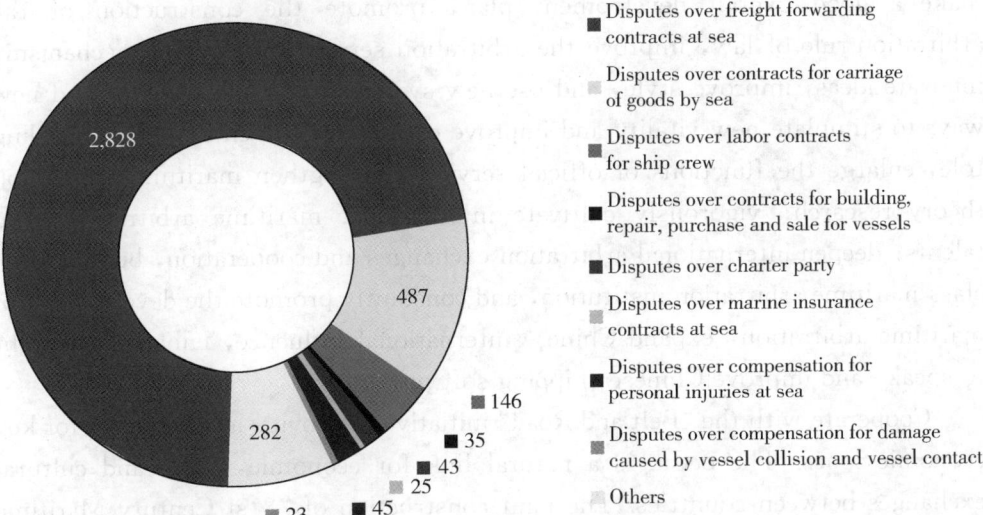

Fig. 2 – 3 Types of Maritime and Maritime Commercial of First
Instance Accepted by Shanghai Maritime Court in 2017

Among the cases concluded: 355 cases were concluded by judgments, accounting for 9.09%, a decrease of 3.25 percentage points year-on-year; 3,260 cases were concluded by withdrawal, accounting for 83.50%, an increase of 6.55 percentage points year-on-year; 277 cases were concluded by mediation, accounting for 7.10%, a decrease of 2.88 percentage points year-on-year; 12 cases were concluded by other means (including rejection of action, transfer), accounting for 0.31%, a decrease of 0.42 percentage points year-on-year.

There were 360 cases being accepted for special maritime procedures and 375 cases being concluded. The types of cases accepted mainly included 91 applications for maritime claims registration, 68 applications for property preservation before litigation, 10 applications for evidence preservation, 84 applications for arrest of ships (before litigation), and 64 applications for confirmation of the effect of mediation agreements.

1.2　China Maritime Arbitration Committee Shanghai Branch

In 2017, China Maritime Arbitration Committee Shanghai Branch continued to serve the national maritime power strategy and the "Belt and Road" initiative, make a good overall development plan, promote the construction of the arbitration rule of law, improve the arbitration service system and mechanism; innovate ideas, improve style, and use new systems, new mechanisms and new ways to stimulate new vitality and improve core competitiveness; play a leading role, enlarge the functions of official services, strengthen maritime arbitration theory research; vigorously cultivate international maritime arbitration legal talents; deepen international arbitration exchanges and cooperation, build a first-class maritime arbitration institution, and constantly promote the development of maritime arbitration, expand Chinese international influence, enhance the right to speak, and improve Chinese shipping soft power.

Cooperate with the "Belt and Road" initiative to provide legal services for key economic zones. The ocean is a natural link for economic, trade and cultural exchanges between countries. The joint construction of "21st Century Maritime Silk Road" brings new opportunities for the development of Chinese marine economy. China Maritime Arbitration Committee uses the established maritime arbitration service network formed by its branches and offices to increase its support for Shanghai, Tianjin, Zhoushan, Guangzhou, Shenzhen, Qingdao, Dalian and other key port cities, and actively provides professional legal services for enterprises and relevant departments to accelerate the construction of pilot free trade zones, the core area of "21st Century Maritime Silk Road", and demonstration zones for marine economic development.

Promote the docking work of action and mediation with the maritime court. The docking business of action and mediation with the maritime court is an important part of the maritime arbitration committee's business. On the basis of consolidating the docking mechanism of action and mediation with Shanghai Maritime Court, it will contact and develop the docking work of action and mediation with Tianjin Maritime Court, Wuhan Maritime Court, Dalian Maritime Court.

Promote the development and construction of the arbitration legal system. With the continuous progress of arbitration, Chinese arbitration law needs to be further revised and improved. Promote the revision of the *Arbitration Law*, at the same time reflect to the relevant departments the necessity and urgency of the revision of Chinese *Maritime Law*, actively promote the revision process of the *Maritime Law*, speed up the pace of Chinese laws in line with the world, and better safeguard shipping benefits of China.

Take advantage of the opportunity of contact and participation with the International Maritime Committee (CMI) to gradually establish friendly cooperative relations with CMI and its national member units to enhance the internationality of the maritime arbitration committee.

Under the new situation, China Maritime Arbitration Committee Shanghai Branch has the courage to act and take the lead to lead Chinese arbitration cause to continue to advance, effectively respond to the competition and challenges of the domestic and international arbitration markets, achieve the goal of a more international first-class arbitration institution to make new contributions to construct China into an international maritime arbitration center.

1.3 Shanghai Arbitration Committee International Shipping Arbitration Court (namely Shanghai International Shipping Arbitration Tribunal)

In 2017, Shanghai International Shipping Arbitration Tribunal (hereinafter referred to as Shipping Tribunal) continued to implement the promotion of shipping arbitration work and promote shipping arbitration through multiple channels. In the year, in addition to insisting on returning to and hearing advice about arbitration work of some parties after concluding the case, and visiting and receiving shipping professionals, Shipping Tribunal also actively participated in various activities in the industry, including docking with Pudong Finance Society, discussed and exchanged views on "Pudong Pilot Free Trade Zone", the "Belt and

Road" initiative, the national strategy of the "Yangtze River Economic Belt", promotion of the construction of Shanghai International Shipping Center, personnel training, cross-industry exchanges, "Internet Finance + Internet Arbitration" and other aspects of the cooperation between court and society; Shipping Tribunal and China (Shanghai) Pilot Free Trade Zone Commercial Committee (Shipping Office), ASEAN Legal Union, China (Shanghai) Pilot Free Trade Zone Overseas Investment Service Platform, Shanghai Maritime University Law School and Shanghai Lawyer Association jointly cooperated and held Shanghai Pilot Free Trade Zone and ASEAN Shipping Investment Legal Seminar under the framework of the "Belt and Road". Focusing on the main line of opportunities and challenges facing the construction of the "Belt and Road", from how to promote international cooperation, assist local governments and enterprises to be actively integrated into the "Belt and Road" construction layout, focusing on the methods and countermeasures of the industry-economic alliance, focusing on the research and creation of exchange and dialogue platform between the pilot free trade zone and ASEAN shipping investment, as well as implementing recommendations between policies and resources, and jointly exploring practice model under the new situation; Shipping Tribunal, in cooperation with Shanghai Shipping Exchange and Pudong Finance Society, conducted study on "the application of smart arbitration in shipping financial derivatives trading", striving to serve the construction of Shanghai International Shipping Center and International Finance Center and support the transformation and development of shipping economy of China.

In 2017, Shipping Tribunal also participated in a large number of shipping forums and exchange activities at the invitation of various agencies and organizations to expand the arbitration influence of Shipping Tribunal; one of the world's most influential legal media, *Asian Law Magazine* published relevant reports of ASEAN Legal Services Shanghai Cooperation Center that Shipping Tribunal participated in the joint construction.

With the approval of Shanghai Municipal People's Government on December 6, 2017, the sixth session of Shanghai Arbitration Committee was formally established. On December 26, 2017, the deputy secretary of Shanghai Municipal Party Committee and the mayor YING Yong issued a letter of appointment for the sixth session of the committee in the municipal government general office. The original fifth member, secretary of the party committee and CEO ZHANG Ye of Shanghai Shipping Exchange was re-appointed as the sixth member.

As a special agency for the professional arbitration of Shanghai Arbitration Committee to hear disputes over shipping, logistics and carriage, maritime and maritime commerce, and port construction, Shipping Tribunal has accepted nearly 1,000 cases involving disputes over logistics and warehousing, carriage of goods by sea, ship leasing, the purchase and sale of ship parts and shipbuilding materials, ship design, and land and air vehicle transactions since it was established, accumulating a wealth of arbitration results. In addition to hiring a large number of legal and economic personnel as arbitrators, the sixth committee also recruited a large number of professionals in the fields of maritime and maritime commerce, air, logistics and carriage, to provide a strong arbitrator team for Shanghai International Shipping Arbitration Tribunal. Shipping Tribunal will actively implement the spirit of the 19th National Congress of the CPC, supported by industry practices, respecting laws and objective facts, and escorting the construction of Shanghai's international shipping center and Shanghai's "free trade port".

2 Selection of Maritime Judicial and Arbitration Cases

2.1 Cases of Maritime Court

1) Disputes over compensation for damages of delivery of goods without original bill of lading

[Case]

The Appellant (the Plaintiff of first instance): XH Logistics Co., Ltd.

The Respondent (the Defendant of first instance): Chile NM Steamship Co., Ltd.

In March 2012, XH Logistics entrusted Shanghai XH to book with NM Steamship (China) Shipping Co., Ltd., the agent of NM Steamship, to ship a batch of medical equipment from Shanghai Port, China to Cabello Port and La Guaira port, Venezuela. Afterwards, NM ships issued 15 sets of original ocean bills of lading. Among them, the shipper recorded in 13 sets of bills of lading was not XH Logistics, the consignees recorded in 15 sets of bills of lading were all Reesika, and the carrier was NM Steamship. The above 15 sets of original ocean bills of lading were all held by XH Logistics.

On March 26, 2012, NM Steamship sent e-mails to booking agents in China through their agents that: "Venezuelan Customs and Port Authority concluded a new regulation that the consignee can take the goods without the original bill of lading. In view of this, the special requirements for Venezuela goods booking and bill of lading are as follows: a letter of guarantee concluded by the consignor should be issued when the EDI booking is submitted; the letter of guarantee requirement for the suspension of the freight of the consignee or the notifier, namely, the blacklisted customer who booked should not be accepted;...". Later, NM Steamship received a letter of guarantee, whose title was HIN - PRO INTERNATIONAL LOGISTICS LIMITED (consistent with the English name of XH Logistics), and the content was that: "... We hereby recognize that we are still willing to send the goods to Venezuela and bear the risk of delivery of goods without original bill of lading at the port of destination by ourselves... We hereby irrevocably undertake, guarantee and agree to compensate and guarantee NM Steamship against any loss, claim, fee, cost, damage or liability that is directly or indirectly suffered as a result of delivery of goods without original bill of lading."

The container goods under the above 15 sets of bills of lading were unloaded at the port of destination between April 26 and August 14, 2012, and were taken by Reesika and other outsiders from May 25 to August 30, 2012. For this, XH Logistics filed an action, claiming NM Steamship to compensate XH Logistics for the loss of value and interest suffered as a result of delivery of goods without original bill of lading.

[Judgment]

The court held that: the legal relationship of contract of carriage of goods by sea between the two parties was established. Since the goods involved were taken at the port of destination, XH Logistics, as the holder of the original bill of lading involved, has the right to claim civil liability against NM Steamship as the carrier. Regarding whether NM Steamship could be exempted from the legal liability for delivery of goods without original bill of lading based on the letter of guarantee involved or relevant laws of our country, even if the letter of guarantee was not authorized as claimed by XH Logistics, its act like adding official seal was binding. However, the content of the guarantee is not of course exempting the carrier from the legal liability of delivery of goods without original bill of lading at the port of destination. Similarly, according to the *Judicial Interpretation of Delivery of Goods without Original Bills of Lading* Article 7, NM Steamship in the case did not provide sufficient and valid evidence to prove that it could comply with the laws and regulations of the location of the port of unloading stated in the bill of lading and must deliver goods of the carrier that arrived at the port to local customs or port authorities. Accordingly, NM Steamship could not be exempted from the legal liability for delivery of goods without original bill of lading at the port of destination according to the letter of guarantee involved or Chinese laws. Since XH Logistics could not prove that it was the owner of the goods involved, nor could it prove that it suffered the loss of payment, so the damages it claimed had no legal basis. For this, the court rejected XH Logistics's claims.

[**Comment**]

a. If the carrier causes loss of the original bill of lading holder due to delivery of goods without the original bill of lading, the original bill of lading holder can require the carrier to bear liability for breach of contract or tort. To claim the loss of payment to the carrier as the owner of the goods involved, the identity of the owner of the goods must be proved. The fact of holding a bill of lading cannot waive the obligation of the holder of the bill of lading to prove that it has suffered an actual loss.

If the carrier must deliver the goods carried to the port to the local customs or port authority according to the laws and regulations of the location of unloading port stated in the bill of lading, the carrier should not bear the civil liability for the delivery of the goods without the original bill of lading, but the carrier should bear obligations stipulated by local laws of the port of unloading.[1]

---

[1] The *Venezuela Customs Organization Law* Article 22 and the *Venezuelan Maritime Code* Article 203 stipulate that there are three kinds of people that goods can be delivered to, namely public warehouses, private warehouses or consignees.

2) Disputes over contract of carriage of goods by sea

[Case]

The Appellant (the Defendant of first instance): GRF Shipping Co., Ltd.

The Respondent (the Plaintiff of first instance): Dalian JY Import and Export Co., Ltd. (hereinafter referred to as JY)

The Defendant of first instance: LH Shipping Agency Co., Ltd. (hereinafter referred to as LH)

On November 25, 2013, JY concluded an agency import agreement with the outsider, YF, agreeing that YF entrusted JY to import 40,000 (+/−10%) tons of laterite nickel ore produced in Indonesia. On November 30, 2013, JY, as the buyer and HY concluded a sales contract for laterite nickel ore. GRF was the owner of the carriage ship. On November 29, 2013, HY (lessee) and GRF (lessor) concluded a charter party. The contract agreed that the freight should be paid USD 100,000 after the contract was concluded, and the remaining freight was paid before the ship arrived at the port of unloading. The delivery conditions agreed in the contract were delivery only after the original bill of lading was provided. On December 27, 2013, GRF issued a clean shipping bill of lading. The bill of lading stated that the shipper was HY, and the consignee provided instructions.

JY obtained a full set of original bills of lading for the goods involved through L/C negotiation. In January 2014, the goods involved was unloaded and stored in Lianyungang. Thereafter, JY issued an original bill of lading to GRF's unloading agent United Company to require to take. On March 1, 2014, GRF recognized that LH was its agent at the port of unloading, and LH exercised the lien on the goods involved according to the instructions of GRF. GRF had not yet delivered the goods involved to JY.

[Judgment]

In the case, JY was entrusted by YF to import the goods involved, but according to the agency import agreement concluded between JY and YF, the ownership of the goods involved belonged to JY before YF paid all the payment. JY concluded a contract in its own name, opened a letter of credit, paid for the documents and declared the goods for import. The bill of lading involved contained the shipper as JY, and after paying the payment to HY, the full set of bills of lading for the goods involved was legally obtained. There was relationship of a contract of carriage of goods by sea between JY and GRF. As the right owner of the bill of lading, JY had the right to claim for disputes and loss suffered during the performance of the contract in its own name. JY required GRF to fulfill the carrier's delivery obligations based on its relationship of a contract of carriage of goods by sea with GRF, and did not claim rights based on the ownership of the goods. In the case that JY issued the original bill of lading to GRF and LH and required to deliver the goods, it had the right to take the goods involved.

GRF and LH claimed detention of the goods involved on the ground that HY owed its freight and demurrage fee. The evidence was insufficient to prove that there was a fact that the freight and demurrage fee were not paid and the exact amount. Even if the fact that freight and demurrage fee were not paid existed, the corresponding freight and demurrage fee were also based on the charter party between HY and GRF. JY was not a party to the charter party and had no obligation to pay the above amounts. According to the *Maritime Law* Article 69, the shipper and the carrier could agree that the freight should be paid by the consignee, but the agreement should be stated in the carriage document. The bill of lading involved stated "freight advance payment", but did not specify that the consignee should pay the freight; according to the *Maritime Law* Article 78, the consignee and the holder of the bill of lading should not be liable for demurrage fee, loss of warehouse fee and other fee relevant to loading happened at the port of loading, except that the bill of lading clearly stated that the above fee were born by the consignee and the holder of the bill of lading, and there was no corresponding record in the bill of lading involved. JY was not the obligor of payment of freight and demurrage fee claimed by GRF, and GRF had no right to retain the goods involved. The goods involved were eligible for delivery. If GRF failed to fulfill its delivery obligations to JY, it should compensate according to the above amount.

LH was the unloading agent of GRF. It handled the relevant matters at the unloading port according to the instructions of GRF, and the corresponding legal consequences should be borne by its client.

[**Comment**]

Foreign trade agency, usually an agent concludes a contract in its own name, rights and obligations of the contract are born externally by the agent, and the disputes arising from the contract are claimed externally by the agent or take other remedies, the rights and obligations between the agent and the principal are determined by the agency contract.

According to the *Maritime Law* Article 87, if the freight, joint average damages, demurrage fee and necessary fees paid by the carrier for the goods and other fee that should be paid to the carrier are not paid in full, and no appropriate guarantee is provided, the carrier can retain its goods within reasonable limits. If the shipper has not paid the freight, demurrage fee, empty storage fee and the necessary fee paid by the carrier for the goods of any voyage, the shipper improperly describes the goods or the private entrustment of dangerous goods causes damage to the carrier or other goods and property and when multimodal transportation is used to ship goods, the land freight or other fee charged by the carrier, or any other debts to the carrier that are not performed on time, the carrier has the right to retain the goods. However, the carrier's lien should not be exercised against the consignee who has no obligation to pay for the fee.

3) Disputes over liability for ship collision damage

[Case]

The Appellant (the Defendant of first instance): TH Shipping Co., Ltd. (hereinafter referred to as TH)

The Respondent (the Plaintiff of first instance): CPIC Shipping Insurance Business Operation Center (hereinafter referred to as TB)

On April 8, 2013, a collision accident happened between M.V. "CHANGFU 6" owned by CF and M.V. "TAIHANG 118" owned by TH in the downstream navigation lane of the Yangtze River, causing damage to M.V. "TAIHANG 118" and M.V. "CHANGFU 6" to sink. After investigation and mediation by Shanghai High People's Court, TH bore 85% of the compensation liability and CF bore 15% of the compensation liability. On April 28, 2012, CF insured all risks for coastal and inland ships for M.V. "CHANGFU 6" to CPIC. On July 5, 2013, CPIC agreed to pay salvage charges, goods removal fee, sinking detection fee and all the insurance compensation for the loss of M.V. "TAIHANG 118" that should be born by proportion of the liability and covered by the insurance. After CPIC paid the CF the actual insurance compensation, it obtained the subrogation right, and filed an action to claim TH for compensation for the above loss.

TH claimed that: ①The collision and salvage operations jointly caused the total damage to the ship. TH did not bear the total damage to the ship and the corresponding wreckage removal loss. ② Part of the facts in the case were wrongly recognized: the entrusted assessment of the market value of the ship had no legal and factual basis, and the residual value of the ship should be deducted from the loss of the ship's value.

CPIC argued that: ①The loss of M.V. "CHANGFU 6" had a direct causal relationship with the accident. ②The underwriting value of M.V. "CHANGFU 6" could objectively reflect the market value of the ship. ③The payment made by TH to CF in advance had nothing to do with CPIC and should not be deducted.

[Judgment]

The case was the dispute over compensation for ship collision damage. After the collision, the reasonableness of the sunken salvage and removal fee paid by CF, as well as the loss of the value of the ship that TH insured to CPIC and the specific amount of the above fee caused the disputes of the appeal parties.

In the case, the two parties of the court unanimously selected an assessment agency to assess the ship's value loss, presuming that the ship was totally damaged. The parties had a lot of disputes involved in the calculation of the loss of ship's value, and the court confirmed that: the compensation for property damage caused by the collision of the ship should reach the principle of restoring to the original state as far as possible. In case of failure to restore the ship to its original state, the reimburse should be based on being restored to the original state. Therefore, the reimburse for the total loss of the ship should be based on the replacement of the damaged ship to resume the relevant operation to make up for the total loss of the ship due to collision.

Regarding the issue of the deduction of the residual value of M.V. "CHANGFU 6", the ship sank in the navigation lane of the Yangtze River due to the collision accident involved, which seriously affected the navigational safety of the ship. The relevant maritime authority required CF to salvage and remove within a time limit. Otherwise, the compulsory salvage and removal would be carried out at the fee of CF. The salvage contract's agreement to change salvage operations to wreck removal operations when the ship failed to be salvages as a whole was to avoid further loss and consider the necessity of salvage. The agreement was legal and valid. The residual value was finally credited to the salvage and removal fee of the ship wreckage as agreed in the salvage contract, and should not be deducted from the loss of the ship's value. Regarding the loss of the value of the ship, the loss was jointly estimated by assessment agency entrusted by both parties. The parties did not clearly have objection to the assessed value of the ship. According to the *Provisions of the Supreme People's Court on Compensation for Property Damage in Cases of Collision and Touching of Ships* (hereinafter referred to as *Ship Collision Provision*) and taking the practice of the ship industry about costs and fee happened after the second-hand ship was purchased and put into actual operation into account, combined with the usual practice that the damaged party should find a replacement ship to make up for the operating loss after the total loss of the ship, therefore, the loss of the value of the ship was the market value of the ship plus the tax, maintenance, and inspection fee of the second-hand ship.

In summary, whereas CPIC's voluntary waiver of the wreck underwater exploration fee, the court of second instance revoked the judgment of the wreck underwater exploration fee. TH's claim to not bear the total loss of ship and wreck removal fee could not be established and should be dismissed. The court of second instance supported CPIC's claim for loss of ship's value, salvage and rescue fee, goods removal fee, and wreck underwater exploration fee, and rejected CPIC's other claims.

[**Comment**]

The case is a case of dispute over a ship collision damage compensation in which the insurer, after paying the insured, requires the other party of the collision to be liable for compensation liability for the collision in proportion to the fault. The *Maritime Law* Article 169 stipulates that both parties of the collision shall bear proportional liability according to the degree of fault in the collision accident, and the *Insurance Law of the People's Republic of China* Article 60 stipulates that giving the insurer the right of subrogation. For this, there is no dispute in the case. The issue in the case was how to calculate the ships value loss accurately and reasonably.

According to the *Ship Collision Provision* Article 3: "Ship Damage

Compensation also includes: reasonable salvage expenses, the fee of detection, salvage and removal of sunken ships, and the fee of setting sunken ship marks." Article 8 stipulates that: "Calculation of ship value loss should be confirmed by the market value of similar ships at the time of the place of the ship collision; if there is no market value of similar ships at the place of collision, confirmed by the market price of similar ships in the port of registry of the ship, or the average price of similar ships in other regions; if there is no market price, calculated by deducting from depreciation from the construction cost or purchase price of the original ship (the depreciation rate is 4% to 10% per year); if there is no value after depreciation, calculated by the residual value. If the ship still has residual value after being salvaged, residual value should be deducted from the ship value." The calculation of ship value loss is of great significance for the correct handling of ship collision damage compensation.

The case involves the estimated total loss of the ship. In practice, the assessment of the total loss price of the ship includes the market price depreciation method, the market price analogy method, the replacement of price method, the current value of income method, and the foreign exchange conversion method. Which method should be accepted for the specific task must be confirmed according to the actual situation of the ship. In addition, the ship's estimation must be applied by the parties to the court or carried out by an estimation agency jointly selected by both parties that the court entrusts. This is to prevent the parties from entrusting the estimation by themselves and the valuer is susceptible to the influence of the parties and has deviation. Taking this purpose into consideration in the case, the domestic ship transaction price information that most closely matched the time of the collision accident was taken, combined with more representative domestic ship listing price information around this time node, and a comprehensive comparison was made to obtain the most suitable price.

4) Disputes over marine insurance contract

[Case]

The Appellant (the Defendant of first instance): Guangdong RK Shipping Co., Ltd. (hereinafter referred to as RK)

The Respondent (the Plaintiff of first instance): ZY Insurance Co., Ltd.

Guangdong Branch (hereinafter referred to as ZY Insurance)

On November 1, 2010, RK and ZY Insurance concluded the Coastal Inland Ship Insurance Contract, underwriting M. V. "×× 1" of RK. The insurance policy agreed that the underwriting conditions were ZY Insurance Coastal Inland Insurance (all risks), ZY Insurance Coastal Inland Insurance plus quarter collision, touch liability insurance clauses, and agreed exemptions: partial loss, total loss, presumed total loss, including collision, touch and rescue responsibilities, the absolute deductibles for each accident was 150,000 yuan or 10% of the loss, which is subject to the higher.

The *ZY Insurance Coastal and Inland Insurance Clause* attached to the insurance contract agreed in Article 2 "All Risks" that only the direct loss and expense caused by collision or touch should be born, and Article 11 agreed that: "the insurer deducts deductibles according to the agreement in the insurance policy for each compensation (except for total loss, collision, and touch liability)."

On February 2, 2011, M. V. "×× 1" had an accident of touching the terminal, causing part of the terminal to be damaged and sinking into the bottom of the river. The comprehensive building built on the terminal was also damaged. Two staff on duty in the building were killed and injured. Three oil transfer arms on the terminal were damaged by falling water. After the accident, RK applied to the court to establish a maritime compensation liability limitation fund.

The dispute between the terminal company and RK went through the first-instance, second-instance and retrial procedure, and a judgment was issued. However, for whether the loss of the five items such as terminal wreck removal fee, accident site and channel care fee, mark setting fee, property loss in the collapsed comprehensive building and purchase fee of temporary terminal duty room caused by the collision accident were covered by the insurance liability; how to calculate the insurance premiums and whether to convert the insurance compensation according to the proportion between the limitation of maritime compensation liability enjoyed and the liability bore before; whether deductibles were deducted from each insurance compensation; the problem about lawyers' fee and litigation fee in the other case and this case; whether the litigation between the two parties exceeded the statute of limitations, RK and ZY Insurance had disputes.

[Judgment]

The court confirmed that the case was the dispute over marine insurance contract. The court confirmed several issues concerning the disputes of the parties as follows: ①Statute of limitations: according to the judicial interpretation on statute of limitations Article 12 and the *Maritime Law* Article 267, the interruption of statute of limitations could be interrupted by the action of the parties and the respondent agreed to perform their obligations. Therefore, the two parties concluded the *Advance Payment Agreement*, and RK's action did not exceed statute of limitations. ②Fees: wreck removal and care fee of terminal involved and mark setting fee were derived from the administrative enforcement measures of the Maritime Safety Administration. The reasons were clear, and the nature was the fee happened to ensure the safety and smoothness of the channel. They were in the scope of exclusions in the annex of the insurance contract. However, other fee was within the scope stipulated in the insurance clauses of the "collision and touch liability", which was limited to the "direct loss and fee happened" of other ships that were collided and the "terminals, port facilities, navigation marks" that were touched. ③About whether ZY Insurance bore the insurance premium within the scope of the limitation of liability: according to the *Maritime Law* Article 206, the insurer enjoyed the same limitation of compensation liability as the insured. Therefore, the amount of insurance premiums of ZY Insurance was paid in full when not exceeding the amount of limitation of liability. ④The courts of the first and second instance held that the lawyers' fee and litigation fee for the other litigation were in nature the fee paid by RK to reduce claims relevant to insurance liability, and combined with the relationship between pleas and insurance liability, it was confirmed to be born by ZY Insurance. ⑤Whether the deductible amount was applicable to the insurance premiums and litigation fee, although the special agreement of insurance contract contradicted with the agreement on deductible amount of Article 11 of the annex, the court held that the special agreement took precedence over the annex agreement—because "special agreement", including "deductible conditions" was the result of mutual agreement between the two parties, the insured was informed of the relevant agreement, the insurance policy involved was a written offer of the insurance contract concluded by the two parties, and the deductible clauses contained in it were also consistent to the insurance policy.

[Comment]

There are two major issues worth noting in the case:

a. The same interpretation of the limitation of maritime compensation liability of the insurer and the insured, from the perspective of the compensation limitation: in confirming the specific amount, the same calculation method applies to the insurer's compensation limitation and the insured's compensation limitation, namely according to the *Maritime Law* Article 210, the calculation is based on the total tonnage of the ship. According to the final results, the insurer's compensation limitation and the insured's compensation limitation are numerically equal in the specific amount. Therefore, in the case, the amount of limitation of maritime compensation liability enjoyed by ZY Insurance Guangdong Branch as the insurer was the same as the amount of limitation of maritime compensation liability enjoyed by RK as the insured, and when the compensation liability bore by the insurer did not exceed the amount, excluding deduction factors such as deductibles, the insurer should bear the insurance compensation liability to the insured in full. In addition, the insurer paid the limit fund amount in advance, which does not mean that the final amount of its external compensation is the amount of the fund. In addition to the review of the plea for the limitation of liability, the agreement between the insurer and the insured in the insurance policy is also an important basis for handling the external compensation of both parties and the amount actually bore inside.

b. When the insurance contract itself has contradiction in the agreement of the deductible, the court will interpret the contract based on the structure and content of the insurance contract and insurance policy. Which is contradictory is sufficient to attract the attention of both parties to the insurance contract. Other materials such as an "insurance policy" that the parties use to agree insurance matters, which are used as a written offer for the insurance contract to determine whether the deductible applies.

5) Disputes over maritime guarantee contract

[Case]

The Plaintiff: CZ Shipbuilding Group Co., Ltd.

The Defendant: Singapore DL Overseas Co., Ltd.

On April 27, 2012, the Plaintiff bareboat chartered its M.V. "CHENGLU 58" to Zhongcheng International Shipping Co., Ltd. In early July 2012, M.V. "CHENGLU 58" was loaded with goods at Bayuquan Port, China. The destination port was Gaoshichang Port, Thailand. The shipper was China National Petroleum International Corporation. The consignee was notified by Thailand Siam Commercial Bank Co., Ltd. The notify party was Mahawang Company, Thailand. The loading goods was 12,250 tons of bulk urea. The outsider HB International Shipping Agency Co., Ltd. issued a bill of lading on behalf of the captain of M.V. "CHENGLU 58" on July 10, 2012. The front of the bill of lading indicated that the charter party was incorporated.

The 12,250 tons of bulk urea involved were loaded on July 12, 2012. Because the loading period of the letter of credit was July 10, 2012, the Defendant, as the charterer of M.V. "CHENGLU 58", issued a letter of guarantee to the shipowner, bareboat charterer and ship management company of M.V. "CHENGLU 58", requiring that the chief officer's receipt and bill of lading be reversed to that date so that the loading date of the bill of lading matched the letter of credit. The letter of guarantee stated that, "as the consideration of the reverse bill of lading issued by your company according to our instructions, our company undertakes as follows: ①compensate your company or your employees, agents for compensation or loss or damage of any nature, and guarantee your company to be exempted from such loss, if such loss is caused by your company issuing a reverse bill of lading to China National Petroleum International Co., Ltd. at the requirement of our company; ②for the litigation of your company, employees and agents caused by issuing a reverse bill of lading, our company will provide sufficient funds from time to time to help your company defend against such litigation; ③if M.V. CHENGLU 58 or other ships or property of your company are arrested or detained or threatened to be arrested or detained, our company will provide bail or other guarantees to release the ship or property, and compensate your company for any loss or fee caused by the arrest or detention of the ship, regardless of whether such arrest or detention is reasonable; ④the liability of any person or any party is joint and inseparable under the letter of compensation, and does not presuppose that your company file an action against a third party, regardless of whether the third party is a party to the contract or is liable for the accident under the letter of compensation; ⑤the letter of compensation will be explained based on the UK laws and people who are relevant to this disclaimer are subject to the jurisdiction of the High Court of England."

On August 6, 2012, Thai Central Intellectual Property and International Trade Court (hereinafter referred to as Thai court) arrested M.V. "CHENGLU 58" at the anchorage of Gaoshichang Port in Thailand on the basis of the application of the consignee Mahawang on the ground that the carriage accident caused the loss of goods. On August 7, 2013, Thai court issued an order to release the ship, released the arrest of M.V. "CHENGLU 58", and actually released the ship on August 14. On March 6, 2014, Thai court issued the judgement for the civil claim case about Mahawang v. the Plaintiff of the case and Weiriya Insurance Co., Ltd., rejecting Mahawang's claims, and each party bore the relevant fee.

The Plaintiff claimed that the arrest of M.V. "CHENGLU 58" was due to the Plaintiff's follow-up to the Defendant's instructions to reverse the bill of lading. The Defendant had clearly promised to compensate all loss happened due to the reverse of the bill of lading. Therefore the Defendant should compensate it for loss.

The Defendant did not reply.

[Judgment]

The court held that the case was the dispute over a maritime guarantee contract. The guarantee object of the shipping letter of guarantee involved, namely, the reverse bill of lading was illegal, and its guarantee content was also illegal. The original illegal guarantee could not be legally valid because the recipient of the letter of guarantee claimed that it was not the subject of the illegal act. The letter of guarantee involved did not have corresponding legal effect, but it did not affect the right of the guarantee recipient to claim damage compensation to the Defendant when it committed an illegal act according to the instructions of the issuer of the letter of guarantee or assumed that the Defendant committed illegal acts and suffered loss. In the case, although the ship of the Plaintiff (recipient of the letter of guarantee) was arrested, it was not due to the reverse bill of lading, and there was no inevitable causal relationship between the two. Therefore, the Plaintiff's claim of the Defendant to bear the compensation liability with the letter of guarantee lacked factual and legal basis. The Plaintiff's current evidence could not yet prove that it was the carrier or the actual carrier in the contract of carriage of goods by sea involved, nor could it prove that it established a contractual relationship of carriage of goods by sea with the Defendant. The Plaintiff, as the owner of the ship, namely, the actual carrier in the contract of carriage of goods by sea, claimed that the Defendant should bear the loss during the arrest of the ship involved, which lacked factual and legal basis. In the end, the court judged that it did not support the Plaintiff's claims.

[Comment]

The reverse bill of lading is an illegal act in the carriage of goods by sea. The shipper issues a shipping letter of guarantee in exchange for the reverse bill of lading of the carrier. Both acts are not in good faith and should be invalid. Although the shipping letter of guarantee is invalid, the recipient of the letter of guarantee can claim damage compensation from the issuer of the letter of guarantee if it commits an illegal act according to the instructions of the issuer of the letter of guarantee or assumes that it commits an illegal act and suffers loss. The premise is that there is an inevitable causal relationship between the behavior of reverse bill of lading and the consequences of damage. In addition, the recipient of the letter of guarantee and the issuer of the letter of guarantee should bear corresponding liabilities according to the size of the fault.

6) Disputes over guarantee contract

[Case]

The Plaintiff: HS Shipping Co., Ltd.

The Defendant: Shanghai PF Bank Co., Ltd.

On December 6, 2006, China-Tanzania United Shipping Co., Ltd. (hereinafter referred to as Zhongtan) and Nantong Huigang Shipbuilding Co., Ltd. (hereinafter referred to as Huigang) concluded a shipbuilding contract. The contract agreed that Zhongtan should pay Huigang shipbuilding payment in installments at a time point during shipbuilding, and Huigang applied to the Defendant to issue a refund letter of guarantee, and the Defendant provided Zhongtan with a refund guarantee, namely, when terminating the shipbuilding contract according to the terms of the contract, if Huigang failed to repay shipbuilding payment to Zhongtan within a certain period of time, the

Defendant should bear the liability of guarantee repayment. Thereafter, Zhongtan transferred the shipbuilding contract to the Plaintiff in the form of an updated agreement. The Defendant issued a refund letter of guarantee on September 11, 2008, and subsequently revised it on March 16, 2010. According to the letter of guarantee, if the seller failed to repay within 15 working days after receiving the buyer's written repayment requirement, the Defendant should irrevocably, absolutely and unconditionally pay the amount the seller should pay as the main debtor rather than only as the guarantor; the letter of guarantee should come into effect from the date on which the first instalment was received by Huigang; any dispute arising from or relevant to the letter of guarantee should be arbitrated in London according to the rules and regulations of London Maritime Arbitrators Association. The Plaintiff paid the first installment to Huigang on November 30, 2009, and paid the second installment on April 22, 2010 according to the contract. Because Huigang failed to deliver the ship within 180 days after June 30, 2011, the original delivery date in the contract, which constituted a delayed delivery, the Plaintiff issued a cancellation notice on January 10, 2012, requiring Huigang to refund all the payment and interest paid by the Plaintiff, but Huigang did not refund it. On February 17 of the same year, the Plaintiff issued a refund requirement to the Defendant, but the Defendant did not pay any payment.

On March 16, 2012, the Plaintiff issued an arbitration application to the Defendant, stating that it had filed an arbitration with the London Maritime Arbitrators Association according to Article 10 of the refund letter of guarantee. The Plaintiff held that it made a refund requirement according to the terms of the refund letter of guarantee, and the Defendant, as the refund guarantor, failed to pay the buyer the installment and interest happened according to the terms of the refund letter of guarantee, which constituted a breach of contract, and therefore claimed the Defendant to pay the debt.

The arbitral tribunal confirmed that the shipbuilding contract and letter of guarantee were unenforceable, and on July 8, 2013, it ruled to reject the Plaintiff's claim.

The Plaintiff claimed that the Defendant was at fault when making the refund letter of guarantee, and required the Defendant to compensate the refund amount recognized by the refund letter of guarantee.

The Defendant proposed a jurisdiction objection, claiming that the dispute involved was settled in arbitration in London, so the court should not accept it. Even if the Plaintiff filed an action based on contractual fault, the contractual fault liability dispute was also a contractual dispute, which was still an arbitration matter agreed in the arbitration agreement and the court should not accept it. The Plaintiff had a malicious action and the action should be rejected.

[**Judgment**]

After the hearing, the court held that the Plaintiff's action was based on the letter of guarantee issued by the Defendant on September 12, 2008. Article 10 of the letter of guarantee agreed that "this letter of guarantee should be interpreted and governed by UK laws, and any dispute arising from or relevant to the letter of guarantee should be submitted to arbitration in London according to the rules and procedures of the London Maritime Arbitrator Committee". The Plaintiff recognized that the arbitration was initiated in London on May 17, 2012 according to the arbitration clause, and its arbitration claim was rejected by the London Arbitration Tribunal. Although the Plaintiff claimed that the Defendant's major fault in the process of concluding the letter of guarantee caused its loss, but the content of its claim was also a dispute relevant to the letter of guarantee, and it should be submitted to arbitration for settlement. The Plaintiff's choice of London arbitration not only recognized the effect of the arbitration clause, but also indicated that it was bound by the arbitration clause, not that the arbitration clause stated in the action was a unilateral expression of the Defendant's intention. According to the law, the parties reached an arbitration agreement, and one party filed an action against the people's court without declaring that there was an arbitration agreement. After the people's court accepted it, and the other party submitted the arbitration agreement before the first hearing, the people's court should reject the action. The dispute involved has been settled by the London Arbitration Commission, and the court had no jurisdiction over the case.

[**Comment**]

The effect of the arbitration clause in the shipbuilding contract as the main contract is not necessarily relevant to the dispute under the guarantee contract. After the dispute happened, the creditor's act of arbitration according to the arbitration clause in the letter of guarantee issued by the guarantor unilaterally recognized the effect of the arbitration clause, indicating that it was willing to be bound by the arbitration clause, and the two parties reached a consensus on arbitration. Once the arbitration clause in the contract is established, it will be valid from the beginning without the revocation of the contracting party. The valid arbitration clause in the contract is still applicable to the disputes of the parties concerning the liability for contractual fault. The *Contract Law Article* 57 *stipulates that no matter whether the final result of the contractual fault is that the contract is not concluded, the contract is invalid or revoked, it will not affect the effect of the arbitration clause legally established.*

7) *Disputes over liability for personal injury at sea*

[Case]

The Plaintiff: BIAN Mou

The Defendant: DONG Mou

On March 24, 2015, when BIAN Mou worked on "SU QI YU 01319" owned by DONG Mou, his back was hit by a cable off the stern, causing cervical bone marrow damage. On March 26 of the same year, the fishing ship returned to Port. BIAN Mou was sent to the Second People's Hospital of Qidong by his family. After examination, he was diagnosed to have high paraplegia. It was recommended to be sent to Shanghai Hospital for treatment. On the afternoon of the same day, BIAN Mou was sent to Shanghai Oriental Hospital for treatment, and was diagnosed with cervical spinal cord injury and quadriplegia. On March 31, BIAN Mou underwent surgery at Shanghai Oriental Hospital. After the operation, BIAN Mou underwent symptoms such as dyspnoea, no sputum out, and fever. After April 18, BIAN Mou underwent a coma.

On November 11, Judicial Appraisal Center of the Institute of Judicial Appraisal Science and Technology issued an appraisal opinion, holding that BIAN Mou was injured on board for some reason and had the basis of injury that caused high paraplegia. After surgical treatment in the hospital, BIAN Mou's physical condition developed into unconsciousness and quadriplegia. According to the provisions of GB 18667—2002 *Disability Assessment of Injured Persons in Road Traffic Accidents*, the sequelae of the residual quadriplegia were equivalent to the first-level disability of road traffic accidents. BIAN Mou suffered from this trauma on the basis of his cervical degenerative lesions, which caused cervical spinal cord injury and left limb paralysis after treatment. Trauma was the main factor, and the trauma participation was determined to be 60% to 80%.

BIAN Mou's son, BIAN Xiaomou, represented BIAN Mou and claimed that BIAN Mou was injured in an accident while working on fish ship owned by DONG Mou, DONG Mou should compensate, so he claimed that DONG Mou should bear medical fee, disability compensation, spirit consolation payments, lost work fee, wages, transportation fee, nursing fee, dependents' living fee.

DONG Mou argued that the casual relationship between BIAN Mou's injury and hospital treatment and BIAN Mou's current condition was unknown, and DONG Mou should not be liable for compensation for BIAN Mou's own injury and medical misconduct. As for medical fee, BIAN Mou did not actually pay, nor could he distinguish the fee of treating his own diseases. BIAN Mou had no right to claim from him.

[Judgment]

The court held that if BIAN Mou was employed by DONG Mou to work on a fish ship owned by DONG Mou, it should be regarded as establishing a labor relationship between the two parties. As a ship owner and actual operator, DONG Mou had the obligation to manage and guarantee the safety of ship operations and the personal safety of the crew. BIAN Mou was injured in the process of providing labor services to DONG Mou, and DONG Mou, as an employer, should be liable for compensation according to law.

The medical fee, nursing fee, transportation fee and other fee actually paid by BIAN Mou due to hospitalization should be borne by DONG Mou. Because BIAN did not actually pay the medical fee, and was still in the process of being hospitalized, he could make a separate claim after paying the corresponding fee. The compensation for disability was calculated based on BIAN's disability level and the median value of 60% to 80% of the participation of trauma given in the judicial opinion.

[Comment]

The crew was injured while working on the ship, and medical damage happened during the hospitalization treatment, resulting in an increase in the final disability. When handling maritime personal injury liability disputes, the maritime court should pay attention to: firstly, the claim for medical damage compensation to the medical institution is a medical damage liability dispute, which is not within the jurisdiction of the maritime court and should not be accepted or incidental hearing; secondly, although the medical damage dispute is not under the jurisdiction of the maritime court, the maritime court may involve the distinction between the proportion of disability due to maritime damage and medical damage in the process of handling disputes over maritime personal injury liability. When entrusting judicial appraisal, an appraisal institution with medical damage appraisal qualifications should be selected to appraise the participation in the results of disability caused by maritime damage, so as to ensure the accuracy of the judgement, and guarantee the rights of the relevant right holders to claim separately for possible medical damage liability; thirdly, the shipowner's or actual operator's liability for compensation should be proportionately born based on the causal relationship between the crew's injury on board and the final damage result.

8) Disputes over contract of carriage of goods by sea

[Case]

The Plaintiff: YG Insurance Co., Ltd. Hangzhou Center Branch

The Defendant: Shanghai LS Trading Center Co., Ltd.

On August 21, 2013, outsider WC concluded a logistics service trading contract with the Defendant. The "Contract Overview" clause agreed that: the property company entrusted the Defendant to ship the goods; the Defendant provided comprehensive logistics solutions and provided professional logistics suppliers according to the plan; the Defendant concluded a valid carriage contract with the designated logistics supplier to provide the necessary guarantee to carriage of goods to ensure the safe, timely and accurate delivery of the goods; the Defendant provided the third-party payment and invoicing services for carriage. The "Service Content and Price" clause agreed that: the name of the goods was strip steel, with a total weight of 5,334.76 tons; the place of departure was Jingtang Port, the destination was Jiangyin Huangtian, the mode of carriage was water carriage, and the ship name was XINHUA. The "Settlement Method" clause agreed that: WC chose the Defendant as a third-party payment platform; WC needed to pay the Defendant's freight of RMB 33,884.84 yuan and transaction service fee RMB 169.42 yuan; upon recognition of the completion of carriage, the property company instructed the Defendant to transfer the above freight to the logistics supplier within 5 days. No waybill was actually issued for the carriage involved.

The goods involved was loaded onto M.V. "XINGHUA" on August 20, 2013, and arrived at Jiangyin Port of the same month. WC found that the goods were damaged on the 29th of the same month, and took inventory with the port operator the next day. According to the record of the inventory situation, the strip steel involved had deformation and loose parts during unloading. On September 22 of the same year, the Plaintiff, Defendant and WC jointly issued a loss recognition letter, recognizing that WC entrusted the Defendant to ship the goods involved. During unloading, it was found that a large number of strip steel were deformed due to extrusion collision, which affected the later sales and processing. The three parties jointly recognized that a total of 113 damaged goods weighed 290.41 tons. The depreciation was calculated based on RMB 200 yuan/ton, and the loss was in aggregate amount of RMB 58,082 yuan. The loss recognition letter showed that the Defendant was the "carrier" and the "person in charge".

The Plaintiff issued a insurance policy of the carriage involved on August 29, 2013, which stated that both the applicant and the insured was WC. The name of the insured goods was hot-rolled carbon steel strip, and the carriage route was from Jingtang Port to Jiangyin Huangtian Port. WC applied for insurance compensation from the Plaintiff on August 30 of the same year. The Plaintiff paid RMB 58,082 yuan to WC on October 18 according to the amount recognized in the above three-party loss recognition letter.

The Plaintiff claimed that: the goods involved were damaged during carriage. The Defendant was the carrier of the carriage involved. The Plaintiff was the insurer who obtained the right of subrogation, and claimed that the Defendant should compensate the Plaintiff for the loss of goods RMB 58,082 yuan and loss of interest.

The Defendant did not respond and reply.

[**Judgment**]

After hearing, Shanghai Maritime Court held that the case was the dispute over contract of carriage of goods by sea. The Plaintiff, as the insurer, obtained the right of subrogation according to law after making insurance compensation. The main issues in the case were: ①the Defendant's legal status in the carriage involved; ②the Defendant's liability for the loss of goods.

About the Defendant's legal status in the carriage involved. Firstly, the Defendant accepted the entrustment of WC to ship the goods involved, and promised to ensure the safe, timely and accurate delivery of the goods. The identity of the Defendant conformed to the legal characteristics of the carrier. Secondly, although the Defendant charged transaction service fees, the Defendant did not actually cause WC to directly conclude a contract with the logistics supplier. Instead, WC first entrusted the Defendant to ship the goods, and then the Defendant concluded a contract with the logistics supplier in its own name. Therefore, there was a carriage contractual relationship between WC and the Defendant, the Defendant was the carrier and not the intermediary. Finally, after the goods damage accident involved happened, the Defendant clearly recognized its identity as a carrier in the tripartite loss recognition letter, and there was no other waybill or other evidence showing that another person had concluded a carriage contract with WC, so the court confirmed that the Defendant was the carrier under the contract of carriage of goods involved.

About the Defendant's liability for the loss of goods. According to the record of the tripartite loss recognition, the goods involved was found to have been damaged when it was unloaded. The goods were deformed due to the extrusion collision during carriage. On the basis of recognizing the above facts, the Defendant also recognized the amount of the damage as the person in charge, so the Defendant should be liable for compensation for the recognized amount of RMB 58,082 yuan to the Plaintiff.

[Comment]

As a new product of the combination of the shipping industry and the Internet, the identification of logistics e-commerce in the sea freight business is a new problem faced in the trial practice. Although the original intention of the trading platform-type logistics e-commerce is to provide a contracting medium for shippers and actual logistics suppliers, if they separately conclude contracts with the shipper and the actual logistics supplier in their own names, it is clearly agreed that they will be entrusted by the shipper to ship goods and then the actual logistics supplier is entrusted to provide carriage services, the logistics e-commerce should be confirmed to be the carrier rather than the intermediary in the sea freight business.

9) Disputes over seafarer labor[①]

[Case]

The Objector (the outsider): Nanjing GR Loan Co., Ltd. (hereinafter referred to as GR)

The Enforcement Applicant: Tan ××

The Person Subject to Enforcement: Nanjing LR Trading Co., Ltd. (hereinafter referred to as LR)

Crew Tan ×× on M.V. "L R 6" owned by LR was delinquent in salary and applied to Shanghai Maritime Court to arrest the ship. On October 9, 2015, the court ruled that the permission was granted and attended on board to carry out arrest on the next day. On November 3 of the same year, the court accepted the case of Tan ×× v. LR crew labor contract dispute and judged on December 18 that LR should pay Tan ×× a salary remuneration of RMB 419,431.05 yuan and interest within 10 days after the judgment came into effect (according to the People's Bank of Chinese six-month to one-year loan interest rate standard, calculated from October 8, 2015 to the date when the judgment came into effect), and confirms that Tan ×× had the maritime lien of M.V. "LR6" for the above payment obligations of LR. After the judgement was pronounced, neither party appealed, and the judgement became valid. Because LR failed to fulfill the obligations confirmed by the valid judgment, Tan ×× applied to Shanghai Maritime Court for enforcement on March 8, 2016. The court accepted the case for enforcement on the same day, and LR failed to perform its obligations after the deadline. Except for five ships including M.V. "LR6", LR did not declare any other property and did not contact the court. On the 28th of the same month, the court made an enforcement ruling to freeze and transfer the corresponding deposits of LR, seal up, arrest, freeze, auction or sell the corresponding property

---

① The case passed the first instance of Shanghai Maritime Court, the case number was (2015) Hu Hai Fa Shang Chu Zi No. 2938.

of LR. Because LR did not always fulfill the obligations confirmed by the valid judgment, nor did it pay off or provide guarantees for the care, transfer, maintenance and other fee happened after M.V. "LR6" was arrested, the court decided to auction M.V. "LR6" and established M.V. "LR6" auction committee. On May 6, Nanjing Liuhe District People's Court (hereinafter referred to as Liuhe Court) accepted GR's application for the bankruptcy and liquidation of LR, and applied to Shanghai Maritime Court to suspend the enforcement of the property of LR. Later on May 10, Tan ×× applied to Shanghai Maritime Court to continue auctioning to realize his maritime lien. After review, Shanghai Maritime Court confirmed not to suspend the auction. After the successful auction, various fee happened during the arrest period were paid. Liuhe Court ruled that GR did not enjoy the mortgage right of the debtor LR.

[Judgment]

After review, Shanghai Maritime Court held that the Objector GR did not enjoy the right of M.V. "LR6" superior to the Enforcement Applicant (person holding maritime lien) Tan ××, so the ship was auctioned in the enforcement procedure and the ship auction money was first paid off for the Enforcement Applicant's creditor's rights. which did not damage the Objector's rights and interests. In the maritime litigation, the procedure of judicial compulsory auction of ships to protect and realize the maritime lien was relatively independent. When the ship auction procedure was initiated, it would not be suspended because the ship owner entered the bankruptcy process. Therefore, after the application of GR's bankruptcy liquidation was accepted, the objection that the enforcement procedure involving the debtor's property should be suspended could not be established. Auction procedure of M.V. "LR6" were carried out strict according to the law, from the formation of the auction ship committee to the organization of ship inspection, evaluations, and determination of auction methods and platforms, from the publication of auction announcements in multiple media to the actual auction, to the final auction transaction, the buyer's payment, ship handover, which had complete links and legal procedures, so GR's objection that the online auction of ships violated the law and the auction should be cancelled could not be established. In summary, the ruling rejected the objection raised by GR. The person subject to enforcement LR disagreed with the ruling and applied for reconsideration. Shanghai High People's Court rejected the LR's application for reconsideration with (2016) Hu Zhi Fu No.8 Enforcement Ruling.

[Comment]

The relationship between the realization of the security right and the bankruptcy process, whether the bankruptcy process should have restrictions on the exercise of the security rights, and the degree of restriction are the quite controversial issues in the theory and practice of the bankruptcy law. The problem of the maritime court auction procedure for ships and the realization of the maritime lien involved (most of the creditor's rights to be realized by auctioning ships mostly have maritime lien guarantee) are more specific than the realization of the general guarantee of real rights. In the case, the judicial auction procedure of the ship for the purpose of realizing the crew's salary was started first, and the bankruptcy procedure of the ship owner was started later. When the announcement of the auction of the ship was issued and it as about to enter the auction link, should the judicial auction process of the ship be suspended and the auctioned ship be transferred to the court that accepts the application for bankruptcy? The courts at both levels agreed that in maritime litigation, the judicial auction procedures for ships that protect and realize the maritime lien were relatively independent. When the auction procedures for ships were initiated, they would not be suspended because the owner of the ship entered the bankruptcy procedures.

10) Disputes over ship sales contract

[Case]

The Plaintiff: ZG Co., Ltd.

The Defendant: XXY (Shanghai) Investment Management Co., Ltd. (hereinafter referred to as XXY)

On December 30, 2013, the Plaintiff and QY (Hong Kong) Co., Ltd. (hereinafter referred to as QY) concluded a ship sales contract, the ship buyer was QY, and the seller was the Plaintiff. The contract agreed that QY would purchase the self-raking dredger "HANGJUN 9002" from the Plaintiff, and the transfer price or contract price of the object ship "current delivery" would be RMB 53,000,000 yuan. On April 24, 2014, the Plaintiff and QY concluded Supplemental Agreement II, which agreed on the matters not mentioned in the aforementioned sales contract. Article 3 of the agreement agreed that both parties agree that the following non-payments should be settled in RMB, including agency fee for export procedures, fuel, fuel oil and detention fee, ship maintenance and relevant testing fee, in aggregate amount of RMB 3,166,375 yuan; the agreement also agreed that if QY failed to pay the above three fees within five working days after May 23, which was guaranteed to pay by XXY.

On April 24, 2014, XXY issued a letter of guarantee to the Plaintiff, which stated that: "although in the Supplementary Agreement Ⅱ and Supplementary Agreement Ⅰ with the contract number of that the buyer and seller under the ship sales contract concluded on April 24, 2014, they made a commitment, but XXY (Shanghai) Investment Management Co., Ltd. further committed as follows: given that the company has transferred RMB 16,098,353 yuan to the seller's account as a guarantee for the buyer to complete the payment obligation, but according to the seller's requirement, the company promises that if the buyer fails to complete the repayment within the dates agreed in the above two supplementary agreements, the company is willing to pay RMB 3,166,375 yuan of it on its behalf."

Since QY failed to fulfill the payment obligation agreed in Supplementary Agreement Ⅱ, from June 15, 2014, the Plaintiff claimed the rights to XXY through e-mails and letters, and required XXY to pay debt RMB 3,166,375 yuan.

The Plaintiff claimed that XXY, as the joint guarantee person in charge of the above-mentioned debts, should bear the corresponding guarantee liability when the debtor QY failed to fulfill its payment obligation.

The Defendant argued that the guarantee provided by XXY to the Plaintiff belonged to the guarantee provided by the domestic institution for the overseas institution, and should be approved or registered by the relevant national competent authority and agency, but the above guarantee was not approved or registered by the national competent authority, so the guarantee contract was invalid.

[Judgment]

Shanghai Maritime Court held that the *Judicial Interpretation of the Guarantee Law* Article 6, Paragraph 2 comprehensively absorbed the invalidity of the contract in the departmental regulations such as the *Administrative Measures* for *External Guarantees of Domestic Institutions* and the *Implementation Rules for the Administrative Measures for External Guarantees of Domestic Institutions*, the original intention was to maintain social and economic order and protect public interests. Its applicable subject and cause were Chinese domestic institutions (except domestic foreign-funded financial institutions) as guarantors, according to the requirements of the law, by guarantee, mortgage, pledge, which promised to overseas institution in China or a foreign-funded financial institution in China as creditors or the beneficiaries that when the warrantee as the debtor failed to repay the debt according to the contract, the guarantor would perform the repayment obligation. In the case, although the enterprise in China provided guarantee for the institution registered in the Hong Kong Special Administrative Region, the creditor was a legal person of a domestic state-owned enterprise. Therefore, the subject and legal fact of the guarantee contract relationship in the case were not in the scope which adjusted and applied by the *Judicial Interpretation of the Guarantee Law* and its absorption of the above-mentioned departmental regulations regarding the invalidity of contract. Based on the above reasons and the facts found in the case, both the Plaintiff and XXY were eligible when forming a guarantee contractual relationship, and their intentions were true, and the content of the guarantee contractual relationship was legal. Therefore, the guarantee contract involved was valid and legally binding. Now the Plaintiff fulfilled the obligations of the ship sales contract and Supplementary Agreement Ⅱ according to agreement, but the debtor QY did not perform the payment obligation agreed in Supplementary Agreement Ⅱ to the Plaintiff. Therefore, according to the letter of guarantee issued by XXY and relevant legal regulations, the Plaintiff's claim that XXY should bear joint and several guarantee liability for QY's unperformed debts in Supplemental Agreement Ⅱ was not illegal, and the court supported this.

[**Comment**]

External guarantees arise from the needs of international economic exchanges and international capital flows. With the rapid increase in the scale of capital flows and the continuous improvement of liquidity in my country, the adjustment of external guarantee policies and regulations must inevitably keep pace with the times. External guarantee is not a pure civil and commercial system. It must comply with relevant guarantee laws and administrative regulations of foreign exchange control and foreign debt management. Therefore, it has significant difference with domestic guarantees in terms of guarantee subject, guarantee method, guarantee effect. Due to the continuous adjustment of the regulatory requirements for external guarantees of domestic institutions by administrative agencies, the same type of external guarantees will have different regulatory requirements at different times, so that the effect of corresponding contract will also have different confirmation results. On May 12, 2014, the State Administration of Foreign Exchange issued the *Regulations on the Administration of Foreign Exchange in Cross-Border Guarantees* (hereinafter referred to as the new regulations) and the *Guidelines on the Administration of Foreign Exchange Management in Cross-Border Guarantees*, and repealed the *Administrative Measures on External Guarantees of Domestic Institutions* and the *Implementation Rules of the Administrative Measures for External Guarantees of Domestic Institutions*, which have a certain impact on the confirmation of the effect of relevant guarantee contracts in judicial practice.

The promulgation of the new regulations and the abolition of the old management regulations have led to the premise of the application of Article 6 Paragraph 2, of the *Judicial Interpretation of the Guarantee Law* no longer existing. The mainstream judgement thinking of confirming unapproved and unregistered external guarantees as invalid should not continue to apply. On the one hand, the unregistered external guarantee contract complies with regulations and takes effect in foreign exchange management practice, but the judicial trial confirms that the contract is invalid, which will inevitably lead to a disjoint contradiction between judicial practice and social practice; on the other hand, the judgment thinking will seriously damage the interests of creditors who conclude external guarantee contracts based on the new rules, which encourages disobedience in disguise. Faced with contradictory and different levels of norms, the Supreme Court has noted the conflict of norms. It is proposed in the *Opinions on Comprehensively Promoting the Strategy of High-Quality in Foreign-Related Commercial and Maritime Trials to Provide Powerful Judicial Guarantee for Building an Open Economic System and Building a Maritime Power* that the court should pay close attention to the impact of the reform of the foreign exchange management system and the opening of the financial industry on the confirmation of the effect of legal actions such as cross-border financing and external guarantee and the court should adjust the judgment thinking in a timely manner, introduce or revise judicial interpretations and guiding opinions in a timely manner, and ensure the smooth progress of relevant reforms.

11) Disputes over contract of carriage of goods by sea

[Case]

The Plaintiff: XSY Co.

The Defendant: HJ Shipping Co., Ltd.

On July 10, 2014, XSY accepted the entrustment of SG Co., Ltd. (hereinafter referred to as SG) to ship 18 containers of goods and issued intermodal bill of lading. The loading port was Shanghai and the unloading port was Prince Rupert Port, Canada. Place of delivery was Edmonton, Canada. On the same day, HJ accepted XSY's entrustment to ship the batch of goods, and issued a sea waybill to XSY. The description of the goods and the transportation information such as loading port, unloading port, and place of delivery were consistent with the record of the intermodal bill of lading issued by XSY. On July 24 of the same year, after the batch of goods was unloaded from the ship, HJ entrusted the Canadian Railways Co., Ltd. to carry 17 of these containers by train to Edmonton, the place of delivery. On July 25, the 17 containers of goods suffered damage due to the derailment of the train.

On July 14, 2015, PICC Tianjin Branch, the insurer of the goods involved (hereinafter referred to as PICC Tianjin) filed an action before the court as a subrogator, claiming XSY to compensate for the loss of the goods involved.

[Judgement][1]

The court of first instance held that: it was found that XSY accepted the entrustment of SG, produced and issued a multimodal bill of lading, charged the whole freight, and then entrusted others to book with HJ and pay the freight, earning the freight difference, and it was the shipper recorded in the HJ's sea waybill and the consignee recorded in the HJ's sea waybill was its agent of the

---

[1] Shanghai Maritime Court heard, upon appeal, Shanghai High People's Court dismissed the appeal in the second instance and affirmed the original judgment (2016) Hu Min Zhong No.321.

destination port Dianxian Co., Ltd. Therefore, XSY was the carrier of the carriage involved, namely, the multimodal transport operator. XSY was the contract carrier of the carriage involved. According to the sea waybill issued by XSY, HJ was the actual carrier of the carriage involved. PICC Tianjin obtained the right of subrogation after paying compensation to SG, so PICC Tianjin had the right to exercise the right of subrogation to claim compensation from the shipper XSY according to the law.

The mode of carriage involved was multimodal transport and the laws of the People's Republic of China should apply. It was found that HJ held that the goods damage involved happened in the railway transportation section within Canada. Therefore, the claim of the liability of compensation and liability limits of the multimodal transport operator should be confirmed according to Canadian law, and the relevant Canadian law should be proofed. However, because the evidence and corresponding jurisprudence provided by it were different from the actual goods damage and the terms of the bill of lading, it was not enough to prove that it could apply the Canadian liability of compensation and liability limits. In addition, because the goods damage involved happened in the railway transportation section, which was during the liability period of HJ, according to the relevant laws of the People's Republic of China, the goods damage involved and relevant fee should be jointly born by XSY and HJ. Later, XSY and HJ appealed to Shanghai High People's Court against the judgment. Shanghai High People's Court issued a judgment on November 2 of the same year, dismissed the appeal, and affirmed the original judgment.

[**Comment**]

The case is the dispute over a multimodal transport contract for goods by sea. SG was the shipper of the carriage involved. XSY issued the multimodal bill of lading involved; HJ issued a sea waybill to XSY. In addition to the information of the shipper, consignee and notify party, other information was consistent with the record of the multimodal bill of lading issued by XSY. SG and PICC Tianjin had a marine goods insurance contractual relationship. After the accident involved, PICC Tianjin paid the insurance compensation to the insured SG, and obtained the right of subrogation of the insurance involved to claim compensation from XSY. In addition, HJ, as the actual carrier of XSY, bore liability to XSY for the entire carriage recorded on the sea waybill. In summary, XSY was the multimodal transport operator under the multimodal transport contract involved. According to the record of the sea bill of lading, HJ and XSY established a multimodal transport contractual relationship of goods by sea. HJ was the actual carrier and liable for the entire transportation process.

Because the parties to the contract did not make a consistent choice regarding the application of the law, according to the principle of the closest contact, both XSY involved and the loading port of the ship involved were located in China. Therefore, the law of the People's Republic of China was applicable in the case. And the sea bill of lading issued by HJ provided by XSY, according to the relevant records, could prove that the two have established a multimodal transport contractual relationship of goods by sea. Although the goods damage involved happened in the railway transportation section, according to the multimodal transport contract of goods by sea, the goods damage happened during its liability period, XSY as the multimodal transport operator should be liable for compensation for the resulting loss. HJ as the full carrier, since the goods damage happened during its period of liability, the carrier should be jointly and severally liable for the loss and damage of the goods involved in the Canadian railway transportation sector.

12) Disputes over supply contract

[Case]

The Plaintiff (the counterclaim Defendant): LB Paint (Shanghai) Co., Ltd. (hereinafter referred to as LB)

The Defendant (the counterclaim Plaintiff): Shanghai AYD Shipping Co., Ltd. (hereinafter referred to as AYD)

In January 2013, LB sent an offer of supporting offer to AYD. The anti-fouling paints ECOLOFLEXSPC2000BROWNA and ECOLOFLEXSPC600PLUM in the business stated instructions that the period of validity of anti-fouling paints was supported by 36 months and the monthly sailing was 0~6,000 nautical miles.

In February 2013, AYD's M.V. "LITIAN" was painted with anti-fouling paints and the plaintiff paid the defendant for the paints payment including two kinds of anti-fouling paints. In November 2014, "LITIAN" was found in South Korea with sea creatures attached to the bottom of the ship. On November 17,

AYD notified the defendant of the ship's fouling of bottom by e-mail, and required the defendant to arrange a inspection. On December 8, AYD again communicated with the defendant about the anti-fouling paint problem via e-mail, and asked the defendant to take a solution or propose a compensation plan. During the court hearing, the defendant LB recognized that no personnel had been sent to conduct the inspection. From November 25 to December 11, 2014, "LITIAN" docked at the anchorage. During the period, Amir cleaned the bottom of "LITIAN" at the anchorage in Busan, South Korea and issued a cleanup report. The cleanup report recorded the cleanup work and the proportion of the bottom of the ship covered by sea creatures. In October 2015, "LITIAN" anchored Shanghai Port Wusong Shipyard for repairs, and AYD entrusted YS to conduct inspections on the failure of anti-fouling paint. According to the inspection report issued by YS, the hull below the waterline of "LITIAN" was attached to large area and high density sea creatures. YS held that no anti-fouling paints that sea creatures attached to was found to have fallen off, and it could be concluded that the failure of the anti-fouling paints was the cause of the fouling of the hull by sea creatures. AYD notified LB the time that "LITIAN" entered the port for dock repair in advance and LB sent its staff to check on October 14.

Ships had a cleaning up fee USD 13,307.91 when the ship was suspended for cleaning up. An anchorage usage fee (including agency fee) USD 6,364.57 and a water diversion fee USD 696.42 happened during the anchorage of "LITIAN". The fuel fee caused by berth shifting was assessed in "LITIAN" inspection report as USD 2,100 for heavy fuel and USD 3,352.50 for light fuel. "LITIAN" inspection report also estimated the loss of shipping schedule during the cleanup period as USD 13,650. During the repair, according to YS report, the boarding pass fee RMB 500 yuan and the crew replacement fee RMB 1,600 yuan were not relevant to repainting the anti-fouling paint, resulting in a port use fee 5,928 yuan; the dock repair fee relevant to repainting the anti-fouling paint was RMB 203,390 yuan and the service fee was RMB 194,667 yuan, in aggregate amount of RMB 398,057 yuan.

In May 2013, LB sent AYD an offer of supporting offer of the ship paint, stating that "the period of validity of anti-fouling paints was supported by 36 months and the monthly sailing was 0—6,000 nautical miles". In June 2013, M.

V. "KAIMOU"was carried out painting work of anti-fouling paints. In May 2014, paints peeled off. According to the records of the CHEXXXX docking paint inspection report (hereinafter referred to as the May 2014 inspection report) issued by LB in May 2014, the area of peeling was mainly: a small amount of anti-fouling paint fell off on the straight bottom, and about 40% of the anti-fouling paint on the flat bottom peeled off. In June 2016, "KAIMOU" berthed at Shanghai Port Wusong Shipyard and docked at ×× No. 1 dock for repairs. AYD entrusted Shanghai YZ Insurance Surveyors & Adjusters Co., Ltd. (hereinafter referred to as YZ) to inspect the failure of anti-fouling paints. According to the inspection report issued by YZ, the hull below the waterline of "KAIMOU" was attached to large area of sea creatures. AYD notified LB in advance about the time to enter the port for dock repair, but LB did not board the ship to participate in the inspection.

The fee associated with the failure of the anti-fouling paint during the ship repair: ①the fee of repainting the paint, the invoice amount was USD 49,084.10, and the actual payment amount was USD 47,246.14. ②Entering and leaving port use fee, the invoice amount was RMB 84,536 yuan, and "KAIMOU" inspection report considered that the fee of the project relevant to the failure of the anti-fouling paints was RMB 73,236 yuan. Because the invoice amount did not match, AYD actually paid the port use fee USD 12,658.93, in aggregate amount of RMB 72,851.34 yuan. ③Shipyard dock repair fee, the invoice amount was RMB 688,047 yuan. ④Spare parts fee and repair labor fee of the main engine, the invoice amount was separate RMB 708,842 yuan and RMB 185,276 yuan.

[Judgment]

The court of first instance held that: the case was the dispute over the contract for the supply of ship materials and spare parts. LB sent a supporting offer to AYD, which constituted an offer. Based on the supporting offer, AYD painted the corresponding anti-fouling paints and paid the offer, which constituted a commitment. The contractual relationship between the two parties for the supply of ship anti-fouling paints was valid. The issues in the first instance of the case were whether LB had breach of contract, the scope of breach of contract and the amount of compensation.

In the case, the offer sent by LB clearly stated that "the period of validity of anti-fouling paints was supported by 36 months and the monthly sailing was 0 — 6,000 nautical miles". In addition, LB should provide technical services during the painting process. However, M.V. "LITIAN" and "KAIMOU" appeared to have large areas of sea creatures attached within 36 months. It could be preliminarily judged that the anti-fouling paint provided by LB failed to achieve the effect agreed by the two parties. Regarding "KAIMOU", according to the information provided by AYD, it could be preliminarily proved that anti-fouling paints were painted by the wrong process because of the wrong product supplied by LB. LB claimed that the paint peeling was caused by unqualified work conditions, but failed to submit valid evidence to prove that there was indeed an unsuitable construction situation, nor failed to prove that AYD was informed that the work conditions were unsuitable, so the court did not support its pleas.

Regarding the scope of liability and the amount of compensation. The fee of repainting advocated by AYD included different types of paint, and the loss involved was caused by the failure of the anti-fouling paint. Therefore, LB should only bear the fee of the anti-fouling paint, and should not bear the fee of other paint products. "KAIMOU" inspection report also used this standard to assess loss.

(1) For M.V. "LITIAN": AYD claimed six main loss, including South Korea's cleaning up fee, repainting fee, port use fee, shipyard dock repair fee, fee of spare parts of main engine, freight and repair fee, and rent and fuel loss. AYD submitted the fee of cleaning bottom, anchorage use fee (including agency fee), water diversion fee invoice and payment voucher. "LITIAN" inspection report was also more reasonable for the assessment of heavy oil and light oil consumption in and out of the anchorage. The five kinds of fee was due to the cleanup of the bottom of the ship, which was caused by the failure of the anti-fouling paint, so the court confirmed the five kinds of fee in aggregate amount of USD 20,580. LB held that the distribution of general service fee was unreasonable. The court of first instance held that the assessor could not give a clear and reasonable basis for the distribution of general service fee. LB could not propose a specific calculation method. Because the ship involved multiple items such as inspection and repainting in the shipyard, it was confirmed that AYD and LB would each bear half of the total, namely, LB would bear RMB 118,251 yuan. Regarding

port fee, as ships entered and left the port and was carried out for inspection and repainting at the same time, the port use fee relevant to anti-fouling paint was confirmed that AYD and LB would each bear half of the total, namely, LB would bear RMB 27,505.50 yuan. Regarding the fee of repainting, "LITIAN" inspection report held that the fee relevant to anti-fouling paint was USD 24,883, which was also recognized by LB and supported by the court of first instance. Regarding the assessment fee and translation fee, LB stated that if the court of first instance accepted the relevant evidence materials, it would be willing to bear the corresponding assessment fee and translation fee. Therefore, it was confirmed that LB should bear the assessment fee RMB 3,650 yuan and USD 1,431.25 and the translation fee RMB 1,080.50 yuan.

However, during the period of cleaning the bottom, "LITIAN" did not have a charter party, so it did not support the loss of shipping schedule claimed by AYD. Regarding the fee of spare parts of the main engine, freight and repair fee, the court of first instance held that: firstly, "LITIAN" inspection report submitted by AYD could not effectively prove that the advance maintenance of the main engine was indeed necessary and necessary casual relationship between the advance maintenance of the main engine and ship fouling; secondly, even if the failure of the anti-fouling paints was relevant to the abrasion of the main engine, AYD did not take reasonable measures to avoid the loss of expansion in a timely manner when it knew the failure of anti-fouling paints, and it should not claim the expansion of the loss to LB; thirdly, because damage of the main engine caused by the failure of the anti-fouling paints exceeded the scope of the loss that could be foreseen when LB concluded the contract. Accordingly, the court did not support AYD's claim on the loss of the spare parts of the main engine, freight and repair fee. Regarding the assessment fee, notarization certification fee and translation fee claimed by AYD, the court of first instance held that the notarization certification fee was a necessary expense for AYD to proceed with the litigation, so the court does not support it.

(2) For M. V. "KAIMOU": AYD claimed four main loss, including repainting fee, port use fee, shipyard dock repair fee, and fee of spare parts of main engine, repair fee. The fee of repainting anti-fouling paints that LB should bear was USD 23,312.12. Regarding port use fee, LB held that "KAIMOU"

docked for compulsory inspection. Therefore, the fee must happen and should not be born by LB. The court of the first-instance confirmed that AYD and LB would each bear half of port use fee relevant to anti-fouling paints, namely, LB bore RMB 36,425.67 yuan. Regarding the shipyard dock repair fee, LB still proposed objection to the distribution of general service fees, and the court had the same reason with "LITIAN" and thought that AYD and LB should bear half of total, namely, LB should bear the general service fee RMB 188,073 yuan.

Regarding the fee of spare parts of the main engine and repairs fee, the court had the same opinion with "LITIAN" and did not support it.

Later, LB appealed to Shanghai High People's Court against the judgment, and neither party submitted new evidence. Shanghai High People's Court held that the facts and supporting evidence of the first instance were clearly and confirmed. The issues were still whether LB had breach of contract, the scope of the liability for breach of contract and the amount of compensation. LB held that the two inspection reports of LB involved could not be used as evidence for finalization. The court of second instance held that YZ and YS both had licenses for operating insurance assessment business, and both assessors held the practice certificate of insurance assessment practitioners. The two inspection reports could be used as evidence to confirm the facts of the case. In addition, LB's appeal reason that the inspection report should be signed and stamped by three assessors had no factual and legal basis, so the court did not support it. According to the content of LB's offer, "LITIAN" and "KAIMOU" had a large area of sea creatures attachments before the 36th month, and LB had a breach of contract. LB held that the time for the two ships of docking was 36 months after the paint was painted, so repainting the ship in the port was inevitable, and the time was also the time for routine inspection of the ship, so the port use fee and the shipyard dock repair fee were general service fee and should not be shared by LB. The court held that LB had breached the contract before and should bear the loss resulting from the breach of contract. AYD's arrangement did not expand the loss the breach of contract that LB should compensate, but it was conducive to preventing the further expansion of loss that might result from breach of the lease, which was in line with the principle of impairment. Since AYD recognized that when the two ships involved docked, in addition to repainting anti-fouling paints and was carried out ship inspection, the court of first instance considered the facts that the ship was inspected and repainted and many items in the shipyard, and confirmed both parties should separately bear half of the port use fee and half of service fee in the shipyard dock repair fee, which was not improper. The court did not support the appeal reason of LB that the distribution of court of first instance in general service fee and the port use fee of the shipyard dock repair fee was unfair and unreasonable. Regarding LB's claim that the first-instance judgement based on the invoice amount to confirm the amount of fee that LB bore, it was a problem of confirming facts wrongly. Therefore, it was held that the court of first-instance made a detailed calculation and fully explained according to specific paid amount.

In summary, LB's appeal claim had no factual and legal basis and should not be supported. Therefore, the appeal was dismissed and the original judgement was affirmed.

[Comment]

The case is the dispute over contract for the supply of ship materials and spare parts. As a bidder, LB issued a offer to AYD, and AYD accepted and paid the price. The contractual relationship between the two for the supply of ship anti-fouling paint was established and valid. LB's agreement on the content of "the period of validity of anti-fouling paint is 36 months" and the fact that AYD's "LITIAN" and "KAIMOU" found a large number of sea creatures on the bottom of the ship within 36 months and LB breached the contract.

The fee of repainting claimed by AYD included different types of paint, and the loss involved was caused by the failure of the anti-fouling paint. Therefore, LB should only bear the fee of the anti-fouling paint for the ship involved, and should not bear the fee of other paint products. The two parties mainly defended the ship involved in the fee of repainting, port use fee, shipyard dock repair fee, fee of spare parts of main engine, freight and repair fee. The ships involved were not rescued by repainting immediately after the seabed attachments were found and there was a problem of paint peeling off, but after 36 months of painting, they were docked and the antifouling paint was repainted and the ship was inspected. LB breached the contract before and AYD's arrangement did not expand the loss the breach of contract that LB should compensate. Instead, it was conducive to preventing the further expansion of loss that might result from breach of the contract, which was in line with the principle of impairment. Relevant service fee was also distributed by average by both parties. The fee of spare parts of the main engine exceeded the reasonable expectations of LB and AYD could not prove that it was inevitable relevant to the failure of anti-fouling paint, so it was not supported. In respect of the amount of compensation for loss, the court insisted on the specific payment amount and insisted on the principle of fairness and reasonableness, so that the two parties involved bore their respective liabilities.

2.2 Cases of Maritime Arbitration
2.2.1 Disputes over ship repair contract
[Case]

On July 16, 2014, the Applicant and the Respondent concluded a contract. The Respondent entrusted the Applicant to repair J ship. On July 18, 2014, J ship was sent to the Applicant's shipyard for repairs. The Applicant completed the repair obligation of the ship according to the agreement. On July 31, 2014, the Applicant and the Respondent concluded a Settlement and Payment Agreement (hereinafter referred to as the Agreement) for the repair fee of J ship. Both parties recognized that the repair fee for the ship was RMB 390,618 yuan. The Respondent paid RMB 100,000 yuan, and would pay RMB 100,000 yuan before the ship left the shipyard, and the remaining RMB 190,618 yuan would be remitted to the Applicant's bank account at one time before August 31, 2014. However, the Respondent only paid RMB 200,000 yuan for ship repair fee, and the remaining RMB 190,618 yuan was repeatedly urged by the Applicant, while the Respondent defaulted up to now.

Therefore, the Applicant claimed the arbitral tribunal to award:

(1) The Respondent should pay the ship repair fee RMB 190,618 yuan to the Applicant and should pay interest at the bank's loan interest rate for the same period from September 1, 2014 to the date of actual performance.

(2) The arbitration fee in the case should be borne by the Respondent.

The Respondent replied that:

(1) The Agreement was concluded by the Respondent under forced

helplessness. At the insisted claim of the Applicant, only after the Respondent concluded the Agreement, J ship could leave the shipyard. Because the ship was within the time charter party, the Respondent had to conclude the Agreement in order to reduce loss.

(2) The Applicant did not perform the repair project of "checking and unblocking the boiler smoke pipe and performing relevant inspections according to the requirements of ship inspection" according to the requirements on the repair project list. After J ship left the shipyard, the main engine was shut down due to a boiler problem. The Applicant refused to call J ship at its dock. The Respondent could only contact Zhoushan Yingshi Ship Repair Co., Ltd. to repair the boiler, which cost RMB 16,661 yuan.

(3) Article 11 of the contract agreed that the power supply fee was RMB 2.2 yuan/degree, however, when the Applicant completed the work and carried out the settlement, the power supply fee was calculated at RMB 2.5 yuan/degree. The Respondent held that the extra amount of electricity fee RMB 1,951.2 yuan should be deducted.

(4) Due to improper repair, deployment and overall management of the Applicant, J ship docked again, and the second docking fee was RMB 21,351 yuan should be deducted.

In addition, the Respondent filed a counterclaim for arbitration:

The dock repair period of J ship was from July 21 to July 27. The repair of the boiler and stern shaft of the ship should have been completed during the period. However, because the Applicant did not comply with the requirements of the contract, J ship left the dock on July 27, and docked again on July 29 two days later. After the repairs were completed on July 31, the Respondent sought other repair factories to repair the boiler until August 8. In summary, due to the negligent repair and poor management of the Applicant, the repair time of J ship was delayed by 12 days, resulting in the Respondent's operating loss reaching RMB 320,000 yuan.

The Respondent claim the arbitral tribunal to award:

(1) The Applicant should compensate the Respondent for the loss of operating income RMB 320,000 yuan;

(2) The arbitration fee in the case should be born by the Applicant.

[Opinion of the arbitral tribunal]

1) Regarding the effect of ship repair contract and settlement and payment agreement

On July 16, 2014, the Applicant and the Respondent concluded a contract for the repair of J ship after negotiation between the parties. The arbitral tribunal held that the contract involved which was concluded by negotiation was on the basis of equality and voluntariness of both parties, and in terms of content and form, complied with the law. The contract should be confirmed to be legal and valid and binding on both parties.

The arbitral tribunal held that after the completion of J ship repair project, the Agreement was concluded on July 31, 2014 after the parties' acceptance and settlement. On the same day, J ship left the shipyard immediately. Accordingly, the procedure for the parties to conclude the Agreement was consistent with Article 4 of the contract. It was not found that the Respondent was forced to conclude the Agreement because of the coercion by the Applicant. The Respondent had the full right to choose to object to the agreement or refuse to conclude. However, the Respondent did not object or refuse to conclude. Therefore, the Respondent's claim that the Agreement was concluded under forced helplessness was not established. The arbitral tribunal held that the procedure for concluding the Agreement was legal, and the content of the agreement was true and was consistent with the contract. The agreement was an expression of the true intention of both parties and should be confirmed to be legal and valid. Both parties should be bound by the Agreement and should perform it seriously.

2) Regarding the increase and decrease of repair projects and unit price of electricity

(1) Regarding the measurement of stern shaft and repair project for replacement of parts of stern shaft.

The arbitral tribunal held that the actual work of the repair project was completed after verbal agreement between the parties. Afterwards, the newly added repair project was recognized by the Respondent's signature. Although when two parties newly added the repair project, they did not comply with the requirements of the contract "if the docking period or the total repair period are affected, after negotiation between the representatives of the two parties, the repair period will be increased according to the actual situation, and a supplementary written contract will be concluded" However, after the completion of repairs of J ship, the two parties negotiated, signed, and stamped to conclude the Agreement, which was the final recognition made by both parties of the repair cycle and the fee of the repair projects of J according to the actual situation. Therefore, the Agreement was a supplement to the original contract.

(2) Regarding repair projects of checking and unblocking the boiler smoke pipe and performing relevant inspections according to the requirements of ship inspection.

The arbitral tribunal held that the Agreement concluded by both parties after consultation had finally recognized that the repair project was not included in the scope of repair projects, nor had it charged the repair fee of the repair project. In fact, the repair project was not actually under work. Based on this, it should be confirmed that the repair project was a reduced repair project that was recognized by both parties through consultation.

(3) Regarding the unit price of electricity.

The arbitral tribunal held that although both parties agreed in the contract that the unit price of electricity was RMB 2.2 yuan/kWh. However, the Respondent recognized that the Applicant calculated at 2.5 yuan/kWh in the summary table of fee of repair project of J ship, and the Respondent did not propose any objection when the parties concluded the Agreement. This was a modification in the content of the relevant clauses of the contract by both parties, and it was a disposition by both parties for their respective rights and obligations. According to this, the unit price of electricity was 2.5 yuan/kWh, which was confirmed.

3) Regarding the amount and interest of overdue debt

The Applicant recognized that after the Agreement was concluded, the Respondent paid RMB 100,000 yuan to the Applicant. Now, the amount of the Respondent's debt should be RMB 190,618 yuan. Accordingly, the arbitral tribunal confirmed the fact.

Regarding the Applicant's proposal to calculate interest at the bank's loan interest rate at the same period. The arbitral tribunal held that the method of interest calculation proposed by the Applicant was not clear and reasonable.

Because there was a central bank and a large number of commercial banks, the Applicant did not specify the interest rate published by which bank to calculate the interest. Moreover, the Applicant did not provide relevant evidence such as the loan contract, the relevancy of the loan contract and the payment involved, and whether the loan contract was actually performed. Therefore, the arbitral tribunal held that the interest loss happened from September 1, 2014 to the date of actual performance should be calculated based on the one-year fixed deposit interest rate published by the People's Bank of China for the same period. This is relatively fair and reasonable for both parties.

4) Regarding the counterclaim for arbitration of the Respondent

The Respondent claimed that the dock repair period of J ship was July 21 – 27, 2014. The repair of the stern shaft and boiler should have been completed during the period. Because the Applicant did not handle according to the ship repair contract, J ship undocked on July 27, and docked on July 29 two days later. After undocking and leaving the shipyard on July 31, it looked for other repair factories to repair the boiler until August 8. Due to the two repairs of the stern shaft and the boiler, the repair time of J ship was delayed by 12 days, resulting in approximate loss RMB 320,000 yuan in the operation income of the Respondent. The Applicant was required to compensate the Respondent's loss.

[Comment]

The issue in the case was on the effect of the contract. During the hearing of a case, the parties sometimes propose that a certain expression they made was due to the helplessness of the other party's persecution or coercion, but not their true expression as the reason for the plea. The *Contract Law* Article 54 Paragraph 2 stipulates that where a party makes the other party enter into a contract against its true will by means of deceit, coercion or taking advantage of its difficulties, the injured party has the right to request a people's court or an arbitration institution to alter or rescind the contract. Coercion in the contract law refers to threat with damage that will happen or directly imposing damage that causes the other party to fear and thus conclude a contract. Constitutive requirements of coercion: ①the subject who has the coercion is intentional; ②the subject who has coercion carries out coercion; ③the subject who is coerced concludes a contract due to coercion; ④coercion is illegal. The *Contract Law*

Article 77 stipulates that: "The parties may modify the contract upon consensus through consultation." According to this, if the parties need to revise or supplement the content of the contract, they should proceed according to the principle of negotiation. If both parties agree on the modification, the modified content replaces the original contract, and the parties should perform the contract according to the modified content.

In the case, the Respondent proposed that the "settlement and payment agreement" it concluded with the Applicant was concluded under forced helplessness, but the Respondent did not provide corresponding evidence to prove that the Applicant deliberately committed illegal coercion. Therefore, the arbitral tribunal could not agree with the Respondent's plea.

2.2.2 Disputes over ship repair contract

[Case]

On May 4, 2014, the Respondent entrusted the Applicant to repair J ship it operated. The two parties agreed to pay RMB 500 yuan/day for terminal fee near the shipyard during the repair of ship. At the same time, it was agreed that the Respondent should pay 30% of the engineering repair fee (RMB 300,000 yuan) before the start of the work, complete the settlement price before the completion date of the contract and pay the full amount before the start of the ship. The two parties concluded a J ship borrowing contract on May 5, 2014, agreeing that the ship was scheduled to enter the shipyard on May 5, 2014 and tentatively leave the shipyard on August 6. On May 12, 2014, the Respondent paid RMB 300,000 yuan in advance to the Applicant for fee of repair projects. On July 15, 2014, July 26, 2014, and September 28, 2014, the two parties concluded two memorandums and a supplementary contract, respectively, and finally extended the end date of the J borrowing contract to October 15, 2014. The Respondent agreed that if the ship repair funds could not be implemented within this date, it should obey the arrangement of the Applicant, settle the payment of the previous period and leave the shipyard.

However, despite repeated urging by the Applicant, the Respondent did not pay the repair fee, the docking service fee arose from it and other fee it owed, the Applicant exercised the lien on the ship, but the Respondent did not pay above-mentioned fee.

Based on the above facts and reasons, the Applicant filed an arbitration claim as follows:

(1) The Respondent should pay the Applicant all the repair work fee RMB 4,177,519 yuan it owed (including pre-repair preparation service fee RMB 163,460 yuan, ship berthing service fee RMB 2,891,500 yuan, and the shifting fee when the ship docked at the shipyard RMB 756,000 yuan, the daily care and maintenance fee when the ship docked at the shipyard RMB 595,800 yuan, and the security maintenance fee when the ship docked at the shipyard RMB 70,759 yuan), and an overdue fine (the overdue fine should be paid at 1.5%/month, calculated from the next month of the day when each unpaid payment should be paid to the day when the award came into effect).

(2) Confirm that the Applicant had the lien of ship on J ship.

(3) The Respondent should bear the lawyer's fee of the Applicant, with a provisional amount of RMB 50,000 yuan.

(4) The Respondent should bear all arbitration fee and other relevant fee in the case.

[Opinion of the arbitral tribunal]

1) Regarding the effect of the ship repair engineering contract and other contracts in the case

According to the facts of the case confirmed by the arbitration tribunal, the ship repair engineering contract involved clearly agreed the conditions for coming into effect. The above-mentioned contract did not have the Respondent's signature and seal, so the arbitration tribunal could not confirm that the contract had become effective. At the same time, the arbitral tribunal noticed that both the J ship borrowing contract, two memorandums of J ship, and the supplementary contract of J ship borrowing contract had the signatures of both parties; the parties' meaning of the limited repair of the ship involved did not change; the requirement claimed by the Applicant were all relevant to the above-mentioned three contracts.

The arbitral tribunal held that the ship repair engineering contract did not take effect. The J ship borrowing contract, two memorandums of J ship, and the supplementary contract of J ship borrowing contract were true and valid.

2) Regarding the arbitration claims of the Applicant

(1) The Applicant's claims for all ship repair engineering fee. The two

parties clearly agreed in Article 3 of J ship borrowing contract that "engineering projects arising out of borrowed refers the offer standard of the offer, whose price basis of settlement was China State Shipbuilding Industry Corporation's 92-year yellow book (*Repair Price List of Domestic Civil Ships* compiled in 1992 by China State Shipbuilding Industry Corporation) and repair price K=1.0". The ship repair engineering fee claimed by the Applicant included: five items including pre-repair preparation service fee, ship berthing service fee (borrowing terminal fee and berthing fee agreed by both parties in contract), the shifting fee when the ship docked at the shipyard, and the daily care and maintenance fee and security maintenance fee when the ship docked at the shipyard, arbitration tribunal confirmed as follows:

① Pre-repair preparation service fee: including the fee of pulling and cutting the anchor chain, using the tug to cooperate with the ship to enter the shipyard, the leaving and docking of the ship, arranging water diversion, escort fee, site inspection fee before repair, and insulation testing engineering in the living area.

The arbitral tribunal held that the ship's entry into the shipyard, cutting the anchor chain and the "preliminary preparation" were completed, and the Applicant and the Respondent recognized that the resulting fee was reasonable fee. The calculation method of the relevant fee should be subject to the agreement between the parties. If there was no agreement, the arbitral tribunal would make a decision based on the principle of fairness and reasonable consideration of the interests of both parties.

In the above preparatory work, the project of untwisting rope twice and building and disassembling up and down ship board ladders twice when the ship left and docked complied with the first and eleventh items of the 92 Yellow Book agreed by the contract. For the ship involved, the unit price for mooring and untwisting rope when leaving and docking should be RMB 256 yuan, and the unit price for building and disassembling up and down ship board ladders should be RMB 350 yuan. The Applicant's requirement for the ship to moor and untwist rope when leaving and docking twice, totaling RMB 512 yuan, and build and disassemble up and down ship board ladders twice, totaling RMB 700 yuan. The two requirement which was in aggregate amount of RMB 1,212 yuan had a clear contract basis and should be supported.

The arbitral tribunal held that the fee claimed by the Applicant actually happened and were reasonable. The above pre-repair preparation service fee which was in aggregate amount of RMB 163,460 yuan should be supported.

② Ship berthing service fee. The ship berthing fee claimed by the Applicant was divided into 3 parts, the calculation basis and calculation standards were different. Namely: from May 5, 2014 (the day when the ship involved entered the shipyard) to August 5, 2014, the berthing service fee of the ship involved was calculated and charged at RMB 500 yuan/day; from August 6, 2014 to October 15, 2014, the berthing service fee of the ship involved should be calculated and charged at RMB 5,000 yuan/day, and the ship should be scheduled to leave the shipyard before October 18, 2014, and October 16, 17 when the ship were not scheduled to leave the shipyard, were still calculated at 5,000 yuan/day. From October 18, 2014 to February 25, 2016 (the date of the original arbitration hearing), the berthing service fee of the ship involved was calculated and charged at RMB 5,000 yuan/day.

From May 5, 2014 to August 5, 2014, in aggregate amount of 93 days, and the amount was in aggregate amount of RMB 46,500 yuan; from August 6, 2014 to the contract termination time agreed by both parties on October 15 was 71 days and the berthing service fee was in aggregate amount of RMB 355,000 yuan; October 16, 2014 to February 25, 2016 was the delay time for the ship to leave the shipyard, in aggregate amount of 498 days, and the berthing service fee was in aggregate amount of RMB 2,490,000 yuan.

The arbitral tribunal held that the berthing service fee claimed by the Applicant should be confirmed as having both the nature of penalty for breach of contract and compensation for loss. The agreement was the true expression of both parties and was not contrary to the law. The above Applicant's claim that the fee to February 25, 2016 was in aggregate amount of RMB 2,891,500 yuan, should be supported.

③ Shifting fee when the ship docked at the shipyard. The Applicant arranged a total of 21 shifts of the ship involved in the 662 days from May 5, 2014 to February 25, 2016. The fee of each shift was RMB 36,000 yuan, and the claimed shifting fee was in aggregate amount of RMB 756,000 yuan.

The arbitral tribunal held that the shifting fee of ships was RMB 36,000 yuan/

time, which was reasonable and the above-mentioned fee actually happened. However, the Applicant had unreasonable arrangements for the ship involved to shift for many days. Based on the consideration of protecting the interests of both parties with fairness and reasonableness, the arbitral tribunal supported the time of Applicant's ship shift as many as 15 times when the ship docked at the shipyard.

④ Daily care and maintenance fee when the ship docked at the shipyard. The arbitral tribunal noted that the length of J ship was 91.5 meters. With reference to the third and fourth items in 92 Yellow Book, the fee of daily fire duty and fire inspection was RMB 112 yuan/person (85 yuan + 27 yuan). The arbitral tribunal held that it was reasonable for the Applicant to arrange three staff members, but the claim that the remuneration should be according to the standard of RMB 300 yuan/person/day, which was significantly higher than the contract. The two parties applied 92 Yellow Book for the ship repair engineering charge project, which was clearly agreed. The arbitral tribunal respected the agreement between the parties. The fee of daily fire duty and fire inspection should be calculated at RMB 112 yuan/person/day. The arbitral tribunal supported the Applicant's claim that the daily care and maintenance fee when the ship docked at the shipyard was in aggregate amount of RMB 222,432 yuan, including 164 days during the borrowing contract period, which was in aggregate amount of RMB 55,104 yuan, and the delayed period for the ship to leave the shipyard outside the contract period was 498 days, which was in aggregate amount of RMB 167,328 yuan.

⑤ Security maintenance fee when the ship docked at the shipyard. The arbitral tribunal held that although the security maintenance fee when the ship docked at the shipyard was not agreed in the contract, the Applicant actually paid the above-mentioned fee to avoid the loss of the Respondent's ship value, which benefited the Respondent. Moreover, the benefit of the Respondent had a direct causal relationship with the payment of the Applicant. Therefore, the security maintenance fee when the ship docked at the shipyard was in aggregate amount of RMB 70,759 yuan that the Applicant claimed, which was supported by the arbitral tribunal.

The above-mentioned fee happened due to repairs was in aggregate amount of RMB 3,888,151 yuan. After deducting RMB 300,000 yuan which was already paid by the Respondent, the Respondent should also pay RMB 3,588,151 yuan to the Applicant.

(2) Regarding the Applicant's claim for the "overdue fine" for the debt of repair engineering fee.

The arbitral tribunal held that, based on the supplementary contract of the borrowing contract concluded later, it was confirmed that all the engineering funds of J should be settled and paid at the latest before the contract termination date on October 15, 2014, which was more in line with the contract purpose and final willing, at that time, the Respondent must pay all the engineering fee, and for late payment, the overdue fine should be born by the Respondent according to the borrowing contract.

The arbitral tribunal held that the Respondent should bear the liability for paying the overdue fine as agreed in the contract from the next month for the failure of settling and paying all fee which was in aggregate amount of RMB 798,823 yuan before the contract termination date on October 15, 2014, namely bore a 1.5% overdue fine for the amount of debt for each month (less than one month was counted as one month) until the effective date of the award in the case. The base for the actual calculation of overdue fine should be RMB 498,823 yuan after the deduction of 300,000 yuan. In addition, due to the Respondent's own reasons, the ship continued to stay in the shipyard, and it did not settle and pay the berthing service fee and other fee that continued to be generated afterwards, which was in aggregate amount of RMB 3,089,328 yuan (as of February 25, 2016). According to the contract between the two parties, the Respondent should still be liable for paying the overdue fine for the part of the debt. In summary, the arbitral tribunal held that the Applicant's claim for the "overdue fine" conformed to the agreement between the parties and was not contrary to the law. The arbitral tribunal supported it.

(3) Regarding the claim for the Applicant's "lien".

According to Article 5 Sub-Paragraph 5 of J ship borrowing contract, the Applicant's claim for "lien" complied with the agreement between the parties and should be supported.

[Comment]

The issue between the two parties is clear, namely, the validity of the ship repair engineering contract, J ship borrowing contract, two memorandums of J ship, and the supplementary contract of J ship borrowing contract. The arbitral tribunal held that the ship repair engineering contract involved was not signed and stamped by the Respondent, so it could not be confirmed that the ship repair engineering contract had taken effect. However, J ship borrowing contract, two memorandums of J ship, and the supplementary contract of J ship borrowing contract had both parties' signatures; the parties' meaning of the limited repair of the ship involved did not change. Therefore, these four contracts were truly valid.

2.2.3　Disputes over arbitration agreement in litigation of contract subrogation rights

[Case]

The Appellant (sub-debtor) and the Third Party (debtor) of first instance concluded the share purchase agreement and the share holder agreement which stated the arbitration clause that agreed the submission to the Hong Kong International Arbitration Center, and to carry out arbitration according to the UNCITRAL arbitration rules and according to the substantive law of New York in the USA. The Respondent (creditor) filed a subrogation action before Shanghai Second Intermediate People's Court for that it held the due creditor's rights under the contract of investment cooperation agreement, termination of investment cooperation, share holder agreement and the Third Party of first instance neglected to exercise its due creditor's rights under the share purchase agreement and the share holder agreement. The appellant was the Defendant.

[Judgment]

The appellant filed a jurisdiction objection before Shanghai Second Intermediate People's Court, and Shanghai Second Intermediate People's Court made a *Civil Ruling* to dismiss the Appellant's jurisdiction objection. Thereafter, the Appellant filed an appeal before Shanghai High People's Court with respect to the above-mentioned *Civil Ruling*.

Shanghai High People's Court held after hearing that: "*Chinese Civil Procedure Law* stipulates that parties to foreign-related economic, trade, carriage, and maritime disputes have arbitration clauses in their contracts or have reached an arbitration agreement afterwards, and submit them to the foreign-related arbitration institution of the People's Republic of China or other arbitration institutions for arbitration, the parties shall not file an action before the people's court. In the case, the appellant and the Third Party of first instance clearly agreed that the disputes involved between the two parties should be submitted to Hong Kong International Arbitration Center and carried out according to the arbitration rules of the United Nations Commission on International Trade Law and the substantive law of New York in the USA. Therefore, the jurisdiction of the court was excluded between the appellant and the Third Party of first instance. The case was a dispute over the subrogation right of foreign-related creditors. Chinese *Judicial Interpretation of Contract Law* stipulates that the sub-debtor's plea which was against the debtor could be claimed against the creditor. The plea included both a substantive plea and a procedure plea. The action of creditor's subrogation right filed by the Respondent in the case was essentially a substitute debtor's claim to the sub-debtor on the due creditor's rights, based on the protection of the position of sub-debtor's jurisdictional interest, the holder of subrogation right should be bound by the arbitration clause. According to the evidence in the case, the Respondent and the Third Party of first instance had clearly known that there was an arbitration agreement between the Third Party of first instance and the appellant when concluding the memorandum of negotiation. Therefore, the court had no jurisdiction." Accordingly, Shanghai High People's Court ruled to revoke the *Civil Ruling* of Shanghai Second Intermediate People's Court, and ruled to dismiss the Respondent's action.

[**Comment**]

In the case of a valid arbitration agreement between the debtor and the sub-debtor, whether the creditor's action of subrogation right will be rejected due to the sub-debtor's plea, the arbitration theory has both support and objections to this. There have been opposing conclusions in justice practice. The reasons for generating different opinions on the issue are based on: ①whether the exercise of subrogation right includes arbitration, and whether the arbitration agreement between the debtor and the sub-debtor can be extended to a third party outside the arbitration agreement; ②*Judicial Interpretation of Contract Law I* Article 18 ("In the litigation of subrogation right, the sub-debtor's plea against the debtor can be claimed against the creditor"), how should it be understood, namely, whether the sub-debtor's plea includes a plea against the procedure dispute resolution method, this also involves how coordinate the fundamental conceptual conflicts behind the design of relevant systems under the current *Contract Law* and *Arbitration Law* in China, and relying only on the relevant confirmation made by the people's court in case hearings, it seems that these conflicts cannot be fundamentally resolved to protect the full realization of the rights of the relevant parties. Therefore, it is still necessary for relevant departments to make up for the conflict through clear amendment opinions.

2.2.4 Disputes over charter party

[Case]

The Respondent issued a bid invitation to the Applicant on August 25, 2008 for the carriage of Brazilian iron ore, listing the specific terms of the invitation to the offer, and submitting a turnaround deadline at 10:00 am on August 27, 2008; on August 27, 2008, the Applicant issued a bid to the Respondent according to the conditions of the bid invitation; on August 27, 2008, the Respondent issued a bid invitation of carriage confirmation to the Applicant to confirm the bid price of the Applicant. During the entire above-mentioned bidding process, both parties expressed their opinions in the form of e-mail, fax and other data messages, and reached the other party's receiving system.

[Opinion of the arbitral tribunal]

1) Regarding whether the charter party was established

The Respondent held that the charter agreement in the case had gone through the bidding procedures and should be concluded in writing. On August 27, 2008, the charter agreement draft submitted by the Applicant to the Respondent was a paper contract in the form of a contract. The contract must be signed and stamped by both parties before it could be established. Regarding the final revised draft of the charter agreement provided by the Applicant on September 5, 2008, the Respondent did not make any expression of commitment and the two parties did not reach an agreement on the "extra insurance" issue. The charter agreement was a negotiating text rather than a legally established contract, so the charter party was not established. The Applicant held that: the bid issued by the Applicant to the Respondent constituted an offer, and the bid invitation of carriage confirmation issued by the Respondent to the Applicant constituted a commitment. The charter party in the case was established when the bid invitation of carriage confirmation arrived at the Applicant, namely established according to law on August 27, 2008. The *Maritime Code* Article 43 required the charter party to be concluded in writing. The written form required by the *Contract Law* Article 11 includes the formation of contracts in the form of data messages such as telegraph, telex, fax, and e-mail. The bid documents of the Applicant in the case and the bid invitation of carriage confirmation of the Respondent were sent to the other party by fax. Therefore, the charter party was legal and valid and in compliance with the legal requirements in "written form".

After the Applicant received the Respondent's bid invitation of carriage confirmation, both parties negotiated on the "follow-up issues of contract clauses" of the voyage charter party. The original draft of Article 27 of the draft of charter agreement was that: "additional insurance: if overage insurance happens due to the age of the ship exceeding 20 years, it should be borne by the charterer. However, the shipowner should compensate the charterer for USD 10,000 in one-time and was deducted from freight." The Applicant revised the draft to that:"If the age of ship exceeds 20 years and overage insurance happened, it should be borne by the charterer. The shipowner is not liable for extra overage insurance."Although the two drafts were not the same, but what they had in common was that: ships which had an age over 20 years could be used, but they only disagreed on who should bear the overage insurance for ships. Regarding the issue of ship age, in the previous bidding process, the Respondent's bid invitation was "... V. Ship age requirements: 20 years MAX...", and the Applicant's bid was "... MAX 20 YEAR OLD...". Obviously, the two parties agreed that the age of winning ship was 20 years. Namely, a ship with a ship age of more than 20 years could not become a carrier ship in the voyage charter party involved. The *Bidding Law* Article 46 stipulates, "... the tenderee and the winning bidder can no longer conclude other agreements that deviate from the substantive content of the contract." Because the content of Article 27 of the charter agreement that the parties negotiated subsequently deviated from the agreement of both parties about the maximum age of 20 years in the bid invitation document and the bid document. Even if the parties finally reached an agreement on the clause, such a clause would be invalid and their actions would violate the law.

The arbitral tribunal held that such a clause that negotiated between the parties violated the *Bidding Law* Article 46 and would not be supported.

Regarding the issue of ship age, which should be subject to the result of winning the bid, namely, the maximum ship age should not exceed 20 years. Apart from this, neither party raised any objection to the other terms of the draft of charter agreement. The arbitral tribunal held that both parties have reached agreement on other terms, so the voyage charter party was established which was concluded on the basis of the bidding results.

2) Regarding the problem of coming into effect of the charter party

The Respondent held that: Article 33 of the charter agreement involved agreed that "this charter agreement should be written in Chinese and English and takes effect by signature". The signature of both parties was a requirement for the agreement to take effect. Since both parties did not sign the agreement, there was no contract binding force on both parties. The Respondent did not bear any liability for breach of contract. The Applicant appointed the ship in advance before the draft of charter agreement was formally established, and any loss caused should be a commercial risk voluntarily bore by the Applicant.

The Applicant held that: in the case, through the bidding method, the contract concluded by the two parties in the form of exchange of e-letters and data messages did not legally require signatures and stamps as the requirements for the establishment and entry into effect of the contract. The establishment of the charter party in the case complied with the requirements of the *Maritime Code* on the written form and was a legal and valid contract. In addition, since the Applicant sent a ship dispatch notice to the Respondent on September 5, 2008, both parties began to perform the charter party, which also showed that the contract was a valid contract.

There was a clause in Article 33 of the charter agreement concerning the entry into force of the signature. The arbitral tribunal held that the charter party in the case was a contract concluded by the parties based on the result of the winning bid. The terms of the charter party were composed of two parts: ①the content in the bidding documents and the conditions agreed in the result of winning bid. In the case, they were the agreed conditions in terms of name and quantity, freight price, loading/unloading port, loading period, demurrage/expedited dispatch, ship age, shipping agency. These conditions constituted the core terms of the charter party. According to the *Bidding Law* Article 45, "the notice of winning the bid has legal effect on the tenderee and the winning bidder". Namely, this part of the charter clause had come into effect and was binding on both parties. Whoever violated these effective agreements would bear corresponding legal liabilities. ②Subsequent terms of the charter party concluded by both parties after winning the bid. However, this part of the provisions must comply with the *Bidding Law* Article 46, namely, "the tenderee and the winning bidder can not conclude any other agreement that deviates from the substantive content of the contract". The purpose was to ensure the implementation of the winning bid, namely, to ensure that the core clauses of the contract in above-mentioned ① could be performed smoothly. Article 33 of the charter agreement involved was a subsequent clause of the charter party in the case, and it was not the condition in the bidding document and the result of winning the bid nor the mandatory provisions of the law. Therefore, it must comply with the *Bidding Law* Article 46, and could not have any "deviations". The meaning of the clause "This charter agreement should be written in Chinese and English and takes effect by signature" was clear. Before the parties signed, the entire charter party had no legal effect. Namely, not only the subsequent clauses of the charter party had no legal effect, but even the core clauses of the contract that had been generated in the previous bidding and had become effective became terms without legal effect. This negated the legal effect of the results of winning bids through bidding. Such a clause violated the *Bidding Law* Article 45 and Article 46. Therefore, the arbitral tribunal did not support the claim of the Respondent that it did not take effect without signature.

[**Comment**]

The case mainly discusses the confirmation of the written form of the voyage charter party concluded through the bidding procedures and the requirements for its entry into effect.

Regarding the confirmation of the written form of the voyage charter party, the arbitral tribunal held that the voyage charter party in the case was concluded by the parties through bidding. According to the relevant provisions of the *Contract Law*, the bid invitation issued by the Respondent constitutes an invitation of offer to the Applicant; the bid issued by the Applicant to the Respondent constitutes the Applicant's offer; the bid invitation of carriage confirmation issued by the Respondent to the Applicant should be the confirmation of the winning bid for carriage in substance, which constituted the Respondent's commitment to the Applicant and had reached the Applicant. The commitment comes into effect when it reaches the offeror. When the commitment comes into effect, the contract is established, namely, the legal relationship for bidding in the case was established, resulting in a result of winning bidding including the content of the bidding document. The *Bidding Law* Article 45 stipulates that "the bid winning notice has legal effect on the tenderee and the bidder. After the bid winning notice is issued, if the tenderee changes the result of the bidding or the winning bidder renounces the winning project, it shall bear legal liability". Therefore, the result of the winning bidding, which contained the main clauses of the voyage charter party, had legal effect on both parties. Article 46 stipulates that: "the tenderee and winning bidder shall, within 30 days from the date of issuance of the bid winning notice, conclude a written contract according to the bidding invitation documents and the winning bidder's bidding documents. The tenderee and winning bidder can not conclude any other agreement that deviates from the substantive content of the contract." Both parties should conclude a written voyage charter party in the case according to this Article.

According to the *Maritime Code* Article 43, "the voyage charter party shall be concluded in writing. Telegram, telex and fax have written effect". For the form of voyage charter party in the case, these laws all stipulate that it must be in "written form". As for what "written form" should be used, there is no mandatory choice requirement in the law. In addition, during the entire bidding process, both parties did not agree that the subsequent voyage charter party must be concluded in the form of a written contract. Therefore, the Respondent held that the contract concluded based on the bidding results must be in the form of a "written contract". The claim was neither a mandatory requirement by law nor a consensus of the parties, and the arbitral tribunal did not support it. The arbitral tribunal held that the voyage charter party in the case was concluded in a written form other than a "written contract", which did not violate the law.

Regarding the requirements for the entry into effect of the written form of the voyage charter party, the arbitral tribunal held that the parties in the case established a winning bid legal relationship that was binding on both parties through the bidding process. According to the *Contract Law*, the legal relationship established by the parties through this process was the contractual relationship. As far as the content of the contract involved was concerned, it was a voyage charter party carriage contract. It was established by the exchange of data messages between the parties via e-mails, fax. This was in full compliance with the *Maritime Code* Article 43, "the voyage charter party shall be concluded in writing. Telegram, telex and fax have written effect". For contracts concluded in the aforementioned form, the law does not stipulate that the establishment of such contracts must be signed and stamped by both parties. Therefore, the conclusion of the charter party in the case complied with the law. "Contracts established according to the law shall take effect from the time of establishment." In addition, according to the *Bidding Law* Article 45, when the Respondent issues a bid winning notice, the bid winning notice "has legal effect on the tenderee and winning bidder", namely, the winning bid is valid and binding on both parties.

2.2.5 Disputes over ship repair liability insurance contract

[Case]

On September 6, 2005, the Applicant and the Respondent concluded a ship repair liability insurance policy, agreeing that the Respondent should cover the Applicant's ship repair liability insurance, and the insurance period was from 0:00 on September 11, 2005 to 24:00 on September 10, 2006. Article 15 of the insurance policy agreed that disputes should be resolved by arbitration by China Maritime Arbitration Commission of Beijing. From September 11, 2005 to October 28, 2005, the ship involved was repaired by the Applicant, and one of the repair projects was the overhaul of the No.5 cylinder of the main engine.

On November 25, 2005, when the ship involved was sailing from Singapore to the Malacca, a repaired main engine No.5 cylinder suffered a mechanical accident. After being informed of the accident, the Applicant contacted the Respondent in a timely manner, and the Respondent appointed an assessor to investigate and survey. Subsequently, the Applicant negotiated with the shipowner of the ship involved and reached a reconciliation agreement on May 29, 2007. The Applicant paid USD 145,000 to the shipowner as financial compensation. The Applicant also reported the process to the Respondent in time and filed a claim for compensation. The Respondent sent a notice of refusal of insurance compensation to the Applicant on March 6, 2008, stating that the accident was not covered by insurance.

The Applicant held that the insurance in the case was professional liability insurance. According to Article 3 of the ship repair liability insurance agreement, the basic risk insured by the Respondent was "the loss caused to the ship under repair that the insured person (Applicant) should be liable for according to the ship repair contract and relevant agreement". Under the ship repair contract, the Applicant was liable for compensation to the shipowner, and the Applicant had the right to obtain insurance compensation from the insured according to the ship repair liability insurance agreement.

The Respondent held that, according to the scope of insurance liability in Article 3 of the ship repair liability insurance agreement, "the direct loss caused to the ship under repair due to fire accident caused by the fault of the ship repair worker or technician and ship's machinery damage that the insured shall be liable for according to the ship repair contract and relevant agreements, but for the damage of the machine itself, it is not liable". In the case, the main engine No.5 cylinder did have a mechanical damage accident, but it did not cause loss of any part of the ship except the machine itself. As for the damage of the No.5 cylinder of the main engine, the insurance liability scope had clearly agreed that "for the damage of the machine itself, it is not liable". The reason for the accident in the case was that during the repair process, the Applicant discovered the defect of the No.5 cylinder of the main engine and proposed to the shipowner to make adjustments on the lathe. The shipowner refused to adjust and refused to sign the memorandum. The relevant components were assembled at the request of the shipowner, and the entire assembling process was carried out under the supervision of the shipowner's representative. In addition, the single cylinder did not have sufficient cooling, and the crew failed to detect the abnormal temperature of the cylinder in time, which caused the accident to happen and expand. These were the shipowner's own reasons, and none of them belonged to the Applicant's liability. Therefore, there was no factual and legal basis for the Applicant to bear liability.

[Opinion of the arbitral tribunal]

In the ship repair contract of the case, the ship repair liability bore by the shipyard (Applicant) was the underwriting basis of the ship repair liability insurance agreement. The size or scope of the ship repair liability were agreed by the shipyard and the shipowner in the ship repair contract. In the ship repair liability insurance agreement, the insurance company (the Respondent) underwrote all ship repair liability or part of ship repair liability belonging to the shipyard. The scope of the ship repair liability insurance was agreed by the insurance company and the shipyard in the ship repair liability insurance agreement. As far as the case was concerned, in the ship repair contract concluded between the Applicant and the shipowner, the scope of ship repair liability of the shipyard was relatively wide, and the types of liabilities were correspondingly large, and the scope of insurance liability in the ship repair liability insurance agreement concluded between the Applicant (shipyard) and the Respondent was relatively narrow. The ship repair liability insurance agreement was a ship repair liability insurance contract in which the Applicant and the Respondent agreed liability. The underwriting risks were "fire accidents" and "machine damage accidents", and the liability for compensation was "direct loss caused to the ship under repair", and not all ship repair risks of the shipyard were underwritten and it not bore corresponding compensation liability. Therefore, for the claim of the Applicant namely "the Applicant was liable to the shipowner under the ship repair contract, the Applicant had the right to obtain insurance compensation from the insured according to the ship repair liability insurance agreement", the arbitral tribunal did not support.

[Comment]

Regarding the confirmation of the scope of insurance compensation of the ship repair liability insurance contract, the arbitral tribunal held that the ship repair contract and the ship repair liability insurance agreement were two contracts of different nature, but there was a certain relationship between the two. In insurance practice, the "scope of ship repair liability" in the ship repair contract and the "scope of ship repair liability insurance" in the ship repair liability insurance contract can or can not be the same. It all depends on the contract between different parties.

3 Summary

Maritime rule of law is an important part of constructing an international shipping center. It is our goal to improve Chinese maritime rule of law level and its right to speak in international shipping, and to gain an advantage in the future global international shipping center construction competition. Continue to improve the maritime justice mechanism, improve the justice capacity of Chinese maritime trial, focus on the establishment of the "Belt and Road" dispute settlement center, better serve the strategy of maritime power, at the same time, Shanghai should play a core cohesion to construct an international shipping financial rule of law center and improve research level and influence to better guarantee the construction of the "Belt and Road" initiative.

Chapter 3 Administrative Enforcement of Shipping Policies and Laws

Maritime administration is part of the administrative management of a state, which is the management activity conducted by maritime safety supervision and administration organs and their staff for the purpose of safeguarding state sovereignty, water traffic safety, protecting the safety of human life and property on water and preventing vessels from polluting the waters through taking measures like administrative licensing, administrative penalty and administrative compulsion according to the law. This kind of management activity involves every aspect of vessels, seafarers and management of sea areas, mainly including: ship registration and safety management, seafarer management, navigable water management, arrangement and management of navigation marks, management of hazardous cargoes loaded on vessels, maritime search and rescue, etc. This chapter is going to introduce the administrative enforcement cases in 2017 of Shanghai Maritime Safety Administration, Shanghai Rescue and Salvage Bureau of the Ministry of Transport, Shanghai Fishery Supervision and Administration Division, Shanghai General Station of Immigration Inspection and so on.

In 2017, closely focusing on the major decision deployment of the Municipal Party Committee and the municipal government, the central work of the bureau and the concerns of the general public, Shanghai Maritime Safety Administration promoted to carry out the *Notice of the General Office of Shanghai Municipal People's Government on Issuing the Key Tasks in Promoting the Transparency of Government Affairs of Shanghai in 2017*, and according to the requirements for transparency of government affairs of the Ministry of Water Resources, the Ministry of Housing and Urban-Rural Development and the State Oceanic Administration, combined with the actuality of maritime and water affairs in Shanghai, Shanghai Maritime Safety Administration insisted on reform and innovation and demand orientation, further improved the system construction of the institution for transparency of government affairs, boosted five aspects of transparency, respectively of decision, enforcement, management, service and consequence, enhanced the interpretation of response, enlarged the public engagement, continuously strengthened the credibility and execution, and further improved the capacity of public services and industry administration level in water affairs and ocean.

Shanghai Maritime Safety Administration actively promoted the information disclosure of the operation of administrative power, making efforts to establish rule by law for maritime affairs. It fully met the relevant requirements of Internet Governmental Services and managed the openness and transparency of the power and the public acknowledgment of how affairs were handled, by putting the reform action of public promotion of "Fang Guan Fu" into practice. It timely updated the power list and the responsibility list according to the cancellation and adjustment of the power and responsibility items. It promoted the formulation and publication of evaluation and assessment methods for intermediary services and further improved the disclosure of the process for handling administrative examination and approval. It promoted the access of governmental service items to the online government affair hall and intensively disclosed them via the portal website of Shanghai China and of the bureau. It explored measures for online handling of administrative examination and approval, continued to deepen online handling, improved online service experience, and promoted the integration of online and offline services.

Shanghai Maritime Safety Administration actively promoted the openness and transparency of credit and regulatory information. According to the requirements of double publicity of administrative license and administrative penalty, it timely published the information of administrative license and administrative penalty to the society. Cooperating with relevant municipal departments, it further expanded the coverage of legal person information and updated the enterprise information that should be published in real time. It worked in a coordinated way to build a platform for interim and ex-post comprehensive supervision and to coordinate cross-department supervision of dishonest judgment debtors. It expanded the application of credit information in the field of water affairs and ocean administrative management, strengthening the initiative to inquire credit information, and innovated the management and service mode of administrative examination and approval; according to the credit situation of administrative counterparts, it explored to establish the credit rating supervision methods, such as random sampling, classification, and dynamic detection of frequency, and explored the implementation of departments' cooperative supervision, joint punishment, and advance warning mechanism, so as to further improve the level of the interim and ex-post supervision.

The report of the 19th National Congress of the Communist Party of China made it clear that we should insist on planning the land and sea as a whole and should speed up efforts to build China into a maritime power, which sufficiently indicated new requirements of the Party Central Committee about the construction and development of marine industry, sufficiently indicated the new target and task of marine industry given by securing a decisive victory in building a moderately prosperous society in all respects and striving for the great victory of socialism with Chinese characteristics in the new era, which pointed out the way forward for the construction and development of marine industry. In 2017, according to the strategic deployment of the 19th National Congress of the Communist Party of China, Shanghai Maritime Safety Administration fully understood the new era, new situation, new strategies and new requirements, and accelerated efforts to build China into a maritime power.

In 2017, East China Sea Rescue Bureau completed 8,368 ships on duty at sea, carried out 629 rescue and emergency missions of various kinds, dispatched rescue forces for 850 times, rescued 1,035 people in distress of various kinds and rescued 42 ships in distress, with a direct value of rescued property of an estimated 1.903 billion yuan. The reform of the management system achieved remarkable results, and the rescue center made outstanding achievements. It took concrete actions to implement China's maritime project of benevolent rule, strengthening the last ditch for maritime safety.

1 Administrative Enforcement Cases of Shanghai Maritime Safety Administration

1.1 Inspection units at Chongming Port implemented joint boarding inspection through the single window for the first time

On December 6, 2017, more than 10 law enforcement officers of the four port units, Chongming Maritime Safety Bureau, Chongming Customs, Chongming Entry-Exit Inspection and Quarantine Bureau and Chongming Entry-Exit Frontier Inspection Station, boarded the Italian cruise liner Costa neoRomantica located in Chongming Huarun Dadong Shipyard to conduct the joint boarding inspection, which was the first time of Chongming Port to implement joint boarding inspection though the single window.

In recent years, with the economic development of cruise liner at Shanghai Port, Chongming Huarun Dadong Shipyard, the initial Chinese ship repair enterprise into the cruise liner repair market, had successively completed the maintenance work of 10 luxury cruise liners like Costa Atlantic, Costa Serena, Sky Sea Golden Era, etc., becoming the major cruise liner repair basement in the far east area. This was the first time of the luxury cruise liner Costa neoRomantica to be repaired and maintained in Shanghai.

During the inspection process, whereas the inspection contents such as ship's safety condition, cargo and personnel, the four units stuck to the principle of efficiency in accordance with law, convenience for the sake of ships, division of labor of the joint boarding system, boarded the ship and carried out the on-spot inspection towards various items at the same time, which lessoned the repetitious boarding for inspection and shortened the time of port inspection on the whole. Meanwhile, in the light of requirements of information exchange, mutual recognition of supervision and mutual assistance in law enforcement, it avoided the repetition of inspection contents, raised the clearance efficiency of port inspection and minimized the influence on the maintenance of the cruise liner.

This single window joint boarding inspection provided strong support for ship repair enterprises at Chongming Port to accelerate the transformation and upgrading in response to the national supply-side structural reform, and to carry out luxury cruise liner maintenance, special ship repair and construction and other new business forms. As the joint boarding convening unit, Chongming Maritime Safety Administration would further summarize experience, optimize the joint boarding inspection mechanism of Chongming Port units, and constantly improve the port inspection capacity and service level, so as to get it well prepared for the upcoming peak tourist season.

1.2 Shanghai Maritime Search and Rescue Center urgently organized the traffic after 30 containers fell into water

At 15:25 on November 18, 2017, Shanghai Maritime Search and Rescue Center was reported that, the multipurpose vessel "PENG AN SHENG" carrying more than 400 containers (Fujian company, 148.78 meters long, gross tonnage of 9,977, 17 people on board, loaded with 153 20-feet containers, 258 40-feet containers, Yantai-Shanghai) was affected by the cold wind in the northern water near the buoy light D3 in the Yangtze Estuary, 30 40-feet containers on the ship falling down into the water. The containers were filled with auto spare parts, with no hazardous cargo in it. Shanghai Maritime Search and Rescue Center assigned "HAI XUN 012" of Wusong Maritime Safety Administration and coordinated 4 salvage ships of "DONG LEI 5", "DONG LEI 12", "DONG LEI 16", "DONG NAN QI 12" to the spot. Shanghai Maritime Search and Rescue Center informed Yangshan Port, Chongming and Pudong Maritime Safety Administrations for coordination and broadcasted the sailing warning.

As of that night, the Yangtze Estuary deep-water channel was normally navigable and the import international cruise liners were normal as planned. Shanghai Maritime Search and Rescue Center organized the traffic at the water of the incident, reminding the ships passing by of cautious navigation and to follow the instruction of the traffic control.

Whereas this frequent accidents of container falling into the sea, Shanghai Maritime Safety Administration suggested that: ①Ships should pay attention to the container fastening scheme of each loading and unloading port and should implement the container fastening operation in accordance with the scheme, and regularly inspect and maintain the ship's movable fastening equipment; ②when the ship encountered a big storm, the master should take effective measures as soon as possible, such as slowing down, altering orientation, in order to reduce the shock of waves to the front of the ship, lower the level of the ship and reduce its rolling. Through the above measures, reduce or avoid the ship damage or container falling into the sea accident.

1.3 Shanghai Maritime Safety Administration comprehensively carried out 2017 Mid-Autumn Day and National Day ship safety major inspection activities

With Mid-Autumn Festival and National Day in 2017 about to come, for the purpose of facilitating the safe travel of the general public and ensuring the stability of security situation of water traffic in the jurisdiction, Shanghai Maritime Safety Administration, in accordance with the spirit of the relevant notice of its superior departments, combined with the requirements of the *Long-term Mechanism of Shanghai Maritime Safety Administration for Passenger Ships' Security Administration*, comprehensively launched a ship safety major inspection in the jurisdiction from September 11, 2017.

The major inspection activities mainly aimed at the passenger ships and hazardous cargo ships operated in the jurisdiction of the bureau and gave priority in ship safety inspection of all the passenger ships, traffic boats and other ships carrying more than 12 passengers which had been put into operation. All the defects that were inspected should be corrected and followed up for review to guarantee the rate of inspection on passenger ships and of the defect correction as 100%.

Major inspection activities this time focused on the actual operational ability of the seafarers, the implementation of the duty system, the outfitting and availability of the ship's fire protection and life-saving equipment as required, and the conduct of emergency drill. The safety inspection of passenger ships would last until the end of September, urging the full implementation of the entity responsibility for safety production, strengthening safety management and land-based support for the ships belonging to them, and urging them to earnestly carry out the prohibition and limitation of passenger ship's navigation under severe weather and the on-duty and emergency disposal of the companies' administrators. Shanghai Maritime Safety Administration, through strengthening the joint law enforcement with the government, transportation department, safety supervision department and other departments, maintained the proper operation order, and tried its best to ensure the safe operation of passenger ships.

1.4 Ships breaking rules and regulations would hide nowhere now that technological measures could arrest them immediately

On June 21, 2017, Yangpu Maritime Safety Administration Command Center found during its electronic patrol that the vessel " * * 207" entered the dock of Fuxing Island Timber Company in its jurisdiction for loading and unloading. The system showed that the ship had been suspected of illegal behaviors of not following the prescribed route and not following the prescribed speed for many times, but had not yet been dealt with. Whereas this situation, the commander immediately verified the ship's position again and informed the on-site law enforcement officials to investigate its illegal behavior. Through the extraction and verification of evidence such as the voyage log and AIS track, the ship finally admitted its illegal behavior. On the afternoon of the same day, the shipowner of the vessel took the initiative to accept the investigation of Yangpu Maritime Safety Administration, and admitted that there was a fluke mentality after receiving the illegal notice, tending to escape punishment by delaying time.

This was the first ship seized by Yangpu Maritime Safety Administration relying on the newly added function of alarming the arrival of the ships of the electronic patrol system, which had been found to have many illegal acts. Since then, Yangpu Maritime Safety Administration continued to carry out in-depth electronic patrol, strengthen the coordination and interaction with the on-site law enforcement, and severely crack down on all kinds of illegal acts.

1.5 Minhang Maritime Safety Administration discovered the first case at Shanghai Port of foreign vessel's detainable deficiencies and continuing navigation without correcting them

On May 15, 2017, Minhang Maritime Safety Administration discovered a case where a foreign vessel sailed to Shanghai Port when ill without correcting its detainable deficiencies of the supervision inspection at its port state.

On that day, Minhang Maritime Safety Administration discovered when investigating the inspectable foreign vessels in its jurisdiction using the ship safety supervision assistive decision-making supportive system developed by Shanghai Maritime Safety Administration that: one of the remaining items of past PSC inspection records of a foreign vessel which ported at the berth of Guan Gang 4 in the jurisdiction was a detainable deficiency but it showed on the system that this defect had not been corrected, which was suspected of sailing to Shanghai Port when ill without its severe security defect being corrected. Minhang Maritime Safety Administration right away assigned the law enforcement officials to make further verification of supervision inspection of this vessel at the port state.

It was discovered after inspection that, this foreign vessel used to be detained in Osaka in Japan for its hatchway cover not being able to be weather tight, and the action code for the detainable deficiency was the new code 46 in the new edition of PSC Manual. The code 46 did not mean the release of ship detention. The vessel should, within the appropriate time limit, sail to Yantai, the repair port designated at that time for repair to correct the detainable deficiency. However, after inspection, the law enforcement officials found that the ship did not sail to Yantai to repair the serious defect, but still sailed in sickness and seriously violated the corresponding requirements of the new code 46 of the supervision procedure at the port state. Meanwhile, the uncorrected detention defect also indicates that the ship seriously violates the relevant requirements of ISM code. In view of the seriousness of the problem, Minhang Maritime Safety Administration imposed detention of the ship according to the law.

1.6 37 containers fell into the river in Wusong Estuary and Shanghai Maritime Search and Rescue Center spared no efforts to clear the barriers in the main channel

At 21:57 on May 10, 2017, Shanghai Maritime Search and Rescue Center received a report that 37 containers fell into the river in the warning area of Wusong Estuary, with no hazardous cargo in the containers. The center immediately organized search and rescue and emergency response forces to the scene to search, locate and salvage containers, and gave priority to scanning and surveying the main channel to ensure the safe navigation of vessels entering and leaving the Yangtze River.

On the night of 10th, when the vessel "SHUN GANG 19" loaded with 129 containers sailed to the warning area of Wusong Estuary, 37 containers overturned and fell into the river, with waste paper inside. It is verified that there were no hazardous cargoes in them. After receiving the report, the center broadcast navigational warnings to ships in the surrounding waters, and Vessel Traffic Services (VTS) strengthened safety information broadcasting and traffic organization, set up special emergency response stations, and implemented temporary traffic control in relevant waters. The center organized 11 maritime patrol boats, 6 tugs, 11 salvage ships and 2 surveying vessels to search, locate and salvage at the site of accident. At that time, 6 containers were salved from the river.

"HAI XUN 1668", a surveying vessel of East China Sea Navigation Support Center, conducted a survey of relevant waters, giving priority to the main channel of the Yangtze River and waters of Wusong Estuary to ensure the safe navigation of vessels entering and leaving the Yangtze River and the Huangpu River. It was Southeast wind, level 3, slight sea, good visibility at the spot.

Wusong Maritime Safety Administration launched an investigation into the accident. Shanghai Maritime Search and Rescue Center formulated a detailed plan for the clearance of obstacles, intensified the strength of scanning, and increased the salvage force to speed up the clearance process.

1.7 Shanghai Maritime Safety Administration comprehensively launched the special safety supervision work of ships entering Xiamen

According to requirements of the *Notice of Maritime Safety Administration of the Ministry of Transport concerning Launching Special Safety Supervision Work of Ships Entering Xiamen Recently*, after careful study and thorough planning in the early stage, Shanghai Maritime Safety Administration officially launched the special safety supervision work of ships entering the controlled waters of Xiamen on June 1, 2017, and steadily promoted the implementation of various supervision measures.

Firstly, strengthen organizational leadership. In combination with the actual work of Shanghai Maritime Safety Administration, specific work plans were formulated, human resources and law enforcement equipment were reasonably deployed, and various work requirements were clarified to ensure that the leaders, responsibilities, measures and personnel were in place for special safety supervision work of ships entering Xiamen.

Secondly, carry out internal learning. It organized on-site law enforcement personnel to conscientiously study the relevant requirements of special safety supervision work of ships entering Xiamen, unified the work standards, specified and clarified the implementation date, special safety inspection requirements and public security inspection requirements, etc.

Thirdly, publicize outwards extensively. Through VTS broadcast, government window, on-site boarding and Microblog, WeChat and other channels, the special safety supervision requirements of ships entering Xiamen were extensively publicized to the administrative counterparts, and the consultation hotline was set up to do a good job in relevant publicity and interpretation.

Fourthly, strengthen ship monitoring. The dynamic monitoring and reporting information verification of ships entering Xiamen were strengthened by means of electronic patrol and entry and exit reporting system, and effective management measures were taken in time for ships that fail to receive special inspection as required.

Shanghai Maritime Safety Administration continued to strictly implement the requirements of the special safety supervision work of ships entering Xiamen, and combining with the previous remote-control work experience, conscientiously implemented it and put the supervision in place, so as to successfully complete the special safety supervision work.

1.8 Shanghai Maritime Safety Administration made great achievements in the construction of the Service Free Trade Zone: To issue the qualification certificate of the first wholly foreign-owned seafarers' assignment agency in Shanghai

Shanghai Maritime Safety Administration had made great achievements in the construction of the Service Free Trade Zone. Chinese-English China Vessel Shipping Management (Shanghai) Co., Ltd., accepted and preliminarily reviewed by Shanghai Maritime Safety Administration, had obtained the qualification certificate of wholly foreign-owned seafarers' assignment agency issued by Maritime Safety Administration of the Ministry of Transport.

On May 24, 2017, Chinese-English China Vessel Shipping Management (Shanghai) Co., Ltd. went to the government affairs center of Shanghai Maritime Safety Administration to receive the qualification certificate of seafarers' assignment agency issued by Maritime Safety Administration of the Ministry of Transport, becoming the first wholly foreign-owned seafarers' assignment agency in the China (Shanghai) Pilot Free Trade Zone, which was a major achievement of Maritime Safety Administration of the Ministry of Transport and Shanghai Maritime Safety Administration in constructing the China (Shanghai) Pilot Free Trade Zone.

According to the approval of Maritime Safety Administration of the Ministry of Transport, Chinese-English China Vessel Shipping Management (Shanghai) Co., Ltd. was limited to dispatch seafarers for ships managed by Chinese-English China Vessel Shipping Management (Hong Kong) Co., Ltd. Allowing a wholly foreign-owned enterprise within the free trade area to carry out the seafarer export experimental unit was an important action of Maritime Safety Administration of the Ministry of Transport and Shanghai Maritime Safety Administration for constructing the Service Free Trade Zone, hoping with the help of the advanced experience, management advantages and rich resources of seafarer management of international advanced ship management companies, to promote more Chinese seafarers to world, coming back with international ship management experience at the same time, realizing enterprises' own development and the win-win of construction of the free trade area.

1.9 Wusong Maritime Safety Administration actively carried out special rectification of fishing-related vessels, effectively guaranteeing the safety and smooth of the Yangtze Estuary deep-water channel

For a long time, Wusong Maritime Safety Administration had always insisted on ensuring the water traffic safety of "Two Ports and One Line", especially the safety and smooth of the Yangtze Estuary deep-water channel, as the main task and core mission of the "Sanhua" construction. March and April were the peak season for fishing, and fishing nets of fishing-related vessel in the Yangtze Estuary occupied waterways and anchorage ground frequently, which affected the navigation safety of ships passing by. In view of it, Wusong Maritime Safety Administration earnestly performed its duties, gave full play to the joint efforts of various parties, innovated working methods, and actively carries out special rectification of fishing-related vessels, effectively guaranteeing the safe, smooth and efficient operation of the Yangtze Estuary deep-water channel.

Firstly, play a good "offensive move", to find out the rules before action. In early 2017, Wusong Maritime Safety Administration organized dragnet inspections of anchorage grounds and waterway areas in its jurisdiction and carried out information registration for fishing-related vessels that had been berthing for a long time or frequently to mater the shipowner's information and contact way, understood and mastered various information such as the berthing, navigation and operation rules of relevant fishing-related vessels, and conducted systematic analysis and research, laying a solid foundation for orderly follow-up actions later.

Secondly, say the "Incantation of the Golden Hoop" well, to try peaceful means before resorting to force. According to the investigation situation, Wusong Maritime Safety Administration had organized forces to go deep into the relevant anchorage ground, concentrated berthing point and other waters, and conducted publicity education to relevant fishing-related vessels on the risks of water safety accidents and legal consequences that may be caused by acts such as illegally crossing the channel or setting up fishing nets; as for fishing-related vessels that did not listen to the persuasion, key management was to be carried out by the alliance of water public security and fishery administration departments.

Thirdly, focus on the "key points", because long-term management showed results. In order to prevent the rebound of illegal operations of fishing-related vessels, Wusong Maritime Safety Administration, in conjunction with fishery administration and other relevant departments, actively established and improved a long-term management mechanism and focused on strengthening patrol, joint law enforcement, publicity and education in waters. During the first quarter of 2017, Wusong Maritime Safety Administration dispatched 132 law enforcement officials in the rectification and the patrol boats cruised for 190 hours and sailed 1,780 nautical miles, drove away and educated 48 vessels and cleaned up fishing nets and gear in the channel for 10 times, achieving phased results in the rectification.

In 2017, Wusong Maritime Safety Administration, closely surrounding the target of preserving the safety, smooth and high-efficiency operation of the Yangtze Estuary deep-water channel, further deepened the rectification, focused on cracking down on the illegal phenomenon of fishing-related "Three Noes" and small fishing boats setting fishing nets in waterways, which actively created a favorable navigation environment and laid solid foundation for comprehensively advancing the "Sanhua" construction.

1.10 More than 500 ships were stranded at Shanghai Port and the cruise liners were given priority to evacuate the port orderly

In the evening of April 15, 2017, a heavy fog hit Shanghai Port. Visibility in some waters was less than 500 meters, and Wusong Jurisdiction Area conducted temporary traffic control. The fog did not clear until the morning of April 17, 2017. The fog, which lasted for several days, stranded more than 500 ships in the Yangtze Estuary, including large-scale cruise liners Costa Serena, Sapphire Princess, Sky Sea Golden Era. Wusong Maritime Safety Administration started the tense and orderly work of port evacuation at 1100 on April 17, 2017.

The evacuation work arranged the vessel import and export in according with the major principle of "passenger ship first; channel first, then anchorage ground; export first, then import; cargo ship and container ship first, then hazardous cargo ship and oil tanker". In order to carry out the evacuation work in a safer and more orderly way, Wusong Maritime Safety Administration continuously strengthened the linkage with its upstream and downstream sibling units, and set VTS intensive training classes to assist the man on duty in evacuating the port. The system of reporting and queuing was adopted upon the ships of north and south passages to maximize the navigation efficiency of the channel.

During the heavy fog, three cruise liners were stranded at Shanghai Port at the same time, involving tens of thousands of passengers. However, Wusong Cruise Terminal had only two berths. How to properly arrange the berthing of these three cruise liners was the most important in this evacuation. Wusong Maritime Safety Administration paid close attention to the restoration of visibility on the waters, and urgently opened up a green channel for the cruise liner, and gave priority to its entry in combination with the navigation environment. Sapphire Princess and Sky Sea Golden Area firstly went to the cruise terminal for berth. Costa Serena anchored in the emergency anchorage ground in the Triangle Area, waiting to pull out the anchor after the berth was vacated. The maritime department completed the safe berthing of three cruise liners in the shortest time.

1.11 The special governance of navigation environment of Minhang Maritime Safety Administration achieved initial success

With the vigorous promotion of the regulation of floating cranes in the

Chapter 3 Administrative Enforcement of Shipping Policies and Laws

upstream of the Huangpu River, all floating cranes under the jurisdiction of Minhang Maritime Safety Administration had been evacuated, and sand and gravel vessels had been discharged at the jurisdiction wharf. Due to the limited discharge capacity of the wharf, the large-scale sand and gravel ships were stranded in the jurisdiction area of the bureau, 42 ones when at most. Whereas the new trend of floating crane regulation, Minhang Maritime Safety Administration attached great importance to it and took active actions to organize and carry out special governance work of navigation environment to ensure the safety and stability of navigation in its jurisdiction.

Firstly, it made use of the electronic patrol systems such as CCTV and AIS to timely monitor the channel situation. When finding illegal anchoring, it urgently assigned patrol boats to the spot for publicity and comparison and expelled the large-scale sand and gravel ships which did not specify their operation plan, time and wharf. In total, 31 large-scale sand and gravel ships were expelled in April 2017, which effectively improved the navigation environment.

Secondly, it strengthened the information communication with the wharf management center, implemented the reporting work of large-scale sand and gravel ships, which effectively reduced the phenomenon that the sand and gravel ships blindly sailed into the port or anchored in disorder. At present, the number of large-scale sand and gravel ships stranded in the bureau's jurisdiction area had been reduced to 15.

Thirdly, it strengthened the on-site inspection of patrol boats on the waters, resolutely investigated and punished the sand and gravel vessels that anchored illegally, and severely cracked down on violations of laws and regulations that would affect navigation safety. From March to April in 2017, 53 violations of all kinds of sand and gravel ships were investigated and dealt with.

Fourthly, it strictly implemented the wharf management system and urged wharf management enterprises to strengthen the management of ship berthing order, to scientifically and reasonably arrange ship import plans according to the discharge capacity of the port and to put an end to the blind and disorder import of sand and gravel ships.

Minhang Maritime Safety Administration would continue to carry out comprehensive control of navigation environment in its jurisdiction area, eliminate safety hazards, and do its best to maintain the navigation order of the Huangpu River in the post floating crane period.

1.12 Reducing ferry suspension and facilitating the public to travel, Wusong Maritime Safety Administration actively carried out navigation order rectification in the Huangpu River

In order to effectively alleviate the impact on people's living caused by the forced suspension of ferries during the overlapping period between the ship sailing peak and the water passenger flow peak, it effectively provided more convenience for the general public on both sides of the Huangpu River to travel safely on water. Wusong Maritime Safety Administration officially launched the special rectification of navigation environment of the Huangpu River in 2017, and severely cracked down on all kinds of water traffic violations in the Huangpu River section under the jurisdiction of Wusong Maritime Safety Administration.

In the special rectification, Wusong Maritime Safety Administration actively promoted the orderly launch of the governance activities from three aspects based on the current situation of navigation environment in its jurisdiction and in accordance with the policy of "combining education with punishment and maintenance with governance".

First was to make a plan and defining the responsibilities, working the overall situation up and down a web. Before activities, it carefully schemed, thoroughly made the activity plan, further refined the key period of governance activities and the focus of each stage, made clear the division of responsibilities among the departments concerned and organically combined VTS supervision, site patrol, government affair acceptance, logistical support and other aspects of work, setting the general tone for opening the governance activities and weaving the responsibility wet.

Second was to pay attention to the propaganda and grasping the governance, leaving no stone unturned in the game of chess. In the early stage of publicity and education, it made full use of banner slogans, electronic display screen, WeChat short message platform and other publicity methods to release publicity and education materials and strengthen warning education for ships. In the stage of centralized governance, on the one hand, it focused on enhancing the investigation and punishment towards water traffic violations of daily ship import peak period in the Huangpu River. On the other hand, the site patrol boats timely carried out division guidance and order maintenance, preventing the ship from excessively entering the Huangpu River at the same time which would have caused channel congestion and making sure that the navigation safety of the ships that had entered the Huangpu River, trying its best to monitor the safety of this water.

Third was to strengthen linkage and setting up institution, being banded together like strands of a rope via a multitude of things. During the rectification activity, all law enforcement departments cooperated closely to form a joint force, and each law enforcement ship exchanged information to cover position in a timely manner, and comprehensively used electronic patrol system track, CCTV real-time picture monitoring, VTS monitoring playback and on-site maritime patrol boat photos to achieve the collection and solidification of illegal evidence. Meanwhile, the daily investigations and punishments towards violations made by various law enforcement departments were summarized, analyzed and compared, and the rectification activities were evaluated on a weekly basis to timely revise the specific plans, so as to further explore and establish a working mechanism for long-term governance.

The rectification activity aimed to create a safe and smooth, stable and orderly water environment for the ferry navigation within the jurisdiction. Wusong Maritime Safety Administration continued, in accordance with requirements of the scheme, to compact responsibility, strictly execute the functions, and ensured the rectification activities in order to promote long-term effective governance results, and made the next step to related ferry companies for interview, urging the enterprises to reasonably shorten the suspension time, under the premise of fulfilling the responsibility of the security subject and ensuring the safety of navigation, so as to provide practical convenience for people on both sides of the Huangpu River.

1. 13　Shanghai Maritime Safety Administration launched a comprehensive governance campaign to control the safety of vessels carrying hazardous cargoes and a special rectification activity to regulate oil tankers and bulk liquid chemicals ships of domestic voyage

In April 2017, the Ministry of Transport and the Maritime Safety

Administration of it respectively issued the *Notice of the Ministry of Transport on Issuing the Comprehensive Governance Action Scheme of the Safety of Ships Carrying Hazardous Cargoes (2017—2018)* and the *Notice of the Maritime Safety Administration of the Ministry of Transport on Issuing the Special Rectification Activity Scheme of Oil Tankers and Bulk Liquid Chemicals Ships of Domestic Voyage*, planning to pass the special activity lasting for one year, which would effectively prevent and restrain the occurrence of serious and major accidents involving ships carrying hazardous cargoes, ensure the safety of people's lives and property, and consolidate the achievements of the "Safe Shipping" campaign.

Shanghai Maritime Safety Administration promptly implemented the requirements of the superior documents, formulated the work plan of comprehensive safety governance actions and special rectification activities based on the actual work, clarified the division of responsibilities of each unit/department, and put forward relevant work requirements. According to the work plan, Shanghai Maritime Safety Administration, from April 1, 2017 to May 31, 2018, carried out the special action in three stages, through which it realized domestic hazardous cargo ship's special safety inspection coverage as 100%, special inspection rate of safety management system or regime of shipping companies of hazardous cargo ship's safety management as 100%, urged self-inspection rate of oil tankers and bulk liquid chemicals ships of domestic voyage as 100%, urged the ship inspection institutions to realize the inspection and verification rate of the oil pollution prevention certificate of oil tanker and the cermet of fitness of bulk liquid chemicals ship as 100%.

Related service divisions of Shanghai Maritime Safety Administration would guide and assist each brand maritime safety administration. Through strengthening leadership, well organizing, clarifying rights and responsibilities, enhancing supervision, comprehensive governance, joint prevention and control, strengthening propaganda, completing the summary and other measures, it effectively carried out the safety comprehensive governance actions and special rectification activities, focused on the supervision and inspection of the company's safety management, ship inspection quality, ship operation, seafarer quality and other aspects, forming an effective combination of source management and on-site inspection supervision mode; focused on investigating and punishing acts such as concealing and falsely reporting hazardous cargoes, illegal discharge of tank washings, and unseaworthy vessels carrying hazardous cargoes, so as to form a tough stance of cracking down on illegal acts of hazardous cargoes carried by ships and realize the goal of sustained and stable improvement of the safety situation of ships carrying hazardous cargoes.

1. 14   Shanghai Maritime Safety Administration carefully implemented the cancellation of requirements of the port entry and exit visas of inland navigation vessels

To facilitate the ship to arrive at and depart from the port, according to the amending decision of the *Regulations of the People's Republic of China on Administration of Traffic Safety in Inland Rivers*, the Maritime Safety Administration of the Ministry of Transport issued the *Notice concerning the Implementation of the Reporting System for Inland Navigation Vessels Arriving at and Departing from Ports*, stipulating that, from March 22, 2017, the port entry and exit visas for inland navigation vessels had been abolished, and the entry and exit reporting system for vessels was to be implemented instead. In order to ensure the smooth and orderly development of the work, Shanghai Maritime Safety Administration issued a notice and took multiple measures to actively implement the notification requirements of its superior.

First was to require each window unit to do a good job in the propaganda, and use a variety of effective ways to comprehensively publicize the important significance and convenience measures of the vessel entry and exit reporting system, the operation process of vessel entry and exit reporting and matters needing attention to administrative counterparts, and announce the contact way convenient for the administrative counterparts to consult at the same time.

Second was to do a good job in the registration work of the vessel entry and exit reporting platform. Each window unit would guide the ships that came to handle maritime services to complete the registration application of the platform. The registration application of ships registered by Shanghai Maritime Safety Administration would be examined and approved as soon as possible.

Third was to establish and perfect the checking mechanism of vessel entry and exit reporting information, strengthen the on-site inspection of the ship and master the ship navigation dynamics in the whole course via various methods.

Fourth was to adjust the documents of ship management quality system, delete the relevant system documents of the original port entry and exit visas for ships, and establish and improve the relevant system documents of the ship entry and exit report.

1.15 Shanghai Port conducted joint inspection in the anchorage waters outside the port

On March 9, 2017, Wusong Maritime Safety Administration, in conjunction with Wusong Customs, Huangpu Inspection and Quarantine Bureau, Wusong Entry-exit Frontier Inspection Station, and Yangshan Entry-exit Frontier Inspection Station, boarded the vessel "ZHANG JIAN", an international navigation ship berthing at the anchorage ground of Luhua Mountain, at the same time, to carry out a joint inspection. This was the first time for Shanghai Port to carry out joint boarding inspection in the anchorage waters outside the port.

According to the requirements of the *Notice concerning Establishing Working Mechanism of Joint Boarding Inspection of International Navigation Ships* of the Ministry of Transport, the Ministry of Public Security, the General Administration of Customs and the General Administration of Quality Supervision, in accordance with the principles of efficiency in accordance with law, convenience for the sake of ships and division of labor, the law enforcement officials of each port unit carried out on-site inspection of the ship's equipment, cargo loading, personnel situation and other items according to their respective duties, and issued relevant documents and went through relevant procedures. In accordance with the principle of "information exchange, mutual recognition of supervision and mutual assistance in law enforcement", the joint boarding inspection greatly shortened the time for port inspection, effectively improved the efficiency of vessel entry and exit inspection, and further enhanced the competitiveness of Shanghai Port, favoring the construction of an international shipping center.

Wusong Maritime Safety Administration, in conjunction with various port units, continuously perfected the joint boarding inspection mechanism, further improved the entry-exit inspection efficiency and port operation efficiency of international navigation ships, making the joint boarding inspection more convenient and efficient.

2 Administrative Enforcement Cases of Shanghai Rescue and Salvage Department

2.1 Salvage of the vessel "MIN LONG YU 66822"

On February 6, 2017, the fishing boat "MIN LONG YU 66822" from Zhangzhou, Fujian, was about 60 nautical miles southeast of Xiamen when its engine room was flooded because of the rough sea and the ship was sinking. 11 fishermen on board met with a mishap, whose situation was quite severe. What's worse, this dangerous case occurred during the key guarantee period of the Spring Festival and the Spring Festival travel rush and the distress position was located in the sensitive waters of Taiwan, which was characterized by great difficulty in coordination and strong regional sensitivity. After receiving the report, the second rescue flight team of the East China Sea immediately activated the contingency plan and dispatched two rescue helicopters, B-7310 and B-7328, to give the first aid.

At 1553 on February 6, the helicopter B-7310 first took off from Gaoqi Airport in Xiamen. At 1617, the helicopter B-7328 followed up and took off for the sea area. At that time, the second rescue flight team of the East China Sea notified the Chinese Search and Rescue Association of Taiwan of the two helicopters, and Taiwan said it would not send helicopters for the time being. At 1634, when the helicopter B-7310 was within the range of the target of 2 n mile, the visibility on the spot was only about 3 km. In order to facilitate the search for the target, the helicopter reduced its airspeed to about 80 knots, opened the airborne radar to assist the detection of the target, and began the search and rescue procedures. About 1 n mile from the target, the aircrew found a fishing boat tilting at the orientation of 2 o'clock under the influence of wind and waves. They immediately went to the boat and identified it as a vessel in distress, beginning to rescue it at the same time. Since the aircrew had completed all search and rescue/lifting tasks on the airway, the aircrew directly dropped its height to the holding point (4 – 5 units away from the vessel in distress) for rescue. Considering that the fishermen had no experience in lifting, the aircrew first tried to lower a lifeguard to the leaning ship in distress and asked the lifeguard to assist the fishermen to use the life jacket for lifting. But when the lifeguard was lowered onto the ship, he found that the wind and waves were too strong, and that the fishing boat was anchored to its forward side and that the boat was floating up and down too fast, where the lifeguard could not stand safety for operation. After successfully assisting a seafarer in lifting, the aircrew decided to try to use the method of high-rope assistance lifting operation. In the first high-rope lifting, the high-rope broke since the fisherman used the rope with an excessive force, and the aircrew immediately prepared the backup high-rope for operation. At this point, the helicopter B – 7328 arrived at the scene. The two helicopters carried out the rescue according to the division of labor. The helicopter B – 7328 provided backup support and observation tips in the left rear of the helicopter B – 7310 and the helicopter B – 7310 normally carried out the lifting operation, two helicopters supporting each other, maintaining the visual flight safety intervals to ensure the safety of operation.

At 1650, the fishing boat in distress capsized at a larger angle under the influence of wind and waves and might sink at any time. After confirming the remaining power of B – 7310 was safe, the helicopter B – 7310 and B – 7328 cooperated with each other in a coordinated way, and all the 11 people in distress were rescued into the helicopter b – 7310. By this time, the fishing boat in distress had tilted at a 90-degree angle. At 1705, helicopter B – 7310 returned. At 1715, helicopter B – 7328 returned.

At 1737 and 1751, the helicopters, B – 7310 and B – 7328, landed safely at Gaoqi Airport in Xiamen and transferred all 11 people in distress to the maritime authorities. The rescue came to a successful conclusion.

In this rescue, the distress position was the Taiwan Strait, which was the traffic artery along the southeast coast of China, where there was a large vessel flow, affected by the "channel effect" to be with many big winds and big waves and complicated weather sea conditions. This successful rescue mainly benefited from the timely alarm of the fishermen in distress and the rapid response and

Chapter 3   Administrative Enforcement of Shipping Policies and Laws   339

coordination of relevant rescue forces. Otherwise, the consequences would be unimaginable under the circumstance of low air and water temperature.

2.2   Vessel "DONG HAI JIU 102" headed for the north embankment of the Yangtze Estuary to rescue the sinking vessel "QI CHENG XIAN FENG"

At around 0400 on December 4, 2017, the 54-meter-long vessel "QI CHENG XIAN FENG" ran aground near the north embankment of the Yangtze Estuary, with its main deck flooded and 9 people on board in distress and in urgent need of rescue. The East China Sea Rescue Bureau immediately activated the emergency rescue plan and ordered the vessel "DONG HAI JIU 102", which was on standby near the Chicken Bone Reef at the Yangtze Estuary, to go for rescue. The vessel "DONG HAI JIU 102" arrive at the spot at 0500 on the same day after a full-speed sailing for 1 hour. During the voyage, the vessel "DONG HAI JIU 102" maintained real-time communication with the ship in distress, understood the situation of the ship and its personnel in distress, and combined with the on-site sea conditions, formulated rescue plans, and promptly instructed the personnel on board to close all valves and pipelines, to prevent the occurrence of secondary disasters such as oil spill inside the ship.

As the ship in distress was stranded in the reef area when at low tide and the water was too shallow, neither the vessel "DONG HAI JIU 102" nor professional rescue boat could get close to it. According to the established rescue plan, the vessel "DONG HAI JIU 102" guided the personnel in distress to safely tow to it one by one along the life rescue guidance ropes built between the ship in distress and the rescue boat after wearing life jackets and life rings. After the efforts of two hours and a half, all the nine people in distress were accessed onto the rescue boat and safely transported to the vessel "DONG HAI JIU 102" of the East China Sea Rescue Bureau for proper disposal.

Ships of all sizes travelled frequently along the waterway of the Yangtze River, where there were more than 1,000 ships passing by every day. These ships not only carried fuel oil that provided energy for the ship, but also waste oil, and some were even specialized in transporting diesel, gasoline or edible oil. In case of accidents, these ships might cause oil leakage and then polluted water resources. In the process of this rescue, the East China Sea Rescue Bureau not only quickly formulated rescue plans to rescue the seafarers in distress, but also well prevented the occurrence of oil spill from ships for a good sake, which reflected the emergency support ability of the East China Sea Rescue Bureau in the face of possible sudden pollution accidents from ships.

2.3 Vessel "DONG HAI JIU 111" went to rescue the leaning cargo ship "FU SHUN 67" at about 12 n mile southeast of Dinghai Bay

In the wee hours of August 20, 2017, the fishing boat "BIN HAI YU 19868" capsized at 10 n mile off the coast of Yancheng, Jiangsu. Many people were in distress, and one fisherman was capsized along with the boat in the cabin to be rescued. After receiving the dangerous case, the East China Sea Rescue Bureau ordered the vessel "DONG HAI JIU 111" and the emergency response personnel of Lianyungang Rescue Basement to rush to the waters of Yancheng, Jiangsu. The search and rescue personnel overcame various difficulties, such as severe current, poor visibility at night, and numerous fishing nets. They made on-site investigation, cleared the fishing nets, turned over and fixed them, and emergency response personnel dived into the cabin. Finally, they successfully rescued a person trapped in distress for 21 hours from the cabin of the capsized fishing boat.

Under the influence of severe convection weather, the eastern sea area had been plagued by dangerous situations and many accidents had occurred recently. Under the coordination of search and rescue centers of relevant provinces and cities, the East China Sea Rescue Bureau had successfully dealt with many dangerous situations and effectively ensured the safety of the area under its jurisdiction.

On August 18 and 20, professional rescue helicopters respectively rescued two fishermen in distress in Wenzhou and Zhoushan; from August 19, the vessel "DONG HAI JIU 111", the professional rescue helicopter "B－7345" and the emergency response team members of Fuzhou Rescue Basement searched for 9 missing drowning people of the sunken cargo ship "XIN DONG YUAN" in the southern waters of Aoqian, Pingtan; from August 20 to now, the vessel "DONG HAI JIU 204", the professional rescue helicopter "B－7361" searched for 2 missing drowning people of the sunken cargo ship "SHUN HANG 9688" near the water of the anchorage ground No.4 in Wusong, Shanghai.

　　The rapid dispatch which headed off the danger of the professional rescue force of the East China Sea Rescue Bureau was attributed to the active exploration of the East China Sea Rescue Bureau to strengthen the comprehensive management and development mode of the rescue basement under the new situation, and continuously expanding the functions of the rescue basement. But precautions should also be taken in the event of inclement weather at the same time: the first was to strengthen the emergency guard, further allocate superior on-duty forces and improve personnel responsibility awareness; the second was to keep close track of weather changes, strengthen information communication with port and shipping enterprises, and release safety information in a timely manner; the third was to strengthen management of anchoring order, enhance supervision of key vessels, and tighten supervision of tourism vessels and boats to prevent collision accidents; the fourth was to specifically deploy ice breakers to effectively respond to the impacts of sea ice.

2.4　Shanghai Salvage Bureau worked for 590 days and the "Sewol" was brought in to light again after three years

　　The South Korean Ferry "Sewol" was 145 m long, 22 m wide and 14 m deep. The empty ship weighed 6,113 t, having a deadweight of 3,794 t and a displacement of 9,907 t. 295 people were dead and nine were missing after the "Sewol" sank in the waters off Jindo County, Jeollanam-do. In July 2015, in the international commercial bidding jointly participated by 19 most powerful salvage companies in the world, Shanghai Salvage Bureau won the bid with its overall strength and humanized salvage scheme of "steel beam bottoming", concluding a salvage contract with the Korean side, and went to Korea to carry out the salvage mission on August 12, 2015.

　　The overall lifting of the sunken "Sewol" was completed by barge lifting, including four operational steps of lifting out of the water, towing and shifting, semi-submersible barge and lifting out of the water as a whole. After the whole shipwrecks emerged from the water, it was bound at the operation site, and then transported to Mokpo New Port of South Korea for final rolling unloading ashore.

　　During the 590-day salvage operation, the Shanghai Salvage Bureau put into operation over 3,000 ships and 2,170 personnel. Among them, more than 6,000 person-time was completed in the diving operation which took up a large proportion of the operation, and the total underwater operation time was nearly 13,000 hours, which created the record of the longest project time and the hardest task in the world. The successful salvaging of the "Sewol" created a miracle in the world salvage history and demonstrated the strength of the China salvage.

3 Administrative Enforcement Cases of Shanghai Fishery Supervision and Administration Division

3.1 Fishery Administration and Water Services jointly attacked to clean up illegal nets and gears in the channels

In order to strengthen the management of fishery resources in the waters of rivers and lakes, in October 2017, the law enforcement brigade of the Agriculture Committee of Minhang District (Fishery Administration Station), together with the waterworks department of Pujin Street, jointly carried out the special action of "net cleaning" in key rivers, and continuously consolidated the foundation of ecological civilization in the waters.

In the special operation, 3 law enforcement boats and 26 people were dispatched to inspect illegal fishing along the coast of 1.8 km of the Zhoupu Pond. The joint law enforcement team members spent 2.5 hours in the rain to conduct detailed investigation on both sides of the river. A total of 37 basket nets were seized, effectively outlawing illegal nets and gears and restoring the river to a clean and navigable ecological environment.

The law enforcement brigade of the Agriculture Committee of Minhang District (Fishery Administration Station) continuously allied with relevant functional departments of the streets and towns to maintain the tough stance of severe cracking down the acts of illegal fishing in the riverways in its jurisdiction, which jointly protected the fishery resources and ecological environment within the scope of its water jurisdiction.

3.2 Shanghai Pudong Fishery Administration launched a special rectification of illegal fishing nets and gears, giving back the cleanness and smooth navigation of the inland riverways

In order to further strengthen the management of inland riverways in Pudong New District and rectify medium and small riverways, from July 11 to 18, 2017, Pudong Fishery Administration, together with relevant functional departments of Nanhui New Town, carried out special channel rectification for illegal fishing nets and gears in the regional riverways. Braving the scorching sun during the dog days of summer, a total of 77 person-time of the law enforcement officials, 11 vehicle-time of cars and 11 law enforcement boats were dispatched to clear more than 150 basket nets in the region.

Clearing up illegal fishing nets and gears was an important measure to implement the long-term mechanism of river management. In 2017, the Fishery Administration of Pudong increased the supervision of inland riverways and completely eliminated all kinds of illegal fishing nets and gears by increasing the number of inspections, strict control and management. Through special rectification actions on illegal fishing nets and gears, the riverway environment was further improved, giving back the smooth navigation of the waterway and its cleanness, so as to maintain the ecological health of the river and keep the channel unblocked.

3.3 The Municipal Fishery Division organized and carried out the special law enforcement action "2017 Qing Jiang No.4"

In order to severely crack down on illegal fishing in Shanghai's inland waters and effectively strengthen the protection of fishery resources and the ecological environment in the waters, the Municipal Fishery Division organized fishery departments at all levels to carry out the "2017 Qing Jiang No.4" fishery special rectification action from September 12 to 13, 2017. The action accumulatively dispatched the law enforcement officials of 301 person-time, law enforcement ships (boats) of 56 ship-time and law enforcement cars (vehicles) of 40 vehicle-time, seized a total of 22 cases (10 electronic fishing cases among them), confiscated 138 illegal nets and gears of various kinds, 9 electric fishing tools, 33 kg of catches, 15 cases settled, 15,350 yuan fined, with another 7 cases being handled.

Before the action, aiming at the waters where there were more concentrative illegal nets and gears and more tracking down on cases of illegal fishing reported by the citizens and the public, the fishery departments determined the key points, well-orchestrated and carefully deployed. Three features were highlighted in the action. First, the municipal and regional fishery departments connected with each other in the action. Through the comprehensive analysis of composition of the time, place and law breakers of recent illegal fishing, the key period and key waters of law enforcement were divided, so as to rationally allocate law enforcement resources, optimize law enforcement methods and enhance law enforcement efficiency. Second, in the action, the fishery departments cooperated with the local public security, municipal appearance and water service departments of Chongming District to jointly carry out the fishery administration law enforcement work, so as to achieve multi-department linkage. The illegal fishing nets and gears found in Dongping Town and Chenjia Town and other waters of riverways were cleaned in time, relevant laws and regulations were publicized to nearby residents and their support and understanding were obtained, all kinds of illegal fishing acts were cracked down on, and the fishery resources and ecological environment of inland waters were protected. Third, during the consecutive action of two days and one night, the law enforcement officials basically adopted an action plan of continuous law enforcement from day to night, especially during the periods of high incidence of illegal fishing in the second half of the night and early morning to carry out key inspections, so as to enhance the pertinence of law enforcement actions, effectively crack down on relevant law breakers and achieve good results.

3.4 Shanghai Fishing Port Supervision Bureau carried out maritime law enforcement and emergency drills

From August 29 to September 2, 2017 Shanghai Fishing Port Supervision Bureau launched the "Lijian - 2017" special fishery maritime law enforcement action. The law enforcement officials focused on checking the captain's failure to ensure that the fishery vessels met the minimum manning standard and the fishery crews carry the certificates that met the legal requirements in the waters of Hengsha Fishing Port, Beigang and deep-water channel. A total of 5 fishery administrative law enforcement cases were handled in this voyage, with a fine of RMB 10,000 yuan. When handling the cases, the law enforcement officials used the new version of electronic law enforcement documents and recorded the whole process of law enforcement with law enforcement recorders to ensure the law enforcement actions as being strict, standard, fair and civilized.

China Yuzheng 31005 and China Yuzheng 31006, in combination with this special maritime law enforcement action, organized the manoeuvre training and the all-ship emergency drill of vice captains. In the manoeuvre training, the vice captains improved their independent manoeuvre level through berthing and navigation training under different meteorological conditions. The emergency drill of the two law enforcement vessels included lifesaving, firefighting and towing (side and tail towing) deployment training, etc. Through the training, the overall training level of the seafarer was improved, laying a solid foundation for the implementation of various rescue tasks.

Shanghai Fishing Port Supervision Bureau continuously strengthened the law enforcement inspection of fishery safe production, continued to enhance the emergency drill work, made great efforts to improve the awareness of the law enforcement officials, fully performed the duties of fishery safety supervision, gave play to the positive role of law enforcement inspection in fishery safe production, and promoted the healthy development of modern municipal fishery industry.

3.5 Shanghai Fishing Port Supervision Bureau carried out joint law enforcement actions in the waters of Hangzhou Bay

On August 15, 2017, Luchao Port Branch of Shanghai Fishing Port Supervision Bureau, together with Pudong Fishery Administration, carried out a joint maritime law enforcement operation in the waters of Hangzhou Bay in order to practically implement the fishery safe production in the waters of Hangzhou Bay after the fishing began.

The inspection of this law enforcement action focused on: whether the seafarers were wearing life jackets, the availability of lifesaving, firefighting and navigation equipment, the manning of the vessel and the entry and exit visas of the it, etc. During the inspection, the law enforcement officials found that after the publicity and education in recent years and regular law enforcement inspection, the fishermen in this city greatly improved their awareness of production safety, which was mainly reflected in: crew members could take the initiative to wear life jackets to protect their own safety when working by the water; in case of inspections, the captain actively cooperated and relevant certificates were submitted in full. But at the same time, the law enforcement officials also found that some foreign fishing boats were not properly manned and did not wear life jackets when operating by the water.

As the first joint law enforcement in the waters of Hangzhou Bay after the fishing ban, this actions effectively troubleshooted safety problems in the fishery production process, powerfully guaranteed the safety of life and property of fishermen, laying a good foundation for the orderly development of fishery production in the waters. Shanghai Fishing Port Supervision Bureau, in conjunction with the fishery administration of all districts, strengthened law enforcement and further did a good job in the supervision of fishery production safety in the waters of Hangzhou Bay.

3.6 Shanghai Railway Transport Court pronounced the judgment of the case of illegal electric fishing

On July 27, 2017, ZHANG Mou, HU Mou and SHEN Mou, three criminals who illegally harvested aquatic products from the Yangtze River, were concentratively sentenced in the second tribunal of Shanghai Railway Transport Court, who were respectively sentenced to penalties as the respite of set term of imprisonment, criminal detention and so on, which symbolized the initial success of Shanghai Branch of Yangtze River Shipping Public Security Bureau in combating illegal fishing and maintaining the ecological environment of the River in 2017.

In the first half of 2017, Shanghai Branch of Yangtze River Shipping Public Security Bureau continuously strengthened its efforts to crack down on illegal fishing in the Yangtze River, jointly carried out several joint law enforcement actions with the departments such as Fishery Administration, and through positive investigation and evidence collection, it, successively in the Yangtze river, such as the waters of Chongming, Changxing, Hengsha, continuously uncovered 75 cases suspected of illegal fishing for aquatic products, capturing 17 criminal suspects such as ZHANG Mou, HU Mou, and seized on the spot of hundreds of kilograms of illegal fishing games of Yangtze River coilia ectenes, coilia mystus, black carp and weever, and seized hundreds of items of illegal nets and gears. In the morning of July 27, ZHANG Mou and other 2 people were concentratively sentenced, with other people involved in the case to be sentenced on another day selected by the court. Through the connection of administrative law enforcement of the fishery departments with the judicial work of public security organs, procuratorial organs and people's courts, a case handling mode featuring "case investigation and handling accordingly", "unified prosecution" and "centralized sentencing" was formed, which not only effectively cracked down on illegal fishing, but also enhanced the deterrent power of the law.

Since 2002, in order to better protect the environment of the Yangtze river and promote the green development of fishery, the Ministry of Agriculture had issued a notice every year banning all fishing of aquatic products in the Yangtze River during the period. Even so, there were still a few outlaws, driven by huge interests, ignoring the relevant provisions, repeatedly used the methods which violated the principle of sustainable development such as placing deep-water fishing nets and doing electric fishing to catch aquatic products like Yangtze River coilia ectenes in the Shanghai section of the Yangtze River, and benefited from this, which undoubtedly brought catastrophic consequences to the Yangtze River, not only probably influencing the navigation safety of ships in the channels, but also worsening, on account of the heavy fishing, the biological chain of the Yangtze River, where the fishery resources might severely decline, resulting in the extinction of rare fish.

Ecological and environmental issues were related to the overall economic and social development. Shanghai Branch of Yangtze River Shipping Public Security Bureau would continue to cooperate with relevant administrative law enforcement departments to take effective measures in the future to severely crack down on all kinds of crimes that damaged environmental resources within its jurisdiction, thus to protect the Mother River of the Yangtze River, and to promote harmony between people and water.

4 Administrative Enforcement Cases of Shanghai General Station of Immigration Inspection

4.1 Wusong Frontier Inspection Station carried out routing inspection in the waters of anchorage grounds

In order to effectively manage the vessels in the anchorage ground, prevent and crack down on all kinds of illegal acts, and promote the regularization and institutionalization of the routing inspection in the anchorage ground, on November 16, 2017, the law enforcement inspection group of Wusong Frontier Inspection Station took the boat "bianjian 3166" to carry out the routing inspection in waters under the jurisdiction of Wusong Anchorage, Baoshan Anchorage and other areas.

Meanwhile, the law enforcement inspection group of the station took the boat "bianjian 3166" to patrol Wusong Anchorage, Baoshan Anchorage and other waters, and compared the information of the ships anchoring along the line, paid attention to finding any law and regulation violating case, conducted key routing inspection to a certain vessel of Ethiopia and inquired and inspected about the personnel aboard and offboard, the availability of the seafarers and so on.

In the course of routing inspection, due to the rainy day, poor visibility, poor sailing conditions and more difficult tasks of the routing inspection than before, all the personnel of the law enforcement inspection group and all the seafarers of the boat "bianjian 3166" overcame the adverse factors and successfully completed various tasks, laying a solid foundation for the completion of the routing inspection of the anchorage ground in the severe weather.

4.2 Waigaoqiao Frontier Inspection Station issued the first electronic boarding permit at Shanghai Port

On October 23, 2017, Waigaoqiao Frontier Inspection Station issued the first electronic boarding permit of Shanghai port through the Shanghai "single window" frontier inspection permit service platform. Holding the electronic boarding permit and his own id card, YE Mou, an employee of shipping agency

Chapter 3   Administrative Enforcement of Shipping Policies and Laws   349

company, successfully boarded a Hong Kong vessel to work after being inspected by police on duty.

According to the relevant deployment of Shanghai Frontier Inspection Stations, Waigaoqiao Frontier Inspection Station took multiple measures to effectively promote the platform measurement work. Firstly, internal training was carried out to ensure that the people's police were proficient in the functions of the platform. Secondly, it organized some shipping enterprises and shipping agents to carry out platform measurement and guided relevant units to carry out information registration. Thirdly, it gave feedback timely, collected, sorted out and reported all kinds of problems found in the actual test operation.

4.3   Wusong Frontier Inspection Station opened up the "Green Channel" to rescue the injured seafarers

At 0600 on July 6, 2017, Wusong Frontier Inspection Station received a phone call from Xinhaifeng Agency Company, saying that a Vietnamese seafarer of the Palau vessel "JI XING 9" operated by the company was injured carelessly. According to the initial diagnosis of the ship's medical staff, it was a comminated fracture of fingers and needed to be sent to the hospital for emergency treatment. It was hoped that the frontier inspection authority could provide emergency assistance.

After receiving the report, the station immediately responded and dispatched the police to quickly rush to the traffic boat dock. In the first time after the seafarer arrived, it carried out the identification to the injured seafarer. After verification of relevant conditions, the injured seafarer was allowed to go to the ground first for medical treatment and then reapply for relevant entry procedures, thus gaining precious time for the injured to get treatment.

4.4   Waigaoqiao Frontier Inspection Station and maritime departments investigated and treated by joint law enforcement the first case of a vessel violating the frontier inspection and maritime provisions at the same time

In May 2017, Waigaoqiao Frontier Inspection Station and Pudong Maritime Safety Administration carried out a joint boarding inspection of a foreign ship berthing at the pier I of Waigaoqiao, Shanghai. During the inspection, it was found that the ship moored to a small oil tanker with no obvious name or mark of home port on. After investigation, the vessel was verified to be a Chinese oil tanker "SU ××" and moored to the foreign vessel with the illegal use of foreign vessel mooring permit of the vessel "HU ××". After finding out the facts of the case, Waigaoqiao Frontier Inspection Station punished the ship manager in accordance with the relevant provisions of the *Exit and Entry Administration Law of the People's Republic of China*. According to the relevant provisions of maritime law, Pudong Maritime Safety Administration punished the illegal act of the ship.

This case was the first case where Waigaoqiao Frontier Inspection Station and maritime departments investigated and treated by joint law enforcement it of a vessel violating the frontier inspection and maritime provisions at the same time.

4.5 Shanghai Frontier Inspection Stations carried out the security routing inspection at the anchorage ground during the "Belt and Road" International Cooperation Summit Forum

To ensure the safety of the waters of the anchorage ground during the "Belt and Road Initiative" International Summit Forum, Shanghai Frontier Inspection Stations made a unified deployment to designate a law enforcement group travelling by the boat "bianjian 3166" to carry the tasks of routing inspection of the anchorage ground and vigilance patrol at the waters of Wusong, Jinshan anchorage ground. The mission lasted two days and one night, with a total voyage of nearly 300 nautical miles.

In the course of routing inspection, the law enforcement group conducted the routing inspection on international ships berthing at the anchorage ground through various methods such as radio call verification, AIS tracking and radar search of the boat "bianjian 3166". The Panamanian vessel Yokohama Pioneer and the Korean vessel Royal Senfter berthing at Jinshan joint inspection pilot anchorage were inquired for information and reminded of caution, emphasizing the laws and regulations on exit and entry administration and the frontier administration regulations during anchorage. After the routing inspection, the law enforcement travelled by the boat "bianjian 3166" to carry out the vigilance patrol to the relevant waters.

The routing inspection this time further enhanced the frontier inspection authorities' management of the vessels berth at Wusong and Jinshan anchorage ground, improved the maritime law enforcement and guard ability, and reached the warning effect, laying a solid foundation for ensuring the safety and order of the waters at the anchorage ground during the "Belt and Road" International Summit Forum.

4.6 Pujiang Frontier Inspection Station, Tourist Administrations and Cultural Market Administrative Law Enforcement Department of Jiangsu, Zhejiang, Shanghai and Anhui, carried out joint law enforcement

On April 26, 2017, Pujiang Frontier Inspection Station, Tourist Administrations and Cultural Market Administrative Law Enforcement Departments of Jiangsu, Zhejiang, Shanghai and Anhui, formed a joint law enforcement group of 26 people to carry out the joint law enforcement action at the international cruise liner port of Wusong Estuary.

Before the action, the joint law enforcement group was briefed by Pujiang Frontier Inspection Station on the basic information of cruise liners operated at Shanghai Port and the innovative handy measures like the simplified entry of cruise liners and the self-service customs clearance of exit, focused on understanding the procedures, methods and problems of the customs clearance of tour groups at Shanghai cruise liner port, and conducted in-depth exchanges on enhancing information sharing, strengthening administrative law enforcement and deepening regional law enforcement cooperation.

During the action, according to the information of cruise liner group travel agencies and problems existing in the process of guest gathering and group leading obtained by the station in the early stage, the joint law enforcement group mainly comprehensively inspected the qualification certificate of the tour guide who led the tour group, the list of group passengers on that day, and about whether the tour group leader left the country with the tour group, and ordered the travel agency to make rectification on the existing problems.

Since the establishment of the linkage and coordination mechanism, Pujiang Frontier Inspection Station and the municipal cultural law enforcement departments had carried out the joint law enforcement for many times, effectively bringing charter travel agencies into the comprehensive control scope of the port, which achieved substantial results. This joint law enforcement further integrated the superior resources of Jiangsu, Zhejiang, Shanghai and Anhui, enhancing the ability of all parties to unite and cooperate in the law enforcement of cruise liner tourism.

4.7 Waigaoqiao Frontier Inspection Station participated the first joint boarding inspection of international navigation ships at Waigaoqiao Port, Shanghai

On April 26, 2017, Waigaoqiao Frontier Inspection Station, Waigaoqiao Customs, Waigaoqiao Inspection and Quarantine Bureau, and Shanghai Pudong Maritime Safety Administration conducted a joint boarding inspection on the American vessel "Marsens Pfeiffer" docking at the pier II of Waigaoqiao, Shanghai.

Waigaoqiao Frontier Inspection Station carefully organized and deployed, formulated work plans in advance, dispatched backbone forces to form a joint inspection team with the joint boarding inspection units to jointly carry out relevant inspections on ships and seafarers, achieving the expected results. This inspection was the first time for departments of Waigaoqiao Port, Shanghai, to carry out joint boarding inspection on international navigation vessels. It was one of the important measures to implement relevant measures of the State Council, strengthen the coordination mechanism of large-scale customs clearance, and comprehensively promote the "one-stop operation".

4.8 Wusong Frontier Inspection Station actively completed the border inspection work on duty under the heavy fog weather

On April 6, 2017, Shanghai Meteorological Administration issued a yellow alert for heavy fog. Visibility of ships in the waters of Yangtze Estuary was reduced to less than 100 meters due to the fog, affecting the frontier (port) entry and exit of most international navigation vessels at the anchorage grounds of Yangtze Estuary and Wusong. Sixteen ships, including the vessel "Ocean Domination" which was scheduled to enter the port in the early hours of the morning, altered their port entry and exit plans on account of rain and fog.

Wusong Frontier Inspection Station actively responded to the situation and

Chapter 3 Administrative Enforcement of Shipping Policies and Laws 353

took effective measures to ensure the smooth of customs clearance at the port under bad weather. Firstly, it tightened the service organization, increased the frequency of routing inspection and the force of port inspection, ensured that the management measures were in place. Secondly, it paid close attention to the dynamic changes of the vessels, strengthened the communication and contact with ship agency, maritime departments and frontier inspection stations of sibling ports, and grasped the dynamic information of ships. Thirdly, through information platforms such as the bulletin board system in the service hall and WeChat official accounts, it released timely ship information and reminded the service objects to adjust their travel arrangements in time to avoid long waiting at the port. Fourth, according to the duration of the fog and the time of the tide, it deployed the police in advance to ensure that after the elimination of the fog, the frontier inspection procedures during the peak hours of vessel entry and exit would be handled quickly and the port clearance would be smooth.

4.9 Pujiang Frontier Inspection Station successfully completed the frontier inspection task of the cruise liner "Aida Bella"

On April 2, 2017, the Italian visiting cruise liner "Aida Bella" docked at the international passenger transport center of Shanghai Port from Ishigaki, Japan, carrying more than 1,900 passengers and 600 seafarers. The ship berthed at the port for three days and wholly changed the passengers in Shanghai, carrying nearly 2,000 passengers and leaving the country for Naha, Japan On April 4, 2017.

The vessel was owned by Costa Cruises and this was its first visit to Shanghai. In order to ensure the smooth customs clearance of passengers, Pujiang Frontier Inspection Station took multiple measures, ensuring the smooth customs clearance of passengers: first was to make all the preparations. It contacted with the ship and the agent in advance to accurately grasp the information of the passengers who need to go through the 24-hour or 144-hour exit and whether any passengers applied for the 15-day visa-free procedures, and deployed sufficient police strength and opened the manual verification channels. Second was to additionally open the spare channel. In view of the fact that nearly 2,000 passengers were foreigners and more than 600 seafarers need to collect information pages of documents, the station set up quarantine measures, temporarily adjusted the trends of passengers and activated four spare channels in addition to opening all the manual inspection channels, thus greatly shortening the waiting time for passengers. Third was to increase the police strength outside the platform. Whereas the characteristics of "too many elderly passengers with limited mobility" of the ship, the on-site inspection team increased the police strength at the post of consultation and guidance to help passengers fill in the entry cards and provide necessary help. Fourth was to ensure the safety of the port. The police on duty at the ladderway of the ship used the relevant information system to accurately count the personnel boarding and leaving the ship, and did a good job of checking the personnel and certificates, ensuring the safety and order of the personnel boarding and leaving the ship during the ship's berthing at the port.

4.10 Jinshan Frontier Inspection Station and Jinshan Maritime Safety Administration carried out joint enforcement action

In order to further strengthen the management of anchorage ground and ensure the safety and stability of the coastal waters of the chemical terminal, Jinshan Frontier Inspection Station and Jinshan Maritime Safety Administration carried out joint enforcement action on March 16, 2017.

During the action, the frontier inspection police and maritime law enforcement personnel inspected the coastal waters of Jinshan by patrol boat, and combining the management status of Jinshan anchorage ground and the current situation of port control, conducted detailed discussions and extrapolations on jointly cracking down on illegal acts such as illegal mooring and boarding without license and coordinatingly responding to the emergency situation of the chemical terminal. Later, the two parties boarded the vessel "Atlantic Goddess", a Hong Kong Chinese ship docking at the anchorage ground of Jinshan. According to the respective division of labor, they carefully inspected all parts of the hull, comprehensively examined the ship's safety management, and timely reported the problems found to the ship to urge the implementation of the rectification.

This joint law enforcement action was the concrete implementation of the cooperation agreement and law enforcement coordination mechanism between the two parties, and laid a foundation for the joint boarding inspection of international navigation ships in the next stage. The joint law enforcement further improved the communications and contacts, enhanced synergy in law enforcement, and provided a strong guarantee for better responding to emergencies at ports, jointly preventing extreme terror events, and maintaining the stability and order of the ports.

5 Summary

Maritime administrative law enforcement departments maintained the order of water traffic, took the responsibility for the supervision and management of ships, investigated and mediated water traffic accidents occurred by ships, organized water safety patrol and escort, and directed and coordinated water search and rescue work. Their business covered all aspects of administrative licensing, administrative compulsion and administrative penalty. Maritime administrative law enforcement departments and law enforcement teams were being constantly strengthened, and law enforcement and law enforcement supervision systems were being improved day by day. The standardization of maritime administrative law enforcement departments was conducive to comprehensively improving the level of maritime culture construction, and blending the concept of " humanity ecology management " into maritime administration, so as to build a healthy maritime internal and external environment and provide strong support for accelerating maritime modernization.

Chapter 4　Literature Review with regard to Shipping Policy and Law

2017 is the second year for China to implement the "13th Five-Year Plan", and it is also a crucial moment for Shanghai to further build an international shipping center. While building the "Yangtze River Economic Belt", implementing the "Belt and Road" initiative and the national strategy of "Shipping Power", as well as major practices in building Shanghai Free Trade Zone, it also drove the research and development of shipping policy in academia, and professional scholars followed the process of development of the shipping industry, carried out in-depth research combined with practice, and achieved gratifying research results, which provides theoretical support for the shipping industry, but also provides strong support for the formulation and innovation of policies and legal systems.

The *"Belt and Road" Construction and Development Report* (2017) summarizes the 5th anniversary of "Belt and Road" from multiple perspectives and proposes constructive ideas for future development. The book studies the issues and prospects of China and the countries along "Belt and Road" in the areas of cooperation between central enterprises, Central Asian cooperation, butt joint alliance, overseas interest protection, and international public opinion. The *China Free Trade Zone Development Report* (2017) reviews and prospects the development of Chinese pilot free trade zone. On the basis of introducing the background of world and Chinese economic development, the paper analyzes and prospects Chinese current free trade zone strategy. It focuses on the analysis of the development of China's pilot free trade zone in the field of financial innovation, looks forward to the development of the expanded pilot free trade zone, and analyzes the strategy of Chinese free trade zone combined with "Belt and Road" initiative, and finally focuses on the summary and prospect of achievements of Shanghai Pilot Free Trade Zone since the third anniversary of the establishment of it and the future development. Based on the analysis of the concept, characteristics, constituent elements, driving forces and industrial chain of the international shipping center, the *International Shipping Center Development under a Global Perspective* studies and compares the key features of Singapore, Hong Kong, Shanghai and different international shipping centers in China through case analysis and evaluates international shipping centers with global influence by constructing a scientific indicator system, so as to explore the future development direction, trend and core competitiveness of the international shipping center, and provides reference for Shanghai to buildthe international shipping center with a global resource allocation capability. Based on a grand perspective, the *Shipping Finance Handbook* introduces ship finance concepts and operating models from all angles and perspectives, collects a variety of conventional and practical ship finance models and practical operation cases, covering legal treatment, German KG model and ship valuation pricing and risk control of equity capital market financing, ship finance loans, sorts out various types of ship finance methods, provides new ideas and concepts for the maritime and ship finance industry, and provides solutions to common problems facing the industry.

The *Connotation, Research Status and Research Significance of the Basic Theory of Maritime Code* through the introduction of the content of the basic theory of maritime code shows that Chinese maritime code scholars lack comprehensive, systematic and in-depth research on the basic theory of maritime code, while the basic theory research of civil law, criminal law, economic law and other legal department has reference value for the basic theory research of maritime code. It shows that researching the basic theory of maritime code is of great significance for improving the maritime code theory system, improving the maritime code theory research grade, correctly guiding maritime legislation and maritime judicial practice and correctly guiding shipping practice. The *Construction of the International Maritime Justice Center under the Background of "Belt and Road"* analyzes the reasons proposed by the International Maritime Justice Center and draws on the British experience to make recommendations for the establishment of construction of maritime justice center in my country. It calls on China to actively and steadily advance the construction of an international maritime judicial center, and strive to achieve the transformation from a maritime judicial major power to a maritime judicial great power.

1 Book Review for Publication in 2017

1.1 "Belt and Road" Construction and Development Report (2017)[①]

The "*Belt and Road* " *Construction and Development Report* (*2017*) is divided into four parts: the general report, the international cooperation chapter, the domestic regional chapter and the special chapter. The general report points out that the achievements in the construction of "Belt and Road" are beginning to take shape. The international cooperation chapter focuses on the cooperation between China and Turkey, Iran, the Czech Republic, Uzbekistan, Azerbaijan, ASEAN and other countries and regions in the construction of "Belt and Road". The domestic regional chapter studies Gansu, Henan, Heilongjiang, Hainan and Yunnan participating in the planning and implementation of regional chapter initiative. The special chapter studies the issues and prospects of cooperation between China and countries along "Belt and Road" in the areas of legal risk, capacity cooperation, cross-border trade, railway transportation, and financing and investment.

The report consists of a total of 25 articles. It summarizes the 5th anniversary of "Belt and Road" from multiple perspectives, and proposes constructive ideas for future development.

On the 5th anniversary of "Belt and Road" initiative, China and the countries along "Belt and Road" have made remarkable achievements in the field of investment cooperation. Not only have they greatly improved the liberalization and facilitation of Chinese investment, but Chinese foreign investment has also become an important engine for the growth of global foreign direct investment.

The construction of "Belt and Road" is a major move to coordinate the two major domestic and international patterns. The report focuses on the analysis of Beijing, Jiangsu, Fujian, Sichuan, Shaanxi, Inner Mongolia, Guangxi and Ningxia's participation in the planning and implementation of "Belt and Road"

[①] LI Yongquan. "Belt and Road" Construction and Development Report (2017) [M]. Beijing: Social Science Literature Press, 2017.

initiative. Based on the city's positioning, Beijing takes advantage of its own advantages and continues to accelerate the transformation of the city's functions. It will play a demonstration and vanguard role in the construction of "Belt and Road" initiative. Focusing on the construction of "Belt and Road" intersection point, Jiangsu strives to promote the interconnection of facilities, strengthen the linkage between the river and the sea, and coordinate the land and sea. Fujian insists on equal emphasis on economic and trade cooperation and cultural exchanges, and comprehensively develops multi-field cooperation with countries and regions along "Belt and Road". Based on the construction of a complete transportation network, Sichuan organically combines its own economic and cultural resources with the countries along "Belt and Road" to implement Sichuan's "251" economic development. The proposal of "Belt and Road" initiative has transformed Shaanxi from inland to an open frontier. In the overall situation of the national "Belt and Road" initiative, Inner Mongolia is given the task of the era of "playing the regional advantages of connecting Russia and Mongolia". Guangxi has achieved positive results in promoting the new international land-sea trade channel and China-ASEAN Information Port. Ningxia takes the opportunity of the inland open economic pilot zone and the China-Arab Expo as a platform to continuously strengthen exchanges and cooperation with countries along "Belt and Road".

Along the Silk Road Economic Belt, the enthusiasm and desire of various countries to participate in the construction of "Belt and Road" is increasing, especially in Central Asia, the Caucasus, and Central and Eastern Europe. These efforts have achieved positive results. The National Development and Reform Commission spokesperson once cited the media's initial achievements in the construction of "Belt and Road" initiative: firstly, it strengthened strategic integration, united consensus on cooperation, strengthened communication and consultation with countries along the route, and promoted the work of strategic integration and planning with the countries along the route. He especially mentioned that the *Outline of the China-Russia-Mongolia Economic Corridor Planning Plan* and signed the corridor planning outline with Poland, Czech Republic and other countries. Secondly, to strengthen interconnection and the construction of land and sea passages. In addition to the China-Russia-Mongolia Economic Corridor, he also mentioned China-Europe Railway, the achievements made in the construction of China-Central Asia-West Asia Economic Corridor. Thirdly, to deepen production capacity cooperation and expand investment and trade. In 2016, the scale of various bilateral and multilateral production capacity cooperation funds exceeded USD 100 billion. China has cooperated with France, Germany, South Korea, the United Kingdom, Spain and other countries to reach an important consensus on jointly developing third-party markets along "Belt and Road", and has launched nuclear power cooperation with Russia, Kazakhstan, Pakistan, Iran and other countries. Chinese companies have built 46 cooperation zones in countries along "Belt and Road". Fourthly, to cooperate with forces of all parties to form a joint force and achieved remarkable results in the areas of local cooperation, financial cooperation, and humanities and education cooperation.

The report also studies the issues and prospects of China and the countries along "Belt and Road" in the areas of cooperation between central enterprises, Central Asian cooperation, joint alliance, overseas interests protection, and international public opinion.

1.2 China Free Trade Zone Development Report (2017)[①]

In 2016, the world economy has not yet emerged from the shadow of the global financial crisis. The overall performance is that the economic growth rate continues to decline, the potential economic growth rate continues to decrease, international trade and investment continue to decline, "black swan events" occur frequently, trade protectionism and anti-globalization trend rises and the volatility and vulnerability of the global financial markets have increased, which has exposed the world economy to more risks and challenges.

Since entering 2016, China has faced challenges brought about by changes in the international economic and political situation. In terms of foreign trade, as the external economic situation continues to deteriorate, Chinese export growth rate gradually declined, and even negative growth happened in 2015; in terms of exchange rate, the expectation of RMB appreciation reversed with the advent of the Fed's interest rate hike cycle. In order to stabilize the exchange rate and avoid

---

① WANG Li. China Free Trade Zone Development Report (2017) [M]. Beijing: Social Science Literature Press, 2017.

a significant depreciation of the RMB, Chinese foreign exchange reserves are also declining; while the domestic economy, financial and real estate market fluctuations, couples with that the real economy has not seen a significant improvement, Chinese economic downward pressure is greater.

After entering the new normal with structural adjustment and development mode as its core, Chinese economy also urgently needs to cultivate new kinetic energy, and the combination of "Belt and Road" and the construction of free trade zones provides ideas and ways for China to deepen reform by further opening up. Especially when the overall external environment is not conducive to the liberalization of trade and investment, it is more necessary to expand the international market by promoting multilateral and regional trade negotiations, and at the same time vigorously build a pilot free trade zone, explore the system innovation, serve national strategies and create new models of reform and opening up through independent expansion of opening up.

The report mainly reviews and prospects the development of China pilot free trade zone. The book is divided into three parts. The first part is the general report, based on the background of the introduction of the world and China's economic development, which analyses and prospects China current free trade zone strategy; the second part is a review of the development of the free trade zone, and on the basis of the review of the development of the current four major pilot free trade zones in China, it focuses on the analysis of the development of China pilot free trade zones in the field of financial innovation; the third part is the development prospect of the pilot free trade zone, which prospects the development of the expanded pilot free trade zone. At the same time, combined with "Belt and Road" initiative, it analyzes China free trade zone strategy, and finally focuses on the summary and prospects of achievements since the third anniversary and future development of Shanghai Pilot Free Trade Zone.

1.3 *Foreign Media Watch"Belt and Road"*(*2017*)[①]

The *Foreign Media Watch"Belt and Road"* (*2017*) excerpts from dozens of

---

[①] WANG Hui. Foreign Media Watch "Belt and Road" (2017) [M]. Beijing: Social Sciences Literature Press, 2017.

foreign media's views, opinions and predictions on "Belt and Road", provides an important perspective for "others" to watch "Belt and Road", and also helps domestic understanding foreign attitude and response of "Belt and Road" initiative, so as to better provide information reference and governance services for the construction of "Belt and Road".

"Belt and Road" initiative was first proposed in 2013. In 2014, "Belt and Road" initiative was fully implemented. In 2015, "Belt and Road" initiative was implemented. In 2016, "Belt and Road" initiative was promoted with great achievements. Over the past four years, policy communication between China and participating countries in the construction of "Belt and Road" has been continuously deepened, facility connectivity has been continuously strengthened, trade has been continuously improved, capital and financial links have been continuously expanded, and people-to-people links have been continuously promoted. "Belt and Road" initiative, which is full of Chinese wisdom, has received positive responses from more and more countries and international organizations, and has reached broad consensus worldwide. In October 2017, "Belt and Road" was mentioned five times in the report of the 19th National Congress of the CPC, emphasizing the active promotion of "Belt and Road" international cooperation, striving to achieve policy communication, facility connectivity, trade flow, capital and financial communication, and people-to-people link, creating a new platform for international cooperation and adding new momentum for common development. The promotion of "Belt and Road" construction was written into the Party Constitution, which fully demonstrates the determination and confidence of China under the leadership of the Communist Party of China to attach great importance to "Belt and Road" construction and to promote "Belt and Road" international cooperation.

The media is the narrator, communicator and interpreter of "Belt and Road" initiative. Domestic reports on "Belt and Road" are overwhelming. In 2016, as "Belt and Road" initiative took root, foreign media have responded more and more strongly. Percentage Data Science Ministry released the *"Belt and Road" International Public Opinion Big Data Report* in May 2017. Since 2015, the volume of international discussions on "Belt and Road" has been increasing year by year. In 2016, it increased by 330.2% compared with 2015. What is the purpose of Chinese "Belt and Road" initiative, how is the construction of "Belt and Road" project, whether it should join in "Belt and Road", what are the risks and challenges of "Belt and Road", and what impact will "Belt and Road" bring? A series of issues have become the focus of attention of overseas media.

"Belt and Road" initiative has received great attention from the international community after it was proposed. Most foreign media welcomed and applauded "Belt and Road" initiative, holding that "Belt and Road" initiative was a stream of cleansing at the time of civilized conflict, and it would be beneficial to job creation, improve people's living standards and promote trade and economic exchanges, also help to enhance regional understanding, eliminate prejudices, and achieve integrated development; however, individual media expressed doubts and vigilance on "Belt and Road" initiative, holding that "Belt and Road" is a tool for China to expand its region and world influence, pointing out that China aims to achieve the purpose of link through a unilateral decision; there were also media hinting that during the construction of "Belt and Road" project, Chinese companies ignored the actual needs of the country where the project was located and lacked respect for the independent choice of the country where the project was located; there were also media suggestions and suggestions on the construction of "Belt and Road", and they proposed unique and well-intentioned construction opinions.

The selection of the book highlights the media's attitudes, viewpoints and observation perspectives, which can help readers quickly understand the foreign media's reporting and interpretation of "Belt and Road". The book aims to help domestic understanding of foreign media's response and attitude to "Belt and Road", and to better provide information reference and political services for the construction of "Belt and Road".

1.4 *China Cruise Industry Development Report (2017)*[①]

In his speech at the opening ceremony of the 2017 "Belt and Road" International Cooperation Summit Forum, General Secretary XI Jinping pointed

---

① QIAN Yongchang. China Cruise Industry Development Report (2017) [M]. Beijing: Social Science Literature Press, 2017.

out that "in-depth development of economic globalization, social informatization, and cultural diversity", "the people of the world have never strongly yearned for a better life like today", the cruise industry has become an important support for people in the world to pursue a better life, an important driving force for economic transformation and upgrading, an important leading industry for the construction of ecological civilization, and an important carrier for displaying the country's comprehensive strength.

2017 is a year of great significance in the development of the party and the state. It is also a year of deepening the supply-side structural reforms. It is also a key year for the steady development of Chinese cruise industry. The *China Cruise Industry Development Report* (*2017*) is an annual research report prepared by Shanghai International Cruise Economic Research Center and domestic and international industry experts, based on the latest developments and changes in the international cruise industry. The whole book is composed of four parts: the general report, "Belt and Road" special feature, the industry chapter, and the policy recommendation chapter. The content system is richer and more comprehensive than before, and has more research depth. The general report provides a comprehensive and in-depth analysis of the cruise industry environment at home and abroad in 2016—2017, the development status and problems of Chinese cruise industry, and researches and judges the development trend of the cruise industry, explores the internal laws of the cruise industry, and discusses countermeasures for the steady and far-reaching promotion of Chinese cruise industry; the latest developments in Chinese cruise industry are presented in the form of "Top Ten Hotspots", showing the latest developments in Chinese cruise industry; under the national "Belt and Road" initiative, a special "Belt and Road" initiative was set up to deeply analyze the new opportunities, new paths, new models, and new strategies for the development of the international cruise industry under "Belt and Road" initiative; the industry chapter studies the strategic path for the transformation of the entire cruise industry structure in order to promote the transformation and upgrading of the cruise industry; policy recommendation chapter, under the global background, discusses to explore the innovation of Chinese cruise industry policy and realize the sustainable and healthy development of Chinese cruise industry.

The scale of the international cruise market continues to grow. It is expected that the total number of tourists will reach 25.8 million. China has continued to steadily increase on the basis of exceeding 2 million for the first time in 2016. The status of cruise tourism in Chinese tourism industry continues to increase, and its international influence continues to increase. As a result, the economic radiation effect of the entire cruise industry chain has also increased significantly. Shanghai's influence and reputation in the global cruise market have been strengthened. On the basis of the Asia-Pacific's No.1 in 2016 and the world's fourth-largest cruise home port, the international ranking is expected to enter the top three and become one of the world's most influential cruise home ports. Governments at all levels in China have paid more attention to the cruise industry, continues to pay attention to and support the cruise industry, and continues to increase their confidence in the cruise industry. In 2017, two new cruise tourism development zones in China, Fuzhou and Dalian, were added to fully support innovative exploration of China's cruise industry. International cruise companies have accelerated their strategic adjustments in the Chinese market. 18 home port cruises serve China. In 2017, NORWEGIAN Cruise opened a new season in China. The new "customized" cruise "JOY" was launched on the Chinese market. "SHENGSHI PRINCESS" that Princess Cruise "tailored to Chinese guests" came to China after a 49-night "Sea Silk Road Journey". Star Dream Cruise "WORLD DREAM" was also launched in China in November 2017. The arrival of the new cruise has added new vitality and development momentum to China cruise market.

Looking forward to 2018, Chinese cruise market will gradually undergo a comprehensive transformation towards maturity during the rapid development. The development of the national cruise tourism industry will pay more attention to integrity and coordination, more robustness and sustainability, and more characteristics and differentiation. International cruise companies' confidence in the Chinese cruise market will continue to increase. China will continue to be the leader of the Asian cruise economy and an important promoter of the global cruise market. It will gradually become the benchmark of the global cruise market and create new laws for the development of the international cruise economy. China is taking advantage of the trend and taking advantage of the situation, participating in the global cruise industry governance and the supply of new cruise products, promoting the stability of the international cruise economy under "Belt and Road" initiative, seizing the new opportunities of the development of the times, and cultivating new formats of the international cruise economy, maintaining the vitality of international cruise ship economic growth, and advance Chinese cruise ship economy towards a better future.

1.5 *China Customs Development Frontier Report* (2017)[①]

Three years after the establishment of the China (Shanghai) Pilot Free Trade Zone, the customs has ushered in important reforms while participating in the national test. In terms of the legal status of the free trade zone, the customs should learn from the international prevailing rules, establish the status of the customs supervision zone "within territory and outside customs" in the free trade zone, and establish the full power of the customs to supervise the goods in the free zone (including infringing goods). In the context of a free trade zone network strategy based on the surroundings and radiating "Belt and Road", customs should further expand the depth and breadth of cooperation with regional logistics companies to provide good environmental support for the construction of international logistics channels and regional trade development. Meanwhile, the establishment of the free trade zone puts forward new requirements for cross-sector cooperation and supervision system innovation of the foreign trade supervision and management department. The innovation of the customs supervision system should focus on the issues of legal basis, collaborative innovation, and innovation path. The construction of the international trade single window should be the starting point in practice to explore the establishment of new mechanisms and breaking the bottleneck of coordination and innovation. On the basis of the innovation of the supervision system, as the promotion of the innovation of the free trade zone system to the development of manufacturing and cultural trade, the customs should further use the experimental field of Shanghai Pilot Free Trade Zone, and continue to promote

---

[①] GAN Chunhui. China Customs Development Frontier Report (2017) [M]. Beijing: Social Science Literature Press, 2017.

and clarify measures that involve manufacturing to play a guiding role in the transformation and upgrading of the manufacturing industry and should learn from the experience of cultural trade development in developed countries, and broaden the development path of cultural trade from the aspects of cultural product export trade and cultural service trade.

The promotion of comprehensive deepening of customs reform also needs to be based on an analysis of Chinese foreign trade situation in recent years. The book is divided into three parts. It summarizes the customs supervision policy from the aspects of culture, system, foreign trade and points out problems and puts forward valuable suggestions. The first part analyzes the development status of Shanghai's cultural trade from the four aspects of development scale, comparison of cultural services and cultural products trade, the proportion of core cultural products and services, and comparison with other cities in the country, pointing out that the development momentum of Shanghai's cultural industry is less than that of Beijing, Jiangsu and other places and the overall size is relatively small, compared with the international metropolis is a big gap. The second part shows that the innovation of the customs system plays an important role in promoting the transformation and upgrading of the manufacturing industry by data, especially the policy guidance and help of the free trade zone including the innovation of the customs system. The large inflow of foreign capital in the manufacturing industry has not only brought about the capital, which is a necessary foundation in development for development of the manufacturing industry, it will bring foreign advanced technology, production management experience, and promote the development of the logistics industry. The mutual promotion and common development between them will better promote the development and transformation of the manufacturing industry. The third part emphasizes that the implementation of the modern ship tonnage tax system has a positive significance for promoting Chinese trade and shipping development. Ship tonnage tax is the tax levied by the customs on ships entering or leaving a country's customs territory. The essence of the modern ship tonnage tax system is the company tax based on ship tonnage. The major shipping countries in the world have all implemented the modern ship tonnage tax system. Chinese current ship tonnage tax system has caused certain obstacles to the development of shipping companies. The implementation of a modern ship tonnage tax system in my country is of positive significance to the promotion of Chinese trade and shipping development. The customs should act as a performer of constructive voice and cooperate with tax authorities to form a perfect shipping tax system and improve the effectiveness of law enforcement.

Under the background of a free trade zone network strategy based on the surrounding and radiating "Belt and Road", the book takes the theme of "Customs Comprehensive Deepening Reform", adopts a combination of theoretical research and practical issues, and uses the latest theoretical results to have a in-depth analysis of major real issues in the process of comprehensively deepening customs reform, with comprehensive content and detailed data.

1.6 Innovative Practice of Shipping Industry under the Background of Free Trade Zone[①]

Weak demand from the world's major economies, slow recovery of international trade, excess shipping capacity in the shipping industry tends to be normal, coupled with continued increase in operating costs, the shipping industry's long-term sluggish pattern is difficult to break. The construction of free trade zones and the introduction of global supply chain concepts will bring new development opportunities to shipping companies. The book systematically introduces the policies and influences of the shipping industry in the context of the free trade zone, the shipping industry development strategy based on supply chain innovation, the optimized shipping operations of delicacy management, and the innovative application of the Internet of Things technology in the shipping industry.

The book starts with the analysis of the shipping policy of the free trade zone and combines with the application cases of the shipping policy of the free trade zone and proposes that: the first trial of the coastal piggyback business of foreign trade import and export containers between domestic coastal open ports and Shanghai Port will trigger a series of coastal carriage authority issues. In

---

① HU Jiankun, HAO Yangyang. Innovative Practice of Shipping Industry under the Background of Free Trade Zone [M]. Shanghai: Shanghai Pujiang Education Press, 2017.

addition, the WTO's trade in services mainly requires that discrimination should not happen and it can not have difference between inside and outside and between two outside.

The second part focuses on shipping management issues: at present, Chinese ship management companies are facing many difficulties, and the first issue is the issue of crew income tax. Taking a ship management company as an example, the cost of crew accounts for 15% of the total cost of carriage (including fuel consumption) and 50% of management costs (excluding fuel consumption). The on-board income is usually more objective. Taking the captain as an example, the monthly income is 50,000 to 70,000 yuan, while the on-shore income is the lowest income of location labor wages where the crew belong. The tax threshold for ocean-going crew is 4,800 yuan. Taking the captain as an example, the monthly tax is 25% to 30%, namely, 15,000 yuan. The average crew is on board for 8 months a year. The personal income tax to be paid is very high. In the context of globalization of international shipping, Chinese ship management companies that manage five-star red flag ships are not very competitive. Singapore and the Philippines implement a complete tax exemption for crew, and India exempts crew for more than 50% of the days spent on board overseas (namely, 183 days of work on board within a year). Another thorny issue is that the wholly foreign-owned ship management enterprises do not have crew management qualifications. For ship management companies, their main businesses include: technology, commerce and crew management. At present, newly registered foreign-owned ship management companies do not have expatriate qualifications and cannot dispatch and manage their own crews, which affects their business development. In addition, there are the problems of introduction of talents, taxation of debit and credit and transit of maintenance of spare parts; the convenience of high-level exit visas for ship management companies and entry visas for overseas crew; the formation of POEA regulatory authorities similar to the Philippines, these issues all bring great troubles for ships management enterprises. Although it is convenient to conduct business in Shanghai Pilot Free Trade Zone, many of the provisions have not yet been implemented, the speed of policy implementation is obviously too slow, and many areas need to be further opened up.

The book finally emphasizes that the shipping policy of the free trade zone needs to be broken through: the shipping industry of the free trade zone is still mainly port-dependent shipping industry, low-end and traditional shipping functions (such as port loading and unloading, ship carriage, freight forwarding, ship agency, collection sparse transportation) dominate, and high-end and emerging shipping service functions (such as shipping finance, international transit consolidation, financial leasing, supply chain management, shipping transactions, ship management, shipping headquarters economy) urgently need to be expanded and upgraded. The industry generally holds that there are more low-end labor in the shipping industry and a serious shortage of high-end professionals (only about 1% of the total number of employees); the grouping of international high-end shipping organizations is insufficient, and the internationalization level of Chinese shipping organizations and enterprises is low; the main body of market lacks diversity and lacks vitality for innovation and development.

In terms of professional shipping services, including shipping finance, insurance, legal services, information services, there are generally problems such as weak service capabilities, small market size, weak professionalism and authority, and facing multiple institutional and policy obstacles. At the initial stage of development, the comprehensive development environment needs to be improved.

1.7 Development of International Shipping Center from a Global Perspective[①]

Openness and integration will become a new trend in the development of international shipping centers. The international shipping center is an important port city with high-quality port facilities, a developed logistics system, and key geographic locations as the basic conditions, with a highly comprehensive shipping service as the core drive, and the allocation of shipping resources on a global scale. From the perspective of "Belt and Road", the development of international shipping centers is facing new trends, and ports have become an

---

① ZHANG Jieshu. Development of International Shipping Center from a Global Perspective [M]. Shanghai: Shanghai Pujiang Education Press, 2017.

important fulcrum for supporting "Belt and Road" maritime cooperation.

Based on the study and analysis of the concept, characteristics, components, driving forces and industrial chain of the international shipping center, the book uses case analysis to study and compare the key characteristics of different international shipping centers in Singapore, Hong Kong, Shanghai and others in China. It constructs a scientific index system to evaluate international shipping centers with global influence, so as to explore the future development direction, trends and core competitiveness of international shipping centers, and provide reference and examples for Shanghai to build an international shipping center with global resource allocation capabilities.

The book points out that the major domestic port companies are still facing many challenges such as "unaccustomed when going out". In terms of benchmarking national missions, most ports are still low on internationalization and do not yet have the ability to go out alone. In the future, it is necessary to explore how to strengthen the coordinated efforts of local governments and port enterprises, help Chinese ports accelerate their integration into "Belt and Road" initiative, and play a pivotal role as a shipping center. At the same time, the current economy is in a period of major turning point adjustment, and carriage by sea and shipping are facing new trends. The rapid development of technology led by informatization and the Internet will further promote the integration and development of various industries. From a global perspective, the entire port and shipping industry are paying more and more attention to safety and the protection of the environment. Enterprise alliances have gradually become a trend. Ports have started to integrate port resources along the coast, greatly changing the ecology of shipping and ports.

The book proposes that: maritime interconnection, port-city cooperation mechanism, and marine economic cooperation can greatly expand Chinese economic development space. Te open development concept is on the one hand conducive to China's international shipping center attracting multinational companies, R & D centers, settlement centers, and logistics centers to settle, and generating agglomeration effects; on the other hand, China's international shipping center uses the combination of its competitive advantages in the field of finance, insurance and logistics and the long-term overseas operation experience of shipping and port companies, which will become the "springboard" for Chinese companies to go abroad and the highlight of "Belt and Road" initiative, and will provide a broader market and development spacefor the construction of Chinese international shipping center.

1.8 *Yangtze River Shipping Development Report* (*2017*)[①]

The book strictly implements the spirit of the Nineteenth National Congress of the CPC and the five development concepts of innovation, coordination, green, openness and sharing, as well as the "traveling power" strategy and new ideas, strategies and goals for the modernization of the Yangtze River Shipping in the new era. And it summaries and shows the operation and development trend and highlights of the Yangtze River shipping industry in 2017, gathers current hot topics such as green development, intelligent development, and industry governance, analyzes the effectiveness of the Yangtze River golden waterway service national strategy, and looks forward to the development prospects and goals of the new era.

The book first introduces the development process of the Yangtze River Shipping in 2017: the Yangtze River Maritime Safety Administration completed the approval of 32 projects "workable", 34 projects "initial establishment" approval systematically; completed 15 projects "workable"department review, 3 "initial establishment" ministry reviews; more than 80 construction projects have been arranged, and the budget enforcement rate has reached more than 95%. The appearance of the Yangtze River shipping infrastructure continued to improve, and the foundation for serving the construction of the Yangtze River Economic Belt was continuously consolidated. A number of key projects have given the Yangtze River golden waterways a greater vitality. The "645 Project" and other key projects are steadily advancing. The "workable" report of the 6 m deep water channel regulation project from Wuhan to Anqing passed the review of the National Development and Reform Commission; the fishery evaluation topics of the "3.Sheng 2 Project" project received environmental protection approval; the main body of the projects under construction such as the digital channel of the

---

[①] Yangtze River Navigation Administration of the Ministry of Transport. Yangtze River Shipping Development Report (2017) [M]. Beijing: People's Communications Press, 2017.

section from Dabu Street to Liuhekou, the second phase of the traffic control of the Three Gorges reservoir area, and the Zhenjiang oil spill emergency equipment library were completed; the Jingjiang waterway renovation project was rated as the "inland waterway ecological environmental protection demonstration project".

Meanwhile, the book closely follows "Belt and Road" initiative: introducing the reform of the Yangtze River shipping administrative system. The reform is not only a "first move" that focuses on the construction of golden waterways and serving the economic and social development of the Yangtze River, but also is an implementation of decisions and arrangements of the State Council and Ministry of Transport, and a "tough fight" that must be won. On the basis of comprehensive law enforcement, the reform of the administrative management system of Yangtze River Maritime Safety Administration is also steadily advancing, promoting the reform of the water monitoring system of the Sichuan section of the Yangtze River trunk line, the adjustment of the management relationship of Jiangsu Maritime Safety Administration and the integration of the water monitoring of the Yangtze River trunk line. The maritime management system of the Yangtze River trunk line has basically been rationalized; The reform of the management system of the Yangtze River Waterway has separated government functions from enterprises, clarified the functional positioning, promoted the transformation of functions, improved the organizational structure, and further improved service efficiency.

The book comprehensively introduces the achievements of the development of Yangtze Shipping, provides important intellectual support for the scientific decision-making of the industry management department, provides useful help for the public to understand the development status of Yangtze Shipping, and also provides scholars engaged in the theoretical research of Yangtze Shipping development and actual participants of Yangtze Shipping with certain reference.

1.9 *Handbook of Shipping Finance*[1]

As a large-span and multi-disciplinary field involving shipping, finance and law, the healthy development of shipping finance is becoming increasingly

---

[1] Oratis Sinas. Handbook of Shipping Finance [M]. Beijing: CITIC Publishing House, 2017.

important for China, which is building a shipping and marine power under "Belt and Road" initiative. Based on a grand perspective, the book introduces the concept and operation model of ship finance in a comprehensive and multi-angle manner, and collects a variety of conventional and practical ship finance models and practical operation cases. The content covers the legal treatment of equity capital market finance and ship finance loans, German KG model, ship valuation pricing and risk control, sorts out various types of ship finance methods, provides new ideas and new concepts in the maritime and ship finance industry, and provides solutions to common problems facing the industry.

The book is divided into six parts: the first part introduces some basic knowledge of traditional ship finance; the second part focuses on equity finance; the third part focuses on asset pricing issues; the fourth part focuses on the institutional framework and its impact on ship finance; the fifth part sorts out the existing solutions to the common challenges facing the industry, such as restructuring, risk management, and alternative ship management and finance methods; the sixth part focuses on the introduction of services closely relevant to ship finance. The content focuses on the views of more than 30 experts from international and Hamburg, whose knowledge and expertise are transformed from industry practice.

The book introduces a series of relevant businesses arising from economic activities such as finance, insurance, currency custody, exchange, settlement, and risk management that happen during the operation of shipping companies, involving the shipping industry, shipbuilding industry, and financial industry. The German KG model is introduced to be a limited partnership model. There are five elements that make up the KG model: one is the fixed tax rate, which is a favorable tax model for investors; the second is the limited liability company model, which is the legal structure of the KG model; and the third is the German shipping banks, which provide loans for the KG model; the fourth is shipping companies, which carry out ship management; the fifth is scattered investors, which make equity investments. The KG model is profit paradise based on the commission. The sponsor of the KG fund protects the interests of the bank and the right to mortgage; the broker and the sponsor protect the interests of the shipbuilding enterprise; the ship manager protects the assets; the charter broker protects the time charter contract; the KG fund protects the interests of investors, trusts and general partners with limited liability.

The book also mentions that: compared with the relatively mature shipping finance industry in Europe and America, Chinese shipping finance industry is still in its infancy, and it is one of the important ways to develop Chinese shipping finance industry to study and draw lessons from the rich experience and failure of European and American countries in shipping finance. The book draws on successful experiences from abroad, which is conducive to Chinese establishment of an effective shipping industry organization structure, optimization and upgrading of the shipping industry structure, rational layout of industrial productivity and improvement of benefits; drawing lessons from foreign failures can appropriately avoid the cyclical and instability, to avoid repeating the mistakes of foreign financial institutions in the field of ship financing.

1.10 *Guidelines and Legal Interpretation of China Shipping Trust Fund* [1]

Shipping trust fund is one of the important ways of shipping finance innovation. Studying the shipping trust fund is conducive to expanding shipping finance channels, promoting the upgrading of the shipping industry and the integration of the industrial chain, and promoting the realization of Chinese "Belt and Road" initiative, the construction of international shipping centers and international financial centers, and the strategy of a marine power.

Based on the particularity of the shipping market and Chinese capital market, the book makes an in-depth analysis of the legal status of China Shipping trust fund, the legal relationship of subjects, the ownership of the trust fund property and the rights and obligations of the parties involved in the establishment of China Shipping trust fund.

This book summarizes the successful experiences of many foreign and domestic companies in the field of shipping finance, and is a practical tool for a comprehensive understanding of the characteristics of foreign shipping finance industry, investment operations, financing channels, and risk management. It

---

[1] JIN Haisi. Guidelines and Legal Interpretation of China Shipping Trust Fund [M]. Beijing: CITIC Publishing House, 2017.

takes the shipping finance industry as an organic whole "industry" and starts from this, discussing the interaction between financial institutions and industries, the development laws of the industry itself, and the methods of studying these laws in the economic development centered on industrialization. In order to promote the development of the shipping finance industry, China needs to strengthen financial policy support for the shipping finance industry, encourage and support financial institutions to actively develop innovative financial products and service methods suitable for the characteristics of the shipping and shipbuilding industry, and effectively expand the financing channels of shipping and shipbuilding industry enterprises, in particular, increase credit support for the high-end ship and sea engineering equipment manufacturing industry. The book can provide readers with answers and ideas with reference value for the above aspects.

Ship finance is still a relatively new field in my country. There is very little literature and the theory and practice are far from being qualitative. The book fills a gap in the regard. The industry operations and trends mentioned in the book will allow domestic shipping companies to see more possibilities, which will lead to innovative thinking and unprecedented modes of operation in the field of shipping finance.

2 Journal Article Review for publication in 2017

2.1 *Connotation, Study Status and Study Significance of Basic Theory of Maritime Code*[①]

Based on the study status of basic theory of Chinese Maritime Code, the author points out that there is no comprehensive, systematic and in-depth study on the basic theory of maritime code in Chinese maritime code circles. The basic theory study of other legal department has reference value for the basic theory study of maritime code. At the same time, it is of great significance to study the basic theory of maritime code for perfecting the theory system of maritime code,

---

① HU Zhengliang, SUN Siqi. Connotation, Study Status and Study Significance of Basic Theory of Maritime Code[J]. China Maritime Law Study, 2017 (1): 3-12.

improving the theory study grade of maritime code, correctly guiding maritime legislation and judicial practice, and correctly guiding shipping practice. They call on China to attach importance to the study of the basic theory of maritime code.

The basic theory of a specific law discipline reflects the basic framework of the maritime code discipline and has a supporting basic role for the maritime code discipline. It is followed by the theory study, legislation, judicial and even practical fields of the discipline. Since the *Maritime Code of the People's Republic of China* (hereinafter referred to as the *Maritime Code*) was passed in 1992, the theory study of the Chinese Maritime Code, especially in the practicality of the maritime code, has made great progress. However, there has been a lack of systematic study on the basic theory of maritime code for a long time in the maritime code circles. The main reason is the lack of understanding of the importance of the basic theory of maritime code. The lack of the basic link has affected the qualitative improvement of the theory study of Chinese maritime code.

The authors use the relevant principles of legal basic theory in jurisprudence, draws on the study of basic theory of other legal disciplines, discusses the connotation of the basic theory of maritime code, analyzes the study status of the basic theory of maritime code in China, and expounds the significance of the study of basic theory of maritime code.

The authors hold that Chinese maritime code circles lacks comprehensive, systematic and in-depth study on the basic theory of maritime code. The reason is that after the promulgation of the *Maritime Code*, the study of maritime code mainly focused on the interpretation of the application of the existing maritime code rules based on the provisions of the *Maritime Code*, which has a strong "annotation jurisprudence" color of medieval Roman law. In addition, the situation that interpretative theory of maritime code actually dominates the theory study of maritime law has not changed significantly so far, and the study on basic theory of maritime code has not received much attention from the academic circle.

Therefore, the authors introduce in detail the reference value of the basic theory study of other legal departments to the basic theory study of maritime code. Most of the provisions of the current *Maritime Code* are provisions for adjusting rights and obligations between equal subjects, and they are special laws of civil law. civil law theory is an important theoretical support for the theory study of maritime code. The study results of the basic theory of civil law provide a good theoretical basis for the study of the basic theory of maritime code. The correct understanding and attention to the role of basic theory study is an important reason why economic law can quickly form a relatively complete theoretical system in China, and it later surpasses the formers and occupies a place in the legal study. This kind of consciousness of basic theory study may be the source of the lack of basic theory study of Chinese maritime code.

Finally, it summaries the significance of the basic theory study of maritime code lies in that: perfecting the maritime code theory system and enhancing the grade of maritime law theory study; correctly guiding maritime code practice; correctly guiding shipping practice.

2.2 Study on Jurisdiction Conflict of Bill of Lading: An Example of Sino-British Jurisdiction Conflict of Bill of Lading[1]

The authors take a case of Sino-British jurisdiction conflict of bill of lading as an example to analyze the reasons why Chinese and British courts have different confirmation over the effectiveness of jurisdiction clause of the same bill of lading and the different basis for obtaining jurisdiction, pointing out that they are the superficial reasons for the conflict of bills of lading jurisdiction, and revealing the root cause of bill of lading jurisdictional conflicts is the consideration of self-interest by various countries. Finally, it points out that the coordination of conflicts of jurisdiction over bills of lading must rely on both international and domestic channels. Although coordination at the international level has achieved certain results, the limitation of the scope of application of international conventions has made it possible for the improvement of coordination mechanisms for jurisdictional conflicts at the domestic level of all countries to have a useful complementary role.

After introducing the basic case, the authors raise the issues involved that: firstly, the effectiveness of jurisdiction clause of the bill of lading, which belongs to the perspective of the parties choosing the court; secondly, the issue of

---

[1] NIU Yuan, LIN Aimin. Study on Jurisdiction Conflict of Bill of Lading-An Example of Sino-British Jurisdiction Conflict of Bill of Lading[J]. China Maritime Law Study, 2017 (1): 60-70.

obtaining the bill of lading jurisdiction, which belongs to the dimension of the court's confirmation of jurisdiction.

The authors introduce the concept of the bill of lading jurisdiction clause and explains the reasons why the Chinese and British courts have different confirmation on their effectiveness. The Chinese and British courts have different confirmation on the effectiveness of the same bill of lading jurisdiction clauses. The main issue is the applicable law of the bill of lading jurisdiction clause. The bill of lading jurisdiction clause is often regarded as the agreement jurisdiction clause in judicial practice, and the effectiveness of the agreement jurisdiction clause may be adjusted by different local laws. The question of whether the bill of lading jurisdiction clause itself is effect (namely, the question of the limitation of the effectiveness of the bill of lading jurisdiction clause) involves the limitation of the effectiveness of the bill of lading jurisdiction clause by different countries. The common limitation is as follows: firstly, the jurisdiction clause of the bill of lading excluding the jurisdiction of the domestic court is noneffective. Secondly, the jurisdiction clause of the bill of lading that is about choosing the court without objective and actual contact is noneffective. Thirdly, the "equivalence principle" restricts the effectiveness of the bill of lading jurisdiction clause. Fourthly, limit the effectiveness of the jurisdiction clause of the bill of lading on the ground that the carrier's liability is exempted or reduced. Whether the bill of lading jurisdiction clause is exclusive is another important aspect of the effectiveness of the bill of lading jurisdiction clause. Based on the protection of national jurisdictions by various countries, most countries do not recognize the exclusive effectiveness of the jurisdiction clauses in bills of lading. The bill of lading jurisdiction clause has certain special features. It is not entirely the agreement of the parties. If the text of the clause does not clearly specify "exclusivity", it is not appropriate to make a presumption of "exclusivity". Otherwise, it is unfavorable to the shipper who passively accepts the jurisdiction clause of bill of lading. The *Rotterdam Rules* take the view that only when the jurisdiction agreement itself expressly stipulates as exclusive jurisdiction, it has exclusive effect.

Finally, the authors put forward his own suggestions on the resolution of jurisdiction conflicts from both international and domestic perspectives. Internationally, it is recommended to unify the criteria for judging the effectiveness of the jurisdiction clause of the bill of lading. The *Rotterdam Rules* fully confirm the effectiveness of the agreement on the choice of court. It is not only respect for the autonomy of the parties, but also an effective means to avoid jurisdiction conflicts. However, there are limited signatories, and there are limitations in the scope of application. In the domestic coordination system of various countries, it is recommended to adhere to and improve the first-action jurisdiction system, introduce the necessary refusal jurisdiction system and give priority to the suspension of domestic actions, so as to reduce improper interference with foreign jurisdictions in the form of "injunction orders".

The conflict of jurisdiction in the international civil field is a manifestation of the conflicts of political and economic interests of various countries. Both domestic legislation and international treaties have certain limitations in solving and preventing conflicts of jurisdiction. Therefore, the conflict of international civil jurisdiction must rely on both international and domestic channels, cooperate with each other, and resolve together. The same is true for the coordination of conflicts of jurisdiction over bills of lading. On the one hand, the international community is committed to coordinating the conflict of jurisdiction in the field of carriage of goods by sea including the conflict of jurisdiction over bills of lading, and has achieved certain results; on the other hand, due to the limitations of the scope of application of international conventions, the coordination of jurisdiction conflict is also inseparable from the establishment and improvement of the mechanism of conflict of jurisdiction of various countries. The coordination at the domestic level is a useful supplement to the coordination at the international level. The author, through a specific case analysis, aims at the different confirmation of jurisdiction in the maritime litigation process between China and Britain, concludes that the coordination of jurisdiction conflicts needs to be improved by both international and domestic countries.

2.3 *Study on Complaint Mechanism of Chinese Crew*[1]

Regarding the crew complaint mechanism, there are still some gaps between

---

[1] CAO Yanchun, TANG Shuyuan. Study on Complaint Mechanism of Chinese Crew [J]. China Maritime Law Study, 2017 (2): 3 – 11.

Chinese relevant laws and regulations and the MLC 2006. The author proposes to improve on-board complaints, establish an on-board ship complaint handling committee, and strengthen contact with shore. Establish a supporting complaint mechanism on the shore, improve the complaint handling and settlement procedures, provide consultation, mediation, liaison, arbitration and other services to the society, effectively protect the privacy of the complaining crew, and provide comprehensive support for the protection of the rights and interests of the crew.

MLC 2006, known as the "Fourth Major Convention of the Shipping Industry", came into effect on August 20, 2013. More than 90% of the world's fleet has operated according to the requirements of the convention, and 77 countries around the world have ratified the convention and guarantees decent work and living conditions for crew according to the convention, whose gross ship tonnage accounts for more than 90% of global ships. China has submitted to the ILO Director General Guy Ryder the approval letter for China's approval of MLC 2006 on November 12, 2015. According to the provisions of the convention, MLC 2006 would formally enter into force on November 12, 2016 for China. Chinese current task is to modify the corresponding domestic laws to meet the requirements of the convention. China still has many problems and difficulties in protecting the rights and interests of crew, especially in the crew's complaint handling mechanism, China has a certain gap with the requirements of the convention. China stipulates a shipboard complaint procedure, but it does not specify the shore complaint procedure. Summarize the current situation of domestic and British crew complaints mechanism and compare it with the relevant provisions of the convention complaint, so as to make recommendations on the conversion of the convention into domestic legislation and the construction of Chinese crew complaint handling mechanism.

Problems with the Chinese crew complaint mechanism: firstly, many crew do not know how to complain, to whom, or how to make complaints. The shipping company also does not provide channels for the crew to complain. Secondly, after the crew complained, the problem could not be resolved and delayed processing, and there was no good complaint handling mechanism. Thirdly, there is no effective protection mechanism. Crew who complained are often faced with serious problems such as being excluded, retaliating that are difficult to stay on. Fourthly, the supervision and inspection duties of the competent authority are unclear. Establishing an active and effective crew complaint and dispute resolution mechanism is an important task.

The authors detail the advantages of MLC 2006 rules: the provisions for crew complaints are also not previously stipulated by the ILO, and provide separate procedures for shipboard complaints and shore complaints. In terms of content, the convention fully absorbs the outstanding achievements of the ILO and other international organizations in terms of legislation, and reflects the humanistic spirit of respecting and protecting human rights. The biggest advantage is its enforcement mechanism. The convention stipulates the inspection and certification system of the flag state and the supervision and inspection system of the port state, and the *Maritime Labor Certificate* and *Maritime Compliance Statement* are issued to ships through inspections. This is a strong enforcement mechanism established to ensure the effective implementation of the convention and an enforcement system supported by a certification system for compliance with the convention. The "non-concessionary clause" of the convention specifies that no preferential treatment should be given to ships of non-ratified countries, which is also a strong provision to ensure the implementation of the convention.

After comparing the Chinese crew complaint procedure with the convention complaint procedure, the authors hold that drawing on the convention should also address issues such as Chinese failure to establish an onshore complaint mechanism. It is necessary to investigate the pros and cons of domestic and foreign dispute resolution mechanisms and establish an onshore complaint mechanism suitable for China.

Finally, the authors put forward suggestions that: strengthen the construction of the crew complaint handling team; standardize the crew complaint handling procedure, establish the onshore supporting complaint mechanism while improving the ship's complaint handling procedure; standardize and unify the relevant crew legislation.

As a special laborer, the crew is the backbone of the shipping industry, fully protecting the rights and interests of the crew and establishing a sound complaint handling mechanism is of great significance to promote the smooth development of the shipping industry. China is a major shipping country and a crew country. Taking the opportunity of joining the convention, we can learn more about the experience of handling complaints from foreign crews, improve relevant legislation and systems, and better protect the rights and interests of Chinese crew. It is of great significance to realize crew's decent work and life on board and to improve their economic and social status and to better promote the development of Chinese shipping industry.

2.4 Looking at the Rationality of the Shipping Industry's Anti-monopoly Exemption System from the Rise and Fall of Modern Liner Conference[1]

As a special monopoly industry, some of shipping industry's monopoly organizations play a positive role in promoting the steady development of international trade. Therefore, they are granted some antitrust immunity privileges. The Liner Conference is the most typical monopoly organization. In the history of the development of modern shipping in the world, the appearance of the Liner Conference is undoubtedly a halo. Through the rise, prosperity and declining development process of the Liner Conference, the author makes a detailed analysis of the positive and negative significance of the Liner Conference on the entire shipping industry, so as to make an in-depth discussion on the changes of some antitrust immunity systems in the shipping industry.

The author starts with the analysis of the significance of the modern Liner Conference to the shipping industry. The positive significance of the modern Liner Conference to the shipping industry is that: ①the Liner Conference will unify the freight rate, agree on the rates that all enterprises should abide by, and not allow members of the Conference privately increase or decrease freight. ②The Liner Conference stipulates the voyages and call ports of each member company on the routes it controls, and arranges operations in a unified manner; in order to balance the interests of each member company, the Liner Conference will distribute the income as a whole and distribute the income of the member

---

[1] WANG Hui. Looking at the Rationality of the Shipping Industry's Anti-monopoly Exemption System from the Rise and Fall of Modern Liner Conference[J]. China Shipping, 2017 (5): 11-12.

companies in proportion intensively. It not only centralizes the original scattered team, avoids the vicious competition, is advantageous to the further development of shipping industry. ③The Liner Conference has also adopted a deferred kickback system. This system not only benefits each member company in the Liner Conference, so that it can obtain a stable supply of goods for freight carriage, and it also benefits the goods owner. As long as they deliver all their goods to a certain liner company to ship of a certain Liner Conference, they will be able to get the corresponding kickback from the Liner Conference at the end of the calculation period. The establishment of the Liner Conference not only benefits each member company, but also the goods owner, and achieves a "win-win" situation.

However, the Liner Conference also has a negative significance to the shipping industry: due to the monopoly nature of the Liner Conference, its existence has greatly inhibited many national shipping companies in developing countries. Take modern China as an example. At that time, in Chinese Liner Conference, most of the member companies were foreign shipping companies or some foreign banks. The Liner Conference was only beneficial to their member companies. At that time, some national shipping companies in China were refused by the Liner Conference, so many Chinese shipping companies dissociated from the Liner Conference did not enjoy the preferential policies of the Liner Conference. Instead, they lost a lot of goods due to the delayed kickback system implemented by the Liner Conference, making their operations difficult. This kind of monopoly organization not only violates the basic principles of fair competition, but also is not conducive to the formation of a maritime free competition system, and it is more harmful to the competition of the entire shipping market.

The author discusses whether to cancel the antitrust immunity based on the positive and negative significance of the Liner Conference on the development of the shipping industry. In Europe, the Council of Ministers of the European Union announced on September 25, 2006 that the antitrust immunity of the Liner Conference would be cancelled from October 18, 2008; in America, the provisions of its *Shipping Reform Act of 1998* carried out limited antitrust immunity system to the Liner Conference stipulates that conference member companies must not enjoy antitrust immunity during domestic transportation; in Japan, its new antitrust law stipulates that the anti-competitive behavior of the Liner Conference should be minimized. For our country, as a shipping country rather than a strong country, the international competitiveness of the shipping industry still needs to be improved. Therefore, in order to maintain the stability of the shipping industry, a monopoly organization such as the Liner Conference still needs to exist within a certain period of time. It is necessary to implement antitrust immunity system for shipping industry. It is too early for my country to cancel the antitrust immunity enjoyed by the Liner Conference. The first task should be to improve the laws and regulations relevant to the antitrust immunity system of the shipping industry as soon as possible to improve the international competitiveness of the domestic shipping industry.

The author analyzes the development course of the modern Liner Conference, and also discusses from domestic and foreign perspective about the rationality of the antitrust immunity enjoyed by the Liner Conference and whether it should be cancelled. In general, as a typical monopoly organization in the shipping industry, the rise and decline of the Liner Conference reflects the rationality of the antitrust immunity of the shipping industry in countries with different national conditions. The rise and fall of modern Liner Conference is an indispensable page in the whole history of shipping industry

2.5 *Looking at the Risks and Countermeasures of Fuel Supply for Chartered Ships by Ship Fuel Enterprises from the Perspective of Compensation for Oil Pollution Damage*[①]

The risk of ship oil pollution faced by ship fuel supply enterprises is a major risk that cannot be avoided. The author starts from the scope and principle of ship pollution compensation, introduces the mechanism of International and domestic ship pollution compensation, and analyzes the present situation of oil pollution compensation in China, and discusses the risk of ship pollution damage

---

① SONG Zhaoguo. Looking at the Risks and Countermeasures of Fuel Supply for Chartered Ships by Ship Fuel Enterprises from the Perspective of Compensation for Oil Pollution Damage[J]. China Ocean Shipping, 2017(8): 74-76.

compensation for oil supply of chartered ship and puts forward some countermeasures and suggestions.

The author introduces the three main modes of ship oil pollution damage compensation mechanism in the world: ①join the two international conventions of the *Convention on Civil Liability for Oil Pollution Damage* (CLC) and *Convention on Fund for Oil Pollution Damage Compensation* (FC), and establish ship oil pollution damage compensation mechanism according to conventions. By accepting and joining the International Oil Pollution Fund, the parties to conventions establish a compensation mechanism for ship oil pollution damage. ②Set up domestic ship oil pollution damage compensation mechanism through national legislation. The most representative of the model is America. America did not participate in the International Oil Pollution Fund, but established its National Oil Pollution Fund Center (NPFC) and Oil Spill Liability Trust Joint Fund (OS LTF) by enacting the *Oil Pollution Act* 1990 (OPA 90). A domestic oil pollution fund of up to 1 billion USD was set up, along with stricter liability for ship owners. ③Both acceding to international conventions and establishing a compensation mechanism for ship's oil pollution damage through national legislation. The most representative of the model is Canada. Canada not only accepted FC 92, joined the International Oil Pollution Fund, but also established the SOPF through amendments to the country's *Shipping Law*. The two sets of mechanisms operate simultaneously and complement each other.

The *Regulations on the Prevention and Control of Ship Pollution to Marine Environment* is of great significance to the prevention and control of ship pollution damage in my country. Compared with the previous laws and regulations on the liability of ship oil pollution, the regulations further clarify the liability principle and exemption situation of the ship pollution damage compensation system. It identifies the civil liability subject of ship pollution damage as a party to the ship, and takes the owner of the ship and bareboat charterers as the civil liability subject according to the principle of "who inflicts harm, who is responsible", and they bear the joint liability for ship pollution damage on the basis of no fault liability. The author holds that the company is in the position of being both the goods owner and the ship operator in the oil supply operation under the time charter status. Therefore, if an oil pollution accident occurs, it will be jointly liable as the subject of civil liability.

The author puts forward corresponding countermeasures and suggestions for the safety and anti-pollution work of the oil supply operation by chartering ship: ①establish a ship condition assessment mechanism. Before chartering, comprehensively understand and evaluate the ship's condition, crew operation level, experience, company safety management qualifications and management status, implement a comprehensive evaluation of the risks that may be encountered when chartering ship to implement the oil supply operation, and propose relevant control measures. ②Select a lessor with a high level of safety management. When choosing to rent a ship, it must carefully analyze and evaluate the company's safety management. ③Increase the insurance coverage of oil pollution insurance. According to the *Regulations on the Prevention and Control of Ship Pollution to Marine Environment* and its supporting regulations, the *Implementation Rules on the Collection and Use of Ship Oil Pollution Damage Compensation Fund*, the amount of oil pollution insurance should be according to the limitation of liability requirements of international conventions to which the country is a party. The insurance amount for heavy oil vessels under 5,000 gross tonnage should be 451 SDR, which is about RMB 48 million. The provisions of the insurance amount are based on the protection of shipowners' interests and the limitation of ship's liability. The current environmental protection situation is becoming more and more serious. In the case of pollution incidents that are less and less tolerant, once a major pollution accident happens, the compensation for pollution damage must be huge, and ship charterers and goods suppliers cannot escape liability.

With the development and changes of the ship fuel supply market and the inevitable trend of social cooperation and division of labor, ship fuel supply enterprises reduce their own ships and implement chartered ship to supply oil, which is as a new open operating mode, and have practical significance for effectively using market resources and improving efficiency and reducing enterprise costs. However, it is undeniable that chartering ships to supply oil has certain specificities and disadvantages compared with using company's own ship to supply oil. When chartering a ship to supply oil, it is necessary to make overall considerations, weigh the pros and cons, and better play the role of the type of oil supply operation.

Ship fuel supply enterprises always deal with oil products. The operation of enterprise involves oil storage, transportation, distribution, supply and many other links. Marine pollution caused by ship accident oil spills is a major safety and environmental protection risk for enterprise. The author studies and analyzes relevant liabilities of compensation for ship pollution damage, especially the relevant liability of compensation for ship fuel enterprises in the case of oil supply by chartered ships, which is of certain practical significance for the audit and management of chartered ships.

2.6 Construction of the International Maritime Justice Center under "Belt and Road"[1]

China is a big marine country and has extensive maritime strategic interests. Maritime justice is an important part of managing and controlling the ocean. At present, China is the country with the largest number of maritime judicial organs, the largest number of maritime judges, and the largest number of maritime cases. The advancement of national strategies such as maritime power, shipping power, and the construction of international shipping centers has provided historic opportunities for the development of the shipping industry, and also put forward higher requirements for maritime justice. The author analyzes the reasons for proposal of the International Maritime Justice Center and draws on the British experience to make recommendations for the establishment of a maritime justice center in my country. It calls on our country to actively and steadily advance the construction of an International Maritime Justice Center, and strive to achieve the transformation from a maritime justice country to a maritime justice power.

The report of the Eighteenth National Congress of the CPC put forward the strategic tasks and objectives of "improving the development capacity of marine resources, developing the marine economy, protecting the marine ecological environment, resolutely safeguarding the national marine rights and interests,

---

[1] ZHANG Wenguang. Construction of the International Maritime Justice Center under "Belt and Road" [J]. China Ocean Shipping, 2017 (11): 68-70.

and building a strong marine power". The Third Plenary Session of the Eighteenth Central Committee called for "promoting the construction of the Silk Road Economic Belt and the Maritime Silk Road, forming a new pattern of all-round opening". The Fourth Plenary Session of the Eighteenth Central Committee put forward the overall goal of comprehensively advancing the rule of law. By 2020, Shanghai will basically build an international shipping center with global shipping resource allocation capabilities; China will initially realize the transformation from a shipbuilding country to a shipbuilding power; China will achieve the phased goal of building a modern shipping system with international competitiveness, and on this basis, it will move towards building a shipping power. Against the above background, the author holds that the proposal to construct an International Maritime Justice Center is in line with China's development for two main reasons: ①the maintenance of marine rights and interests requires maritime justice protection. At present, Chinese marine rights and interests are facing severe challenges. The particularities of jurisdiction and jurisdiction cases make the maritime courts of particular importance in safeguarding and proclaiming national judicial sovereignty. ②Promoting the construction of "Belt and Road" requires maritime justice escort. With the implementation of "Belt and Road" initiative, maritime economic activities will become more frequent, marine ecological and environmental problems will become more prominent, and the trend of rising maritime disputes is inevitable. Without a good maritime justice environment and without strong judicial jurisdiction as a backing, the construction of "Belt and Road" will lack the assistance of the rule of law, and our national interests will not be fully guaranteed.

The UK is a world-recognized international maritime dispute resolution center. The judgments of the British courts have received extensive attention from the international trade, maritime, judicial and academic circles, and have been invoked or followed in some countries. In the field of maritime arbitration, London is even more dominant. 75% of the world's maritime arbitrations are conducted in London, more than 90% of shipbuilding contracts choose English law as the applicable law, and more than 80% of shipbuilding contracts choose London arbitration. The author holds that the main reasons are that: firstly, the stability of the law and the predictability of the judgement are strong. Britain is a case law country with a long maritime culture. After years of development, the meaning of English law and important maritime conventions is relatively clear. The overall level of judges is relatively high, and the judicial credibility is strong. The parties are willing to choose English law to resolve disputes. Secondly, a large number of international shipping organizations have gathered in London, and the standard contracts developed and recommended by them usually agree "apply English law" and "London arbitration". Thirdly, the British shipping finance sector is very strong. Banks are investors, insurance companies and mutual insurance associations are usually the final payers of maritime disputes. It has a strong say in the formulation of contract terms, so it is a rational choice to choose familiar laws and settle disputes at home. Fourthly, London has a gathering of talents and a complete industrial chain, which can play a synergistic effect and resolve disputes quickly and economically. Fifthly, path dependence is difficult to change in the short term. In order to clarify the specific meaning of British law and the international maritime convention, the maritime circles and the trade circles have paid huge lawyer fees. For businessmen, costs are important, but risk control is even more critical. Unless other options have obvious advantages or are derived from mandatory provisions of the law, businessmen are usually reluctant to change their original practices.

The author proposes advice for specific measures for China to build an International Maritime Justice Center: firstly, to improve the maritime legal system. The revision of the *Maritime Code* and the *Maritime Special Procedure Law* should focus on absorbing Chinese judicial experience, embodying Chinese judicial wisdom, and forming "Chinese experience" and "Chinese rules" that are generally accepted by the international maritime circle. Secondly, to reform the maritime justice system. The establishment of a high maritime court and the establishment of a complete maritime specialized court system are of great significance for further strengthening the professionalism of maritime justice, better integrating maritime justice resources, and unifying the adjudication scale of maritime justice.

With the advancement of the construction of "Belt and Road", Chinese maritime justice strives for a higher international status and international influence, actively participates in the formulation of international rules and leads the development of international rules, which is an urgent practical need and a responsibility of a major power. China should establish the judicial concept of a great power and accelerate the construction of an International Maritime Justice Center.

2.7 Conflicts between Procedural Rights and Substantive Rights in the Issuance of Chinese Maritime Injunctions and Solutions[①]

In order to resolve conflicts between procedural rights and substantive rights when the maritime court decides to issue the maritime injunction, the author analyzes the factors that hinder the exercise of the entity right of the respondent due to the abuse of maritime injunction in judicial practice and legislation, and puts forward the problems and suggestions in legislative and judicial aspects that: there are currently problems with the formulation of the maritime injunction in China; the *Maritime Special Procedure Law* lacks specific provisions regarding the review of applications for maritime injunction by the maritime court; the content of the maritime injunction is not clear enough; the implementation of the maritime injunction can prevent the respondent from exercising substantive rights according to law; the filing of a maritime injunction case must follow certain principles; the introduction of hearing procedures is in a timely manner; and use reasonably the maritime litigation guarantee system.

In judicial practice, some applicants basically do not consider whether they should apply for a maritime injunction or whether they should apply for evidence preservation when applying for a maritime injunction, or to solve the problem by advanced enforcement or through substantive trial. The author holds that the reasons for the phenomenon are that: ①the parties' factors, because of the lack of legal expertise, it is impossible to distinguish the different application situations between the maritime claim preservation and the maritime injunction system, resulting in the abuse of the maritime injunction; ②there is an understanding of the possibility of relevant legal provisions, and there is a coincidence between the application conditions of the preservation of evidence and

---

① SHEN Xiaoming. Conflicts between Procedural Rights and Substantive Rights in the Issuance of Chinese Maritime Injunctions and Solutions[J]. Water Transport Management, 2017 (7): 22 – 25.

the maritime injunction, both of which are only raised when the maritime claimant is in an emergency, and can be applied to the maritime court before the action or arbitration.

In judicial practice, the applicant's maritime injunction prevents the respondent from being able to realize its legally substantive rights. The kind of application can be regarded as an abuse. There are many cases of abuse, and compulsory delivery is a common situation in maritime judicial practice. In the case, the implementation of the maritime injunction can prevent the respondent from exercising its legally substantive rights. The author holds that it is mainly a problem of the *Maritime Special Procedure Law* in the legislation of the maritime injunction. Firstly, there are problems in the formulation of the maritime injunction in my country. The *Maritime Special Procedure Law* Article 51 stipulates that a maritime injunction refers to a compulsory measure in which the maritime court orders the respondent to act or not in order to protect its legal rights and interests from damage according to the application of the maritime claimant. The biggest problem in the article is to solve procedural issues through substantive norms, namely, in the procedural provisions, it considers it to "in order to protect its legal rights and interests from damage" and order the respondent to act or not. Secondly, from the perspective of procedural law, as a maritime injunction procedure for initiating special procedures for maritime litigation, in addition to reviewing the decision or ruling to the application for the maritime injunction procedure, the maritime court also has to review the decision or ruling to refuse maritime injunction namely reject the application procedure. At present, the *Maritime Special Procedure Law* only stipulates the conditions for applying for a maritime injunction, and does not have any provisions on the procedural rules for the maritime court to accept applications for maritime injunctions. Finally, the implementation of the maritime injunction can prevent the respondent from exercising substantive rights according to law. Although the *Maritime Special Procedure Law* requires the applicant to submit relevant evidence, the maritime injunction has procedural features and does not involve the sharing of the ultimate liability of the parties. The maritime court only conducts general surface evidence review when reviewing the evidence provided by the applicant. Therefore, the approval of the maritime injunction can cause undue loss to the respondent or defendant due to wrong application or wrong trial.

The author puts forward some suggestions on how to solve the problem that the implementation of maritime injunction can lead to the incapacity of the claimant to exercise its legal substantive rights: the hearing system is applied to make up for the vacancy in the law on maritime injunction in my country. The implementation of the hearing system must have a reasonable applicable hearing procedure rules, only to help judges make a fair judgment on the basis of a comprehensive analysis of the facts, improve judicial transparency, and truly protect the interests of both parties.

The maritime injunction has the characteristics of urgency and confidentiality, and the relevant maritime injunction legislation and judicial system in China are not yet perfect. As a law, it gives the parties procedural rights, and the issuance and exercise can lead to the other party's substantive rights being deterred, even the complete loss of substantive rights, or causing litigation burden or waste of judicial resources to the parties. The author recommends that the relevant maritime injunction system in my country should be modified from both legislative and judicial aspects to achieve a balance between the parties' substantive rights and procedural rights.

2.8 *Impact of the General Principles of Civil Law on Shipping Laws*[①]

In order to further clarify the possible impact of the *General Principles of Civil Law* on shipping laws, the author analyzes: the establishment of green principles can guide the legislation of marine environmental protection systems such as compensation for ship pollution damage in China; as for the provisions of convention as the source of civil law, shipping practice is endowed with the effect of dealing with shipping disputes as the official source; the applicable relationship between the *General Principles of Civil Law* and the *Maritime Code* needs to be further clarified in practice.

The *General Principles of Civil Law* Article 9 stipulates that: "any civil activity conducted by civil subjects shall be conducive to saving resources and

---

① SUN Siqi. The Impact of General Principles of Civil Law on Shipping Laws[J]. Water Transport Management, 2017 (9): 33-36.

protecting the ecological environment." The content of the article is called the "green principle", and it is also the first time that Chinese civil and commercial legislation has introduced the establishment of protection of environment and resources as one of the basic principles. The green principle established in the *General Principles of Civil Law* Article 9 are in line with the development direction of contemporary shipping laws. Marine environmental protection is one of the key points of contemporary international maritime legislation. The value objective of shipping laws, especially the *Maritime Code*, shows a trend of increasing emphasis on marine environmental protection. The author holds that: the *Maritime Code* lacks a compensation system for ship pollution damage, and the *Marine Environmental Protection Law of the People's Republic of China* also has only Article 89 and Article 91 concerning liability for compensation for marine environment pollution damage. The law has the function of guiding people's behavior, and the function of the basic principles of civil law is to fill legal loopholes and guide civil legislation. Therefore, the *General Principles of Civil Law* Article 9 establishes the green principle as one of the basic principles of the law, which has positive significance for guiding people to pay more attention to marine environmental protection in shipping activities, as well as guiding the establishment of relevant systems in the maritime legislation such as the revision of China's *Maritime Code*.

The entry into force of the *General Principles of Civil Law* will have a relatively obvious impact on shipping laws. Many legal issues need to be clarified gradually in the course of practice. The author holds that the kind of influence is mainly manifested in: ①for cases where there is no provision in the *Maritime Code* as a special civil law, many provisions of the *General Principles of Civil Law* will be directly applied to the social relationships arising from shipping activities; ②for the problems that the *Maritime Code* does not stipulates clearly, the court will use the *General Principles of Civil Law* as the basis for its interpretation, or give due consideration to the basic principles and specific provisions established by the *General Principles of Civil Law*; ③when the *Maritime Code* is revised in the future, under the premise of maintenance of a special maritime legal system, it will fully consider the integration and harmonization with the *General Principles of Civil Law*, including the creation of some special rules adapted to the development of shipping.

Since the *General Principles of Civil Law* adopts the method of "extracting public factors" to make general provisions for civil activities, most of the impacts of shipping laws are not reflected in the legal regulations of specific shipping activities. The author analyzes the legal use relationship between the *General Principles of Civil Law* and the *Maritime Code*, which shows the impact of the compilation of the Civil Code on shipping laws. Therefore, the shipping industry should pay full attention to the *General Principles of Civil Law* and the compilation of future chapters of the Civil Code.

2.9 Recommendations for Improving Chinese Ship Pollution Damage Compensation System[1]

The authors start from the role of ship pollution damage liability insurance, analyzes the current status of Chinese ship pollution damage compensation system, compares the current ship pollution damage compensation systems, and points out the necessity and urgency of improving Chinese ship pollution damage compensation system. The thesis puts forward suggestions to improve Chinese ship pollution damage compensation system from three aspects, such as carrying out research, revising the relevant laws of ship pollution damage compensation and revising the supporting system.

The authors introduce the compensation system for oil pollution damage of ships in Chinese sea area and inland rivers. As China implements a separate management system for rivers and seas, the liability for ship pollution damage compensation systems are also independent of each other. Divided by pollution area, the system can be divided into inland waters ship pollution damage compensation system and sea area ship pollution damage compensation system; divided by pollutant, the system can be divided into oil pollution damage compensation system and dangerous chemical pollution damage compensation system. The construction of oil pollution damage compensation system for ships in sea area is earliest, which provides a good example for the construction of

---

[1] ZHOU Fangzhen, ZHU Yiyi. Recommendations for Improving Chinese Ship Pollution Damage Compensation System[J]. Water Transport Management, 2017 (11): 30-35.

other damage compensation systems.

The authors clearly show the necessity and urgency of improving Chinese ship pollution damage compensation mechanism through charts. China places ecological civilization on a prominent position and places ecological environmental protection at a strategic height, striving to prevent environmental pollution and ecological damage from the source of decision-making, and solve the problem of environmental restoration. Obtaining adequate compensation for environmental damage is a prerequisite for the successful implementation of environmental restoration measures. The International Maritime Organization has adopted the *International Convention on Liability and Compensation for Damages of Carriage of Toxic and Harmful Substances by Sea*, which establishes an international toxic and harmful substances compensation system similar to the international oil pollution damage compensation mechanism. Perfecting Chinese ship pollution damage compensation mechanism is not only an urgent need for the coordinated development of Chinese shipping industry and marine environmental protection, but also in line with the development trend of the international ship pollution damage compensation system.

The authors put forward suggestions to improve Chinese ship pollution damage compensation mechanism: ①carry out research on the subject. Carry out research on the subject of ship pollution damage compensation liability, find out the situation of ship pollution damage in our country, study and analyze the current status of ship pollution damage compensation in our country, and propose solutions to improve Chinese ship pollution damage compensation mechanism. ②Revise relevant laws on compensation for ship pollution damage. On the basis of the *Environmental Protection Law of the People's Republic of China*, amend the *Prevention and Control of Water Pollution Law of the People's Republic of China*, the *Marine Environmental Protection Law of the People's Republic of China* and the *Maritime Code of the People's Republic of China* to improve relevant laws of the compensation system for ship pollution damage in Chinese waters, and add relevant content such as implementation of oil pollution damage compensation liability insurance in Chinese domestic river waters and dangerous chemical pollution damage compensation liability insurance in coastal waters to provide legal basis for Chinese comprehensive implementation of the ship pollution damage civil liability insurance system. ③ Modify and perfect the supporting system. After the higher law stipulates the basic system of ship pollution damage compensation, appropriate supporting implementation rules will be issued in due course to ensure the smooth operation of the ship pollution damage compensation liability insurance system and the ship pollution damage compensation fund system.

2.10 *Reference Value of Legislation of Carriage of Goods by Sea in Other Parts of East Asia to China* [1]

By examining the main jurisdictions of maritime legislation in other parts of East Asia, South Korea completed the revision of its domestic maritime code in 2007. Japan is undergoing relevant revisions. Its shipping legislation presents the trend of an expansion of the carrier's liability period, maintenance of liability exemption of nautical fault and diversification of transportation document. The author holds that the Fourth Chapter of the *Maritime Code of the People's Republic of China*, "contract of carriage of goods by sea" should be modified to comply with this trend, extending the carrier's liability period to "receiving to delivery", retaining liability exemption of nautical fault, and stipulating relevant provisions about the shipping bill and electronic transportation records.

The authors introduce the premise of the East Asia region's national legislation of carriage of goods by sea that can be used by China for reference: namely, because any law formulation needs to combine with the economic situation of the country (region), the formulation and modification of shipping-related laws cannot ignore the country's (region) shipping economic situation. Countries in East Asia have similar shipping economic situations. In the maritime legal systems of various countries in East Asia, taking Japan as examples, the overall structure of the maritime code is similar. The legislation of carriage of goods by sea in other parts of East Asia is similar to that in China, and has a relatively sufficient basis for reference.

The authors describe in detail the carrier's liability period, the carrier's

---

[1] CAO Shan, JIANG Zhengxiong. Reference Value of Legislation of Carriage of Goods by Sea in Other Parts of East Asia to China [J]. China Maritime Law Study, 2017 (3): 32 – 39.

liability principle and exemption, transportation documents and other rules, compares the maritime law of East Asia with the *Maritime Code*, and proposes suggestions for amendments to the *Maritime Code*: ① regarding the carrier's liability period, the shipping legislation in other parts of East Asia is showing an expanding trend. When the *Maritime Code* is amended, the carrier's liability period should be extended to "receiving to delivery". ②Regarding the principle of liability and exemption for carrier's liability, the shipping legislation in other parts of East Asia retains the liability exemption of nautical fault. The principle of liability for incomplete fault based on the *Hague-Visby Rules* should also be maintained in the present and future revision of the *Maritime Code*. ③Regarding transportation documents, the shipping legislation in other parts of East Asia shows a trend of diversification. When the *Maritime Code* is amended, the relevant rules of the shipping bill and electronic transport records should be stipulated.

Due to the similarity of the shipping economic situation and the maritime legal system, the trend of the legislation of carriage of goods by sea in other parts of East Asia has reference value for China.

3 Summary

The Chapter brings together comprehensive study achievements of many experts and scholars who have drawn the essence of study from home and abroad and studied hard, which involves the study of the forefront of maritime theory and the discussion of major difficult issues, providing valuable contributions to maritime justice norms and maritime dispute resolution, strengthening the synergy between theory study and judicial practice, providing wisdom for the healthy development of Chinese shipping industry.

Chapter 5　Annual Shipping Focus

In 2017, the long-depressed international shipping market came out from the bottom and showed signs of recovery. The continuously growing Shanghai International Shipping Center is actively exploring the construction of a free trade port, testing fully automated terminals, improving the high-end shipping service industry chain, and strengthening the linkage with "Belt and Road" and the Yangtze River Economic Belt... A series of new measures towards "deep blue" have attracted worldwide attention.

The report of the Nineteenth National Congress of the Communist Party of China stated that: "give the pilot free trade zone greater reform autonomy and explore the construction of a free trade port." Shanghai has worked hard to prepare a free trade port construction plan. Constructing a free trade port in Shanghai will not only promote the prosperity of trade, but also promote the development of a large number of modern service industries such as ship supply, shipping finance, insurance and maritime law.

At the beginning of 2017, China's first shipping self-insurance company, COSCO Shipping Captive Insurance Co., Ltd. was established in Shanghai, and shipping insurance formed a complete industrial chain. In October, China Shipowners Mutual Insurance Association entered Shanghai International Shipping Service Center. As various shipping insurance operation centers and intermediary service organizations have settled in succession, Shanghai provides increasingly rich insurance service options for the international shipping industry.

In May 2017, C919, a domestically produced large passenger aircraft developed by COMAC, made its first flight at Pudong International Airport. In December, the first 21,000 TEU container ship built by Waigaoqiao Shipyard was successfully docked. The China International Maritime Exhibition held in Shanghai has become one of the world-class maritime exhibitions that is as famous as the Hamburg Maritime Exhibition. Based on the high-end shipping equipment industry, the business cards of "Made in Shanghai" and "Shanghai Service" in the shipping field complement each other, providing a solid material foundation and technical support for the construction of Shanghai International Shipping Center.

In June and September 2017, COSCO Shipping Group concluded an agreement with Spain's largest terminal operator and Maersk Group successively, to acquire relevant terminal assets. In July, Shanghai Shipping Exchange released "Belt and Road" shipping trade index, which comprehensively and timely reflected the development effectiveness of "Belt and Road" initiative in terms of smooth trade and transportation. The construction and operation of infrastructure such as ports and terminals directly affect the smooth flow of "Belt and Road" trade channels. In Shanghai, port and shipping enterprises settled overseas, which not only achieved a breakthrough in the enterprise's internationalization strategy, but also promoted the interconnection of infrastructure along "Belt and Road".

Shanghai continues to attract and nurture international shipping functional institutions, and the maritime service system is increasingly improved. Asian Maritime Technical Cooperation Center, authorized by the United Nations International Maritime Organization, was established at Shanghai Maritime University in May 2017. This is China's first substantive functional institution authorized by the International Maritime Organization, with the goal of becoming a model platform for leading the green development of the global shipping industry. The Supreme People's Court has confirmed Shanghai Maritime Court as the Shanghai base for international maritime justice. Shanghai Maritime Court issued the outline of the five-year development plan and proposed to construct Shanghai into an international maritime justice center with global influence. Through the construction of Asian Maritime Technical Cooperation Center and International Maritime Justice Shanghai Base, Shanghai continues to attract and nurture international shipping functional institutions and accelerate the formation of a complete maritime service system.

In 2017, the construction of shipping culture achieved great progress. The holding of "Belt and Road" Cultural Round table and other activities, the holding of relevant exhibitions and seminars have enhanced the influence of shipping culture, and made the whole society pay more attention to the development of shipping.

In 2017, Shanghai's legal construction of shipping continued to advance. In order to better serve and guarantee the strategy of the maritime power, the construction of "Belt and Road", Shanghai Free Trade Zone and the construction of Shanghai International Shipping Center during the "13th Five-Year Plan" period, the *Outline of the Five-year Development Plan of Shanghai Maritime Court (2017—2021)* was issued to comprehensively plan the work of Shanghai Maritime Court in the next five years.

A series of meetings and events were held in 2017. It provides a platform for communication, sharing and learning for shipping professionals from Shanghai and all over the country, and deepens cooperation and exchanges in the shipping industry. Bringing together the wisdom of many parties to provide new ideas and new horizons for international cooperation in the current new situation.

1 Yearly Hot Issues

1.1 COSCO Shipping Captive Insurance Co., Ltd. officially announced its establishment

On February 17, COSCO Shipping Captive Insurance Co., Ltd.(hereinafter referred to as COSCO Shipping Insurance) was officially announced in Shanghai. COSCO Shipping Insurance is a secondary subsidiary of the group established by the sole proprietorship of China COSCO Shipping Corporation Limited, with its registered place in Shanghai and registered capital RMB 2 billion. PAN Liang, Chairman of the Supervisory Committee of the State-owned Assets Supervision and Administration Commission of State Council, LI Tianbi, Director of the Water Transport Bureau of the Ministry of Transport, and XIE Feng, Director of Shanghai Municipal Transportation Committee, attended the inaugural meeting, and jointly with XU Lirong, Chairman and Party Secretary of COSCO Shipping Group, and WAN Min, General Manager inaugurated COSCO Shipping Insurance.

In his speech, WAN Min stated that as the first true financial license of COSCO Shipping Group's shipping financial strategy, the establishment of COSCO Shipping Insurance marked the deepening reform of both horizontal and vertical of strategic layout of COSCO Shipping Group's "6+1" industrial cluster was more effective. This was a very important financial strategic layout of COSCO Shipping Group's strategic blueprint, and it had a milestone significance for helping the group build a multi-industry cluster and a global leading comprehensive logistics supply chain service group with shipping, comprehensive logistics and relevant financial services as the pillar. As the first self-insurance company in Shanghai and the first shipping self-insurance company in China, COSCO Shipping Insurance had a profound impact on the shipping industry and insurance industry in Shanghai and even the whole country. As an insurance management platform, risk management tool and cost management center of COSCO Shipping Group, the self-insurance company will make full use of and integrate insurance resources in the group, provided guarantee for the upgrade of the group's risk management capabilities and levels, and provided escorts for strategic security and asset security of the country and provided escorts for the country's "Belt and Road" initiative and "Maritime Power" strategies.

In his speech, ZHANG Lin of Shanghai Municipal Transportation Committee said that shipping enterprises were important participants and performers of "Belt and Road" initiative and the "Going Global" national strategy. While achieving the strategic efficiency goals, they must pay attention to national strategic safety and personnel safety, asset safety, and environmental safety, strengthen identification of risks in safe production and take effective measures to prevent and control risks. Self-insurance company, as a new thing that closely connected China's shipping industry and insurance industry, would surely have a strong vitality and development prospects, would surely escort the specialization of risk management level, the refinement of operational management capabilities and the chain development of business development capabilities of COSCO Shipping Group, and would accumulate more active and rich experience for the exploration and promotion of new forms of China's shipping industry and insurance industry and would provide even more beneficial risk guarantee for the implementation of "Belt and Road" and "Going Global" national strategies. It is hoped that COSCO Shipping Insurance could gradually become a characteristic, capable and highly professional self-insurance company in the domestic insurance industry, and also hoped that the company could develop into a model of the domestic insurance industry and a leader in the global self-insurance field.

Finally, ZHENG Xiaozhe of COSCO Shipping Insurance, thanked the guests for coming and thanked all levels of government agencies, groups and units within the system, as well as colleagues from all walks of life who gave concern and support during the company's preparation! As a tribute to the first anniversary of the establishment of the new group, COSCO Shipping Insurance would innovate and operate according to laws and regulations and fully implement its strategic positioning as the group's "risk management tool, insurance management platform, and cost management center" definitely according to regulatory requirements, and provide a customized risk management special program that would be more suitable to the actual situation of the company for the group and each member unit, wholeheartedly do a good job in service, build the self-insurance company into a domestic leader, and the leading company which would lead the development of the self-insurance company in the international shipping industry.

1.2 9 major port groups and 5 shipping companies jointly established the "Yangtze River Economic Belt Shipping Alliance" in Shanghai

On July 20, 2017, the founding meeting of the Yangtze River Economic Belt Shipping Alliance was held in Shanghai. The Yangtze River Economic Belt Shipping Alliance, jointly established by 9 port groups including SIPG, Ningbo Zhoushan Port Group, and 5 shipping companies such as CSC, is a non-profit industry organization that aims to implement the Party Central Committee and State Council's major strategic deployment to promote the development of the Yangtze River Economic Belt, and adhere to the ecological priority and green development concepts, and exerting the synergistic interaction of the alliance.

The alliance focuses on strengthening regional port and shipping information integration, container, bulk goods, liquid goods and ro-ro goods and other river and ocean combined transportation of goods, ship type standardization, green port and shipping system construction, and maintaining orderly and stable development of the shipping market and cooperation among different fields, relying on the pilot function of Shanghai International Shipping Center and the service radiation function of the shipping centers along the river, innovating business service models and service connotations to meet the market needs of convenience, efficiency, transparency and low cost for the Yangtze River shipping, and strive to create smooth, efficient, safe, green and modern Yangtze River shipping system, and further enhances the support for the development of Yangtze River Economic Belt.

The alliance is guided by the port construction and shipping development of Yangtze River Economic Belt. It promotes the optimal allocation and coordinated development of shipping resources in Yangtze River. It strives to enhance the function of the golden waterway, realize the smooth flow of the channel, the interconnection of the hubs, the connection between the river and the sea, and the direct inspection and customs clearance. It will reduce the cost of comprehensive logistics of enterprises and serve the growth of trade in Yangtze River Economic Belt and promote economic development. The establishment of a shipping alliance in Yangtze River Economic Belt, giving full play to the pilot role and the service radiation function of Shanghai International Shipping Center, promoting the optimized allocation and coordinated development of shipping resources in Yangtze River, strengthening the division of labor and cooperation among ports, and improving modern shipping services are essential for accelerating the development of green shipping playing the role of the golden waterway and serve the national strategy of Yangtze River Economic Belt.

1.3 The world's largest automated terminal, Shanghai Port Yangshan Deepwater Port Phase Ⅳ opened

On December 10, 2017, Shanghai Port Yangshan Deepwater Port Phase Ⅳ opened.

As the world's largest automated terminal-Shanghai Yangshan Deepwater Port Phase Ⅳ Terminal officially opened for trial production, injecting new impetus into Shanghai Port's acceleration into the forefront of the world's shipping center. Shanghai Port Yangshan Port Area, designed and constructed by CCCC and built by China State Construction Engineering, is the world's first island-type deep-water container port area, with container throughput accounting for more than 40% of Shanghai Port, which becomes an important support point for Shanghai to be an international shipping center.

Yangshan Deepwater Port is the world's largest island-type artificial deepwater port and a strategic and pivotal project for the construction of Shanghai International Shipping Center. The first to third phases of the Yangshan Port project have now been completed, with a total of 16 deep-water container berths of 70,000 to 150,000 tons, releasing the annual production capacity of container throughput of more than 15 million TEU. Yangshan Port Phase Ⅳ Terminal can be equipped with 7 large-scale container deep-water berths, with a design capacity of 4 million TEUs in the initial period and 6.3 million TEUs in the long term since the construction from 2014. The first batch of 10 bridge cranes, 40 rail cranes, and 50 AGVs that have completed commissioning will be put into port trial production. According to the plan, 26 bridge cranes, 120 rail cranes, 130 AGVs will be equipped in Yangshan Phase Ⅳ finally. It is unprecedented for an automated terminal of such a large scale to be built and put into operation at first time. After the opening of Yangshan Port Phase Ⅳ Terminal, the annual throughput of Shanghai Port will exceed 40 million TEU. This figure is the total throughput of all ports in America, and it is also one-tenth of the current annual throughput in global ports.

Yangshan Phase Ⅳ is also known as "Devil Terminal". Compared with the traditional container terminal, this unmanned "Devil Terminal" has the biggest feature of realizing the intelligent operation of the whole process of container loading and unloading in the terminal, horizontal transportation and yard loading and unloading. This means that there will be no more people in the entire terminal and storage yard. Not only the shore bridge does not need to be driven, but also the container truck does no longer need. The container will be directly transported to the storage yard by the automatic driving unmanned AGV car. The bridge crane in the yard is also unmanned. The original terminal operators are all transferred to the monitoring room, and all operations can be completed by facing the computer screen.

The fully automated terminal in Phase Ⅳ will reach 40 boxes/hour, far exceeding the operating efficiency of the manual terminal and reducing labor by 70%. The terminal can operate 24 hours a day, ensuring the personal safety of the operators, the working environment has also been greatly improved, and it is electrically driven to save energy and protect the environment. The TOS system of the terminal independently developed by SIPG and the ECS system independently developed by ZPMC command the fully automated terminal. The two constitute the "brain" and "nerve" of Yangshan Phase Ⅳ terminal. The development and application of these two systems have enabled the fully automated terminals in China to truly use the "China Core".

Yangshan Phase IV fully-automated terminal is the world's largest single fully-automated container terminal and the world's most comprehensively automated terminal. Its completion and commissioning mark a milestone upgrade in the operation mode and technology application of the China port industry, and provide a guarantee for Shanghai Port to consolidate the world's No.1 position in port goods throughput.

1.4 Shanghai Shipping Exchange officially released "Belt and Road" shipping trade index

On July 11, 2017, under the guidance of Shanghai Municipal Transportation Committee, the 2nd "21st Century Maritime Silk Road" Construction Summit Forum co-sponsored by China Maritime Museum and China Financial Information Center was held in Shanghai. Shanghai Shipping Exchange officially released "Belt and Road" shipping trade index at the forum.

In order to comprehensively and timely reflect the achievements of "Belt and Road" construction, especially the achievements in the areas of unimpeded trade and transportation, Shanghai Shipping Exchange, under the guidance of Ministry of Transport and Shanghai "Belt and Road" Promotion Working Group Office, researched in 2015 and carried out external trial operation and released the index in 2015. After the index was released, it was highly concerned by many domestic and foreign governments, finance, and media organizations, and also received high evaluation and recognition from the industry. Some port and shipping enterprises consulted the index, checked the index, and ordered the index. After two years of trial operation, the index structure was continuously adjusted and optimized, and was officially released on July 11, 2017.

"Belt and Road" shipping trade index is formally released to the outside world, which consists of 3 major categories of indexes including "Belt and Road" trade volume index, "Belt and Road" freight volume index, and "Maritime Silk Road" freight index, four major types of goods including subdividing coal, ore, crude oil and containers, and the transportation method is not limited to sea carriage, but also includes railways. In the future, it will expand and increase a variety of transportation methods such as aviation. "Belt and Road" shipping trade index takes January 2015 as the base period, and the base period index is 100 points. Shanghai Shipping Exchange released on the last Wednesday of each month.

"Belt and Road" freight volume index includes a composite index and five component indexes (respectively, the railway freight export volume index from China to the countries along "Belt and Road", the export container shipping volume index from China (Shanghai) to the countries along "Road", and import coal shipping volume, iron ore shipping volume, crude oil shipping volume index from China to the countries along "Road") and sub-regional index. "Belt" freight volume index reflects the changes in railway freight volume from China to Mongolia, Russia, Central Asia, Southeast Asia, and Europe along the Silk Road Economic Belt; "Road" freight volume index reflects the changes in sea freight volume of major goods such as mines, coal, oils, and tanks between China and countries along the side, involving many regions in Southeast Asia, West Asia, South Asia, Europe, Oceania, and North Africa along "Maritime Silk Road".

"Maritime Silk Road" freight index includes a composite index and four component indexes (respectively, "Maritime Silk Road" export container freight index, import container freight index, import dry bulk freight index and import crude oil freight index) and subdivision route index. The index covers the main goods types and main routes of "Maritime Silk Road" connecting Asia, Africa and Europe.

ZHANG Ye, President of Shanghai Shipping Exchange, said that, "'Belt and Road' initiative is an important foundation for China to build a new pattern of opening up to the outside world. It is organically linked to strategies including the construction of free trade zones, coordinated development of Beijing, Tianjin and Hebei, and Yangtze River Economic Belt and mutual supported. It is also inextricably linked to the comprehensive deepening of reforms and the strategy of a shipping power. The most important manifestation of the shipping industry in 'Belt and Road' initiative is the freight volume and freight rates. Based on the volume and freight rates, the shipping element information in 'Belt and Road' initiative will be disclosed by Shanghai Shipping Exchange, which will enhance the transparency and influence of the market".

"Belt and Road" shipping trade index not only reflects the development of trade, but also directly reflects the changes and interrelationships among trade volume, freight volume, and transportation prices; it can not only give full play to the construction of Shanghai International Shipping Center and "Belt and Road" bridgehead advantages, but also can more fully reflect the implementation effect of "Belt and Road" initiative at the national level. In the future, relying on "Belt and Road" index, Shanghai Shipping Exchange will actively promote the application of "Belt and Road" shipping trade index, and build a shipping trade index cooperation platform for "Belt and Road" countries jointly participated.

1.5 Shanghai Shipping Exchange released FDI

On November 28, 2017, the 2017 Shanghai Shipping Trading Forum was held in Shanghai, and the theme of the forum was set as "Shipping decision in the era of big data". People from all walks of life from Ministry of Transport, Shanghai Municipal Transportation Committee, Shanghai Pudong New District, and the shipping industry talked about the breakthroughs and innovations in the era of big data from multiple perspectives.

After nearly 20 years of development, the "Shanghai Shipping Index" has covered major market segments relevant to shipping, such as containers, dry bulk goods, oil tankers, trading ships, "Belt and Road", crew remuneration, and prosperity of shipping enterprises, forming a overall, authoritative and comprehensive index system. The brand series of "Shanghai Shipping Index" has become a barometer of the trend of the shipping market, providing objective basis for the government to grasp the market trend and corporation decision-making. Some of the indexes play an innovative and decisive role in many fields such as index-linked agreements and freight derivatives with index as settled objects.

Shanghai Shipping Exchange announced at the forum that: "Shanghai Shipping Index" has added a new member, FDI, which has been officially put into external trial operation. CCTFI was independently commissioned from CBFI and put into trial operation, and CDFI has also been adjusted and optimized.

In the past ten years, the global shipping center has moved eastward to the Asia-Pacific region, and the Far East has become increasingly prominent in the global dry bulk trade. The Far East market has become a top priority for global shipping. In order to adapt to the trend of the eastward movement of the shipping center, under the guidance of Ministry of Transport and with the support of the editorial unit of the China Import Dry Bulk Freight Index, Shanghai Shipping Exchange conceived that based on CDFI, developing the Far East dry bulk index. The significance of moving from China to the Far East is not only to provide more and more comprehensive information references to the market, but also to lay the foundation for China's shipping enterprises to go out and further participate in the international division of labor and enhance international competitiveness; the significance of moving from China to the Far East is also to take index as a basis, accelerate the formation of "Far East Prices" and form influence and voice in the entire Far East market and even the Asia-Pacific market.

1.6 Fully implement ship-to-shore oil change in Yangtze River Delta Ship Emission Control Area

From September 1, 2017, Yangtze River Delta Ship Emission Control Area implemented the relevant requirements of Ship Emission Control Area 2018 in advance, namely, all ships should switch to low-sulfur fuel oil as required after arrival, or adopt shore power, tail gas reprocessing and other alternative measures.

According to the requirements of Ship Emission Control Area plan issued by Ministry of Transport, from January 1, 2018, ships should use fuel oil with a sulfur content of 0.5% or less during docking at all ports in the emission control area. Yangtze River Delta Ship Emission Control Area advances this requirement to September 1, 2017 and implement it four months ahead of the original plan to further promote the development of green shipping and ship energy conservation and emission reduction.

In addition, the core ports of Yangtze River Delta Ship Emission Control Area, Shanghai Port, Ningbo Zhoushan Port, Suzhou Port, and Nantong Port have taken the lead in implementing the Ship Emission Control Area plan on April 1, 2016. So far, Yangtze River Delta Ship Emission Control Area has been fully implemented ship docking oil change measures. Over the past year, monitoring data from the environmental protection department has shown that air quality has improved in all parts of Yangtze River Delta, and the concentration of sulfur dioxide in regions near ports has dropped significantly. From April to December 2016, compared with the same period in 2015, the sulfur dioxide concentration of Shanghai Donggaoqiao Monitor Station decreased by 52% year-on-year; the sulfur dioxide concentration of Xinjiangwan Monitor Station decreased by 23% year-on-year. In the first half of 2017, the sulfur dioxide concentration at Ningbo Zhenhai Air Quality Monitor Point decreased by 31% year-on-year; the sulfur dioxide concentration at Beilun Air Quality Monitor Point decreased by 21% year-on-year.

1.7 Waigaoqiao Shipbuilding launched its first 21,000-TEU container ship

On December 25, 2017, the first 21,000-TEU container ship (H1416) built by Waigaoqiao Shipbuilding for COSCO Shipping Group was successfully docked at Changxing Heavy Industry. This is by far the largest container ship under construction with the largest main scale and the largest container capacity in China, and it once again sets the record of shipbuilding for the largest container ship in China. This is another breakthrough in China's shipbuilding industry, marking the success of Waigaoqiao Shipbuilding as International "building club" for super-large container ships.

The total length of the container ship is about 400 meters, the width is 58.6 meters, and the depth is 33.5 meters. It is equivalent to the longitudinal arrangement of 4 football fields. The design draught is 14.5 meters, the structural draught is 16 meters, the speed is 22 knots, and the number of containers is 21,237-TEU, among which the number of cold boxes is 1,000-TEU.

As a typical representative of super-large container ships, the container ship is tailor-made for COSCO Shipping Group by CSSC, developed and designed by MARIC, which fully considers the individual requirements of shipowners, custom-designed combined with the shipowner's operating characteristics, and its loading performance and hydrodynamic performance have been comprehensively optimized. It has broken through the key technology of super-large container ship structure design, and has excellent technical and economic indicators and environmental protection indicators.

In order to improve the intelligent level of ships, for the first time in China, the real ship application of intelligent system is realized on 20,000-box class container ships, equipped with intelligent system, and the i-ship (N, M, E, I) intelligent ship class symbol of CCS Classification Society will be obtained. In addition, the ship conforms to the LR Classification Society's GR (A, S, E (M)) classification symbol design technology to meet the feasibility of future dual-fuel conversion at a minimum cost, while using an efficient host and optimal advanced design, to achieve excellent energy efficiency and emission control.

The construction of container ship has not only successfully completed many technical breakthroughs, such as the use of TOFD new technology, the entire ship positioning flaw detection no left; also successfully accumulates such as multi-island construction in the dock, large section shift, digital test box, rail frame precision control, medium voltage power testing, quality inspection and control and key technologies in the construction of super-large container ships, have provided valuable experience for the Chinese shipbuilding industry

1.8 Shanghai became the world's third city with annual air goods volume exceeding 4 million tons

On December 15, 2017, the annual air goods volume of Shanghai Airport (including Pudong Airport and Hongqiao Airport) exceeded 4 million tons for the first time. As a result, Shanghai became the city with global third annual air goods volume of more than 4 million tons after Hong Kong, China and Memphis, USA.

This is another great event for Shanghai to become the world's fifth billion-air passenger city in 2016. It is a milestone for the construction of Shanghai Airport's aviation hub. It is also an important achievement for the construction of Shanghai International Shipping Center. It is an important manifestation of the comprehensive strength of Shanghai, an internationalization metropolis.

In 1998, after the completion of Shanghai Airport Group, it began to seek the development of air freight business. In 1999, Pudong International Airport was completed and put into operation, and the first-stage goods facilities started operations simultaneously. In 2004, the *Shanghai Aviation Hub Strategic Plan* was formulated, which put forward the strategy of developing freight and passenger transport simultaneously, with equal emphasis on international and domestic development, and further clarified the status of air freight in the development of urban economy. In 2011, an action plan for "building a world-class air freight hub" was compiled. In 2012, it put forward the Pudong Airport Freight striving for the "World No.1" goal. In 2015, Shanghai Airport Aviation Logistics Development Company was established to integrate the airport's internal goods resources, actively promote the construction of an air freight hub, and proposed the goal of building the most attractive world-class air freight hub.

In 2002, Shanghai Airport's goods volume exceeded 1 million tons; in 2005, Shanghai Airport's goods volume exceeded 2 million tons; in 2008, Pudong Airport's goods volume ranked third in the world's airports; in 2010, Shanghai Airport's goods volume exceeded 3 million tons; in 2017, Shanghai Airport's goods volume exceeded 4 million tons.

In recent years, the compound growth rate of goods and mail at Shanghai Airport is 5%, goods and mail throughput accounts for 1/4 of the national airport goods and mail throughput, and international goods and mail throughput accounts for nearly 1/2 of the national airport international goods and mail throughput. The goods and mail volume of Shanghai Airlines Port only accounts for about 0.8% of the total goods throughput of Shanghai Port, but it creates 34.2% of the total value of import and export cargo value of Shanghai Port.

In terms of hardware, Shanghai Pudong and Hongqiao have a total of six runways and three goods and mail international (regional) transshipment centers. It is the first airport in the country that freight functional area are included in the comprehensive bonded area and pilot free trade zone, leading the construction of dedicated freight infrastructure to major competitors. In terms of software, the utilization rate of electronic waybills of Shanghai Airport reached 52% in 2017, ranking second in the world's airports and first in the country. The air goods freight information integration system is maturing, and the construction of smart logistics parks is actively promoted.

Shanghai Airport Group "built a nest to attract the phoenix". In 1999, Shanghai Pudong International Airport Freight Station Co., Ltd. (PACTL) and China Eastern Freight Station Company settled in Pudong Airport and put into operation; in 2000, Pudong Airport International Express Center was put into operation. Fedex, UPS, DHL and TNT gather in Pudong; in 2009, Shanghai Pudong International Airport West District Public Freight Station Co., Ltd., the largest operating entity of the Asian single public freight station, was formally established and put into operation; in 2008, the UPS transshipment center was put into operation; in 2013, DHL North Asia Hub was put into operation. In November of the same year, DHL started the project of international transit transportation gathering of air express as a free trade zone system innovation; in 2017, Fedex International Freight Express Center was put into operation, and then Pudong Airport has become the world's only airport that global three major international logistics integration business entered.

Shanghai Airport actively seeks strategic cooperation with new domestic carriers. In May 2016, Shanghai Airport and SF Express formally concluded a contract, and SF Express Domestic Express Distribution Center project landed in Pudong Airport Express Center. Shanghai Airport is currently negotiating with strategics customers including Post and SF Express to explore the feasibility of further building air freight facilities at Pudong Airport in the future.

By building a world-class aviation integrated cargo hub, Shanghai Airport is further building a route network connecting major airports along "Belt and Road", serving industrial transfer and economic and trade cooperation along "Belt and Road", and enhancing the international competitiveness of "Belt and Road" countries. In recent years, Shanghai Airport has witnessed a rapid increase in goods volume entering and leaving major airports along "Belt and Road". In 2017, Shanghai Airport Group also concluded a memorandum of strategic cooperation with Russian Air Bridge Aviation to jointly assist in the construction of China-Russia air corridors and establish a closer collaboration mechanism.

In recent years, Pudong Airport has been awarded the title of Best Freight Airport in the World and Best Freight Airport in Asia. In 2017, it also won the title of Best Green Airport in the World.

As of the end of 2017, more than 100 airlines operate scheduled flights in Shanghai to carry out freight operations. Among them, the Pudong Airport route network covers 279 cities on five continents, and the Hongqiao Airport route network covers Japan, South Korea, Hong Kong, Macao and Taiwan and 87 domestic cities. Shanghai Airport Group strives to build a comprehensive international aviation hub with outstanding hub advantages, high-end element clustering, and complete functional layout, becoming a world-class aviation integrated freight hub that radiates the world and faces the Asia-Pacific region, providing strong support for Shanghai to move towards global cities.

1.9 Asian Maritime Technical Cooperation Center was established in Shanghai

On May 15, 2017, Asian Maritime Technical Cooperation Center (MTCC Asia) authorized by the United Nations International Maritime Organization was established at Shanghai Maritime University.

This is China's first substantive organization authorized by the United Nations International Maritime Organization and the only cooperation center in Asia with global maritime technology coordination qualifications and capabilities. It aims to promote China's shipping industry and the global shipping industry to achieve green development and sustainable development.

The construction of "Belt and Road" service is an important topic of Asia Maritime Technical Cooperation Center. The center will promote Shanghai to become the leading city in the construction of the "21st Century Maritime Silk Road", and enhance Shanghai's level in the construction of global shipping think tanks and global influence science and innovation centers. It will exert a far-reaching influence on the development of Shanghai International Shipping Center and even the whole Chinese shipping industry.

The center aims to accomplish five important tasks: implement the mission and tasks of the International Maritime Organization, grasp the advanced concepts and culture of shipping environmental protection, make full use of the development of shipping technology and management, and focus on the capacity construction of reduction of emissions and energy efficiency of ships in the Asian shipping industry and achieving sustainable development of the global socio-economic.

In the past 30 years, the United Nations International Maritime Organization (IMO) has been committed to constructing a global regional maritime technical cooperation center, carrying out extensive technical exchanges and cooperation, and promoting the global shipping industry's emission reduction and energy efficiency improvement concepts and strategies. IMO decided to construct a global network of ship emission reduction and energy efficiency technical cooperation centers, and on April 15, 2016, issued an invitation to the world to apply for hosting the maritime technical cooperation center.

As a direct link of Asian shipping industry to IMO, the world's highest maritime legislature, and its international platform on advanced environmental protection concepts, the center is carefully guided by IMO and coordinated with the other four MTCCs in the world. It is planned to be established as an important platform for international communication and cooperation in Asia and global shipping professional technical field.

1.10 Shanghai Maritime Court was confirmed as the "Shanghai Base for International Maritime Justice of the Supreme People's Court"

On March 23, 2017, Shanghai Maritime Court formally held the *Outline of the Five-year Development Plan of Shanghai Maritime Court* (2017—2021) (hereinafter referred to as the *Outline of the Five-year Plan*) consultation symposium, experts and scholars from shipping departments, research institutions, large-scale shipping companies and Shanghai High People's Court were invited to participate in the conference, and a larger and deeper solicitation of opinions was launched again. Shanghai Maritime Court sorted out all the feedback at the symposium, and after repeated pondering and research, finally formulated the official *Outline of the Five-year Plan* and was issued on April 12, 2017.

This is the first five-year development plan issued by national maritime courts. It has forward-looking guidelines and development goals and refreshing planning tasks and implementation requirements comprehensively and systematically improves the strategic positioning and service level of Shanghai Maritime Court in the future.

The purpose of formulating the *Outline of the Five-year Plan* this time is to provide Shanghai Maritime Court with a strategic, forward-looking, and guiding program of action in the overall interests of service in order to better condense, enhance, and release the inner vitality, and promote the continuous innovation of the court.

The *Outline of the Five-year Plan* clearly clarifies the overall goal of the Shanghai Maritime Court's development by 2021: with characteristics of "modern", "innovative", "professional", "wise", "transparent" and build the domestic advanced and international first-class maritime court that is judicial functioning, justice and efficient and has distinctive professional characteristic, solid talents foundation, advanced information technology, can all-round adapt to that service guarantees national major strategic implementation and economic and social development judicial requirements and match the status of Shanghai International Shipping Center, meet with requirements that speeding up the construction of Shanghai into the socialist modernization international metropolis, and take the lead in fully realizing the modernization of maritime trial system and maritime trial capacity.

Shanghai Maritime Court "self-pressurized" in the *Outline of the Five-year Plan* to further clarify the specific goals of the maritime trial work in the future, and strive to achieve "more effectively serve for the strategy of the country, a substantial increase in the credibility of the justice, an increasing international influence of the justice, judicial supply capacity significantly enhances, and judicial innovation practices continue to deepen".

In recent years, Shanghai Maritime Court has been committed to creating a new model of "Internet + Maritime Trial", which has successively launched a series of initiatives such as online filing, online mediation, remote court trial, mobile case handling, online overseas evidence review, online ship data analysis, and online ship auction and creating a new pattern of maritime trial work that integrates intelligence, network, sunshine and mobile.

On March 13, 2016, ZHOU Qiang, President of the Supreme People's Court, clearly stated in his work report that it was necessary to continue to deepen judicial disclosure and speed up the construction of a "smart court". In July of the same year, Shanghai High People's Court researched and formulated the *"Data Court" Construction and Development Plan* (2017—2019), and continued to promote the in-depth development of the informatization of Shanghai courts. Shanghai Maritime Court tightly focuses on the requirements for constructing a "data court" and also puts forward clear development goals in the *Outline of the Five-year Plan*.

On April 19, 2017, Shanghai Maritime Court Maritime Linkage Command Center was officially opened. Maritime Linkage Command Center is composed of eight modules: trial management, team building, overall service, information centralized control, police support, command center, intelligent analysis with deep maritime characteristics, and linkage coordination. Among them, ship data analysis system in the intelligent analysis module is the first of its kind in national maritime courts, and it has the functions of ship positioning analysis and dynamic simulation of ship collision at sea.

Shanghai Maritime Court will conscientiously implement the objectives and tasks set out in the *Outline of the Five-year Plan* and strive to construct Shanghai into an international maritime judicial center with global influence, providing a strong forceful maritime judicial service guarantee for the implementation of major national strategies and the economic and social development of Shanghai and its surrounding areas.

2 Free Trade Zone and Modern Shipping Service Products

2.1 Ministry of Commerce carried out work to promote the establishment of free trade port zones

On October 26, 2017, Ministry of Commerce, together with relevant provinces, cities and departments, actively worked on establishing a free trade port area on the basis of building high-standard and high-level pilot free trade zones.

The report of the 19th National Congress of the Communist Party of China proposed that the pilot free trade zone should be given greater autonomy for reform and explore the construction of free trade ports. Gao Feng, a spokesman for the Ministry of Commerce, said that this put forward higher requirements for the construction of the reform and opening-up test field, pointed out new directions, required us to benchmark higher standards, and promotes a more comprehensive and in-depth new pattern of opening up.

In the *Comprehensive Deepening of the Reform and Opening-up of China (Shanghai) Pilot Free Trade Zone* issued by State Council in March, it was clearly proposed to set up a free trade port zone to benchmark the highest international level and implement a higher standard trade supervision system. Ministry of Commerce is working with Shanghai and relevant departments to study and formulate relevant construction plans.

In addition, Zhejiang Pilot Free Trade Zone has also formulated the development goal of the preliminary establishment of a free trade port zone pioneer zone, docking with international standards, and promoting the liberalization of international bulk commodities trade with oil products as the core.

In the next step, Ministry of Commerce will study and implement the spirit of the 19th National Congress of the Party in depth, work closely with relevant provinces, municipalities and departments to closely follow the core task of system innovation in the pilot fee trade zone, intensify efforts to explore the construction of a free trade port, and further highlight the comprehensive deepening of reform and expand the role of the opening test field.

2.2 Shanghai Free Trade Zone released the 2017 action plan

State Council has officially issued the *Comprehensive Deepening of the Reform and Opening-up of China (Shanghai) Pilot Free Trade Zone* (Version 3.0). It was mentioned in the press conference of Shanghai Municipal Government on April 2, 2017 that Shanghai will clarify the subject responsibilities and implementation responsibilities according to this "Version 3.0" plan, and drive the overall advancement with key breakthroughs, further refine the measures, and come up with 2017 action plan, form a joint effort to promote implementation, and comprehensively deepen reform in a larger scope.

When formulating plans, it insisted on taking institutional innovation as the core, and took the lead in establishing an institutional system that was in line with international economic and trade rules, striving to obtain more replicable and scalable institutional innovation results, and further demonstrate the role of comprehensively deepening reform and expanding the opening test field. Adhere to the highest standards to find weaknesses and shortcomings, with the goal of constructing the most open and free trade park, and according to the highest international standards and the best level, comprehensively deepen the reform measures to promote trade and investment liberalization and facilitation and show the world China's distinctive attitude of opening up in all respects.

The "Version 3.0" plan proposes that Shanghai Pilot Free Trade Zone should target the highest international standards and implement a higher standard "first-line liberalization" and "second-line safe and efficient control" trade supervision system. Shanghai will combine the construction of a free trade port zone to further promote the construction of the single window of the highest international standard, including efforts to achieve full coverage of port law enforcement and trade management; and docking with the single window system of national ministries and committees, and all the permits and qualification certificates of various ports are included; all links of port logistics are fully penetrated, and all links of port logistics are included in the single window of international trade.

Meanwhile, Shanghai Pilot Free Trade Zone focuses more on the system integration of reforms, enhance the systemicness, integrity, and synergy of institutional innovation, and strive to improve the "four systems"; investment management system with equal access and orderly competition for various market players; a trade supervision service system that promotes the transformation and upgrading of trade and facilitates customs clearance; a financial service system that deepens financial innovation and effectively prevents and controls risks; a government management system that meets the requirements of market economy rules and modernization of governance capabilities, forming a comprehensive reform situation.

LU Fangzhou, Deputy Head of Pudong New District, said that in order to strengthen the system integration of trade facilitation reform measures and promote the transformation of trade development methods, Shanghai Pilot Free Trade Zone would benchmark high international standards and establish and improve a set of institutional innovation system of links with international investment and trade regulations, to gradually shape, mature, and improve, "Key tasks include promoting comprehensive customs supervision reform, deepening classification supervision system of goods status, comprehensively optimizing the 'single window' of international trade, enhancing trade and shipping functions, and serving the construction of Shanghai International Trade Center and Shipping Center".

PENG Wenhao, Deputy Director of the Municipal Industry and Commerce Bureau, said that in 2017, the reform of the "multiple certificates in one" registration system will be further promoted. According to the *Opinions on Promoting the Reform of the "Multiple Certificates in One" Registration System* issued by the State Administration of Industry and Commerce, it will be connected with Municipal Commerce Committee, Municipal Public Security Bureau, People's Bank of China Shanghai Branch, Shanghai Customs, Shanghai Entry-Exit Inspection and Quarantine Bureau and other departments, and integrate more enterprise-related certificates, realize inter-departmental information sharing at a deeper level, reduce repeated certificate issuance and repeated submission of materials, and facilitate the masses to do business and start businesses.

Standing at a new starting point, Shanghai Pilot Free Trade Zone focuses more on linkage development in the next step, focusing on strengthening the linkage between the reform of the pilot free trade zone and the reform of Shanghai, the linkage with Shanghai International Financial Center and Science and Technology Innovation Center, and actively serving the construction of national strategies like "Belt and Road" and the development of Yangtze River Economic Belt, giving full play to the role of radiation of the pilot free trade zone.

"At present, Shanghai Pilot Free Trade Zone has become an important channel for the country to go out. The demand of enterprises is very strong. It can take advantage of the trend and closely focus on the construction of serving 'Belt and Road', with the purpose of global resource allocation and core of international production capacity cooperation. It can rely on the interconnection of infrastructure and be supported by the public service system and treat the construction of the free trade zone as an important hub for various enterprises and factors to go out". YANG Chao, Deputy Director of Municipal Commerce Committee, said that Shanghai would continue to improve the management system of foreign investment cooperation with convenience as the core, and promote the Ministry of Commerce to relax the conditions of free trade pilot zone for investment and construction of high-tech, infrastructure, biomedicine, high-end manufacture in countries along "Belt and Road", explore breakthroughs in qualification management system focusing on project contract, and carry out relevant explorations and pilots.

Regarding the field of financial reform, LI Jun, Deputy Director of Municipal Finance Office, said that, in order to promote the implementation of the "Golden Reform 40", Shanghai would further deepen the pilot free trade zone financial opening innovation pilot, and at the same time benchmark the national strategy and the overall deployment of financial reform and opening up to serve construction of "Belt and Road" and the RMB internationalization strategy to strengthen linkages with the construction of science and technology innovation centers and international shipping centers, continuously amplify the "Golden Reform" effect of the pilot free trade zone, and continuously enhance the real economic function of financial services.

LU Fangzhou revealed that on the linkage between Shanghai Pilot Free Trade Zone and Science and Technology Innovation Center, in 2017, it promoted the establishment of a fast-authorized, fast-defined, and fast-protected intellectual property protection center in Pudong, China, and promoted the arrival of the new deal policy "double self" talent entry and exit policies by Ministry of Public Security to attract more overseas high-level talents to the region for innovation and entrepreneurship.

2.3 2017 China Free Trade Zone Development Index was released

At the 5th China Pilot Free Trade Zone Forum held on September 16, 2017, Shanghai University of Finance and Economics released the 2017 "Shanghai University of Finance and Economics China Pilot Free Trade Zone Development Index". The results showed that Shanghai Free Trade Zone Index was 81.35, which was ahead of Guangdong, Tianjin and Fujian Free Trade Zones, and had certain first-mover advantages. Guangdong, Tianjin and Fujian were 80.58, 79.71 and 79.90 respectively. The development gap between free trade zone established later with Shanghai is narrowing.

Professor ZHAO Xiaolei, Dean of the Shanghai Development Institute/Free Trade Zone Institute of Shanghai University of Finance and Economics, said that the index was the result of a comprehensive survey of more than 2,000 enterprises, the public, relevant experts and publicly disclosed economic data by the Shanghai University of Finance and Economics project team. At the same time, it considered the changes and interactions in the areas of investment, foreign trade, public finance, finance and employment in the free trade zone, combined with the characteristics of the development of the free trade zone to judge the comprehensive development status of the free trade zone and sought the periodic development law of the free trade zone.

The "Development Index" examines the development of the free trade zone from the subjective and objective dimensions, and defines and evaluates index system from the three levels of confidence, innovation and impact, which are used to evaluate the development of four free trade zones in Shanghai, Tianjin, Guangdong and Fujian. "Development Index" includes development confidence index, innovation index and influence index.

The confidence index is compiled based on the subjective judgments and psychological feelings of enterprises and the public on the development of the free trade zone, reflecting the public and enterprises' confidence in the future development of the free trade zone. The results showed that the comprehensive development confidence index was 80.96. It shows that the free trade zone can bring about a significant positive impact on reform and opening up, regional economy, enterprise development and public life. At the same time, the enterprises' sense of gain is further strengthened.

The innovation index is used to measure the optimization effect of the business environment of the free trade zone. It mainly targets five aspects such as the transformation of government functions, the expansion and opening up of investment fields, financial innovation, trade facilitation, and management system innovation. The results showed that the innovation index of the free trade zone development was 81.04, which was slightly higher than the confidence index. This shows that the development of the free trade zone in terms of institutional innovation has accelerated, and it has been unanimously endorsed by enterprises, the public and experts. From the perspective of the four free trade zones, Shanghai was 81.98, Guangdong was 81.39, Tianjin was 80.49, and Fujian was 80.41. Shanghai and Guangdong are in a leading position. They take the lead in institutional innovations such as "license separation" and post-event supervision several free trade zones.

The influence index reflects the influence and spread of the free trade zone on regional economic development and public life. The index showed that the free trade zone's influence index was 80.73, Shanghai was 81.62, Guangdong was 79.82, Tianjin was 77.88 and Fujian was 77.53. Zhao Xiaolei held that Shanghai Free Trade Zone, as the first pilot, was more prominent in economic development. The free trade zone has a significant impetus for the economic development of the area where it is located, but the impact on the surrounding areas still needs to be improved.

However, during the investigation, the project team also found that the confidence and satisfaction of enterprises located in the free trade zone were significantly higher than those outside the zone, and the scale and establishment time of the enterprise had a negative impact on confidence and evaluation.

In addition, the public does not understand the concepts of "license separation", "negative list" and "market access", which reflects to a certain extent that the transparency of the free trade zone policy interpretation, development planning and publicity efforts needs to be improved. Service industries such as culture and education, tourism and leisure have relatively low evaluation of the development of free trade zones, which reflects the need for the free trade zones to be more open to related service industries.

On the whole, it is necessary to further strengthen the reform and opening up, improve the legal system construction of the relevant system of the free trade zone, and increase the economic influence of the free trade zone, which is an important development direction in the future.

2.4 Under the framework of "Belt and Road", Shanghai Free Trade Zone and ASEAN Shipping Investment Law Seminar were successfully held in Shanghai

On June 27, 2017, sponsored by China (Shanghai) Pilot Free Trade Zone Commercial Committee (Shipping Office), undertaken by Shanghai Arbitration Commission International Shipping Arbitration Court, and ASEAN Legal Alliance, China (Shanghai) Pilot Free Trade Zone Overseas Investment Service Platform, the Law School of Shanghai Maritime University and Shanghai Bar Association jointly cooperated under the framework of "Belt and Road" and Shanghai Pilot Free Trade Zone and ASEAN Shipping Investment Law Seminar were successfully held at Shanghai Shipping and Financial Industry Base.

Focusing on the main line of opportunities and challenges facing the construction of "Belt and Road", the seminar started with how to promote international cooperation, assist local governments and enterprises to actively integrate into "Belt and Road" construction layout, focused on the methods and countermeasures of the industry-economic alliance, and focused on researching and building a communication and dialogue platform between the pilot free trade zone and ASEAN Shipping Investment and realizing the connection between policies and resources, and jointly exploring the practical model under the new situation.

The seminar was chaired by LU Qixing, Deputy Director of the Commercial Committee of China (Shanghai) Pilot Free Trade Zone and Deputy Director of the Commercial Committee of Shanghai Pudong New District, and CHEN Xi, Deputy Director of Shanghai Pudong New District, gave a welcome speech at the opening ceremony. Deputy Director CHEN Xi said that according to the latest requirements of the central government on the functional positioning of Shanghai Free Trade Zone and the deployment of tasks to serve the national "Belt and Road" initiative, Pudong New District Government would focus on enhancing the global shipping resource allocation capability, the main line to arrange relevant work about shipping, including efforts to improve the functional layout of shipping comprehensive services, strengthen the gathering of international shipping functional institutions and leading enterprises, and further improve the soft environment for business services in the Shanghai Free Trade Zone. Shanghai Free Trade Zone and Pudong New District would participate in international economic cooperation in a more open attitude, and welcome more international enterprises and institutions to find partners in Pudong to expand business and markets.

President of Shanghai Bar Association YU Weifeng made the keynote speech "thinking about the Internationalization of Legal Services Under the Framework of 'Belt and Road'". How to establish new international trade standards and dispute resolution mechanisms under the framework of "Belt and Road". This is an issue that the entire Chinese legal community needs to consider. Facing the general background of internationalization, Chinese lawyers should fully grasp such opportunities and bravely face the challenges that modern technology posed to the traditional legal service industry.

At the seminar, LIU Xu, Deputy General Manager of Shanghai Wailianfa Business Consulting Co., Ltd., and YU Yaodong, associate professor of the Law School of Shanghai Maritime University, talked about "policies and innovations related to overseas investment by Chinese capital" and "risk, challenges and responses of building the 21st Century Maritime Silk Road", the two core topics, and actively interacted with the guests. Nearly 20 legal professionals in shipping, finance, and investment fields from China, Singapore, Malaysia, Philippines, Cambodia, Thailand also focused on role of "Belt and Road" and ASEAN Economic Zone investment, dispute management, and arbitration in above-mentioned activities and the characteristics of the professional development of the International Arbitration Court of the Shanghai Arbitration Commission in recent years and started a heated group discussion.

The successful holding of the seminar effectively strengthens ASEAN economic partners' deep understanding of "Belt and Road" initiative, further demonstrates the good legal environment of Shanghai Free Trade Zone to the industry, and deepened sense of identification among major economic transaction entities of the resolution mechanism of arbitration that is accepted by the whole world for disputes. It is believed that with the continuous deepening of "Belt and Road" initiative and the continuous upgrading of the construction of Shanghai Free Trade Zone, arbitration will surely provide more professional legal protection for domestic and foreign shipping and trade entities.

2.5 Press Conference of Shanghai Municipal Government: introducing the situation of deepening reform and innovative development of Shanghai Pilot Free Trade Zone

Municipal Government Information Office held a municipal government press conference on September 12, 2017. Zhu Min, Deputy Director of Municipal Development and Reform Committee, introduced the measures and results of deepening reform and innovative development since the establishment of Shanghai Free Trade Pilot Zone. LU Fangzhou, Deputy Head of Pudong New District and Deputy Director of Shanghai Free Trade Zone Management Committee, introduced the annual work priorities of Shanghai Free Trade Zone. SHEN Weihua, Deputy Director of Municipal Commercial Committee, PENG Wenhao, Deputy Director of Municipal Administration for Industry and Commerce, LI Jun, Deputy Director of Municipal Finance Office, and WU Wei, Deputy Director of the Municipal Port Office attended the press conference and answered questions from reporters.

The construction of China (Shanghai) Pilot Free Trade Zone is a strategic measure by the Party Central Committee with XI Jinping at the core to comprehensively deepen reform and expand opening-up under the new situation. By the end of September 2017, Shanghai Pilot Free Trade Zone will be operated for four years. In the past four years, under the strong leadership of the Party Central Committee and State Council, the relevant departments of the state have actively promoted, actively served, and fully supported and coordinated the implementation of the overall plan, deepening plan and comprehensive deepening plan of Shanghai Pilot Free Trade Zone. Shanghai adheres to emancipating the mind, boldly practicing, firmly grasping the core task of institutional innovation, strengthening overall planning and systematic innovation, and focusing on serving the national strategy, striving to build Shanghai Pilot Free Trade Zone into the benchmark and engine to lead the comprehensive deepening of reform and acceleration of innovation-driven development under the new situation. In the past four years, the reform and innovation of Shanghai Pilot Free Trade Zone has mainly manifested in three aspects.

Firstly, institutional innovation further stimulates market innovation vitality and economic development momentum.

According to the requirements of the combination of expanding opening and reform system and the combination of cultivation functions and policy innovation, Shanghai Pilot Free Trade Zone actively promotes the process of transforming the advantages of institutional innovations into industrial functional advantages and industrial functional advantages into industrial development advantages.

The bonded area is the first area in Shanghai Pilot Free Trade Zone to operate. In the past four years, institutional innovation has played a significant role in promoting the transformation and upgrading of the economic structure of bonded areas and improving the quality and efficiency of economic operations. Since 2013, the bonded area has achieved a sustained and stable development in which the regional economic scale has grown at an average annual rate of 9% and the import and export volume has increased at an average annual rate of 5%.

For more than two years since the expansion of Shanghai Pilot Free Trade Zone, institutional innovation has shown a positive effect on improving the quality and efficiency of the economic development of the new expansion zone.

The financial opening and innovation functions of Lujiazui Financial District have been further improved. There are more than 8,000 new enterprises in the region, which is more than double the same period before the expansion. Jinqiao Development Zone continues to promote the coordinated development of "Jinqiao Manufacturing" and "Jinqiao Service", promote the extension of advanced manufacturing to both ends of the "smile curve" such as R & D, design, sales and service, and accelerate the cultivation of Internet+, Internet of Things+, virtual reality and cross-border integration of productive service industry emerging formats and economic development quality and efficiency have improved significantly. Zhangjiang High-tech Zone continues to promote the "double self-linkage", and has made major breakthroughs in the drug market permitter system, overseas talent entry and exit policies, and intellectual property protection mechanisms. The ecological environment for innovation and entrepreneurship has been continuously improved.

Secondly, build an institutional system that is consistent with international investment and trade rules.

The central government requires Shanghai to set a good benchmark, give play to its first-mover advantage, and take the lead in establishing an institutional system that is in line with international investment and trade regulations. According to the requirements of the central government, Shanghai has a global vision, based on national conditions, maintains the courage to innovate, the drive to be pioneer, and vigorous to pursue, with the new development concept as the guide, focusing on investment, trade, finance, and post-event supervision and management, forming basic and core institutional innovations, and continue to mature and finalize in practice. Institutional innovation promotes a fundamental change in the way the government manages the economy. It has made significant progress in taking the lead in forming a legal, international, and convenient business environment.

Thirdly, it has played a leading role in demonstrating and breaking through for overall reform.

Over the past four years, the reform and innovation concepts and system innovation achievements of Shanghai Pilot Free Trade Zone have been replicated and promoted across the country at differentfields and levels. The 116 administrative licensing items for "license separation" reform pilot program will be promoted and implemented in 10 other free pilot trade zones across the country, as well as qualified national independent innovation demonstration zones and national high-tech industrial development zones. 37 reform measures in the investment field, including foreign investment filing management and "single window" for enterprise access, were replicated and promoted nationwide. 34 reform measures for trade facilitation such as enter and then take customs declaration, batch entry and exit centralized declaration have been implemented in stages in an orderly manner across the country, in the Yangtze River Basin, and in areas under special customs supervision. 23 financial institutional innovation reform achievements such as cross-border financing and interest rate liberalization have been replicated and promoted across the country at different fields and levels. The active opening and independent reform of Shanghai Pilot Free Trade Zone explore new ways to promote comprehensive deepening of reforms and wider opening-up under the new situation, and provide experience and models for the construction of the national pilot free trade zones.

In the end of 2016, General Secretary XI Jinping made important instructions on the construction of Shanghai Pilot Free Trade Zone, fully affirming the effectiveness of the construction of Shanghai Pilot Free Trade Zone. In early 2017, State Council issued the *Comprehensive Deepening of the Reform and Opening-up of China (Shanghai) Pilot Free Trade Zone*. The 98 reform tasks detailed in the comprehensive deepening plan and the 24 key tasks in 2017 have all been launched.

Shanghai has studied, understood, and implemented the spirit of General Secretary XI Jinping's important instructions in depth, with the goal of building the most open free trade park, with "three districts and one fort" and "three linkages" as the starting point, in contrast to the free trade zone with international highest standards and best level, will continue to make new actions in deepening the reform of the pilot free trade zone, give full play to its leading role, better serve the national strategy, and further highlight the effect of comprehensive deepening of the reform of Shanghai Pilot Free Trade Zone and the expansion of the open pilot field.

3 Legal Construction of Shipping

3.1 Shanghai Maritime Court and Shanghai Insurance Regulatory Bureau cooperated to promote the reform and innovation of shipping insurance industry

On October 13, 2017, Shanghai Maritime Court and Shanghai Insurance Regulatory Bureau jointly held a press conference to launch maritime litigation security liability insurance and the recommended format of the letter of guarantee in the country firstly.

The maritime litigation protection liability insurance and the recommended format of the letter of guarantee launched this time has obvious maritime litigation characteristics. It is the result of many consultations and discussions between Shanghai Maritime Court, Shanghai Insurance Regulatory Bureau and Shanghai Shipping Insurance Association.

The recommended text lists the types of security that are common in maritime trials, which is convenient for insurance companies to determine the rates and charging methods based on the differences in the risks of different types of security, and for the maritime court to review. The applicant for maritime litigation security should apply the security liability insurance to the insurance company, and the insurance company should issue a letter of guarantee, and should bear the liability for damage compensation to the respondent or the third party according to law in case of wrong security. At the same time, the recommended text is more precise and concise on the name and validity of the letter of guarantee, and there are also clear regulations on the level of the insurance company that issues the letter of guarantee.

The recommended text has been applied for the first time in a financial loan contract dispute heard by Shanghai Maritime Court, and had good results.

3.2 Shanghai Maritime Court issued a white paper on maritime trials involving the protection of the rights and interests of the crew

On June 22, 2017, on the occasion of the "June 25th World Seaman's Day", Shanghai Maritime Court held a press conference to publish the 2016 Chinese and

English version of the white paper on maritime trial with the protection of the rights and interests of the crew as the topic, focusing on the notification of the trial and enforcement of cases involving the protection of the rights and interests of the crew in the past 3 years. This is the seventh time the court has notified the society of the maritime trial work since 2010.

The white paper released this time continues to use the form of bilingual publishing in Chinese and English, continues the characteristics of "normalization of publication, serialization of topics, and refinement of content", and focuses on hot issues in the field of shipping and livelihood, focuses on the professional development and rights protection of crew groups. It fully and thoroughly reflects the trial and enforcement status of cases involving the protection of the rights and interests of the crew and the implementation of various working mechanisms related to judicial protection of people's livelihood of the court, and provides effective judicial practical experience for regulating and guiding the healthy development of the crew industry and shipping industry.

The white paper shows that: in 2016, Shanghai Maritime Court received a total of 5,054 cases and concluded 5,101 cases, up 7.49% and 8.28% year-on-year respectively; the total amount of subject matter involved was RMB 4,590 million; of which 983 foreign-related, Hong Kong, Macao and Taiwan-related cases involved 36 countries and regions; disputes over contracts of carriage of goods and contracts of freight forwarding in maritime and open sea areas are still the main types of cases, accounting for 69.79% of the total number of cases received in the first instance.

On the basis of maintaining a good overall situation in the trials and enforcement, Shanghai Maritime Court also concluded a number of high-quality cases. By legally exercising jurisdiction over disputes over shipwreck accidents near the South China Sea Huangyan Island, China's national sovereignty over the South China Sea was declared to the international community; a case of ship collision damage compensation liability dispute was included in Supreme People's Court Gazette Case and "2016 Ten Typical Cases of Maritime Trial by National Courts", "2016 Ten Typical Cases of Shanghai Court"; two cases of disputes over contracts of freight forwarding on sea were published by the French authoritative legal journal *French Maritime Code Journal* and highly praised by the French industry.

The white paper also informs Shanghai Maritime Court that in-depth implementation of the trial quality strategy, actively participates in the comprehensive governance of the shipping field, deepens the professional trial mechanism, establishes a fast-filing, fast-security, fast-hearing, and fast-enforcement "four fast" green channels, improves the work and achievements of the six aspects of the ship network judicial auction mechanism and the expansion of the application of network information technology.

In response to the new situation and new issues in maritime cases, the white paper informs that there were many disputes over ship operation loan contracts. After the abolishment of the Domestic Waterway Goods Carriage Regulations, the actual carrier's identification and liability bearing are difficult. Export carriage disputes over textile happened frequently in emerging markets, disputes arising from cruise travel entered into litigation and oil spills from ships caused the relative concentration of clean-up and anti-pollution enterprises to argue operating fee cases, and corresponding risk warnings were given.

The white paper not only informs Shanghai Maritime Court of the basic situation of the 2016 maritime trial, but also conducts a special summary and analysis of the relevant cases concerning the protection of the rights and interests of the crew heard by the court in 2014—2016, and publishes the typical cases concerning the protection of the rights and interests of the crew. The implementation of trial enforcement work provides more complete judicial protection for the crew, creates a good legal environment, and promotes the healthy development of China's shipping industry.

The white paper shows that over the past three years, Shanghai Maritime Court has accepted more than 2,000 cases involving various types of crew disputes, including 790 cases involving disputes over crew labor contracts. Affected by the market operating conditions, the number of cases accepted fluctuates greatly each year. The cases distributed in the range of less than 60,000 yuan of the subject matter were relatively concentrated, and most of them appeared in the form of collective litigation by the crew. Among 804 cases concluded during the same period, 49.62% of the cases were concluded by judgment, and 55.47% of the cases were concluded within one month. In addition, there were a significant increase in disputes over foreign-related, Hong Kong, Macao and Taiwan-related crew labor contracts.

The typical cases concerning the protection of the rights and interests of the crew published in the white paper involve the types of cases such as the disability of the crew due to injuries, the casualties of multiple crew in shipwreck accidents, and the personal injury of expatriate crew, as well as the green channels for judicial protection involving crew and the enforcement involving crew. Mature and unified judicial judgment standards, regulate and guide the behavior of market subjects, optimize the legal environment for the performance of crew, and promote the orderly development of the shipping industry.

Shanghai Maritime Court has carried out a lot of work in providing judicial protection for the rights and interests of crew, forming a relatively mature mechanism and experience. The white paper specifically introduces the working mechanism and main practices of the court to protect the rights and interests of the crew according to the law, such as establishing a "four fast" green channel, shortening the realization cycle of crew's rights and interests, and actively advancing the network judicial auction of the ship to achieve a faster and better victory for rights and interests of the crew.

3.3 The first case of "ownership" ship oil pollution damage was compensated

On June 15, 2017, Ministry of Transport held the 2017 annual meeting of the China Ship Oil Pollution Damage Compensation Fund Management Committee in Beijing. The meeting reviewed and approved three claims reports for ship oil pollution accidents, involving compensation of nearly 16 million yuan. Among them, M.V. "Shanhong 12" oil pollution accident claim was the first time that China's ship oil pollution compensation fund compensated "ownership" ship oil pollution damage case, marking a new breakthrough in the work of China's ship oil pollution compensation fund.

The meeting reviewed and approved the annual work report of the Secretariat of China Ship Oil Pollution Damage Compensation Fund Management Committee, the 2017 annual revenue and expenditure budget report of China Ship Oil Pollution Damage Compensation Fund, and the *Management Measures of Experts for the Ship Oil Pollution Damage Compensation Fund* and the list of the first batch of claims experts. XU Ruqing, secretary general of China Ship Oil Pollution Damage Compensation Fund Management Committee Secretariat and Director of maritime safety administration of Ministry of Transport, issued letters of appointment to the first group of claims expert representatives.

In his concluding speech at the meeting, XU Ruqing pointed out that the use and management of China's ship oil pollution damage compensation fund was a brand new practice, which must be combined with reality, exploration and practice, and step by step. Through two years of hard work, the fund's rules and regulations have become more sophisticated, the fund's benefit to the people has become increasingly evident, the fund's management system has matured, and the fund's social impact has grown. In order to better promote the use of funds, we must take precautions, further improve the fund system, and do a good job in related policy reserves; we must adhere to the problem-oriented, give full play to the role of expert think tanks, and promote the scientific and healthy development of fund use management; we must strengthen publicity and communication work, give full play to the radiation effect of the fund; we must summarize experience, further improve the decision-making and operating mechanism, and enhance the effect of use of the fund.

3.4 Law School of Shanghai Maritime University was approved to establish the nation's first maritime arbitration research center

On May 19, 2017, China Arbitration Law Research Institute formally approved the establishment of a maritime arbitration research center in the Law School of Shanghai Maritime University, and submitted that the center was a professional committee of China Arbitration Law Research Institute to the competent department of Ministry of Civil Affairs, Chinese Law Society and China International Trade Promotion Committee to be filed.

The Law School of Shanghai Maritime University integrates professional resources and invites authoritative experts to join in. It has been approved to establish the country's first maritime arbitration research think tank. The Maritime Arbitration Research Center will rely on a capable scientific research team and a solid research foundation under the guidance of China Arbitration Law Research Institute to carry out academic exchanges, teaching guidance, subject research, membership services and strengthen communication and exchange between theoretical and practical circles in the field of maritime arbitration, track the cutting-edge developments of legislation and practice in various countries, explore academic innovation, gather excellent achievements to promote the development and improvement of China's maritime arbitration system, and promote the construction of China's arbitration rule of law.

3.5 Shanghai Maritime Court and Jiangsu Lianyungang Intermediate People's Court jointly issued the *Framework Agreement on Cooperation in the Service Guarantee of Construction of "Belt and Road"*

On August 29, 2017, Shanghai Maritime Court and Jiangsu Lianyungang Intermediate People's Court jointly held a press conference to release the *Framework Agreement on Cooperation in the Service Guarantee of Construction of "Belt and Road"* concluded by the two courts. Vice President of Shanghai Maritime Court JIA Zhenkun and Vice President of Lianyungang Intermediate People's Court GU Changzhou attended the press conference, informed the relevant situation and answered questions from reporters.

In May 2017, General Secretary XI Jinping reviewed the fruitful results of "Belt and Road" construction over the past four years at "Belt and Road" International Cooperation Summit Forum, and made a forward-looking deployment for the future development of "Belt and Road". At present, the construction of "Belt and Road" is continuously deepening. China is taking advantage of the geographical advantages of coastal ports, actively building cross-border multimodal transport corridors, and carrying out the construction of a land-sea combined transport corridor connecting Maritime Silk Road and Silk Road Economic Belt. Shanghai is an important port city on the "21st Century Maritime Silk Road". It is actively using additive advantages of the "four centers" of international economy, finance, trade and shipping, and the construction of pilot free trade zones and the science and technology center to further enhance the service level of the linkage of the construction of "Belt and Road". Lianyungang has a unique position in "Silk Road Economic Belt". As the main node city of the New Asia-Europe Continental Bridge Economic Corridor, the Sino-Kazakh logistics transit base and the SCO overseas base, it is actively constructing the

"Belt and Road" east-west two-way open portal, and continuously strengthen the construction of the pilot area in the core area of the intersection. Shanghai and Lianyungang have obvious regional advantages in the construction of Maritime Silk Road and Silk Road Economic Belt, and their responsibilities are becoming increasingly prominent. The Lianyungang dispatched court, as Shanghai Maritime Court's dispatched office in Lianyungang, Jiangsu, has formed an effective connection with Lianyungang Intermediate Court in the construction of the judicial service guarantee "Belt and Road" land-sea combined transport corridor. Shanghai Maritime Court and Lianyungang Intermediate People's Court concluded the *Agreement* in order to deeply implement the spirit of General Secretary Xi Jinping's important instructions on "Belt and Road" initiative, and to implement Supreme People's Court's work requirements of providing judicial services guarantee for the construction of Lianyungang. Through exerting their respective advantages, forming a joint force of work, comprehensively docking the judicial needs in the construction of the Maritime Silk Road and Silk Road Economic Belt land-sea combined transport corridor, and jointly providing more quality and efficient judicial services guarantee for the construction of "Belt and Road".

According to the agreement, two parties should strengthen communication on the trial work related to "Belt and Road" cases, improve the level of foreign-related trial work, and create a good business rule of law environment; actively resolve conflicts and disputes, and jointly promote the construction of a diversified dispute resolution mechanism and maintain harmonious and stable social environment; strengthen enforcement work, establish an all-round and three-dimensional enforcement cooperation mechanism, protect the parties' rights to win the litigation; give full play to the jurisdictional advantages of the two places, launch mutual assistance measures for touring trials and facilitate litigation of the parties, and extend judicial service functions.

The press conference introduced the basic situation, scope of jurisdiction, working characteristics of Shanghai Maritime Court and the work of Lianyungang dispatched court, the work plan and outlook of Shanghai Maritime Court's service guarantee for the construction of "Belt and Road", and cases of the cooperation and enforcement collaboration between Shanghai Maritime Court and Lianyungang Intermediate Court.

3.6 Shanghai Maritime Court and Shanghai University of International Business and Economics concluded a cooperation agreement to jointly build the "21st Century Maritime Silk Road Research Center"

On November 28, 2017, Shanghai Maritime Court and Shanghai University of International Business and Economics held the opening ceremony of the "21st Century Maritime Silk Road Research Center". ZHAO Hong, President of Shanghai Maritime Court, and XU Yonglin, Vice President of Shanghai University of International Business and Economics, respectively delivered speeches and concluded a cooperation agreement on behalf of the two units to jointly unveil the establishment of the research center.

According to the agreement, two parties cooperated to establish the "21st Century Maritime Silk Road Research Center", focusing on the construction of "Belt and Road", a maritime power, a trade power, Shanghai free trade zone, a free trade port and an international shipping center and carry out all-round cooperation in the fields of decision-making consultation and academic research, international dissemination of Chinese maritime judicial cases, foreign academic exchanges, foreign law identification, and big data service sharing.

In recent years, Shanghai Maritime Court has actively explored the construction of a high-end international maritime justice think tank, promoted the improvement of the maritime trial theory and practice level with first-class think tanks, and successively concluded cooperation agreements with Tsinghua University, Shanghai Maritime University and other universities to continuously deepen the construction of judicial think tank-type research platforms.

Shanghai Maritime Court takes the opportunity of the contract to sincerely cooperate and support each other with Shanghai University of International Business and Economics to promote the implementation of various cooperation matters with high standards and high quality, and strive to build the center into a first-class legal policy think tank with concentration of research resources, prosperous research activities, a broad research horizon and rich research achievements to contribute more wisdom and strength to the implementation of major national strategies and the economic and social and economic development of Shanghai.

3.7 Shanghai Maritime Court was formally confirmed by Supreme People's Court as the "Shanghai Base for International Maritime Justice of Supreme People's Court"

In April 2017, Shanghai Maritime Court was formally confirmed by Supreme People's Court as the "Shanghai Base for International Maritime Justice of Supreme People's Court".

In order to give full play to the advantages of Shanghai maritime trial, through the practice and exploration of regional first-ahead trials, improving and innovating maritime litigation mechanisms and trial methods, and forming more replicated and promoted trial experience, Shanghai Maritime Court formulated the *Opinions on the Implementation of the Construction of "Shanghai Base for International Maritime Justice of Supreme People's Court"*, further advances to the goal of "constructing China into an international maritime justice center with high international influence".

The *Opinion* clearly stated that Shanghai base would take the construction of an international maritime dispute resolution center as its core function and the construction of a high-end international maritime justice think tank and an international maritime justice exchange platform as its auxiliary functions.

As the main function of the international maritime dispute resolution center, it is the main and core goal of constructing an international maritime justice center. Shanghai Maritime Court relies on its advantages in the internationalization of shipping entities, the scale of disputes, and the diversification of dispute types, in-depth implements the maritime trial high-quality strategy, takes efforts to improve the international credibility of maritime justice and makes creation of rules led by fair, transparent and predictable judges to attract more and more domestic and foreign shipping market entities to choose Shanghai Maritime Court to resolve litigation disputes with the international, attractive and convenient maritime litigation mechanism.

As one of the auxiliary functions, the high-end international maritime justice think tank aims to find the integration point and focus point of maritime justice and major national strategies. It gathers international maritime legal talents and resource around maritime justice theory and major hot practice issues that are generally concerned by the international community to provide high-quality maritime justice service guarantee and professional think tank support.

As another auxiliary function, the international maritime judicial exchange platform aims to use Shanghai's international advantages to build an interconnected maritime justice information exchange and sharing platform to better integrate with the international maritime legal field and expand international influence of China's maritime justice.

Shanghai Maritime Court has implemented the International Maritime Justice Center in recent years. The main performances are as follows: ①give full play to the maritime trial function, and actively promote the legalization, internationalization, and convenience of the shipping operation environment. ②Justly and efficiently resolve disputes in the shipping field and enhance the international credibility of maritime justice. ③Innovate convenient litigation mechanism, and actively create a preferred maritime litigation. ④Deepen international maritime justice exchanges and cooperation and build a new platform for maritime judicial think tanks. ⑤Strengthen the construction of the maritime court team and cultivate international high-end maritime justice talents.

3.8 Shanghai Maritime Court was confirmed by Supreme People's Court as the "Practice Base of Smart Maritime Court (Shanghai)"

In June 2017, Shanghai Maritime Court was confirmed by Supreme People's Court as a "Practice Base of Smart Maritime Court (Shanghai)". As the first smart court practice base in the country, Shanghai Maritime Court has formulated and issued the *Implementation Opinions on Promoting the Construction of the "Practice Base of Smart Maritime Court (Shanghai)"*, making full use of modern scientific and technological means to focus on solving the key and difficult issues which impact and restrict the development of maritime trials, and comprehensively serve and guarantee that various work of court that taking the law enforcement as the first priority.

The *Opinion* proposed that the construction of smart maritime courts should promote the comprehensive application of artificial intelligence, as well as the deep integration with maritime trials and maritime litigation services, and strive to make "smart maritime courts" an important measure to lead the development of maritime justice and promote innovation in maritime trials. An important means of development. By building a smart maritime court, a "model room" will be built to effectively enhance the capacity and level of maritime adjudication services to guarantee the national strategy and Shanghai's economic and social development.

The *Opinion* makes it clear that the main task of the construction of the smart maritime court is to create a "1+2+X" information construction template. To build a "one center", namely build a safe, stable, advanced and controllable big data exchange processing center to realize the integration of data collection, exchange, processing, display and release. To build "two platforms", namely, build an intelligent case-handling platform, improve the quality and effectiveness of trial enforcement, and improve litigation service capabilities; build an intelligent office platform, improve judicial administrative capabilities, and improve judicial security. To build a number of intelligent auxiliary systems to realize the transformation and upgrading of the "artificial intelligence +" working mode of the smart maritime court.

Shanghai Maritime Court has many highlights in recent years in building maritime characteristic big data platforms, exploring "Internet + maritime trials", advancing the improvement of the network judicial auction of ship, and building intelligent auxiliary case handling systems.

3.9 Shanghai Pudong New District Court issued the 2016—2017 white paper on the trial work of cases involving free trade

On November 19, 2017, Pudong New District People's Court issued a white paper on the trial work of Shanghai Free Trade Zone (November 2016—October 2017) and ten typical cases, and showed the research results of judicial big data related to free trade cases.

The white paper disclosed that from November 2016 to October 2017, Pudong Court accepted a total of 33,708 cases involving free trade. From the perspective of the types of cases, there are 26,847 civil and commercial cases, 565 criminal cases, 12 administrative cases and 6,284 enforcement cases.

HU Yongqing, Vice President of Pudong Court, said that Pudong Court was always committed to providing fair and efficient judicial services for the construction of the free trade zone. In the past year, with the progress of the construction of the free trade zone, the cases involving the free trade trial by

Pudong Court have also shown corresponding features and changing laws. Firstly, the number of accepting and concluding cases slowed down, and disputes involving litigation stabilized; secondly, the case withdrawal rate rose, and the mechanism for diversified dispute resolution involving free trade achieved remarkable results; thirdly, the adjustment of the case type structure reflected the continuous improvement of rule of law environment in the pilot free trade zone; finally, the types of foreign-related cases were diversifying, and the opening of the pilot free trade zone would be further deepened.

In the white paper, Pudong Court also made a typological analysis of cases involving free trade, and had an in-depth analysis on general review and basic characteristics of the trial of criminal, general civil, investment and trade commercial affairs, financial commercial affairs, intellectual property, labor disputes, administrative and enforcement cases.

In March 2017, State Council issued the *Comprehensive Deepening of the Reform and Opening-up of China (Shanghai) Pilot Free Trade Zone*. In this context, the construction of free trade zone requires more powerful and efficient judicial service guarantees. On the one hand, it is necessary to conduct high-quality trials of new types of difficult cases that are constantly emerging, to promote the establishment of free trade zone rules and value guidance; on the other hand, we should boldly use "Internet+", big data and other technologies to improve the quality and efficiency of trials and facilitate litigant parties.

On November 19, 2017, Pudong Court also issued the ten typical cases involving free trade in 2016—2017, and gave a live demonstration of the research results of judicial big data concerning free trade cases.

CAO Kerui, President of Pudong Court Free Trade Zone Court, introduced that the ten typical cases included 4 commercial cases, 2 intellectual property cases, 1 administrative case, 1 labor dispute case, 1 criminal case and 1 enforcement case. Most of these cases were new types and difficult cases, and the trial results have a strong demonstration effect.

The ten cases involved multiple disputes including equity transfer disputes, securities brokerage contract disputes, unfair competition disputes, and competition restrictions. Among them, "Public Comments v. Baidu Unfair Competition Dispute" was also selected as the "2016 Ten Typical Cases of *China*

Trial" and "Ten Influential Cases of China's Internet Rule of Law from 2014 to 2016". These cases have high social attention and have important reference value for promoting the healthy development of the industry and the trial of similar cases.

Pudong Court demonstrated a big data analysis system involving free trade cases. This system is the first of its kind in the country, and can automatically collect and analyze the distribution and case information of free trade cases involving Shanghai and the whole country to form a free trade case analysis database. The system can also use key entities, key industries and new fields in the free trade zone as keywords to discover new and typical cases in a timely manner and realize dynamic supervision and prevention of risks in the free trade zone.

3.10 The Supreme People's Court issued the second batch of typical cases involving the construction of "Belt and Road"

On May 15, 2017, the Supreme People's Court held a news briefing and released the second batch of ten typical cases involving the construction of "Belt and Road". LIU Jingdong, Vice President of the No.4 Civil Trial of the Supreme People's Court, introduced the situation and spokesman for Supreme People's Court Lin Wenxue presided over the news briefing.

The typical cases issued this time were the types of disputes common in the construction of "Belt and Road", involving letter of credit issuance, equity transfer contracts, intermediary contracts, independent letters of guarantee, compensation for marine pollution damage, contracts of carriage of goods by sea, recognition and enforcement of foreign arbitration, recognition and enforcement of foreign commercial judgments, and law issues involving cases were highly representative. For example, China Construction Bank Co., Ltd. Guangzhou Liwan Sub-branch and Guangdong Lanyue Energy Development Co., Ltd. letter of credit issuance dispute retrial case were a long-term documentary letter of credit issuance dispute with foreign-related factors. The Supreme People's Court interpreted the contract system and protected the preferential right of reimbursement enjoyed by the issuing bank that held the bill of lading according to law, and at the same time clarified the dispute over the legal nature of the bill of lading voucher that had long plagued judicial practice.

Most of the cases involving the construction of "Belt and Road" are foreign-related cases. During the trial of such cases, we often encounter issues such as the application of conflict norms to confirm the applicable law, the identification and application of foreign law, the application of international conventions and international practices, and the preservation of public order. For example, in the case of dispute on compensation for pollution damage to the sea area of Dalian Ocean and Fisheries Bureau, it involved the interpretation of the *1992 International Convention on Civil Liability for Oil Pollution Damage*. The case was strict according to the *Vienna Convention on the Law of Treaties*, which made it clear that compensation for environmental damage under the Convention was limited to the cost of reasonable restoration measures. The case of Siemens applying for recognition and enforcement of foreign arbitration award was a contractual dispute between the wholly foreign-owned enterprise in the pilot free trade zone. This case confirmed the validity of the arbitration clause and specified "estoppel", which was in practice the concept of "conducive to the enforcement of award" in the *New York Convention*.

In the process of advancing the construction of "Belt and Road", the types of transactions involved are becoming more and more abundant. On the one hand, there will be more legislative gaps, which requires China to improve the corresponding legal system. On the other hand, it will involve more legal conflicts and coordination between China and countries along the routes.

In 2017, the Supreme People's Court focused on judicial services and guarantees for the construction of "Belt and Road". It issued judicial interpretations on the recognition and enforcement of foreign civil and commercial judgments, external guarantees, and other difficult issues that needed to be urgently resolved in foreign-related trials and go about judicial interpretation concerning disputes over crew's labor and compensation for maritime resources and ecological pollution damages. Meanwhile, it issued regulations on the jurisdiction of foreign-related civil and commercial cases, further improved the foreign-related litigation jurisdiction mechanism, promoted the pilot work of the maritime courts in jurisdiction of maritime criminal cases, safeguarded the blue homeland security, and ensured the smooth flow of Maritime Silk Road.

4 Shipping Culture Construction

4.1 In 2017, "Sail to Distance" Navigation Culture Forum was successfully held

On July 10, 2017, the Ninth "Sail to Distance" Navigation Culture Forum was successfully held at Ningbo Museum. As one of the special forums for this year's China Maritime Day, the forum was hosted by the Organizing Committee of China Maritime Day Forum and was jointly undertaken by Baode Institute of Ancient Ships, Qing'an Hall, Ningbo Museum and Ningbo Port and Shipping Administration.

The forum was mainly held in the form of photo exhibitions, keynote speeches, expert forum. The "Silk Road Sailing Shadow" UK Royal Greenwich Museum's image and photo exhibition began its first exhibition in Qing'an Hall in Ningbo. The photo exhibition truly recreated the symbiosis of ships, people and ports in China's coastal areas in the 1930s.

At the opening ceremony of the forum, Deputy Secretary-General of Ningbo Municipal Government WANG Jianyun delivered a speech explaining the development and achievements of China, especially Ningbo in the history and culture of navigation, and looking forward to Ningbo as an important node city of "Belt and Road" to make new breakthroughs and contributions. Kevin Fewster, British Deputy Consul General in Shanghai, Curator of UK Royal Greenwich Museum, and SUN Jian, Technical Director of the Underwater Cultural Heritage Protection of National Bureau of Cultural Heritage, delivered keynote speeches respectively. Relevant leaders from the British International Museum, Ningbo Museum, Hong Kong Maritime Museum and China Overseas Transportation History Research Institute exchanged speeches on international cooperation in the museum industry and interacted with guests on site. In the special session of "China's Modern Navigation and Trade", more than 20 well-known experts and scholars in the industry launched professional academic reports and exchanges based on their own research fields.

Themes of this forum were "China's Modern Navigation and Trade under the Vision of Maritime Silk Road" and "Maritime Silk Road and Museum", bringing together the wisdom of experts, gathering consensus of all parties, and conducting professional academic exchanges and discussions, so that everyone could feel the voyage cultural charm, enhance nautical and marine awareness and achieve good social effects.

4.2　Construction of the North Bund Terminal Culture Museum

A new bright spot will be added to the riverside area of the North Bund, and a "promenade", open air museum of terminal culture that reflects Shanghai's centuries-old terminal cultural history has been constructed.

Thew aterfront of Huangpu River in Hongkou District was once an important distribution center for freight and passenger carriage in Shanghai. As early as 1845, the British East India Company built a humble barge terminal in Xujiatan (now East Daming Road and Gaoyang Road). In 1860, the British Baoshun Foreign Bank built the Baoshun terminal, which was the first steamship terminal in Shanghai. In 1861, American Qichang Foreign Bank built the Qichang Terminal. In 1864, the British Blue Chimney Steamship Company rebuilt the Hongkou Terminal and changed it from a barge terminal to a steamship terminal.

Before the founding of New China, Huangpu Terminal, Yangshupu Terminal, Huishan Terminal, Huashun Terminal, Gongping Road Terminal, Gaoyang Road Terminal, Waihongqiao Terminal and Yangtze River Terminal were mainly along the Huangpu River in the Hongkou District.

The open air museum of terminal culture opened in Hongkou District is an open terminal culture and history corridor that organically combines Shanghai's urban culture with terminal culture, tradition and modernity. The museum uses a 600-meter-long glass wall as a display carrier, plus sculptures, Leshi inscriptions, historical landmarks and personal mark, and architectural components, using appropriate sound, light, and electricity technical methods, combined with the rich historical humanities resources of Hongkou District, starting with the opening of Shanghai in 1843, to the establishment of modern industry in Shanghai, and then to the opening of advanced social civilization, with the main line of recalling the history of Shanghai's urban development. The open air museum of terminal culture not only shows the city spirit of Shanghai's "all rivers run into sea, humble quality", but also the inheritance and development of overseas style culture.

According to the plan, the glass wall was made up of three parts, namely, "Terminal Evolution", "Western Learning to the East" and "Celebrity Trail", mainly using historical pictures and QR codes to show the historical changes including Shanghai's terminals along the Yangtze River and scenarios that early Chinese intellectuals traveled across the ocean, embarked on the road to study abroad, sought truth, learned advanced foreign knowledge, participated in cultural exchange, and scenarios that many world cultural celebrities and scientists, such as Tagore, Einstein, Chaplin came ashore to visit China and give lectures.

The open air museum of terminal culture also sets up several riverside landscape point sculptures and models, including a schematic diagram of the distribution of the Huangpu River in old Shanghai, a schematic model of the distribution of the old terminals in the North Bund, tether rope piles, and 20 terminal annual rings. Meanwhile, there is a group of Einstein and children's landscape sculptures called "relative", which means that Einstein invented the theory of relativity.

4.3 2017 "Belt and Road" Cultural Roundtable

On August 24 – 25, 2017, "Belt and Road" Cultural Roundtable jointly organized by the China Song Ching Ling Foundation and Lanzhou University was held at Lanzhou University and nearly one hundred experts and scholars from 21 countries including China, Russia, the United States, Japan, India, Pakistan and Australia attended the meeting and discussed in depth how to play the role of non-governmental organizations and universities, promote exchanges and cooperation among countries in the "Belt and Road" region, and build consensus and wisdom for peaceful development, exchanges and mutual learning, and win-win cooperation.

"To jointly defend the human spirit and the value of civilization, to advocate constructive dialogue among civilizations, and to actively respond to various new challenges is the mission of the era of non-governmental organizations." QI Mingqiu, party secretary and Executive Deputy-Chairman of the China Song Ching Ling Foundation, said that in the construction of "Belt and Road", sincere cooperation between the governments, mutual benefit and mutual trust were dominant, and unofficial exchanges and dialogues also had a unique and irreplaceable role. As a link and bridge between the government and society, non-governmental organizations in various countries are playing an increasingly important role in international affairs, especially in some areas of common concern to mankind.

DU Yubo, former Deputy Secretary of the party group and Deputy Minister of Ministry of Education, pointed out that in the process of promoting the construction of "Belt and Road", it was necessary to better promote educational exchanges among countries along the route, especially the exchange and cooperation of higher education, in order to play the role of higher education as a bridge in the cultural and humanistic exchange among countries along "Belt and Road", the role of higher education communities as a think tank in the construction of "Belt and Road" among countries along the route, and the catalytic role of higher education in enhancing mutual trust among countries along the route.

WANG Cheng, President of Lanzhou University, said that in the process of revitalizing Silk Road Economic Belt, various exchanges and cooperation in education, culture, science and technology would certainly play an important leading role. Lanzhou University, as a national key comprehensive university located in the core node city of Silk Road Economic Belt, would integrate more scientific research forces and carry out research and service with a broader perspective and more pragmatic cooperation in the future.

At the keynote forum, Chinese and foreign experts and scholars gave speeches around the theme. They discussed the concrete path of practically carrying out cultural, regional and university cooperation, and analyzed how to promote "peaceful cooperation, openness and tolerance, mutual learning and mutual referring, mutual benefit and mutual victory"Silk Road spirit to be carried forward in all countries along the route.

During the meeting, three sub-forums of "cultural exchange", "regional cooperation", and "college cooperation" were also organized, and the participating experts carried out in-depth discussions and exchanges on topics in related fields.

During the two-day discussion and exchange, the participating experts reached the following consensus through equal dialogue, frank communication, and brainstorming:

First was to promote the construction of "Belt and Road" with the principle of "co-consultation, co-construction and sharing". It was not only necessary to actively promote regional economic and trade exchanges and cooperation, but also to explore and appreciate the cultural heritage and humanistic spirit contained therein. It was necessary to further deepen the non-governmental friendship and pragmatic cooperation among the countries along the route. Through cross-border and cross-civilization exchange activities, to encourage countries along "Belt and Road" to promote exchanges, integration, dialogue, cooperation and win-win results, and make the Eurasian space a region of prosperity, development, peace and tranquility.

Second was that to promote the construction of "Belt and Road", it must jump out of the traditional regional economic model and explore a new type of regional cooperation model. Under the premise that all countries agree on the same concept and rules, expand economic exchanges in an equal, mutually beneficial, and win-win manner, and advocate higher-level and wider-content cooperation, not only for industrial transfer, to strengthen trade exchanges, and to deepen investment cooperation. It was necessary to deepen cooperation in the fields of humanities, education, science and technology, ecology, and environment, and finally realize the normalization of policy communication and the liberalization of trade and investment.

Third was that in an era of closer integration of knowledge and economy, higher education has become an important force for countries to promote social and economic development. In the process of advancing the construction of "Belt and Road", it is of special significance to better promote educational exchanges among countries along the route, especially higher education exchanges and cooperation. Countries along the route should further encourage and expand various forms of personnel exchanges in the higher education community, and provide more talent support and innovation driving force for the construction of "Belt and Road" through higher frequency and level of educational resource sharing, scientific and technological cooperation, and personnel communication.

4.4 Shanghai held a number of activities to celebrate the 13th China Maritime Day

July 11, 2017 was the 13th China Maritime Day. With the theme of "Ship · Port · People - Connectivity", Shanghai held a variety of publicity and commemorative activities to promote the spirit of navigation, promote the culture of navigation, and create a good atmosphere where the whole society commonly care for and support the navigation cause.

On July 11, the North Bund Shipping Service Center, which gathers shipping functional institutions and bears the history and culture of shipping, was officially opened to further enhance the energy level and status of the North Bund shipping industry. The launch ceremony of *Hand Drawing of Shanghai Shipping Cultural Landmarks*, "Post Road Silk Road Renaissance Road Walking New Silk Road" theme exhibition was also held at the newly completed North Bund Shipping Service Center.

In the newly completed North Bund Shipping Service Center, there are now a number of national key shipping functional agencies settling such as China Shipowners Association, China Ship Oil Pollution Damage Claims Center, Shanghai International Shipping Research Center, and China Shipping 50-person Forum Secretariat. In 2016, shipping industry has accounted for 31% of the entire fiscal revenue of Hongkou District, making it a veritable pillar industry of Hongkou.

For this, Hongkou District put forward a "one line, two circles, four centers" strategic pattern, costal area along the river focused on attracting the development of shipping industry headquarters, cruise, yachts, crow boat; Huoshan Road Circle focused on the gathering of shipping functional elements to promote the exchange of shipping information to attract relevant functional institutions and various shipping conference forums to settle down, Shanghai Bund Shipping Service Center was the image symbol of Huoshan Road Circle; Miyun Road Circle relied on the national-level Shanghai Crew Evaluation Demonstration Center to develop Shanghai Navigation Talent Public Training Base, Shanghai Port Safety Training Base, focusing on crew services.

The *Hand Drawing of Shanghai Shipping Cultural Landmarks* released this time collects about 39 shipping cultural landmarks in Shanghai, focusing on displaying the connotation and characteristics of Shanghai's shipping culture. It was available to citizens from July 11 at Shanghai airports, terminals and ferries free of charge, and Shanghai Post also specially distributed exclusive souvenir covers.

In order to actively respond to the country's "Belt and Road" construction, to explore how the maritime industry can seize new opportunities, seek new impetus, and expand new space, how Shanghai can connect with the national strategy in the process of building an international shipping center to play a supporting and leading role in the context of "21st Century Maritime Silk Road", the 2nd "21st Century Maritime Silk Road" Construction Summit Forum was held in Lujiazui. Nearly 400 industry experts, business representatives and government representatives from the shipping and financial sectors participated.

"In 2016, the scale of the global economy reached approximately 80 trillion USD, of which world trade totaled approximately 32 trillion USD, accounting for about 40%. Among them, most of them depend on shipping. Which is the important value and significance of shipping". JIN Yongxing, Secretary of the Party Committee of Shanghai Maritime University, said that the history of Shanghai confirmed the development trajectory of that port was used due to the city and the prosperity of city was due to ports.

Under the guidance of the principles of mutual consultation, joint construction and sharing, 21st Century Maritime Silk Road provides new opportunities, new impetus and new space for the expansion of transportation methods, trade content and coverage under the goal of building into a "road of peace, prosperity, openness, innovation, and civilization". Discussing how to seize new opportunities, seek new impetus, expand new space, and combine regional and industry reality to promote the development of navigation under the background of the New Silk Road became the main thrust of the forum. At the forum, experts and scholars delivered keynote speeches from the perspectives of macro policy, shipping development, "Belt and Road" and free trade zone, port development, maritime law, shipping finance, and international cooperation to discuss opportunities in Shanghai.

At the forum, after two years of trial operation and continuous adjustment and optimization of the index structure, Shanghai Shipping Exchange officially released "Belt and Road" shipping trade index. The index was composed of three major categories of indexes: "Belt and Road" trade volume index, "Belt and

Road" freight volume index, and "Maritime Silk Road" freight index with subdivide coal, ore, crude oil, container, 4 kinds of goods. The transportation methods included shipping and railways, and a variety of transportation methods including aviation would be added in the future.

5 Shipping Talent Service

5.1 Foreign high-level talents in Shanghai Free Trade Zone can directly apply for the "China Green Card"

Foreign talents in Shanghai Pilot Free Trade Zone apply for permanent residence in China, and now there are more convenient and faster channels. The foreign talent identification standard and identification process have been approved by Ministry of Public Security a few days ago: from April 13, 2017, foreign talents could according to *Recommendation Letter of Application of for Permanent Residence in China of China (Shanghai) Pilot Free Trade Zone Foreign High-level Talents* issued by Shanghai Free Trade Zone Management Committee, applied for a permanent residence permit for foreigners at Municipal Exit-Entry Administration Bureau, and their foreign spouse and minor children could also apply with them.

The permanent residence permit for foreigners is called the "China Green Card". To support the construction of the Shanghai Science and Technology Innovation Center, Ministry of Public Security has introduced the "new ten" entry-exit policies. The first of these is clear that: "for foreign high-level talents who meet the recognized standards, they can apply for permanent residence in China directly upon recommendation by Shanghai Zhangjiang National Independent Innovation Demonstration Zone or Shanghai Free Trade Zone Management Committee." Now that the talent confirmation standards and confirmation process are released, it means that this reform measure has officially landed. From April 13, 2017, universities, scientific research institutes, enterprises and other units within Shanghai Pilot Free Trade Zone can apply to the free trade sector zone administration they locates, and after being reviewed by the New District People's Insurance Bureau, it will recommend to the relevant departments about foreign high-level talents who meet the confirmation standards.

The criteria for the identification of foreign high-level talents are divided into three categories: one is the winners of well-known awards or high-level talent program candidates, including winners or nominees of internationally renowned awards such as Nobel Prize, Fields Prize, Wolf Prize, Krafford Prize, Turing Prize and Pritzker Architecture Awards; Chinese government's "Friendship Award", "International Science and Technology Cooperation Award" and other national commendation award recipients; central "Thousand Talents Program", "Foreign Special Thousand Talents Program" candidates; National Outstanding Youth Science Fund recipients; recipients of the "Changjiang Scholars" award program of Ministry of Education, "Hundred Talents Program" and "Introduction of Outstanding Technical Talent Program" of Chinese Academy of Sciences. Recipients of "Hundred Talents Program" of Pudong New District and "500 Chief Scientist" plan of Pudong New District and recipients of major talents programs are also included in this category.

The second category is well-known foreign experts, scholars, and professional technical personnel, including foreign academicians of Chinese Academy of Science or Chinese Academy of Engineering, foreign academicians of National Academy of Science or National Academy of Engineering; "National High-Tech Research and Development Plan" (863 Program), "National Key Basic Research and Development Plan" (973 Plan) chief scientist; the main accomplisher of the National Technology Invention Award and the National Science and Technology Progress Award. The person in charge of the National Laboratory, National Key Laboratory, National Engineering Laboratory, National Engineering Research Center, National Certified Enterprise Technology Center, National Engineering Technology Research Center, and Foreign Investment R & D Center in Shanghai Pilot Free Trade Zone (Deputy Director and above) can also apply.

The third category is foreign high-level talents for enterprise innovation and entrepreneurship. This type of talent mainly reflects the characteristics and needs of the Shanghai Free Trade Zone and talents of different types of enterprises encouraged by the free trade zone, especially key financial, shipping, trade institutions, headquarters-type enterprises and "four new" enterprises, and other foreign talents have special expertise and superb skills and are urgently needed in Shanghai Pilot Free Trade Zone.

The opening of Shanghai Free Trade Zone permanent residence policy is very strong. It believes that the implementation of this policy will provide overseas talents with convenient and fast channels for work, innovation and entrepreneurship in Pudong, as well as more convenient, efficient and high-quality service for overseas talents. The service will play an active role in improving the opening of Shanghai Free Trade Zone and the concentration of international talents and promoting the construction of the Shanghai Science and Technology Innovation Center.

5.2 Measures of Shanghai Free Trade Zone increase the success rate of overseas talent entrepreneurship and settling in Shanghai

On September 11, 2017, China (Shanghai) Pilot Free Trade Zone Overseas Talents Offshore Innovation and Entrepreneurship Base Work Coordination Group Office held a press briefing, announcing the situation of "Second Overseas Talents Entrepreneurship Exchange in Shanghai Free Trade Zone" large-scale docking exchange activities at offshore bases.

The construction of an overseas talent offshore innovation and entrepreneurship base in Shanghai Pilot Free Trade Zone is an important project for the cooperation between China Science and Technology Association and Shanghai. It is one of the first batch of offshore base pilot projects in China. It is a brand new exploration and experiment based on the talent introduction mechanism and innovation and entrepreneurship model, which was unveiled in August 2015, and was put into physical operation in the second half of 2016. The headquarters space was officially opened.

The offshore oversea talent innovation and entrepreneurship base in Shanghai Pilot Free Trade Zone has signed 75 contracts or registered overseas projects in just one year; introduced 44 domestic and overseas partners, including 28 professional groups and 16 third-party service organizations; 7 signed cooperation space, 2 development intention cooperation space, and set up the first overseas service station in Beersheba, Israel.

The second oversea talents Shanghai Free Trade Zone entrepreneurship exchange Activity under the theme of "Creating a Free Trade Link to the World" was held in Shanghai Pilot Free Trade Zone from September 17 to 20, 2017 as an international comprehensive innovative and entrepreneurial platforms. Offshore bases attract talents, start-up incubation, professional service guarantee and other advantageous functions are gradually being played.

XU Minxu, Deputy Director of the Shanghai Pudong New District Science and Technology and Economy Committee, introduced that entrepreneurship exchange aimed to gather a large number of high-quality overseas talents and projects through activities to achieve "attract talents". The offshore base was oriented to overseas talents. Registration in the district, internal and external operations, based on low-cost, convenient, full-factor, open, and mature supporting space carriers, building an international comprehensive entrepreneurial platform with functions such as business incubation and professional service guarantee.

In 2017, the offshore base focused on creating an upgraded version of the "1+N" entrepreneurial exchange series of activities, relying on a large-scale docking exchange event, combined with N series of special activities, to create an internationally influential entrepreneurial feast, forming the mechanism that overseas projects dock with and communicate with the normalization of local capital and technology, which would guide more overseas high-end talents to innovate and start businesses in the pilot free trade zone, and promote the cross-border flow of various innovation resources.

In addition to policy promotion, roadshow demonstrations, park inspections, and traditional capital docking, the event was the first to set up the "top 500 enterprises in the world technology demand release and capital, technology docking", which will invite large and medium-sized enterprises and investment institutions to participate, and by "capital + technology" dual docking mode to promote the win-win cooperation between the innovation advantages of small enterprises and the industrial resources advantages of large enterprises, and improve the success rate of overseas projects settling.

In terms of project solicitation and selection, it emphasizes technological innovation and encourages originality. The activity requires that the project must have certain technical advantages and a strong willingness to start a business in Shanghai Pilot Free Trade Zone, focusing on key industries fields in pilot free trade zone such as electronic information, biomedicine, and artificial intelligence.

In terms of talents invited to participate in the conference, "younger, highly educated and elite" has become a distinctive label. Talents participated in the event came from 12 countries and regions around the world, foreigners accounted for more than 2/3, the average age was 41 years old, master's degree and above accounted for 83%, 70% had senior management positions in well-known international companies or had research experience in well-known universities, who were very familiar with overseas technology and economic environment.

Entrepreneurial exchange arranges inspection activities every year to help overseas talents to understand the macro-policy through different arrangements of activities, to connect with technological capital, to feel the atmosphere of innovation, to have a more comprehensive understanding of the high-quality and relaxed entrepreneurial environment in the free trade zone, and to attract more overseas talents to come to start businesses.

5.3 2017 seminar on talent training and dispute resolution strategies for "Belt and Road"

On May 8, 2017, China Academy of Aeronautical Engineering Technology Development Strategy held a seminar on talent training and dispute resolution strategies for "Belt and Road" at Beijing University of Aeronautics and Astronautics. More than 40 people from relevant units and departments such as Chinese Academy of Engineering, the Supreme People's Court, National Railway Administration, National Remote Sensing Center, China Council for the Promotion of International Trade, Academic Exchange Center of the Chinese Law Society, and AVIC, CASC, COSCO, Zhejiang University, Shijiazhuang Railway University, Belt and Road International Research Institute, Beijing University of Aeronautics and Astronautics attended the meeting. The meeting was chaired by Professor TAO Zhi, Vice President of Beijing University of Aeronautics and Astronautics and Vice President of Aviation Strategic Research Institute.

Academician ZHANG Jun pointed out in his speech that more than 60 countries along "Belt and Road"were countries with diverse legal systems, rule of law environment, historical and cultural characteristics, and the establishment of dispute resolution mechanisms and institutions that were suitable for "Belt and Road" features is the necessary guarantee for promoting the implementation of

"Belt and Road" initiative. In order to serve "Belt and Road" and the "Beidou Going Out" national major strategies, Beijing University of Aeronautics and Astronautics and the first-class universities along "Belt and Road" jointly built the Beidou Silk Road College to cultivate international, high-level and innovative talent for countries along the route.

Professor HUANG Haijun introduced the situation of talent training and construction of the Beidou Silk Road College for "Belt and Road", and reported on the background, positioning, goals, mechanism innovation, existing foundation and progress of the establishment of Beidou Silk Road College. Professor Wang Guiguo, President of "Belt and Road" International Research Institute, reported on the current status of international dispute settlement, the necessity, urgency and feasibility of establishing a "Belt and Road" dispute settlement institution, as well as plans and recommendations.

The academicians and experts at the meeting conducted in-depth exchanges and discussions on the current status, urgent needs, and urgency of talent training and dispute resolution in "Belt and Road", as well as plans and recommendations for establishing "Belt and Road" dispute settlement agency. Everyone agreed that during the implementation of "Belt and Road" initiative, it was of great significance to demonstrate "Belt and Road" dispute resolution mechanism, and to accelerate the demonstration and consulting work of China's "Belt and Road" dispute resolution agencies.

5.4　2017 "Belt and Road" Initiative Implementation and Talent Training Forum

On June 4, 2017, "Belt and Road" Initiative Implementation and Talent Training Forum held by the School of Economics and Management of Tongji University and the Literature and Science of School was held.

The forum launched an in-depth and fruitful discussion on how to face the construction of "Belt and Road", continuously improve the international running level of universities in China, and create high-quality talents suitable for the construction of "Belt and Road".

Participants believed that the construction of "Belt and Road" was a new round of open development in China. We should strengthen the building of soft power, such as the interconnection of people's hearts, and realize the "soft connectivity" between Chinese and foreign people through systematic and long-term social responsibilities, and promote local economic development and talents training to help shape the country's image with a responsible and respected corporate brand.

Participants emphasized that overseas development was inseparable from the cultivation of international talents. International talents should have a global perspective and an international thinking model, be familiar with international business rules, technical standards and related legal and financial knowledge, and have strong cross-cultural communication capabilities and have a high level of foreign language. In addition, it could subsidize foreign students studying in China, and cultivate local technical and management talents through "passing, helping, and bringing".

Participants at the forum talked freely, brainstormed ideas and suggestions for the construction of "Belt and Road" and talent cultivation, and discussed how colleges and universities could create management talents with a global perspective to provide continuous and solid human resources support for "Belt and Road" construction.

5.5 The "Pilot Program" 2017 was held successfully for the first shipping youth talent exchange meeting

On March 16, 2017, Shanghai Lujiazui Financial City Development Bureau supported the launch of the first event of the 2017 Lujiazui International Shipping Elite "Pilot Program", a shipping youth talent exchange meeting.

The theme of this event was "Leadership and Career Development of Shipping Women". The event invited three women representatives and experts from the industry to attend, including Ms. Banu Kannu of the Wärtsilä Group, Ms. LIU Qianwen of Yihailan and Ms. GU Jiayu of Lloyd's. They shared their own workplace experience and life experience with the participants in the form of group discussions. Nearly 100 young talents in the shipping field including COSCO Shipping Containers, DHL, Drewley Maritime Services, Lloyd's Register of Shipping, AVIC International Leasing, Denmark Tok Shipping, Germany Saire Heavy Parts Transportation participated.

The event created an opportunity for Lujiazui's Shipping young talents to interact with various experts and colleagues in various fields. The atmosphere on the scene was lively and won wide recognition and praise from the participants.

5.6 Interview meeting for talent development and talent training of shipping logistics enterprises

On November 9, 2017, interview meeting for talent development and talent training of shipping logistics enterprises was held in the COSCO lecture hall of Shanghai Maritime University. The event was sponsored by the Shanghai Maritime University Youth League Committee, the Propaganda Department, the Student Office, and the library and co-organized by Transportation School Youth League Committee and the College Students Career Development Association of the Transportation School. Ms. HUANG Yihua from China-Philippines International Logistics Group and Mr. ZHENG Xulong, Sales Manager of Demei International Freight Forwarding (Shanghai) Co., Ltd. were present as guests.

During the interview, the issue of shipping logistics market was discussed. The current downturn in the market and a consolidation in the shipping industry were both a crisis and a turning point. For the question the socially concerned whether artificial intelligence could enter the shipping field and whether that Ali would get involved in the shipping industry would bring a shock, Mr. ZHENG emphasized that it should be optimistic. Intelligent development replaced part of the manpower and also brought the convenience of big data. However, in the end, the intelligence was still mainly based on serving people, and the analysis and application of data still depended on people. With regard to dealing with the relationship between internship and academics, Ms. HUANG gave valuable advice on her own experience: attach importance to the organic combination of theoretical learning and practice. We must have a willingness to learn and a humble and studious attitude, and treat ourselves as a brand.

Interview questions and answers, gave patient answers to questions such as the impact of AI on logistics, the most desirable quality of enterprise employment, academic qualifications and degree of recognition of overseas learning experience of enterprises, and encouraged everyone not to ignore the learning of professional knowledge. Educational qualifications were a stepping stone. Talents who were eager to learn and have positive attitudes were the most fancy of enterprises.

6 Exchange Activities and Meetings

6.1 The 4th International Shipping and Internet Summit Forum was successfully held in Shanghai

On May 18, 2017, sponsored by Shipping Industry Network, co-organized by Lujiazui Shipping Association and Lujiazui Shipping Internet Professional Committee, Changjiang Hui, Where to Ship, and Intercontinental Shipping as the supporters, with the theme of "New Journey of Data Shipping and Smart Shipping", the 4th International Shipping and Internet Summit Forum was successfully held in Shanghai.

At the forum, TANG Hongbin, Deputy General Manager of Yihaitong Supply Chain Co., Ltd., gave a keynote speech on "Thinking and Practice of Carless Carriers", and pointed out in detail that the ideal logistics industry should be the coincidence of logistics and information flow, which was a development direction for the logistics industry in the future. The basic spirit of the Internet was open sharing. Enterprises could efficiently use resources, improve efficiency and reduce costs through the use of the Internet. The development of information technology brought innovation and transformation to traditional enterprises.

ZHOU Shihao, the founder and CEO of the "Where to Ship" platform, took the theme of "The Unchanging Logic of the Changing Market" and comprehensively explained the "new shipping" under the Internet. He held that excellent international logistics companies were generated on the premise of high efficiency and expanding scale. "The Internet can sell all commodities that cannot be sold". What could not be sold in the original scene + the Internet was equal to the commodity in the new scene + to meet more market needs created new services, and new value.

WU Yunlong, a partner of Zero One Venture Capital, talked about the thinking and insights of *Investment Logic of B2B Companies*. He held that although B2B was currently experiencing some cold winters or bottlenecks, there were still opportunities for improvement in the long run. The business model itself was traditional and did not change even in the long term. However, the means of completing business processes has greatly improved with the advancement of technology, and the efficiency has been improved unprecedentedly.

YANG Lei, Deputy General Manager of the Legal Affairs and Risk Management Division of COSCO Shipping Group, discussed the current risks and potential risks of shipping and the Internet with "Prospects and Risks of Shipping Internet+". The main risks of Internet + Shipping were that: strategic risk based on "transaction" or "tradable"; strategic risk based on "box" or "goods"; operational risk of "capability" & "capability"; financial risk of "resources" VS "targets"; legal risk of compliance supervision.

LIU Qianwen, Senior Deputy CEO of Yihailan (Beijing) Data Technology Co., Ltd., comprehensively explained the viewpoint of "Innovation and Collaboration of Shipping Logistics Big Data" from the big data side. In the current shipping market, the big data revolution was under way. The container market was a very interesting market, not only on the sea, but also on land. Hope to make this market better through more transparent information, to give customers the services they really needed, and to get the data on the industry chain while serving customers, these data could be provided to upstream and downstream, let them do what they should do.

FANG Baoli, chairman of Nanjing Changjiang Ship Service Electronic Commerce Technology Co., Ltd., discussed with the theme of "How to Transform Yangtze Shipping into Smart Shipping", from the Yangtze River Inland shipping about what kind of smart shipping was innovation and could be called transformation. And from many aspects and multiple angles to tell the current status and pain points of the Yangtze River shipping. Three driving factors for smart shipping were platformization, intelligence and sharing. The development of "smart shipping" must embrace the technology of the times, innovate new service paths, and build a new shipping ecosystem.

CHEN Zhiqing, founder of 56cargo.com, delivered a keynote speech on the theme of "Innovation and Upgrade of Shipping E-commerce". He said that: "shipping company + third platform is a direction for the future development of shipping e-commerce. Success depends on the one hand, the third party platform's comprehensive resource capabilities and integrated logistics service capabilities, on the other hand, it also depends on shipping company transaction regulations. After all, the shipping company makes a balance and choice between its traditional mainstream goods providers—freight forwarders and emerging third-party platform with unpredictable goods volumes."

HUANG Xianming, the founder of the Chuanlaoda.com, delivered a keynote speech on "Opportunities of the Yangtze River and the Internet" from another angle. He held that the domestic water freight rate exceeded 500 billion and the entire industry chain exceeded 3 trillion. Therefore, the Internet + the Yangtze River and the inland river faced rare opportunities. Wang Yiqiu, the co-founder of Jijiyun, discussed in detail "How the Internet can Promote the Development of a New Business Model for LCL" in specific LCL business. He shared his thoughts on the integration of the application of Internet: establishing a standardization system and price rules of online transactions; to achieve the improvement of per capita efficiency and comprehensive efficiency; to penetrate the entire logistics chain based on the application of cloud technology to achieve collaboration, interaction and sharing; combine fourth-party logistics to build a logistics flexible supply chain; establish customer positioning on big data, precise demand; combined with B2B's own financial attributes, connected transactions to realize corporate credit and financial services.

6.2 Shanghai Shipping Trading Forum was successfully held in 2017

2017 Shanghai Shipping Trading Forum was held at China Financial Information Center on November 28, 2017, and the theme of the forum was set as "Shipping Decision in the Era of Big Data". Experts from Ministry of Transport, Shanghai Transportation Committee, Shanghai Pudong New District, as well as financial, economical, shipping and other industry and macro and industry experts talked about the breakthroughs and innovations in the era of big data from multiple perspectives—from "Belt and Road" trade data to look at the development opportunities and challenges of the shipping industry, the future development trend of the port and shipping industry in the context of the big data era, the application of "block chain" in the supply chain, big data in port layout and innovation, and big data logic in the coastal container capacity layout, use big data to build a leisure town on the Yangtze River cruise and look at the trend of the port and shipping industry from the operation data of listed port and shipping companies in the capital market.

Standing on the tide of the era of big data, Shanghai Shipping Exchange announced at the forum that FDI and CCTFI were officially put into trial operation, and the "Shanghai Shipping Index" was added a new member.

Big data has been deeply integrated with the shipping industry, and the long economic wave of the information age is coming. The mining of big data and the rapid development of shipping technology have brought about the upgrading and transformation of the information service platform, which will trigger a revolution in the shipping industry's service model and profit-making methods, and eventually realize the leap-forward development of the shipping industry's operating system.

Shanghai Shipping Exchange Forum is a professional, international and large-scale shipping boutique forum that Shanghai Shipping Exchange has been building since 2010. The forum selects a key issue related to the future of shipping every year. Elites from all parties gather together and their wonderful views and innovations and practice will lead the market.

6.3 2017 China Maritime Day Forum was held in Ningbo

According to the gradual advancement of the implementation of the national maritime power strategy, the topics and agenda of the main forum of 2017 Maritime Day were adjusted in time to make the main forum consciously integrate into the national strategy. The main forum would promote Chinese views, listen to industry concerns, make international friends, create a cooperative atmosphere, and make new contributions to the construction of the 21st Century Maritime Silk Road.

2017 Maritime Day Forum activities were held from July 10th to 12th, 2017. Among them, there were 2 thematic forums held on July 10th: one was the Sail to Instance Navigation Culture Forum, and the other was shipping 50 people forum. There were 5 thematic forums held on July 11th, including the Crew Forum, Haishi Port Forum, Pilot Forum, Small and Medium Shipping

Enterprise Forum, International Shipping Service Industry Forum. There was one thematic forum held on July 12th: Ocean Emerging Industry Forum. The guest speakers invited by the 8 thematic forums were mainly composed of well-known experts of government officials, high-level enterprises, and scientific research institutions. The third round table of port management agencies and the Ningbo Zhoushan Port and Central and Eastern Europe Port Cooperation Conference were also held in Ningbo at the same time.

The main theme of the forum was "Raise the Sails of the Silk Road and Build a Blue Dream Together". It was composed of a main forum and 8 thematic forums such as China International Crew Forum and Haisi Port International Cooperation Forum. Deputy minister of Ministry of Transport HE Jianzhong delivered a keynote speech at the main forum. Deputy-governor of Zhejiang GAO Xingfu, Deputy Secretary of Ningbo Municipal Committee and Mayor QIU Dongyao attended the main forum and delivered a speech.

HUANG Youfang, chairman of China Maritime Society, presided over the main forum of China Maritime Day Forum. CAO Di, Executive Deputy Chairman of China Maritime Society, secretary-general WANG Qun, and Deputy Secretary-General GU Weiguo participated in the main forum and related activities.

In his speech, HE Jianzhong pointed out that in the new development period, President XI Jinping proposed "Belt and Road" initiative, which opened up a new path for cooperation for countries around the world, and has received positive response and broad support from the international community. Shipping was an important carrier and guarantee for "21st Century Maritime Silk Road". While strengthening the construction of "hardware" such as infrastructure interconnection, it was necessary to strengthen the construction of "software" such as the integration of shipping development systems, rules, policies and standards, and deepen cooperation mechanism, highlight planning and guidance, promote project implementation, and take the lead in the construction of "Belt and Road".

GAO Xingfu said that: "in order to implement the new requirements put forward by General Secretary XI Jinping during the G20 summit and the spirit of the 14th provincial party congress, the goal of our province's marine port work in the next few years is to work hard, lead new development, and focus on implementation of '5211' marine strong province action and vigorously implement five strategic measures to build five platforms including Zhejiang Marine Economic Demonstration Zone, Zhoushan River-Sea Combined-Transportation Service Center, and Shanghai Cooperation Develop Yangshan Port, focusing on building a strong marine province and an international strong port. By 2020, we will initially achieve the goals of strong marine province with strong marine comprehensive economic strength, marine scientific and technological innovation capacity, marine ecological protection capacity, and marine management and control capacity. We will achieve a world-class modern hub port, a world-class shipping service base, and a world-class commodity trading base. And fully implement 11 Chinese measures such as planning to lead major projects, marine industry, and marine ecological innovation system and mechanism."

SHI Qingfeng said in his speech that since the "Twelfth Five-Year Plan", China's marine economy has generally maintained a good development trend. The marine economy has played an important role in expanding development space, building ecological civilization, accelerating power conversion, and maintaining sustained and stable economic growth. According to statistics, in 2016, China's marine GDP reached 7.0507 trillion yuan, accounting for 9.5% of GDP, with a growth rate of 6.8%, which was 0.1 percentage points higher than the GDP of the same period. The marine economy has become a driving force for national economic growth. Facing the future, with the implementation of major strategies such as the construction of a maritime power and the construction of the 21st Century Maritime Silk Road, China's marine economic development space would be wider, the prospects would be better, and the contribution rate to the national economic development will continue to increase.

ZHENG Xinli said that President XI Jinping's speech at the summit of the G20 leaders on July 7, 2017 not only pointed the way for world economic development, but also proposed new tasks for how domestic economic development could adapt to the requirements of economic globalization. We must expand foreign investment and trade in an active construction of an open world economy, lead economic globalization through the development of mutually beneficial and win-win foreign economic relations, and strive to set an example for all countries in the world in terms of domestic economic development and global economic governance.

6.4 2017 Maritime and Maritime Commerce Seminar and Seminar on Legal Issues Related to Bankruptcy of Shipping Enterprises was held

On May 12, 2017, All-China Lawyers Association Maritime Commerce and Maritime Professional Committee—"2017 Maritime and Maritime Commerce Seminar and Seminar on Legal Issues Related to Bankruptcy of Shipping Enterprises" was held in Zhoushan, Zhejiang. Sponsored by All-China Lawyers Association Maritime Commerce and Maritime Professional Committee, co-hosted by Wintell & Co., Jingheng Law Firm, Dacheng Law Firm, Zhejiang Lawyers Association Corporate Bankruptcy Management Committee, Shanghai Lawyers Association Maritime and Maritime Commerce Professional Committee, Zhoushan Lawyers Association co-organized.

The meeting took the form of a round table. After the keynote speakers and subject-matter speakers made special speeches, experts and scholars present at the meeting discussed the topic, focusing on four issues of "the status and solution of conflicts between the maritime court and the people's court under the bankruptcy case of shipping and shipbuilding enterprises", "conflict between arbitration procedure and bankruptcy case procedure", "the dilemma of bank creditors of shipping and shipbuilding enterprises in bankruptcy cases", "Research on the legal issues of bankruptcy law of multinational shipping enterprises—analysis from Hanjin bankruptcy" to carry out in-depth discussions, and the results were quite fruitful, which had far-reaching significance for promoting practical innovation and theoretical research on improving relevant system of bankruptcy of shipping companies.

Chaired by Judge WU Shengshun of Ningbo Maritime Court, Lawyer REN Yimin, the arbitrator of China Maritime Arbitration Committee Shanghai Branch ZHANG Lirong gave opening speeches focusing on the enforcement of arbitration awards; the jurisdictional court that revoked the awards; whether the review of the non-enforcement of the arbitration awards continued; whether the disputes over bankruptcy revocation, right of set-off of bankruptcy, right to recover of bankruptcy could be arbitrated; foreign-related arbitration and other issues and their solutions were discussed.

DONG Dengyong, a senior partner of Dacheng (Ningbo) Law Firm chaired, Lawyer DONG Jie, Director of Dacheng (Zhoushan) Law Firm, Lawyer Ren Yi of Dacheng (Ningbo) Law Firm, and Lawyer CHEN Xiangyong, Director of Wang Jing & Co. (Shanghai), gave opening speeches focusing the influence and exercise of bank creditors' rights in shipping and shipbuilding enterprises, had an in-depth discussion on the influence of ship possessory lien on the mortgage of ship under construction, the influence of ship lien on the realization of mortgage rights, and the degradation of ship value.

Chaired by Professor HU Zhengliang of Shanghai Maritime University, Judge WANG Lei of Shanghai Maritime Court, WANG Yang, Senior Manager of Legal Affairs of COSCO and FANG Yi, lawyer of Wintell & Co., gave opening speeches. Judge WANG Lei made introduction on the hearing situation of derivative litigation in Hanjin bankruptcy in China. Lawyer FANG Yi of Wintell & Co., as an experienced person, introduced the overall process of Hanjin's bankruptcy case, the procedures for declaring claims, and the general situation, as well as the problems and reflections encountered in Hanjin's bankruptcy case. Among them, representatives discussed about foreign-related bankruptcy cases in China's confirmation and implementation and foreign-related bankruptcy enterprises in China's property enforcement and other issues.

In recent years, shipbuilding industry and shipping industry have continued to slump, and bankruptcy of shipbuilding enterprises has entered a period of high incidence. The bankruptcy reorganization or liquidation of shipping companies, on the one hand, caused many ships to be arrested and auctioned, which led to a large number of maritime and maritime commerce disputes; on the other hand, between bankruptcy proceedings and maritime litigation, from case jurisdiction to liquidation distribution, regardless of entities and procedures, there are still great differences and conflicts and at the same time, the conflicts between bankruptcy and arbitration procedures, and cross-border shipping bankruptcy issues have also become increasingly prominent, bringing many difficulties and challenges to the development of bankruptcy work and related trial work. How to deepen theoretical research, strengthen communication and coordination, and properly resolve the conflicts and connections between different legal systems and different countries' bankruptcy systems are common issues faced by courts, maritime and maritime commerce lawyers, and shipbuilding bankruptcy managers.

6.5 The third China Maritime Finance (Dongjiang) International Forum was held in Tianjin

On May 16, 2017, the third China Maritime Finance (Dongjiang) International Forum was held in Tianjin. The forum was jointly organized by Tianjin Dongjiang Bonded Port Management Committee, Baltic International Shipping Association and Financial Times. Tianjin Deputy Mayor Yan Qingmin attended the forum and delivered opening speeches. Relevant leaders of CBRC, Foreign Exchange Administration, General Administration of Customs, Maritime Safety Administration of Ministry of Transport, China Classification Society, China Shipowners Association, China Internet Finance Association, China International Chamber of Commerce attended.

The theme of the forum was "New Opportunities, New Changes, and New Forms: The Road to Diversified Development of China's Maritime Finance", adhering to the spirit of "openness, innovation, pragmatism, and cooperation", and had a in-depth discussion of new needs, new changes and new trends in the development of maritime finance to promote win-win cooperation in all aspects of the industrial chain. It was strongly supported by China Foreign Investment Enterprise Association Leasing Industry Working Committee, China Shipowners Association, and China Financial Leasing 30-person Forum, attracting 250 institutions and 42 media including People. com at home and abroad, the conference scale exceeded 600 for the first time, which aroused great attention from the industry.

The level of participating enterprises has improved significantly, and the full coverage of the upstream and downstream of the maritime finance industry chain has been achieved. Including 47 leasing enterprises, 49 financial institutions, 42 shipping and manufacturing enterprises, 10 international classification societies, 36 intermediaries and Royal Caribbean, Costa Cruise, Carnival Group, Mediterranean Cruise and other large international cruise companies. China Maritime Finance (Dongjiang) International Forum has become an annually renowned maritime finance professional event, building an efficient business negotiation, exchange and cooperation platform for participating enterprises.

More than 50 speakers at home and abroad on the main forum discussed 60 topics, including the analysis of the global shipping economic situation, the new ecology of maritime investment and financing, innovative maritime financial services, legal risk prevention and control, maritime asset management, maritime financial tax planning, maritime financial internationalization strategy, shipping fund, shipping insurance.

As a national leasing innovation demonstration zone, Dongjiang attaches great importance to the deep integration of the development of the maritime financial industry and international capital, and actively builds a leading zone for the development and pioneering of maritime financial innovation in China. It adheres to policy innovation, functional innovation, model innovation, product innovation and service innovation, constantly improves the financial environment, judicial environment, talent exchange environment, and creates a new ecology of the maritime financial industry in line with international standards. It has become a gathering place for China's maritime financial cross-border leasing business and offshore leasing business, and a comprehensive platform for China's maritime financial leasing asset registration, publicity of creditor's rights, trading, and circulation. As of the end of April 2017, Dongjiang had registered a total of 2,230 leasing companies with a cumulative registered capital of RMB 288.8 billion yuan; Dongjiang had registered a total of 160 single-ship companies, and international ship leasing assets reached 5.2 billion USD, accounting for 80% of the country; offshore drilling platform leasing assets was 2.5 billion USD, accounting for 100% of the country.

In 2016, all the 90 reform tasks of the *China (Tianjin) Free Pilot Trade Zone Overall Plan* were initiated, 175 system innovation initiatives, 151 were implemented, and 9 system innovations became the national replication and promotion pilot experience. With the level of investment and trade facilitation of free trade zone significantly improved and the increasingly improved international business environment, Dongjiang maritime finance has ushered in new development.

Under "Belt and Road" initiative, "Made in China 2025" and other national strategies, Dongjiang will actively explore and boldly innovate in the future, build China's largest overseas engineering export base, build China's maritime finance and offshore financial innovation zones, and continue to promote China maritime finance industry to develop rapidly.

6.6 Round table discussion on the construction of "Belt and Road" dispute settlement mechanism

In order to further study and practice the spirit of the 19th National Congress of the Communist Party of China, implement XI Jinping's series of speeches and instructions on advancing the construction of "Belt and Road", sponsored by the Supreme People's Court and Xi'an Jiaotong University. Siting, organized by the No.4 Civil Trial of the Supreme People's Court, the institute of international law and comparative law of the Silk Road and the legal governance research center of the free trade zone research institute of Xi'an Jiaotong University "round table discussion on the construction of 'Belt and Road' dispute settlement mechanism" was held on October 24, 2017. LIU Guixiang, vice-ministerial level full-time member of the Supreme People's Court Judiciary Committee, DU Hangwei, member of the Standing Committee of the Shanxi Party Committee, Secretary of the Political and Legal Committee of the Provincial Party Committee, and Deputy Governor, WANG Xiaoli, Executive Deputy Secretary of Xi'an Jiaotong University, and more than 40 leading experts and scholars from Supreme People's Court, Ministry of Commerce, Shanxi Provincial Committee, Shanxi High People's Court and other government departments, academic institutions and China International Economic and Trade Arbitration Commission and other practical departments gathered in Xi'an, to provide suggestions and support the construction of dispute settlement mechanism of "Belt and Road" and judicial guarantee were made.

DU Hangwei said in his speech that Shanxi, as the new starting point of Silk Road Economic Belt, had a unique geographical advantage in integrating with "Belt and Road" initiative. Shanxi Provincial Party Committee and Government attached great importance to docking "Belt and Road" in promoting the economic and social development of Shanxi. With the spirit of the instruction of XI Jinping's important speech in Shanxi and the requirements of the report of the 19th National Congress of the Communist Party of China, efforts are being made to build the core area of "Belt and Road", including the core area of "Belt and Road" dispute settlement. Du Hangwei encouraged relevant departments, colleges and universities in Shanxi and the Supreme People's Court to further contact and cooperate with each other to jointly promote the docking and coordination of major issues such as "Belt and Road" dispute settlement mechanism and the construction of "Belt and Road" legal services and rule of law innovation demonstration zones to make greater contributions to the national "Belt and Road" initiative and the building of a rule of law China.

LIU Guixiang said in his speech that building a just, efficient and convenient dispute resolution mechanism for "Belt and Road" was the core of "Belt and Road" rule of law and a long-term systematic project. The practice and law circles should thoroughly study the spirit of the 19th National Congress of the Communist Party of China, work together to strengthen research, consolidate the theoretical basis of the "Belt and Road" dispute settlement mechanism, strengthen international judicial cooperation, actively participate in the formulation of international rules, and promote coordination and integration of cross-border disputes settlement mechanism, build a "three-in-one" one-stop dispute resolution mechanism organically connected by mediation, arbitration and litigation, strive to create a new situation in international commercial maritime trials, and effectively improve the level of services and guarantees for the construction of "Belt and Road".

Focusing on the construction of "Belt and Road" dispute settlement mechanism, discussing three topics, including demand and design, supporting innovation of the rule of law, and investment arbitration reform. Experts at the meeting agreed that the establishment of a fair and reasonable dispute settlement mechanism was a major and urgent issue facing the process of the rule of law in "Belt and Road"; properly handling and resolving commercial maritime disputes and investment and trade disputes in the construction of "Belt and Road" not only was the premise and guarantee for the smooth progress of the construction of "Belt and Road", but also an inevitable requirement for creating "Belt and Road" legal business environment; the construction of "Belt and Road" dispute settlement mechanism was a systemic project of great significance and required an integrated international and domestic two resources, required the benign interaction between the international rule of law and the domestic rule of law, and the mutual cooperation between the international dispute settlement mechanism and domestic justice; the construction of "Belt and Road" dispute settlement mechanism should comprehensively use mediation, arbitration, trial and other mechanisms, with particular attention to give full play to the leading role of the mediation mechanism; in order to better serve the construction of "Belt and Road" dispute settlement mechanism, China needed to make legal and institutional innovations on issues such as the revision of the arbitration law, the effectiveness of mediation agreements, and the confirmation and enforcement of arbitral awards.

Whereas Shanxi's outstanding historical position and contemporary geographical advantages in "Belt and Road", it is necessary to actively explore the establishment of a national "Belt and Road" legal service and rule of law innovation demonstration zone in Xi'an based on the Shanxi Free Trade Zone to serve "Belt and Road" initiative dispute settlement and at the same time to explore for the country the internationally competitive legal service and rule of law innovation path with mediation, arbitration and justice.

6.7 2017 Seminar of "Construction of 'Belt and Road' and Maritime Justice Response"

On September 26, 2017, 2017 Annual Meeting of the Maritime and Maritime Commerce Trial Theory Professional Committee of China Trial Theory Research Society was held at Shanghai Maritime Court. The theme of the annual meeting was "Construction of 'Belt and Road' and Maritime Justice Response".

ZHAO Hong, Deputy Director of Maritime and Maritime Commerce Trial Theory Professional Committee of China Judicial Theory Research Association, Chairman of Maritime Code Research Association of Shanghai Law Society and President of Shanghai Maritime Court, delivered a welcome speech at the meeting. CAO Shouye, Executive Director of China Judicial Theory Research Association, Deputy Director of the Institute of Applied Law of Supreme People's Court, and SHI Jixiong, Full-Time Deputy Chairman of Shanghai Law Society, attended and addressed the meeting. Five units including the Institute of International Law of Chinese Academy of Social Sciences, Tsinghua University, Shanghai Municipal Transportation Committee, Shanghai Branch of China

Maritime Arbitration Committee, and COSCO, respectively made keynote speeches on the construction of Shanghai International Shipping Center and International Maritime Justice Center and maritime arbitration development and other content under "Belt and Road" initiative.

Participants discussed three topics: "legal innovation in the connection between 'Belt and Road' and the construction of free trade zone", "improvement of the maritime legal system and diversified settlement mechanism for maritime disputes", and "maritime judicial needs and trial hot issues". The Secretary-General of the Maritime and Maritime Commerce Trial Theory Professional Committee of China Judicial Theory Research Association, Deputy Chairman of Maritime Code Research Association of Shanghai Law Society, and Vice President of Shanghai Maritime Court, JIA Zhenkun presided over the meeting. About 60 representatives from the Supreme People's Court, China Applied Law Institute, Shanghai Law Society, Shanghai High People's Court, maritime courts across the country, and related scientific research institutions, competent authorities, arbitration institutions, and port and shipping enterprises participated in the seminar.

6.8　2017 first high-end forum on "Belt and Road" and construction of maritime rule of law

On June 20, 2017, the first high-end forum on "Belt and Road" and construction of maritime rule of law was held at Shanghai Maritime University. Units like China Law Society, Legislative Affairs Office of State Council, Supreme People's Court, China Arbitration Law Research Association, Shanghai Law Society, Shanghai Maritime Court, China Maritime Arbitration Commission, China Shipowners Mutual Insurance Association, China University of Political Science and Law, Dalian Maritime University, Shanghai Jiaotong University, COSCO, China National Aviation Fuel Group Limited and other experts and scholars from well-known law firms attended the event.

ZHANG Mingqi, Deputy Chairman of China Law Society, member of the Standing Committee of the National People's Congress, and Deputy Chairman of Law Committee, LU Yunhua, consultant of China Arbitration Law Research Association, Deputy Leader of the preparation and leadership group of China

Arbitration Association of Legislative Affairs Office of State Council, LIN Guoping, Executive Vice President of Shanghai Law Society and HUANG Youfang, President of Shanghai Maritime University, delivered speeches respectively.

President HUANG Youfang said that under "Belt and Road" initiative and the great environment, background and strategy of goal of constructing an international maritime justice center, the holding of this high-end forum on "Belt and Road" and construction of maritime rule of law would be of great significance to promote the development of Shanghai Maritime University and the construction of Shanghai International Shipping Center.

Vice President LIN Guoping pointed out that the establishment of a maritime arbitration research center would further deepen the reform of the diversified dispute settlement mechanism, enhance China's shipping soft power, and help the construction of Shanghai International Shipping Center.

Consultant LU Yunhua said that the maritime arbitration system was an important guarantee for the implementation of the national maritime strategy, and the establishment of the maritime arbitration research center was an important measure to implement the maritime power and "Belt and Road" initiative.

Deputy Chairman ZHANG Mingqi pointed out that the maritime arbitration research center should give full play to its role as a think tank, systematically carry out academic exchanges, teaching guidance, and research projects to further promote the development of China's maritime arbitration.

At the forum, the nation's first maritime arbitration research think tank, Maritime Arbitration Research Center, was officially established. GUO Feng, Executive Deputy Secretary-General of China Arbitration Law Research Association, read out the *Response on the Establishment of a Maritime Arbitration Research Center at Shanghai Maritime University* and the list of the first batch of senior researchers employed by the center. ZHANG Mingqi, LU Yunhua, LIN Guoping, and HUANG Youfang jointly unveiled Maritime Arbitration Research Center, and issued letters of appointment for the center's directors, consultants, and senior researchers.

LIU Jingdong, Vice President of the No.4 Civil Trial of the Supreme People's

Court, CHEN Bo, Deputy Secretary-General of China Maritime Arbitration Commission, and Vice President of the Arbitration Court respectively centered on themes of "Full Play of the Role of Arbitration in the Construction of Belt and Road" and "New Development of China Maritime Arbitration—Transformation and New Attraction" and delivered speeches. Experts attending the meeting conducted in-depth discussions on "Belt and Road" and hot issues in the construction of maritime rule of law.

6.9　2017 International Shipping and Financial Summit Forum was successfully held in Shanghai

On November 10, 2017, sponsored by BIMCO and Shipping Industry Network, and co-organized by Lujiazui Shipping Association, Lujiazui Talent Golden Port, Qingdao Intercontinental Shipping, China Air & Shipping Exchange, and Wintell & Co. were supporters, with the theme of the "Market Recovery, Where Shipping finance to Go?" 2017 International Shipping and Financial Summit Forum was successfully held in Shanghai. More than 150 guests from shipping industry chain such as shipping, finance, law, insurance, and news media attended the meeting. Executive Vice President of China Shipowners Association ZHANG Shouguo made an opening speech for this forum.

The organizer of BIMCO and the Shipping Industry have successfully held four consecutive international ship financing summit forums. On this basis, the organizer and Lujiazui Shipping Association held this forum in Shanghai, inviting various experts from ports, shipping and shipping finance companies to gather together and brainstorm: to discuss together in the context of that the shipping industry has become a national strategic industry, how to promote the strong support of financial institutions for the shipping industry, and how to constructively develop the relationship between shipping and finance.

HAN Ning, Director of Drewry Maritime Consulting China, pointed out from the analysis of the supply and demand data of the container transportation market that 22,000 TEU ships would be the largest in the market, but the upgrading of ships would lead to the expansion of the scale of all routes, and the balance of supply and demand would not happen in 2020. Market freight rates would increase but volatility would increase. JI Wenyuan, Chairman of Seamaster

Shipping Group, explained the status and characteristics of the bulk dry goods market. Freight rates of the bulk dry goods shipping market were characterized by short change periods and large relative changes. The fluctuations were inextricably linked to bulk commodity trade (prices, imports). LU Chengyun, Deputy Director of the Comprehensive Transportation Research Institute of National Development and Reform Committee, explained the development opportunities for Chinese shipping companies. Chairman of Qingdao Intercontinental Shipping Group GUO Jinkui explained how traditional shipowners responded to the new normal of the market from three aspects: operation, management and capital.

Although the future prospects of the shipping market are not smooth, the linking and integration of shipping and finance are always topics of concern. JIN Hai, Executive Director and General Manager of Yuanhai Xinda Investment Management (Tianjin) Co., Ltd. admitted that although the bank was the largest provider of shipping capital, there were still huge opportunities for those capital resources interested in and capable of investing in the shipping industry. Each type of shipping investment financial institution had a unique set of criteria. Shipowners seeking funds must understand and decide which correct source to choose. Financial shipowners have become an important force that could not be ignored in the shipping market. GUO Fangmeng, Executive General Manager of ICBC Leasing and Shipping Division, said that financial shipowners needed to pay attention to the diversified combination of ship types in terms of investment, taking advantage of characteristics of different cycles of each ship type; it needed to be put in rhythmically, especially in the operation of leasing business, to avoid a large number of ship leases to expire at the same time; it was necessary to pay attention to customer selection, customer default rate should be controlled below 10%, and bad lease rate should be controlled below 5%. COSCO Haifa Shipping Leasing Division which has successfully transformed into a shipping finance company GONG Ling also held that under the weak shipping cycle, the shipping leasing industry was ushering in new opportunities. Yingtai Maritime Law Firm partner LU Yujia explained the new format and legal risks of shipping financing.

For small and medium shipping enterprises, they were facing severe survival challenges. LI Duozhu, Chairman of Shanghai Dingheng Shipping Co., Ltd., gave advice on how small and medium-sized enterprises could overcome difficulties in the shipping industry chain of the new era. Most of the participants in the inland shipping market were individual shipowners. The transaction scale was small and the transaction data was scattered. However, traditional financial institutions were insufficient to sink in subdivided industries. They lack effective monitoring of dynamic assets such as ships. In particular, there was a serious imbalance between supply and demand in the inland waterway shipping financing market of Pearl River and Yangtze River. HUANG Fenglin, Vice President of China Air & Shipping Exchange, said at the meeting that China Air & Shipping Exchange relied on the shipping asset management platform to gradually accumulate and form an inland river shipping risk database with authoritative reference value through the development of shipping financial services, ship asset technical services and payment settlement services and initially established a business model for shipping asset management. On the one hand, China Air & Shipping Exchange built a bridge between financial institutions and inland small and medium-sized shipping companies. On the other hand, it has also laid a solid foundation for China Air & Shipping Exchange to build China's largest NVOCC platform and intelligent ship and goods matching platform.

6.10 2017 Shanghai International Shipping Rule of Law Forum was held

On October 25, 2017, 2017 Shanghai International Shipping Rule of Law Forum co-sponsored by Shanghai Law Society, East China University of Political Science and Law and China Maritime Arbitration Committee was held. Experts and scholars jointly discussed issues such as the construction of the international shipping dispute settlement mechanism under "Belt and Road".

YE Qing, President of East China University of Political Science and Law said that the forum focused on "Belt and Road", "Shipping", and "Rule of Law" and closely connected with the national development blueprint in the report of the 19th National Congress. In the construction of "Belt and Road", shipping was the interconnected link, and the rule of law was the guarantee for the development of shipping. "Belt and Road" initiative has provided new opportunities for the development of the rule of law in shipping and also raised new challenges. He said that East China University of Political Science and Law would continue to deepen the research on the legal guarantee of the construction of Shanghai International Shipping Center, and provide theoretical support and intellectual support for the construction of Shanghai International Shipping Center.

GU Chao, Secretary General of China Maritime Arbitration Committee, held that at a time when China's economy was ushering in new development, China's shipping legal service industry was also ushering in new opportunities. China International Maritime Judicial Center and International Maritime Arbitration Center complement each other's advantages, which was conducive to enhancing China's voice on the international stage. China's maritime arbitration ushered in unprecedented opportunities and space for development, strengthening the top-level design, establishing and improving a diversified dispute resolution mechanism, and developing the maritime arbitration cause were of great significance for the construction of Shanghai International Shipping Center. In the special discussion, more than 100 experts and scholars from domestic legal circles and related practical departments centered on the theme of the forum: the new trend of the development of the international shipping rule of law under the background of "Belt and Road", the construction of International Maritime Justice Center and the theoretical study of maritime trials, International maritime legislation trends and improvement of China's maritime legal system and the construction of the international shipping dispute settlement mechanism under "Belt and Road" and had in-depth discussions and exchanges.

6.11 Conception on the Construction of Maritime Cooperation in"Belt and Road" was released

On June 20, 2017, National Development and Reform Committee and State Oceanic Administration formulated and released the *Conception on the Construction of Maritime Cooperation in "Belt and Road"*.

This "Conception" was the first time that the Chinese government has proposed China plan for the promotion of construction of maritime cooperation in "Belt and Road" since the *Vision and Action to Promote the Joint Construction of Silk Road Economic Belt and 21st Century Maritime Silk Road* was released on March 28, 2015, which was also one of the achievements of the leaders of "Belt and Road" International Cooperation Summit Forum.

The "Conception" proposed to cooperate with all countries along 21st Century Maritime Silk Road in all-round and multi-disciplinary maritime cooperation, jointly create an open and inclusive cooperation platform, establish an active and pragmatic blue partnership, and forge "Blue Engine" for sustainable development.

In terms of thinking, the "Conception" proposed that according to the key directions of 21st century Maritime Silk Road, the construction of maritime cooperation in "Belt and Road" was supported by the Chinese coastal economic belt, and close cooperation with the countries along the route, connecting the China-Indo-China Peninsula Economic Corridor, from the South China Sea westward entering the Indian Ocean, connecting the China-Pakistan, Bangladesh-China-India-Burma Economic Corridor, and jointly building China-India Ocean-Africa-Mediterranean Blue Economic Channel; from the South China Sea southward entering Pacific Ocean and building China-Oceania-South Pacific Blue Economic Channel; active promoting the joint construction of a blue economic channel connecting Europe via the Arctic Ocean.

The "Conception" clarified five areas of cooperation focus: build a mutually beneficial and win-win blue partnership, innovate cooperation models, build a cooperation platform, jointly formulate a number of action plans, and implement a number of exemplary and driving cooperation projects, take the road of green development, create the road of prosperity by the sea, build the road of safety and guarantee, build the road of wisdom and innovation, and seek the road of cooperative governance.

In terms of creating a road of prosperity by the sea, the "Conception" proposed to actively participate in the development and utilization of the Arctic. The Chinese government was willing to work with all parties to carry out a comprehensive scientific investigation of the Arctic waterway, cooperate to establish an Arctic shore-based observatory, and study the Arctic climate and environment changes and its impact, carry out waterway forecast service, support the countries surrounding the Arctic Ocean to improve the transportation conditions of the Arctic waterway, and encourage Chinese enterprises to participate in the commercial use of the Arctic waterway. We were willing to cooperate with relevant Arctic countries to carry out resource potential assessment of the Arctic region, encourage Chinese enterprises to participate in the sustainable development of Arctic resources in an orderly manner, and strengthen clean energy cooperation with Arctic countries.

The "Conception" proposed to take active actions in five areas, including high-level guidance and promotion, building a cooperation platform, increasing capital investment, promoting internal and external docking, and facilitating project implementation. Among them, with regard to capital investment, the "Conception" proposed that the Chinese government would coordinate domestic resources, establish the China-ASEAN Maritime Cooperation Fund and the China-Indonesia Maritime Cooperation Fund, and implement the *South China Sea and Surrounding Ocean International Cooperation Framework Plan*. The Asian Infrastructure Investment Bank and the Silk Road Fund would provide financial support for major maritime cooperation projects.

7 Summary

After experiencing a low freight rate in 2016, the shipping industry embarked on a path of bottoming out in 2017. In 2017, State Council, Ministry of Transport and related departments made important instructions regarding the long-term development of the shipping industry and the current grim situation. As the largest port city in China, Shanghai has superior hardware and software conditions, and should bear the responsibility to shoulder the historical responsibility for realizing "Belt and Road" initiative. Vigorously develop modern shipping construction, strengthen the construction of the development and innovation of shipping technology, shipping finance, shipping transactions, maritime justice and other modern service industries. Enhance the international competitiveness of the shipping industry, construct an international shipping transaction center, and accelerate the construction of an international shipping center.

Chapter 6　Prospect

2017 is the fifth year of Shanghai's construction of Pilot Free Trade Zone, and a key year for the deepening of the reform and opening up of Shanghai Pilot Free Trade Zone. As the "Belt and Road" initiative is fully launched, the construction of Shanghai Pilot Free Trade Zone has entered a new era. The development goals of the Shanghai Pilot Free Trade Zone are free entry and exit of goods, convenient flow of funds, highly opening up of transportation, free practice of personnel, and fast connection of information. The core of development is to benchmark international trade, shipping, and financial centers, and formulate and implement a liberalization and facilitation system, and gather domestic and foreign companies to build a resource allocation platform.

Throughout the development of international trade, shipping, and financial centers such as London, Singapore and Hong Kong, China, if Shanghai is to transform from a Chinese center to an international center, it must vigorously develop offshore service industries including offshore shipping. The so-called offshore service refers to the provision of services by residents of the country (such as enterprises, organizations, individuals) for residents of the other countries for transactions of goods, technology, services and other transactions that are not actually relevant to the country. Offshore services are broadly divided into intermediary, middle man and exchange services. The exchange type is a high-end format for offshore services. The best example is the London Lloyd's Insurance Market (hereinafter referred to as Lloyd's), which has accumulated shipping and other insurance companies and applicants in more than 200 countries and regions, and more than 85% of insurance transactions are concluded between non-UK companies.

The development level of the offshore service industry is the main indicator to distinguish domestic, regional and international trade centers. Only by mastering the offshore (between other countries) transactions can we obtain the right of speaking, pricing, rule-making, and the ultimate distribution of rights in the international market, and thus have a substantial impact on the market. For example, in 2018, Lloyd's insurance transaction amount was approximately RMB 320 billion, of which offshore was approximately RMB 270 billion yuan, accounting for 30%~40% of the global transnational total. The premium rate in the market is regarded as a standard in the international market, and the format clause of the insurance contract formulated has become the norm in the international market.

The offshore service industry is an important part of modern international trade, and the vigorous development of the industry is what the party and the state should approve to set up a new area. The reasons are as follows:

(1) Offshore service is an ideal carrier to achieve the goal of free trade zone construction. The objective of the free trade zone is the free flow of goods, funds, talents and information. Offshore services precisely involve the aforementioned four elements in and out of China's borders and free trade zone areas. Offshore services are the only high-end service industry that can simultaneously promote "free flow of the four elements".

(2) The Pilot Free Trade Zone takes the national "Belt and Road" initiative as its own responsibility, and the primary service targets for offshore services are Chinese enterprises that and are deployed along the "Belt and Road". Offshore services will eliminate the worries of "Go Out" companies developing in other countries and enable them to use reasonable means to reduce the adverse effects of Sino-US trade frictions.

(3) The development of offshore industries is in line with the historical mission given by the state to build "five centers" in Shanghai and enhance the country's international influence. The development of the industry cannot only create new growth points for Shanghai's economic transformation, but also eliminate the huge deficit of my country's service trade to a certain extent. The benign interaction of offshore trade, transportation, finance, insurance and other relevant industries will make our country stand at the center of the world stage.

Compared with the recognized international trade center, Shanghai's offshore service industry is in its infancy, and statistics on the offshore industry have not yet been published. According to the new requirements put forward by the Central Government on Shanghai Pilot Free Trade Zone, and whereas the development status of Shanghai's offshore service industry, the writing team recommended that: Shanghai Municipal Government seeks the authorization of the national ministries and commissions to use the new area as a sandbox and creates offshore service industry center under the premise of controllable risks and pilot the policy measures that facilitate development of offshore shipping and other offshore industry. The specific recommendations are as follows:

(1) Top-level design. Shanghai Municipal Government can establish the "Shanghai Offshore Service Industry Development Office" (hereinafter referred to as Office), which is jointly operated with the new area management committee to promote the overall development of the offshore service industry. Office should formulate the *Measures for the Development of the Offshore Service Industry in the New Area of Shanghai Pilot Free Trade Zone (Trial)* to create an appropriate business environment for offshore service companies from the aspects of registration of commercial subjects, operation, foreign exchange payment and settlement, taxation, and introduction of talents.

(2) Exchange-based offshore services. Office can organize large state-owned trading companies, together with more than 20 existing exchanges in Shanghai, large domestic and foreign trading companies and e-commerce platforms, to jointly establish the "Shanghai Offshore Service Center (Exchange)" (hereinafter referred to as Center) in the new area, including online and offline trading platforms, providing display consulting, intermediary agents, contract delivery, futures trading, payment settlement, financial leasing, logistics transportation, credit assessment, insurance risk controlfor, dispute resolution and other services for foreign companies participating in offshore services and domestic and foreign companies providing offshore services. Encourage institutions that already have offshore capabilities such as Shanghai Shipping Exchange, Shanghai Insurance Exchange, Shanghai Futures Exchange (Shanghai International Energy Exchange Center), and China Foreign Exchange Trading Center to play a leading role in developing the central platform, providing offshore trade, shipping and finance and other product and service models.

(3) Enterprise introduction. With the help of the integration process of the Yangtze River Delta and the broad economic hinterland of the Yangtze River Basin, we will focus on the introduction of "Belt and Road" and "Go Out" enterprises, Yangtze River Delta foreign trade headquarters and foreign trade and

e-commerce enterprises to establish offshore service companies in the free trade zone and provide trade, shipping, finance and other offshore services for their overseas (associated, customer) companies on the central platform. Encourage domestic and foreign business and trade enterprises and e-commerce to provide offshore trade services on the central platform. Actively explore cooperation with foreign offshore trade service providers, especially those overseas exchanges that have institutions in China, such as Lloyd's, London Baltic Shipping Exchange.

(4) In order to facilitate international payment and settlement and avoid being injured by the Sino-US trade war, Center can encourage offshore traders to use offshore RMB for transactions; to avoid exchange rate fluctuations, it can consider issuing an anchoring offshore RMB or digital, stable currency or token vouchers with special drawing rights, but must be based on real transactions, and only used for central transactions; to avoid transactions and systemic risks, it can consider purchasing policies or commercial insurance.

(5) Shanghai tax authorities can grant a certain percentage of "service export tax rebates" to foreign exchange service income obtained by enterprises that provide offshore services on the central platform.

The writing team firmly believes that the development of the offshore service industry is an indispensable sector in the construction of Shanghai Pilot Free Trade Zone. It is also an important part of building Shanghai's international trade, shipping and financial center, and an important entry point for China to reshape the world economic structure.

Shanghai Shipping Policy and Law Development Writing Team
Shanghai International Shipping Institute Shipping Policy & Law Institute
January 1, 2018

Appendix

1

Contract for Ship Repairs

This Contract for Ship Repairs (hereinafter referred to as this Contract) is made on this _____ day of _____ by and between the following parties:
Name of Principal (hereinafter referred to as the Ship Owner)
And
Name of Contractor (hereinafter referred to as the Shipyard)
The parties are collectively referred to as the Parties, and separately each Party.

The Ship Owner agrees to entrust the Shipyard to repair its ship "_____" (hereinafter referred to as the Ship), and the Shipyard agrees to repair "_____". The Parties hereby agree on the terms and conditions as follows:

Clause 1   Description of Ship

Name of Ship: _____
IMO No.: _____
Flag: _____
Name of Registered Owner: _____
Whether under demise charter: ☐No
  ☐Yes, Name of charterer: _____
  Period of charter: _____
  Whether registered: ☐No ☐Yes

If the Ship is under demise charter, a copy of the demise charter and a certificate of demise charter (if applicable) shall be provided by the Ship Owner as ANNEX 1 to this Contract.

Clause 2   Performance of Works

2.1   Before or upon the execution of this Contract, the Ship Owner shall furnish the Shipyard with specifications for the work (including alterations or modifications subsequently made by the Parties, hereinafter collectively referred to as the Works) and the key drawings (including but not limited to the docking plan, general arrangement, capacity plan and mid-ship section) and necessary technical data for the Works, and the Shipyard shall perform the Works in accordance with the provisions of this Contract and the usual work standards prevailing in the ship repair industry.

2.2 If any alteration or modification of the Works is requested by either Party, the requesting Party shall promptly notify the other Party in writing and the Parties shall mutually decide whether such alteration or modification should be included into the Works. If any alteration or modification of the Works is agreed by the Parties, the Contract Price as defined in Clause 8 and the Working Period as defined in Clause 3.2 for the Works shall be adjusted accordingly.

2.3 If the alteration or modification of the Works is necessary or indispensable to the performance of the Works, the Ship Owner shall not unreasonably withhold its consent to such alteration or modification as requested by the Shipyard. If the Ship Owner fails to give its consent to the alteration or modification of the Works within 2 days of its receipt of the notification of the same from the Shipyard, the Shipyard is entitled to suspend the Works and extend the Working Period accordingly and any extra expenses and losses incurred therefrom shall be paid by the Ship Owner.

2.4 During the Working Period and with the Shipyard's prior written consent, the Ship Owner is entitled to appoint qualified repair service providers other than the Shipyard (including but not limited to the Ship Owner itself, the master or the crew) to carry out any other relevant works to the Ship provided that such works are beyond the Shipyard's capacity, but the Ship Owner shall advise the specific scope of such works to the Shipyard, remain responsible for all of such works. If such works interfere with or delay the progress of the Works, the Shipyard is entitled to extend the Working Period accordingly. The Shipyard is entitled to, before the commencement of the aforementioned works, refuse the service providers appointed by the Ship Owner with reasonable causes. If the Working Period is delayed due to the Shipyard's unreasonable refusals, the Shipyard is not entitled to extend the Working Period.

2.5 During performance of the works by the Ship Owner's appointed service providers mentioned in 2.4 above, the Shipyard is entitled to charge reasonable management fees against such service providers before the commencement of relevant works. If the service providers fail to pay such management fees, the Shipyard is entitled to refuse such service providers to undertake relevant works, and is entitled to extend the Working Period accordingly if the Working Period is therefore delayed.

2.6 The Shipyard is entitled to appoint sub-contractors to perform all or any part of the Works, provided that the Shipyard shall remain responsible for all of such sub-contractors' performances. The Ship Owner is entitled to, before the commencement of the aforementioned works, refuse the sub-contractors appointed by the Shipyard with reasonable causes. If the

Working Period is delayed due to the Ship Owner's unreasonable refusals, the Shipyard is entitled to extend the Working Period accordingly.

Clause 3   Delivery, Working Period and Redelivery

3.1   The Ship shall be delivered by the Ship Owner to the Shipyard's designated safe water or work site (hereinafter referred to as Repair Site) on _____ (D) _____ (M) _____ (Y) as agreed between the Parties, and shall be safely afloat, gas free, free of cargo, slops or sludge, excessive ballast water and of any substances which are dangerous or harmful to health (hereafter referred to as Delivery). After inspections, the Shipyard will take delivery of the Ship from the Ship Owner and commence the Works. All expenses and risks related to dockage, towage, pilotage and mooring etc. prior to Delivery shall be borne by the Ship Owner.

3.2   The estimated working period, including the period in dry-dock, shall be _____ calendar days (without guarantee, and hereinafter referred to as the Working Period), and shall be counted from 0800 hours (local time of the Shipyard) on the next day of Delivery or the day when the Ship Owner has provided the complete set of key drawings and necessary technical data for the Works (whichever is later). If the Shipyard has commenced the Works, and the Ship Owner delayed in providing the key drawings and necessary technical data, the Shipyard is entitled to extend the Working Period accordingly.

3.3   Conditional upon the Ship Owner's performance of its contractual obligations, the Shipyard shall timely redeliver the Ship to the Ship Owner at the Repair Site or other agreed locations (hereinafter referred to as Redelivery). If the location of Redelivery is a place other than the Repair Site agreed between the Parties, the Ship Owner shall bear the expenses and risks in moving the Ship to such location.

3.4   As per the Ship Owner's requests, the Shipyard shall keep the Ship Owner informed of progress of the Works and the expected date of Redelivery.

3.5   In case of any change of the Ship's Delivery or Redelivery time, either Party requesting such change shall obtain the prior consent of the other Party.

3.6   The Shipyard is entitled to terminate the Contract if the Ship Owner fails to deliver the Ship as agreed in Clause 3.1 above without prior written consent of the Shipyard. The Shipyard's termination of this Contract shall not prejudice its claims against the Ship Owner for its losses suffered thereby.

3.7   If, at the date of Redelivery, the Ship Owner fails to take delivery of the Ship, the Shipyard is entitled to charge against the Ship Owner at the rate of [____] per day, and such expenses shall be deemed as a part of the Contract Price. If the Shipyard could provide evidence which indicates that its actual losses exceed the aforementioned expenses, such losses shall be borne by the Ship Owner.

Clause 4   Dry-Docking

4.1   The Parties may agree on the dry-docking of the Ship. Nevertheless, in the event that there are unexpected underwater damages or defects on other ships lying in the Shipyard's dock, wharf or berth, and if, in the opinion of the Shipyard, immediate and continuous repair is indispensable for the such ship's safety, the Shipyard is entitled to adjust the schedule for the Ship's dry-docking. In the meantime, the Shipyard is entitled to extend the Working Period accordingly provided that it had timely notified the Ship Owner that the Ship's dry-docking schedule has to be adjusted. Under this circumstance, the Shipyard shall arrange the Ship's repair in the dry-dock as soon as reasonably possible.

4.2 In the event that the alterations or modifications in the Works are agreed by the Parties and thus the period for dry-docking has to be extended, the Shipyard is entitled to undock the Ship according to the Shipyard's schedule upon the expiration of the initial dry-docking period and then re-dock the Ship at the earliest possible opportunity. The additional costs and expenses incurred for the docking and undocking shall be on the Ship Owner's account. If the Works could only be conducted during the dry-docking period, such waiting time during the un-dock period of the Ship, which is caused by the aforementioned alterations or modifications, shall not be calculated into the Working Period.

Clause 5 Supervision and Confirmation of Works

5.1 The Ship Owner shall appoint and designate its superintendent(s) to the Shipyard throughout the Working Period to supervise the Works. If the Ship Owner fails to designate its superintendent(s) or the superintendent(s) is (are) unable or refuse(s) to perform duties during the Working Period, the master of the Ship shall be deemed as the Ship Owner's superintendent.

5.2 Unless the authority of the superintendent(s) is expressly restricted by the Ship Owner, the Ship Owner's superintendent(s) shall be entitled to deal with all matters under this Contract, including but not limited to the approval of plans, drawings, calculations, documents, giving instructions to the alterations or modifications in the Works, confirming the progress of the Works, executing the Works Completion List, the bill(s) of account and Final Contract Price Agreement on behalf of the Ship Owner.

5.3 If the Ship Owner's superintendent(s) fail(s) to perform duties properly, including but not limited to willful or unreasonable delays in giving relevant approvals, instructions, confirmations or opinions, the Shipyard is entitled to request the Ship Owner to replace its superintendent(s) immediately. If such replacement has adverse effects on the progress of the Works, the Shipyard is entitled to extend the Working Period accordingly.

5.4 The superintendent(s) shall confirm the completion of the Works by way of executing the Works Completion List prepared by the Shipyard before Redelivery; the Shipyard may also prepare the Works Completion List for particular Works for the Ship Owner's execution during the course of the Working Period. If the superintendent(s) fail(s) to confirm and execute the Works Completion List within [   ] working days upon its receipt of the same, and also fail(s) to raise any written objections, it shall be deemed that the Ship Owner has confirmed and accepted the Works Completion List. If the superintendent(s) raise(s) written objections against the Works Completion List, the Parties shall negotiate or jointly appoint a third-party surveyor or survey organization (hereinafter referred to as Surveyor) to make a decision on the disputed items in the Works Completion List. The Surveyor's decision shall be binding upon the Parties. If, according to the Surveyor's decision, the Ship Owner's objection does not stand, the Ship Owner shall bear the Shipyard's losses suffered thereof and also the Surveyor's costs; if the Ship Owner's objection stands, the Shipyard shall make adjustments to the Works, re-submit the Works Completion List, and shall also bear the Surveyor's costs.

5.5 The Ship Owner, its superintendent(s), crew or employee(s) shall be cooperative and are obliged to provide assistances in the completion of Works. If the Works could not be completed due to non-cooperation of the aforementioned parties, the Shipyard may demand the Ship Owner to perform its obligations within a reasonable period and is entitled to extend the Working Period accordingly; if the Ship Owner fails to fulfill its obligations within such a period, the Shipyard is entitled to terminate this Contract and claim damages.

Clause 6   Disposal of Waste and Scrap Materials

6.1 The Shipyard is entitled to dispose of all waste and scrap materials generating from the Works. If such materials are categorized as solid wastes or hazardous wastes in accordance with Chinese environmental laws or regulations, the Shipyard's costs and fees incurred in storing and disposing of such wastes (including entrusting qualified and licensed third parties in storing and disposing of such wastes), after deducting the Shipyard's earnings in disposing of such wastes, shall be borne by the Ship Owner.

6.2 If the Ship Owner requires to retain any specific scrap part or equipment disassembled from the Ship, the Ship Owner shall notify the Shipyard in writing to obtain the Shipyard's prior consent before disassembling from the Ship and shall have the same moved away as soon as possible after disassembling and in accordance with Chinese environmental laws or regulations. The Shipyard's storing costs incurred thereof and losses suffered as a result of the Ship Owner's failure to dispose of the aforementioned scrap part or equipment in proper manners (including but not limited to penalties imposed by local environment protection authority) shall be borne by the Ship Owner.

Clause 7   Ship Owner's Supplies

7.1 The Ship Owner shall timely deliver all materials of the Ship Owner's supply items to the Shipyard's designated locations as requested by the Shipyard. If the Ship Owner delays in providing its supply items, the Shipyard is entitled to extend the Working Period accordingly or decline any particular work, and also entitled to claim damages against the Ship Owner for losses or damages sustained thereof.

7.2   All paints necessary for the Works shall be supplied by the Ship Owner.

7.3   All of the Ship Owner's supplies, which are in the custody of the Shipyard at the Ship Owner's request, shall be at the sole risk and responsibility of the Ship Owner, provided always that the Shipyard shall perform proper duty of care.

7.4   The Shipyard shall not be liable for any fault, defect, breakdown and/or whatsoever occurrences in the course of or after completion of the Works insofar as they are attributable to the Ship Owner's supply items.

Clause 8   Contract Price and Payment

8.1   Unless otherwise agreed in writing, the Contract price shall be determined in accordance with □ the tariff as attached to this Contract (Annex 2) □ *China Shiprepair Tariff* (2016 edition) without its attachments which was published by China Association of the National Shipbuilding Industry and became effective since 1 June 2016 (hereinafter referred to as the Contract Price). The discount ratio of the Contract Price is [   ]. The Ship Owner confirms that it is fully aware of and agrees the contents of the Contract Price and the discount ratio.

8.2   The estimated Contract Price is [   ]. The final price for this Contract shall be determined by the bill(s) of account or the Final Contract Price Agreement signed by both Parties.

8.3   Upon the Ship Owner's execution of the Works Completion List, the Shipyard shall timely issue bill of account or bills of account in instalments to the Ship Owner. The Ship Owner shall confirm and sign the bill(s) of account within [   ] calendar days of receipt of the same, or sign Final Contract Price Agreement (see Annex 3, and the Final Contract Price Agreement shall be deemed as a part of this Contract) with the Shipyard.

8.4   Unless otherwise expressly agreed in writing by the Parties, the Ship Owner shall pay the full amount of the Contract Price in U.S. Dollars or any other currency acceptable to the Shipyard without set-off, deduction and not subject to foreign exchange control. All taxes and bank charges etc. related to the Contract Price shall be borne by the Ship Owner.

8.5   The Parties agree that the Ship Owner shall pay [   ] within [   ] calendar days of the execution of this Contract as deposit for the Works. In the event that the Ship Owner fails to pay the deposit, the Shipyard is entitled to suspend the Works, and to terminate this Contract and lodge claims against the Ship Owner for losses sustained thereby.

8.6   The Shipyard is entitled to request the Ship Owner to pay the estimated Contract Price in [   ] installments before completion of the Works, provided that Parties agree alterations or modifications in the Works and such alterations or modifications are considered to be material to the Works by the Shipyard. In the event that the Ship Owner fails to pay the installments as per the Shipyard's request, the Shipyard may suspend such alterations or modifications until the Ship Owner's payment of the installments and the Ship Owner shall be responsible for the Shipyards' losses sustained thereby.

8.7 If the Shipyard completes the Works prior to the last day of the Working Period, the Ship Owner shall pay to the Shipyard [   ]% of the final Contract Price per day pro rata; if, due to causes not attributable to the Ship Owner, the Shipyard fails to complete the Works within the Working Period (including the Working Period as extended by the Shipyard in accordance with this Contract), the Shipyard shall pay to the Owner [   ]% of the final Contract Price per day pro rata. Under whatever circumstances, the aforementioned payments shall not exceed [   ]% of the final Contract Price. If the difference between the actual completion date and the last day of the Working Period is within 5 days, both Parties shall not bear payment liabilities to each other.

8.8 Unless otherwise expressly agreed in writing by the Parties, the Ship Owner shall pay the total or [   ]% of the final Contract Price to the Shipyard within [   ] calendar days of the completion of the Works or before Redelivery (whichever comes earlier). In the event that the Ship Owner fails to make payment of the Contract Price in accordance with the aforementioned agreement, the Shipyard is entitled to exercise lien on the Ship or otherwise detain the Ship for all sums due until the payment is made in accordance with the relevant agreements under this Contract; The Shipyard shall not assume any liability or responsibility for its exercise of lien on or detention of the Ship and shall be entitled to claim against the Ship Owner for any expenses, losses and/or damages sustained thereby; during the period of the lien or detention of the Ship, the Ship Owner shall be responsible for maintaining the Ship properly and shall be responsible for the safety of the Ship and preventing the Ship from polluting the environment in accordance with Clause 10.4. If the Ship Owner fails to pay the outstanding debts within 1 month of its receipt of the notice of exercise of the lien from the Shipyard, the Shipyard is entitled to realize its lien by way of auction or sale of the Ship through the court and to the priority of having the debts paid with the proceeds from such auction or sale.

8.9 Upon confirmation of the final Contract Price, the Parties may agree that the final Contract Price be paid in several installments. In the event that the Ship Owner is in default of payment of one of the installments, all the following installments shall immediately become due, and the Ship Owner shall immediately pay all the amount thus become due together with interest accrued thereon in accordance with Clause 8.10.

8.10 If the Ship Owner fails to pay the full or the agreed amount of the Contract Price on the agreed due date, it shall pay interest at the rate of [   ]% per annum on the unpaid amount from the due date to the date of full payment. If the Contract Price is paid in a currency other than Chinese yuan, and if the Ship Owner fails to pay the Contract Price on the agreed due date, the Ship Owner shall indemnify the Shipyard against any loss arising out of the conversion including any discrepancy between the rate of exchange, which is used to convert the aforementioned Contract Price into Chinese yuan, on the agreed due date and the actual payment date.

8.11 All the classification services, technical service engineers and sea trials shall be arranged by the Ship Owner on its own account, unless otherwise agreed by the Parties.

Clause 9　Shipyard's Liability and Responsibility

9.1 The Shipyard shall not be responsible for any loss of or damage to or in connection with the Ship or her part(s), cargo aboard or any other properties of the Ship Owner and/or its employees, unless such loss or damage is directly caused by willful misconduct or gross negligence of the Shipyard or its employee(s) or sub-contractor(s) in conducting the Works, the employment activities or authorized activities.

9.2 Liability Limitation: The Shipyard's aggregate liability to the losses or damages of the Ship Owner or any other party (including insurers and any other third parties, whether such party has interest in the ownership or operation of the Ship or not) shall be limited to US Dollars [　　]. The Shipyard's aforementioned liability shall include all the losses or damages of the Ship Owner or any other parties, including but not limited to all direct or indirect losses or personal injuries or death, and whether such losses or damages were caused under contract, in tort or by any other reason, or by the fault of the Shipyard, its employees, agents or sub-contractors. Such limitation shall apply to single or a series of incident(s), losses or damages which was/were caused by a single or a series of cause(s) or incident(s). The Ship Owner agrees and undertakes that it shall be responsible for liabilities for any losses, damages, claims or costs which exceed the limitation of US Dollars [　　], and shall hold the Shipyard harmless under this circumstance, regardless of the causes of the aforementioned liabilities and whether such liabilities were caused by the fault of the Shipyard, its employee(s), agent(s) or sub-contractor(s).

9.3 Any tests, sea trials or movements of the Ship shall be at the Ship Owner's sole risk. Any offshore repairs of the Ship shall be at the Ship Owner's sole risk. The Shipyard, its employee(s) or any sub-contractor(s) shall not be under any liability to the Ship Owner for any expenses (excluding repair costs) incurred during the course of, or defaults, losses and damages caused by the sea trials or movements or offshore repairs.

9.4 Upon completion of the Works, any and all responsibility of the Shipyard shall be discharged save as provided for in Clause 9.5.

9.5 The Shipyard shall take quality warranty responsibility for the defects of its furnished equipment, parts or materials or its workmanship. For fixed parts, the quality warranty period is [　　] months from Redelivery; for moveable parts, the quality warranty period is [　　] months from Redelivery. The Ship Owner shall serve the Shipyard with a written notice within [　　] days of occurrence of the aforementioned defects and shall describe such defects with supporting documents to prove that such defects were completely caused by the Shipyard's negligence. In the event that the Ship Owner fails to serve the aforementioned written claim notice within the aforesaid period, it shall be deemed that the Ship Owner has unconditionally and completely waived its claims.

9.6 Upon receipt of the claim notice in 9.5 above, the Shipyard is entitled to investigate the causes of such defects through its authorized representatives, and the Ship Owner shall provide necessary assistance. If the Shipyard confirms that such defects were caused by the Shipyard's negligence, it shall undertake, free of charge, to repair or replace such materials or rectify such defective workmanship at its Repair Site. If it is not practicable or cost effective for the Ship Owner to bring the Ship to the Shipyard's Repair Site, the Ship Owner may cause the necessary repairs or replacement to be made elsewhere subject to the Shipyard's prior written consent and the Shipyard shall, subject to all the foregoing conditions and upon the Ship Owner's written request, reimburse a sum equivalent to the cost of making repairs or replacement at such other places, but the aforementioned sum shall not exceed (the Parties may choose one of below) □ [   ] times of the Contract Price; □ [   ] times of the price for the same repairs or replacement at Chinese leading shipyards; □ [   ] times of the price for the same repairs or replacement at shipyards in China, Singapore or Middle East areas.

9.7 The Shipyard's liability for guarantee repair is limited to Clause 9.5 and 9.6 above, and the Shipyard shall in no event be liable for any other losses, damages or expenses, whether direct or indirect, including but not limited to salvage, towage, dockage, wharfage, any other non-routine service fees charged by the shipyard who actually carried out the guarantee repair, port dues, any other expenses for inspection and supervision, consumables, insurance and transportation etc., or for any loss in the operation of the Ship and/or for any loss of time and profits due to repairs, which were caused by any fault or defect. The Shipyard shall have no liability against any fine or penalty imposed on the Ship Owner and the Shipyard shall have no liability against any third party having an interest in the ownership, operation of the Ship or the ownership of cargo on-board etc. for any liability against any latent or worsening damages.

9.8 In any event, any claim in connection with guarantee repair shall not affect the payment obligations of the Ship Owner. Any outstanding Contract Price shall be paid on time, and the Ship Owner shall not withhold such payment in partial or in whole or set off the same with its request for guarantee repair.

9.9 The Shipyard did not guarantee the workmanship, quality and/or condition of any painting if the same, which was conducted under the requests of the Ship Owner, was improper and not in accordance with the requirements of the paint maker.

9.10 Within the Working Period, the Shipyard shall have adequate ship-repairer's liability insurance, and shall timely provide copies of the policies, evidences and detailed statements in accordance with the Ship Owner's requests.

9.11 The Shipyard's obligations and liabilities set out in this Clause are not meant to be exhaustive.

Clause 10　Ship Owner's Liability and Responsibility

10.1　The Ship Owner shall be responsible for obtaining all necessary approvals and certificates relating to the Ship, and shall maintain the effects of the same.

10.2　During the Working Period, the Ship Owner shall procure relevant insurance for the Ship, crew, equipment on board and other properties owned or controlled by the Ship Owners, including but not limited to the Protection and Indemnity Insurance, the Hull and Machinery Insurance and War Risks Insurance. Upon the Shipyard's request, the Ship Owner shall furnish the Shipyard with related documents such as copies of the insurance policy, evidence, and detailed statement.

10.3　The Ship Owner shall solely be responsible for any losses or damages resulting from disregard or non-observance by the Ship Owner or its crew or its employee(s) or other repair service providers appointed by the Ship Owner of the prohibitions specified in the General Regulations at Shipyard attached hereto as ANNEX 4 or of the Shipyard's safety requirements during the Ship's stay at the shipyard.

10.4　The Ship Owner shall at all times solely be responsible for the safety of the Ship, and shall take all necessary measures to protect the safety of the Ship and to prevent the Ship from polluting the environment. The Delivery and Redelivery in this Contract shall not discharge the Ship Owner from the aforementioned liabilities. During the Working Period, the Shipyard may, at the request of the Ship Owner, assist in maintaining the safety of the Ship and preventing the Ship from polluting the environment, and all the expenses related thereto shall be borne by the Ship Owner. The aforementioned expenses shall include but not limited to the labor and material costs the Shipyard incurred in maintaining the safety of the Ship or taking pollution prevention measures, expenses the Shipyard incurred on behalf of the Ship Owner to meet relevant regulations regarding ship safety and pollution prevention, and expenses actually incurred and losses actually suffered by the Shipyard as a consequence of assisting the Ship Owner or taking necessary measures in accordance with the Ship Owner's instructions.

10.5　The Ship Owner shall at all times solely be responsible for death, personal injury and disease of the Ship Owner's employee(s) or the Ship's crew or passenger(s) or the employees of sub-contractors appointed by the Ship Owner onboard, unless the death, injury or disease is directly caused by the willful misconduct or gross negligence of the Shipyard and/or its employee(s) or subcontractor(s) in conducting the Works or the employment activities or authorized activities. The Ship Owner shall hold the Shipyard harmless of and indemnify the Shipyard against any claims in respect of the aforementioned death, personal injury or disease.

10.6　In the duration of this Contract, if the Ship Owner intends to transfer the ownership of the Ship, or terminate the demise charter of the Ship, it shall give the Shipyard prior written notice. In this circumstance, the Shipyard is entitled to request the Ship Owner to pay off the amount of Contract Price already incurred and to provide security acceptable by the Shipyard for the uncompleted Works. Unless the Ship Owner provides security according to the Shipyard's requests, the Shipyard is entitled to terminate this Contract and cease the uncompleted Works.

10.7 The Ship Owner's obligations and liabilities set out in this Clause are not meant to be exhaustive.

Clause 11   Extension of the Working Period

11.1 In the event of Force Majeure, which refers to events that are unpredictable, and the occurrence and consequence of the same could not be overcome or avoided at the time of the conclusion of this Contract, such as fire, flood, typhoon, earthquakes, extreme weather, orders of the government etc., the Shipyard shall notify the Ship Owner within [   ] calendar days of the occurrence of the same in writing, and shall also notify the Ship Owner within [   ] calendar days after such Force Majeure event ends in writing. The Shipyard is entitled to extend the Working Period accordingly, and its expenses in avoiding or reducing the impacts of Force Majeure events on the Works shall be borne by the Shipyard.

11.2 Besides the provisions of Clause 2.3, 2.4, 2.6, 3.2, 4.1, 5.3, 5.5 and 7.1, if the Working Period is delayed by other reasons attributable to the Ship Owner, the Shipyard is entitled to extend the Working Period accordingly.

Clause 12   Termination of Contract

12.1 Besides the provisions of Clause 3.6, 5.5, 8.5 and 10.6 of this Contract, this Contract may be terminated under the following circumstances:

12.1.1 if the occurrence of Force Majeure event makes it impossible for the Parties to realize the purposes of this Contract, either Party is entitled to terminate this Contract;

12.1.2 if an order or an effective resolution is passed for the dissolution, winding up or bankruptcy of one Party, or if a receiver/administrator is appointed over the whole or any part of the property of one Party or any similar process or proceeding is initiated under the laws of any relevant jurisdiction, or one Party ceases to carry on its business or makes any special arrangement or composition with its creditors, the other Party is entitled to terminate this Contract;

12.2.3 if one Party clearly indicates by its word or action that it will not perform this Contract, the other Party is entitled to terminate this Contract.

12.2 Even if this Contract is terminated, the Ship Owner shall still pay to the Shipyard the Contract Price already incurred as well as the actual costs incurred including the materials purchased and the goods supplied by the Shipyard for the purpose of completing the Works, within [   ] days of the termination. After termination of this Contract, the Shipyard is entitled to move the Ship from the Repair Site to other locations, and all costs and risks incurred as results of the wharfage, towage, pilotage, docking and berthing shall be borne by the Ship Owner.

Clause 13　Trademarks and Patents

In the event that the Works involves manufacture or renewal of machinery, equipment, fittings or their parts in accordance with drawings, specifications, models or other data/information supplied by the Ship Owner, the Ship Owner shall solely be responsible for infringement of trade mark, patent or similar rights of any third party, and shall hold the Shipyard harmless of and indemnify the Shipyard against any claim by the third party in respect of such infringement. The Shipyard shall have the right to suspend the manufacture and renewal and to lodge claims against the Ship Owner for the losses and damages sustained thereby.

Clause 14　Confidentiality

Drawings, designs, diagrams and other documents prepared by the Shipyard shall remain as the Shipyard's property and shall not be disclosed to any third party without its written consent. Likewise, the Shipyard shall not disclose drawings or information which belongs to the Ship Owner to any third party without the Ship Owner's written consent. It is the Parties' obligations to maintain confidentiality.

Clause 15　Assignment

Save as that provided in Clause 2.6, neither Party shall be entitled to assign its rights and obligations under this Contract to any third party without prior written consent of the other Party.

Clause 16　Cooperation in Legal Requirement

Where it is necessary for the Shipyard to comply with certain procedures of government authorities to satisfy any requirement under the applicable laws and regulations to perform this Contract, the Ship Owner shall, upon request of the Shipyard, cooperate with the Shipyard to facilitate such procedure.

Clause 17　Notice

17.1　Any and all notices and communications in connection with this Contract shall be addressed as follows:

　　For the Ship Owner:　　　　　　　　Address:
　　　　　　　　　　　　　　　　　　　Attn.:
　　　　　　　　　　　　　　　　　　　Tel. No.:
　　　　　　　　　　　　　　　　　　　Fax No.:
　　　　　　　　　　　　　　　　　　　E-mail Address:

　　For the Shipyard:　　　　　　　　　Address:

Attn.:
Tel. No.:
Fax No.:
E-mail Address:

17.2 Any change of one Party's address shall be communicated in writing by the Party to the other Party and in the event of failure of such notice of change, communications addressed to the Party's last known address shall be deemed sufficient.

17.3 "In writing" or "written" in this Contract shall mean any method of legible communication. A notice may be given in any effective means including but not limited to cable, telex, facsimile, email, registered or recorded mail, commercial courier or by personal service etc.

17.4 Any and all notices and communications to the Ship Owner's superintendent(s) and the master shall be seen as served to the Ship Owner.

Clause 18 Effectiveness of Contract

18.1 The undersigned warrant that they have proper authorities to execute this Contract for and on behalf of the relevant Parties.

18.2 This Contract may be executed by facsimile or via email with full legal effect.

18.3 This Contract shall become effective upon the executions by both Parties' representatives. If this Contract is not signed by the master, the validity of this Contract shall not be affected.

18.4 If the Delivery has taken place before execution of this Contract, any written agreement between the Parties shall be deemed as an integral part of this Contract. If there is any conflict, the provisions of this Contract shall prevail.

18.5 All the annexes to this Contract together with the executed Works Completion List, bill(s) of account shall constitute integral parts of this Contract, and shall have the same force of law as this Contract.

Clause 19 Arbitration and Governing Law

This Contract shall be governed and construed in accordance with the laws of People's Republic of China. Any dispute arising from or in connection with this Contract shall be submitted to China Maritime Arbitration Commission (CMAC) for arbitration which shall be conducted in accordance with CMAC's arbitration rules in effect at the time of applying for arbitration. The arbitral award is final and binding upon both parties

IN WITNESS WHEREOF, the Parties have caused their respective authorized representative to execute this Contract on the date first written above.

Ship Owner's Representative(s):

_____ (Signature)

Signed by Name and Position of the signatory

As authorized representative of_____
(Name of Company), as Ship Manager (/Ship Operator) (/agent)
For and on behalf of
Ship Owner (/Demise Charterer)_____
(Name of Ship Owner or Demise Charterer)
Company seal:
Date:

_____(Signature)
Ship Master:_____
For and on behalf of
Ship Owner (/Demise Charterer)_____
(Name of Ship Owner or Demise Charterer)
Ship seal or master seal:
Date:

Shipyard's Representative(s):
_____(Signature)
Signed by Name and Position of the signatory
For and on behalf of_____(Name of Shipyard)
Shipyard seal:
Date:

2

Notice of the State Council on Issuing the Plan for Comprehensively Furthering the Efforts of Reform and Opening Up in the China (Shanghai) Pilot Free Trade Zone

Establishing China (Shanghai) Pilot Free Trade Zone (hereinafter referred to as SHFTZ) is a strategic measure adopted by the CPC Central Committee and the State Council to comprehensively deepen reform and expand opening up under new conditions. Since the construction of the SHFTZ commenced over three years ago, significant progress has been made, and the expected objectives have been generally accomplished. This Plan is developed for purposes of implementing the decisions and arrangements of the CPC Central Committee and the State Council, with an eye on international free trade zones of highest standards and at top level, comprehensively deepening the reform and opening up of SHFTZ, accelerating the development of an open new economic system, and further making use of the leading and demonstrating role in a new round of reform and opening up.

I. General requirements

(1) Guiding ideology. We shall comprehensively implement the spirit of the 18th National Congress of the Communist Party of China (CPC) and the Third, Fourth, Fifth and Sixth Plenary Sessions of the 18th CPC Central Committee, carry out in depth the spirit of a series of important speeches and new concepts, thoughts and strategies of managing state affairs of General Secretary XI Jinping, conscientiously implement the decisions and arrangements of the CPC Central Committee and the State Council, advance the overall layout for "economic, political, cultural, social, and ecological progress" in an overall manner and the Four-Pronged Comprehensive Strategy in a coordinated manner, adhere to the general work principle of making progress while maintaining stability, firmly uphold and practice the new development concept, persist in institutional innovation as core, continue freeing our mind, being bold to make breakthroughs and setting examples, further follow highest international standards and discover shortness and weakness, make audacious experiments and adventures, independently make changes, stick to all-around opening up, promote liberalization and facilitation of trade and investment, strengthen stress testing, and practically and effectively prevent and control risks, so as to promote reforms, development and innovation; further enhance the interaction with the

building of Shanghai international financial center and science and technology innovation centers with international influence, constantly magnify the policy integration effect, voluntarily serve the building of the "Belt and Road" and the development of the Yangtze River economic belt, and establish new momentum for economic transformation and development and new international competitive edge; more vigorously transform government functions, accelerate the exploration of the innovation on the administration system of first-level local governments, and comprehensively improve the governance system of the government; and make use of first-doer advantage, strengthen the integration of the reform systems, make efforts to have more achievements in system innovation that can be replicated and promoted, and further highlight the role of the experimental field in comprehensively deepening reforms and expanding opening up.

(2) Building objectives. By 2020, an institutional system connected with common international rules for investment and trade will have been first developed, SHFTZ will have been developed to an international high-standard free trade zone park featuring freedom of investment and trade with open and transparent rules, fair and efficient regulation and convenient business environment, the investment administration system of equal access and orderly competition for various market participants, the trade regulation service system promoting the transformation and upgrading of trade and the facilitation of customs clearance, the financial service system deepening financial opening and innovation and effectively preventing and controlling risks, and the government administration system consistent with the requirement for the modernization of the market economic rules and governance capability will have been improved, and a law-based, internationalized and facilitated business environment and a fair, unified and efficient market environment will have been first created. The interactions between reforms in SHFTZ and those in Shanghai will have been enhanced, and each task of the pilot program of reforms, if with good conditions, will have been comprehensively implemented in Pudong New Area or promoted on a trial basis in Shanghai.

II. Strengthening the integration of the reform systems and building a comprehensive reform pilot zone combining opening and innovation

The systematicness, integrity and coordination of institutional innovation shall be enhanced, centering on deepening the reform of the investment administration system, optimizing the trade regulation service system and improving the innovation promotion mechanism, overall arrangements shall be made for the reforms of all parts, the cooperation of all departments shall be strengthened, attention shall be paid to the combination of reform measures, the bottleneck restricting innovation shall be effectively removed, and market dynamism shall be sparked to a greater extent.

(3) Establishing a more open, transparent market access administration mode. The market

access negative list and the foreign investment negative list system shall be implemented. On the basis of improving the market access negative list, for various market participants subject to consistent administration, matter-handling links and process shall be further optimized and simplified, and the review standards and periods for business licenses and application for qualifications shall be unified, so as to promote fair competition. The transparency of the foreign investment negative list and the predictability of market access shall be further improved. A fair competition review system shall be carried out, and differentiated treatment in the aspects such as qualification attainment, bidding and protection of rights and interests shall be reviewed and canceled, so as to enable various market participants to lawfully and equally access the industries, fields and business not on the lists.

(4) Comprehensively deepening the reform of the business registration system. The enterprises' independent right of registration shall be protected, and enterprises' right of independent business operation shall be respected. The enterprise name registration system shall be reformed, and an enterprise name is no longer subject to pre-confirmation unless the department responsible for the involved pre-approval matter or confirmation of the enterprise name is not the one responsible for enterprise registration. The conditions for the registration of domiciles (places of business) shall be relaxed so as to effectively release field resources. The mode of registration of business scope stated in business licenses shall be optimized. The pilot program of the reform of whole-process electronic registration and electronic business licenses shall be promoted. A market participant leaving system featuring mutual support of ordinary and summary deregistration systems shall be researched and established. The pilot program of the reform of "one license, multiple addresses" shall be conducted.

(5) Fully realizing "separation of permits and licenses". The reform of "business licenses before government permits" shall be deepened, and exploration shall be further strengthened. Permit approval matters involving market access shall be included in the pilot program of reforms in good time, whatever can be canceled shall be canceled, further optimization and adjustment shall be made according to notification and commitment plus enhancement of market access administration and other modes if approval is required to be retained, and, on the basis of the reform of permit administration mode and improvement of risk prevention measures, the fields subject to notification and commitment shall be further expanded. The connection between permit administration and registration administration of enterprise establishment shall be strengthened, and the application of the unified social credit codes in all permit administration parts shall be realized. "One permit for one enterprise" as for manufacturing permits shall be implemented, and the removal of the inspection of products manufactured with permits shall be explored.

(6) Building international trade "single windows" at advanced international level. The UN international trade "single window" standards shall be learned from, and trade data shall be

coordinated, simplified and standardized. The functions of logistics operation included in harbors, airports and areas under special customs supervision shall be integrated with payment and billing functions through banking institutions or non-banking payment institutions so as to facilitate enterprises in making payment and inquiry. The exchange and sharing of the information on logistics and regulation, among others, shall be realized so as to facilitate the inquiry into and administration of the traceability information on the quality safety of import and export goods. The fields covered by international trade "single window" shall be promoted to be expanded to trade in services and gradually to trade in technology, service outsourcing and maintenance services, among others, and the application for export tax rebates (exemption) of trade in services shall be gradually included in "single window" administration when the conditions are mature. State-level "single window" standards and specifications shall be integrated and connected, cross-regional customs clearance in Yangtze River economic belt shall be advanced, and data connection and coordinated regulation shall be strengthened.

(7) Establishing a safe, efficient and convenient new mode of comprehensive customs regulation. The measures such as national customs clearance integration, supervision through inspections of randomly selected entities by randomly selected inspectors and the public release of inspection results, and "Internet plus customs" shall be implemented in depth, the mode of customs business administration shall be further reformed, international trade "single window" shall be connected, and an integrated, intensive, intelligent, smart, efficient and convenient new comprehensive customs regulation mode unifying powers and responsibilities shall be established. Big data, cloud computing, the Internet and the Internet of Things shall be comprehensively applied, and the scope of the pilot program of "independent tax filing, self-help customs clearance, automatic inspection and release and verification of key points" shall be expanded. The reform of "opening up the first tier" and "safely and efficiently controlling the second tier" shall be deepened, comprehensive law enforcement shall be enhanced, coordinated governance shall be advanced, and a supporting administration system adapting to the need of the development of "integration of the zone and neighboring port areas" shall be explored and established. The mode of guaranteed release in disputes over patents of export goods in processing trade shall be innovated. Enterprises from outside areas under special customs supervision shall be supported in conducting high value added, high-technology and zero-pollution maintenance business. Classified supervision of state of goods shall be implemented in depth, the expansion of the pilot program from logistics and storage enterprise to trade, production and processing enterprises shall be researched, and when conditions are met, the pilot program shall be promoted and implemented in other areas under special customs supervision in Shanghai.

(8) Establishing an inspection and quarantine risk classified supervision and comprehensive assessment mechanism. The import goods risk early warning and quick response mechanism shall

be improved, the disqualification risks of import goods shall be better monitored, and the consumer goods and other goods recall system shall be implemented. A new qualification assessment mechanism of comprehensive application shall be established, and a national quality and basic inspection and quarantine comprehensive application demonstration park shall be constructed. On the basis of developing and issuing catalogs and lists to which the admission of third-party testing results is not applicable, the admission of third-party testing results of goods and items shall be vigorously advanced and expanded. The expansion of the scope of international recognition of inspection and appraisal results shall be explored.

(9) Developing an internationally competitive innovative industry regulation mode. The access permit for special articles used for experiments in global coordinated research and development of biological medicine shall be optimized, and the content and modes of access permits shall be improved. A customs regulation mode helpful to enhance the international competitiveness of the whole industry chain of integrated circuit shall be improved. A catalog allowing the import of old electromechanical devices for re-manufacturing shall be researched and developed, and, on the premise of controllable risks, the pilot program of the import of numerically-controlled machine tool, engineering equipment and telecommunications equipment, among others, for re-manufacturing shall be conducted. The introduction of a market-oriented insurance mechanism shall be explored, and the regulation efficiency in the fields such as medicine production shall be raised.

(10) Optimizing the market allocation mechanism of innovation factors. The system of the holders of drug marketing licenses shall be improved. The applicants for the registration of medical instrument in SHFTZ shall be allowed to entrust medical instrument manufacturers in Shanghai with the manufacturing of products. The talent determination standards and recommendation modes more conforming to the patterns of the socialist market economy and the growth, development and flow of talents, the permit system of foreigners working in China with unified standards and regulated procedures, and the efficient and convenient talent visa system shall be improved, more high-level foreign talents shall be attracted to participate in innovation and entrepreneurship, provided with more convenience of entry into and exit from China, stay and residence, and entitled to the relevant policies issued by China to encourage innovation and entrepreneurship according to the provisions. Under the laws and regulations, high-level foreign national talents with permanent residence permits for foreigners shall be supported in establishing science and technology enterprises and granted the same treatment as Chinese nationals. The pilot program of "science and technology innovation board" at the Shanghai Equity Exchange shall be deepened, and the financial services for science and technology innovation enterprises shall be improved. Foreign-funded enterprises shall be supported in establishing united innovation platforms and cooperating with homegrown micro, small and medium-sized enterprises in

advancing projects industrializing innovation achievements. The innovation on the mode of scientific and technological finance combining the building of financial centers and science and technology innovation centers shall be deepened and advanced.

(11) Improving the intellectual property right protection and use system. The leading role of patents, trademarks, copyrights and other intellectual property rights shall be fully used, the whole chain from the creation, use, protection, administration and services of intellectual property rights shall be opened up, and the quality and profit of intellectual property rights shall be improved. With several advantageous industries as key points, the process of the examination and registration intellectual property rights shall be further simplified and optimized, and the quick intellectual property right protection working mechanism shall be innovated. The rules for the protection of intellectual property rights in the fields of the Internet, e-commerce and big data, among others, shall be researched. The standards for intellectual property right services shall be developed and improved, and the intellectual property right service system shall be perfected. The diversified intellectual property right dispute resolution mechanism shall be improved. Enterprises shall be supported in using intellectual property to make overseas equity investment. Intellectual property right financial services shall be innovated and developed. The intellectual property right ownership system helpful to encourage innovations shall be deepened and improved.

Ⅲ. Strengthening the connection with common international rules and constructing risk stress test areas of the open economic system

According to the highest international standards, fuller stress test shall be made in order to promote the implementation of a new round of high-level opening up, new development areas of the open economy shall be explored, and systematic experience from the pilot program, meeting the requirement of a more open economy, shall form.

(12) Further relaxing investment access. The SHFTZ foreign investment negative list shall be reduced as much as possible, and the opening up of specialized services such as financial services, telecommunications, the Internet, culture, cultural relics, maintenance and shipping services and the field of advanced manufacturing industry shall be advanced. Except special fields, the special administration requirements for the period of business operation of foreign-funded enterprises shall be canceled. A new mode of administration shall be explored for qualified foreign startup investment enterprises and equity investment enterprises conducting investment projects in China. National security review, anti-monopoly review and other investment review systems shall be improved.

(13) Implementing new rules for trade facilitation. The process of port customs clearance shall be optimized, the reform of the supervision modes at all parts shall be advanced, and the

average time of goods clearance in all parts shall be explored and published. Whole-process paperless work covering at all links such as arrival and leaving of vessels, port operation, customs clearance of goods, and other port operations shall be realized as much as possible, and the administration of electronic certificates and proof in the trade field shall be advanced. The pilot program of Asia-Pacific demonstrative electronic port networks shall be deepened. The implementation of the pre-ruling system of place of origin shall be prompted. According to free trade agreements, the implementation of the independent declaration system of place of origin shall be promoted. Cross-departmental sharing of enterprise credit rating shall be advanced, and the inspection rates for enterprises with high credit ratings shall be lowered. The industrial security guarantee mechanism issuing security early warnings and improving international competitiveness shall be deepened and improved.

(14) Innovating on the administration modes of cross-border trade in services. On the premise of controllable risks, the advancement of trade facilitation in high-end service fields such as finance, insurance, culture, tourism, education and health shall be accelerated. The facilitation of temporary import of goods relating to trade in services shall be improved, the scope of the application of the ATA carnet system shall be expanded, and the term of carnet shall be extended. A mode of the regulation of trade in digital products, taking security and efficiency into account, shall be explored. The trade in traditional Chinese medical services shall be vigorously developed, the international market access of the trade in traditional Chinese medical services shall be increased, and the overseas innovative development of traditional Chinese medicine shall be promoted. The innovation on international ship registration system shall be deepened, and international vessel administration enterprises shall be further facilitated in providing overseas seaman employment services. The restrictive measures for cross-border delivery, movement of natural persons and other modes of trade in services in proper fields shall be gradually canceled or relaxed on a level-by-level basis. The statistics system of trade in services shall be explored and improved, and a monitoring system of the trade in services shall be established.

(15) Further deepening the opening up of and innovation on finance. The interactions with the building of Shanghai international financial center shall be strengthened, and the Plan for Further Advancing the Pilot Program of the Opening up of and Innovation on Finance in China (Shanghai) Pilot Free Trade Zone and Accelerating the Building of Shanghai International Financial Center shall be vigorously implemented in an orderly manner. The development of a financial market system orienting to the international arena shall be accelerated, a global Chinese currency service system shall be established, and the pilot program of convertible capital account shall be advanced in an orderly manner. The establishment of a financial regulation coordination mechanism shall be accelerated, and the capability of financial regulation shall be improved, so as to prevent financial risks.

(16) Constructing free trade port areas. Free trade port areas shall be constructed in Yangshan Bonded Port Area, Shanghai Pudong Airport Comprehensive Bonded Zone and other areas under special customs supervision. Top international level shall be connected, and a higher-standard trade regulation system of "opening up the first tier" and "safely and efficiently controlling the second tier" shall be carried out. An intensive administration system based on national authorization shall be implemented, on the premise of effective prevention and control of port risks, depending on information-based regulation means, the trade control measures for goods entering the areas shall be canceled or simplified to the maximum extent, and front declaration formalities shall be simplified as much as possible. A financial, foreign exchange, investment and immigration administration system consistent with common international practice shall be explored and implemented, and a risk prevention and control system shall be established and improved.

IV. Further transforming government functions and building pilot zones to improve the governance capability of the government

The interactions between the building of SHFTZ and the transformation of the functions of first-level local governments in Pudong New Area shall be enhanced, the reform of simplification of administrative procedures, the delegation of powers, combination of decentralization and control and optimization of services shall be systematically advanced, and reforms and innovations shall be made in the aspects such as the reform of administrative bodies, innovation on administration systems, optimization of operation mechanisms, transformation of service modes and other aspects, and the governance capability of the government in an open environment shall be fully improved.

(17) Improving the administration system with simplification of administrative procedures, the delegation of powers as priority. The advancement of simplification of administrative procedures, and the delegation of powers shall be accelerated, and the reform of the administrative approval system shall be deepened. With sorting out the relations among the government, market and society as priority, approval matters shall be further canceled and simplified, and powers shall be delegated to the market to the maximum extent. The transformation of the administration mode in the fields of market access and practicing qualifications shall be prompted. The reform of the big department system shall be deepened, and a cross-departmental coordination mechanism shall be developed according to the principle of simplification and efficiency in the five functional modules: market regulation, economic development, social administration and public service, reform and legislative affairs, and environmental protection and urban construction.

(18) Deepening and innovating on interim and ex-post supervision systems and mechanisms.

According to the requirement for exploring and establishing a new governmental economic administration system, the reform of classified comprehensive law enforcement shall be deepened, and centering on the proper separation of approval, regulation and law enforcement, the reform of comprehensive law enforcement in the fields of market regulation and urban administration shall be improved. The reform of comprehensive administrative law enforcement in transport shall be advanced, and coordination of law enforcement shall be strengthened. The scope of the collection of abnormal directories and information shall be expanded from market regulators to other administrative departments, and the cross-departmental permit handling mechanism of "double notification, feedback and following" and the regulation coordination mechanism of "double random, assessment and publication" shall be improved. The market participant first responsibility mechanism shall be implemented, and a market participant social responsibility report system and responsibility traceability system shall be established in the fields of work safety, product quality and environmental protection, among others. Social resources shall be encouraged to participate in market regulation, and institutional arrangements for third-party specialized institutions of accounting, audit, law and inspection and testing, among others, to participate in market regulation shall be made and improved.

(19) Optimizing the government service system featuring interconnection and sharing of information. The development of an "Internet plus government service" system oriented on the demand of enterprises and supported by the analysis of big data shall be accelerated. An information sharing mechanism featuring coordination between the Central Government and the local governments and connection between strips and blocks shall be established, and the border rules for the interconnection of information among departments shall be specified. Based on data sharing, business process shall be reshaped, and "single window" and "whole networks" for handling market access, "whole district" for handling individual affairs, and "whole personnel cooperation" in government services shall be realized. A public credit information and financial credit information complementary mechanism shall be researched and established. Market participant credit rating standards and systems shall be explored and developed, and a specialized credit information service market shall be fostered and developed.

V. Innovating on modes of cooperation and development and becoming a bridgehead serving the building of the State's "Belt and Road" and promoting market participants in heading overseas

The organic combination of "introduction" and "heading overseas" shall be adhered to, the mode of economic, trade and investment cooperation, research and development of essential industrial technology and internationalized financing shall be innovated, a new open cooperation platform of the "Belt and Road" shall be researched and established, pivots with the functions allocating resources and market factors serving the "Belt and Road" shall be built, and SHFTZ shall be allowed to play a radiating and driving role in serving the "Belt and Road" initiative.

(20) Promoting economic and trade cooperation with high-standard facilitation measure. Asia-Pacific demonstrative electronic port networks shall be connected, and information exchange and service sharing between Shanghai "single window" and ports along the "Belt and Road" shall be vigorously advanced. A new mode of interconnection and regulation cooperation shall be first explored, and bilateral and multilateral cooperation and exchange shall be made in the aspects of certification, accreditation and standard measurement, among others. The building of international hub airports shall be accelerated. The cooperation and connection between Shanghai ports and the ports along the 21st Century Maritime Silk Road shall be promoted, and a central hub on Asia-Pacific supply chain connecting key ports at home and abroad shall be developed. Comprehensive outbound investment promotion institutions and overseas investment public information service platforms shall be established, and business operation shall be made in the aspects of inquiry in law, lawyers' services, commercial dispute mediation and arbitration, financial accounting and auditing services, among others. The "Belt and Road" property rights exchange centers and technology transfer platforms shall be established, and cooperation in the "Belt and Road" industries and technology shall be prompted. International cooperation in production capacity and construction capacity in the fields of energy, ports, telecommunications, high-end equipment and manufacturing, among others, shall be advanced.

(21) Enhancing the "Belt and Road" financial service functions. The in-depth cooperation and interconnection between Shanghai international financial center and the financial markets in countries and regions along the "Belt and Road" shall be promoted. Strategic cooperation with offshore Chinese currency markets shall be enhanced, overseas institutions and enterprises shall be advanced steadily and properly to issue bonds in Chinese currency and assets securitization products, quality overseas enterprises shall be supported in using Shanghai's capital markets to grow, the central banks, sovereign wealth funds and investors from countries along the "Belt and Road" shall be attracted to invest in domestic assets in Chinese currency and provide financing services for major projects of the "Belt and Road". Overseas investment insurance, export credit insurance, cargo transport insurance, project construction insurance and other business shall be vigorously developed, and comprehensive insurance services shall be provided for enterprises' overseas investment, export of products and technology and undertaking major projects of the "Belt and Road". The development of the New Development Bank shall be supported.

(22) Exploring internationally competitive offshore taxation arrangements. Adapting to the demand of enterprises participating in international competition and services for the construction of the "Belt and Road", on the premise of not resulting in the erosion of tax bases and the transfer of profit, tax policy arrangements for the expansion of the scope of the pilot program of

innovation on trade in services shall be researched and explored, on the basis of true trade and service background, taking into account the pilot program of innovation on trade in services.

Ⅵ. Serving the big picture of national reform and opening up and making more achievements in institutional innovation that may be duplicated and promoted

The basic orientation of SHFTZ shall be closely grasped, the launch of pilot programs shall be adhered to, the initiative and creativity of reform and innovation in all aspects shall be fully used, and more achievements in institutional innovation shall be obtained for comprehensively deepening reform and expanding opening up.

(23) Accelerating the forming of systematic reform experience and mode. With innovation on concepts, systems and mechanisms and policies, the strengthening of risk prevention and control and the experience in the pilot program of reforms in other aspects as priorities, the summary of the experience in pilot programs and system integration shall be strengthened. The forming of experience in reforms in fields such as market access, trade facilitation, and innovation on and development of systems and mechanisms which can be duplicated and promoted across the country shall be accelerated. The experience in stress test matters such as further expansion of opening up and connection with high-standard international economic and trade rules shall be vigorously explored, and policies shall be effectively reserved for the state to advance the building of a new pattern of bilateral and multilateral economic and trade cooperation. As for reform matters such as innovation on the mode of government administration, reform experience in reform concepts, organization advancement and other aspects which can be learned from by other regions shall be obtained.

Ⅶ. Effectively ensuring the implementation of the work

Under the overall arrangements and coordination of the inter-ministerial joint meeting for pilot free trade zones of the State Council, the local governments and departments shall be fully motivated and ensure the implementation of reform measures. According to the principle of overall arrangements, implementation by steps, first breakthroughs and gradual improvement, all relevant departments shall vigorously give their support, develop detailed rules or measures for the implementation in a timely manner, and strengthen guidance and services; and, as for reform matters involving the adjustment of laws and regulations, intensify legal guarantee in a timely manner, effectively make connections with the revision, repeal and interpretation of the relevant laws, jointly advance the innovation on the relevant systems and mechanisms, and pay attention to enhancing regulation and preventing and controlling risks. Shanghai shall grasp the basic orientation, intensify mission and obligations, innovate on thinking, seek patterns, solve problems, accumulate experience, improve the working mechanism, systematically advance the implementation of the tasks of the pilot program of reform, and continue acting as a leader of national reform and opening up and pioneer of innovative development. All significant matters shall be reported to the State Council in a timely manner.

3

Shanghai Cruise Travel Contract Model Text (Edition 2015)

Formulated by Shanghai Industry and Commerce Administration Bureau and Shanghai Tourism Administration

Instructions

I. This contractual model text is for tourists to use when signing organized travel contracts with travel agencies for the cruise tour. Tourists shall choose travel agencies with corresponding qualifications for tourism business. A travel agency shall have the *Travel Agency Business License* issued by the tourism administration department and a *Business License* issued by the industry and commerce administration department. A travel agency operating overseas tourism shall have the qualification for operating overseas tourism; in addition to the above-mentioned qualification for overseas tourism, a travel agency operating tours to the Taiwan region shall also have the qualification for organizing mainland residents to travel to the Taiwan region.

II. Prior to the tour, a travel agency shall conclude a written travel contract with the tourist, and the contract and its attachments shall be in Chinese. The travel agency shall issue an invoice after the tourist pays the travel costs.

III. Tourists shall choose the activities on the cruise liner according to their physical conditions at free time arrangements. Tourists shall choose ashore tourism products and programs suitable for their physical conditions.

IV. Where a travel agency authorizes any other travel agency to organize the group, it shall inform the tourists in advance and indicate the basic information in this contract.

V. An electronic version of this contract may also be used by the tourists and travel agencies.

VI. When filling in the Article 2 of "Itinerary and Standards" and "The Itinerary List" of this contract, a travel agency shall express in accurate and clear language, and such vague and uncertain terms as "quasi X star class", "equivalent to X star class", "for reference only" and "the same class as × ×" shall not be allowed.

VII. Tourists shall have the right to independently choose tourism products and services, and the right to refuse compulsory transactions with travel agencies.

VIII. At the time of conclusion of the contract, both parties shall, in light of the specific circumstances, select the option provided in the terms of the contract. If there is a "□" symbol before the terms, both parties shall select such option through negotiation. For terms selected by both parties, the "□" shall be marked with the "√"; for terms not selected by both parties, "□" shall be marked with "×"; if there is any blank space in the terms, it shall be agreed by both parties and filled in completely. For the blank space not agreed by both parties, "×" shall be marked to indicate that there is no special agreement.

IX. Where a travel agency formulates supplementary terms and other contents agreed by both parties on their own to supplement and refine the contents of the relevant terms in this contractual model text, the contents agreed on their own shall not mitigate or exempt the responsibilities that shall be born by the travel agency.

X. This contractual model text shall be used as of August 25, 2015. This edition shall continue to be used until a new edition is formulated in the future.

XI. Travel consultation and complaint institutions

1. Shanghai Tourism Quality Supervision Institute

Address: Building B1, No.2419, Zhongshan Southern Second Road

Postal code: 200232

Complaints phone number: 64393615, 962020

2. Shanghai Consumer Complaints Reporting Center

Reporting and complaints phone number: 12315

3. Shanghai Cultural Market Administrative Law Enforcement Department

Address: No.383, Yongjia Road

Postal code: 200031

Phone number of reporting the law and regulation violations in tourism: 12318

Contract number: _____

Shanghai Cruise Travel Contract
(Edition 2015)

Party A (tourist or tour group): _____
Party B (travel agency): _____
Business license number: _____
Business scope: _____

In accordance with the *Contract Law of the People's Republic of China*, the *Tourism Law of the People's Republic of China*, the *Regulation on Travel Agencies*, the *Tourism Regulations in Shanghai* and other relevant laws and regulations, both parties conclude this contract on the basis of equity, free will and negotiation for agreement.

Article 1　Contract Object

Name of cruise product: _____
Group number: _____
Ways of forming a group (choose one of two)
☐ Form a group on its own
☐ Form a group by authorization (full name of the authorizing travel agency and its business license number: _____)
Departure date: _____, departure spot: _____
Port of call on the way: _____
Tour spots ashore: _____
Ending date: _____, return spot: _____

Article 2　Itinerary and Standards (the itinerary list provided by Party B shall contain the following elements)

Type and standard of cabins on the cruise liner and accommodation days: _____
Number of meals on the cruise liner, standard: _____
Name of tour spots ashore and time for sightseeing: _____
Round transportation ashore: _____, standard: _____
Sightseeing transportation ashore: _____, standard: _____
Tourists' free time arrangements ashore: _____, number of times: _____
Accommodation arrangements ashore (name) and standard and number of days: _____
Number of meals ashore: _____, standard: _____
Name of the local travel agency ashore: _____, address: _____, contact person of the local travel agency ashore: _____, contract phone number: _____

Article 3   Insurance of Tourists

Party B shall prompt Party A to purchase personal accident insurance and cruise travel accident insurance. Upon the recommendation of Party B, Party A has read and clearly known the insurance terms of the above-mentioned insurance and contents of the policy. Party A _____ (shall be filled with agree or disagree, tick invalid) entrusts Party B to handle the personal accident insurance insured by individuals; Party A _____ (shall be filled with agree or disagree, tick invalid) entrusts Party B to handle the cruise travel accident insurance insured by individuals.

Insurance company and name of the product: _____

Insurance expenses: RMB _____ yuan/person

Relevant insurance information shall be subject to the policy and its insurance terms

Article 4   Travel Costs and its Payment (Calculated in Terms of RMB)

The travel costs include: ☐ cruise ticket price (including the designated cabin, catering, sightseeing and entertaining programs and facilities on the cruise liner); ☐ service charge aboard (tip) ; ☐ harbor dues; ☐ visa fee; ☐ endorsement fee; ☐ admission fee for ashore sightseeing scenic areas and spots uniformly arranged by Party B, ☐ transportation fee, ☐ accommodation charge, ☐ meal fee; ☐ other expenses: _____

Party A shall pay the travel costs of _____ yuan, _____ yuan in capitals.

Payment deadline of the travel costs: _____

Ways of payment of the travel costs: ☐ cash; ☐ check; ☐ credit card; ☐ other ways: _____

Article 5   Rights and Obligations of Both Parties

(1) Rights and obligations of Party A

1. Party A shall have the right to know the true information of the tourism products and services on the cruise liner and on the shore purchased by Party A, and shall have the right to request Party B to provide products and services as agreed; shall have the right to refuse party B to designate specific shopping places or arrange additional paid tour programs without agreement through negotiation; shall have the right to reject Party B to entrust the tourism business to other travel agencies without prior agreement through negotiation.

2. Party A shall consciously abide by the norms of civilized behavior for tourism, comply with the requirements specified in the description of cruise tour products, respect the etiquette on the cruise liner and the manners and customs, cultural traditions and religious taboos of ashore tourism destinations, preserve tourism resources and protect the ecological environment; abide by the norms of civilized behavior such as the *Guidelines for Civilized Behavior of Chinese Citizens Traveling Overseas*. Party A shall abide by the team discipline in the travel activities and cooperate with Party B to complete the travel itinerary agreed herein.

3. When concluding the contract or filling in the materials, Party A shall use valid identification documents, provide the contact information of family members or other emergency contacts, and be responsible for the authenticity and validity of the filled information. If a person with limited capacity for civil conduct participates in a travel alone or accompanied by a non-guardian, the written consent of the guardian shall be obtained; guardians or other persons under the obligation of guardianship shall protect the safety of accompanying minor tourists.

4. Party A shall comply with the cruise travel product description and safety warning requirements in the travel activities, voluntarily participate in and complete the marine emergency life-saving drill, and cooperate with the safety prevention and emergency treatment measures taken by relevant departments, institutions or Party B.

5. Party A shall not carry with it or carry in its luggage any contraband prohibited to be taken aboard by laws, regulations and the cruise travel product description. Party A shall comply with the no-smoking provisions of the cruise. Smoking is prohibited in all other places except the designated smoking area.

6. During the cruise tour, Party A shall properly keep the belongings with it.

7. During the activities freely arranged by party A on the cruise liner, Party A shall carefully read and choose the meals, sightseeing and entertainment programs on the cruise liner according to the *Daily Notices* and activity arrangements of the party of the cruise ship. During the activities freely arranged, Party A shall, within the scope of its ability to control risks, select activities whose risks can be controlled, and be responsible for its own safety.

8. Party A shall comply with the departure and return time of the cruise liner and arrive at the assembly place on time for the cruise tour and ashore sightseeing.

9. Where a dispute happens in the tour, Party A shall resolve it in accordance with the methods agreed in the Article 7 and Article 11 of this contract, shall not harm the legitimate rights and interests of Party B and other tourists and the party of the cruise ship, shall not delay the itinerary or withdraw from the group on terms of behaviors such as refusing to get on or off the cruise liner (aircraft, vehicle, ship), shall not interfere with the normal order of ports, docks, otherwise it shall bear the liability for compensation of the expanded losses.

10. The entry and exit documents submitted by Party A to Party B shall comply with relevant regulations. Party A is not allowed to illegally overstay overseas, and shall not divide the group into sub-groups or leave the group without permission when travelling overseas in a touring group.

11. Where Party A fails to make the trip, it may ask a third party qualified to participate in the cruise tour to perform the contract on behalf of Party A and timely notify Party B. Both parties shall settle the increased or reduced expenses incurred for the performance of the contract according to practical.

(2) Rights and obligations of Party B

1. Party A shall confirm the cruise ticket or voucher, cruise travel product description, embarkation related documents and the list of ordered services provided by Party B, as an integral part of this contract.

2. The itinerary list provided by Party B shall be an integral part of this contract after being signed or sealed by both parties.

3. Party B shall not organize travel activities at an unreasonable low price, deceive Party A, and obtain kickbacks or other improper benefits by arranging shopping or other separately paid tour programs.

4. Party B shall, prior to the departure of the cruise tour, truthfully inform Party A of the cruise tour service programs and standards in the form of a illustration meeting, and remind Party A to comply with the norms of civilized conduct for tourism and the requirements specified in the cruise tour product description, and respect the etiquette on the cruise liner and the manners and customs, cultural traditions and religious taboos of ashore tourism destinations. During the conclusion and performance of the contract, Party B shall give true explanations and explicit warnings to the situations that may endanger the personal and property safety of Party A during the tour, and take appropriate measures to prevent the occurrence of such hazards.

5. In event of any delay or failure to reach the port, Party B shall timely release information to Party A and inform party A of the specific solution.

6. Party B shall properly keep all certificates submitted by Party A and keep party A's information confidential according to law.

7. In event of any change in the total contract price caused by policy-based price adjustment of aviation, port charges, fuel prices and other expenses, both parties shall make the settlement according to practical fees.

8. Where Party A falls under any of the following circumstances, Party B may terminate the contract:

(a) Party A suffers from any infectious disease or any other disease that may endanger the health and safety of other tourists;

(b) Party A carries articles endangering public security and does not agree to hand over the articles to the relevant department for handling;

(c) Party A conducts any activities in violation of law or social morality;

(d) Party A conducts any activities which seriously affect the rights and interests of other tourists and does not stop the activities after being persuaded; or

(e) Other circumstances as prescribed by law.

Where the contract is terminated due to any of the circumstances as prescribed in the preceding paragraph, Party B shall refund the remaining money to Party A after deducting necessary fees; and if any losses have been caused to Party A, Party B shall be liable for compensation in accordance with law.

9. Number of people for forming a group and agreement on not forming a group (choose one of two)

☐ Minimum number of people for forming a group: _____ person(s); where the number is below the minimum and the group cannot be formed, Party B shall notify Party A 30 days in advance that this contract is terminated and refund all the expenses already collected to Party A.

☐ This group shall not be subject to the minimum limit.

Article 6 Situations of Party A not Suitable for the Cruise Tour

Where no specialist physician and medical facility is on the cruise liner and the first aid and treatment cannot be obtained in time after the cruise liner leaves the shore, to prevent an accident on the way, Party A, when purchasing the cruise tour products and accepting the travel services, shall truthfully provide personal health information related to cruise travel activities and participate in cruise travel activities that suit its own conditions. In event of concealing personal health information to participate in the cruise tour, Party A shall bear the corresponding responsibilities.

Article 7 Termination of Contract and Necessary Expenses of Party A

Where the contract is terminated due to Party A's own reasons, Party B shall refund the balance to Party A after deducting necessary expenses according to the following standards:

(1) Where the contract is terminated by Party A ahead of the itinerary, the standard agreed by both parties of how necessary expenses are deducted is:

1. _____ day(s) to _____ day(s) before the itinerary, _____ % of the travel costs;

2. _____ day(s) to _____ day(s) before the itinerary, _____ % of the travel costs;

3. _____ day(s) to _____ day(s) before the itinerary, _____ % of the travel costs;

4. _____ day(s) to _____ day(s) before the itinerary, _____ % of the travel costs;

5. The day when the itinerary begins, _____ % of the travel costs.

Where Party A delays in paying the travel costs for more than _____ day(s) before the itinerary, or Party A fails to arrive at the agreed assembling departure place or join the tour in the middle, Party B shall have the right to terminate the contract. Party B may refund the balance to Party A after deducting necessary expenses according to the provisions of this paragraph.

(2) Where the contract is terminated during the itinerary by Party A due to its own special

reasons such as diseases, the deduction standard of necessary expenses is: (choose one of two)

☐ 1. Both parties may reach an agreement which shall be abided by:

Travel costs—(　　)—(　　)—(　　)—(　　)

☐ 2. Where both parties fail to reach an agreement, following standards of deducting necessary expenses shall be abided by:

Travel costs × deduction rate on the beginning day of the itinerary + (travel costs - travel costs × deduction rate on the beginning day of the itinerary) ÷ number of days of the tour × number of days already traveled.

Where the necessary expenses deducted according to the preceding standards (1) or (2) are lower than the actual expenses incurred, they shall be deducted according to the actual expenses incurred, but the maximum amount shall not exceed the total amount of the travel costs.

Where the contract is terminated before the itinerary, Party B shall refund the rest of travel costs to Party A within _____ working day(s) as of the date of termination of the contract after deducting the necessary expenses.

Where the contract is terminated during the itinerary, Party B shall refund the rest of travel costs to Party A within _____ working day(s) after deducting the necessary expenses and assisting Party A in returning to the departure spot or arriving at the reasonable spot designated by Party A.

Article 8　Responsibility Reduction and Disposal of Force Majeure

(1) A travel agency shall be exempted from responsibilities under the following situations

1. Where Party A suffers from personal damage, property loss or loss to others due to its own reasons, Party A shall bear the corresponding responsibility, but Party B shall assist in dealing with it.

2. Where Party A suffers from personal damage, property loss due to force majeure, Party B shall not be liable for compensation but shall positively adopt rescue measures.

3. Where Party A's personal and property rights and interests are damaged during the free time arrangements, Party B shall not be liable for compensation if Party B has fulfilled the necessary warning and explanation obligations prior to the event and has fulfilled the necessary rescue obligations afterwards.

4. Where the personal damage and property loss are caused since Party A participates in the activities not arranged or recommended by Party B, Party B shall not be liable for compensation.

5. Where Party A's personal damage and property loss are caused by the public transport operator, the public transport operator shall be liable for compensation and Party B shall assist Party A in claiming for compensation from the public transport operator. Where the contract cannot be performed as agreed due to the delay of public transportation, Party B shall not be liable for breach of contract but shall refund the expenses not actually incurred to Party A.

(2) In event of force majeure or unavoidable events where Party B or the performance assistant has already fulfilled the duty or reasonable care, which may result in the change of cruise itinerary or cancellation of part of port of call, the following procedures shall be followed for disposal.

1. Where the event happens before the itinerary, Party A may make the option according to (1) or (2) (choose one of two)

☐ (1) Where Party A agrees on the change of cruise itinerary or cancellation of part of port of call, the following procedures shall be followed for disposal:

①Delay of departure, shorter port call time and delayed arrival of return without reducing the number of natural days of the itinerary: meals and various services shall be provided by the ship, and Party B shall refund _____ % of the total amount of travel costs.

②Unable to call at the port of destination: refund the port charges of this port and the ashore sightseeing expenses not incurred.

③Number of natural days of the itinerary is reduced: refund the travel costs according to the percentage of natural days of the itinerary reduced among the planned itinerary after deducting the non-refundable expenses that have actually been paid.

☐ (1) Where Party A does not agree on the change of cruise itinerary or cancellation of part of port of call as agreed, this contract shall be terminated; Party A shall refund the balance of _____ yuan to Party A after deducting the non-refundable expenses that have actually been paid.

2. Where the event happens during the itinerary, the disposal shall be proceeded according to the preceding agreement of (1).

Article 9 Responsibilities for Breach of Contract

(1) Where Party B raises the termination of contract within 30 days before the itinerary (including the 30th days, similarly hereinafter), it shall refund the full amount of travel costs (expenses for the visa/endorsement shall not be conducted) to Party A and shall pay the liquidated damage to Party A according to the following standards:

1. _____ day(s) to _____ day(s) before the itinerary, pay _____ % of the full amount of travel costs as the liquidated damage;

2. _____ day(s) to _____ day(s) before the itinerary, pay _____ % of the full amount of travel costs as the liquidated damage;

3. _____ day(s) to _____ day(s) before the itinerary, pay _____ % of the full amount of travel costs as the liquidated damage;

4. _____ day(s) to _____ day(s) before the itinerary, pay _____ % of the full amount of travel costs as the liquidated damage;

5. The day when the itinerary begins, pay _____ % of the full amount of travel costs as

the liquidated damage.

Where the preceding payment of the liquidated damage is not adequate to compensate for the actual loss of Party A, Party B shall compensate Party A in accordance with the actual loss.

Party B shall refund in full the collected travel costs and pay the liquidated damage to Party A within _____ working day(s) as of the arrival of the notice of termination of contract.

(2) Where Party A delays in paying the travel costs, it shall pay Party B a liquidated damage equal to _____ % of the delayed part of travel costs on a daily basis.

(3) Where the personal information and relevant materials provided by Party A are not true, Party A shall be liable for any losses caused thereby. Where any loss is caused to Party B, Party A shall also be liable for compensation.

(4) Where Party A does not follow Party B's advice and prompt and affects the travel itinerary, which causes losses to Party B, Party A shall be liable for compensation accordingly.

(5) Where Party B fails to provide transportation, accommodation, catering and other services according to the standards agreed in this contract, or arbitrarily changes the travel itinerary in violation of this contract, which causes losses to Party A, Party B shall be liable for compensation accordingly.

(6) Where Party B authorizes its tourism business to other travel agencies without the consent of Party A, Party A shall have the right to terminate the contract upon receipt of such information prior to the itinerary (excluding that day), and Party B shall refund the collected travel costs in full and pay a penalty equal to 15% of the travel costs. Where Party A is informed at the beginning of the itinerary or after it begins, Party B shall pay a liquidated damage equal to 25% of the travel costs. Where the liquidated damages are insufficient to compensate the actual loss of Party A, Party B shall compensate Party A according to the actual loss.

(7) Where Party B designates specific shopping places or arranges additional paid tour programs without consultation with Party A or without party A's request, Party A shall have the right, within 30 days after the end of the itinerary, to request Party B to handle the return of goods and pay for the return of goods in advance, or refund the expenses for the additional paid tour programs.

(8) Where Party B meets the conditions for performance and still refuses to perform the contract at the request of Party A, causing serious consequences such as personal injury or detention of Party A, Party A may, in addition to requiring Party B to bear the corresponding liability for compensation, also require Party B to pay _____ times (more than one time and less than three times) of the travel costs.

(9) Other responsibilities for breach of contract: _____

Article 10　Voluntary Shopping and Participation in Additional Paid Tour Programs

1. Party A may independently decide whether or not to participate in the shopping activities

or additional paid tour programs arranged by Party B.

2. Party B may, on the premise of not organizing tour activities at an unreasonable low price, not deceiving Party A, not obtaining kickback and other improper benefits, and not affecting the itinerary arrangements of other tourists, reach a supplementary agreement on shopping activities and additional paid tour programs with Party A through consultation in accordance with the principles of equality, voluntariness, honesty and credibility.

3. The arrangement of shopping activities and additional paid tour programs shall not conflict with the itinerary list.

4. Where the local travel agency and its employees arrange shopping activities or additional paid travel programs during the itinerary, the responsibility shall be born by Party B who has concluded this contract.

5. For specific agreements on shopping activities and additional paid travel programs, refer to the *Supplementary Agreement on Voluntary Shopping Activities* (Attachment Ⅰ) and the *Supplementary Agreement on Voluntary Participation in Additional Paid Travel Programs* (Attachment Ⅱ).

Article 11　Dispute Resolution

In case of any dispute between both parties, the dispute may be settled through negotiation, or the parties may apply to the tourism quality supervision organization for mediation within 90 days after the end of the travel contract, or the dispute may be submitted to the Shanghai Arbitration Commission for arbitration (if both parties choose to bring a lawsuit to the court instead of the arbitration, the parties shall delete this arbitration clause when signing the contract).

Article 12　Supplementary Provisions

This contract shall come into force upon being signed or sealed by both parties. The itinerary list, description of cruise tour products, supplementary terms and supplementary agreements appended hereto shall be the attachments of this contract and have the same legal effect as this contract.

Supplementary Terms

Party A's signature (seal): _____　　Party B's signature (seal): _____
Domicile: _____　　Place of business: _____
Party A's representative: _____　　Party B's representative (transactor): _____
Contact number: _____　　Contact number: _____
Postal code: _____　　Postal code: _____
Date: _____　　Date: _____

Attachment Ⅰ

Supplementary Agreement on Voluntary Shopping Activities

1. Party A may independently decide whether to participate in the shopping activities arranged by Party B;

2. Party B may, on the premise of not organizing tour activities at an unreasonable low price, not deceiving Party A, not obtaining kickback and other improper benefits, and not affecting the itinerary arrangements of other tourists, reach an agreement on shopping activities with Party A through consultation in accordance with the principles of equality, voluntariness, honesty and credibility;

3. The arrangement of shopping activities shall not conflict with the *Itinerary List*;

4. Specific shopping places shall be open to the public at the same time;

5. Where the local travel agency and its employees arrange shopping activities during the itinerary, the responsibility shall be born by Party B who has concluded this contract;

6. Specific agreements on shopping activities are as follows:

Specific Time	Site	Name of Shopping Places	Main Commodity Information	Maximum Residence Time (minute)	Other Description	Party A's Signature
Date Hour						Signature:
Date Hour						Signature:
Date Hour						Signature:

Party A's signature:
Date:

Party B (transactor)'s signature:
Date:

Attachment II

Supplementary Agreement on Voluntary Participation in Additional Paid Travel Programs

1. Party A may independently decide whether to participate in the additional paid travel programs arranged by Party B;

2. Party B may, on the premise of not organizing tour activities at an unreasonable low price, not deceiving Party A, not obtaining kickback and other improper benefits, and not affecting the itinerary arrangements of other tourists, reach an agreement on additional paid travel programs with Party A through consultation in accordance with the principles of equality, voluntariness, honesty and credibility;

3. The arrangement of additional paid travel programs shall not conflict with the *Itinerary List*;

4. Sites for business operation of additional paid travel programs shall be open to the public at the same time;

5. Where the local travel agency and its employees arrange additional paid travel programs during the itinerary, the responsibility shall be born by Party B who has concluded this contract;

6. Specific agreements on additional paid travel programs are as follows:

Specific Time	Site	Program Name and Content	Expense (yuan)	Program Duration (minute)	Other Description	Party A's Signature
Date Hour						Signature:
Date Hour						Signature:
Date Hour						Signature:

Party A's signature: Party B (transactor)'s signature:
Date: Date:

Issued by the Office of Shanghai Industry and Commerce Administration Bureau on August 25, 2015.